Africa in the Ancient World and Today

The Wealth of a Nation is the Excellent Education and Skills of Its Honestly Hardworking Citizens

Nung Uko

To Mr Umoh
from Author Akpaneyen' Akpan-Essien'
25/07/10

AuthorHouse™ UK Ltd.
500 Avebury Boulevard
Central Milton Keynes, MK9 2BE
www.authorhouse.co.uk
Phone: 08001974150

First published by AuthorHouse 12/7/2009

ISBN: 978-1-4490-0127-8 (sc)

This book is printed on acid-free paper.

AFRICA IN GLOBALISED AND ANCIENT WORLD.

The world is facing grave crisis in wise, rational and selfless leadership, leaderless Africa virtually excluded in all global affairs and business, religion and religious intolerance, racial intolerance, politics, economy, lands and resources, travels and immigrations, family control, law and order, social order and human relations and self-discipline, confusion in defining civilisation, wealth distribution, environmental degradation and pollution, increasing greenhouse gases, sudden financial meltdown, Economic collapse, unemployment and poverty, social and Economic exclusion of Africa and most black people and the underclass, corruption, crimes and graft, lack of mutual trust, lack of integrity, virtue, dishonesty in high places, disregard of compassion and human sympathy for the sick and dying, and youth crimes; individualism is fast suffocating common interest of the community. Individual strife to gain a place in History is corrupting civic loyalty, subverting, eroding and tingeing leadership crucial decisions in critical situations. Cronyism is silencing free speech and freedom. Leaders lie to the citizens to start war without counting the costs of war in lives and damage to properties. People cannot trust their leaders to guarantee their security. The criminal youths are totally lawless and beyond control. Corruption, graft, crimes, greed and blatant selfishness and self-aggrandisement are commonplace. The leaders of Businesses, financial and fund managers pay greater attention to paying themselves huge bonuses in managing Businesses than running businesses to grow to support the Economy. They ignore the benefits of the investors, the Economy and the community at large. Business and Commerce are lacking in mutual trust and dignity. The Economy is collapsing around the expert specialist managers and administrators. Unemployment is rife. Families are suffering. Global youths are fleeing to Western Europe in search for better life. Human trafficking in women and children for criminal purposes, prostitution and child abuse by criminal fraternity is refractory to all efforts by security agencies to stop it. Criminal money laundering in secret banking havens persistently promotes the criminal fraternity activities and corruption. All is happening at a time when the world is rich enough to settle down to consolidate on its gains in trade and Economic Growth. Technological advances have globalised the world. This has promoted waves of Economic migrants among less privileged youths travelling mainly to Western Europe and the US in search of work and better life. Many of our youths and children are wild and beyond control; they missed family education and discipline due to family disintegration and breakdown. Even the adults lack self-discipline and inhibition. Scientists lie in the name of Science and poorly performed Research. Self-interest has biased and polluted Scientific facts

Greed is hampering wealth distribution. Lack of self-discipline is destroying families and communities. Our children and youths are pulling out guns and knives to kill and settle issues at least provocation. Our leaders go to wars to enhance their status against all people's disapproval to show that they are strong leaders without thinking about the damage by war. Religion is becoming a platform for sins against God and man, hostilities and violence. Religious intolerance is promoting riots, chaos and crises. Religious rioters are burning down churches, schools, and people's properties and slaughtering people all in the name of their religion and faiths. Financial and fund managers pay themselves huge bonuses even when the Business is losing money. Daring conmen are ripping-off investors. They rob the public and Businesses of huge amounts of money. Expanding industrial capacity, increasing travels and commerce are increasing greenhouse gases and environmental pollution. Climate change is causing havoc. Drought and uncontrollable bush fires are destroying woodlands and properties. Floods are submerging farmlands and properties. Underwater earthquakes and tsunamis and land earthquakes are causing havoc in destruction of lives and properties among people with greater number living below poverty line. Economic meltdown, recession, redundancy and unemployment are making people and families desperate. Failure to re-integrate colonial dismembered Africa before independence and correcting the tragic disasters that sub-Saharan Africans went through in slave trade, slavery and brutal and oppressive colonisation, and during the recent West and East European Cold war had turned their misery into catastrophe. While it was cold war in Europe and the West that were directly involved that ideological contest in Africa it was continuous hot proxy war. The world finds it difficult to understand the behaviour of the current regime in Australia that found it difficult to apologise to the indigenous native black Australians that they and their ancestors decimated by brutal genocide. If this is not racial xenophobic discrimination against global black people and insult to them and Africa, what then would be the interpretation of this behaviour? He had moral obligation and strength to apologise to fellow British white children subjected to their traditional child abuse culture. They find it unimportant to apologise to black native Australians that had the roughest edge of their brutality and decimation by cruel genocide. Even now the cruelties are still going on. The people are isolated for slow elimination by poisoning with alcohol and drugs while the world is being deceived and fooled with phantom projects for their resettlement. Which is a priority slow and subtle elimination or resettlement?

Right now the wealthy world countries are closing their eyes to what international criminal and vice fraternity Businesses and cartels are doing in Africa in places like Democratic Republic of Congo (DRG). They are sponsoring never-ending brutal civil wars while mining on the cheap, the two metals essential for making mobile phones. Rich mineral resources in DRG had exposed that part of Africa to persistent abuses and torture from Leopold the second of Belgian, the tyrant and blood sucking monster of DRG, to European cold war atrocities until now. They have deliberately excluded Africa and its rich resources from global Economy and single her out for pillaging by Western con Businessmen. They have ignored our call for urgent re-integration of Western colonial dismembered Africa and pooling the earnings from its resources together to open up Africa by rail and roads to the world to prevent free for all pillaging of the continent by unscrupulous Western European Businessmen. The West has ambivalent and ambiguous policy towards Africa. The non-existent leadership of sub-Saharan Africa representing the region with huge flowing gowns only has failed to take up human form to speak for the tormented and tortured people. When will Africa be represented with real people who will plead its case with the world as other people do for their regions?

Social and Economic exclusion has damaged a lot of black people and Africa despite its rich natural resources. Chronic racial segregation and unspoken institutional subtle racial xenophobia had enforced social exclusion of black people from good Education and genuine skills training and jobs. Abandoning the African resources in the hands of its corrupt illiterate leaders and freelance foreign fortune seekers (Pseudo-investors) had decimated its Economy. Corruption, graft, lack of leadership and total resource mismanagement and the Economy and everything had completely destroyed jobs in Africa. This has equally destroyed Education, Health and reduced the standard of living much lower than what colonialism could offer. Poor leadership and bad Governments have fostered Anarchy and loss of initiatives and dampen the desire and urge in the young to work hard to distinguish themselves. Mediocrity has replaced talents. Embezzled public funds have created a class of illiterate socialites in Pseudo-elitism. This has damaged the value of Education and good scholarships to develop talents. Talents are not rewarded. Criminal and corrupt wealth has powerful societal influence and respectability. The foundation of human community is the existence of compassion and sympathy in human beings for the sick, the suffering, the dying and the poor. But today human beings are blood thirsty. They take comfort in the disaster and catastrophe confronting their assumed enemies. They psychologically lynch those they deem are guilty of offending them. They are itching for blood of those they suspect to be guilty of hurting them. They conduct shambolic trials and condemn the suspects by legalistic judgement to severe penalty. They are hilarious in harming those they disagree with. They kill people to demonstrate their might but shout at the rooftops when any of their group is harmed. They cry, "Vengeance, vengeance we want vengeance."

The release of terminally ill Libyan Abdelbaset Ali Mohamed Megrahi from Scottish gaol on compassionate grounds by Presbyterian Scots has exposed the hypocrisy of the Christian West, American mass hysteria and paranoia. It also revealed the level of cronyism and the fear to speak the truth to avoid losing friends and votes among politicians. It is sad that the rich Christian West has been collecting compensations from various nations and Khedafi's Libya which is poor Africa's money but it has resolutely refused to pay even a token amount for what it did to Africa and the black people. Is this a world of the rich and powerful where the rich is above having compassion and sympathy for the poor they tormented and wronged? The poor deserves no mercy, compassion and rewards for his labour. The rich complains loudly, demands and collects damages from the poor they deem had offended them. Ronald Reagan sending planes to bomb and rocket-fire Libya and killing Khedafi's adopted daughter received applause and raised no eyebrows in the USA. Lockerbie was an evil deed. May a just world denounce all bravado evil deeds regardless how rich and powerful or how poor and weak the victim might be. Is might right to abuse and torture the weak? People express concern over the plight and miserably poor state of Africa but yet they continue to pillage the continent and practise social exclusion of Africa and black people from vital human activities to improve the lot of Africa and its people. The ruthless cruelty and brutality of capitalist free market has hurt and damaged Africa severely. Evil deeds by Angel and Mr Right that cannot do any wrong is the same as evil deeds by the devil that always does wrong. The Public must dispense justice and denounce any wrong without fear or favour. This is why this book strives to be even handed in apportioning blame and praises where they can be found. Unseen snoopers on my screen had wiped of most copies of this book. They had even altered its content several times. Silencing people who say what you disapprove is totalitarian dictatorial autocracy and tyranny. What you hear would not damage you but what you do not hear would damage. Banning and restricting free speech deny the tyrants the privilege of hearing what his supposed enemies say about him. They force the autocratic and security paranoid dictators to rely on rumours and intelligence reports for information. Some of these may be falls and misleading.

People have started to question the Market capitalism and Private enterprise as the only means of wealth creation. They are asking if they must either be regulated or modified to suit a rapidly changing world or be replaced by something more humane and stable than the Bubble Economy of Market Capitalism to prevent frequent boom and burst and its accompanied recession. Strong argument is that Economic collapse and recession affect all in Private Enterprise, owners of the capitals, managers, administrators, employers and employees. Why should the community leave the Economy in the hands of private individuals while Economic collapse affects everybody in the community? Hence the Economy should best be managed by the community. The whole community and the world suffer the effects of Economic collapse in the hands of a few people managing and administering private Business and the free Market. They also argue that huge Public Funds were used to rescue Private Businesses. Without this the financial meltdown and deepening recession should have damaged the Economy permanently. They also observed that the rescue efforts did not discriminate between the sources of funds, private, public, socialist or capitalist. They noted that a world confronting disaster needs all hands on deck without ideological cleansing and selectivity.

They also observed that people in planned Socialist free Market like China came out with substantial funds to rescue the global Economy. Russia and several middle Economies all contributed to the rescue of the global Economy in near collapse and deepening recession. Many people are now convinced that it is not Ideology and slogan that help the Economy. Neither private ownership and free Market dictatorship nor Socialist command Economy that will create wealth and raise the standard of living of the people. It is high standard of Education and good and genuine skills training and civic responsibility and total commitment to honesty and hard work among all citizens that generate wealth and prosperity for the community. It is the dignity and conscientiousness of all the workers, the managers, the administrators and Business leaders and meticulous and careful planning that make the Economy successful. Corruption, graft, bad habits and practices damage the Economy. Honesty and selfless good management protects and stabilises the Economy. The real culture of the people and respect for integrity protect a healthy Economy. The G20 should not rush to regulate the free market or management of the capital alone. It should also look into the monopoly of one system dominating business. The new system should be the melting pot of all safe and free systems that must make human beings and the safety of their jobs and businesses the centre of all activities. Human beings should not be mere numbers. Each has life, families and commitments. Treating them as mere numbers that can be decreased or raised at will is callous. Redundancies and unemployment are destructive to industries and detrimental to employees. Spreading out the available funds to retain workers is good. Retraining young employees and diversification of jobs must always be tried. Employers and trade Unions must always work together to save jobs. Making each other enemies is bad practice in market capitalism. They should always reach some understanding of the situation. They should always find some solutions together.

They also argue that what we have now is joint Public and Private ownership. Private Business now is all but in name. Majority of people would rather to go for mixed Economy involving Public and Private Funds and investments. They would prefer conscientious and honest people with good management and planning skills to manage the Businesses and the Economy. They would like the regulations to be revised and tightened. The statute Books should define Economic crimes and stipulate stiff penalties for them. Equally they are starting to feel that by abandoning Business in private hands Government is evading its responsibilities. It is allowing politicians to take over public assets to make fortunes while they resort to public funds to launch rescues in Economic disasters. Therefore public funds should always form part of investments in Business to protect public interest and jobs. The pro-nationalisation camps and trade unions for years had frowned at the free marketers giving privatised Companies subsidies to run the Businesses. It is now very clear that the best way to run the Economy is joint Private and Public joint management. Success does not depend on Private efficiency or Public Profligacy. Success depends on conscientiousness and integrity of the managers, administrators and Business leaders. Good regulations are excellent provided the top officials and leaders in charge of Businesses keep them.

Unfortunately Capitalism seems to be striving to commercialise and monetarise our way of life and all methods of natural production and breeding including human reproduction to gain absolute control of human life. The Doctors seem to be offering assisted Pregnancy to everybody who can pay. Designer babies are gradually being offered to customers. Patriarchal cultures are slowly acquiring Pregnancies bearing males in preference to girls, a practice that may in future upset the ratio of males to females in the population. Same sex males and females co-habit as homosexual gay people and lobby to defend their weird and strange lifestyle. They harass governments to legalise their lifestyle by legislation. No governments ever decreed on man being a man or woman being a woman. Nature made them that way. Government had to decree for recognition of homosexual and what is acceptable for them to do in the community. Some members of the group denounce the lifestyle as a folly and opt out to lead normal life. They marry and get families. They stay with their families and are wife and husband in the proper and natural way.

They are now accepted to adopt unfortunate children from children's homes. Nobody seems to care how such unfortunate children would feel seeing same sex people living and sleeping together and cuddling and kissing themselves. The homosexual say that their lifestyle is normal and natural. They style their existence as natural minority creation. Yet they cannot breed normally. They have to buy IVF at very high price and may have to hire surrogate mothers to bear them children that would live in shame and embarrassment all their lives. It is time for us to review capitalism and its Business conduct critically if it is worth the credits attributed to it. Capitalism is erroneously bound to individual choice, freedom and Democracy. Yet capitalist free Market tolerated slave trade and slavery. It allowed Apartheid for years in South Africa and a handful of white farmers to farm fertile land in Zimbabwe. Capitalism requires cheap materials, capital and cheap labour and easily guaranteed regular profits. It does not seem to bother if crimes are involved in this. Crime syndicate money from illegal drug and human trafficking is frequently laundered in Capitalist free Market without objection. There is meek response and differential treatment and acceptance of such funds. The massive corrupt money from corrupt African leaders laundered in European Banks and Switzerland are received with gratitude and protected. Leaders like Mamuar Khedafi who bank Libyan funds in Libyan name are hounded. They are accused of unproven crimes and bullied to pay damages and compensations for the West to gain access to these funds. The morality of the West receiving compensations from poor Africa through Khedafi while refusing to pay compensation to descendants of African Bantu Negroes for the tortures and deaths of slave trade, and slavery and for their labour and brutal pillaging colonisation of Africa is left to the probing scrutiny of Christian West conscience. At the same time the West confiscates funds from known drug traffickers. The capitalist free market practises selective Democracy and rationed freedom and social exclusion.

Just like any competitive game Capitalism badly requires regulations, rules and referees. Capitalism and free Market are not sacrosanct and no go area. Other methods of doing Business must be examined and tried. Any system the world finally adopts must recognise that it is to help human beings and their families to work efficiently to support themselves. No system should ignore the human factor, element, and needs in life. The system must aim to make human beings accept responsibility of working together to improve their lot and peaceful co-existence without unnecessary rivalry and strife. It must realise the importance of the family as the basis of sustainable and orderly continuity. It must integrate human beings, machines, Science and Technology to work together. Technology must be viewed as an easy way and means for human beings to do things to increase and improve production. It should never be seen as means to get rid of human labour. Human beings will continue to eat. They essentially have to work to provide for themselves and their families regardless of Technology or no Technology. All Technology must plan ways of incorporating and absorbing human beings into its operations to keep and sustain human beings at work.

Perhaps an all inclusive method that respects the family and the welfare of the community may be a good way of developing the Economy .Every free citizen must be encouraged to work conscientiously hard and regard the work as his genuine civic duties in the community. Public and Private ownership deserves being tried as at the moment. Public and Private ownership managed by devoted and conscientious, experienced and honest managers and Business leaders is ideal. The limit to what one person should invest in any Business should not be fixed. It is total ruse to say that private ownership creates and protects jobs. It is a shame that for almost over a century the West contested communism in the Eastern Europe and told the citizens in the East that their salvation would come from Capitalism, Private Business, free Market and Democracy. It never occurred to them that culture of the people defines the way they prefer to be ruled. This defines the type of Democracy they practise. It also defines their meaning of Democracy. The human being is a complex machine.

The human communities and cultures are equally different and complex. What one community and culture would tolerate and practise is different from what another community and culture would accept. Cunningly enough everybody in the world, today, is conscious of their wellbeing and healthy Economy. They are willing to co-operate in matters concerning their Economic interest. It is worth examining all the Economic systems and taking all good characteristics in each system to build up a global system that will be a reference point for good practices. This must recognise the diversity in Ecology in different places on earth. This will form the basis of global regulations of trade, commerce and Business. It will also make sense of Economic Advice to nations under the stress of Economic Depression. Already national interest has replaced discussion of the Economy with Politics of National vested Interest. Paying fixed salaries to Bankers and curbing Bonuses are no longer a priority in banking reforms. Politicians are now evasive in their answers to questions by the Press and the Media. Each country is now plotting how to acquire dominance of global Stock Exchange Market. Therefore every suggestion of reforms and regulations of global Banking, funds and finances management is viewed with suspicion. The communiqué and answers to questions from the Press and the Media were deliberately made vague. The leaders tended to give the impression that while supporting the reform and regulation they objected to all the proposals so far made. The capitalist free market seems to be anti-human beings. It pays, bribes and campaigns against Health reforms. This is led by Insurance business to defend the lucrative Medicare thriving in sharp practices in service to the sick.

The subtle threat to the UK Government of capital flight from the UK to soft spots in the world is typical of the recent Hedge Market announcement. The Conservative Party in spite of announcing pre-election tough fiscal policy and stiff austerity is still wobbling over regulating against sharp practices in financial management in the capitalist free market. Nobody proposes a nanny state but there must be regulations over the way the way the UK and all others should encourage fair wealth distribution and conscientious labour. The Media kept on asking the Conservative leaders where the fit dole takers would find jobs but they were mischievously evasive. The truth is that at the current rate of high salaries there would be no jobs. The truth is that in the global world the West and the whole world should open up new job frontiers all over the world. Africa in the South of West Atlantic should be opened up for jobs. The West did this in the last millennium by colonisation. This time it should use the current high Technology to open up Africa as it used Industrial Revolution to open up Europe and the USA. Asia is already opening up even though huge population load and culture would continue impede some places like India. The West and nobody should be to blame for the current plight of Africa. The brains of Africans heavier than what their bodies can carry are mainly to blame. The great American President Barack Obama that may be described as the world President delivered an address in Ghana to all Africans.

Till today none of them has answered the question he asked Africans. Half of this book is delegated to Africa. Its publication was in progress when he asked this question. This book is riddled with the same question to the Africans. Many Bantu leaders now parading as Presidents of the fifty four colonial African Bantustans are ignorant illiterates. Many of them were globe trotting in Europe in financial meltdown and living on what is described as quantitative evaluation (QE) that means officially approved printing of dud money by the Central Bank to circulate for business and payment for goods after failure of qualitative evaluation (QE). The illiterate African leaders did not know that Europe was in recession. They came with their begging bowl to ask for money. The UK announced that it had given the IMF some billions of the QE money to lend out to money hungry Africans that perhaps would not know that laundered money might have melted away with the financial meltdown or were clandestinely coming to check if the financial meltdown affected their stolen and laundered money." What are Africans doing to join others in the world to alleviate miserable poverty in Africa? What are they doing about credible high standard of Education in Mathematics, Science, Technical education, Engineering, Agriculture Biological Science, Genetics, Medicine and genuine skills training to apply in rapid development of the continent? Would they still choose to remain indifferent to changes all around them in the world? Would they continue to kill each other for flimsy reasons as establishing Muslim Islamic Sharia law, religious intolerance and feuds or ethnic intolerance, war and violence? What is Africa doing when Asia with fewer resources is racing away at the front? Yes the illiterate Geriatric Africans leaders lacked ability to transform their opportunities at School into achievement. But they have no right to deny African youths the opportunity of having up to date modern Science Laboratory and Technological facilities for their studies.

The Eastern citizens rioted under rampant orange flags in orange revolutions. They acquired freedom and Capitalism. Yet each one of them grabbed whatever he or she could get from collapsed Socialist Economy and rushed to the West to start a new life. They were shocked to see that the West had some homeless and poor people. They quickly settled into capitalist culture, crimes, vice and greed. Some quickly took to Bank card identity data theft to fiddle with depositors' accounts. Others took to gun running and human trafficking deceiving young girls with false offers of jobs in the West to bring them out to enlist in Prostitution and vice to make money for pimps and male criminal bosses. They also continue to consume excessive amounts of Vodka and Scot whisky. Surprisingly they have better work culture than the West but heavy drinking reduces their productive capability substantially.

Hence capitalist free market and Democracy are synonymous with corruption and daring crimes. They have introduced new problems, feuds and conflicts to the global world. Ideological rivalry is not worth the energy, time and resources devoted to them. The West had rushed to claim victory but this was premature. There was no basis for the strife in the first place. Each group has some inbuilt weaknesses and is guilty of some sort of crimes and no group is perfect to offer itself to the world for adoption and emulation. Perhaps the world would benefit if human beings would learn from each other and modify their behaviours and cultural habits for the good of peace and making progress and improving our existence on earth. Interplanetary trips the world is planning need no rivalry but planetary unity. Whatever global elements would confront would have dare consequences on the whole world.

Back in the homelands the leaders resorted to corruption and murders of their opponents. They hired paid assassins as private security guards men who frequently dealt with any perceived threats. Late Yeltsin a well-known drunkard and opportunist mounted artillery guns and shelled Parliament full of his opponents. They specialised in consuming excessive amounts of Vodka and other alcohol beverages. Yeltsin was a typical example and remnant of what was wrong with Communist leadership, drunkenness and negligence of duties. Some of the ordinary citizens took to crimes synonymous with capitalism and the free Market. Many continue to consume large amounts of Vodka. From these practical observations we have seen that any system, Communism or Capitalism would fail if we use wrong tools (wrong people) to operate it. Capitalism is not a panacea. Free Market is not the solution. The solution lies in human culture and behaviour in the community. The community must recognise human fallibility. It must strive to develop the strength of good and honest character and trustworthiness in managing Business and strong sense of responsibility in leading the community. A high sense of responsibility is needed in leadership in politics, public affairs and human communities.

The community must regulate human behaviour by binding law and order. People must behave and keep the rule of law to prevent upsetting the slim balance between the scarce resources and poverty. In Physiology the interneur milieu and in Biology and Biochemistry the optimum pH for optimum reactions and functions of molecules are essential for life and healthy existence. It is worth observing that the same applies to the human community. Darwinian evolution law and natural selection and Genetics all confirm these principles in nature and natural selection. We must recognise that these principles are in dynamic equilibrium with external stable conditions. Therefore adopting one system to wrap it around all others upsets the balance. Our new Economic system must be flexible. It must involve everybody in working conscientiously hard to produce the results and managing it to avoid lapses and bad practices and mistakes that individual private Business may make to cause collapse of the Business. The argument that Private Business creates jobs is not proven. It is yet to be proven. "Community Management Board" (CMB), of honest and well-educated conscientious citizens with experience in Business, selected to manage the Business is a new concept worth considering. The CMB should be the house keeper in Business. Similarly there must be established a national finance management board (NFMB). Both these bodies must be managed by honest responsible highly qualified Personnel on fixed salaries commensurate with their qualifications and duties.

This is not a Quango but a body of very experienced, respectable, honest, conscientious and trustworthy highly educated citizens on good fixed salaries to take charge of national funds and finances and the treasury leaving the politicians with the duty of governing. The argument that Bankers, funds and finances managers and Business leaders should not be on fixed salaries but should always have bonuses is flimsy and wrong. It is an indirect way for the politicians to tell the world that they cannot legislate over what they can pay themselves and this group of workers. They legislate and regulate what salaries and remunerations other workers get. What is impossible about doing the same with Bank managers, funds and finances managers, administrators and Business leaders? Is it because most Western politicians moonlight as non-executive Directors in these Businesses and benefit from Bonuses? They also work in these Businesses on retirement and get fat bonuses.

The politicians come for a short period with their policies but the NFMB should be a permanent institution managing the finances and funds for the community to fund and finance the political programmes without avoidable profligacy. The politicians should form the Government and appoint the Ministers. They make and approve the budget with the active assistance of the NFMB. The NFMB has the duty of advising the Government on how much is available in the coffer for spending on various projects. It must also advise the Government on types of taxes to raise money. It must advise the Government on savings. It has to strive to avoid large budget deficit. It must protect Pension funds. It has to advise the Public and Private enterprises on funds available for salary increases. It must avoid inflation. It must audit Government expenditures. The Government in turn must audit the NFMB funds and finances to guarantee efficient management of public funds and finances. This method will guarantee continuity in fund and Economic Management regardless of which Government is in charge. Any political Party voted in comes in with its Programmes. The Public through the

NFMB funds them within the limits of what the nation can afford without excessive budget deficits and bloated national debts. It is the duty of NFMB to maintain good housekeeping to protect jobs.

This will be an antidote to current head hunting bonus-laden specialist Managers and Administrators that nobody can fix their salaries. Why should we hire people that we do not know how much we need to pay them? Are we telling the world that there are a set of workers who have to fix what they must earn as remunerations for their services? The community has no power to place the limit on what they pay themselves for their services. The community must be the Guardian of Business. Business is the lifeline of the community of developed industrialised countries. It is risky to leave it in the hands of private individuals alone. Equally "Community Management Board" does not exclude Private Capital. The Private Capital owners and the Public must jointly own future Businesses. The Public must essentially own shares. Each shareholder essentially has a single vote. Each share essentially has dividend. Shareholders are paid dividends according to the number of shares they hold. They must have a single vote each as other members. They have to argue and sell their arguments to the other members in the shareholders' conference. The Board must not be a lead shot to delay the speed of Business but must have means for Business to act fast. Time is the essence of Business. "Community Management Board" is not a Socialist harbinger. It is a body of Technocrats well educated in various branches of Business and expert specialists in their various fields that must work with Business managers, administrators and Business leaders to regulate how Business must be run to avoid disasters. The question of taking over Business is destabilising and should not arise.

Investors injecting more funds into a Business must make their suggestions on improvements to the CMB that must examine the quality of their suggestions for improvement and present it to the management for execution. Rampant shedding of staff and redundancies must be avoided. Human beings working for a Business have a lot of serious commitments and should not be treated as cast away stones. Business must be managed to be stable to retain staff. It must always look out for sensible and safe expansion. It can freeze employment from time to time. It must make its employments flexible to achieve a balance between replacements by retirements and wastes. It is acceptable for staff to be paid moderate sustainable salaries rather than to be made redundant. Experience from the current recession has shown that staff would accept reasonable pay reduction rather than Business closing down or being made redundant. Business involved in trading and manufactures must keep an eye on what is currently selling and what manufactured goods are popular in order to diversify punctually before it loses its Market. CMB may advise against squatter Businesses offering cheaper services and low prices opening close to long established Businesses to freeze them out to seize the Market to gain monopolies to finally regulate and control the services and the prices all in the name of competition and open Market. Instead of take over and redundancies the would be new suitor should use his funds to expand the business in partnership. He may run the expansion as outsourcing extension. He should be free to pay the staff what he considers would be suitable salaries for them in the new environment. He must present to the whole Board and the CMB, the reforms in the Business he considers necessary for it to succeed. The Business must take the funds the new partner invests as shares. The Business must also invest some funds in this new extension to acquire some shares. The extension must pay dividends to its shareholders according to the profits it makes. The main Business does the same. The main Business benefits from the extension by getting some dividends from the shares it holds. Any part that makes no profits or losses would not pay dividend. The whole parts of the Business should have grand share holders' annual conference to discuss the problems the group is experiencing in each part. Any reforms are discussed here. Staff reduction is made by retraining young employees either to diversify or for a new career. The retained staff may need retraining and exchange with any successful parts.

It is regulated body of housekeepers to manage Business to prevent mistakes from individuals damaging Business. They must be on good fixed known salaries. The community must be protected from Business leaders with tendency to bend the rule. This frequently makes the Business crash to go into bankruptcy and liquidation. The CMB must examine the books and see how Business spends its money. Its auditors must audit Business funds and finances to ensure that there is no misappropriation. The CMB ensures that the Business is in positive balance before it pays out benefits to staff and dividends to share holders. Published statements of Accounts must be true representation of the Company funds and finances. Prudent investments of Business funds and finances must be insisted upon. Business must make savings. It must not tamper with pension funds. Every worker must make some savings. No Business should be allowed to make austerity out of the employees. Fiscal discipline must be encouraged at all times. Business must expand and diversify. It must review the state of Business and the Economy daily. Its surveillance must strive to spot any oncoming danger. The Government must in turn supervise the way CMB does things by regular inspection and auditing of its finances.

The politicians of developed industrialised West seem to conduct wars in distant countries to maintain unity at home. They fail to recognise that free travels, business, trade and commerce and global Economic stability require peaceful and friendly atmosphere in the world for everybody's security and safety. They seem not to care about the damage and social convulsions they had inflicted on these countries and their people. They arrogantly flout all international laws and ignore the global community to mount offensive wars against weak and poor nations. Another thing that has to be considered is where management of the Economy should start. Should it be at the top or from the bottom? Should regulation cover all levels or just certain levels of Business? These questions are on how do global nations regulate small Businesses? How do they support small Businesses? How can they support the self-employed in health and ill-health? Finally how do they integrate all levels of Business to support each other? Already people are aware that farmers have arrangements with the supermarkets but can CMB be involved in order to guarantee and support the arrangements? I feel uneasy when politicians offer incentives to any Businesses new or old, small or large. With people living longer everybody, employers and employees must start savings from day one at work. The present is employment and earnings for a fit person. Retirement and old age lay emphasis on the way to look after a frail old person. The savings become handy.

CMB would arbitrate if there is a problem to be resolved. Similarly which is cheaper and improves the quality of the products; private individual or small Business suppliers of parts to factory or factory mass production of parts? The objective of Business should be to support the Community to lead a decent level of living by deployment and integration of skills in the community to ease employment. It should not be insensitive to what happens in the community it supplies its needs and services but it must be sensitive to stimulus to spur the individuals in the community to work conscientiously hard to increase the quality and quantity of the products of the Company and maintain good delivery time to the customers.

These people complain of third world corruption. Yet they use huge bribes to buy supporters in the countries they invade. They claim to be selling Democracy to these people. They conduct shambolic and rigged elections for them. This is a brand of democracy fraught with crimes. It is Democracy delivered from the barrel of the gun. The West used bribery and corruption to build and expand their colonial territories. Illiterate and totally ignorant African chiefs were given Whisky and other alcohol Brands, cloths and gunpowder to fingerprint documents they knew neither the language nor the contents. This was the Democratic Business conduct Western colonialism sold to Africa. Today bribery and corruption are endemic in most postcolonial countries and their trails follow capitalism all over the world. It is just fair to say that the West has helped to spread corruption in the world. This new brand of democracy is just a ruse. Bribery and corruption are evident every where in the spread of this new Gospel, Democracy from the barrel of the gun and money bag.

Nobody in the world can understand Dick Tierney why he was justified to use torture to extract information from their victims. How can Government violate the USA constitution and set up bad example to their invaded countries' pseudo-democrats telling them it is acceptable to use tortures on prisoners. The backbone of Democracy is the right of people. They had privatised killings in wars by engaging Security firms of ex-SAS and French Legions Mercenaries to do the killings. They carry out kidnappings of innocent people in their so-called rendition practice. They fly them out to world notorious global Dictators and tyrants to be tortured in their torture chambers and dungeons. How can a country that prides itself on Democracy, freedom and Human Rights do this without any regard to world opinion and its reputation?

Torture violates the right of people. Nobody should break the law and claim to practise democracy. The Government is not beyond the law; the law is the Constitution and breaking the law is violating the Constitution. This is not a matter to be resolved by document release to the Media. It is a legal matter. If Dick Tierney feels comfortable breaking the law and violating the Constitution of the United States, he should go to court for a redress. What is Dick Tierney afraid of; war crimes? A fearless and confident world should rein in the Bush war council, George Walker Bush himself, Dick Tierney and Ronald Rumsfeld before a tribunal for war crimes. A timid world is now silent over the damage. It is now pushed up to the front to pretend that it has the power and authority to repair the damage caused by these amateur warlords and toothless bulldogs. It was powerless to restrain the warlords. The UN is a Western Quango. It is totally spineless.

US and the West commit several atrocities in the world in its name. They use it to harass and molest their opponents. Sanction is a siege of war. Nations with means must view UN sanction as an act of war. It cannot apply sanction on the US or its ally. It should not apply it on others. The world needs an organisation fearless to speak out against any nation guilty of violence against its citizens and other nations. It can fine nations substantial amounts for breaking its laws (International Laws). Power must be on continental basis. Corruption and bribery in forms of aids to any group must be strictly prohibited. No vote buying in such a world organisation. There should be open ballot; no secret ballot. Every continent fearlessly supports its interest and draws strength from the authority of the world that gives it freedom to do so. That authority comes from the creator itself,

The USA conservative right always makes mistakes and does not learn from its past mistakes. There is one thing US observers learn. Almost all the people who finally threaten US security had been US alien operative assets. They always turned against the US and threaten its interest. These ranged from Noriega of Panama, Iran under the Anglo-American installed Shah and later (Iran gate), Saddam Hussein (Iraq) and Osama bin Nadin and Al Qaida. The USA flew round the world and lifted fanatical Muslim extremist fighters and brought them to Pakistan; placed them under Osama bin Nadin; trained them in weaponry to drive the Russians out of Afghanistan. The mission was accomplished. What happened then? Today the USA is confronting the very people in Afghanistan. It is very provocative and insulting to observe the USA conservative right criticizing the Democratic Party Policy of Barack Obama. You do not have to be a mad dog and a killing hawk to show the strength and fire power of America to be a strong President leading a Patriotic Government in the USA. A bully is a coward. It is an inapt Conservative Government in the USA without experience in managing domestic and global emergencies that had thrown the world into this crisis and confusion.

They go around the world as a cartel of brigands and mobs knee-capping people when they fall out with their assets just to abandon them for the Democratic Party to run round to apply suiting plaster on the wounds to heal them. The only fault and mistakes of the Democratic Party and Obama are their failure to end the wars on taking over the Government. They were afraid of political repercussions. They should make the soldiers, people and the population know that theirs was not in search of an illusory victory to prove the might of the USA but to guarantee true security and safety of the American people by mutual understanding and friendship. Republican conservatives have every reason to be ashamed. They had always damaged the USA. Now they had damaged the world by causing global Economic collapse and deep recession. The US operative assets in Iraq and Afghanistan that the US now uses would in future become enemies of the US.

Capitalism or any system for that matter is operated by fallible human beings that must be regulated by the law. What we are dealing with is failure of the free Market Capitalism coming on the back of failure and collapse of command Economy of Eastern European Communist Socialism. The world now has reason to think and select what is consistent with human cultures and behaviours. But ensuring that human beings behave according to the rule of law is essential for the health of any systems it chooses. There must be bodies like the CMB to help Business managers, administrators and leaders to steer the course of good Business management. Business must be regulated. Flouting regulations must carry penalty. As capitalism is synonymous with corruption and crimes, vote rigging at sham elections, all malpractices must carry heavy penalty. All vehicles need a brake to bring it to stop.

The brake controls the vehicle. In the same way the society needs regulatory body to control it. This is not advocating for a nanny state. This is not canvassing for restriction of human freedom. One person's freedom must not interfere with the freedom of others. Individual freedom should never meddle with other people's liberty. Similarly the justification of current wars as national efforts and sacrifice to protect people against terrorists is a political slogan for the gullible. Security is safe when it does not involve conflict, violence and war. Even victorious war cannot guarantee security as war leaves bitterness in people. The Eastern culture has vengeance as a priority for murder. The best way to resolve current conflict is by jaw, jaw and not war, war. Talk over the problems; discuss religious intolerance, social female freedom and sober and civilised way to spread of Islam without violence, imposing it on non-believers and restricting the spread of education. Sharia Laws and other religious laws should not be used as a legal system. The UN should make it very clear that the only law it recognises is secular law from a popularly approved secular Constitution.

All free eligible voters in a place must vote to approve autarky (autarchy) in their autarkic state once in a decade. No interest group must be allowed to escape by hijacking the popular vote by feeding false Economic statistics to the people. The voting in Board meetings of privatised Public Utilities at the moment has room the CEOs and business leaders to flout and ignore the decisions of the investors. The investors cannot oust the poor-performing top executives. They use bulk votes to neutralise total votes of members attending the annual share-holders' meeting and stay back on their jobs even when share holders want them out. The "Community Management Board" (CMB) is a new concept of a regulatory body ensuring that Business CEOs and leaders operate according to regulations and directives on the conduct of Business. It will regularise the voting system and each share holder will have one vote. There should be no bulk votes for the CEO. This is essential as we have seen that the Minister in HBOS Board Meeting could not take in what remuneration the CEO was entitled to. CMB is a body that will work with Business regularly and knows its rules and commitments. Already, RBS bailed out of bankruptcy and liquidation by Government with Public funds has returned to the old culture of paying senior officials huge bonuses. Capitalism does not create more jobs than any other well managed Business. It supports a bubble Economy. It supports boom and burst. Whenever there is a hint of any hitch in the Economy, the investors take to capital flight. The Economy collapses and mass unemployment occurs. Unemployment alternates with employment.

The advocates of Capitalism and the free Market were always strong and powerful lobbyists in the days of European ideological debate. They seem to have oversold the values of Capitalism and the free Market to the people. They bound Capitalism to freedom just as they do with war even when it is unjust pillaging war of resources. They make people who doubt the value of pillaging and looting war feel hollow and uncertain and unsure of their patriotic stance and democratic credentials by doubting the values of such wars. They actively canvass for support for war efforts and for the fighting soldiers. Sending soldiers out to fight avoidable war is treason and criminal act. It is political subversion of the military and the Army. It deserves severest form of punishment. It is criminal and treasonable act to abuse fighting a war with undeclared clear purpose. Leaders without ability to manage national emergency, crisis and conflicts declared war as a short cut to bully innocent citizens over their patriotic stance and war efforts. Similarly people who doubted some sharp practices in the capitalist free Market were bullied to re-examine their Democratic credentials.

Placing hard drinking communist Party conveners over Business destroyed the Eastern European Economy. CMB takes Business away from political control and places it in the hands of experts answerable to the Government and the community. "Community Management Board" is a team of Experts involved in day to day running of the Business but in Advisory and Supervisory capacity in planning, development and expenses. Discipline is the lifeline of Business. The CEOs who manage the Businesses daily have the CMB to consult for advice at all times. Equally the CMB has some restraining influence over the Business. It can halt very risky investment that may sink the Business like recent purchase of HBOS by Lloyds TSB. The rapid return of Royal Bank of Scotland to the Bonus culture is not very encouraging. Existence of an Institution like CMB would prevent this regardless of what the politicians may say. The hard right conservative fanatical extremist hawks have tactics of keeping the community busy while they do their own things. They make their opponents doubt their patriotic and Democratic credentials. They make light opinions incompatible with theirs.

Cronyism and sycophancy harm Business. They are bad for Business as corruption. Success in Business depends on discipline and hard work. Business should run as a good family. Workers should be confident of their job security. If they see that the Business is running properly they will take it as their family enterprise. Good teamwork is important in efficient Business management. Bloated bonuses for top management are very discouraging to the ordinary workers. Business Management must make the team see that the senior management makes genuine sacrifice for the success of the Business. They must be conscious of its success. They should all be conscientious and aware of the fact that failure of the Business will make them redundant and unemployed. They must see the Business as a vital part of their lives and occupation and support it with honest hard work provided everybody from the top to the bottom does so and makes essential sacrifice to achieve this.

Free market capitalism gives the illusion of affluence during boom time. It creates temporary jobs but both employers and employees are vulnerable to boom and burst and recessions. Joint ownership of Capital and Business and good planning of growth and expansion by both the employers and employees and other citizens is important for the Economy. Lean period must be recognised and planned for. Community consumption must be regulated by taxes and interest rates. Citizens must review the statute Books and Economy in every decade. Every free citizen must have a vote and vote to approve the result of the review. This is what we call social stream down or down-size of the Economy. We must avoid living in an artificial world in the name of modernism and free enterprise. We waste our scarce resources when we live above our means. People can live comfortably within their means at current level of Western Wealth without corruption, vice and crimes. It is greed, corruption and crime and misbehaviour that create scarcity and failure of the Economy.

The price of Economic ideological rivalry has been high and costly to the whole world. It encouraged a lot of people and nations to live above their means. Theft of resources and pillaging were commonplace. The poor world became victims of bullying, harassment and name calling. Corruption, crimes and bribery caused crises, chaos, war and violence. The opposing Economic ideological camps armed most poor nations to fight proxy wars. This resulted in massive destruction and damage to the environment and waste of resources. There was unregulated environmental degradation. There are, even at the moment, strange new diseases spreading like wild fire and difficult to control. Previously well controlled diseases like Tb, Typhoid, poliomyelitis, measles etc are gradually returning.

We are gradually losing our senses of the differences between the sexes and are succumbing to intensive pressure and lobby of lifestyles of powerful minority perverts justifying their behaviours in a consumer-materialistic society as being natural. We are facing grave dangers to humanity and the world by *relentless adherence to modernism. Children, nature's investment for continuity of the future are being reared and brought up in deceit by single sex phantom marriages between two same sex co-habituating males* or females. Governments are busy passing laws legalising such trespasses on natural institution of marriage. We all seem to confuse Technological advancement with civilisation and culture.

Civilisation rejects the barbaric and lawless behaviours and actions we are now witnessing in several parts of the world. Sophisticated Industrialisation is not a mark of civilisation. Our observation, today, seems to be that the more Technological the community is the more degenerate it becomes and the further it is from true civilisation. Technological advances do not intoxicate the community and make the people arrogant and wild. They do not make people intolerant of people Technologically less developed. They do not make people incapable of taking rational and sensible decisions. Similarly, civilisation does not constitute people into bully gangs or create supermen out of human beings. Technology that had improved human life on earth beyond belief should not challenge nature. It should respect nature and try to unfold the natural wonders. Unfortunately it seems it has equally given the people false confidence that they can get away from all crimes and illegal activities and human life is worth nothing in high Technology communities.

Money which is metal, paper or plastic had assumed the position of the deity. People deify it and feel everything on earth has a value in money mere tokens we use to fulfil our promises in acquiring goods and services. It is worth killing for in brutal and irrelevant wars. Compensation in money seems to settle all criminal neglect and even murders. The damage and destruction of war are worth huge contracts and wealth. Therefore it pays to go to war if need be to make money. High Tech gadgets are adequate to guarantee easy victory. Any lies and spin can be offered as reason for conflict. It is equally interesting to observe that it is the conservative right that always start war leaving the Democrats to sort out their mess. The conservative Republicans had already awarded themselves huge contracts. They control munitions factories and the arms trade. Wars increase munitions manufactures and sales. They deceive the people that they are vital for employment. Many peaceful industries also provide employment. Why it is munitions manufacture only that is singled out to provide jobs? The truth is that munitions manufacture is associated with research to improve the quality of these lethal weapons and find new ones. The Republican conservative rights always have enemy threatening their security. This time is terrorism an invisible enemy.

Coming to Africa, the black people and sub-Saharan Bantu Negroes, it is now time for them to decide their fate and future in a dynamically fast changing world. They must decide if life is for them to live independently or depend always on unreliable sources such as the global NGOs for support and help. The choice is Africa's to continue always waiting for new masters to take over their affairs while they continue in lawlessness. It is already neck deep in all manners of crimes, vice, corruption, social decadence in high places, wasteful bush wars, destruction of innocent lives and property, destroying jobs and sabotaging wealth creation and the Economy. It is guilty of indolence and lack of genuine initiative and leadership.

The leaders are morally decadent and corrupt. The youths do not want to work. They had been inducted to believe that success is impossible without cheating and malpractice. They do not study but buy examination papers from teachers. They join killing mob cults and harass female students and gun down any male students going out with the girls they fancy and want. They bully teachers to pass them in examinations. They frighten the invigilators and students in the Examination halls by discharging live munitions. They fake certificates. They fake everything and cheat in all their deals.

It is difficult to find the way to teach Nigerian youths how to work hard for good results without cheating. Children of politicians and soldiers had grown up to learn from their parents that to make money is to swindle the oil money. Everybody is involved in embezzling public funds and receiving bribes for performing their duties. Government Ministers pass the budgets for various programmes. They disburse the money from the treasury and share among themselves. Government officials obtain the money. Each Minister shares the money so that each important member of the Government including the President has a share. This may be christened "Budgetary theft from Public coffer or budgetary recycling of Public funds among the officials and top politicians and leaders of Government". At the Federal level the officials and Government Ministers share the money among themselves including a share for the President. At the State level the Local Government chairmen share the money including share for the state Governor. Each Governor ensures that the President has a share.

Those children of the Government officials who have no access to substantial oil money by doing business depending on oil and gas smuggle themselves to Europe to apply for asylum from Government of their parents. They are actually economic migrant refugees. Some of them become professional students. They take up lowly paid jobs and pay owners of private Tuition schools to have papers for visa. Those who cannot reach Europe the easy way pay human traffickers to smuggle them across the Sahara. Several of them die in the Desert. Why do they run away from a country they and their parents had ruined? People make Europe great by hard and honest work. It is sad that some Nigerians and Africans with access to Local Government contracts have started to massage the system to abuse Public funds in the UK. It is speculated that some acquire social housing and rent out and collect rent. It is worth checking this type of fraud. This is an obnoxious abuse of generosity. It is worth probing to ensure that it does not exist.

This is abuse of generosity. Those with access to dole and social security and housing abuse the system. Perhaps the State should take such conducts seriously. They should strip the culprits of their evil gains, jail them for a term of imprisonment and nullify their residential status and repatriate them back to their homeland in Africa. This will be a deterrent and demonstration to would be scroungers that dishonesty and corruption do not pay. It will also confirm Government determination to tackle scam ruthlessly. There is no room for witch hunting. The locals equally abuse the Social Security system. Nobody therefore should lay the blame on such abuses on some Nigerians and Africans alone to justify racial xenophobia. The Social Security System in a Welfare State is an Institution supporting the whole community in a civilised Society. It supports everybody in job and financial difficulties until they can stand on their feet again if they are young and fit to return to work. It is not for swindlers. It is everybody's duty to support and protect it. No scams and cheats should be tolerated. Such is abuse of Societal Generosity and sabotage of the community effort to cater for the poor and deprived.

Technological Skill is not civilisation:

As a matter of fact the more sophisticated the Science and Technology become the more primitive and retrogressive the people seem to become. They become degenerate and bolder in doing queer and weird things. Permissive and perverse sexual habit becomes bolder. It harasses Government to legalise its lifestyle by legislation even though it is neither genetic nor minority ethnic trait but very dirty corrupt lifestyle. It is against the rule of law. It is against the rules of personal hygiene. It is against the rules of nature, Biology and Science of breeding.

It is not a benchmark for freedom or liberal lifestyle. It is an argument that has won a place for criminals because minority powerful and influential people in the society are equally involved. Criminalising it will equally criminalise them. Hence make it acceptable lifestyle by law but it is not biological or genetic. It is not seen in the wild. Wild males are possessive and maintain and defend their harems and territories. They constitute dominant males in the harems totally excluded to other males. Why then try to corrupt Biology and Science to justify this queer and strange lifestyle of weird males and females corrupting the natural way of breeding to keep the human society in continuity? Some members had seen the futility of this lifestyle. They had opted out to lead normal life. This is a proof that it is neither biological nor genetic trait. It is a social lifestyle with some Psychological addiction. The members also use some form of bullying and threat such as naming and shaming members that do not declare their involvement. The recent case of the French Minister, Misseur Mitterrand abusing rent boys in Thailand is evidence of moral decadence and degenerate European culture. This is incompatible with civilised conduct.

Perverse lifestyle, therefore, does not need societal approval. Let it not lie to corrupt Biology and Science to give it acceptable face. It is grossly dirty lifestyle fraught with deadly diseases. Human secular laws may approve it but natural laws still deny it natural approval. It is perverse criminal pervasive and permissive lifestyle unnatural to normal human behaviour. Let us in our rush to queer, weird and strange lifestyles not lay claims to civilisation. Arrogance and bragging are not trademarks of civilisation. Racial xenophobia, segregation against people of different skins and physical features are not a mark of civilisation. Greater fire power and wars of conquest, ethnic cleansing and genocide are not attributes of civilisation. Humane genuine compassion and sympathy for the suffering and the dying are clear marks of civilisation. Ability to forgive your fellow human beings and not always demanding and bidding for vengeance and a pound of flesh from those you feel had wronged you is blueprint of civilisation. Tolerance regulates a civilised community. Civilised people do not dash out to attack their provocateurs as a fowl defending its chicks.

Ability to resist being overwhelmed by anger and emotion to demand vengeance and retribution for people you feel had wronged you at all costs is display of mature civilisation. Philanthropic generosity is mark of deep rooted civilisation. Resistance to temptation and attraction to rich resources in a foreign land that you feel that you can bully and intimidate its people to pillage and plunder the resources is excellent display of acknowledgement and respect for right of others to own property regardless of their social status. Conscientious hard work, good education, successful skills training and excellent apprenticeship to create wealth, promote prosperity and improve the societal standard of living is sign of responsible civilisation. This gives improvement to the culture and enhances civilisation. Finally ability to tolerate other people's cultures, religions, ethnicity and habits and live in peace with your neighbours is a sign of refined civilisation. Bullying is degenerate behaviour and cowardice not civilized.

Civilisation is the humane human culture that stands human beings out as different from other primates. It has abandoned the wild traits of other primates. It has built up from changes in human behaviours and gains from work and self-propagation. It is tolerant of other human beings and their cultures. It develops the rule of law and obeys the rules and regulations. It rejects obnoxious practices and banishes them from the community. It respects human life and right of man to his life, family, and property. It is able to take accounts of its gains and co-relate them to build on them for further progress. It borrows from other cultures. It has compassion and sympathy for fellow human beings. It makes learning its core principle to educate the community to progress in mastery of the nature and the eco-environment. Civilisation is a sobering humbling mood that makes human beings think and show character and behaviour different from other primates. It thinks rationally.

Greater firepower and killing index are incompatible with democracy and civilisation. Sexually transmitted diseases, (STDs) including AIDS/HIV are common and take their current potency in this weird and queer sexual habit. The Gay community is a powerful lobbying machine. It makes it a duty to make homosexual practice look innocuous and completely innocent and even scientists are guilty of hypocrisy of silence and suppression of the facts and the truth.

They bury their heads in the sand. New resistant strains of the HIV/AIDS are found so far in the so-called Gay Community. The writer is not homophobic. He is expressing his views. He is telling the Gay community what they should know. They are free people. They can abuse their bodies for pleasure. Homosexual practice started among the Greeks perhaps among the Spartans. Male Spartans stayed together in camps to train and fight wars. Females stayed at home. Prolonged clustering together of males might have started homosexual practice among the Spartans. It is, however, a feature of the whole of that region, Christians and Muslims and others. It may be a culture of minority of people in Europe but it is not our place to chastise and criticise them in this land of the free. Equally they have no right to harass us to accept them to places where they are not needed like most of the African places of worship and homes. Most Africans still find it difficult to accept this strange and weird lifestyle as normal. It is abnormal.

We have been here before. The world is evolving around old events taking place in changing times and changing events and generations. The Romans took the world by storm and exerted their influence all over their known world. They claimed to know more about the world than all other people in it. They became overstretched and finally their empire collapsed and threw the world into chaos. The Romans generated collaborators all over their empire and showered them with special privileges including violating and flouting the laws. The Marmertines were mercenary soldiers. They broke the ancient laws of military engagement that protected families, mothers and children. The Marmertines went into towns; they slaughtered the fathers and males and took their wives and children. They looted their properties. Ancient laws stipulated stiff penalties for such behaviours against non-combatants. Pompey their leader even accepted responsibility. The Romans protected them. They used them to fight against African Carthaginians. From these might have developed the offspring of the Sicilian Mafioso, the Cosa Nostra. It is easy to introduce long lasting evil into the world by taking advantage of objectionable situation. The West particularly the USA has repeatedly done this with devastating backfiring results.

Today we are gradually seeing the warlords in Afghanistan and the Kurds, Iraqi national congress and religious militant fanatics sheltering under the umbrella of military occupation-sponsored democracy to support expanding slaughters of their fellow human beings. The inbuilt instability of this unholy alliance frustrates any hope for an end to this human carnage and tragic catastrophe. We do not fail to recall that the current crisis has evolved from the alliance the West made with global Muslim Islamic league to vanquish former Soviet Union in Afghanistan. They flew them into Pakistan from all nooks and corners of the world, trained and equipped them to fight the Soviets. It was here that global Muslim Islamic federation had the opportunity to see the injustices in the world and recognised their potential to fight against them. I am not in a position to justify the right or wrong of this concept. It is equally difficult to blame people who sacrifice their lives for a cause. The success the Muslim fighters made of their mission in Afghanistan also encouraged them that they could take on anybody in a sword-free jihad. Just as the West from Alexander to the Romans and Europeans of all generations fighting has become a tradition and culture, the Muslims from AD 208 when the Prophet Mohamed resurfaced in Mecca with swordsmen on horses' backs had not stopped fighting jihad. All their aggressions and hostilities are named jihads. Their land grabbing and Sharia law imposition wars are all christened jihads. The world has changed. This aggressive fighting culture has to change too. They must change. They must armament and fighting. The Muslims are now acquiring modern weapons and are fast in learning how to use them.

Today, the Anglo-American power axis and their allies in the coalition of the willing are battling against their erstwhile allies. It is difficult to apportion blame and justify the slaughter. It is, however, obvious that previous Western manoeuvre had backfired. In my short life time all dangerous dictators and global tyrants had had overt support from the West. Why it is always like this; is it because of armament manufactures and sales? From the current crisis will finally evolve future bloody dictators and tyrants of this century and millennium. The US may also be involved in a row with them claiming to protect democracy.

There is absolutely no justification for either NATO or the UN to intervene in the current crisis. The combatants should use the resources of conflict resolution to settle their differences and sue for lasting peace, safety and security. This is a conflict of religion, clash of cultures, ways of life, racial groups, rich resources, and differences in the levels of wealth, wealth distribution and development, people traditionally aggressively pugnacious with different visions of the world. Therefore, let us not pretend that we are purely innocent. We raised up our current assailants by error of judgment and seizing advantage of short term benefits.

The world love America but it amazes many people that a nation with a breed of very intelligent scholars and some of the best brains and brightest minds on earth, today, lacks people who can detect crooks and conmen, very unintelligent people who are foolish enough, to take chances to take on the global giant by trick and con but are always lucky enough to fool the mighty America. They can recall late Mobutu and Jonas Sivimbi in Africa. These two conmen and tricksters fooled the US for decades to rule by despicable tyranny, gruesome murders, corruption and flagrant abuses of basic fundamental human rights and systematic destruction of their homelands and people under the very nose of America but both managed to sustain US support and protection until God at His good time took them off the surface of this earth. They fooled the US that they were fighting for democracy that they flouted, disdained and ignored its basic rules.

Yet the CIA found them very useful agents and assets. They died and left trails of devastated and ruined countries. We know that the US benefited from mineral wealth. The proceeds from these could have been used by the US to give good education and skills training to the youths that the criminal tyrants used as fodder for their gunpowder of cruel brutality and atrocities. Truly, if the US adopted generous mass education and skills training of the youths in these countries the money the US wasted on them could have transformed these places. Today, the whole US could have gained credit as a credible and genuine spreader of democracy and defender of freedom.

The money the West and the US had made from pillaging African resources could have built road and rail network across the continent to open up the continent to the outside world to make life a bit easy for sub-Saharan Bantu Negroes after several years of torture, cruelty and brutality from naked greed and xenophobic tyranny. The

US has always left behind trail of tyranny and ruins of crimes and corruption. The Middle East is starting to unfold. Yes the West and US want energy but can the US do clean business and gain world respectability as an honest broker? It should withdraw its troops from Iraq. The troops are there to protect the traitors the US has installed in power to allow them to pillage Iraqi energy resources. Use of tax payers' money to provide protection to a few renegade politicians and traitors in Iraq and Afghanistan to protect the business interest of some of its powerful and influential businessmen in politics is betrayal of public trust.

The spin that the troops are there to protect the West from terrorists is unconvincing and totally false. The troops are there to save the face of cunning and crafty politicians to protect them from public anger, ridicule and disgrace for lying to take the West into fruitless wars because they did not know how react to situations in national Emergency and world crisis. George Walker Bush has yet to tell the world that if Saddam Hussein had included the USA in the list of those who were to benefit from the lucrative oil contracts after the so-called UN sanctions that devastated Iraqi Economy and children, he would have still invaded and occupied that country. He just could not bear being excluded from Iraqi rich energy contracts. His main business is listed as dealer in Energy.

It is obvious glancing at this man, Ahmad Chalabi, his carriage, body language, gestures and the number of I's in the speech purported to have been delivered by him to the UN, he fails to come across as a person, an innocent market woman food trader can do business with, not to talk of the top US leaders or an Institution like the CIA. This man comes off as a crook and a conman. The way he talks before thinking does not portray an intelligent man in a critical situation. It would not be safe to dismiss him outright but the first impression he gives several people even his posture in photos would make many think hard before they come to his aid and open the door to him to have a drink of water on a hot day. He is not persuasive. A man who claimed to have been tortured looked much healthier than his supposed torturer. His Rolex wrist watch and silk suit and tie should make a fool think that this is not a liberator of his people in chains of tyranny. Moses did not go to Pharaoh, Ramesis11, dressed like that. There is no shred of humility in him. He is typically macho

Arab person. Most people involved in a fight for life and death never bore such carriage. The air of seriousness does not smell like that. Even the leaders of very affluent America do not do that. Those who embraced him perhaps had never been first class students at School or taught students to evaluate their attitudes towards life and their goals in life. Chalabi came off as a high society man for wealth, affluence and leisure.

A very tidy soldier appearing at the end of bloody and severe battle, perhaps, had not taken part in the fight. He had been hiding just to emerge from his hiding place to claim victory. The world is yet to see when America will take care to have leaders that will have analytical mind that sees through people introduced to them. The US is well known to walk in the shadow and darkness of intelligence alone. It can give itself time to learn more about the people and countries it does business with. We are all fallible but should not be prone to repeat the same mistakes. They cost lives and huge amounts of money to offer crooks and conmen protection and comfortable lives. The politicians would defend their role and score high the Iraq enterprise but it was all futile and a waste of life and resources. It was a flash in the cups of hasty and thoughtless leaders. Failure to know the culture of the people you are dealing with or ignoring it and relying on firepower is a mistake and serious threat to world peace.

The Iraqi National Congress (INC) is a false promissory note printed in the US and a charade. It is the Greek horse. "I fear the Greeks even though they may bring gifts". The Latin Trojan Horse stories fooled the Romans to open the city door for them to attack the city. The US as the only lone superpower has a great responsibility on its shoulders for world peace. It is a geopolitical economic conflict. They may have their prejudices, bias, grudges and grievances. Intervention by a third party may not resolve these deep seated differences. The best way to resolve this dispute is for the parties to recognise the futilities of their actions and behaviours. It is the recognition of the folly of this feud by the parties involved that is important in its resolution. If US claim to be a world leader it must realise that leadership embraces everybody in the world but not only the willing. It must learn to deal with everybody as a benign leader without bullying them tyrannically. The USA will be a better leader than at present, by abandoning arrogance and bragging and dealing with global nations as equals and humans demanding mutual respect. It must avoid bullying other people with name calling even when they have some differences and problems to resolve. It should not form alliance of the willing.

It will also guard against future similar incidents and adventures. Using a third party like the UN will be an encouragement for any aggressive military power to attempt this type of conflict ignoring world and UN advice in the hope that the UN will bail them out at the end. Who will pay innocent Iraqi citizens the indemnity they rightly deserve. What guarantees does the world have for peace if the Anglo-American alliance is let off the hook in this mess? In the last millennium they devastated the world and left most parts in a mess and chaos in South East Asia and South America, their backyard. It appears the USA is deliberately using other people as cannon fodder for testing their new weapons and military wares. This would be incomprehensible and deplorable. The way US pours 500lb incendiary bombs into highly populated areas of cities does not portray civilised people with human touch and respect for the lives of other people. US appear to have no punctum of compassion for fellow human beings. How would you claim humanity if you are so merciless? Human sympathy and forgiveness of fellow human beings you feel had offended you is important for civilised conduct and peace. The US must learn that in human community someone has essentially to sue for peace regardless of how hurt he may feel. Craving for winning and victory in some conflicts may drive some people to commit crimes of genocide and transformation into murderous monsters. Nobody or any serious minded Americans, neither members of the NATO, Western Europeans nor alliance of the willing would at this juncture take victory in Iraq or Afghanistan seriously. The first decisive failed to deliver the knock out. What they are doing now is patching up. Patching up is not victory.

The warriors had already been clubbed and damaged. They had failed to show their ferocity and invincibility. They had battered their Economy and global Economy. They are heavily indebted with huge budget deficits. Prolonging the war will show how callous the leaders are with human lives. They sacrifice the lives of their soldiers and people in the occupied countries. Even if it has been a clean victory it would not fetch the West the shield they are craving for as these are small poor and weak countries. The West could have offered them peaceful aids instead of war. The leaders have an opportunity now to show us that they have respect for human lives by stopping the war and suing for peace. They cannot stop terrorism by becoming terrorists themselves. The world is now harassed by two groups of terrorists, Western NATO and Muslim terrorists. The best the world can do now is to seat down the two groups and settle the feud and restore peace.

They had started again in this millennium. They paid for their war machines. They must pay for the damages they cause. The clockwork conflict, war and violence are shrouded in shrivel fur coat of fleece-laden wool concealing lice and lies. The Anglo-American alliance may be the most powerful in the world. The leaders lied to themselves, to their fellow citizens, the world and God. They lie to their teeth and bear false witness against their neighbours. They lack the courage and ability to tell the truth about their real global intention. They are insulting our intelligence by lying to us when we know the truth. They equally debase themselves by lying over the truth that everybody knows. In these days of IT revolution they seem to be living in a different age from us. They invented these things. What persuades them to believe that we would ignore what we see and hear to believe in their lies? This is the age of high Technology and Information Technology (IT) and it is difficult to hide information from the Public. Information is no more frequent casualty of what the politicians and leaders do. What they do is under Public eye and scrutiny.

Fallujah showed the extreme of Anglo-American barbarity, brutality, cruelty, atrocities, inhuman touch and ruthlessness. Do they not know that we all knew that the fire and live munitions from their helicopter gun-ships and artillery guns were dropping on innocent human beings, women, the elderly and children below? Would any Western leaders accept their wives and children to be in Fallujah under those fires? Persistent lies will not cure our hurt, revulsion and disgust. The duty and integrity-conscious Western diplomats had summarised the feelings of all honourable, virtuous and respectable people of conscience and integrity. It is insulting hypocrisy and cowardice for some traitors to admonish that we

African Negroes should not tell the truth the way we see it to avoid offending their white masters. It is not what we say that damages their white imperial colonial masters. It is what their white masters do. We are innocent reporters and recorders of what their white masters do. We are witnesses of the truth.

If their white masters do not like us to write about the truth of what they do to damage the world, it is just simple that they stop doing it. As a scholar I am a fan of the West and America. There is age-long tradition. Well educated people think constructively in a balanced way and owe some loyalty to their group regardless of racial divide. The Western white males are yet to stop fraudulent wealth gathering. They brutalise people in alien lands calling them savages. The Western white males are unfortunately savages judging by the records of genocides they have been guilty of in the world. They did these all in the name of wealth and escaping from poverty. Can they now adopt a policy of sharing the wealth of distant lands with the natives and educating them instead of eliminating them by genocide?

Evidence of the crime of genocide by the West abounds everywhere in the world. How did they come to own America, Canada, most of South America and Oceania? The best the West can do now is to change their habits. Let the wealth they acquired through brutal and ruthless brigandry not make them mad. They must now show some human touch, compassion and sympathy. The victims of Western global atrocities and the world had forgiven the West. The West must show some sense of responsibility and remorse. Nature never released them as a scourge on the world. Consumer-materialism is damaging the world. The West must equally learn to forgive others. Assuming that the world does not mention these things because they can punish them if they do is wrong. The world would not tolerate Western empire building or genocide in this millennium.

We Africans do not forget this type of Anglo-American tyranny of greed in slave trade, slavery, racial xenophobia, Negro bashing, lynching and brutal colonisation, pillaging and looting of Africa. It was free for all, for money in consumer-materialistic, greedy society not afraid to hurt and damage their fellow human beings to earn wealth and money. The Anglo-Americans do not forget their wars.

What makes them believe that we will forget their brutalities and hostilities against us in our homeland? Is the concept of democracy an afterthought after over five hundred years of greed and extremes of tyranny and cruelties of endemic racial punitive xenophobia?

The West had a very long time to introduce and teach the world about Democracy and set examples in Democracy but all our exposure and relationship were based on extreme tyranny, bullying, intimidation, cruelty, atrocities and racial xenophobia, name-calling, abuses and arrogance. But today the Western leaders talk of Democracy as an after-thought. The way they used religion to deceive and brainwash us makes us hesitant over this new concept of Democracy. It is a new deceit. How democratic are Western white males who send their Armies to invade and occupy poor and weak foreign countries slaughtering their people, women, the sick children and elderly in phantom war against terrorists? Does Democracy make a terrorist not a terrorist any more? Equally people's cultures determine the type of Democracy they practise. Therefore there are diverse forms of Democracy even the Athenians had their own model. Even the West is unable to define their own model but pay lip service to Democracy and use it to molest their opponents. On the whole Democracy and right of man are very good socio-political conduct for maintaining discipline, Justice, Peace and law and order in the community. It should, however, not be delivered from the barrel of the gun.

Today spin and persistent lying and pretending of ignorance of what most of them fully know and their current behaviours do not convince us that they have any feelings of remorse. They give us the impression that they have the right to bully, abuse and dehumanise their fellow human beings on earth. They give us the impression that we are trespassing on their property, the earth. We have right to be here to share this world with them. It is easy to define Economy as prudent management of resources without wastage. Wastage is Economic madness. It is an attempt to display wealth that we lack. It cannot be overemphasized that we all must work, get good education, acquire good skills, excellent apprenticeship and be ready to sacrifice to achieve the results of our work objectives to provide for ourselves and make contribution to the community to live in dignity and virtue without corruption and crime. It is time everybody on earth labours and toils to feed his and her people. Reliance on US sponsored NGOs to feed them is abuse of US farmers. They work long hours to produce the food for world food programme, (WFP). Sub-Saharan Africans should stop bush wars and work to feed themselves. They deserve better leadership than what they have at the moment. Their ancestors were able to feed themselves and families. The generations, today, cannot do that. They are degenerate and parasitically dependent.

It is easy to interpret my writing as anti-Western sentiment. Superficially, it looks like a tirade against the West. Far from it, it is a series of questions our Anglo-American brothers and sisters must answer to live at peace with themselves and the wider world. They must see where they have got it wrong in the world. Africa has many cowards unwilling to tell our friends and neighbours in Western Atlantic that they had got it wrong several times and hurt most people in the world. This millennium is not for that old bravado culture. It is neither acceptable way of life nor a mark of civilisation. Times have changed but the Anglo-American axis still wants reason to justify its armament. Why not use the money and the resources to improve the plight of tormented human beings on earth? Constructive and not destructive trade is what the world in crisis of uneven development, paucity of wealth distribution, poverty, starvation, hunger, malnutrition and diseases wants. Constructive trade provides more jobs than war and violence. A rude BBC Hard talk interviewer tormented crony and timid African leader. He bullied and cowed the leader. This was not an interview. It was a sort of repudiation for failing to do what the UK wanted him to do. Adverse events that would subject Africa to unending colonial and imperial tutelage were praised as rescue for Africa. It amazed me that several white petty journalists still moan for lost British Empire. They display wrong concept of patriotic zeal and loyalty to past exploiting lost brutal empire. They are longing for the return of ruthless pillaging, looting and impoverishing brutal colonial rules in Africa. They are hostile to any indigenous decisions. How on earth would these deride Robert Mugabe and expect South Africa and other Africans to castigate him? Have they forgotten Ian Smith in former Southern Rhodesia and South African Apartheid regime? How short are our memories of events in History?

Imperial powers have no sympathy for Africa. They fail to realize that they had fatally wounded and hurt us. They interfered with and suspended our progress and development in the world for several centuries. They battered our economy and frequently sabotaged the same under unjustified open and concealed sanctions. They swaggered away abandoning us in crises and chaos and genocide as in Rwanda due to abnormal border resulting from dismemberment of Africa 15th Sept 1884 in Berlin. They walked away without re-integration of dismembered Africa before independence; just to put it back the way they saw it before 15th September, 1884. They knew that without re-integration of colonial dismembered Africa independence would be a colossal failure. Any path disadvantageous to us is the one they push us into to perish to satisfy their desire to see us fail.

They want white farmers to own and farm fertile lands in Zimbabwe. Why not help black people to own and farm the land of their ancestors, their land? It is obvious Education, today, what the depressed areas of the world want. Good skills for most parts of the world would improve their lot. It would improve their basic food production and nutrition. This is what the world needs. The body needs food. The first human activity on earth involved food. They were hunters and food gatherers initially, later farmers and livestock keepers and finally settlers. This shows the place of food in human life. Therefore everybody should be able to grow enough food on his land to feed himself. Sadly, generations of Africans in recent times had been too parasitically dependent on outside help to do so. A handful of white farmers using African labour on peanut salaries could farm the land to produce enough to feed the whole Zimbabwe and export food. The whole Zimbabwe cannot produce enough to feed itself. Global black people are behind President Mugabe. Let them die. Let hunger teach them self reliance. Freedom demands people to look after themselves and their needs.

When the world is able to produce enough food to feed itself and is certain of reliable source of food supply, it can then start to look for other sources of minimum essential comforts.

The world needs reliable accommodation, good road and railway communication network. This will engage Western Technological know how. It will preserve friendship and more Western jobs than war and violence. Africa has been excluded from global Economic Activities for several centuries. Its rich mineral resources have been fragmented to be exploited by private individuals, freelance alien fortune seekers (gold diggers) and recently ignorant illiterate leaders of African Bantustans. This has been convenient for Western Europe and past colonial masters. Their transnational corporate conglomerates like the Belgian de Biers, mine them for their shareholders in Western Europe. The Bantustans are small and economically weak or non-existent. They have no good Education, no skills training, neither capital nor good communication network to be able to participate in exploiting the mineral resources. The past colonial masters had mischievously walked away at independence abandoning Africa without re-integrating Africa they dismembered on 15th Sept, 1884 in Berlin Germany. They even re-integrated Germany divided by brutal war. They left Africa so that it may never become a viable country again to be able to take charge of its resources to use to open up the continent to the outside world for trade and development of its Economy and the land. A viable strong and united Africa is not what they would tolerate. Africans themselves have no good Education and skills. The bulk of them are illiterates and ignorant of what is good for them.

Africa is in the South of Western Atlantic. It has shared the Atlantic and the Mediterranean with the West for a long time. The belligerent Western culture can no longer be approved as efforts to defend freedom. It is open hostility towards freedom of other people the West wants to bully, intimidate and subjugate and continue to pillage their resources. Unless the West is fighting for freedom to pillage resources from alien lands, it cannot say it is not free and its way of life is under threat. This is totally unacceptable. Regardless of all fabrications and spin Western freedom is not under threat. The principle of first strike of weak poor third world country is desperate attempt to find soft spot to re-start empire building. The world is not in mood to tolerate the expensive project of empire building. Africa must get its acts together. It must ignore and disregard the fears raised by past colonial masters and the European Union (EU) that are reaping very rich rewards from their own Union, over re-integration of Africa they dismembered in 1884. Africa must form Union of African States (UAS).

The States spoken about must be viable States that will evolve from re-integrated Africa from the Africa that the European colonisers dismembered in Berlin, Germany on the 15th Sept, 1884. It is not the current unviable arid Bantustans. Our salvation lies on re-integration and formation of the UAS and pooling our earnings from our mineral resources together to raise some capital to open Africa up by good road network and rail network to allow free movement within the continent and out of the continent. This will allow the development of trade. It will also create jobs and employment. If small Arabs States are able to achieve so much from their oil why should Africa not succeed? Uniting Africa is a necessity of the features of our land. We have two massive deserts and extensive savannah. Economic viability of Africa depends on Union to unite its fertile land and its water resources, the savannah and the desert.

It is time to declare the two camps in the debate on "RE-INTEGRATION OF COLONIAL DISMEMBERED AFRICA,"

1. AAGAINST:
   (a) The corrupt illiterate and ignorant present African leaders solely out of ignorance and selfishness.
   (b) The former colonial masters led by Britain and France and the European Union all defending their vested interest in reaping rich reward from a weak and powerless Africa.
2. THE PROS: PEOPLE ADVOCATING FOR RE-INTEGRATION OF COLONIAL DISMEMBERED AFRICA:
   (a) Educated and intellectually enlightened Patriots.
   (b) Africans in the Diaspora. They know that a viable Motherland is a United Africa able to control its resources to use in developing and opening up Africa to the world. They also know that at present it is foreigners and corrupt African leaders who are pillaging these resources while Africa remains a dark continent. (Joseph Conrad)
   (c) The genuine Pan-Africanists. They know that a truly independent Africa is a United Africa.

What about the ordinary people in Africa? Several Africans are uneducated but they are quick to absorb what will benefit Africa if it is honestly explained to them. They will support a United Africa. How do we go about to achieve our objectives? The Pros and against must get their gunpowder dry. They must acquire resources for daredevil global campaign. A reformed United Nations but not current Western Quango must organise the campaign. The referendum votes for two things:

Homogeneous Groups like the Yorubas, the Hausas, the Swahili speaking groups who should stay together and those who want to join them to form their countries. The minor groups who would like to join together to form their own country but they must be close to each other. They must have a secular constitution that recognises every citizen as equals in security and safety and in opportunities. No monopoly of capable leadership.

Then the United Africa or Union of these new African States (UAS) proper is voted. This is the picture of a viable continent of Africa rescued from the ruins we see, today. This is the vision and the desire of all global Africans. My failing health will deny me opportunity of seeing this in my life time. It is a guarantee for future security of our children and our land, Africa.

The Western leaders are blaming their soldiers for hostilities of this senseless war and its fatigue. It is the conduct of Anglo-American leaders that is to blame. They, the leaders must have the courage to tell the truth. It is their action and lack of foresight that is to blame. They sent the soldiers there to torture and kill the Iraqi people. To blame and put down a dog trained to bite strangers is not a right judgement. When the Anglo-American leaders rushed to attack Iraq under all disguises, falsehood and fabrications, it was obvious that they would soon become the terrorists while the Iraqis would be their victims. The military aggression against Iraq and illegal occupation of that country were all acts of terrorism. It is not only a rogue state that commits acts of terrorism but a superpower involved in war of bullying, intimidation and illegal occupation of a third world country is equally guilty of terrorism by killing innocent citizens and damaging their properties. The Iraqi people are fighting resistance war against invaders and occupiers of their land. The French did it in the last world war. Most European countries also fought resistance war but not terrorist war against Germany. They were patriots and not insurgents. Justice demands that the guilty should be pronounced guilty regardless of how powerful he may be. Yes he can hurt but cowardice should not suppress the truth. The Anglo-American alliance is the aggressor. Iraqis are victims of brutal aggression.

This war is still raging in spite of the fact that Anglo-American terrorist fighters murdered Saddam Hussein's sons without arresting them for a fair trial under the rule of law and now they have their father in their illegal dungeon. All the reasons given for this unprovoked war had come to pass without the war ending. It is now obvious that all those reasons were completely false. The Anglo-American leaders lied to the world and their people. Can they do the decent thing now and leave Iraq and pay them indemnities to repair the damage they had inflicted on the country and people? This will give the Anglo-American aggressors the credit as democrats and freedom lovers and respecters for the rule of law. Short of this they will leave Iraq as gamblers without any respect for democracy, freedom and the rule of law. They have no support from genuine Iraqis except from a few political renegades and gamblers. History will not pardon Anglo-American divide and rule for fragmenting Iraq into hostile loyalty camps, the Shiites, Sunnis and the Kurds and demoting a middle grade country to a third world country. They did this to weaken its resistance. They wanted to seize Iraqi energy resources.

Political gamblers subvert democracy, freedom and the rule of law. It is only criminal traitors that betray their fatherland to foreigners for conquest. It is sad that the Anglo-American leaders had killed Saddam Hussein by proxy pre-meditated murder. Their hands are dripping with blood of those they had slaughtered in this war of greed, hatred, jealousy and envy and arrogant abuse and display of power. Chalabi is a known criminal conman who does not mind what he sells to make money. This may be his homeland, Iraq or false information about his country that he knows nothing about, to foreign Intelligence agencies to provoke war, violence and total destruction of his homeland that he cares nothing about as long as he gains his personal ambitions. The Iraqi National Congress is a false stamp and a false promissory note printed in the US to justify this oil and gas energy-theft war in Iraq. Is it any surprise that the US has now fallen out with their great and useful asset, a well-known gambler and a perfect liar just as the West? They are corrupt criminals.

The Anglo-American politicians sent out this formidable war machine to hunt down and eliminate terrorists. Unfortunately, the Anglo-American politicians and the personnel manning their formidable and deadly war machine are fast becoming terrorists. Soldiers on expeditionary military aggression to subdue foreign lands and their people to seize their resources as loots are mercenary terrorists and outlaws. They break the law to fight an unjust and illegal war to seize foreign lands and their resources under false pretences. Oil and gas war has been dubbed "war against terrorists." The metamorphosis of names and reasons for war in Iraq has no comparison in history of sanity. It went through war to dismantle the weapons of mass destruction (WMD) now dubbed weapons of mass deception or fabrication.

Now it is campaign to remove Saddam Hussein from power. Now Saddam Hussein is done with and gone. At present it is life and death struggle to find a safe home and base for US Army in the Middle East, the lifeline of Western Economy for energy supply. I am not fond of anybody or any group in this conflict. It is the smart action of the combatants that has baffled me and landed us here. This is a conflict of land grabbers. The Arabs grabbed the whole of North Africa and the Mediterranean seaboard and Palestine when they had power and means to do so a long time ago. They were ruthless in the Arab Muslim Islamic Conquest of Palestine and North Africa. Now some other people are stronger than the Arabs. They are now doing the same thing that the Arabs had been doing to others over the years but two wrongs cannot make a right. The Arabs should recall the Arab Conquest of these lands. But this time the Arabs are victims of Anglo-American tyranny of greed. They deserve world sympathy.

They should be humble to accept the changing times. They are no more the conquerors but victims of their previous war of land grabbing and conquest. Palestine existed before that conquest. The Jews lived and owned that land. Humility and magnanimity are not beyond what the Arabs require in the stalemate in the Arab-Israeli conflict and crises. They should please spend sometime to review scattered Jewish History as they travelled round the world from AD 642 to the holocaust. The Jews before that time also had horrid times as captives in Babylon (Iraq) and Persia (Iran). Of course religious myth ascribes this to Deital punishment for their sins. When knowledge was not as advanced and deep as now every bad thing including diseases and illness was punishment from the Deity. But the problem of the Jews (Israel) has been the magnetic attraction to its location by all nations and people on earth. Being a home to three powerful and popular global religions has not helped either. It has reduced Israel to focus of tension. The Jews (Hebrews) had a raw deal in Europe. They suffered from lynching, persecutions, and frequent confiscations of their properties, banishments and expulsions. Arab-Israeli conflict has caused suffering among the Arabs but it is not as bad and long as the Jewish travail. Yet both had suffered. Both of them deserve Peace and security now. They are victims of events dating back to their ancestors beyond their control. They live in a changed and different time. They should never think of eliminating Israel, the original owner of the land. They should accept the reality of the changing times. They must forget the past and its emotions and embrace the present. They must plan for the future. They must accept Israel as a reality. Both Israel and Arabs should be compassionate and accommodate each other. Dwelling in the past and holding unto past emotions have no wound healing power. They cannot solve the current problems. Finding reliable solution to current problems is what everybody involved in this conflict wants. Maximum humane Human compassionate compromise and sacrifice are required.

Everybody wants and deserves genuine security. Everybody wants to live in true safety without harassment and violence. All should now look forwards to the future of their children. They should feel content that they had sacrificed and invested their lifetime to secure safety and freedom for them. They should denounce war and violence and end all conflicts. Each of them must conscientiously accept the responsibility of guaranteeing peace, security and safety for one another. The concept of having a disarmed separate state is not a seasoned or a serious proposal. You cannot make peace by disarming your undefeated enemy by fiat. Israel would not accept that from the Arabs. One state solution under very strong secular Constitution and independent Judiciary equally represented by both is ideal. The House of Elders with equal representation and the Parliament must be in charge of the Army. Everybody, Arabs or Israelis must be equal before the law and must have equal opportunity. Merits and talents must count. Hard work and achievers must be rewarded. Group interest must be backed up with conscientious hard work.

The Constitution must make rioting illegal. There must be laws to control ownership of weapons and guns. Importing weapons by private groups or individual citizens must carry stiff penalty. The country or foreign merchants sending the merchandise must suffer penalty from the United Nations. The Police must be demilitarised and trained to be friendly. They must provide true security for every citizen. They must prevent corruption and crimes. They must always be a step ahead of trouble shooters and nip any plot in the bud. They must see the folly and wastage of wars and violence. It is a folly to bury their heads in emotions of religious myths. God made us to live under secular laws. He never regulated us to live under laws written in His name by ancient religious authorities. These laws are incompatible with rapidly changing times and the world and secular public societal life. God is a Deity of Peace. He wants us to live in Peace in this world. We must have the human touch and compassion to live in Peace with one another. Emotions and holding unto the past cannot rescue us from current stalemate. Love for fellow human beings and acceptance of the human nature are essential for resolving long standing conflicts. Our life time on earth is not long enough and is too inadequate to resolve all conflicts. We have to be realistic to make room for resolution of our conflicts with one another by reaching out to our foes. The challenge is for us to approach settlement of long standing feud with open mind. The Arabs must avoid the lure of using any resolution as an opportunity to continue the conflict, war and violence.

Everybody loves justice and humane and compassionate treatment of the weak. Ahab was a king and Jezebel, a queen but they had no justification for seizing Nabot's land because it was fertile and Nabot was weak and poor. This is what Anglo-American aggression against Iraq is all about. The rich and powerful has no right to seize the only asset of the poor and weak because the poor is vulnerable. The Anglo-American power had indulged in land seizure by force and genocide for centuries. It is totally unacceptable at this time. The tedious programme of empire building in this century is a costly and bloody project too expensive to contemplate upon. Colonisation is a bygone word in this generation. It is stupid of human species to refuse to use its God-given senses to learn the rules of co-existence.

If we lay our dirty hands on claims to civilisation, we must learn to live peacefully together. We have to tolerate one another. We must learn to resolve all conflicts peacefully. The money invested and wasted on war is more than enough to buy friendship and peace. Unfortunately Bush and Blair war and violence have no place in good leadership. Good leadership could have resolved most of the issues involved in this conflict by behind the scene negotiation for the safety of our innocent citizens and global business. Safety and security are no longer the objective of the West alone but the whole world needs it. Travels in the global world are a great feature of change in our own time. Air travel has virtually made the world a global village. In a global village security and safety cannot be overemphasized. War and violence cannot guarantee these. Global peace is the only guarantee for security and safety in free travels. Armed marshals are no use for security and safety. They may offer false confidence for security and safety. There is temptation to take up gun if you have it in a situation such as the Sept 11 but a hasty decision is very risky here. Any decision and action must prevent any future occurrence and guarantee security and safety for all.

The West must abandon the culture of bullying, intimidating and assaulting and pillaging foreign lands for loots under very false pretences. It must devise means of living in peace with the rest of the world. The posture of threat of use of force and aggression against those who refuse to conform to its wishes and orders is unacceptable. Hostile attitude is unfriendly. It does not command respect. Fear of Western fire power is not a safe deterrent. True security and safety for all are the rewards of friendship, respect for others without arrogance and name calling. Mutual help is cheaper and better than force and war. The world, today, is crying out for even development to enable everybody in every region to have at least one balanced meal a day, good drinking water, secure roof over his head and good communication for people to move about their businesses without fear of danger to their lives. It is wrong for the West to invest the huge amount of the resources it spends on the military. This investment is world resources. It should be used to develop the lot of all global human beings.

Rapid communications and global travels and business all need safety and security. It must be acquired peacefully but not by forceful pacification, subjugation and humiliation of others deemed weak and unable to resist naked aggression. The US has a duty to learn humility, compassion and genuine consideration for the poor, weak and ignorant. It must resist the temptation of being dragged into hopeless and avoidable war through arrogance and ignorance of its leaders. There are a lot of good and rational people in the US. Unfortunately the free democracy in the US has the loophole that can allow people like George W Bush to seize power to play Adolf Hitler or Napoleon Bonaparte. Even these two might have had in their own times reasons for fighting for gallantry and victory. Today, we are living in a different age in a changed time in a changed world. Our actions should reflect these things. We have nothing to lose by sharing the lands and their resources.

It is unwise to insist on all or nothing when it comes to issues of land where several races and ethnic nationalities live. The world had been here for millions of years before our time. People had lived, passed through and returned to various lands. It is not exactly right for people to emotionally claim permanent attachment and ownership of particular lands. But where History convincingly with certainty associates groups of people with ownership of the land and losing it by war and conquest as the Arab conquest of Palestine and North Africa in AD 642-698, the best thing is for the contestants to reconcile and seek for means to live with each other in peace and share the land for safety and security without emotions and hatred.

Human habitation had changed hands several times in the past. All or nothing theory of conflict resolution in habitation and lands would rake up the past. The past always finds that in most cases the two have claims to the lands. Usually we find that one might have driven the other out of the very land in the past as in the case of Arabs and Israelis and black Africans. The best thing is for the two to bury their pride and hatred. They must learn how to forgive each other for the suffering and the dead and several victims of the atrocities and concentrate on how the living can learn to live and accommodate each other in peace. Tolerance is not timidity in the wisdom of interethnic and inter-racial and across-the-religious divide sharing. They must learn how to share the land and life together without contemplating on how to vanquish each other for victory far beyond their reach. Only God can cause extinction of one group over the other. Unfortunately God does not do this because people hate each other. He it is that allows each group to continue breeding and procreation to populate the land. It is our duty to recognise that we have to acknowledge every person's right to live on this earth. We equally must accept to share the land together. It is equally every person's duty to keep the peace. The community has a duty to make binding acceptable secular Constitution and laws for peace.

Palestine is too small for two countries. It is the home of three main religions that teach, "Love your neighbour as yourself." Bury religious bias and prejudice. Ignore self-pride and arrogance and learn to love, live and accommodate your neighbour in peace. Let the rule of good secular law of "live and let live" written down in a binding secular constitution determine the way to maintain law and order. There is no real sense in claiming lands that had seen changes of hands several times in the past. We should allow our civilisation to take charge of our using civilised conduct and law and order to share the land without resorting to primitive and barbaric slaughter of each other for the land we shall leave behind when we die. The safety and security of the land for our progeny should be enacted in unambiguous binding secular constitution and strict observance of the rule of law. I do not know how Sharon would feel when he was a child if he were an Arab Palestinian child to be roused up by debris of their house being bulldozed down with all members of his family dead? Definitely he would not like it. He should not do it to the Arab children.

If Yahweh is a merciful God full of justice and love, He would definitely take no part with Sharon's scourge earth policy and child murder. His hands are soaked wet with Palestinian Arab blood. David was a warrior. He was not a blood thirsty beast of war and violence without morals. The Palestinian lives are as precious to God as the Israeli lives.

The burden of doing God's will lies on the shoulders of the leaders of the two groups that had taken to the way of war and violence. The Palestinians must realize and recognise that the longer the violence the bitter the anger and the more painful the hurt. Hatred and violence would eliminate neither the Jews nor the Palestinians. Victory of one over the other would bring neither peace nor land. Suppression of one group by the other, Israel knows creates a perpetual state of war, hostilities and violence. The Koran says, "Allah is merciful." That mercy is for the whole human beings but not only for Muslims. The true peace can come only from determination of the combatants in the conflict to put aside their bitterness and differences and make genuine peace protected and guaranteed by binding genuine laws capable of defending their lives and properties regardless of race or religious belief. It sounds doctrinaire and incredible but human instinct overcoming our animal rage and emotions and the desire to live can overcome any insoluble conflict.

The truth is that over the years the US got its energy needs from this source without any hindrance. Several industrialised Western countries equally acquired their energy needs from this source without war and violence. They all bought and paid for the oil and gas they got from the Middle East without this level of destruction of lives and properties by war and violence. Right now the non-members of the coalition of the willing are still buying their energy needs from the Middle East. Why then does the US need safe bases for its Army in this zone? This chameleonic posture and continuous and persistent fabrication and lies cannot justify this broad day light murderous genocidal action of the Anglo-American alliance. There must be some ulterior motive behind this mad action beyond what they give us as the reason for their mad and irrational violent action. The objective of empire building now is irreconcilable project too costly for the damages it has inflicted on global peace. The ambition of a few misguided leaders has brought us here. How do we move out of this trap? Fortunately, the finest in man comes out of tragedies and catastrophes. Right now we see that people of good conscience across the political divide are rallying up to the challenge of conscience and civic responsibilities to question the justification for the hostilities and actions of their leaders. We will have a lot to learn from the current conflict.

It would be foolish for anybody to argue that the US reason may be genuine but does it deserve the amount of intrigues, fabrications, lies, deception and above all war and extreme violence, the massive destruction in lives and properties, the deaths of children, women, elderly and disabled persons? You do not need to be a genius or President of America or Prime Minister of Britain to know that it is not worth it. It is immoral. The Arabs are not going to drink the oil. The US has enough money to buy the oil. They do not have to fight for it. Nobody should die for US energy needs. Equally no religion has direct injunction to fight war for its deity or die as a martyr for the same. Those who shed blood for religion are violating God's law. No deity accepts war and violence. Most religions bless adherents with "Peace be with you always". God is peace and truth. The Anglo-American alliance must not compare the Arabs to the post world war two Japan. Diversity of culture makes the comparison and assumption far-fetched.

There are photos of Anglo-American soldiers torturing helpless Iraqi prisoners. This war has been based on repeated denial and accusations. The world has come to recognise one thing that the powerful Anglo-American establishment can lie persistently to destroy the world to get their way. It is regrettable to note that with all the power and resources at their disposal they continue to lie. They lie to themselves. They lie to their citizens. They lie to their soldiers. They lie to the world. They continue to lie their way through crimes. They live by intrigues and deceits. This is not the path to democracy and freedom. The rate of slaughters and atrocities by this Anglo-American war machine has far outstripped whatever Saddam Hussein did to his people. He would gain a gold or platinum medal if he slaughtered and murdered his people at this rate. Most Iraqi people confess that they did not have to undergo what they are now enduring in American hands under Saddam. It is not the Anglo-American power that is in doubt. It is their credibility that is damaged by their persistent spin and lies. People who went out with a banner of civilisation and Democracy are now behaving as savages and terrorists.

Why do the leaders involved in this unholy war not do a single honourable thing and come out and apologise to the world, the Iraqi people and their own people for lying and deceiving them to involve them in avoidable war and damage to their reputation? The Abu Ghrain Prison need not be pulled down. Could you imagine what the world would miss, if the London Tower Bridge Prison had been destroyed? We need this as a future Tourist attraction in Iraq and the Middle East. This famous torture Chamber, to me should be made a world heritage. Attempt to destroy this Anglo-American torture chamber in Iraq is a revelation guilty conscious of the leaders of this war. They have nothing to fear or feel guilty about.

It is their credibility and real intention that are in doubt. They had fed us all with dubicity (dubium, dubiousness, see dubiety) and so many lies that we cannot believe what they tell us any longer. They raised up and supported in the past the people they now condemn and take out several innocent lives in their pursuit of these very people. The dog trained to bite will always bite. Putting down that dog for biting is just unfair. The Anglo-American alliance in the past had been guilty of all the crimes they condemn the people they engaged to execute them for them. Why should genuine people rise up in condemnation of these very people who acted under their influence and authority? I have just alluded to Anglo-American cruelties to the African Negroes. They dehumanised and abused them as beasts of burden. They slaughtered and murdered them at will.

They persistently deny the atrocities in spite of all the abundant evidence in the British Museum and all over the West including our Obelisk in London and Washington. The West seems to have brains impervious to the truth and guilty conscience but impregnated with lies, deceits and denials. They have no memory for their wrong doings. The Anglo-American leaders mobilised their war machines to take democracy and civilised conduct to Iraq and the Middle East. They were to defend their ways of life. If what we see in pictures on Television in Abu Ghraib Prison, Guantanamo Bay in Cuba and Kandahar International Airport in Afghanistan, are what they went out to deliver and defend, it is worth asking the question. "Are these barbaric conducts worth defending?" The worst terrorists are well armed barbarians and mob. It is not worth condemning anybody. It is just right to ask the Anglo-American leaders to examine their consciences and stop feigned emotions but come out with the truth on who now genuinely qualifies to be called terrorists? The Anglo-American Armies went out to chase terrorists but they are now the worst terrorists and killers. This is not civilised conduct in democracy. The Arabs have a lot to learn from one another. They must learn not to hire the most formidable and powerful Armies to fight their wars. They essentially must learn to live in peace with each other. They must live in Peace with their neighbours. They must accept religious tolerance. Religious tolerance is vital for the Economy, commerce and trade in Globalisation. Arab intrigues and fabrications equally stand condemned. Their willy-nilly business dealing no longer has a place in today's world.

Unfortunately, the English whose ancestors committed the most heinous crimes and atrocities in the world to acquire wealth hate anybody who mentions or claims to know their past. The Anglo-American Alliance and the West are not very wise to form the NATO to use in intimidating the world to suppress any mention of their past atrocities. The blood of those they had slaughtered all over History is sufficient to float the largest liner in the world. Let them pray to the creator (God) for forgiveness. Resorting to intimidation and punishment of those who mention their past savage atrocities to their hearing is no solution to their horrible past. Why should they worry if they know that they and their ancestors did the right thing? When they talk of war as Olympic Games they must remember that they killed several people and destroyed many properties to win victory. The most important thing is for them to examine their conscience if they would approve and accept the atrocities they had inflicted on everybody in the world.

What I can now say as an African and I believe I am speaking for all genuine Africans and equally the whole world the West has traumatised the whole world to gain wealth and power. The West was awake while the world was sleeping. It went about rampaging and pillaging the whole world. The world is no longer asleep except people in Africa still in deep slumber. The West should not assume the mantle of purity. They are impure as most other human beings. We all are at the same learning curve. Western atrocities are totally unacceptable to the world as all other atrocities. The Western hands are soaked in blood of their innocent victims. The massive destructions of lives and properties at the altar of consumer-materialism may be acceptable way of life and civilisation to the West but decent men and women, the world over reject them. This is Western god. It is their way of life. Are they sure that the world accepts this destructive way of life? We should now learn from each other. The safest thing is for everybody to live within the rule of binding laws. The West talks about democracy. It behaves undemocratically and acts in violation of basic fundamental human rights totally outside the law. They lie to gain credibility while everybody now knows that they are liars.

They give doubtful value to democracy, freedom and the rule of law. The West is doubly guilty of what they accuse other people of. They are quick to accuse others of the very crimes they are guilty of. They have no moral justification to level accusation on other people. They are always smart to accuse the victims of their crimes of the same crimes. It is Western tactics and strategy we, all now know. Unfortunately it is their very credibility that they have damaged irretrievably. It was easy to lie and deceive strangers when we did not know ourselves well. Now we know each other very well. Intrigues and deceits can no longer work. We have to bring some decency into the way we do business and improve our business conduct radically. Ill-treating and murdering strangers you deem too weak to harm you to pillage their resources is not gallantry or a show of your power and strength. It is cowardly criminal act. It is a savage brigandry. The bully is a coward. The resource pillaging alien aggressor is a criminal rogue.

The conclusion here is that from all our observations, past and present experiences we all are at a learning curve, how we should live with each other in this world. We have a lot to learn from one another. We should share our knowledge. Human life on earth needs two vital things: Education for genuine knowledge of our world both good and bad things in it and skills to work our land and live comfortably in it. It is the skills and labour with our hands that will create our long desired wealth and prosperity. It is the genuine knowledge of our land and its full potentials and the world that we share with other races of human beings and other living things that will give us full comprehension of the world and the good and evil in it. Having genuine knowledge to understand the world and living things in it is vital for us to appreciate our weaknesses as living things and human beings. We are fallible and mortal human beings. We should strive to do good in this life. Watching wildlife had taught me many things about other living things on earth. They have their families. They look after and teach their young. They also live in relative peace with their neighbours. War should if at all be the last resort but in the current conflict war seemed to have been the first resort. History would remember Bush and Blair (BB) as trigger happy leaders. They were completely tactless in handling emergency and crisis. War closes the door to security and safety.

Having the skills to work our land consumes our time and takes us away from idleness and mischief. We must accept the doctrine of co-existence and tolerance as the key to world peace. The West must know that the world cannot settle all its problems by war and violence. Education and genuine skills training are the tools we need to rehabilitate humanity on earth and make our existence here eco-friendly. We are all here by right. That right is direct from God our creator. We have to share the earth and its resources that God gave to us free. Each of us regardless of status has the right to be here. Each of us has the responsibility to acquire some appropriate Education and genuine skills training to labour on the land to achieve his heart desires in wealth and prosperity. The right to genuine Education and creative skills training is the same as the right to be here on earth and share it with other living things in it. It is, therefore, our responsibility to acquire genuine Education and creative skills training. We all on earth should share genuine Education and creative skills training. It is our collective responsibility to make the earth user-friendly and eco-friendly. The right to excellent genuine practical Education and skills training with active apprenticeship training should now be regarded as the right of man. Every Government and national leaders should make their Educational policy compulsory. They must devise means of public funding of Education. It may be a special Education Tax per head is worth thinking about. Everybody male and female from the age of eighteen years should pay the flat rate until the age of sixty. It is sad that the British Commission for Industries (CBI) has suggested that University students should pay tuition fees. The CBI always laments that Britain does not produce students ready for work in the Industry. Post High School University students should pay no tuition fees. The Pubic should fund their Education. Funding should depend on good performance. Course must be completed in the scheduled period. Beyond this the students pays the tuition fees. There must be arrangement for mature students in Adult Education Scheme. The same arrangement should be made for Health as in Education. Wastage must be avoided. Throwing money at these essential Public Utilities is a waste of Public Funds. No Institution should be allowed to operate on deficit. The Health Service must have drug recovery Programme. Patients not using the drugs for one reason or the other must return it to the Pharmacy. Relatives of the deceased should return the drugs. Drug return must be prompt. Any drugs the patients no longer want must be returned immediately. Patients must be warned not to mix tablets and capsules. They must leave them in their original packages.

Each one of us has that sacred responsibility to toil and labour to create wealth and prosperity to his or her heart's desire. Genuine Education for effective knowledge of the world around us is the responsibility of all responsible governments and authorities to offer every citizen. It is equally the civic duty of each citizen to acquire good education and adequate skills to contribute positively to the orderly and sustainable development of the people and their homeland. Peace gives people restful mind to think and concentrate on their work. It allows the growth of wealth. Charity must start at home. People must first learn ways of developing the land where they live to support them. They must grow enough food on their land to feed themselves, families and population. Everybody is just passing through this world. "Our end is written at our birth". Why do we pretend to own the world? It does not belong to us. Killing with 500lb incendiary bombs and rocket shells still delivers one thing, "death" the end of life. Killing with mines or roadside bomb is still "death", end of life. Why are we in a rush to kill while death will surely come to us and our foes?

It is a great challenge to Africa in a world in crisis to define its goals and objectives and vision of the world. We may wonder why Africa has been so low in the ladder of world events that it pioneered and led for several millenniums. We started with Education and delegated search for the truth and understanding. We embarked on massive skills training and apprenticeship for special skills. Then we embarked on labour to create wealth and prosperity. We exploited rich mineral and natural resources of this vast land. We then took to selfish living that flouted the rule of law and common justice. We detracted from paying the right reward for labour, goods and services. We took to cheating and defrauding our workers. We finally embraced slave labour. We cheated our fellow human beings and God. We started to dehumanise our own kind to own them as slaves and private property. We finally dehumanised the whole African Negro race and demoted ourselves to subhuman beings. Hence we Africans have a role in our demise. It is our duty to correct some mistakes we had been making all our lives. The argument goes. Our ancestors did these things. Our generations are not involved. Have we abandoned selfishness and damaging individualism? We still project individual name and fame at the expence of the community. Our leaders are still corrupt. They embezzle Public funds and deprive several millions of Africans of their shares of the money. Our ancestors did these. Hence we are not different. We have not changed but the world had changed and left us behind. The aeroplane is a hundred years old. Our independence from colonial rule is fifty years old. Aeroplane was about fifty years by then. What efforts have we made to establish our basic Industrial Base? How many Africans can repair a plane?

Our Bantu divisive culture of disunity must abandon selfish and greedy individualism and adopt group and community culture of being our brother's keeper. Globalisation uses cosmopolitan towns and cities to settle peoples of diverse backgrounds and cultures. To get on and succeed we essentially must adopt community spirit. We are part of the community in providing the infrastructures for recreation. We form teams that participate in the exercises, games and athletics of the community. We work and desire success for the community. The scandal of Sub-Saharan Africans to re-integrate their colonial dismembered Africa at independence is still haunting us as people who do not know where their interest lies. We are ignorant of our community interest. Bantu individualism is incompatible with the rough terrain where we live in Africa. Does this mean that we lack the ability to build and expand a community? We have to re-integrate dismembered Africa in our Economic interest. In a world where most people are attempting to integrate, Africa cannot win without total re-integration. EU is virtually ruling Europe. The same EU is using bogus scare tactics to frighten Africans off re-integration of colonial-dismembered Africa. They benefit from Disunity in Africa. Africans and their corrupt leaders need courage to learn from the Europeans the benefits of Unity. In the presence of EU in the global village the only Independent Africa with Authority is a re-integrated United Africa (UAS).

By the time the foreign invaders arrived at our doorstep we were too divided and weak to offer any effective resistance. The greatest damage to any group of human beings is tyranny of the leadership and the divisive tendency that delights in disasters, tragedies, and catastrophes affecting the sections of the community they hate. This destroys the ability of the people to defend their land from alien intruders and invaders. Africa is a land of traitors and very disloyal citizens because of divisive behaviours of the citizens and the tyranny of greed and selfishness of its leaders. The Africans saw nothing wrong with slave trade and slavery by the time Europeans were campaigning for abolition. Today Africans see nothing wrong with corruption and poor leadership.

Some us then placed ourselves above others and pretended immortality to be equal to the gods of our imagination. We then embarked on creating places of solace in the immortality of the after life. We took to violence and intimidation and extortion of wealth from the weak and frail. We neglected our culture of searching for the truth and training for skills. We made our fellow human beings created in the image of God have monetary value. We had several women, concubines for our pleasure. We adopted the licentious pleasures of the Hittites (Turks) and the Persians. We lost our tract in life. We lost continuous Education and regular creative skills training. Our reserves and barns grew thin and empty. Africa lost tract of growth and progress. We became condemned to antiquity. We became the objects of ridicule bullying, intimidation, humiliation and dehumanisation because we fail to keep the simplest African basic law of humanity. We lack dignity and respect for life and property of our fellow Africans. This takes dignity and respect out of our lives. Humiliating and dehumanising our fellow black people equally humiliates and dehumanises us. We have no respect for ourselves. Nobody takes us seriously as we are not serious in life. Sub-Saharan Africa is populated by Bantus. Bantus are described as people of several languages. No wonder why this has more mini-ethnic groups than most regions of the world. The ethnic groups are disunited. They have no loyalty for Africa. The word, "Patriotism" has no meaning to them. But they have to unite for survival. They have to sacrifice and unite to form Africa. They must be loyal to African Flag. They must demonstrate self-respect by civic Patriotic Duties. The African Bantus are not above self-respect. They must not do things that show them as irrational people incapable of planning and choosing their priorities rather than people acting by the flash of the pan. Stealing public funds and laundering them in safe Banking havens abroad while asking for debt pardon and alms shows that you have no confidence in the safety of investment in your country, and that you are a dishonest person. You are behaving as a gypsy and dishonest person. If you cannot invest in your country why should foreign investors invest there? The stock of uncompleted projects represented by large signboards confirms that you cannot plan and manage your Economy.

All human beings deserve by right humane human treatment without subjugation and subjection to torture, torment and humiliation. We are all subject to the rule of law. Each person deserves a place under the sun that gives life to all. This was the basic concept of the worship of the sun-god, Osiris Ammon Ore, Mel kart, Baal hakim and Astarte, the great mother of the creation. God is inclusive and not exclusive. African festivals included all together with strangers in our midst. This is the same way King Solomon prayed for all foreigners who came to the Temple at Jerusalem and asked God to grant them their requests. Today, the Jews would despise black Africans but surprisingly we have more in common than modern History would like to accept. Our modes of worships and beliefs were close and tolerant of one another. We even shared Judaism together until Islam came to force people with threat of pains of death and torture to switch to Islam and swept away indigenous faiths. Hiram was the architect of Solomon's Temple modelled along the structures of the Temples of the sun-god in Egypt. David arranged this with King Hiram, his friend and confidant. Solomon gave Hiram infertile land for the reward but the friendship continued uninhibited even though Hiram was not very impressed by the reward Solomon gave him. There was genuine bond of friendship despite the previous chaotic push into the land by Israel. The Biblical story says that Israel had a difficult time in Egypt but they learnt a lot in Egypt. The Ancient leaders practised Religious tolerance. The sources of information on problems the Jews in Egypt had were the books of faiths, the Torah and the Bible. No reliable secular History offers tentative information on this.

Global crisis:

It is no exaggeration the world is in crisis. It is in crisis of environmental pollution and contamination with toxic chemicals and risk of global warming with emission of carbonaceous greenhouse gases. It is in crisis in wealth distribution and scramble for control of scarce resources. The world is in crisis in disparity of wealth distribution and welfare facilities. One section of the world is in abundance of wealth and food. Some of its citizens suffer from overfeeding and over-nutrition, obesity and its associated diseases. They invest a lot of money to produce drugs and facilities for treating these self-inflicted scourges of man. The rest of the world is in dire poverty and ignorance. They all have land but lack the right type of Education and effective creative skills training to develop their land and resources to create the wealth that they require for their orderly and sustainable development and the manufacture of goods that they consume. These problems had left them all in abject poverty and grinding ignorance.

They suffer from disparity of wealth distribution within and without. They suffer from starvation, under nutrition and malnutrition and all their associated diseases. They lack both the drugs and the facilities for treating the diseases. The world is in deep crisis of wealth distribution. We are in crisis of lacking leaders with understanding of the problems confronting the world. The leaders seem to live in the past ignoring the present and strive to repeat the acts of gallantry of the past leaders to guarantee themselves positions in history. They place themselves above human fallibility. They ignore the fact that they are leaders in a different age, at a different time. They ignore the fact that time had changed and they all are living in a changing time requiring different solutions and approach to problems.

In Africa, most leaders give the impression that they owe their positions to past colonial masters and powerful Western nations and their leaders. Once they are able to keep these people sweet, they owe no duty to their people. This has led to abuse of office by the leadership and negligence of duty of governing. The citizens lack education and skills. The leaders have no serious Education plans for their youths. They blame others and not themselves for their fate. Unfortunately, the West freely selects its leaders without any interference or contribution from the world and its people that some Western leaders come to regard as their legitimate subjects. African leaders should demonstrate that they are capable of uniting to lead Africa. They must show that they love Africa and are loyal to Africa by their actions and behaviours. They are the face of Africa. They must show some self-respect to demonstrate to the world that responsible and respectable people lead Africa. Unfortunately misbehaviours of African leaders, today, make the world not take Africa seriously. They shame Africa. They make the world treat Africa with levity and Africans as people without direction and purpose in life.

The Western leaders should not regard Africa and poor nations of the world as their extended borders. They pretend to speak for them. Yet they do not know their problems. Their assumption comes from lost past colonial heritage. They tend to forget that they no longer have overseas territories. They act out of delusion of grandeur. Their current war against terrorists is a show of strength and a warning to the poor and weak. It is frank use of force to intimidate the poor and weak countries. They just do not know the conditions under which most of these their victims are living. They do not know where they live except by looking at the map. They do not know what they eat as food and how many times a day they and their children eat and what type of water they drink and where they draw that water from. They do not know in what type of environment they live in yet they claim to have control over them just because they have the military machine to subdue and pacify them. They claim that they are defending their way of life and civilisation. They fail to accept that these people may be poor but they also have a way of life and civilisation to defend. They claim that they are transporting democracy to the people without asking the people if they would accept it. They fail to consider their religion, faith and culture. They want to impose everything from the top with superior firepower. These leaders may be good for their various homelands but they must have the understanding to recognise that their homelands are not the foreign lands they invade and occupy.

The world is not in mood for that costly project of empire building and colonial rule. The resistant fighters in France were not terrorists but patriotic defenders of their homeland. The Arab gallant fighters are not terrorists but courageous defenders of their homeland, Iraq. What is good for the gander is also good for the goose. Anybody whose homeland is invaded and occupied by aliens has the right to offer resistance. They are rejecting alien rule in their homeland. Definitely they are not insurgents. Anglo-American occupation forces have no right to be there. Factually, every generation of Anglo-Americans had resisted alien boots trotting their streets. They fight them at sea, on their beaches, land, and in the air. They resist alien invaders and occupiers. They would never speak to them. Britain frowned at French Administration that accepted co-operation with German occupiers. They supported French resistance fighters. Therefore, name calling and abuse of resistant fighters in any occupied countries are absolutely wrong. They are heroes of their nations. They are courageous warriors. War is destructive and bad. Victims have the right to fight back and give the bullies bloody noses. Any Governments ordering its Army into offensive action against a foreign country should give them many body bags.

The world has acquiesced to flagrant violation of democratic principles. It is government by the people for the people. Unfortunately there are so many forms of democracy. It is, however, not government by superpower for the lesser folks. The West started foreign military expeditions from Alexander, son of King Philip of Macedonia. It was followed later by the Romans. Scipio Cornelius Publius invaded Africa. Later Marcus Cato instigated the invasion and extinction of Carthage by genocide in North Africa. This left that vital gate of Africa to the world outside open. Later Julius Caesar and Marcus Antonio came and made pack with Cleopatra in Egypt. This was rejected outright by the ultra-conservative right led by Octavius. This group wanted extension of the Roman Empire into Africa. They killed both Julius Caesar and Marcus Antonio by bloody conspiracy. They took home whatever they could carry back to Rome. Later the leader of the conspirators, Octavius that removed Marcus Antonio, the man who later christened himself Caesar Augustus entered Egypt by storm. This shows that Africa had become a football and a playground for Western adventurers and invaders for a long time. The most recent had been the Western European colonisers. They are traditionally bullies and molesters of the weak. They like wars and violence. Their armies fight for loots and land grabbing. They seize foreign lands to plunder and loot. These people reject integration. They chose military conquest, subjugation and tyrannical terrorising imperial rule. Egypt was made Roman Province in Africa.

They had frequently violated the peace in Africa and used its resources to fight their ethnic and global wars. They did this in their first global war and second global war. Africa is always commandeered to fight completely alien wars. Unfortunately, no coconut-headed power-drunk and corrupt African leaders or African people consider this intolerable situation as abnormal and something to think about. You frequently hear them, talk of the United Nations, a Western Quango that they abuse at will and violate and ignore its rules and regulations but yet use it to molest their opponents and rivals. This is the crisis confronting the world. The arrogance and ignorance of some Western leaders are driving the world towards a third world war. The world must have the moral courage to denounce the bullies and defend the weak. The West have neither right nor justification to overthrow a foreign government to replace it with a puppet Government to restore democracy. The West makes the already bad problems of the citizens more complex by adding their own.

The Palestinian conflict and crisis have faced intractable failure of conflict resolution because nobody has seriously considered the issues involved. Neither the Palestinians nor the Israelis have taken seriously the problems of living in a state of indefinite hostilities, war and violence. The basic thing they have to consider is that they have found themselves, today, living side by side. Whether you are Palestinian Arab or Israeli, you are neighbours and have responsibility to protect your neighbours. Therefore, since you both are the victims, it behoves all of you to talk to each other and find a compromise solution to the current stalemate. The two state formula is not a wound healing solution. My fear is that each Free

State would seize the privilege to pile up arms and prepare for war for victory by proximity of the states. The natural facilities like water are limited. They can spark of new conflict between the states in the two state formula. Equally the two state solution doubles the cost of running a small patch of land. Good persuasion to the contesting parties to examine these facts and see the use of one state as a solution. Power, authority and freedom are good; equally one state solution with reliably assured guarantee of security, safety and equal opportunities provided by a valid strong secular Constitution approved in a referendum voted by everybody from the two warring contestants in a free one man one vote is worth considering. This will provide the rare opportunity for the contending parties to police their peace, reconciliation and cessation of hostilities. It will also allow the people to reach out to make friends across the religious and cultural divide. It will also make them aware and conscious of common security and safety. Eventually they will grow to love with pride and loyalty for their homeland and nation.

The best solution to this stalemate is for both the Israelis and the Palestinian Arabs to accept the uneasy reality of their current situation that they live together in Palestine now. None of them would be able to eliminate the other. This is nevertheless unacceptable. The world would disapprove of it. They must lick their wounds and since each of them desires to continue to live on that land, both of them have a duty to resolve their differences. They should not leave it to a third party to resolve it for them. This is a form of self neglect. The burden lies on their shoulders and not on those of the third parties. The discussion of this massive destruction of lives and properties had been transformed into a talking shop blowing hot air while people are dying and properties damaged. The Palestinian Arabs and Israelis must have genuine respect for each others lives. They must respect truth and justice to induce genuine trust in each other for safety and security.

All of them want to live and not to die. They want to live in peace but not at war and violence. They want progress. Why do you not make a binding treaty declaring genuine end to war and violence and accept the principle of one State of Palestine governed by the rule of law binding on both the Arabs and the Israelis regardless of religion Judaism or Muslim Islam. They all accept Jerusalem as the home of the God. Why do they not respect the God and the Holy place they delegate to Him and accept the message of peace and goodwill and accept to live in peace with one another? The concept of starting a new religion and faith came to Mohammed from conversation he had with a Christian Monk, Beharas in AD 200 in Syria where he visited with his uncle, a businessman on a business trip and in AD 228, the Prophet established the Islamic faith. The closeness of the two faiths should not divide the people. It should promote friendship. It is clear that Mohammed loved the Christian way of life he saw in the Hermit monk, Beheras. This is why he adopted it. He finally founded the Muslim faith and established Islam Religion in AD 228.

Modern nation states are governed by strong and credible article of secular rule of law known as the constitution that must be binding on all its citizens. The judiciary must be independent and a House of Elders made of equal numbers of Palestinian Arabs and Israelis of high integrity, fearless and ready to defend the truth without any prejudice must also be established to supervise what the politicians do. Peace under the rule of genuine secular law is better than war and violence. The responsibility of supervising and keeping the peace between the Palestinian Arabs and the Israelis is theirs and not that of the third party intervention-members. The role of this article is not to apportion blame but to appeal to the inner instinct of human beings in dealing with a very nasty and objectionable situation that has to be contained. One state solution and settlement are simple to negotiate. It offers everybody equal security, access to common facilities and nobody feels cheated in the settlement. The participants settle any problems they may have as a domestic issue. They are all bound by secular Constitution and a common code of Laws. They also have a common Programme for development. There is no need to duplicate things. This reduces the cost of running the state. It also provides funds for rapid reconstruction and rehabilitation to enhance reconciliation.

No group should be favoured in land distribution. The constitution, the law, the socio-political culture and religion and societal conduct should all discourage ghetto culture. The population should be encouraged to mix. The greatest thing is avoidance of religious segregation. Mixed marriages must be allowed and written into the constitution. Islam in particular and Judaism to some degree must never be allowed to have veto over this; it is a fundamental of the right of man that must not be compromised. Neither religion nor culture should be allowed to decree on the way people choose their spouses. The way the children are brought up should not be religious choice but that of the parents. There should be no honour killing. Such is murder punishable by death in the Law and Constitution. Freedom of choice must be enshrined in the Law. Religion must be free choice and not a way of life. No religion should be imposed on anybody directly or indirectly. It must be individual choice and conviction but not by harassment. Nobody should be allowed to impose religious laws, Sharia or the Torah's Ten Commandments on the people. Religious festivals and observations should be allowed and made national holidays.

The House of Elders must have equal numbers of dignified religious leaders from both sides among other distinguished citizens from all walks of life. They must vow to defend the truth and the Constitution and the common people of the state regardless of their social, religious or ethnic background. Every citizen must sign a charter of loyalty and allegiance to the new state denouncing violence. There must be a binding treaty signed by all Arab countries that they would not support external terrorism and sabotage of the new state. Any state that violates the treaty does it at the risk of war with the Palestinian State and world sanction and exclusion as punishment.

Capital punishment may not be out of place for terrorists until things calm down. This concept sounds far-fetched but both combatants want one thing, the land of Palestine. Let them share it under the rule of secular law and well-supervised trust. The Muslims would like Sharia Law while the Orthodox Jews would prefer theocracy from the Torah but Modern world requires Secular Constitution written by constitutional expert lawyers that can be reviewed and mended from time to time and approved by the people in a free referendum. One state solution is an expression of absolute sincerity of mutual trust in total ending of hostility. It will allow sharing of common facilities and infrastructures so that nobody or group would feel cheated or favoured over the other. It will guarantee security and safety for everybody and all groups so that nobody or group feels insecure and be tempted to re-arm.

Refusing to acknowledge the truth as it is neither the monopoly of Israel nor of the Arabs. It is foolhardy and refusal to see the truth open on the table. We fail to see it because we hate it so much that we acquire temporary blindness so that we may not see what we detest. We read foolishness into great wisdom because the truth does not suit our wishes. The world is dodging its duties in failing to advise both Israel and the Arabs to stop violence and invest both their resources and energy they waste in wars, violence and destruction in preparing this land both of them love to accommodate and feed them. At the end, this may be a miraculous way that God wants to show the world that there is no room for religious intolerance and bigotry. It may be the first genuine peaceful religious co-existence and co-habitation. The Holy place of God or Allah should welcome and tolerate all religions. They all are in the service of God or Allah. Why then do we refuse to live peacefully in the house to serve the Master we all love dearly and volunteer to serve him? These powerful conservative orthodox religions must accept the truth of changes in time and lifestyles and embrace living together in peace to serve Yahweh, the one God or Allah all of them know and love. They must avoid the temptation of using religion and God to foment trouble.

Our objective should be to avoid war and violence and use the scarce resources to invest on Education and skills training. The world has enough for everybody but not enough for the greedy and selfish ones. They should not be allowed to take the world into avoidable and senseless war and violence. The world cannot make orderly and sustainable development and progress without peace. The disruption of war and violence is costly. They affect human progress and expansion of prosperity. War destroys lives and the very things that we want and fight for. War and violence are no solution to our misery. It is a shame that the world has failed to follow the example of the Europeans. They have decided to talk their problems over instead of resorting to war, violence and hostilities. This stands to be applauded. Unfortunately, the West is now embarking on exporting war and conflicts to foreign lands to maintain their armament manufacture and sales to save jobs and their terror charge. This is what we should resist by ensuring that we make peace and talk our problems over instead of resorting to open hostilities, war and violence. The cold war is over. There must be a new reason to justify armament. It is war against terrorism.

Africa is a strange case. They seemed to have completely neglected the defence of their homeland. This seemed to have been the period of decline and Dark Age in Africa. It appears everybody was conscious of individual survival rather than Public defence and security. The Persians overwhelmed Egypt and made a dependency. Ever since, Africa had not been able to free itself from dependency. It seems unable to manage its own affairs. It lacks credible leadership. It waits for a new overlord when it loses one. It tolerates being ill-treated, humiliated, subjugated and enslaved. It is this mean and meek behaviour that has belittled Africa. They give the world the impression that they cannot think for themselves and appreciate freedom and evolve as united people with a purpose in life. Each African wants to go it alone but the world moves in groups. Africans must learn to unite and go in their group. Security and safety are acquired in groups. Defence is best in a united group. Re-integration of colonial dismembered Africa is best for interest of Africa. Those that oppose it are ignorant of what is excellent for Africa and how the global community works. People move in united teams for safety and security. Africa in its current form, cannot provide security for Africans and global black people while a smaller Europe can protect its people. This has resulted in individualism and failure of Africans to work in united teams. Failure to work in united teams and leaderlessness make Africa irrelevant. Usurpers of leadership in Africa are floating about the world while Africa is virtually excluded from all global activities. Colonial dismembered Africa as at now is confused, directionless and completely irrelevant in this global world. The global trade, today, is container ship borne. The containers carrying the real global goods call at ports in all continents except Africa. The container routes exclude Africa. The ships calling at African ports are totally outside the core global goods trade.

Complete aliens took control of our land. We offered no resistance. Alexander, son of Philip, King of Macedonia encountered no resistance when he entered Egypt. Egypt was already the slave and property of the Persians that Alexander routed in the battle fields. We were already too weak and intoxicated with intrigues and feuds. We lacked cohesive rallying point for the defence of our land and interest. By the time the Romans came to our land selfish, private and individual interest had taken over and Massinissa and off-spring of the Royal household of Ancient Libya was a spy and a traitor betraying Africa and his homeland and the seat of his ancestors to Scipio Cornelius Publius, the Roman General that drove Africans out of Spain and Europe and entered Africa. This shows the status of Africa at this time of World History. Any slave seizes the opportunity of a cruel master coming to harm to escape. Africa (Egypt) was too weak and complacent to revolt against Persia and resist Alexander. Even the Arabs in Gaza did this heroically though they were finally routed by Alexander' Army.

Can you imagine a royal blood betraying and sailing his throne to aliens because he disagreed with the royal council because of his unroyal behaviour? Massinissa badly desired Saphonisa for his bride but he was unsuitable suitor. The Romans promised him that they would help him to get Saphonisa provided he betrayed Africa to them. He loved a woman more than Africa. This is Africa where the leaders are traitors spying on our land for foreigners. They are called assets. It is treason to betray and sell your homeland and people to aliens to get what you cannot get from them by honest service and merit. This is criminal corruption, betrayal and disloyal.

Even at the decay of the evil Roman Empire, Africa was hopelessly frail and dependent but there was no alien power to depend on. Hence by the time Arabs from Gaza came for Arab Conquest there were nobody to defend the homeland. Later the fond loving Ottoman's Turks came for Muslim Islam conquest, Africa was neither at peace with God nor with itself. The Arabs had previously seized the whole of North Africa, our vital outlet to the world at the Mediterranean seaboard and link with Asia and Europe. The problem of Sub-Saharan Bantu African people is that every one of them works for his individual personal interest and security but not for that of the community. Look at the nature of the feeble Businesses the black African people have. There is no corporate Business. They have no sense of corporate Business even if they were educated in the Harvard Business School. Black people will have to abandon individualism to adopt corporate culture and community spirit in order to get along with others. It is astonishing that Africans tolerate the massive corruption in their leaders but they are intolerant of very small margins their business partners may make. This hinders their acceptance of corporate business. It encourages "Go it alone". Unfortunately this is unsuitable for the age of pan-national, globalisation and transnational corporations.

It buckled and went into deep recession and decline. When the Europeans from the West arrived it was a fertile ground for criminal and corrupt practices. Slave trade took off with full swing. It was a land of decadent people. The wild Europeans called them savages. Each of them concocted horribly frightening stories to frighten others off Africa for them alone to continue pillaging the continent south of the Sahara. Africa became a land nobody cared to defend its interests or borders. Today we lack vision of our world and its future. We are totally overwhelmed by poverty, ignorance and diseases. Why are we in this position? We lack the sense of direction. An educated, skilled, progressive community with selfless leaders is lacking.

Individualism has been enthroned as a carbuncle that damages everything.

We developed split personality. Our souls, spirits, hearts and minds, desired the world and its wealth. Our physical bodies and beings loathed toil and labour to create the wealth and prosperity our psyche very badly needs. Our psychosomatic existence fail to catch failed to catch up with others. We forget God's injunction that by our labour, toil and sweat shall we eat. We are at that critical point to re-examine our priorities. We inherited this land at the centre of the world from God. We have binding treaty with God to keep this land as centre for the spread of Education and skills training and to keep his laws. We owe it to our spirits, soul, hearts and minds to live within the rule of law. We must do unto others what we expect from them. The ten commandments of Moses are basic African laws he studied and knew them by heart. We must merge our split image together. We must get our spirit, soul, heart, and mind merged and united with the physical body to make it labour and toil with sweat to create the desires of our psyche. It is the psychosomatic labour and toil with sweat that will enable us to confront the challenges we now face in life in this world. Merger and union to form that critical mass we require for our progress what we need. We must swallow our pride and merge and unite together to form that critical mass effective for survival in the world today.

We must learn from our past mistakes. We cannot build world peace around fragile alliances created by intrigues and corruption. The West from the Romans on had been persistently guilty of this. It may even date back to the Greeks but the Greeks were disciplined Europeans. They were liberal thinkers but were subject to the rule of law. They were not opportunists as the Romans. The Romans were totally lawless opportunists. They developed a crack military machine that was ruthless. The rules of engagement were totally ignored and flouted. These were the long established ancient military laws. The Roman Army had three divisions, the fighting, the looting and the occupation divisions. The fighting division was to kill every moving thing in sight until the leader of whatever was left finally came to kiss the toe of the Roman commander to surrender. The slaughter stopped only after this act.

Thereafter, the place became an extension of Roman Empire and a province of Rome. The looting battalion then went on full-swing offensive to pillage and plunder and loot whatever they could loot. They were under strict orders to keep the loots. These were transferred to Rome to be shared among the Senators. These included human beings, women and children. The few surviving men were sold out as slaves. They were used for gladiatorial shows fighting ferocious wild animals in Imperial games. The females were for sexual pleasure of the morally decadent licentious pleasure-loving and fond-loving Roman senators. This was a very brutal inhuman regime and empire. The senate gradually became crony and sycophant to the Emperor that frequently became an arrogant tyrant.

The Romans were famous for carrying out the first recorded genocide in the History in Carthage in Africa. Marcus Cato shouted the infamous “Cartago est. délente.” This changed the conduct of Western warfare permanently. In the last millennium Western countries jointly and separately eliminated or decimated several races of human beings and seized their lands in North and South America, Australasia (Oceania) and several Ocean islands. From Alexander, son of Philip of Macedonia to the Romans and current Europeans white males had never ceased fighting wars. They fight among themselves and against alien lands for loots. The Western military machine had equally grown relentlessly. The US alone had spent several trillion dollars that could have developed the world fifty times over on its military machine. The West in all has spent several thousands of trillion dollars on Army and military forces. The money and resources and funds for these are global funds acquired as loots from brutal colonisation, unfair trading practices, crimes and corruption. At this juncture, it is time for all sane and wise human beings to pause and ask, "Is it not time that human beings stopped devising means of destroying each other and the eco-environment and searched sincerely for means of peaceful co-existence instead of assured mutual destruction either in the name of deterrent or search for illusive victory. It is time that all the global leaders decide if we are to take the risk and open up the world including Africa using the funds we use for wars.

Such victory unfortunately contributes nothing to the safety and security of our world. It does not help human beings. If it did we would neither be fighting wars nor preparing for wars, today. We now have a world where some eat and die of overeating and obesity while others suffer from hunger and starvation and die of malnutrition and diseases. We shrug off this state of affairs "as events in a cruel world". Yet all of us in our feud claim that we are fighting in the name of God to defend our ways of life in a world that we are just passing through. We have to listen to our conscience and be sure that our actions are telling it the truth.

Unfortunately, we seem to be living at a time when mediocrity is challenging talents, foolishness is challenging wisdom, ignorance is challenging knowledge and negative and destructive human assets are taking over from positive human virtues. Intelligence is exploited for graft. Minority wise people are shouted down. The mediocre majority are weeping up fears and emotions to drown the noise from a few concerned intelligent and wise vocal minorities. The desire to have and own possessions is getting out of control. It is threatening human existence on earth. Before darkness falls can we recover our sanity and humanity? We should listen to each other and not to our conviction. None of the things that divide us has succeeded to take away our being human beings. We still have the characteristics of human beings. Neither our divisiveness nor our disunity has succeeded to free us from poverty and misery. In Africa team work may rescue us from our current demise. Unity and unquestionable loyalty to the land of Africa will free us from the present poverty trap. We must abandon the culture of human weakness and fallibility that desire it all for an individual selfish and possessive self. Freedom is a factor and reward of a united solid community that is ready and willing to sacrifice all to protect and defend its freedom, independence and security. Genuine wealth is not what an individual has but what the corporate body of the community or a nation has.

It had failed to secure us true freedom, wealth and genuine prosperity. It had corrupted our independence, degraded merits and talents and promoted the ascent of mediocrity, corruption and vice. Africa can never develop with most of its current leaders. They would be totally unfit for leadership in most African communities even before the advent of the European white colonisers. We have semi illiterate leaders without any sense of value for merits or talents. They have no value for education or investment in essential infrastructures. They have no value for merits or talents. Education suffers without talents. Hence examination abuses, leakages and other malpractices are rife. Qualifications are totally worthless. I read of the mighty acts of leaders, great men of wars and heroes. I equally read of the rich and poor and the rejected in life. I read of the victorious Armies. All of them have unavoidable two points in life in this world. They were born into the world. They served their times in life and finally died and left the world. We all are doomed to this fate. Why do we all not allow a little wisdom to take precedence over self-conceit at this time? It is not war, violence and destruction alone that can create heroes and gallant men.

Negotiating durable peace and establishing sound basis for good Education and skills training to make people in different parts of the world work their lands to earn genuine living are yelling at us. Ideology, democracy and religion are empty slogans. Working correctly to create wealth and prosperity to improve the living standards of people in different parts of the world is the challenge we are now facing. Ignorance sponsors confusion and conflict. Knowledge allows rational thinking and actions. Arrogance affects wise decisions and actions. The world, today, is totally spineless and too timid to defend decency and civilisation. |The victor always writes History of conflicts and war. The vanquished has a story rebuffed by the triumph and conquest of his victor. We need leaders with initiative to preserve the peace and free the world from crushing poverty and ignorance.

The world misses the story of the vanquished and defeated lot. Arab-Israeli conflict is escaping beyond the reach of conflict resolution and human solution. It is equally too distant from religion and is fast becoming beyond heavenly settlement. None of the warring factions is willing to listen to God. They claim to fight in the name of religion to defend the way they worship God but are not prepared to listen to God. The forces of darkness want to seize power from God on earth. Unfortunately none of them will be here forever to judge the damage they had inflicted on the world. Africa and the black race had had lethal dose of this human destructive arrogance. We are in a position to tell the power-drunk world that we have right to be here in this world with them. But all Africans must know that achievements in wealth and prosperity that live on in the world are corporate community possession and not mortal individual achievements or fame. The nation lives on when individual dies and is no more.

We are not trespassers on other people's estates. We are no party to violence and war. We need Education and skills to work constructively to repair the damage inflicted on us by past wild behaviours of other people. The West seems to be closing its doors to other people while poaching on their lands riding on the back of war against terrorists to erode the rule of law. The world cannot sustain this type of behaviour as it is self-destruction. Nobody can claim to have the model of what is acceptable to the world. The world had existed for several million years with certain rules and regulations governing human beings. It is not safe to bend the rules and ignore the rule of law. Democracy cannot be delivered from the barrel of the gun and violation of human rights. Tortures and rendition are illegal and lawless acts of savages and wild people.

Most people claim to practise and appreciate civilised standards. They should all be ashamed of these barbaric acts of savages. No civilised people would kidnap husbands and fathers and fly them away from their families to alien countries to be tortured in tyrannical tormenting dungeons of notorious global dictators.

The simple African Negroes' response to all these frustrating events is that we have had raw deals both from the West and the Arabs. Our renegade, corrupt, ignorant and illiterate leaders had equally damaged Africa immensely. Africa is totally exhausted. Africa is facing a very difficult time and is exhausted. Africans ask to be spared the problems of a world in crisis. Let us be neutral. We are not in the business of apportioning blame. We strongly feel that the world has enough for everybody provided each of us is willing to share both the labour and the wealth. But the world has not enough for the acquisitive and possessive greedy ones.

Appropriate Education and adequate skills will share the labour and the knowledge to do things. Unlimited consumer-materialism may be justified by free enterprise and hard work but human instinct of possession and sharing should not be ignored. People's desires and demand are fallibly limitless but global resources are limited. Each of us has right to be here in this world. Each of us is equally mandated to share this world. That mandate comes directly from our creator. Conception is still taking place. Children are still being born. Research in new methods of treating infertility and assisted pregnancy are advancing to new heights. It makes nonsense of abortions and contraception. We may have to devise means of sharing this world and its resources just the way we have done in researches in other areas of human activities. This may sound foolish but there is wisdom in this concept. We have means of killing each other but we do not have means of stopping each other being human beings or being born into this world. We have to share it. Today, the problems in Africa, poverty, AIDS-HIV, hunger, starvation, war and violence are on every leader's lips, which cares to speak about this miserable but very rich continent defiled by foreigners and Africans alike.

There are several excuses given for the chaos on this continent. Unfortunately, nobody mentions the role of the West in pillaging and looting this continent to a standstill and slow extermination of human beings on this continent by wars, mass human trafficking and inveterate racial discrimination and long standing socio-economic exclusion of the black race from human activities and failure of our white masters to recognise and reward our goods and services fairly. For several millenniums the white people from the West kept on abusing us, insulting us with name calling and describing us as savages while what they did to us were beyond acts of savagery, exploiting us and dehumanising us with the active collusion of some of our ignorant people. Racial xenophobia is the most brutal exclusion and humiliation of human beings. It had brutalised the black race and Africa. Today, most people in the West are claiming credits for dismantling Apartheid in South Africa. Yet they supported and armed Apartheid to the teeth including giving them nuclear weapon to use in wiping off black people in Africa. They stealthily smuggled this back once Apartheid exclusive and oppressive regime was over. Whom do they think they are fooling? Africa looks stupid in looking after itself and interest but it knows its friends.

Let the world not forget that Apartheid picked up where Western European colonial masters, administrators, religious preachers and cruel traders left off in Africa. How can people excluded from the affairs of their land and the world for so many years progress? Tell me the morality and justification for the crusade to install Democracy, the rule of law, the fundamental human rights led by white leaders from the West in Africa and the third world, today? These are the very people who spent several thousand years destroying these pillars of human civilisation and development in Africa. Their transnational traders are still involved in criminal and corrupt activities on the continent even now. Shell cannot say its actions in Nigeria were clean without contributing to the confusion of that country. They sponsored fratricidal and ethnic cleansing brutal civil war. Today, ethnic strife is rife in oil and energy politics. Back in the West the white people and their leaders are still practising subtle institutional racial xenophobia. This is inequality of opportunities in Education, justice, jobs and social facilities.

Yes respect for fundamental human rights is yet to pass the obstacles and labyrinths of legalistic justice of the white authorities in the West. The black people are yet to have the same justice as the white people. Is this rush to Democracy, the rule of law and fundamental human rights, a new concept or an afterthought after several years of brutal colonisation, slavery and exclusion of black people by white rulers who failed to apply these principles to their colonial rule in Africa? The black people in Africa themselves cannot go without blame for what has happened to them and their land. They tolerated the loss of human freedom on their land. They collaborated with the greedy and cruel Arabs and Europeans to sponsor mass human trafficking of their children to depopulate their land to promote slave trade and slavery without realising that they were selling their liberty, self-esteem, dignity and integrity to total brutal and hostile aliens.

They sold the freedom and opportunities of the black race to brutal, greedy and cruel Arabs and Europeans for bowls of porridge in the presence of enormous wealth in Africa. We developed into decadence and total indolence. They failed to realise that death is better than slavery. They developed sharp taste for consumption of the goods from the European factories without bothering to find out how these things were made. They essentially must have education and skills to produce the goods. They developed the mentality of consumer-materialism even when that meant selling their children into slavery. The behaviours of the black people in dealing with the white people from the West were despicable and disgraceful. Even, today, the greatest enemy of the black people on earth are their fellow black people themselves. Some black leaders are agents to foreign intelligence. Late Mobutu and Jonas Sivimbi were CIA operative for their countries and leaders. Many black people are thoughtlessly selfish and individualistic. They aimlessly chase individual security and safety instead of unity and group security.

The very leaders of the continent are traitors selling the secrets of their land to foreign enemies to help them in their security and business in their land and destruction of their very homeland. This is the mentality and loyalty of the black person that still make them typical slaves. Our behaviour in loyalty and patriotism to our land of birth is deplorable. It lacks self-esteem and respect. We sell ourselves and our land to total foreigners. We have respect for neither our land nor ourselves. The worst thing is that the foreign buyers do not pay with money from their homelands. They seize our resources and funds to pay these traitors that betray us and our homelands to them to rape and abuse. How can a black person be free when he or she lacks self-esteem and loyalty to the homeland? The black person is timid. He accepts mere existence without living life and accepting the responsibilities of living in freedom and democracy. He barters his treasures for food. The African Academy could not be established at a better time than this when Africans are like sheep without a shepherd and ultra nationalist European xenophobic Aryan racists' politics has resurfaced in the open and is on the rise. Open declaration of racial hatred of the black people is on the increase. Of course, these people have the right of freedom of association. They are very free not to welcome black people as long as they make it clear that they are uncomfortable with black people. The problem is denial of this discomfort. This gives the wrong message to the black people. They become complacent innocent victims of this ambiguity. Dismissing this new manoeuvre as action of minority maverick people is spinning scam; it is risky and dangerous. The world seems to be gullible to swallow lies and revised lies. Are they fooling themselves? The idiots may swallow the lies and fool themselves but every intelligent person has the right to think as a human being. It is action but not words.

Are we honest to ourselves by accepting being lied to when idiots and fools go to war to kill and defeat their enemies but return to tell us they won the war without killing anybody. Yet we watch and see several corpses of children being buried by wailing parents. I would wish the leaders with responsibilities for lives and properties of fellow human beings as ministers of government would speak about lives and losses in war less callously. The ease with which the black person is killed in the US still makes Africans uncomfortable with the much heralded fundamental human rights, freedom and democracy in the US. Even professional black people offering essential useful services to the community, like Doctors and Police are still subject to racial xenophobic prejudice and bias. They are prone to discriminatory treatment and miscarriage of justice. I am an excellent Doctor. I came into the Profession to offer true humanitarian service. I honestly believe that what a genuine Doctor does is beyond financial reward or prestige. Medical Practice is a vocation and a calling.

It needs full commitment. My ethical conduct is exemplary. Yet when I had cancer of the Prostate in 1997 the Boss wanted to kick me out. He engaged a novice GP as a Consultant and an Indian Doctor as a locum Consultant, a good crony and a dangerous creeper. They conspired to kick me out by deliberate bullying, smear campaign, character assassination and provocation. They sent me to the Hospital Occupational Therapy Doctor for Medical Examination. The Doctor reported that he found nothing wrong with me. They wrote secretly to the GMC that I had Psychiatric illness. This was completely false. My clinical practice was impeccably clean. They got the GMC to suspend my registration. I appealed against the GMC action. By this time the cancer had affected my spine. I had to have operation. I could not attend the GMC meetings. I told the GMC that as I never had any Professional misdemeanours and was too ill to be in active practice, I would prefer that they left my registration in tact. They refused as some them were too stupid to work for Doctors. Of course I am impatient of people ignorant of what Medical Practice is involved ordering Doctors about. Most of these people wanted to be Doctors but they could not make it. The hormonal refractory Prostate carcinoma (HRPC) is the first illness I have had since birth.

Unfortunately it is familial as my late father had it. My grandfather seemed to have had it. My God father and name sake, my father's uncle died at tender age of it. My disciplined peasant family background and very high achievement at School till graduation as a Doctor and successful Postgraduate Training in the UK had no room for any distress not to talk of Psychiatric Illness. I am always happy about the rare opportunity I had that children of richer parents in my time never had. I made success of it. I wonder how many of my readers went to start high School with £10 (Nigerian pounds in 1956) my elder brother took one whole year to deposit with the Headmaster of the Primary School I attended who took to me as he saw signs of a brain that should not be wasted? This kind master kept the money in a cigarette tin. He brought it and opened it the day I was going to start High School. I did so well during the first year that my late father who made it a policy to hang around wherever my affairs told me that when they read my results at the Council everybody stood up and clapped. He told me that I was offered instant partial Scholarship. Mr Etim Akpan Enang, the deputy

Headmaster and philanthropist supplemented my fees. With these I completed my High School. Thereafter, a fleet of Scholarships saw me through to the highly coveted final FRCS of the Royal College of Surgeons. Anybody that reached that level with very meagre resources had no reason to suffer from depression in life even with disseminated cancer. I am happy 24 hours daily till death which is the conclusion of every life takes me away.

I was referred to the Law Court. There I saw lawyers who told me that the GMC has taken decision to remove my name from the register and they could do nothing. This looked like sham justice. It was all legalistically managed. Of course, I was too ill to stand. I just could not practise. Registration was not my clinical skills. This is always excellent. I have used my clinical skills to treat myself of this highly hormonal refractory cancer of the prostrate (HRPC). When my Doctors tell me that they had reached the end of the road, I start reviewing the Literature racking my clinical knowledge. Usually I would see very simple thing that I could try. They always work. When the Doctors review my case they are always amazed the way my illness behaves. They are excellent clinicians. I first used Aromatase Inhibitors to control the Disease for over four years. At that time the Disease was resistant to everything the Doctors threw at it. I came by the inhibitors through my personal research. The GMC is a funny body. I am very confident of my Medical knowledge and clinical skills; GMC or no GMC. The intrigues and readiness to slander a Doctor by the GMC and its indulgence in character assassination of Doctors is amazing and criminal.

Its supervision of Doctors is mechanical and biased at times. Its decisions can be artificial and out of tune with the conduct of Medical Practice. An Indian Doctor that wanted my Post as a Locum Consultant in A&E told me that he was fighting for his right. He had reported to the GMC that I had Psychiatric illness by false whispering campaign. GMC is encouraging smear campaign. It runs like a cult doing its business in secret. One thing is true I never had Psychiatric illness. I had never been ill since I was born. My first illness is this cancer. I do not drink or abuse drugs. I was very bright at School. There was no reason for Psychiatric illness. It was GMC Indian inspired gossip to damage me. This man was a poor quality Doctor and ignorant of duties in A&E. The job was offered to me an outsider in the first place because his employers did not find him fit for the position. Establishment whispering campaign and slandering of disaffected staff to damage him or her to justify getting rid of the staff and persuade industrial tribunal to view the staff with some suspicion seem to be a common practice. The shocking and saddest thing in this practice is attempt by Hospital Trust Authorities to use some unscrupulous Doctors to make some false diagnosis in deceased patients from Medical blunders to avoid or reduce damages they pay to the relatives. The Doctor is the only voice of the patients they treat. They are professionally bound to tell the truth in disasters and blunders in patient treatment. Doctor lying over the cause of patient's death is terrible dishonesty. Risk management and damage limitation are lying tactics that should not be used in Medical treatment errors and blunders. This is done to dilute Coroner's inquest decisions.

He was working under me and was a truant. He was always late. I had insisted that all my junior Doctors attend the Study session. I am a disciplinarian. Medicine is a discipline. Hence I insist that the juniors must obey the rules. The unsocial period was not pleasing to the junior Doctors and their spouses. Hence all of them ganged up with the post-hungry Indian to kick me out. The Indian Doctors behave as though they own the NHS. Their conduct and clinical competence are costly to the NHS. They give me the impression that Sub-Saharan African Doctors in the NHS are intruders and blockers of their jobs. A lot of Indian Doctors are good and excellent. But the bullying and hostile attitude towards non-Indian and non-European Doctors and their crony behaviour are unattractive to most people. This takes away their concentration from the duty of care for their patients. Their campaign for jobs and positions at times can be embarrassing to their colleagues. Many of them are hard working but they are good at eye-service to impress. Most of their performance lacks originality. Other nationality Doctors are very good. They respect camaraderie. It is difficult to understand if the Indians know and understand that spreading false gossips and rumours to oust colleagues from work and take over their positions is bad practice and manners. It is true Indian Doctors form the lifeline of the NHS and will continue to be so as the new generation of Indian Doctors are locally trained and Medical Schools are full of them.

The GMC should not act on unproven rumours and gossips. It is bad practice to encourage Doctors to gossip to the GMC on their colleagues. Respectable and excellent Doctors would not do that. They would rather approach a defaulting colleague and speak to him or her directly. The Doctors who gossip about some of their colleagues are poor quality Doctors. I am very aggressive in treating allergy (Anaphylaxis) and severe acute Asthma. As a Trauma Surgeon I do delay attacking bleeding once I have established safe conditions for controlling it in a well-lit theatre with the trauma staff complement in place for support; the same goes for dirty sloughing gaping trauma wound. The timid ignorant Doctor rushes away from these. He uses his tongue to gossip to discredit the brave and the bold that attacks them with excellent results. A number of my timid and ignorant colleagues would gossip without understanding a clue of what I am doing even though the result is excellent and instant.

A few days ago I was highly impressed the Professional way the British Emergency Flying Doctors treated a patient in Anaphylaxis from insect bite. They established quick airway with oxygen running venous line with saline running. They gave him Piriton iv and hydrocortisone (200mg) he was hypotensive; they gave him 0.5 ml of 1 in 1000 adrenaline subcut. He was still hypotensive; they repeated subcut adrenaline 0.5 ml 1 in 1000. He was not responding; they started him on iv adrenaline (special iv prep). This is what I learnt as Medical student in Nigeria and had been using all my life. I used it once here in the UK in one backyard Hospital in treating an acute anaphylactic patient that responded instantly and I sent her home. The nurses told my Consultant; he told me he did not treat his patients that way. Of course, he lost a patient with traumatic splenic rupture; he kept on fiddling and missed the diagnosis. PM the final court of appeal revealed his inaptitude. I never missed this as a Medical student let alone as a Doctor. The truth is that what they do not know does not exist.

There is one culture I learnt from my mentor and role Model Prof Fabian Udekwu. Most GMC officials have no clue about what Doctors do. It takes years to train a Doctor and very few

years to qualify as a clerk. Some panicky clerks can damage the Doctor's career. I wanted the GMC to leave my registration for posterity as I never broke the GMC rules. Striking a Doctor's name off the Register places a big question mark on his clinical skills and professional character. I am neither clinically unskilled nor guilty of professional misconduct. The GMC policy of accepting gossips allows rubbish Doctors to gossip their colleagues out of jobs for them to over their positions. Malicious slander is damaging. Unscrupulous people would not mind doing this with an objective.

I did assure them that I was too ill to work. My ethical conduct is exemplary. I am outspoken against racial discrimination. I am very strict against poor clinical practice and indiscipline among Doctors. I love knowledge, reading and writing. I spend my time doing what I like. The GMC could be better than it is if it had better Staff than what it has at the moment. The current staff hate being asked if they are Doctors? It is not wrong question. The way clinical issues are discussed with a Doctor is different from the way it is done with a clerk. The GMC secretly engaged Doctors to write reports on me without my permission. This was assault. Such reports were fraudulent and criminal. It was invasion of my person without permission.

Unfortunately everything they wrote to justify deleting my name from the register of Practitioners was false. Whoever wrote those false reports never interviewed me or spoke to me let alone coming near to me as to examine me. It is professionally criminal to write report on someone you have not examined or treated but this is GMC UK. I was just too ill with disseminated carcinomatosis. Hence it never bothered me. I was always in pain and taking analgesics to control my pain. Equally I had cord compression and was paralysed. I could not walk. I had to have open back operation.

I discovered this when I requested for my files under right to know. The job-hungry Indian was one of the GMC secret Doctors. The whole thing looked as staged by the Indian clan. It seems interest groups have implants in the GMC. They do the dirty job for the interest group like the powerful Indians in the NHS. Everybody that dealt with in the case from the GMC clerk to the Chairman of the "Fit to Practice" was an Indian. Those I left behind in the Hospitals were mostly job-hungry Indians. All these observations make me anxious over the GMC as a neutral supervising body. The Judiciary is used as a false stamp to render sham justice to victims of injustice. Engaging secret professionals as spoof to write positive reports on a Doctor they had not examined is criminal and dishonest. It came at a time I was too ill. The conduct of the GMC made me lose my young daughter. Invading and splitting my family is not a credit to the GMC. To me GMC is a scam. It has a number of criminals who should not be there. Hiring secret unscrupulous Doctors to write reports and fill the forms to authorise deletion of a Doctor from the register is criminal. Shame to the shambolic GMC biased Doctor supervision because my excellent clinical skills had kept me alive from 1997 till now; it has given me time to write my story. The GMC Consultants must accept the inevitable fact that because of the way the NHS appointments are made and positions fixed when they involve most black highly qualified Doctors, they would frequently have black Doctors with superior skills to theirs working under them. They should not regard such black colleagues as snobbish and arrogant.

I am just too ill to deal with this. Those who become Doctors for jobs, money and prestige are in the wrong jobs. This was not my intention for becoming a Doctor. My idea is to bring relief to the patients and relatives at no extra cost if I am employed to care for them. Every patient has the same quality of treatment in my Practice. The GMC is unscrupulous and breaks the law by slandering Doctors in the name of maintaining high standard of clinical Practice. Some Doctors are more decent than people from Mumbai Ghetto eager for permanent escape from poverty in India. I am a Doctor to be a Doctor in honest conduct, integrity and performing my duty of care. I have no reason to be arrogant because I have done nothing extraordinarily. I am just a citizen with some skills to offer services to the community. The Doctor should be honest and dignified through and through. The Doctor should not be involved in any strife. The Doctor should command confidence and make everybody relaxed in his presence. The Doctor should be tension and stress free at all times. The Doctor should be calm and cool when everybody has lost his or her nerves. Finding a Doctor in a murky deal with involvement of the GMC throws me off my feet. It is just mean.

How can someone that repairs and fixes God's machine behave like a devil? The Doctor is calm and quiet because he knows what the problem with the sick is and he knows what to do. The Doctor keeps his head when all have lost theirs. The Doctor should not be involved in the scramble for jobs. "I am fighting for my right" is a much undignified statement for a Doctor. Scheming for jobs and positions has no place in Medical Clinical Practice. I feel very uncomfortable with Doctors who do this. Where do they get the time for this?

Middle Grade Indian Doctor under me on day I volunteered to cover the unit as there was no senior cover saw a chronic asthmatic 29 years male in acute attack that could not complete a sentence during history taking. He gave him only a shot of salbutamol nebuliser and discharged him home without seeking my advice. The faithful girlfriend brought back this poor asthmatic a second time. This Indian again failed to call me. He started to argue with the junior Anaesthetist that came to take charge of the airway. They finally inserted needle into the chest without accompanying chest drain. The Anaesthetist continued to vent the patient. I leave the rest to all good Trauma Surgeons and Emergency Medicine Doctors. Of course they murdered the poor man with iatrogenic tension pneumothorax. Post-mortem confirmed this.

The lady Pathologist was very badly upset. I also had every reason to be upset. I took it up with the Hospital Trust Administrative Authorities. They told me that there was nothing the could do about the dead as he had already gone. They were to protect the career of the Doctors. They talked of risk management and damage limitation. This was against my conscience and what my mentors taught me. The Doctor represents the patient in life and death. If he comes to harm under his care he must tell the truth of the circumstances of death. I opted to leave the job. They gave it to the job-hungry Indian Doctor. This man started to recruit even my patients and their relatives to slander me before them. He joined the Hospital Authorities to write blackmailing and damaging letters to the GMC about me to pre-empty any action I would take.

This seems to be a common tactics adopted by the employers confronted with uncompromising employees and whistle blowers.

With terminal cancer there was no strength in me pitch my oars with anybody. The Hospital in Midland must examine their conscience. My habit is to be meticulous in all I do. Asking for senior help in difficult situations is not exposure of one's ignorance. It is an excellent safety valve. I am now too ill to practise but the death of 29 years old (RH?) still pains me. They hid the deceased folder from me so that I could not photocopy what happened. Now management of my disease is a joint clinical affair. My Doctors decide on treatment and tell me their decision. I administer the treatment to myself according to my clinical knowledge and the result I feel. I joggle the treatment until I obtain satisfactory results. I report any adverse results to the Doctors and stop the treatment. This is the way I managed all my patients in clinical practice.

I had personal experience of this racial harassment at work as a Doctor in the UK. Even my superior qualifications, skills and experience could not protect me from harassment from mediocre white and even my subordinates. To be fair to them my father brought me up to be a darling of friendly people and snob snobbish people for them to feel how those they snob feel. Their reaction is to see no good in me but they get no evidence in rubbishing me except to embark on malicious character assassination and slander. God blessed me with so much success and skills to be a victim of their blackmail. Today, immigration is a very hot topic in the West. Immigration created prosperous affluent West. Unfortunately, this is happening in the face of migration from the West to various parts of the world. Perhaps the world requires strict rules on immigration to protect innocent people in their homelands.

The whole world cannot believe that the US lacks the means of giving black people good education, skills training, positive trade and apprenticeship training. Such well-developed manpower with some white American volunteers can be injected into Africa for positive mass education and skills training where for several years they depleted its able bodied fit young people. Unfortunately some white people still flirt with tolerance and acceptability of the black people but their mind of racial xenophobic discrimination, segregation and social exclusion of the black people is not there. It is this pretence that is the problem. The black people are good at talking but they lack the courage of taking positive steps to solve the problems confronting them. There is still frequent outburst of some depressed white xenophobic segregationist seeing a person half white, half black in the white House. They must all remember that if Anthropological History is right everybody black, white, yellow and red originated from Africa. Genetics and Biological Science confirms this. In Medical Practice all human beings can receive well matched blood and organ grafts from each other. Africa still welcomes you all his children. The globalised world admonishes the racists that xenophobia is no longer rewarding. Divide and rule they applied to Iraq and are now striving to apply to Afghanistan would finally collapse. They would be the hated ones. Obama is God's gift to the world. His white mother and her family were Christians and his black father was a Muslim. No divisionist can foul him. Congratulations to his white American mentors. They, it is that really care about the USA and the world. Short sightedness abandons some people in old habits. Foresighted wise people see through the dynamically changing times and the future. High Technology IT has changed the world. Global world demands everybody to change with the changing world.

They all know these problems well but they fail to find means to tackle them. They are good at complaining and offering excuses for their failure and inability to face the problems. They know about unity and critical mass for action but fail to explore the methods and means of raising up such a mass. Unfortunately most of the black people are traitors, informers to those who are prepared to harm their progress. They frequently betray our cause to our enemies. It is the duty of the Sub-Saharan Bantu Africans to convince the world that they can plan their Economy and development. We should not pretend that we have no problems so that we may not be challenged by ways to fix them. It is wrong for us to gloss over our problems and ignore them.

How can you be free when you do not believe in freedom? They have no business to treat a black person who exercises leadership and fails to behave meekly like a slave with any sympathy. They have stereotype for any black colleague by making bogus and expensive jokes and they have no courtesy in their record when it comes to dealing with a black colleague. Yet they expect a black person to be courteous and friendly in the face of continuous provocations and insults. The first blow is deliberate efforts to mutilate your name by giving you any provocative and derogatory name of mockery and abuse. They claim that they cannot pronounce your name. Yet you are expected to address them by their names properly.

As students in Africa we were expected to know the names and correct spellings of the white officials in charge of our countries. What then is the basis of my white students and junior Doctors not learning my name and its correct spelling? They are white and just do not care showing courtesy to the black official. What an insult to be given a completely new name at the age of forty at workplace so that you can work? Is this not another attempt at tattooing a black slave to make him lose his identity? What is this human right; is it the right to die with ease in the hands of racial xenophobes without value for black lives? The myth of US being the land of opportunities and freedom will continue to sound hollow until black life has greater value and genuine purpose than what it has at the moment.

Tokenism is dangerous cosmetic action and deceit. It is a divisive action targeted to split our unity and weaken our consensus and popular resolve to be free. There is so much to be done to make this world comfortable for the black person on earth that the word boredom has no meaning for a black person. Boredom is self-neglect to the black person who feels bored. Problem-solving education and creative skills training are yelling at our youths to apply themselves to study and acquire creative skills to do things for themselves. The black child needs education, knowledge and skills to work efficiently to improve his chances in life. Tokenism has made black opportunities into lottery but life is certain and its demands are beyond gambling of lottery baiting. It is an expression of white European power. It warns black people to behave and respect their authority so that they would be rewarded with token privileges.

The Western political opinion and temperature are controlled by what the voters believe. The Western voters, today, seem to go for anti-immigrant racist parties. Yet the whole History of the West and its achievements had been built around immigration. I would hope that these papers were legitimately presented under the right to free speech, freedom of information and liberal education. It is just fair that in the same breath these people will accept my observation not as a chip on my shoulders but as essential contribution from the black people to free speech. It is cardinally important that the human being can be made into a beast to kill without provocation or into a top scientist capable of producing the tools to go to the moon. Human being can be made into a rational wise ruler or into a tyrant capable of killing his subjects. Education offers the tools to do all these. We must not ignore that it is our responsibility to offer the best education to our youths for the safety, security and prosperity of the community. In the day when money, base metal and paper promissory notes had captivated the humanity we must read the Proverbs Chapter four for wise counselling from the Holy Bible. Nobody loses by getting information from any available source; be it the Holy Bible, the Torah or the Quran.

Knowledge and understanding are greater assets in life than all other wealth. The Old Testament of the Holy Bible is African history concealed in religious myth. It is perhaps the most factual written form of our History. Before the advent of the Europeans, the African child went through education in various social organisations before being initiated into the community. Education then was mandatory but today it is optional. The colonial masters and European missionaries branded these organisations as pagan and satanic. Now we see that they were not pagan or satanic but essential social education to bring up our children under social discipline and the rule of law as we knew it then. They were the only forms of education we had at the time. Now education is a global language. The Africans and the black race must learn this language and make it their own. High quality Education is essential for developing the mind and intellect of the child and youth. Mathematics and Science are stimulatory to the mind. They challenge the intellect to comprehend solutions to complex problems.

There is so much information in this language to learn that the whole lifetime is not enough to complete it. All of us must learn and specialise in particular aspects of it as modern Economy demands everybody to have sound understanding of this language and skills in order to do things easily. Effective lifelong education is essential for social order, discipline, and adherence to the rule of law in the community. It is equally essential for high calibre manpower and efficient workforce. This is important for wealth creation and prosperity. It is sad the rivalry of religion and politics had denied most Africans the opportunity of reading and learning this unique History of mankind and humanity. The Muslims are economical with the story of Beheras, a Christian monk meeting the teenage Prophet Mohammed that accompanied his merchant uncle on business to Syria that was a Christian country by then. The monk Beheras revealed God's message to the young Mohammed. On return to Mecca Mohammed continued to abide by the word. He proceeded to establish the Arab version of the good news in the name of Allah. Both Christians and Muslims regarded the old ways as idolatry.

They got rid of them. Hence during Western Renaissance the Muslims freely released all Byzantine records to the West. It equally seems that some Christian converts to Islam continued perhaps secretly to practise their education, in Science and Mathematics. Recall that Christianity was intolerant of them. It persecuted and punished them harshly, e.g. Astronomers like Galileo never had it easy under Christianity. The scholars and their teachers lived secretive life then. They professed Christianity and when Islam came those of them that converted to the new faith continued with their way of secretive life. Hence Islam probably later relaxed control and contributed to knowledge. We owe Mathematics like Algebra and some Science to them.

Our basic moral laws are still relevant for peace. Western influence and alien adulterated religion had damaged Africa and the black race a great deal. Sadly we seem to have lost our sense of self-development and self-recognition acquired from effective social education and apprenticeship that initiates individual citizen into the community. Proper induction of the individual citizen in discipline, self-esteem and integrity by sound and effective education and skills training has no replacement in building up a viable and virile community with stable economy. People create wealth and prosperity. Natural resources are not wealth. They are wealth to people with Industrial Base and the skills to convert them to the products they consume and sell to other consumers. They are curse; disaster and tragedy to those that rely on them as the only source of income and mortgage them for what they consume. They cause indolence, poverty, ignorance, corruption, crises, violence and war.

They generate instability, violence, and war. Africa had stagnated for several years because of its enormous natural resources. High quality Education and Skills are essential for mastery of the environment and security of life. You may be hungry even though you are sitting on plenty of food if you do not know that what you are sitting on is food. Worst still you may know that you are sitting on food but you lack the skills to turn it into consumable form to eat. This is the dilemma of the Africans and the black race. They need effective focused education to know their wealth. They equally need the skills to convert this wealth into consumable form. The African and the black race must know that they need widespread education to understand their environments. They essentially need the skills to gain mastery of their environments and make them user-friendly, secure, safe, healthy and prosperous. There is something affecting our learning. We seem to be always in a rush.

We want it all at once. Politics is dangerous for the patience and concentration needed for studies and orderly and sustainable learning. We are impatient to invest time and money in learning. Education and good skills make people and groups realise their potentials. In the same spirit we write to mobilise our intellectuals, scholars and Academicians to mount concerted efforts to liberalise focused education targeted to overcome the apparent indolence that make black intellectual ability seem inferior

We do not threaten anybody by doing this. We equally do not feel offended by the comments. Rather they challenge us to action to dispel this impression. Africans traditionally are great travellers but not migrants and colonisers. This is why we did not colonise Southern Europe after over half millennium of living there and doing business. This introductory paragraph is not meant to cause racial tension or disharmony rather it is stating a fact of life. The failure of African scholars and educators to have a forum and a body to take charge of this vital sector of our mental development is damaging our community and its economic potentials. The African scholars and intellectuals and all people with concern about the plight of Africa in the world must see the need of coming together to take action to give their popular concern, practical expression and credibility. Our privileged position is not a safe escape from the people we had left behind in the slums of poverty and desolation. We know what education had done for us. We must let education reach more of our people. Public funds must sponsor youth Education in Higher Institutions.

The Academy of Africans in Africa and Africans in the Diaspora (AAAD)should be inaugurated to accomplish this purpose. It is sad that in the West discussing the common ills of the community is no-go area and a taboo for the middle class; it is politics. It is not for their class that is well covered by the economy. It is the exclusive club of the politicians that are not responsible for the plight of the poor and the down-trodden. As for the middle class elites they have reason to be grateful to the professional politicians. They have all reasons to be grateful and content and enjoy their extremely corrupt lifestyle and support the type of leadership and lifestyle the politicians offer them and the poor and the deprived should be content with empty promises of future development and changes in their plight. In Africa it has become the duty of the desolate poor and the deprived to listen to two classes of people, the religious and political leaders. They all promise them good times in future. The politicians demand their loyalty and support in return for development and changes in their miserable life. Of course, these are empty promises. They always return at election times. The religious leaders require obedience to God in return for luxury in God's kingdom and Paradise. They may lose out on earth but Heaven belongs to them. The desolate poor is indoctrinated to live in hope and not to look for ways to change his fortune. AAAD would not have promises.

We want to make good education and adequate skills training accessible to all citizens. They should not be the privilege of the chosen few. The investment in education and skills training must provide the students the means to work to earn decent living standards. The Education and skills training must be related to our land. They must be relevant to the needs of our land. They must be relevant for the problems the student faces in the Community daily. The African child must spend a third to half the study time on Practical work. This may need African Institutions to increase the length of time of studies in years to complete requirements for Matriculation.

It must provide adequate manpower for development. It is shocking that racist counterfeit scholars have been delivering papers in international Sociology conferences on superiority of Aryan white intelligence and inferiority of black intelligence in bogus Sociological and Anthropological debates. These debates totally fail to mention the role of white detrimental activities in the problems the black race had encountered all over history in its development. Brutal unprovoked aggression, conquest and dehumanising asset stripping, looting, plundering and ruthless pillaging colonisation and xenophobic oppression and total socioeconomic exclusion had virtually stopped the growth of knowledge and creative skills for several millenniums. Several centuries of European centralised institutional dehumanisation, segregation, abuses and oppression of the black race widely practised in Europe and among the Arabs in brutal enslavement and exclusion of the black people from active and viable economic activities and politics could not help us to keep abreast with other races of human beings. Despite Arab brutalities against black people and unceasing open hostilities, we do not wish any evil to confront the Arabs. Knowledge and initiatives can spread among people in freedom and liberty without outside control. For almost three millenniums Africa had been under very destabilising colonial rule in one form or the other. Presenting any paper without taking these things into consideration and the free privileges the black people had had to concentrate on their mental development is an expression of ignorance on the way intelligence develops, grows and knowledge spreads. It actually exposes the ignorance of the people of what makes black people seem intellectually inferior to the white people. Given the privileges and the opportunities the white people had and are still having the black would be intellectually equivalent to the white or more than the white.

We wish that they should learn the tragedy of intrigues, betrayal and deceit. In the past the Jews and Africans were the victims of Arab victories. Today, the Arabs are victims of their treachery, previous cruelties, injustice, greed and cunning past victories and Conquest. True History does not give them Palestine or our homeland in North Africa and our Mediterranean seaboard. They took them by religious intrigues, deceit and brutal conquest, as their original homeland was Gaza. Alexander, son of Philip, King of Macedonia saw the Arabs during his march in Gaza only. Let them accept a just settlement that would correct their past cruelties and injustice. What was seized by force, violence and brutalities is returning to the owners with superior force and victory of justice previously denied. The Arabs should settle for a just settlement that does not make them or Israel homeless.

The Arabs in collaboration with other foreigners threw out the Jews from their homeland one and a half thousand years ago. Now the Jews are back. The Arabs have no choice but to make safe and secure room for them. Justice for both the Jews and Arabs would demand and accept this as a just settlement. I would like to suggest a new opening sentence in a protracted global conflict resolution: "Do you accept to live together in peace and security for each other and the fact that nature would continue to multiply each of you in population growth and expansion to share this land and if you love this land you have no choice but to share it in peace and security for each other without the emotions of memory of past suffering as two of you have stories of suffering, religion and ethnic loyalty?" If the answer to this question is "Yes", the next vital question is the challenge: "Do you want a settlement and resolution of this conflict to guarantee permanent settlement and peace and security for all of you and devise means of ensuring that each of you live in peace and security and absolute respect for human rights, law and order and maintain the rule of law according to the secular charter approved by each citizen that constitute the rule of law that is your "Constitution" and written promise to live together in this land without fear and suspicion of each other?" The final question is the offer of choice and limitation:

"1. You have first choice to form a country and look forwards to the future to make it safe for both of you. This is safe and challenges you to make the new home safe, prosperous and safe for all of you. Proximity provides additional safety and security while separation offers a false sense of security and fails to prevent future conflict over sharing of resources." Jerusalem would not have to be contested for. It is the capital of the State. There must not be any ghetto. Population must mix. No segregation is allowed. These must be stated clearly in the Secular Constitution. The constitution must be approved and adopted by a referendum or plebiscite by one man one vote. Open ballot watched by the whole world is preferred.

"2. The two state solution is an illusion of cursory settlement and conflict resolution with volatile hidden future conflict over sharing of the resources and the land." The choice is yours and you have time to think about it and pick your choice. I sincerely and humbly beg the Establishment in the West to take their feet off the brakes of African progress and development for wealth creation and prosperity. Help us to stop corrupt illiterate leadership in Africa and money laundering in the West and Banking havens. Let us join hands and educate Africans to appreciate the value of honest labour, self-esteem and integrity. Let us stop global transnational corporate "Cosa Nostra Africana Mafioso" money making, quick buck mentality in Africa and the third world. Viable functional livelong focused education targeted to solve our multifarious problems must replace cheap money, cheap comfortable and easy living among black people. This is asylum and refugee seeking mentality. Appreciating beauty and comforts without means to achieve them is dangerous. There is no Eldorado in the West. Money does not grow on trees in the West. The West works hard for its wealth, beauty, comforts and affluence. It is easy money by living on crimes. It amazes the whole world, the speed at which the Sub-Saharan Bantu Africans master the benefits system and rapidly develop the dole culture and settle down to milk the taxpayer after being granted residence permit as refugee or dubious marriage status. It is an expression of African Bantu reluctance to work to support the system but selfish individual determination to milk it. Unlike the Asians they do not want to learn so that they can copy and support their community. On the other hand there are some white people who persistently pillaged Africa e.g. were the three Musketeers led by led Tiny Rowland, the De Biers and Energy Mining Groups etc.

AAAD would need help to educate the black people and Africans to acquire self-discipline and avoid crimes and drugs. Africans must learn the value of honest labour and legitimate wealth creation for comforts. AAAD would establish learning cells to offer education and training in skills in trades to our youths hanging around in the street corners in city ghettos all over the world in utter despair and desperation. There are a lot of jobs to be done in the black homelands all over the world. These youths need the knowledge and skills to return to them. It is criminal to destroy jobs the way African leaders had done through massive corruption in the last fifty years. They achieved this with active collaboration and connivance of the corrupt transnational corporate conglomerates. These sponsor resource jungle wars and violence instead of jobs. Africa is not a violent continent. The manufacturers of the weapons, the guns, the missiles, the RPGs and mines and the arms merchants are the violent people who kill Africans. The nonsense that if we do not sell them others will do does not hold any longer. These merchants of death can stop arms delivery to Africa in exchange for its rich resources. They can offer Africa education and skills training instead. It is unpardonable crime to hook young people with illegal addictive drugs to destroy them. Equally young people who take to these drugs should know that they are destroying their lives on earth. Socialising with your pars does mean you should accept all they do. You can reject some of their habits or leave their groups.

Constructive trade instead of destructive trade is what the world and Africa want. AAAD would target and train them to accomplish this task. AAAD aims to return our people to work after several years in the wilderness of joblessness and despair. The way is through our own moderate active Science and Technology skills and education. It is criminal for a child to grow up without skills to work and look after himself or herself. The society has civic duty and responsibility to ensure that it gives every child this means through active and effective education and skills training and viable apprenticeship. Africans must acquire a sense of civic responsibilities and duties. All black people must have mandatory livelong education to acquire social discipline and skills to achieve means of living and safe initiation into the community. Our ancestors had various societies for every age group and sex for proper initiation of the people into the community and proper social order. People were thrown out for misbehaviours.

Criminal behaviours were absolute taboos from membership of these societies. Cheating was objectionable. Fraudulent behaviour and faking of documents carried heavy penalty. This prevented criminals from gaining positions of responsibilities. Modern education in Science and Technology is adequate replacement for the past ancient all engaging societal life. Research and the work involved are all engaging to consume the time our people spend on mischief or hanging around at street corners. The rich resources of Africa and the amount of work needed to develop this original home of human beings on earth can sustain all Africans and black people on earth and a lot more people for a long time. Reforestation and recovery of land from the desert alone will require a lot of long time of research. Civil Engineering projects will need enormous work and research. African industrial revolution will require tremendous research to produce environment-friendly Science and Technology.

Recent very hot summer in Europe has stressed the fact that Science and Technology in Africa may be vital for human survival on earth in case of global warming. It was obvious that most electronic equipment failed to function properly in hot weather. We must produce equipment that will work in all weather. We must use the surplus labour currently being wasted in Africa to initiate reforestatation of the continent and learn new water preservation techniques. The current resource grabbing attitude towards the continent may turn out to harm our planet. The two vast deserts may take over that continent in a number of millenniums. This may be disadvantageous to the whole earth. It will affect its water reserves. Already expansive deforestation and logging had caused a number of rivers to dry up in Africa. Some large rivers that could not be waded through in the past are now wadable. The earth may be Marsisized and made barren as the planet Mars. Re-integration of colonial dismembered Africa to form proper countries with real authority and ability to collect revenues for development projects is an integral part of doing all these.

Educate Africans and stop indolence, poverty and ignorance. Cultural and religious brainwashing and colonial propaganda of several millenniums and progressive deprivations, poverty-induced ignorance and lack of opportunities had reduced the black people to static, negative and retrogressive development. Yet our brains and creative minds are as good as those of other intelligent and educated human beings on earth. Fragmentation and Balkanisation and dismemberment of Africa and its resources and placing these under mediocre and corrupt leadership to fit the colonial objectives of "impera et divide" (divide and rule) to weaken the colonies to make it easy for them to rule damaged the continent in several ways. It strangled the Economy of Africa and weakened the continent, making it dependent on foreign handouts to survive almost permanently. Dependence on others to take charge and do most things for them is virtually a cultural habit among black people and Africans as a whole. A re-integrated and united Africa needs brave and bold enlightened leaders with independent mind and initiative to do things. It is worth comparing Africa's position in the world now as a continent without face among others. It has to get itself in order by re-integrating and getting the sort of leaders described above. It would then rudely without shame force its face through the crowd to be recognised. People would immediately realize that Africa is ready and means business to assume its position and take responsibilities in the world.

Let us say it frankly. The Union of African States (UAS) is not beyond what our ethnic and religious divide, (Bantustans) highly exaggerated differences and tremendous problems would allow. It is not beyond our basic comprehension that it is the right thing to do in our current situation in postcolonial Africa. We are approaching half a century since we got independence. We have tried to operate this continent on the bases of what the Western colonial masters left for us. It has not worked. We should ask why the colonial masters divided Africa into these unviable Bantustans. Africa has to be re-integrated to form larger units to provide space from the Desert to the Seas to make it viable.

African Unity is not beyond what we can afford. Now we must start to think of the unthinkable. We must see beyond what others offer as the causes for our failure. We must make the sacrifices and take very bold decisions. We must be focused and take charge of our destiny. A Union of African States (UAS) with readjusted colonial balkanisation boundaries would provide a market too large to ignore. It will avoid unnecessary duplications of facilities. It will pool the resources together and allow orderly and sustainable development. It will allow acquisition of large and viable Technological devices to provide reliable services to the people. It will allow centralising infrastructures. This will reduce the cost of purchasing the equipment and maintaining it. It will also broaden the scope of subscribers. It will avoid unnecessary duplications and wastage. The USA and China are successful because they are very large markets. Their people work very hard and have reliable and high standard of education and skills training for effective manpower. Our greatest disaster in the recent past had been the inflated ego of some people placing them above everybody, communities and Africa itself. Nobody should be above Africa. Everybody should be under the authority of the community and Africa. They must be under the constitution and the rule of law. The constitution and the law must be binding on every citizen regardless of his or her societal status. Everybody is equal before the law. Breach of the law must carry severe penalty. Violation of the constitution is treason.

The Africans are intoxicated with overdose of very corrupt, lawless and vindictive politics. They can do with less politics and more practical and productive work. They must not be shy and timid in doing what is right to guarantee them the path to orderly and sustainable development. The wealth and prosperity of their homeland must take priority over their individual personal wealth. Mass population movement and compulsory and forced depopulation of Africa of its young and fit talented people by slave trade and slavery further weakened the continent. Colonial intimidation and continuous maintenance of dismembered primitive and obsolete statuesque in a fast changing world left Africa behind. Religion, colonialism-mediated servile Christianity and Islamic Muslim dogma further worsened the plight of Africa. These made Africa exist for Economic interest of colonial and imperial countries. Colonial indoctrination and deceit damaged Africa a great deal and Western capitalist propaganda continue to damage Africa. The Western global Quangos masquerading as UN agencies equally continue to damage Africa. So far the so-called world bodies are only in name. They are all Western colonial institutions, Quangos. The West uses them to molest their opponents and dominate the world. They have to be re-organised to reflect global interest and to represent the world. Africans and global black people must quickly re-organise Africa in co-operation with the whole world by re-integration of the colonial dismembered Africa and regain control of the continent. It must draw up a binding secular constitution and establish the rule of law. It must rein in all the warlords, round up alien criminals and lock them up and repatriate them when they are old enough and unable to cause trouble. The leaders must show that they are responsible, honest, virtuous, duty-conscious, hard-working and loyal in their behaviours and utterances.

Africa now needs all hands on deck to rescue it from its current dilemma. Africa is in dire strait jacket and enormous difficulty. It is worth noting that while Christianity is dwindling in the West, it is on the rise in Africa for the wrong purpose. It is open market Christianity. The pastors and the prophets exploit the poverty and misery of the people. They defraud their frustrated followers. They brainwash them with false miracles and promises. They collect tithes and gifts from them. These false religious preachers are milking the poor to build their fortunes and empires. This is happening in the midst of tremendous poverty in Africa and hunger in the affluent Western youths for something real and different from consumer-materialism. In the middle of these two needs and desires the false preachers move in to exploit the gap for their fortunes. The world leaders are chasing trivialities. The Western leaders seem to be young and go for exotic adventures to immortalise their names in History. On the other side the African leaders are illiterate Geriatric mediocre and ignorant people. They are both morally and physically corrupt in most cases. Most Africa leaders are people who would either be in Geriatric homes in the West or spend quiet retirement at home. They should be resting.

There are too many of them ruling over bloated numbers of mini rogue states and banana republics. These are all very poor countries. Many of them lack the resources and means for wealth creation. Others have the means but lack the skills to use their privileges. They persistently ruin any chances with wide spread corruption and total mismanagement of their resources. The leaders are exhausted with moral decadence. This is another reason for advocating for the establishment of the UAS to create something new to replace all these failed states and to start with a completely new slate making NEPAD work.

The Western young leaders would have to ignore spin and childhood dreams from School History lessons and live in the real changing world with its high demands. They have to create a society that satisfies both the consumer-materialism and spiritual needs of their people. They must be very frank with African leaders. They must be told to ensure that their youths have viable education and skills training. They must have means to work for themselves. They must not rely on relief and aids handouts or running to developed Western countries to obtain refugee status under false premises and pretext to live as economic immigrants. The vicious abuses of the rights and freedom of black race by the white people from the West should not be ignored in this debate. The white racial xenophobic scholars have the right of being reminded and they must know that "not too long ago" we black people were owned and kept as working horses and pleasure tools by white people. They deprived us of all opportunities to progress in life. Yet, today, despite all these we black people, to some extent, are able to hold out on our own. We were denied the opportunity for a long time. Having no opportunity to join the rest of the world was a tragic disaster. We were not participating in the race. Non-participants do not win. The world continues to ignore us because we are not ready to assume our responsibilities and our position in the world. We are socially. Politically, commercially and economically we excluded from active participation in world affairs purely because we show the world that we are not ready to assume our responsibilities.

We are not bitter and have no prejudice over what the white people are doing. We now know the value of freedom. We also know that education, creative skills training and freedom and power to get on with our life without white racial xenophobic bullying and harassment should no longer be taken for granted or compromised in our co-existence with the white race. The current exclusion of majority of black people from mainstream Economy has condemned majority of the global black people to life at the fringes of the enormous wealth in the world today. Our young people are stigmatised and stereotyped as violent criminals. Our traditional family culture had been destroyed. Most of us live below poverty line in extreme deprivation and despair even when we have tremendous excellent skills and experience.

Foreign aids must offer Africa the means to use its enormous resources to develop in an orderly and sustainable way. They must work to rescue themselves. There is no such thing as a free meal. The Africans had enjoyed a lot of free meals. All black scholars know that white Aryan race super-intelligence is not true. It is a fallacy, ruse and false propaganda that had failed to gain intellectual seat from the era of the Greeks, Romans and lately Nazi Germany. Equally this new upsurge of this bogus theory will fail. The European white male owe Africa one favour. They must stop money laundering by our leaders and use of African resources to maintain a world Economy from which Africa is totally excluded. It is a cruel world but good conscience and moral justice are not dead.

It has no place in Academic debate but unfortunately it has come at the time of black emancipation and genuine efforts at African Renaissance. We know that we have excelled over the white whenever we have even very slim and lean opportunity for equal competition. We also know that we had excelled in the face of sophisticated fraud and cheating by the white competitors and judges. It is only the black race that had survived the brutal dehumanising atrocities, and cruelties that we had gone through in the hands of white people. Equally they had gone through brutal abuses in the hands of their brutal tyrant African mediocre and illiterate and senescent leaders. Most of these leaders ensure that they use their whole life times and generations to destroy Africa to feed their corrupt and filthy lifestyles before they die to leave their people in penury, abject poverty and misery. Most of our handicaps are white made. We are permanent victims of the white tyranny of greed and selfishness promoted to racial xenophobic hate and arrogance of superiority to justify this odious man's inhumanity to man and flagrant persistent abuse of human rights.

Racial intolerance is conversion of white jealousy and envy for what the black race has. It is deliberate manoeuvre to rubbish the black race to justify the way the white people had abused and bullied them all over history. We have no reason to remain indifferent to race hate and abuses. We are victims of white brainpower. To overcome our travails we must mobilise all our brains and activate them to think of a way out of our current dilemma and predicament. Let us not forget that whatever ill-treatment we are talking about here had always been delivered to us through our fellow black people's hands. The black people always make themselves available as vehicles to convey all manners of dehumanising treatments from white people to their fellow black people. They even regard it as a privilege to torture their fellow black people for white people. Therefore while I deplore white racial discriminatory treatment, segregation and exclusion of black people, it is important to mention and deplore our fellow black people for encouraging and participating in this dehumanising humiliation of their people and destroying opportunities for the black race. In spite of this observation, there is no biological or genetic evidence of black people having inferior brain. Of course, all genuine scholars know that there is no biological, genetic, anatomical or any proven scientific basis for racial super- or inferior intelligence. The difficulty of the black people in Education, skills training, is that they had been detached from these activities for several years.

Knowledge is acquired by steady sustained pressure and continuous practice of learning. The leadership has to awaken the people to the importance of Education, skills and apprenticeship training. They must make youth Education and learning compulsory. They must make the people aware of the importance of making the sacrifice to provide the funds for sponsoring Education and learning. Africans have to re-acquire learning culture. They must make formal Education an essential part of the culture of the African communities. Public funding of Education cannot be over-emphasized in African effort to rehabilitate Education and learning. Africans and black people cannot win if they do not take part in the race. Therefore, premature conclusion on the inferiority of black brain and inability to acquire knowledge does not apply. The black people had been out of the race of Education and active learning for over five to ten millenniums. Non-competitors do not win the race. It is unfair to accuse them of failing to win and losing the race they took no part for years.

The human brain has limitless ability to assimilate knowledge. It has the ability to transform knowledge into creative skills to make tools. The human brains are capable of developing new skills when they are free from the restrictions white tutelage imposes on them. The effect of brutal and oppressive colonialism on the progress of all black people on earth has been disastrously catastrophic. Imperialist goals feed on subversion, sabotage and criminal corruption. Today, foreign covert operations against black interest have assumed several forms. Any imperialist colonial power achieves its objectives by use of intrigues, blackmail and brute force to subdue and weaken its victims to exercise power and authority over them. This is the demise of Africa. Poverty and ignorance have reached phenomenal proportions. HIV-AIDS pandemic and return of lethal infectious diseases in Africa in the face of crippling foreign debt burden have not helped either. Africa has neither the means to acquire drugs nor the Education, knowledge and skills to produce them. Sadly it depends solely on charity to rescue it. It would have the funds if its dishonest and corrupt criminal leaders did not steal them to bank abroad. It would have the manpower to manufacture the drugs if it invested satisfactory amount of its resources in offering very high quality Education and skills training to its youths. It would solve much of its problems if its youths were well-disciplined and grew up under well-disciplined society and communities led by well-disciplined leaders. Self-respect and patriotism are good incentives to promote self-reliance in a nation. In Africa people think of what they could steal from the nation but not what they could give to the nation to make it prosper. Yet prosperity of the nation is the wealth of its conscientiously hard working and honest citizens.

Imperial colonial administrations in Africa had a long History of exclusion of black people from vital educational activities and skills training. The growth and development of these depend on freedom to be included and participate in all aspects of human activities. Africa has over three millenniums of being excluded from genuine learning. This means that millions of their generations missed the continuous handing over of knowledge and skills from one generation to the other. Several millions of generations missed the most important thing in the growth and progress of knowledge, stimulation of the brains, knowledge and skills of people in each generation by available knowledge and skills and teachers to hand over these to succeeding generations. A conducive environmental stimulation is important for the brain to function and acquire new knowledge and skills. Persistent practice makes the skills stick. Alien rule deprived us of this vital opportunity. Alien imperial colonial administrations own colonies for their Economic benefits and not for the colonies' benefits except if the benefits accrue vital Economic values to them.

Therefore, colonial administrators frequently lay no foundation for the Economy. Education, skills training and apprenticeship are ignored. Youth talents are not exploited. Free enterprise is restricted. Colonisers control free thinking and public ideas. Economic developments in the colonies are prevented from infringing on Economic interests of the colonial masters. Hence, Economic foundation in the colonies was always weak and unable to support the community and youths. Self-motivation is important to overcome the underlying weakness in the Economic potentials of the colonial Community. What is the solution?

The British colonial masters called black Africans savages and excluded them from most activities. The Irish General Montgomery wanted white people in South Africa to take over that land to develop it. He was a racist and supporter of Apartheid. He called us savages. Yet he was an Irish not highly rated even though he was a good soldier. Ignorance made some of the officials do what they did. The truth is that most colonial officials were not educated. They were not well-read and knew very little about the world. The only thing they knew was their white skin and the difference between it and black skin and their business. Colonisation holds down the people and their progress. The people held down by colonisation must run to escape from all the disadvantages of being under a colonial rule. They must work conscientiously hard to catch up with others. They must learn how to be independent and free to work with initiative to achieve satisfactory results. They have to develop and progress.

I have, today, proposed the establishment of "AFRICAN ACADEMY, (African Academy for Africa and the Diaspora, AAAD) " to concentrate the attention of our intellectuals, leaders of thoughts and scholars on Education, skills training and definite periods of apprenticeship compulsory for jobs. Higher Education and Research consistent with our needs must be actively developed. Education and Development Programmes must be planned together to allow us feel the vacancies in the projects. This will prevent unemployment. Education must be of very high standard. It may need a year or two longer than what other nations use. We have right to be in this world with other races of human beings. We equally have the same right to do what other races of human beings do to survive in this very competitive world. It is our creative skills and tool production that had suffered a set back for several millenniums. Our creative skills in tool production had been irreversibly damaged. We must learn team work. We must merge together and unite to form that effective critical mass to do things together and avoid unnecessary duplications and wastage of our scarce funds and resources.

We must avoid senseless rivalry and duplications that cause massive corruption and embezzlement of public funds. The council of Elders is a necessity. Respectable elders had always played positive role in African affairs. Today, people that our ancestors would not accept into the society of decent, responsible and respectable people are in politics to form governments. These are people strange to self-esteem, dignity and honour or intelligence. They are in charge of Africa as its leaders. They are not leaders of the people. They lack leadership skills. They damage our land and people. They are ignorant of the responsibilities of leadership.

It is the duty of our scholars, intellectuals and responsible Academicians to popularise education and skills training to raise up fine core of educated youths with sense of civic duty, self-esteem and the ambition to compete with others and win. This is the race we must not lose. Even our feeble efforts at this time had succeeded to produce primitive and inferior tools not matching what other races of human beings are fashioning and making. Education and creative skills training are essentially what we need to regenerate our tool production skills. The youths must know that education is to enlighten the mind and not for a meal ticket for jobs. It needs patience to study and master the subjects the student has to master.

Every black child must study Mathematics, Science and Technology. We must acquire the Technical skills to convert our abundant raw materials into the finished products that we need. This must take place outside the realms of politics and its controversies and budgetary restraints and restrictions. African Academy will be a permanent forum where all our top scholars and intelligentsia would meet regularly to exchange ideas on the ways to do things in modern world in order to survive in the competition. It reviews global world wide progress and changes to avoid being left behind. Our students must be up to date in what is happening in our fast changing world. This is the battle of wits. It is intellectual combat. We must have a forum where our best brains would meet to exchange ideas.

Isolated efforts would be inadequate to rescue us from our current Educational backwardness. A successful team meets regularly to practise and plan their strategy.

Africa must dismantle colonial borders. Re-integration of dismembered Africa is as important as effort to develop and stabilise the Economy. Lay less emphasis on religion, ethnicity and politics. Confine religion to their worshipping places and their believers. Give them freedom to practise their faith without interfering with the freedom of other faiths and nonbelievers. All affairs of State must be secular. The leaders must not be older than sixty. At sixty people must retire from politics. Only the very few selected for the "House of Elders" would have anything to do with politics. Science and Technology and Research must take priority over everything. They must be independent of Government. Education, Health and Communication network must be free from the politicians. They must collect tax through autonomous community management board (CMB) and provide the money used to run them. Independent Bodies must run these services. The Government is effective at supervisory capacity. It must watch what the people do with the money given them. It must have skilled Inspectors to keep the standard high. All the Research must be aimed at achieving national economic and strategic objectives. Education and skills training must from now be the craft to take Africa across the vast ocean of influence and global existence.

Arab macho influence has no place in Africa. We are land of the free. Slavery in all its forms must stop in Africa. Both male and female must be free and equal. We are free to say, "No" to homosexual practice. It is a lifestyle we object to and disapprove of. We must review the past and the march of civilisation with pride. We must also always firmly acknowledge that "Ancient Egypt" is not synonymous with Arab invaders. The Arab invaders that live in what is known as "Egypt", today, are not the owners of Ancient Egyptian civilisation. The Arab invaders came to North Africa barely fourteen hundred years ago about 642-698 AD, long after the Ancient Egyptian civilisation. Egypt was frequently Union of Kush (Sudan) and Egypt. At times it included much of Africa as ancient Libya occasionally defeated Egypt and appointed its Pharaohs to rule over all the land. Also occasionally ancient Ethiopia defeated Egypt and the rest of

Africa and elected its own Pharaoh to rule over the whole people. Therefore Ancient Egypt involved most of Africa at various times. The Pharaohs equally came from both sides. The problem was that they frequently feuded and broke up to re- unite again. Even Northern and Southern Egypt occasionally broke up just to re-unite again.

Therefore, they cannot claim that civilisation as their own. That civilisation is over three millenniums old. Any races of human beings that were not in that place over three thousand years ago cannot, therefore, claim the magic of those human achievements as those of their ancestors. Of course it would be unfair to fail to mention that at a certain time African rule extended as far as Syria and Levant (Lebanon) and the whole of Palestine. Therefore this discourse will be incomplete without mentioning this. But the driving force of Egyptian civilisation rule and power was black people. That civilisation was black African civilisation and other people who lived in Egypt at the time. The black Africans that escaped death from the Roman and later Arab invaders were driven across the desert south. The new invaders and conquerors took over our land and heritage. They even banned our intellectual, educational activities, craftsmanship and manufacture at pains of death. They permitted only those activities a few of our people in captivity could do to enable them learn from the enormous pool of knowledge and skills that were in Africa and Ancient Egypt.

Our education, creative skills training and tool making, decayed with our defeat and loss of freedom. The real truth is that the Arab invaders collaborated with all foreigners that invaded us from across the Mediterranean. They regarded themselves as white people without any relationship with us the indigenous Africans. The Muslim Islamic culture scattered our precious and treasured antiquities. They called them idols that their religion wanted to get rid of. They presented them as free gifts to most of the early European invaders. When they found that most of them were highly sought after, they resorted to selling them for cheap money. It is on record that the Arabs and early European colonisers specialised in tomb robbery and sales of our antiquities. Our obelisks in London and Washington are described as gifts to Nelson for his conquest of Napoleon. The truth is that they were looted as war souvenir.

Nobody had the authority to give what never belonged to him to complete strangers. The Arabs scattered our antiquities because they had no value for them. To their Muslim faith they were idols just as we saw the way they damaged Buddha in Afghanistan. Tomb robbery is repugnant to our culture. It is desecration of the dead. It is violation of the wishes of the dead and insult to our ancestors. The world knows that ancestral worship is the core of our traditional religion. Even in Christianity we still believe that we must always respect our dead ancestors so that they would bless us. It is only people ignorant of this our belief that would violate the peace and quiet of the dead.

The Arabs did this without fear. They scattered our precious antiquities and artefacts they regarded as idols. The Arabs indulged on tomb robbery and desecration of graves that majority of black Africans objected to and deplored. The Pharaohs took enormous steps to secure their bodies and properties in their tombs. Pyramids were built mainly to achieve this purpose. They stole from the living and the dead. They stole our great and valuable manuscripts and forced our people held in captivity to teach them how to read them. Today, UK and US have two of our remaining sacred obelisks. Long before the Roman invasion, Alexander, son of Philip of Macedonia was so fascinated by the scholarship and level of civilisation and high standard of living in Egypt that he chose to make Egypt his home. He built the city of Alexandria solely for this purpose.

For an invader and conqueror to choose residence in an alien land in preference to his throne in Greece meant that Egypt was by far superior and fit for a powerful king as Alexander better than Greece or Macedonia, his homeland. The Romans stopped Education, intellectual activities and boat building in Carthage in 146 BC at pains of death while they used our scholars in captivity in Rome to teach them these things.

The British colonisers stopped brewing of local liquor, (" Akpatasit") and manufacture of hunting guns and gun powder in their West African colonial territories. Colonial rule is synonymous with decay in genuine education and practical creative skills. It is dehumanising debasing of the human beings and human values. It is abuse of the human person. It is an insult and violation of basic fundamental human rights. The world is not fully aware of the damage the Romans inflicted on Africa and its resources. Octavius, that later became Caesar Augustus emptied North African forest of its wildlife to support his flamboyant lifestyle of staging more than normal number of imperial games (wild gladiatorial shows).

He devastated the forest by felling timber for the enormous constructions and countless amphitheatres and boats for its navy and commerce in Rome and grazing his vast numbers of African wildlife he collected for taming to be transferred to Rome. This evil man deforested much of North Africa and promoted the desertification of North Africa. Octavius foolishly made the Sahara expand to cover much of North Africa. The Western European brutal colonisers did the same thing south of the Sahara and allowed the desert to expand to take over much of the land in the South. No colonial History carries this story.

It is always great Greek civilisation and mighty civilised Roman Empire. We resisted Europe until they overwhelmed us with intrigues and betrayal by our own. They seem to use the knife of foreigners to slaughter us and Africa. This is the evil culture we must overcome. In times of danger let us all bury our grievances. Let us rise up as one person to defend and save Africa, our God given heritage. We are powerful enough to ward off all enemies provided we rise up as one person in solid unity and confront the evil monster. We can face poverty and ignorance and defeat them. We have to slaughter them and the people who bring them to us. It is the lifestyles of some people alien and local that makes us poor and ignorant. It is plausible for foreigners to highlight our plight to the world. But what do we do to obviate our deplorable conditions? It is not clear if all the foreign money earmarked for our development is another loan. If it is a new loan we must know very clearly the conditions. If they will impoverish us again we stand to refuse such loans. They do not help us. The plight of Africa from the Cape to Cairo, Tripoli, Algiers, Rabat and Tunis is the same. Separating it is fiction of the European colonisers. A number of confused Arab leaders want to join the EU but people developed the EU and made it work. Africa has the AU; the Arab leaders have a duty to make it work. Do the Arabs accept that they are Africans? They have the Arab league. What is the place of Africa in Arab League? Mamuar Khedafi suggested Africa boycotting Israel. No Africa should court Israel. We should learn to live in peace with Israel. Africa under OAU made this mistake. It boycotted Israel. This was a stupid thing to do. Israel is as important to Africa as the Arabs are. Africa should always play the role of mediator in Arab-Israeli conflict. It has no reason to take sides.

The challenge is ours, the Africans. The most barbaric and cruel people of the ancient world were the Romans. Their atrocities in Africa were incalculable. Perhaps this is why European History of Romans in Africa is sketchy. Memory of Romans in Africa is that of colossal pillaging and vast destruction and damage. Hence the Europeans seem to gloss over it and at times pretend as if the rustic Romans did not reach Africa. Equally they have ambivalent attitude towards North Africa as though it is not part of Africa. Rather they talk of the Middle East.

The Rock of Gibraltar and a number of Mediterranean Islands are now European lands. Africa is shrinking. This is a land where men would go all length to chase away intruders and trespassers in our land. What an indolent and docile generation occupies Africa, today? Let us use education to cross this fragile bridge. The strength of the land depends on knowledge, skills, courage and hard work of its citizens. Africa is weak and frail, today, because its citizens are no longer hard working people eager to let it happen in Africa as in other lands. We are indolent and indifferent to the progress others make even though we admire the same.

In 146 BC the Romans invaded Africa. They destroyed Carthage by genocide. They captured our wealth, Educational Establishments, Technology (the most advanced in the world at the time) our scholars, scientists, engineers, architects, masons and builders across to Europe to be enslaved to build Rome. These are the famous Roman buildings, the coliseum, amphitheatres, temples and famous buildings. This is the origin of European learning. The pioneers had been killed off and the remnants scattered. Any activities to reactivate learning and skills training in Africa were at pains of death. It was regarded as an act of revolt against Rome. The great African Egyptian-Carthaginian boat building and maritime skills became the property and monopoly of Europe. Europe plundered a lot from Africa. It is our place to fight back and replace what they stole from us. The key is Science and Technology. We have seen it in Asia. What are we doing? Religion is ours. St Augustine maintained the momentum when the Vatican was in a state of crises and brought it back to them from Africa. The rule of law is ours.

We built the first Law Court and Law School and run them in Palestine in the Roman Empire to curb the Roman lawlessness. It was there for a hundred years, a whole century before the Romans recognised them and removed them to Rome. Democracy is African. Aristotle took it to Greece to stop the rule of the most powerful feudal lord after the death of one leader. Replacement used to be by war, violence and murders. Aristotle saw how we did it in Carthage. He sold it to the Greeks who christened it "Demos Cras". Education and Science are ours. The Arabs seized North Africa after the fall of Rome. They got it with our Institutions intact. They gave it to Europe and the world as theirs. It was stolen from us with maximal violence, war and murders. The mitre the Bishops wear and in paintings of the angels are all the symbols of the sun god. The black rings the Arabs wear are "Okpono Idiong Ibibio" a religious symbol the Priests wear in ceremonies. We have offered a lot to civilisation, a lot more that the world and our children and the people know.

Let us ignore greed and corruption. We must rise up and make the sacrifice to integrate with this Scientific and Technological advance. Within there lies knowledge. The key to prosperity is hidden there. The resources of Africa can carry us. Our criminal and corrupt leaders had held us back to the pleasure and approval of our former colonisers. There must be a mechanism of choosing leaders. They must be honest and patriotic. They must not have loyalty to political parties. These are subversive instruments of European colonisers. Our loyalty must be to Africa, our God given heritage and land. We must sacrifice to make it rich and strong. Admiral Himilco met humble farmers in the Isles of Cassiterite, the British Isles, tin islands. He was surprised to see such primitive people. How had the roles changed? Today, it is Africans that are primitive. Hanno sailed around Africa at the instigation of the Pharaoh Necho. Africa was the first continent to be mapped. Hanno founded the city of Cerne in West Africa. Many of us are descendants of the thirty thousand Carthaginian founders of that great city. The geographical description would place Cerne at Calabar instead of Senegal. The big difference the world notices between the coastal people and people in the hinterland in West Africa is due the fact that the coastal people are mainly marine culture people and in the bulk descendants from Carthaginians while the hinterland people perhaps are indo-Asian migrants from Southern India that came through Asia Minor to settle there. They were nomads in the main. They roamed around the fringes of the desert in the savannah with their cattle. All these people mixed with the natives to live in West Africa. They had all intermarried to create homogeneous population.

He actually paid for the land in gold. The Romans chased this gold to recover it after their genocidal war and conquest in Africa. Even the recent colonisers were chasing it. They stole a lot of Ashanti Royalty gold furniture and ornament. The remnants of Carthage escaped to Cerne. This is why the level of sophistication and pride in West African coastal region is different from that of the hinterland. We are not apron strings of Europe. The Europeans out of envy and jealousy destroyed Carthage. The Jews felt they could escape the envy and jealousy of Europe. Europe seems to hate success of others. The Jews went through various forms torture and punishments in Europe. The myth that the Jews killed Jesus justified European cruelties .But everybody knows that this is false. The Romans arrested Jesus, tried him and condemned him to death. They allowed the Sanhedrin to interview him. Their soldiers nailed him on the cross. This was the Romans way of executing their condemned. The Jews stoned theirs. The Romans gave the permission for him to be buried. Therefore every act in Jesus death was Roman. Typical European pathological lying, to avoid embarrassment the Romans deny their action. They put the blame of Jesus death on the innocent Jews that were only interested bystanders.

They accused the Jews of all manners of crimes. They descended on them. Everybody knows that the Romans murdered Jesus out of fear. Yet after Constantine converted to Christianity, the Holy Roman Empire was not to be seen as murderers of Christ. It suited them to make the Jews criminals and victims in this Roman crime. Romans arrested, tried Jesus in a mock trial, sentenced him to death and executed on the cross, standard Roman mode of execution different from the Jewish stoning.

The Western European raw lies are not only today. They had always been perfect criminal liars. As the potential for lying to incriminate the innocent is time-old culture of Western Europe. The world must be careful that it is not taken in by their lies. Their threshold for criminality is very low in the face of consumer-materialism and resources to pillage and the potential to lie confidently without shame is high. They talk of Democracy, human rights, freedom of individuals and the rule of law but they do the exact opposite. They say, "We are not racists." Yet they are the worst racists that had institutionalised racism. It is the tyranny of greed and god of consumer-materialism that leads the West. They are ready to fight and die for what is not theirs. They lie about the reason why they fight.

Education and skills training die from disuse atrophy after several generations fail to use them actively. Knowledge decays if it is abandoned especially under threats of pains of death. From 146 BC till today is not a week. It has equally deprived every black African generation from then till today. If the world or the West is serious about helping Africa, it must help us to rebuild and rehabilitate our Education, growth of knowledge and skills training. We must reactivate our learning and acquisition of skills. We must rebuild our battered Economy by active and genuine construction work. We have to engage our unemployed youths in the construction of the South-North African trans-Sahara Railway and Road networks. We must get the Africans to work for themselves. We must remove the restrictions of colonial borders. Re-integration of colonial dismembered Africa to restore its Economic viability is a priority. Africa must be opened to the outside world by road and rail networks.

We must remove the harmful, corrupt and destructive activities of the European transnational corporations and their middlemen the corrupt and ignorant presidents of African rogue Bantu states. The best programme of rehabilitation for all human being is to teach him or her how to look after himself or herself independent of outside help. Teach him to work for himself. Teach him to be free from help and addiction to aids."Factis non verbis" Action not words. The plight of Africa needs action and not words.

The middlemen African presidents are waste pipes on the fragile African Economy. They drain the Economy with their corrupt and wasteful activities. They cause unnecessary duplications and failure of development programmes. Pool the resources together. Develop few viable projects. Expand slowly from these few viable and successful projects. This is what I call "orderly and sustainable development." This is what Africa needs. This is what the world can do to help Africa to do for itself.

Emphasizing diversity and divisions is no use in emergency. In emergency each African must be willing to sacrifice for the good of all. That sacrifice is self-identity and interest. The invading and conquering Arabs lived for several centuries on tomb robbery. They did this to emphasize the power and authority of the victor, perhaps to provoke the remnants of totally vanquished Africans. We Africans regard tomb robbery as desecration of the dead and sacrilege. The Pharaoh Tutankhamen placed a curse on tomb robbers.

The Arabs did this because they had neither loyalty nor value for those who were buried there. Equally they might have known how distasteful tomb robbery was to the Africans. The Europeans equally indulged in this deplorable act because they were excited by the wealth and affluence that was Africa and the elaborate ways we buried our dead with enormous wealth Conquering invading Barbarians have value only for wealth and loots. Envy, jealousy and greed led to their aggression and invasion of Africa. They are famous in record as criminal invaders and illegal immigrants in Africa who stole both corpses from their graves and tombs and living human beings from their homes to take them abroad to sell for money.

Consumer-materialism is religion. The West kills and goes to war to kill for it. Today, we have the mummies in various European Museums and descendants of slaves in various parts of the world to confirm this observation. It is important to stress these facts because the West does not take kindly to any part of history that is distasteful to them. Unfortunately, these acts might have been deplorable but they were deeds of gallantry of pillagers and plunderers of wealth in Africa from the West. They are the major reasons for black intellectual mediocrity, today. This is what brought miserable black people to live in the ghettos next door to the affluent whites.

Yes it is unpalatable part of history of black contact with the white people. But history deserves its place for education of the future generations and posterity. There is no reason for any animosity between us and our bullies and abusers. There is strong need for a resolve to say, "Never again should we abandon ourselves and ignore the importance of Education, Science and Technology for creative skills for tool and material manufacture to find ourselves victims of alien ambitions to dominate over us and our wealth so that we are made poor in the midst of plenty". We do not advocate for African Academy to provoke futile debate on intellectual superiority of the races.

The early Negro leaders and Educators in the US combated the problems of segregation and denial of opportunities of Education and creative skills training by founding of the Negro Colleges. Education, learning, acquiring knowledge and creative skills are not restricted to any special human races or colour of their skins. These colleges slowly broke the myth and false doctrine that black people were not capable of being educated and that they lack the ability and brains to understand the sophisticated sports, games, athletics, arts, music and dance that we virtually lead, today, regardless of whatever impression our detractors may have. We are not advocating for isolation or further exclusion. Education, today, is a global language and the benefits of Science and Technology are real. Fortunately, today, some of the best US institutions in these days of racial integration in education are these pioneering Negro colleges. Equally some of the US best scholars come from them. African American scholars and educators are distinguished in the US.

AAAD must bring them into proper perspective. It must use available educational facilities to provide problem-solving education, knowledge and skills to Africans to help them do things to solve their Economic problems. Wherever they live in the world and in Africa they face difficult Economic problems. The survey chain must link up all African Negroes wherever they may be found. The African cousins must unite. African Academy is not an attempt to segregate knowledge. It is an effort to make the Africans aware and conscious of the importance of education, creative skills training, Science and Technology and their places and roles in fashioning tools and materials for life improvement and comforts. The Western Pharmaceutical houses led by US are rightly opposing the manufacture of cheap generic drugs for HIV-AIDS and its associated diseases in Africa. What are these drugs? They are products of herbs, plants and several living things common in Africa. It is our duty to find them and make our own drugs. Knowledge is free. We have to search patiently for it. If HIV-AIDS threatens our very existence it is our duty to deploy all our available resources to search properly for a cure. Retroviruses constitute an interesting area to research into in Virology. The human papilloma virus is incriminated in cervical cancer while the murine leukaemia virus, (MLV) or xenotropic murine retrovirus (XMRV) is incriminated in Prostate cancer in males. The HIV/AIDS is retrovirus. A detailed study of retroviruses and their roles in causing sexually transmitted diseases (STDs) are worth being undertaken. The ways to produce safe vaccines should be explored. Drug design and manufacture are exciting Research area in the computer age. High quality Education supports strong Research basis. Research is the heart and power house of the nations' intellectual capability. The Research Laboratories of a nation must have their lights burning twenty four hours. Streams of conscientious researchers must be working all day long. They must be provided for adequately.

African Academy is an attempt to bring individual excellence together to form collective excellence to have the clout and the reserve for us to cope effectively with the absence of research in Africa. The African must activate his brain to work. Education, learning and knowledge must no longer be a hobby but a lifelong commitment. They are not beyond our brains. Unlike Negro colleges, the African Academy is not a school. It is an international institution or a body to bring global black and African scholars together to share their experiences and find means of promoting Education, creative skills training and advancement of knowledge in Africa and among all black people in the world. Africa has the richest resources in the world. Africa belongs to all Africans in the world including African-

Americans, the Caribbean, those on isolated ocean islands and the Americas and natives of Australia. Africa has always provided the rest of the world with raw materials. Today we Africans want the knowledge and skills to convert these raw materials into finished goods that we consume and to share with the world. The Academy is to bring our global Scholars together. They should know what each other is doing. They should know how many of them are involved in each area of interest so that they can easily help each other. They should know how many Institutions we have, the quality of equipments and staff they have and where they can call for help. The Academy should serve as a communication line and link between the Institutions of learning. It may also visit these Institutions to see their organisations, equipment and staff. It will also offer some advice on improvement in these aspects. The most important thing is to know the facilities at their disposal and plan for their use. Joint efforts guided by the Academy may create funds for purchase of costly equipment for Advanced Research for career Researchers and Postdoctoral workers.

We do not want to be excluded from this any longer. We face extinction if we fail to acquire the education, creative skills and the knowledge to convert the raw materials abundant on our land and environments into modern manufactured goods and materials that we consume and may share with the world in, today's global village and free market. It is only people who have these goods to sell in this market that will survive. Therefore, it is totally nonsense to encourage us to go to market like mad people without the goods to sell in it. We have neither the goods nor the services to sell in this market. We also have no money to buy from this market. Why then are we encouraged to participate in it?

For over three millenniums African Education, creative skills training, learning and advancement in knowledge had suffered permanent disruption and complete stagnation. It had stopped permanently and retrogressed. It had been replaced by ideas and directives by victorious invaders. The new masters had stolen several of our ideas and adulterated them so much that we could, today, scarcely recognise them as our own. Psychological warfare and sophisticated brainwashing of billions of generations over several millenniums had dealt a fatal blow on African culture of inquisitive mind and learning. The miracle of human learning in Egypt was purely of black Africans. Today, black Africans are strangers in the fields they knew best. The Greeks even created a slogan on the Africans because of this. The Greeks felt we were close to the gods. The Etruscans loved and respected the Carthaginians. They were our allies and friends in Europe. It was only the Romans that we initially trusted and helped that developed the mentality and culture that felt that any good thing should be Roman or made Roman by brutal aggression, conquest and defeat.

We black Africans were very conscious of the role of Education and creative skills training. We invented the art of writing and record keeping. We started arts and science. The Egyptian mummies were preserved by chemistry that was sophisticated beyond what several other people at the time knew. The Science, Mathematics and Technology that built the pyramids, tombs and the temples of the sun god are yet to be rivalled by what we have today. The royal purple the Phoenicians and the Carthaginians developed with murex dye had no match at the time. Here we are? We made great linen. Today, we cannot clothe ourselves because we can make nothing. We rely on others for everything. The world may be generous but it cannot supply all our needs. We are a very vast continent of several people. We have to contribute to global production. We cannot just sit down always to be fed by other people. We must feed ourselves. We must wake up from sleep and acquire genuine practical education and effective job training for valuable skills. We will succeed in feeding ourselves. We also must spread education far and wide. We must not rely on one saviour, even if it is Hannibal. There comes a time when we are old. The young ones must be able to assume power and responsibilities. One man leadership and prominence is dangerous for Africa.

Leadership, valour, courage and strength must be community based but not only in one person. The Sub-Saharan African Bantu Negro is notorious lone operator and failures. We have to operate in groups. Each person works for the group or community. Studies are best done in groups. Success is achieved in community for continuity dwells in community. We are mortal. We die and leave but the world goes on. The community continues. It is the community that must be prepared to ward off the enemy. Whatever we know and do must be community-based to last and be useful and sustainable. The current alphabets we use are the Carthaginian inventions. There is always the bogus debate on the Phoenicians and the Carthaginians to diverse them from black Africa and constitute them into colonisers in Africa. Carthage was in Africa. The Army that Hannibal took across the Alps to fight in Southern Europe was three quarters African warriors and only one quarter our European allies fighting against Roman domination. The Syracusean genius, scholar and Engineer, Archimedes was a pupil of African masters. The Romans executed him because he fought on the side of the Africans in defence of his native land Syracuse in Sicily.

Today, the white minority in South Africa and Zimbabwe claim to be Africans. They had not lived as long as the Carthaginians in Africa. We and the entire world accept them as Africans. The Anglo-Saxons, the Vikings and the Norman conquerors in Britain are credited with the original progress in Britain, today. They were all invaders and occupiers of Britain. The British people are proud of them. We are Africans very proud of the Carthaginians and Carthage. The Romans wounded Africa fatally by destroying Carthage by genocide. This was Grievous European crime against Africa. It is worth recalling Hannibal's comment when the Romans threw the head of his second brother; Hasdrubal wrapped and tied in green leaves. He said that is Africa beheaded. What could be truer than that, today?

Recent limited gene typing, matching and locating origins of black people that were victims of mass human trafficking of slave trade had discovered that there is no such thing as white and black. This found that most black people had white ancestry. The same finding would be the case if we probed the genetic ancestry of some of the white racists. They would be surprised along the line that they had black parentage and ancestry. Human behaviour reckons no colour of the skin. Racial xenophobia comes from political economy, power and control of resources for wealth. Unfortunately the skin colour that seems to be a product of the environment, ecology and the weather of the location of human beings on earth and idiosyncrasy of human choice and selectivity in looks and colour that might have influenced line of breeding has come to be a dividing factor in race relations on earth.

Fortunately Science still links us in blood and organs that we can exchange to save lives. Human Biology has not changed a lot. Therefore, the genuineness of Africanness of a first class African nation in Carthage does not arise. Equally, when anybody observes the Negroid features of the descendants of the Carthaginians cross marriages in Southern Europe it is obvious that the Carthaginians were black people just as the ancient Egyptians. Note that they were there for over five hundred years. The role model of the flare of my African patriotism is Barca. The Barcine dynasty, that brood of African lions, Hamilcar, Hannibal, Hasdrubal, Hanno and Mago, this group of warrior kings and Generals stood firm to defend independence, freedom and integrity of Africa. They all died in defence of Africa. The honour of Africa and its civilisation died with them. Today, Africans had survived massive systematic genocide from slave trade and slavery. The menace of brutal colonisation is still manifest in the current conflicts on the continent. It is the principal cause of our chaos and crisis, today. The WTO global trading guidelines are unfavourable to Africa. If it is true that human beings first lived on the continent of Africa from where they spread to cover the whole world and the population has been dynamic with people moving out and returning to Africa, it would be no surprise that human beings on earth are similar. Africans leaders abroad had always been exemplary.

They damage Africa. The love for Africa floats like oil on top of a deep ocean of hatred and hostility. Remember all the names above are after God and its good acts to us. In this case God was Baal in Aramaic language. The Lord Melkart and the Lady Astarte were various representations of this God, Baal (Abasi in Efik/Ibibio). Today, it would not surprise you that we are still naming our children after an act of God. Hence we have Iniabasi, Imaabasi and Mfonabsi (interpreted respectively as elected time of God; love of God and grace of God). This is African. Africa may be exhausted on the road of human existence on earth. It needs helping hands to climb the hills and the mountains to continue in the journey, from fellow human beings, brothers and sisters regardless of colours, religions and creed.

Most of the advice the IMF and World Bank gave Africa in the last century and millennium had turned out to be poisoned challis. We have to be cautious this time. We just need education and training in skills to do it this time for ourselves. I am a liberal African historian in the Ancient world. My civic duty in patriotism and scholarship is to inform the world that very adverse circumstances robbed Africa of its pride several millenniums ago and brought us to where we are today. The world had changed beyond our recognition during that time.

We had also changed beyond human recognition during that time. African potentials are still enormous. We just have to recruit them and bring them all together from all over the world. Africa can then tap from it to recover from this millennial malaise. Let all of us who live, today, in this wonderful rich land of hope ignore the dividing factors and adopt the true strength of the rainbow continent that seems to work for the Americans and use focused education targeted to solve the problems of our underdevelopment, poverty and misery by coming together in AAAD. We have to rebuild from the ruins of several millenniums. Do you know that the famous Roman authorities that pioneered the infamous Roman Empire had to steal a Carthaginian African boat to dismantle to learn boat building Technology to mass produce boats to mount invasion of Africa from Sicily to destroy Carthage by genocide. The man Massinissa of ancient Libya became a Roman spy? He informed the Romans on Carthage and Africa. He corruptly received bribes from the Romans. Our Technology and education were far more advanced than those in Rome and not to talk of the whole Europe. We must be determined to sit down in patience and work hard to provide what we lack. We would have what we lack by working for them. Global knowledge spreads all over the world the way human beings do. We have to learn from those who have it now.

Find the description of Britain the Isles of Cassiterite by Admiral Himilco of Carthaginian global commercial fleet in Africa and you will find that I am not spinning. The Greeks you must recall had come to Africa to plunder under Alexander, son of Philip of Macedonia who pioneered the first recorded global ravaging army. They had by this time looted a lot from Africa and were in possession of what they had plundered from Africa. Herodotus, an ancient Greek Historian narrated some of these events with flare even though he frequently coloured his narratives with patriotic bias and loyalty. Africa was at its best when Education and skills training took priority over all other things. Apprenticeships and trade standards were taken seriously. Since Archimedes was close to Africans in Syracuse, it would not be wrong to conjecture that Archimedes' Principle was used to test the purity of gold in trade to establish standard by African traders. The basis of our strength and progress was the family. The consumer-materialism of the West had destroyed our family bond as the foundation for education and training in skills. Also note that Africa had abundance of gold it used for trade.

We must develop education, the spread of knowledge and learning to achieve Mathematical skills, Science and Technology to make our tools and achieve economic empowerment. We must not attempt to model our education on what others had done. We must produce our own pattern and shortcuts to load maximum information to our system to achieve maximum results from our knowledge and skills. We have a lot of odds stacked against us. Our challenge is to overcome them. Our target is to develop highly educated and efficient manpower with high sense of civic duty and dignity. We must have citizens content with their work and the salaries they earn. They must know the indignity of corruption. They must know that bribery is not a way of escaping from poverty.

Corruption and bribery are criminal stealing from your own farm or house. Hard work and discipline to live within one's means are both economic prudence and self-esteem. This is the civic duty of all loyal citizens. The African must have viable means of living and be content with what he or she has. Fortunately we still have our fragmented parts all over the world. We have to relink the global survey chain. We all must first reconcile with each other. We must apologise for what had gone wrong and is still keeping us apart. These had alienated us to each other to the advantage of our victorious invaders and looters of our treasures. We must all reconcile and merge together to maximise our efforts. The global Western white cousins are always going out to do things together from America, Canada, Australia and New Zealand despite the deplorable past History of their relationship. The white people had fought and slaughtered thousands of each other. Now they had formed the EU and are working together.

The black cousins too might have had bad History too but all of them suffered from the same brutalities. They must go out together to do things as a group now. Martin Luther King Junior fought and died to offer African-Americans civil rights. Nelson Mandela spent almost his entire active life in jail to offer South Africans the nominal Independence. The next phase of the struggle is total freedom of the black race from slavery, loss of self-esteem and economic empowerment. We have to do this through genuine education and creative skills training to convert all our people into efficient and effective workforce capable of standing on its own productive power. The final phase of this struggle will involve all black people on the surface of the earth and on both sides of the Atlantic. The "House of Elders" must be created as an Assembly for very genuine African leaders on their retirement from active politics and high offices. This must include highly respectable people from the Diaspora. We are not willing to abandon the destiny of the black people on earth to political, religious and economic dribbling. The black race must have a purpose in life even if that means working for white people. The terms of relationship must be well defined so that each person knows his or her role and understands the position and the situation very clearly without any latent ambiguity and confusion.

AAAD will do everything to promote viable education and skills training for all Africans and black people all over the world. Education must never aim to make Africans and black people into Western European affluent white people. It must aim to make Africans and black people capable of making a comfortable living from their homelands and lands of birth. They must understand the world in which they live and the things around them. This is the type of education we need. The education we need must improve our initiative, attitude, work culture and change the way we work to create wealth, prosperity and decent environment without crimes and corruption. This final phase of the struggle will involve every black person on earth without any exception. It should never involve African-Americans only. It should involve every black person on earth. We all require economic empowerment through active focused education and skills training targeted to solve most of the common problems we face and produce positive results.

This time we are not asking others to give us. We are asking all our people to stand up and work very hard to carve out a place on earth for themselves. We must confront all impediments on our way. We must use democratic freedom to remove these obstacles. We must use the rule of law. Stephen Lawrence and millions of his type had perished by legalistic lynching. We have nothing to fear. Death is the inevitable end of all humanity. Why should we allow fear of death to rob us of the unique opportunity to accomplish our mission here on earth? The cry for economic empowerment must be loud and clear from both sides of the Atlantic this time. Let us be very clear in our mind that the world currently treats all black people as underdogs and slaves. The onus is on us to prove to the world that we are not. We can do this peacefully through good programme of education and effective skills training.

The Martin Luther Day should be a day of African and the black race march to freedom through empowerment for focused education and efficient skills training targeted to solve most of economic and developmental problems. It must be a day when the black race will undertake a marathon race and other activities to raise money to promote genuine education for all our people. It should be a day we test our strength and reserve and reflect on our past achievements and failures.

Freedom is self-reliance. It is not equivalent to seeing a black person occupying position previously held by white. It is not licence to be corrupt and amass wealth by corrupt means. The bubble Capitalist Economy started with capturing Sub-Saharan black people to sell for money and enslave for free labour to generate capital for private business. Evidence is abounding everywhere in Western Europe in Mansions the dealers in this muggy business built for themselves. Equally the black collaborators were involved in this criminal trade and practice. People in Ghana are said to actively been involved. But the capitalist Economy it developed needed regular supply of cheap labour and cheap source of capital and cheap raw materials. Once these were in short supply the Capitalist Economy became fragile and bubble Economy of boom and burst. My research has shown that this is regular feature of

Capitalism. There had been countless Economic collapse in the past. Some even led to war and violence. Some caused bloody revolutions.

When the Romans defeated and sacked Carthage in Africa Europe had relief and pride of taking the mantle of guardian of global civilisation and development. It has so far done a lot in this direction. The world is vast and dynamic. It is not static but changes. Its race is a relay requiring handing over of the baton from time to time. It is equally plausible that the West is sensitive to consult the world on its difficulties. The world is equally ready to co-operate. The earth is our planet and home. The Sub-Saharan Region has remained a global problem. Investments and aids in its Economy had failed to produce Economy let alone any positive results. The inhabitants of these Bantu Republics stand to blame for failure of their homeland. The resources in the region are global resources. The world in this difficulty of severe Economic collapse has a duty to tap into these resources to use in opening up Africa. The aim is to use our skills in massive Construction works on the continent to open Africa up as an Economic Front. This will regularise the use of these resources that had been wasted in the past. It will also offer the world the unique opportunity of tackling the Desert. This may help us in the study of the environment. Massive Construction work provides employment in recession. It is equally a period of inventions and discoveries.

The argument against this proposal is that the rough terrain in Africa is almost impassable. The world cannot provide the funds for this type of massive project at this time. The response is that we have adequate Technology to do it. We do it to provide jobs for the unemployed. We do it to open up a new Economic Frontier. We do it to make the Bantu inhabitants join the global workforce. We do it to learn more about the arid parts of the world. Knowledge of the use of the Deserts is important to the world. We may be missing something by ignoring to acquire it. Desert Studies as a discipline is important. The world needs a well funded Institute of Desert Research.

Opening up Africa will deter Bandits from hiding there to plunder the world. There is equally the argument that we need security for such massive construction work as Bandits would exploit the situation. Yes this is true but even the violent people may see some good in the construction and accept it as positive progress. As the Baton of this relay went to Europe between the two contestants, this may be the time to give Africa opportunity and see what it can do for the world. Asia has already made its trademark. It is Africa that had remained unresponsive to all stimulations. They have to sacrifice to help themselves. If the world ignores Africa while its leaders keep on talking about Africa, it will be self-delusion and deceit. It will miss the opportunity to rescue Africa. Every global Region has tried and succeeded. Africa is lost in the Desert. The whole world has to rescue it. It seems to have been fatally wounded by slave trade, slavery and colonisation. It has lost initiative. Why do we propose this now? It is the time the world is returning to the drawing board, to review its slate and see the direction it should go. Yes it appears that what is proposed is for African interest only but global self-interest is equally involved. The constructions should belong to all global major investors and their share holders. The commercial values of these constructions are enormous. Most facilities should charge tow taxes.

Corrupt Bantu leaders had already sold some of the assets from African resources to countries like China. These assets must be reversed to the Central Pool and China must pay the correct prices if it wants to retain them. It can contribute by Technical labour. Equally Africa will have to put aside a fraction of its earnings from mineral resources to pay for the work. All investments should be fixed and secured with Insurance. This sounds like Utopia but it will work. It will allow the world to control this fragile environment of Desert and fast disappearing rainforest. It will help in the fight against green house gases and control of environment. Health and tropical diseases are real threat. Panama Canal Construction yielded the discovery of Quinine. This one may yield more new products for disease control. Africa has some of the rare species of wildlife in the world. This is one of the world assets. This project will allow

the world access to control these habitats. We are asking for global construction funded in the main by Africa and aided by the rich of the world.

It is not opportunity for leaders to have foreign and off-shore Bank accounts. Africa and the whole black race must start a global fund raising relay run that proceed the Martin Luther King Junior freedom day. There should also be a global torch run and each participating country will register its runners with token funds. Each event should have a shield or a cup for the winners and certificates for each contestant. The participating countries should have prizes too. We should consider the establishment of Martin Luther King-Nelson Mandela Brigade (MLKNM) to indoctrinate our youths in religious and civic duties and undertaking Education and skills training teaching missions to various black countries. We should teach self-help and civic responsibilities. We must teach our youths and people to help each other. This is not new to us. We share our food with visitors and strangers. Our culture does not allow us to eat alone in the presence of visitors and strangers. This is good civic practice. We must be loyal and patriotic. The AU or re-integrated dismembered African fusion State, the United Africa, (UA.) must teach its citizens honest labour and virtue. Cheating must be rejected and punished. Faking documents must carry severe penalty. Dishonesty in all forms must be penalised. Work is defined as when force moves through a distance. This movement requires energy. Know that you have not worked if you have not moved a force through a distance.

Freedom is economic empowerment where everybody works hard to acquire a high standard of living for all. Freedom demands that every citizen behaves responsibly and sets a good example for others to follow. Prosperity of the nation is demonstrated in clean environment, good health service, good and effective educational programmes, efficient communications network, good housing and water supply, good lighting, efficient maintenance service and adequate and well-maintained public utilities. A good community is law-abiding. It maintains the rule of law. It is not one with adherence to religious fanaticism and fundamentalism. It is not a club of born again Christians. It is not a haven for religious fanatical fundamentalism and martyrdom. It is a place where each person gets the right type of education and skills to promote a prosperous and healthy environment.

It is a place that lives in freedom under the rule of law and respect for God. Economic empowerment demands that the community educates trains and produces manpower and workforce to accomplish provision of high standards of public and social services. It means that if you need to have more company directors and managers you have to appreciate the strength of merger to build strong businesses capable of competing with others for business. Self-reliance, tolerance and team work are vital components of economic empowerment. We must trust each other. Unity is at the heart of a good community. People must be ready to sacrifice their interest to avoid divisions in the community. We must offer civic education that teaches our children the value of virtue, honesty, integrity and good and trustworthy behaviours. We must have a value for the truth and truth alone. We must have a culture that frowns at and punishes falsehood very severely. We must show our confidence in freedom to talk to each other and to unite form a viable country capable of developing a viable Economy to provide employment for our children and the population. African countries must come together to surrender their so-called sovereignty to unite to form a country that works. We cannot cross our legs and fold our hands in support of leadership that has neither leadership nor improvement in standard living to offer us. Rather they hold our land and people to ransom as their private property for their children, friends and families.

Global Africans and the world are disappointed as Africa stubbornly resists all global efforts to help it out of its Economic demise and woes. The leadership has no initiatives. They are selfish, corrupt and criminal. Ruthless slavery and brutal colonialism had dehumanised the black people. They had made us lose value in what we sincerely believe in. They had inculcated the survival culture in us. We have to re-humanise our children by teaching them the value of truthfulness and trustworthiness. We cannot achieve economic empowerment if we cannot rely on each other to be trustworthy. Freedom is not licence to bend the rule and ignore the rule of law. Freedom means responsibility for your individual existence on earth and all your people and land of birth or your homeland. Freedom means the collective responsibility of the people to cater for the welfare, safety and security of the community and work efficiently and effectively for the prosperity of the community.

War and violence destroy freedom. Tyranny and dictatorship create fear. Fear destroys freedom. Lack of freedom creates lack of initiatives. Lack of initiatives creates dependence. Dependence creates poverty, ignorance and misery. These support reliance on handouts. Reliance on handouts has already resulted on lost of freedom and permanent institutions of NGOs. African wealth, to me belongs to all black people in the world, today, regardless of his or her homeland. It is not the exclusive property of the corrupt Bantu dictators that rule Africa for global transnational corporations and foreign powers nowadays gloriously christened, "international community". This is an amorphous structure that does not like to be identified with any faces, landmass or known structure or organisation. This casts a large shadow on its existence and functions. Those who serve it must pause and think if they are serving humanity. The international community seems to be inert shadowy group created to give tacit approval and legality to illegal actions of the Straussite Western ultra conservative rights' actions in the world. This is purely illegal and undemocratic. The behaviours, conducts and events in the so-called war against terror have shown clearly that the Straussite Right Conservatives do not believe in the Right of Man or Democracy.

They conduct and manipulate elections to accomplish their purpose. Their behaviours in renditions, tortures of Prison inmates in Abu Graib in Iraq and Guantanamo Bay in Cuba cannot be justified as actions by people who believe in Democracy and the rule of law and making their social, political and Economic actions subject to law. They are lawless people and arrogant and treat their victims with scorn and spite. They abuse them as savages unfit for decent treatment and respect.

AFRICA AND THE WEST ATLANTICS:

Africa is world's second largest continent. It is second most populated continent after Asia 30.2 million per sq.km/ 11.7 per million sq mile.

Africa is 6% of Earth's surface area with a population of 922 million people in 2005 in 61 territories of human habitation 14.2% of human population.

Arabs are today described as people who speak linguistic Arab language and practise Muslim Islam Faith. In the West, is the Atlantic Ocean while in the East is the Mediterranean Sea. The real Arabs are Semitic people in origin and spread in the Middle East and North Africa.

The Bantus originally spread over the African Continent. They spoke 513 languages and 681 Bantoid group languages are spoken in Eastern and Southern Nigeria and Central Africa, East Africa and Southern Africa. There are about 400 ethnic Bantu groups in sub-Saharan Africa from the Cameroons across Central to Southern Africa. Initially the inhabitants of Africa were divided into Libyans, Egyptians, and Ethiopians. The Libyans made up all groups including the sub-Saharan Region.

There were convulsions of movements of populations during Arab conquest of Palestine and North Africa. The Nubians occupied the areas of the lower Nile. Not much was written of the Bantus. Later the Tuareqs and Bedouins came into the scene. The Bedouins are nomad Desert dwellers. They occupy both the Arabian and the Sahara Deserts. They live with their families in their community and move about in camel caravans. They are famous for festivities. The Berbers were in Africa before the Arab conquest. This is what is fuelling the crisis Algeria. The Indo-European groups occupied Eurasia. It is now very obvious that Darwinian evolution of Natural Selection maintains mankind along this line with strong genetic diversity and persistent Genetic injection and exchange.

The world is dynamic and not static and people had been moving round to and fro. Land exchanges hands. Culture and civilisation move from place to place. Hence it is inaccurate to say that one section copied from the other. Rather a particular invention or discovery moves from one place to the other. Even here I sometimes make erroneous assertive statement on pioneering inventions and discoveries. It is not accurate because dynamism and population movements to and fro. People move about and see new things and ideas and copy them and take them to different places. This is the way Education, skills and apprenticeship spread. This the way knowledge spreads. Hence it is inaccurate to be assertive that a particular idea started here. Rather it is safe to say that some people also knew some particular skills too. Most skills moved about with travellers and became improved until the age of Patency came to confine inventions and discoveries to their inventors and discoverers.

Merger is the soul of business and success in the global village and free market. The black race and its tin pot Bantu dictators and their fiefdoms the past colonialists created and left to serve their alien colonial interest must think twice if they have to go into a merger of their regions in Africa and merger of the countries in Africa and effective link with all displaced black people in the Diaspora to reconstitute and consolidate our global family in a world where all of us are the lowest of the low and the poorest of the poor even though by all estimations Africa is the richest continent in minerals on earth. What we are doing at the moment in this global village of big is beautiful and merger for unity, strength, global expansion and power, is futile attempt at building a great Cathedral or Mosque with a single named block. We must now know that we are members of the black race first before being Muslims and Christians. We are black Muslims or Christians and not the reverse. We are members of the human community on earth. Our religion should not replace these gifts the Creator Himself gave us. Religion should make us better members of these groups. Our religious beliefs should make us perfect for God but not to destroy lives for God.

Merger and union increase our number and expanse of land we inhabit and control. This makes our home an attractive market. It allows more people access to the facilities we possess. The more the number of citizens using these facilities the greater the funds they generate from users. Above all the African rough terrains require re-integration of colonial dismembered Africa for its Economic health. Without re-integration some people are abandoned in unworkable rugged land difficult to work for it to grow food.

The failure of post colonial Africa to destroy the past colonial borders and merge to form real nations of their own is the scandal of independence in Africa. The Africans rejected colonial rule but opted to retain the backbone of colonial rule. The colonial rule denied Africans freedom of movement in their continent. Colonial rule denied the Africans the freedom and right to pool their resources together for effective and efficient management for developing funds to develop their continent. This is the only way to genuine economic empowerment. Each individual African leader is left with a piece of African land, a fiefdom and a rogue state totally unviable to form a nation state and completely incapable of achieving economic empowerment. It is a very difficult task to persuade Africans to unite in humility and work for the improvement of the continent. It is hard to convince them that they should sacrifice individual interests and unite and merge together to work for their common good. Unity and merger provide greater energy to do the work they have to accomplish to attain orderly and sustainable development of Africa. It is essential to stop unnecessary duplication of projects and wastage of scarce resources and limited funds. It is easier to provide modern infrastructures for more people than for a few. Television and internet network and telephone communications all require a lot more users and larger populations. The road and rail network all require to cover larger areas and serve more people and communities. We may liken this situation to having each African in the continent holding on to a brick block meant for building a castle to protect the entire continent and refusing to bring the bricks together to surrender for the building of the castle for their common security. They deliberately ignore the provision of this secure fortress and castle because they do not want to part with what they assume they have.

Yet what they have cannot give them the security and economic empowerment, development and protection they need to escape from poverty and ignorance. It is a shame that Africans are content to live in alien designed postcolonial rogue states rather than merging to form their own states that will offer them both security and economic protection. The whole continent of Africa is riddled with failed states. These feuding and chaotic arid parcels of land cannot offer us the type of economic empowerment that will resolve our chronic poverty. Economic empowerment means that the people are willing to unite and merge together and make all the sacrifices to work hard to use their resources, limited funds and energy to acquire orderly and sustainable development and progress. There must be people in the community who see beyond immediate individual interest. They have to analyse their Economic interest and find out what would enhance the growth of their Economy. It is from here that they make sacrifice the action to improve the Economy demands.

The continent can be described as a failed continent. Yet nobody seems to care. How do you explain and justify the fact that the most brutal and corrupt tyrants of military rules in Africa are returning to rule as civilians? These are the pioneers of failed leadership in Africa. They should rightly be in prison but yet they want to rule again. There is something wrong here. Genuine people interested in good governance on the African continent have a duty to discourage this wind of stagnation. This is why African Academy is essential for African brilliant minds to meet together to lead our people in the debate on what is the best way Africa should face its problems. The question remains for the Africans to answer. It is they alone that can answer the question: "Are their current illiterate geriatric corrupt mediocre and morally decadent leaders the only persons we have to lead?" Until we acknowledge that we have to unite and re-integrate Africa to realise that great continent of our dream, Africa full of vigour, strength and power and be willing to submit to a viable leadership that works for us, we shall forever remain poor, weak and dominated upon by those who realise the value of unity and re-integration into larger and viable countries.

Unity for strength and power is more important than clinging on to tiny patches of our vast land for the benefits and influences of a few self-centred and selfish individuals. A single block cannot form a house. One pebble cannot constitute the door to progress. Africa is the house and we are the blocks with which it is built. Therefore, African Union must be made real. Its Institutions must merge together to give the continent the scope, strength and power to compete in a world where size and quality count. This is why we are advocating for African Academy. We want to make African Academy an institution of that Union to make our people conscious of the value of good practical education and adequate skills training with formal apprenticeship for orderly and sustainable development and genuine economic empowerment. African youths must shed off that image of confused and chaotic continent and people. Our people must work harder.

We must be very serious with what we do for a living. We must take up one project and successfully bring it to conclusion before starting another. We must focus our attention and energy on what we do. We must ignore all distractions. Every African must make room in his or her mind to think about Africa and what we can do to improve and develop it. The development must be orderly and sustainable. We must concentrate on how we can make things better. We must convert our dreams into reality. Desires and ambitions are the inner instincts that point human beings to what can be achieved by working genuinely to get them. It is the gateway to orderly and sustainable development and progress. We are self-sufficient in everything. We have no good Education and creative skills to make the best of what we have in our land. We have no Science and Technology Education, knowledge and skills to transform what we have into the goods we consume and have excess in goods and services to sell to the world and get only minimum of what we need from the world. To succeed we must reconcile with each other and accept a merger of our resources and skills. Our leaders must have the humility to re-integrate Africa and sacrifice their private interest for the community. They must accept that patriotism and love of the land of birth do not mean leadership but service to the land in whatever capacity one may find himself or herself in the community. Failure to accept merger of our land and people condemns us to fragmentation not even of our own but alien colonisers, into negligible fragments powerless to control our enormous wealth and unable to balance our budgets or feed our children.

Genuine merger into a powerful, strong and virile nation governed by the rule of law and true democracy is economic empowerment. Tyranny is gate to hell and poverty. Corruption is sale of freedom to those who pay the bribes. Corrupt nations are homelands of beggars. Beggars have no choice or respect. There is tendency for some religion to assume that Africa is their home to spread fundamental fanaticism. Unfortunately, the West and the US allowed this concept to thrive during the cold war. The fight to expel the Russians from

Afghanistan brought Muslims together. This concept took a new dimension. The Sept 11 twin tower violent destruction was an eye opener. The World, the UN, the West, US, global religious leaders and world leaders must no longer dodge the issue of influence of religion in global affairs. It is not beyond these people meeting at the global arena to declare that religion must be separate from politics, legal system, Economic affairs and governments of every country requiring international recognition must be purely secular.

There must not be any room for theocratic Governments. God has no armies. We must not tolerate wars and violence in the name of religion. Religions so love life that they created the concept of Paradise and eternal life. Hence killing in the name of religion is false undertaking and unacceptable. Heaven stands for life and not death. Let people not abuse religion to dominate over others. We must respect life and the human person and the properties sustaining people in their homelands. We dehumanise ourselves by dehumanising fellow human beings on earth. The hypocrisy of the true situation is that the West is guilty of frequently exploiting religious emotion and loyalty to achieve its objectives. It did so in Afghanistan during Soviet occupation of that country. Intelligence infiltration of places and groups frequently use religious disguise to achieve its objective. This seems to have backfired in this war against terrorism. The Muslims want freedom to protect their way of life. There is nothing absolutely wrong with this aspiration as long as they recognise that others have their way of life to protect. Hence the urgency of the world confiding religion to the confines of the believers by law to avoid any misunderstanding, confusion and assumption that religious leaders can impose religion on the way their countries should run to dominate the lives of other people. To avoid such confusion, the world must ensure that any government requiring global recognition must be secular. They must adopt just secular laws.

Religion has no right or authority to divide the world into ghettos. Religion deals with issues concerning individual well being, soul and spirit and his or her maker. It is a private matter of the individual and the sect involved. They have no right to impose their faith on others or kill them if they refuse. This took place in the past. The world stressed by activities and violence of religious fundamental fanatics must have the courage to tell the believers that they have the freedom to practise their faith but have no right to impose the same on others not willing to accept their faith or cut off places and countries into religious ghettos or religious iron curtain. The global laws on religion must be simple and clear. There is no more room for us to be vague over religion. Freedom of worship must not deny freedom to others that have nothing to do with such religion.

What is the role of African Academy?

It is a forum or platform for African scholars, intellectuals, intelligentsia and educators in all fields of learning to come together to discuss Education, creative skills training, knowledge and learning in the context of the needs of black race and Africa. This is not racist. It is plan for self-help. We must do things for ourselves. We must take the initiative. We must improve on our Education. Our knowledge and skills must have an active nucleus. This must be the active volcano of African knowledge bailing out molten larva of current knowledge and advances in Science and Technology. Technical Education and formal apprenticeship to improve the quality of our products are important for us to produce efficient craftsmen and women.

AAAD IS A BODY OPEN TO ALL HIGHER INSTITUTIONS IN AFRICA AND THE DIASPORA. ITS OBJECTIVES ARE TO MAKE OUR SCHOLARS ALWAYS CONSCIOUS OF PROGRESS IN EDUCATION AND RESEARCH.

The establishment of AAAD to take charge of these responsibilities is urgent. Africa requires a strong lobby group for its Academic life. Such a lobby group has a duty to generate Academic activities, represent Africa in the Academic world, and follow up progress and advancement in education, Science and Technology. It will bring African scholars together. It will award honour to talented African scholars. It will keep records and maintain archives of names and achievements of African scholars. It will also keep records of ongoing works by African scholars. It will also keep records of centres of excellence in Africa and their fields of specialisation. It will publish its journals. It may undertake inspections of these centres for the purpose of approval and accreditation. It will ensure that we have fewer but adequately equipped centres for our youths to study in. It will avoid unnecessary duplications and wastage. We will encourage the community to be courageous and get rid of dead wood in its leadership. The community must be stronger than the individuals in the community.

At the moment we are operating a fringe economy outside the main global economy. Africa, under neither the Egyptians nor the Carthaginian ever did this. This is suicide for any nation not to talk of a whole continent like Africa. Our ancestors relied on production of top grade goods and services to market in their own world at the time of their existence. African Academy is not a political organisation. It is an Academic Sanctuary to offer African scholars and intellectuals that unique user-friendly forum to share their Academic experiences in all theatres of learning to lift up Africa and take the black people out of the city ghettos. We want to take Africa out of the doldrums of poverty, deprivations and want. We want to abolish poverty and ignorance among our people. We need practical education and effective skills to convert our abundant raw materials into finished products that we need and can sell to the world to survive. One thing that is obvious when one compares sub-Saharan Africa to other global regions is the shortage of earning capacities in various fields of human activities. The Academy can conduct research to find out how most of our social activities can be fee paying in Arts and entertainments. Expansion of our earning capacities is important in globalisation.

The Academy should be intellectual powerhouse for our people and their development. African Academy is solely for purpose of disseminating knowledge. African Academy will exist to evaluate what we have and what we will need in order to build up our Academic base. AAAD will help Africans to produce problem-solving-targeted programmes of research in our institutions to produce people with practical education, knowledge and skills to solve the economic and employment problems in Africa and our various environments all over the world. Any knowledge and skills that cannot be employed to solve teething economic and social problems to improve the standard of living of the people is redundant and useless.

AAAD is out to tackle this problem in Africa. The resources and funds Africa spends abroad to offer education to its youths could be used to improve educational facilities several times more than what we have abroad. It would produce more high calibre scholars and professionals than what we get at the moment by overseas training. Developing facilities at home, would give us opportunity to control the areas we need more manpower and the quantity and quality of the training they should have. It would cost less to train people at home than abroad. Equally the students can help in projects while they are training. Planning is essential. At the moment students go abroad and return to ask for employment but planning would highlight our priority areas where we need manpower. To be able to develop our Economy we must be able to plan the type of manpower we need.

African Academy may be regarded as the Negro think tank in the world. There is tremendous need for this sort of body to fill the gap in our thinking. Other races of human beings have got several institutions to accomplish this purpose for them but so far Africa has no reliable body to fulfil this function. We have to plan. We must have targets to meet and fulfil. We must have definite objectives in life. Drifting along without any aim is disastrously catastrophic for Africa. Africa requires training professionals on the jobs to make them comfortable and familiar with what they would do after qualifying. Practical sandwich courses are what we in Africa need. Persistent work is needed Science and Technology. The Researchers in these areas should find good salary earning careers in the areas. Success in the areas requires full commitment. The work should be consistent and the researcher should make his work a conscious part of him or her. Nothing should disrupt the work. The team working on particular projects must always have people working on them at all times. It is the desire of the Academy to advise and encourage the development of viable and functioning Research facilities and make them permanent. Researchers should always work on various projects. The Research Funds should be free from the Treasury Purse Strings.

It is true that several of us are members and fellows of diverse institutions and learned societies. We share these with dominant majority races. Our ability to influence their activities to improve the lot of Africa and the black race is limited. Our membership of these bodies, therefore, serves as status symbol and social prestige. Our presence in them gives them respectability as international forums. They even tap our scarce knowledge and skills to improve their various communities. Our participation may overtly provide them with our contributions as part of their working tools. Equally no matter how many of our people participate in these alien bodies as members and fellows, we are just acting as punctuation marks in their essays. Our participation does not express any ideas as words and sentences do. We still lack our own forums where we can bring all our ideas together to offer effective response to our problems. The Academy wants to bring our Institutions of Learning together as members, improve the quality of their teaching and equipment they have for teaching and learning, make them education and research conscious and develop a core of scholars committed to Academics as life calling and commitment.

What will African Academy do to Africa?

African Academy will bring African educators; intelligentsia, scholars and intellectuals together to find out how their knowledge and skills can be tapped to solve the enormous economic problems we face in Africa. It may succeed in recreating the lost African culture that accepts that only those with genuine message should address the audience. It will contribute intellectual input now lacking in African debates. It will provide African scholars a forum to debate and discuss African problems in an Academic setting controlled by them. It will form the nucleus of active Academic activities in Africa. It will emphasize the role of Education and effective skills training in the life and orderly and sustainable development of Africa. AAAD would thrive to make good education more popular in Africa than at the moment. AAAD aims to give education and skills' training more prominence than it has at the moment. It will encourage the integration of education and work. We must apply education and skills to our work to improve its quality and make education relevant and applicable in our working life. Education must have both social and job relevance. Equally the Academy emphasises that Education broadens and enlightens the mind. It is not a meal ticket. It is wrong to say that it is no use as it does not solve unemployment. Education is part of our culture we had neglected but now have to improve it to grow.

African Academy will essentially bring out the best in Africa and among all global Africans in the Diaspora in all fields of expertise to show what we have and what we shall require to build Africa of our dream. Africa needs a home for knowledge and African Academy is that home. The African Academy will exist to make all Africans conscious of the importance of education, learning and creative skills training. It will be the African eye and ear at the forefront of new and modern developments in education, learning and advances in knowledge. Science, Technology and Technical skills for fashioning working tools and materials are here to stay and they are vital and indispensable for nationhood. This is vital, today, as high Technology dominates all aspects of our lives. We cannot afford to be left behind.

Academy is the Cathedral or grand Mosque for knowledge but it is independent of religion, ethnicity, family or social status and politics. Membership card is excellent scholarship and expertise in Academics. Knowledge is the key to progress. The Academy is the temple of knowledge. It is an assembly of knowledge. It has no room for wealth and affluence or primitive elitism. That knowledge will be the collection of our learned resources and skills to enable us to control our land, environment, space and deep under the earth and seas and oceans. Geothermal, solar, ocean currents, and various undiscovered energies are awash in Africa. Knowledge is the key to them. We must find means of harnessing this energy to work our land.

Reforestation in Africa and all the lands where we live in the world must gain significance. We had depended on nature and our forest for our food. We have to use knowledge of Science, Technology and Technical skills to control the eco-environment and cultivate the food we need. AAAD growing out of wise counselling and our knowledge of the world is the tool we need to plan for programmes of effective education for our purpose. We need focused education targeted to produce people with adequate skills to solve our problems. We can do this. We are capable of doing this. The land has been kind to us. It has fed us all these years. Now we have to kind to this land. We must promote the spread of Science and Technology education for skills to care for our land and protect its eco-environment. Nature alone cannot satisfy our demands for food and wood. Human beings appeared first in Africa as hunters and gatherers; they grew into farmers and livestock keepers and spread out to people all the world. They had increased in skills to the level we are now.

Nobody can do this for us. Why should our children who should be at School be holding not toy guns that civilised people give to their children to play with but AK rifles with live munitions to kill both children and adults in bush jungle wars? It is almost fifty years, half a century; the world had watched this without action? Residual food had been provided as relief to feed the victims of this carnage. Equally it is criminal tyranny of greed to see well paid retired British Army officers organising mercenary fighters in African bush wars under the names of security organisations earning several millions of pounds and dollars from warlords terrorising poor and miserable people and their dying malnourished children. These also offer protection to tyrants and dictators in the name of security contracts. The governments of these mercenaries' turn blind eyes to their illegal activities. The Anglo-American war in Iraq and Afghanistan is said to be privatised to these mercenaries.

We need this money for proper education of our child soldiers and children dying of malnutrition. These people earn adequate amounts from their pensions. They should know that their extra money earning activities in Africa are killing our people and destabilising Africa. They equally know that they are not providing security but chaos, war and violence. We also know that they do not undertake these roles in their homelands, why then in Africa? I am not out to criticise and blame others for our failures and demise or to antagonise and alienate people to our plight but to be very frank to all people of good conscience and point out that some of their methods of wealth creation impoverish Africa and cripple its Economy.

The debt burden of Africa is a big scandal and challenges the good conscience of the people in the West. This is a form of endless slavery and misery for all generations of Africans. The Western lenders have great admiration for democracy and freedom. Yet they are operating this neo-slavery in Africa. The ways these debts were incurred everybody knows were by very shady corrupt and questionable deals. The borrowers in most cases were illiterate African dictators and tyrants without any understanding of the Western financial world and fund management. The negotiators for the lenders were in most cases young bankers zealous to show results. They benefited from their activities. The terms of lending and borrowing were scarcely well defined. Most of the funds never left Western Banks.

The corrupt dictators banked them in the West for their affluent lifestyles and arms to terrorise and silence their oppositions. Yet we are victims of this criminal corruption. Capitalism to us has become a nightmare. It is synonymous with naked corruption. This is why the concept of AAAD is vital to offer our people practical education to help them to apply their knowledge and skills to do things for themselves without relying on contracts, we can ill-afford to pay for with our lean purse and meagre resources. The reality of life confronts us to do this or perish. We also have to understand our world. We should no longer watch the progress of Science and Technology with excitement but we should be participants in all aspects of their advances and developments.

Out there, someone is producing these arms in the armament factories. Out there people are making fortunes in the lucrative arms markets as arms merchants. This is the shadowy criminal market where the products of African jungle resource bush wars fought by African child soldiers, brought up as brutes and killers in the year, 2003 exchange hands for guns and lethal weapons made in the armament factories of very civilized people.

The owners of this merchandise of death are very civilised and rich people. How civilized is a world where responsible people arm African child soldiers, deny them opportunities for education and teach them to be wild killers, savages and criminals? This is the cream of African future generation being destroyed. At the same time African people are being destroyed and decimated by strange diseases like the HIV-AIDS at the height of genetic engineering and gene manipulation of microbial agents for biological weapons. How safe are we without the knowledge of these advances in Science and Technology? The African has wasted his time on earth feuding about nothing. We must urgently acquire our Science and Technology base and solid foundation. The people with knowledge and skills of Science and Technology are much disciplined otherwise they could wipe us out if they wanted to. We have no knowledge or skills in Science and Technology to analyse what we consume from their industries. We need Laboratories and permanent workers in this area. We must stop leaving ourselves prone to danger. Our analysts should be able to screen what we consume to detect any contamination.

The African has wasted precious lives for nothing. The African must now use these wasted lives and resources to acquire and advance knowledge, promote education of our people for effective creative skills focused and targeted to solve the problems of ignorance, poverty and misery among our people in the world. This is African world war to acquire useful knowledge and skills to control our lives. We should be able to advance the frontiers of human knowledge by the end of this century or millennium. There is so much to learn and know that each African life time joined together, today, will not complete the task before they leave this world. We have to start urgently.

Our world war is against ignorance, poverty and misery. Even the recognition that we are ignorant, poor and miserable is knowledge we have to acquire and do something to prevent starving ourselves of knowledge. Ignorance and lack of education are major disaster and catastrophe to any human group caught in this vicious cycle. It is worse when the human beings involved in this are trapped in acquiring useless knowledge and learning the wrong skills. This is African tragedy at the moment. We should be selective in what we choose to study now. At the moment we need knowledge that we can apply to our work; knowledge that will improve the quality and quantity of our work.

Does the world need African Academy?

Of course, the world is becoming sick and tired of Africa. This is not because the world is not interested in Africa. It is rather due to the attitude and behaviour of the Africans. They just seem not to be interested in protecting their interest. They would rather fight and die in defending other people's interest instead of defending theirs. Therefore if educated Africans can gather to get their acts together the world will listen and will be relieved. The world would love to share knowledge with Africa serious to acquire knowledge and skills to do things to help its citizens. Equally the world academic audience is eagerly waiting for African indigenous Academic activities. The world is eager to listen to Africa telling it of its achievements in Science and Technology. The world is eager to see Africa's positive contribution to Science and Technology.

Africa has to convince the world that it is capable of independent sensible decisions for its own interest. It must demonstrate that it is fit to be independent by taking bold actions to overcome its enormous postcolonial problems. Above all Africa must show the world that it can exist without reliance on past colonial masters. Positive and persistent and successful orderly and sustainable Academic activities with good concentration and consistency constitute the foundation of independent life. A successful system is conscious of the basic needs of its citizens. Good housing, clean environment, adequate food production and good nutrition, adequate clean water supply, fabrics for adequate dressing and good communication network all form the core of modern healthy society. Science and Technology and good local Technical skills are essential to provide and maintain all these basic needs that the people require to maintain basic standard of living for their health and comforts. It is common sense that the nation should make positive use of the energy of its citizens by engaging them in effective education in Science and Technology and creative skills training; always challenging them with new projects to resolve problems that the community needs to improve its standards of living or neglects tapping into this energy and abandons it to be abused in mischief, crimes and social strife and violence as in Africa, today.

Articulation of its intelligentsia and available knowledge and skills is the real starting point in its independent nationhood. There are many Africans out there with knowledge, skills and talents that Africa needs for its development. Absence of a body that gathers them together for recognition condemns them to live in isolation without recognition. It also denies the community the opportunity to tap into this pool of knowledge and skills to advance its social needs positively.

An Academy is the collective mind of our best scholars, educators and experts. Individual expert alone cannot move the stone blocking our way to progress. African Academy will generate adequate intellectual force and that critical mass needed to move this stone. Academy of Africans in Africa and the Diaspora is a clarion call to all black cousins to assemble in front of Academia to revive Education, the chase and quest for knowledge and effective skills. We must release all our energy on assimilation of knowledge. We must be certain that no knowledge and skills available to human beings will pass us by. The resources and energy we had been wasting on irrelevant and unrewarding pursuits and projects should be fully invested in Education and skills training to give us the means to do things independently to develop our homeland, Africa and all the places inhabited by our black cousins and improve our standards of living, currently non-existent and miserable. The white cousins are busy studying Science and Technology and conducting researches in various fields and sharing both the works and knowledge among themselves. The black cousins have seen this. Yet they fail to act and respond to this positive incentive that should persuade us to imitate them and create our own Academic base to compete with them. Sitting and complaining and begging for debt forgiveness are embarrassingly unhelpful and counterproductive. The best way to enjoy a good meal is to learn how to prepare and cook it.

We need genuine Education, knowledge and skills to do things for ourselves and produce what we consume. We should not be involved in disputes, feuds, war and violence. We have no means for these. At the same time we should not compromise with deliberate provocation and bullying. We should not allow any seizure of an inch or centimetre of our land. Our land is our heritage from God. It is our asset. We should not tolerate or compromise with asset stripping and corruption. Unfortunately, we still have a lot of Nigerians public figures that find it difficult to differentiate between public funds and their individual private finances. They are endemically corrupt and dishonest. It is a shame that Shell Company that had been in our country before October, 1960 when Britain left us to manage our own affairs has announced leaving Nigeria in five years. Shell had been forced to tolerate and participate in the chaos of Nigeria. Now this infectious social disease is threatening its business. It is quitting. The structure of Nigeria as at present is the major problem. It has to be dismantled. Nigeria has to be dissolved. We may re-unite even to form much larger union than Nigeria but under our own new arrangement and rules for genuine merger. The current union is based on extortion, crimes, fraud, cheating and corruption. For any union to work in future we must abolish, by effective secular and binding laws these vices that continuously destabilise and make our union a rabble of mobsters. The truth is that the leaders do not respect Africa. They want citizens to respect them.

TOKENISM:

Tokenism is the false impression created by appointing one black person to a high public office or having a few affluent black people around in the midst of several millions of black people living in abject poverty and misery, permanently below the poverty line or the bread line. Tokenism is not racial integration or tolerance. Tokenism is a subtle way of dividing black people into opposing feuding camps of the rich and the poor deprived people. It places a permanent wedge between white and black people and other ethnic minorities. What the black people want in this world is practical education and creative skills training to gain full control of their resources and lives. Education and creative skills training are what we want. Even development is what makes the West rich and affluent. The black race lost its freedom and affluence over five thousand years ago. We need equal opportunity to compete fairly. Affirmative action and its privileges or tokenism fool us into silence and inaction but we need mass practical education and creative skills training in Science and Technology to be able to do things for ourselves and the community. The weapon we need is sound education and effective creative skills training. These are the tools we need for orderly and sustainable development. Africa must lose that image of chaos and the leaders that sustain it. This continent and its people are capable of organising an orderly society and people. Independence of Africa from colonial rule will continue to be nominal and meaningless until the colonial dismemberment of the continent is abolished and Africa is re-integrated. A re-integrated Africa can then create few viable proper countries that will form United African

States (UAS). The United African States will control the African borders and the earnings from rich African mineral resources to use for both internal and external development of the continent of Africa and the Diaspora African homelands. UAS will open up Africa to the world. It will stop and prevent isolation and exclusion of Africa from global activities for abuse and exploitation by interest groups. This is not in the interest of Africa and vast number of people living in the continent and the Diaspora.

The tragic catastrophe of the black race is mistaking cosmetic actions for real. Tokenism is purely cosmetic action. It is neither racial integration, tolerance nor acceptance. It is a clever manoeuvre to isolate a section of black leadership to place it in the uneasy position of sham power and responsibility under the watchful eyes of those who do not fancy black people achieving genuine equality or real power to take care of themselves. Tokenism is a clever manoeuvre to make the black race permanently dependent on the white for progress in life. This makes black people accept their life achievements as promotion from white people. Such promotion in turn depends on the black leaders benefiting from the system of favours doing the bidding of their masters at the disadvantage of the black people. Tokenism is existence with tolerance to live life like parasite. Tokenism is a clever way of the majority white establishment abandoning the bulk of poor black people in the slums and ghettos to handpick one or two black people to join them as leaders. This policy leaves the black community with fringe activists without effective leadership.

Africa cannot survive on freak economy at the fringes of its enormous wealth under the control of the powerful crocodile tail of corruption and crime and its crushing jaws of agonising greed. Such an economy is like a carbuncle or fragile disposable amphibian tail that can be dispensed off and be replaced with a new one. Unfortunately a sound economy is a permanent feature that continues to grow and expand. At the moment Africa depends on freak economy, freak religion and freak culture. Even African nationality has been made freak. We must accept the responsibility and register our presence here on earth. We must reactivate Education and creative skills training and make them our way of life as in the days of the Pharaohs. We must make African nationality a precious security and identity card wherever we may be on this earth. Let us restore that word pride to Africa. It is equal opportunities for all of us to live good life or nothing. Tokenism is deception and fraud to fool the African Negroes to accept existence in place of equality of opportunities and privileges to acquire adequate education and skills to work for ourselves. Tokenism cannot rebuild our family and clan culture that maintained respect for the elders and respected and observed the rule of law. It cannot repair the damage done to the African Negro race. Tokenism subverts our unity. Our strength lies on working as a team in unity.

The aim of the European Union is to bring their already very powerful individual economies to form one block. This allows their resources to be pooled together for effective and efficient planning for rapid development of Europe. Is it not plain common sense that if African countries bring their weak and freak economies together they can evolve a viable growing economy? This will allow the continent to pool their resources together to generate funds for orderly and sustainable development of the continent. This will also avoid unnecessary duplications and waste of scarce funds and resources. If rich Europe embraces the advantages of merger and Union what will poor African countries lose by doing the same? Islam seems to see African Union as an opportunity for the spread of religion and Christianity has genuine reason to fear such concept of Union and its ambitions but religious bias has no place in modern secular government and economy.

US is powerful and rich not because the people are white but because it has that critical mass union and merger to pool its sources together to generate both the energy to work for good results and to reward the citizens that work hard and to hire the best workers all over the world to re-enforce and strengthen its workforce. Africa can do this provided it abolishes both ethnic and negative religious influences. We can adopt open door policy regulated by the rule of secular laws. We can still maintain good aspects of the core of our culture without compromising it to licentious libertarian lifestyles such as sexual perversion and corruption of social standards.

Religion should be free for the believers but it should have no place in politics in secular governments and the economy. Religion must be voluntary. It should not interfere with individual lives of private citizens and non-believers. The believers should keep their faith and beliefs to themselves. They should not allow it to interfere with the affairs of the state. Religious freedom must ensure that it is not a licence to dabble into and meddle with politics and the affairs of government or the economy. Religious politics is a dangerous brand. It threatens the freedom of non-believers. The democratic constitution must be very distinct from religious dogmas. Modern trend is secular government under the rule of secular constitutional laws and fundamental human rights free from religious bias and interference. Our survival hangs on neutral and secular merger and union. Violence and bush wars are no answer to our current problems. Equally Africa must not be spineless over the influence of the warlords and their sponsors.

We essentially must be brave and courageous to confront the warlords and their sponsors by sanctions and boycotts. It is our very existence as human beings that they are threatening and we do not do any justice to our survival by remaining indifferent in the face of such major threats. We must confront them. Africa had been lucky to rid itself of all our former warlords. Bashir has continued to slaughter our children. His day will come.

Africa is our home. Crisis, violence and war in Africa affect us all. The Mobutu kleptomania and Jonas Sivimbi sadistic psychopathic violence should never be tolerated again in Africa. We are not savages. We must deal with warlords turning our youths into savages. Our free constitution must make it a capital offence for any African to kill another African or for any group to start bush wars regardless of territorial integrity.

There should be the House of Elders to settle any dispute between any groups in political and other disputes. Africa can no longer afford the luxury of bush wars and being held to ransom by warlords. The bush wars subscribe to armament manufacture and trials of these lethal products on our people. The foreign armament manufacturers use the warlords to secretly use our scarce resources and limited funds for production of these weapons.

Frequent religious riots must score, any religious groups involved, penalty points. The authorities should have the power to suspend the religious activities of such group until it can learn peaceful co-existence. No religion preaches violence. Violence denies any group the right to religious activities and freedom until it learns to maintain the peace and be tolerant of others. Religious intolerance must forfeit the right to freedom of worship and assembly. The UN and the human right groups must consider this seriously in the light of Sept 11 and current war against terrorists. No religion accepts violence as the standard.

We must produce and make most of the things we need to sustain our lives here on earth. Nobody will do this for us. Therefore we need proper education and skills to be able to do these for ourselves. We should beg for knowledge, problem-solving education and practical creative skills training and not drug and food handouts. We need the knowledge and skills to produce food and drugs ourselves. I was born into this continent, Africa full of hope. I am now departing from a fast disintegrating continent. It is not because it is a dark continent. It is because illiterate generals turned bandits. They embarked on killing and terrorising the people and looting the resources in the continent. People without any potential for leadership turned permanent leaders to mislead the people. We have to educate all our citizens to understand the responsibilities of leadership. One Nigerian ethnic group had used cunning intrigues and deceit to out-manoeuvre all others to seize what it calls national cake and ruined Nigeria. It has made Nigeria the most corrupt country on earth. They fake everything. They have made Nigeria not trustworthy at home and in the world. They had made our youths not work any more at School. They pass out with fake certificates. They falsify all documents including travel papers. They have given Nigeria a bad name.

They, it is that are dark in their total ignorance. May patriotic citizens with a sense of civic duties rally around the call to problem-solving education and practical skills training to create Africans with high sense of duty and civic responsibilities and capable of working genuinely for their living without becoming parasites of the state living on corruption and theft of public funds and crimes. We may say that this is not the place to discuss some of these issues. Unfortunately these are the issues that had persistently brought Africa to its knees. It has made the black race lose its self-esteem and humanity in the whole world. It is essential that proposition for AAAD must highlight them as unacceptable behaviours. Effective education needs good self discipline.

This means we will be well educated and have viable and reliable means of living in the land where we live. This demands that we work hard to release all our raw human energy on the African land to make it once again the fortress of human knowledge and wealth created by our sweat and genuine labour. The African should feel the protective power of Africa in every land where he or she sojourns on earth. Africa has felt the weight and impact of the world on it. The world has got to feel the weight and impact of Africa on it in this millennium. Educated Africans had betrayed Africa. They had collaborated with the enemies of Africa to damage Africa. AAAD is a single organisation, a unique forum and a humble home ready to accommodate educated Africans with a sense of patriotism and civic duties to plan and use their knowledge and skills to make Africa work for all Africans. We educated ones must first rehabilitate ourselves in good self discipline. We must have respect for integrity, virtue, self-esteem and high standards without any compromise. We will lose nothing by keeping pupils longer at School to have proper education.

It is our duty to offer the world a viable and confident Africa free from corruption and crimes. Africa cannot afford to be an appendage to a double-headed hydra with amphibian body capable of chameleonic colour changes sustained by intrigues and deceit. Today, this strange organism, European imperial colonialism is no more. Africa is left as a huge bodiless appendage. It is slowly disintegrating into shapeless fragments known as "rogue states". Rogue states are failed nation states. They fail because they were not up to nation states in the first place. Let us not delude ourselves. Let us face the truth. If Africa is fit for a single economically viable nation state capable of looking after itself and its citizens let it be that single nation state. If Africa can afford to have more economically viable nation states let her have only that number of nation states.

Such nation state must be viable and capable of looking after itself and its citizens. What is objectionable and unacceptable is Africa made up of several worthless rogue nation states. These are failed nation states not profitable to Africa. The sad thing about this situation is that alien colonial powers created these artificial failed nation states and left them behind in Africa. Now they are not working. The world is silent and indifferent. Responsible Africans remain silent and confused. We had the courage to ask for independence. We must have the courage to ask the world to help us to re-integrate and reconstitute Africa into African nation states that will work for us.

A land full of rich natural resources is not essentially rich, wealthy or prosperous. The wealth of any land is the high level of practical education, knowledge and the creative skills of its citizens. The ability and creative skills of the citizens to convert the resources into finished consumable products are wealth. Prosperity grows out of good and efficient management of the education, knowledge, creative skills, highly trained and effective and efficient manpower and the finished products they yield to the community. Africa is poor because it is content to live in freak economy at the fringes of the enormous wealth in the world, today. We are not a sleeping lion. We are a dead lion or elephant. We need radical resuscitation to escape brain death. Group labour is common to all human beings. House building has always been group labour in Africa. Africa re-integration is overdue. We lose nothing from re-integration of this continent. The only things we will lose will be our corrupt leaders and unsolicited past colonial masters' foreign intrusion.

We cannot achieve prosperity by operating freak economy outside the world financial market where wealth and prosperity are created. We had been left with several counterfeit rogue Bantu nations that failed to work for the people in them, Africa or the world at large. It is challenging to ask, "Why do they still exist as nation states when everybody inside them, in Africa and the whole world know that they are failed states and are not working?" They borrow money and cannot pay back. They lack food to feed themselves and go cap in hand to ask for drug and food parcels. They beg their lenders for debt pardon. They are corrupt and frequently engage in conflicts, violence and jungle wars. These days are prone to be hijacked and used as a floating armoured carrier and a safe haven by criminals and evil men. We have no qualms in suggesting that they had outlived their useful purposes. The colonial masters created them to express their colonial possessions.

Now they are no longer colonial possessions of the foreign countries that owned them. They should be dissolved and be re-integrated into the Union of African states to take over their affairs genuinely. It is then that Africa can lay down the rules that it will use in controlling its vast number of citizens. The name Africa is synonymous with chaos, corruption, crimes, poverty, ignorance, war and violence. This type of image is what we can do without. We have to shed off this negative image. We must strive for positive image. We must have self-esteem and avoid doing silly mean things. Positive image is essential for optimism and success. As a successful scholar it never crossed my mine that my Academic work was invincible. It was more difficult to fail my examinations than to pass them. The secret was that I worked with total commitment to success.

AAAD is body ready to resuscitate and revive Africa in education. Africa must be re-integrated to work. Africa is more worrying than its current level poverty. It is gradually eroding the foundation of genuine wealth creation and way out of grinding poverty. It is closing the way to escape from poverty to Africa. Collapses of education and rampant examination malpractice have combined to render our knowledge and all our qualifications fake and counterfeit. Counterfeit coins have no value. They are not legal tender and cannot buy anything. This is a lesson to Africa that its citizens must respect integrity and honesty. They must rid themselves and the continent of Africa of corruption and crimes. They must work hard for their wealth and prosperity. They must avoid cheating.

Postcolonial Africa must re-invent itself and Africans must re-discover themselves, their self-esteem and pride. They must abandon timidity and pessimism and regain courage and genuine optimism to face the future. That future lies in good and well-planned orderly and sustainable education in Science and Technology for easy and efficient ways of doing things. To create wealth and prosperity we must combine hard work with integrity and honesty. We cannot succeed if we continue to cheat our way into false success by corruption and gross mismanagement of our resources just as it is at the moment. These habits cannot encourage hard work and positive results. Hard work and positive results require real labour and genuine sweat with full commitment and good planning.

Good management of both human and natural resources is important for wealth creation and prosperity. Africa is far short of this at the moment. Mediocrity has replaced talents and merits. The leaders are arrogant in gross stupidity and ignorance. Negligence and irresponsibility gloriously pass over as moderation and good judgment. Beware of conditioned and robotised leaders beyond the reaches of knowledge and intelligence in the name of moderation. A rational human being is like good palm wine sweet from the tapper. In Africa everybody likes sweet palm wine and drinks it. It becomes strong over twenty four hours. Like every seasoned wine it is for mature experts with knowledge of good wine. Men who know the value of wine appreciate and drink this type of wine. In Africa again it is the elderly people on whose shoulders lie the affairs of the community, Africa and the world that drink this palm wine to give them strength to deliberate on these matters. It is seasoned wine for seasoned people.

The leader should be a rational, knowledgeable and understanding human being capable of reading and understanding fellow human beings that he or she leads. Being bland is not the role of a leader. The leader must know the rough terrain and be prepared to respond with effective action. Equally a friendly welcoming environment requires reassuring response. Loyalty and patriotism must not be stigmatised as hard-line, harshness, dictatorship, domination, tyranny or no compromise. There must be a zone of compromise. Uncompromising situations must gain adequate response and rejection. In my short lifetime the two most hard-line leaders I have known gained credits as strong leaders. Defending a collapsing Africa from the brim of total catastrophe and tragedy is equivalent to saving your precious house and treasures from burning fire. You fight like a hungry lion for meal. Moderation does not come into question. Speaking this way may expose me to be guilty of approving war and violence in defence of patriotism and loyalty. No! War is failure of leadership and communication and lack of skills for conflict resolution. Worst of all war seems never to have solved any problems satisfactorily. It seems to do completely the opposite of what it is supposed to do.

The leaders prosecuting war do everything to justify the sacrifice in human lives and resources made in war but a close scrutiny of war would show that it has never resolved any conflict satisfactorily. The morality of war is left to the leaders and the people. It is failure of leadership. It is corruption and fraud. It is an attempt to cover up weakness. It frightens the people at home to keep quiet over the failure of leadership. It shelters the leadership from exposure to other leaders to settle contentious issues by sound debate and argument. It is criminal because the leadership sacrifices the people and their resources to protect it. The sharks of war gather the spoils.

We all know that living things resort to fight and violence to defend their possessions and interest when initial remonstration of objection and disapproval fail. We must recognise that fighting and violence take over to advance one viewpoint over the other when talking fails to resolve an issue. It is to defend that viewpoint by brute force. The defender equally has very strong conviction and commitment to defend the opposing viewpoint. War, then, is essentially a strange way of resolving an issue or argument by superior physical force. It has no relevance to human relations. It is a total stranger to human relationship. It is like a bull in the china shop. It does not understand the issues involved. It takes over, assumes control and completely ignores what is at stake. It aims to force the opponent to drop his claim and forget the contest.

War ignores reasoning, sympathy and compassion. Our ancestors confined war and fighting to combatants. We are determined to teach the African Bantus communal socio-political cultures and sacrifice they have to make to develop a functional viable Economy. We must create community and struggle to develop within the community. Good manners mean self-sacrifice and suppressing that divisive individualism promoting disunity out of selfishness. Even though we are black African Bantus made timid by our past terrible bitter experiences that made each of us develop core individual survival strategy, we can change and learn to survive in the community. Our leaders and influential people reaping great benefits from

Disunity and failure of Africa may continue to ignore Re-integration of colonial dismembered Africa; it is not overemphasis to stress that independence from colonial rule makes no meaning without re-integration of Africa to reverse the disadvantages the scramble and fragmentation of Africa exposed us to.

They were, perhaps, for entertainment, amusement and fun. It was the leaders that led out their fighters. It was the leaders that opened up the battle. The fighters joined but if the leaders were vanquished and the opponents could not raise up an immediate replacement the opponents ran away. The opposing team get the trophy of victory. This varied from the issues under argument to taking of slaves. The slaves were initially taken to replace the people the victors lost. Later it became means of dehumanising and humiliating the victims. Ancient gallantry never accepted humiliating the defeated at war. It is a sign of our degeneration by dehumanising our opponents.

Perhaps it was a way nature devised to force people to forget protracted and irreconcilable situation in a contest and argument. The physical punishment forces the combatants and contestants to feel the pain and the effects of war. At the end of war, the victor takes what was being contested for as a souvenir or war booty. The opponents no more exist to argue their claims. It is raw strength and energy that count in war and violence. It is not right or wrong any more. Justice has no place in war and violence. It is complete nonsense to talk of a just war. War has no room or place for justice, good human relations or reasoning. War and violence completely flout and violate basic fundamental human rights. They violate the right to life and property.

War, fighting and violence are the most primitive characteristics of human beings and all living things. Regardless of the sophistication of the weapons deployed war is still barbaric and a crude way of settling issues. Therefore, those who think that war is a way of bringing good to human beings are ignorant. To deliver good things to people, it is important to maintain good relationship. This is the first casualty of war. Hence war destroys and cannot construct. War ignores the rule of law. How then can it enforce the rule of law and deliver democracy? The people that spin these concepts are ignorant of the values of war. War cannot deliver democracy to people. War delivers fear. Fear is not acceptance. It is revulsion and rejection of the concepts.

On the surface, war looks like a competition. The conduct of war clearly shows that it is neither a genuine contest nor competition. It is the vanity of human beings that give the life they do not make to trivialities of life on earth. Competition is to win and be alive to get and enjoy the glories. War is to end life for what some fanatics believe in. The life sacrifice may not believe in the cause. It is similar to the Roman gladiatorial imperial games of spilling blood as long as it is not that of the emperor and his kindred. War displays the brute in man. It is cruel and full of atrocities and ruthless murders.

It is worth condemning war in all its manifestations but the human spirit is violent in nature. It is arrogant and takes a lot of risks. Let those who lose genuine argument to war and violence ensure that what they are contesting for is worth sacrificing lives for. The arrogance of superpower prowling the world with wars is expression of ignorance, callousness and disregard for human lives. It is violation of the rule of law. It is loss of control and self discipline. Above all, just as the war and violence take over from reasoning, it is tacit acceptance by the leaders that they had lost the power of communication, reasoning, conflict resolution and leadership. They recline on their arm chairs and let force and murders do their work. They send in the army to kill and plunder for them to get the glory from terror, war and violence.

Courtesy may count but docility and doubtful compromise are totally out of place. Unquestionable patriotism and loyalty should be total and know no bound. Patriotism and loyalty do not count in competition only but they should also take prominent place in your work, self-esteem and conduct. We all should stand tall and brave to speak with African voice and wrestle with African strength to win for Africa. We can smile to court favour not for ourselves but for Africa. This life that is now spent had trodden the earth as an African. Those who refused to recognise and ignored the footprint of Africa where it reached failed to gain African recognition. They were ignored to take offence at their demise.

There is a place for expression of joy and gratitude. There is equally a place for showing just rage. The word, silent diplomacy is a misnomer of ignorance and cowardice. It is equally true that silence is golden. This is more so in personal relationship to avoid aggressive personality. But permanent silence has no message to deliver. It causes confusion. It abandons the people without any ideas on what to do. It ignores nature that gave you the senses to use in reacting to events and express your opinion. If we are confronted by war we have no choice but to stand firm in our community and fight. The madness of war has no reasoning. Courage and display of human Barbarism are what the violence and atrocities of war know. It would be a disaster for African Bantu to accept abuses and humiliation as in the past. They have to wipe out local collaborators and destroy aliens who defile their human person. Yielding to slave trade, slavery and brutal colonialism is denunciation of your human person in danger and self-abandonment. Do not run away. Organise your community and stand and fight with all your weapons including biting with your teeth. Seize weapons from the enemy and use them on him. Be mad and kill until the enemy knows that you can kill and fears for his life.

Competition requires cheering and noise making. This is why the world came around to applaud Mohammed Ali. In the international arena it is stiff competition. It is equally important to make friends in a democracy. We need friends for support but we must know how to argue our cases and persuade friends and foes to support our cause. The path is not all smooth in life. We must have the knowledge and skills to walk both the smooth and rough paths. This is why the creator equipped us with adequate tools to offer appropriate responses in different situations. Let us no longer be fooled that the terminology, “moderate African leaders” is praise for good performance. It signifies failure and ignorance. Africa had had its fair share of moderate leaders but it had failed to achieve its objectives. The leaders were timid and afraid to take bold decisions. They failed to dissolve mini colonial rogue states after their creators and owners had left. They took wrong advice and continued to run their continent as estates for absentee landlords and estate owners. The leaders became estate managers and supervisors. They travelled frequently abroad for instructions and advice from their estate owners. Today, most of these estates are overgrown with weeds. The redundant estate managers are crippled by both age and shortage of ideas but they would not retire. They salvage a living by scavenging from the neglected overgrown estates.

User-friendly education in Mathematics, Science and Technology is what Africa and the black race need. The black race has the right to be here. It also has the right to accept the responsibilities for life on earth. Africa is just too big to live on charity and handouts. Problem-solving education, creative skills training must be the right of all Africans and every black child on earth to enable the child make a decent living from the land of his or her birth or habitation. The demands of life are associated with work. Every person must have the skills and means to work. Our lone-ranger culture is very destructive to our opportunities here on earth. God created us as a team. That team is called the black race. Africans have villages. In the relationship between the villages in certain cases friction and violence might have been involved but modern economies rely on peaceful co-existence for growth. Business cannot thrive in violence. Violence and its destruction are wasteful to resources. They scare away business essential for wealth creation and prosperity. We cannot be consumers only but we must also produce the product we consume. We are insulting and abusing those who produce what we consume.

We will never make any progress unless we recognise each other as members of the team, the black race. The social level of the individual, what he wears, eats, where he lives or his educational level has no relevance in his being a member of the black race. What is important is the way the black race brings up the individual to reach his potentials to be acceptable to the team and to play constructive role in it. Merger is not a nasty word. We must work as a group. We see the huge multinational transnational Western conglomerates of Western share holders operating in our various countries in Africa. Asia is fast developing theirs but our illiterate leaders specialise in stealing our money to launder abroad in tax-free havens or in Western Banks while their people are destitute. Do we not know that people made these beautiful places we admire? Africans have to work in teams. Merger in African case is the important re-integration of the colonial dismembered Africa. Africans disapproved of colonial rule. Unfortunately, they left the lifeline of colonial rule: the division and fragmentation of Africa into non-viable territories shared among Western European countries in Berlin on 15th Sept 1884 to avoid European countries fighting each other for a share of African land to pillage its resources. For a while, it worked as long as the Western colonisers were around in control of these patches of African land. They suppressed the people and kept their social demands to basic minimum. They took charge of external affairs affecting their overseas African territories. After independence, these territories suddenly became countries. They had to take over all the obligations of every country in the world. A large number of them are unviable patches of land unfit to be a country. They condemn the people to virtual banishment in poverty and deprivation in arid lands. The eco-environment, Geology, soil Chemistry and climate (weather) in Africa essentially requires re-integration of the continent back to the way it was before 15th Sept 1884. Drought is frequent in some places while rainfall is high in other places. Therefore, any division of Africa into countries must not ignore these facts. Water must be high in consideration in such division. Ethnic distribution should also play a role for ease of communication in a common language. Economic viability is also important in the formation of such countries.

Money laundering abroad in safe banking havens and Western Banks is a clear acceptance and recognition that the leaders themselves are dishonest and do not trust the institutions that they are in charge to keep our funds safe. They do not recognise the safety of Africa for their investments. How on earth do they think that foreign investors would trust them to come and invest in their countries? The more money they dump abroad, the more they frighten away foreign investors. Nigerian leaders are stupid enough to launder much of their stolen oil money abroad while asking people to come and invest in their country. How safe is Nigeria if its leaders launder all their embezzled funds abroad? Sadly, these illiterate leaders do not know the significance of their actions in laundering money abroad. They are telling prospective investors that their country is not safe to invest in. This is the simple message they are sending to the world. If they cannot save there why should foreigners do so? This is the dilemma of Africa and its would-be helpers and investors. Fair-minded people all over the world try to persuade people to go and invest in Africa but these people witness huge capital flight from Africa. Its leaders launder huge amounts of their stolen and embezzled funds abroad. If they cannot invest their stolen money in the place why should alien investors do so? Adding to this Africa is always in chaos riddled with violence.

We must have the patience to work as a team for satisfactory results. We must equally accept that we do not essentially have to benefit from every situation. We must allow some people to benefit from some situations even when we fail to do so. We must learn to work for the common good. The Africans have got to learn how to work as a team without expecting immediate reward. We must learn to be patient and work hard for results. The tragic catastrophe of the current culture of the black race is that everybody wants his own share before the investment is made. This has resulted in massive senseless corruption. People escape with the capital to be invested on projects that would yield results to change the lives of many people in the community. We cannot progress in life if each person caters only for his own personal interest at the expense of the communal interest. A tree cannot form a forest. The forest has several trees and is able to protect and provide shelter and food for everything within it. The things in the forest must not destroy it. They lose their home if they make this mistake. They become stranded. The African Negro must love this continent and work hard to make it user-friendly as other places on earth. The illiterate Bantu African politicians pay themselves more than the highly educated elites and fail to recognise the talents. Failure to recognise talents and reward them adequately affects the Economy. The prosperity of the country makes the people prosperous. It creates many jobs and employments. It also promotes several successful businesses. People's purchasing power is increased and stable.

Community projects generate and protect jobs. They promote prosperity. We must be prepared to make the sacrifice for the common good. We can never escape from our current crippling poverty and misery without making adequate sacrifice for the common good. The vision of AAAD is to encourage our scholars to come together under one umbrella to ensure that we all make the sacrifice to offer all our people problem-solving education and practical creative skills training. The pool of knowledge of the AAAD must be the collective maximum intellectual and skills creation of all the Africans and black people on earth. Our genuine work culture must develop to take us out of our current poverty and misery. Team work and real sacrifice are needed. It is our intention and great desire that every black child should have genuine problem-solving education and adequate skills to acquire economic fulfilment in the society in life. We may have to integrate all forms of apprenticeship with formal education to widen the option at School for every youth. AAAD would be formed to bring our scholars and intellectuals together to work in teams. Its major duty is to generate the culture high education and research among the black people. It will advise black governments on the essential equipment each educational institutions needs for the students' work. It will also help them to produce curricula of studies relevant to their needs. AAAD would be an autonomous body. Members may have to pay reasonable member fees. It would also accept genuine donations from responsible, respectable and honest people. It will also charge for projects it undertakes to do for governments and businesses. It may also undertake fund-yielding voluntary activities. AAAD would be intellectual housekeeper charged with the responsibility of developing high standard relevant education for all black community. It should also develop practical skills training for them to help them develop their practical skills. It would encourage the establishment of credible uniform standard of apprenticeship training for youths.

We should integrate formal education with skills training and apprenticeship to ensure that each citizen leaves School with something to fall back on to earn a living. We must make education productive and profitable. Africa had set standards of social education the youths had to go through before they were admitted to the adult society. Today we have seen that Science and Technology, Technical and apprenticeship Training are very important landmarks in education that every African and black youths must have before they are admitted to the adult society. We must replace our ancient social induction education for our youths with this essential new form of social induction education. We risk damaging our youths, our land, families and people by neglecting and abandoning our youths without preparing them well for life in the community on earth. The world relies totally on Science and Technology and good skills, to survive today. Our youths must be equipped with honesty, observance of the rule of law, integrity and trade for survival in the community. They must have lessons on civic responsibilities and working conscientiously in teams. Our youths must know that working hard as isolated individual is unlikely to succeed in a world where youth gangs are predominant and work in teams.

The catastrophic tragedy of illiterate leaders has devastated Africa. The world political and economic discussions no longer include Africa. Africa is in discussion over wars and violence. Africa is mentioned in the devastation of HIV-AIDS and its consequences on humanity and the continent. Yet these empty headed illiterate leaders are busy laundering the scarce money mineral resources of Africa earn in off-shore banking havens and Western Banks. These leaders cannot be described in any other language than the fact that they are stupid and ignorant. A leader that plunders wealth from his land to store abroad from his impoverished and deprived people is stupid and ignorant. Africa has had a fair share of absolute illiterate leaders capable of emptying its treasures without any skills in leadership. Africa has leaders who see their positions as privileges to embezzle public funds. To them leadership means escape from poverty and the group still in it. Unfortunately, these are the very people they were selected to lead and take them out of poverty. Africa will continue to waste away in poverty and chaos as long as this continues. We must develop Academic Research Culture and continuous and sustainable Studies of what is going on in other parts of the world. Knowledge is power. Africa must invest in Knowledge and maintain viable Academic Research Institutions.

The tragedy of the situation is that the few educated Africans are in league with these illiterate leaders to loot the treasury and plunder the African wealth to impoverish their fellow citizens and make Africa desolate and miserable and unfit for a highly competitive world of high Technology global village. AAAD is out to promote problem-solving education and practical creative skills training for all Africans and black people all over the world to help every black person to have reliable means of living to work to restore the dignity and respectability of Africa. Africa is overdue for rehabilitation. The job is to be accomplished by Africans themselves and no-one else.

AAAD will promote mass education for all Africans, effective curriculum of studies, high standards of performance and efficient and responsible use of the limited resources for good results. AAAD is not in confrontation with fabulously rich illiterate Army generals in the grip of leadership in Africa. AAAD is out to make education, knowledge and practical creative skills a top priority in Africa and among all black people in the world. The current concept and practice of taking up security and cleaning jobs in affluent Western cities by highly qualified Africans is a travesty of economic priorities and complete neglect of Africa in absolute distress. Here is a continent needing enormous manpower to build its roads, houses, its communications network and essential infrastructures but yet its scarce manpower is wasting away where it is not needed. Training efficient and effective manpower and managing it to be productive and serve the purpose of development in Africa are important. We must not only sort out trade disparity but must equally tackle the employment opportunities in Africa. We have to stop massive official corruption to save funds for job creation in Africa. Corruption destroys more jobs in Africa than all other factors. Corruption in Africa is self-inflicted injury. It destroys jobs and increases their misery and frustration. Corruption makes Africans and black people poor and deprived. It leaves Africa and black people behind other people making fast progress, today, in the world.

TEAM PLAYER:

This is a sound principle in participatory democracy and social order. This does not mean compromising your sound reasoning on issues of vital importance in human relations. It is not total surrender to dominant militant fanatics that cannot see beyond the screen of immediate vested interests. It does not mean surrender to mediocre leadership that walks the team into avoidable danger. It does not mean acceptance of permanent slave status and inferiority complex of a slave worker. It does not mean ignoring your talent, self-esteem and skills for the mediocre to exploit you to build up his non-existent image. Nobody has be a crony to be a team player. Team player does not prevent you from registering your doubts and disapproval in the midst of bogus convictions and lack of vision in mediocre gullible leadership. Team player does not prevent you from doing your job the way your knowledge and skills allow you to produce better results than others. Team player must know the team and contribute to its health and success. You do not have to be a religious fanatic to be a good team player. A good team player must champion the cause of the team and not individual crusade. The team choice takes priority over individual preference no matter how genuine that may be. Unanimous decision must not, however, compromise sound team principles. Diversity of opinions at times may be enriching to orderly and sustainable development. Participatory democracy requires contributions from all the stake holders.

It must avoid the domino effect of a domineering overwhelming personality. Passive and bland behaviour does not make you a good team player. A good team player makes positive contributions to the success of the team. A good black team player has a duty to recognise tokenism and its objectives. He is under the pull of two forces. The people who want to use him to oppress his suffering people and his poor and ignorant people. He needs wisdom and ingenuity to deal with these strenuous forces acting on him. He must know when his actions are directly opposed to his own group interest. A good team player is not essentially submissive and humble to slavery. He must not compromise his freedom of expression of frank and sound opinion to "good team player". A good team player makes positive contribution for the success of the team.

The thieves, criminals, conmen and law breakers can be good team players in crime but a man of integrity, dignity and virtue has nothing to do with their trade. You do not have to participate in evil action to be a good team player. A good team player is a person of independent mind not taken in by the crowd. He does what he knows is the right thing to do for the good name of the team. He ensures that the team does not bend the rule. He keeps the team within the rule of law and good behaviours. He works for both the good reputation and success of the team. He ensures that powerful domineering people do not hijack the team to advance their hidden agenda injurious to the team or carry out their personal vendetta against other people. A good team player respects integrity and virtue. A good team respects the rule of law. It plays according to the rules.

The world will be thrilled to know that Africa can articulate its knowledge and skills to help its people. We cannot achieve our objectives with fun-loving geriatric corrupt and illiterate leaders. It is disgustingly astonishing that Africa has paedophilic leaders without morality in asking their grand daughters' age group to bed for casual sex. These are polygamous fathers of several children. A lot of them cannot count their children because of those they miss from casual sex.

SUMMARY:

The greatest weapon of imperial colonisation from the Romans down to recent colonial masters has been "Divide and rule------- Impera et divide." Fragmentation to form weak negligible parts that may be encouraged to feud with each other to give the colonising power peace and freedom to rule is a major part of instrument of colonisation. Unfortunately, we do not recognise this in Africa. The multiple postcolonial conflicts in Africa had failed to make us realise this in our continent. Even the massive mergers of the transnational Western corporate conglomerates controlling our economy had failed to make us think. Even the evolution of the European Union has failed to compel us to think of the huge advantages of merger. Rather we had resorted to bush wars in the name of our religion and ethnicity. We still cannot feed ourselves. The current tactics the Anglo-American NATO of recruiting frustrated local people to form security forces to protect renegade local people they handpick to impose on the people in invaded and occupied lands are new methods in empire building and neo-colonisation. It is sad, the UN, obviously a Western subordinate Quango is an active collaborator in this conspiracy. The UN secretary, Banki Moon is hopelessly a Western crony. Are the Anglo-American Alliance Military and NATO the UN standing Army? Why should the UN take up responsibility for tidying up the mess they had made of Iraq and Afghanistan? They should clean up the mess they had made of these places. The UN should not be involved.

Our brilliant Academic minds must come together to find out what the power of knowledge and creative skills can offer us. African Academy aims at making Africans aware of the fact that merger into effective union to pool our resources together is the gateway to strength and knowledge is power. Time is overdue that colonial dismembered Africa should re-integrate to recreate Africa as the Western European colonisers saw it on 15th Sept 1884 in Berlin Conference that divided it by drawing straight lines in a poorly drawn map to create what we have, today, in Africa. Africa Magna should organise and collect the funds from the sales of its rich minerals, currently in private pockets, to use to rehabilitate Africa and open it up within and without. It should build up its Economy. This will rehabilitate our suffering people.

It is extremely difficult to find that most black people are fully aware of our status in this world and what levels of human degradations we had been through from various human races but yet we fail to act in the interest of our people and community as a race of human beings. It is ordinary common sense that each one of us is a black African first before all other considerations we may be given. Ignoring this single fact for whatever purpose is damaging to us as a race of human beings. Today, we have seen the very people who invaded our land as illegal immigrants, exploited, plundered and looted it ensuring that we do not get to their lands. They are bitterly complaining of being swarmed with illegal immigrants, economic migrants, asylum-seekers and refugees. Yet they brutally colonised our land. They fragmented it into unviable dependent countries that they are now calling "rogue states". Nevertheless, the solution to the problems currently confronting Africa, Africans and global black people does not lie in the querulous youths queuing up for asylum in the West.

Yet we continue to lack initiative and vision. We lack the self-esteem to reject being poor and wretched, miserable parasitic rogue states. We fail to recognise that in order to achieve true freedom and stop being rogue states we have to reject the colonial-created rogue states and their artificial borders. We have to merge together for strength and power. Our so-called leaders fail to recognize that unless they make the sacrifice to think less of their individual gains and social status and accept the merger of our minirogue states into a strong and powerful nation in our own right, we will continue to be poor, miserable, parasitic and highly dependent irrelevant units and people. Are we so shameless that we allow the criminals who created these unviable miniunits without our permission or authority to fragment and weaken us for them to rule and dominate to get away with their crime and turn around to label us rogue states and banana republics to insult us without our response? They knew they were creating rogue states and banana republics, why did they create them? Was it to humiliate us and condemn us to social and economic exclusion? Did they create these unviable ministates for derogatory name calling and insulting abuses?

It is worth telling fellow black people and Africans wherever they may be that they are wretched and miserable, today, because the past did not treat them fairly. Egypt was a first class nation. Alexander, son of Philip of Macedonia sacked the kingdom. He brought in the Ptolemy. The Ptolemaic dynasty was a disaster that Africans, today, had failed to notice. The Romans rejected Cleopatra's attempt to establish friendship with Rome. They sacrificed two famous Roman emperors, Julius Caesar and Marc Anthony. They turned around to eliminate Cleopatra herself and her four children including the chosen heir to Caesar that he introduced to the Senate in Rome at the age of ten. The European conservative right whose conservativesm means that there should be no change in white policy and attitude towards Africa, Africans and black people, opted for subjugation of Africa, black people and Africans. The spineless and toothless bulldog corrupt African leaders should know that Africa now has to define its policy towards Europe. If Europe wants radical change in their position, Africa should co-operate. However, Africa should not be timid; it should harden its position if Europe sticks to its former African policy.

THE DISASTROUS CATASTROPHE OF THE ULTRA-RIGHT NEO-CONSERVATIVES:

The world and the true and wise global democrats and compassionate freedom lovers the world over must rally round to defend the banners of our real civilisation and true democracy. The current Western neoconservative right group led by US faction because of the enormous power, wealth and affluence of prosperous United States of America is in the mould of Octavius's Group in the early well-acclaimed powerful Roman Empire that Julius Caesar created and consolidated and Marcus Antonio realised very late that Octavius's group had hijacked the Empire to execute their individual ambitions and tunnelled vision of the world. This Group got rid of Julius Caesar and later Marcus Antonio. They took over the Empire and executed their individual ambitions and visions of the world in their time. Octavius is acclaimed to have accepted Julius Caesar as his father and mentor he accepted Senate to make him "god". He changed his name to Caesar Augustus. He was a self-conscious ambitious man. He cared not what he did to enhance his popularity. He ripped off the Forest in North Africa and built more amphitheatres in several parts of the Empire. He held several shows, Imperial games, to entertain and please his subjects. He caused global warming in North Africa and expansion of the Sahara Desert and destruction of the fauna in that Region. He ruled by decrees and fiat. Mary and Joseph were responding to one of those decrees on census when Jesus was born. This was an Emperor without any sensitivity to the feelings of the interest of the people in the so-called Roman Province. To him the alien Province was for exploitation. Hence he looted North Africa clean and dry.

The Empire running on their newly replaced wheels and tyres finally crashed. Of course, this does not mean that Octavius and his group took the Empire on a joy ride and crashed it immediately. It took some time before the end came long after the most of the neoconservative ultra right had each taken turn to use the Empire to execute his own narrow-minded selfish ambitions. Octavius under the name of Caesar Augustus took over North Africa by storm. To average Roman citizen this was wonderful. A strong man had emerged after Julius Caesar. He had extended the frontiers of the Empire into Africa. But little were there aware that this was Julius Caesar's wise vision and achievement. Julius Caesar had realised the significance of world unity under the expanding Roman influence. Hence his co-habitation with Cleopatra was to achieve this objective. Yes ignorant people would feel that this was expression of Julius Caesar's vanity. But wise and intelligent people would understand that cross bonding had always been the way human beings unite across the ethnic and racial divide, conflicts, violence and war. Equally, Research has surprisingly shown that all significant European leaders including the Generals and military men who fought against Africa and genuine African leaders had always supported integration of Africa into the West instead of subjugation. But the European conservative had always rejected integration.

They wanted subjugation and humiliation of Africa. They fought and seized a weak and disorganised Africa and sacked it. Thank God/ Allah our creator that time is dynamic and changes. The world today is yelling for integration of Africa into the current global Economy. The world wants Africa opened up for both internal and external communication and business. Africa is central and links Asia and Europe and all other landmass on earth. It is a mistake to ignore the heart of the world. The Africans are famous for self-neglect. They failed to join the Europeans to campaign for abolition of slave trade and slavery. The sub-Saharan Bantu Africans should stop ever searching for wealth they cannot make sense of and join others to exploit the rhythm of the dynamic changing times. They must join the debate on integration and lobby the world on the advantages of integration and what they can offer investors for opening up Africa. Global mass construction work can open up Africa. The Technology and skills are there for the work. The argument that the rugged terrains of the African soil are unsuitable for such construction is wrong. The same applies to the argument that sandstorms would make roads across the desert impassable. Already the Bedouin caravan traders are passing across the desert without invincible difficulty. Small innovated Technology can overcome the problem with sandstorms. Challenging problems made Technological inventions and expansion possible.

Julius Caesar was wise and visionary. He saw the benefits of Africa and Europe uniting across ethnic, racial hostility divide. There is absolutely nothing wrong in matching personal Chemistry across this divide expressing itself in any dignified form. Caesar and witty Cleopatra, the last symbol of African diplomacy and vision of the world, saw this. They had the wisdom. Cleopatra, just as Moses had that rare education in ancient African core persuasive diplomacy and the rule of law. This was centre of African concept of democracy. It was always to be all embracive to maintain the peace. Today, we may also add, “participatory” to this. She succeeded in persuading Julius Caesar to accept her vision of the world. The ultra conservative rights in Rome were just as mischievous as they are today. They decided to slander and blackmail both Julius Caesar and Cleopatra. They called Cleopatra, a patriotic Noble daughter of Africa, a whore. They accused Julius Caesar, of betraying the Empire to Africa because of an African whore. The chance of saving the world by long held African vision had been smashed. The ultra conservative European rights always believe that the world should develop around their tunnelled vision of it and each of them should be immortalised and given credit as the heroes of the past. The worst thing about the ultra conservative rights of the West from the Romans to this day is their cravings for immortalisation of themselves for the wrong causes that they sell to their people as positive expression of the greatness of their nations and the people.

Octavius and self-styled Caesar Augustus on the Imperial Throne at Rome at the time of birth of Jesus of Nazareth, having eliminated obstacles to his ambitions in Africa and Rome itself descended to damage the environment in North Africa. He sent his army of men to destroy the forest and wildlife in North Africa to satisfy ever insatiate vast appetite for wood to construct ever expanding amphitheatres and wild animals for games and meat for consumption by the citizens at home and during games. This evil man created enough greenhouses gases and massive deforestation to convert the forest in North Africa into desert to expand the Sahara into its current size. Recent Western European adventure of imperial colonial empire in Africa extended the desert in the South. The Sahara expanded by lips and bounds. Now oil exploration and industry are dealing fatal blows on this poor and unfortunate land, Africa. The damage the Romans inflicted on Africa seems to be escaping the History books. Perhaps the Europeans like praises but hate bad eulogy.

But there was clear difference between the evil Romans and Alexander, son of King Philip of Macedonia. He seized Egypt from the Persians under Ahasuerus. He appointed local nobles to take charge of this jewel in his golden crown. He fell in love with this great land with better civilisation than what he had in Europe. He chose Alexandria to build his city fit for the King. He proceeded on his way to achieve his ambition to conquer the world. Alexander had a short busy life. He had very little time to revisit conquered places but whenever he had any chance to revisit captured places Alexander never failed to punish and discipline people who violated the Greek culture of democracy. He was forced to accept obeisance by Indian crony lords though he was strongly advised against it by his confidants. Alexander even fell out with his chief confidant who expressed displeasure over this. The man was executed for being disloyal to Alexander. After a few days Alexander personally became uncomfortable with obeisance and abandoned the idea. This is to illustrate the differences between the Greeks in Africa and the Romans in Africa. It is irony of History that it was the ultra right conservatives in Rome led by Octavius that murdered both Julius Caesar and Marcus Antonio. They proceeded to destroy Greek heritage left in Africa by Alexander and later advanced by his General that took over as Alexander had no heir. They destroyed Cleopatra and her son Caesar's heir, introduced at the age of ten to the Senate in room as his legitimate heir. They proceeded to destroy the remaining three children of Cleopatra. This is the History of Africa.

East Germany was forty years from frontline Technology but Africa had been five thousand years from Technology starting from when they were leading the world. Our learning and Technology were brought to an abrupt end by repeated invasions from Europe. Each invading horde destroyed as much as it could. It plundered and looted as much as it could. Starting from the Romans they made as much efforts as they could to dehumanise the black people in Africa and destroy as much as they could. They plundered and looted everything in sight. They even removed our holy Obelisks and lie that they were given to Admiral Nelson for defeating Napoleon. By the time East Germany reunited with the West after only forty years it was behind in Technology. This is what has happened to Africa after over five thousand years of persistent destabilisations by alien invaders of all colours. We, however, have no excuse for not standing to fight off the invaders. It is criminal to remain prostrate in the face of demeaning and dehumanising threats. We should unite and plan credible response and fight. It is our civic duty to prepare orderly and sustainable development and defence of Africa.

Whoever, disseminated that lie must know that it was not right for the Arab invaders to give them, our celestial stones and artefacts of our civilisation. Islam regarded these things as idolatry that was to be destroyed. The Arabs called us slaves. It is sad that even, today, the Arab Muslim brothers are still expressing their expansionist policies. Their ethnic cleansing and genocidal action in Darfur is recent reminder of what the Arabs are up to in Africa. This is not to degrade anybody but the fact that Darfur African Negroes are fellow

Muslims belie the previous lies that the Arabs came to Africa to spread Islam. They came for land grabbing and slave hunting. If the African Negroes are human beings, they must warn the Arabs that we are not out to evict them but if they do not value good neighbourliness and tolerance they may stimulate crisis similar to what is happening to them in Palestine with Israel. This is not Islam conquest. It is eviction of previous alien invaders expressing their intention to expand and grab more of our land and kill our people. Islam itself must prove to the world that they are not for global conquest or seizure of the African continent. United determined people can evict any invaders regardless of how long they had stayed in the place if such ancient but recent invaders fail to behave.

It is worth restating the importance our ancestors attached to spoken words and numbers. The Egyptians used Hieroglyphics, studied Mathematics, Astronomy and integrated words by letters and sounds with Mathematics to interpret events in the elements and stars in the study and interpretation in Astrology. Our ancestors in Africa were very conscious of the community, its bonding while observing the independent role of every individual. The Pyramids were designed to signify the social bonding of the community to give honour to the gods and the sun the giver of life and sustainer of everything on earth. Each brick in the Pyramid was independent but regardless of its position played a role in the building of the Pyramid its firm support. The Carthaginians wrote twenty two letters of the current alphabet to represent the popular Aramaic language spoken at the time. It exercised individualism in the community. The Pharaohs allowed individualism to rob them of the opportunity to be universal and uniting leaders.

They were consonants as the Aramaic language did not recognise vowels. It was the Romans that added the rest of the letters now represented as vowels. The Mathematical concept is exciting and intriguing. The binary theory of numbers forms the basis of this thinking. Multiplication expresses addition of one the numbers in the number of places of the multiplicator. Division is the reverse: subtraction of one of the numbers in the number of places of the divisor. Raising numbers to powers means continuous multiplication of the number in the number of places of the power index. Roots mean the continuous division of the number until what is left is the number.

Note the division is continuous until it reaches the number of places of the root index. The same applies to multiplication involving root index. The concept integrates letters into Mathematics in Algebra. Architecture developed out of this concept of order under the rule of strict laws. Mathematics demands the strict observance of the rule of law to get it right. How great is it to know that if you take any number to the power index of zero you get one. This means that if you propose an idea that nobody accepts, you are alone. In the same way whatever number you multiply by zero is zero. Take zero away from any number the number remains the same. Add zero to any number leaves the number the same. This is Mathematical concept of the life and spoken words. Apply this to letters by using Algebra you see the greatness of nature in interpreting itself to fallible mortal human beings how limited we are in our vision of the world. We have the freedom to enjoy it but our understanding of it is limited.

Has it occurred to you that all we have in the world can be counted in different combinations and operations of 0, 1, 2, 3, 4, 5, 6, 7, 8, and 9? These combinations and operations can be expressed in letters, sounds and finally made into spoken language. It is great concept that continuous subtraction of the same number in the number of places to be divided finally yields the answer to the division. The opposite yields the answer to multiplication. Keep on adding to the number of places of multiplier, it will yield the answer to the multiplication. Algebra uses letters to define this concept of Mathematics. Art and drawings are incorporated into Mathematics in Geometry and Trigonometry to define heights and spaces. The Arabs have the credit of Discovering Algebra and numbers while the Greeks are famous for discovering Geometry as Mathematics of solids. We have to recall that all Greek philosophers of substance travelled to Egypt. Of all Alexander's contribution to knowledge and learning the greatest success was in Alexandria. Pythagoras discovered the famous Geometrical theorem. Euclid wrote a textbook of Geometry used by several generations of students.

Trigonometry developed out of the demands of accuracy of Architecture and Astronomy. It was later Inco-operated into Astronomy to calculate the distances between the earth and the stars. The angles of the changes in the positions of these heavenly bodies developed into Astrological Practice and interpretations of earthly events. The need for accurate calculations of the angles developed into Geometry. Applied Mathematics developed out of the combinations of these ideas and playing with concepts. My great ancestors were great thinkers. The brain of the black person can be activated to act and invent things.

We developed Chemistry and used it for tool manufacture, food processing and textile manufactures. We needed metal tools to build boats to challenge the seas and Oceans and build the temples and the great tombs. Later it was necessary to design tools to fight wars to ward off intruders into our homeland. Brass became a very useful ornament and bronze precious war tool. Equally the metals soon took important position in designing musical instruments. Metallurgy developed out of the useful roles they played as tools and ornaments. We made fortunes out of mining but Rome seized all the money and wealth we made out of our skills and ingenuity. Why should I not shout the little that I know of our ancient fate from the roof tops and ask our youths that it does not pay to see wealth in the stars? We have to return to the drawing board and concentrate to spread education and skills training to get the means to work and find our path again on earth. We are lucky we have several sources to acquire knowledge from but the duty to do so falls on our shoulders and the leaders who are blind to the real world in our time.

Africa had major role in the development of the first two major religions in the world. We were almost pioneer members of the evolution of Judaism. Abraham was a nomad that worshipped one God pioneered by Akhenaton and his mother Neferreti. At the dawn of Christianity and the beginning of the Gospel of Jesus Christ, there were two proud people the Romans had trampled upon their pride and freedom. The Jews and the badly wounded African Carthaginian remnants from the 146 BC genocide were eagerly looking for a saviour, a warrior of the calibre of late Gen Hannibal, a hundred years before. Appearance of Jesus of Nazareth on the scene was a great hope. But his message did not appeal to the orthodox Jews. His claims were wild and did not conform to the Torah. Hence the Jews were neither enthusiastic nor impressed by the upstart that made too many wild claims. To them he was a dangerous impostor. The Messiah was to come as a direct descendant of the nobility of David not from the village carpenter of questionable origin even though Mary was definitely a Jewish lady. Therefore, from all considerations the early followers of Jesus were in the main displaced African refugees. The lifestyles of the new sect suited them. The fiery and defiant message of Jesus gave them confidence and hope.

Therefore most of the very reliable followers of Jesus of Nazareth were Africans. Unfortunately the Bible written with the bias of the Jews and the Gentiles did not dwell a lot on the Gentiles and followers. The Romans were mortally frightened by this new preacher. They were unsure if he was preparing to give them trouble as Hannibal over a hundred years previously. The Jews that frequently followed this charismatic preacher with very sharp messages and great knowledge of the Torah and the law but delivering a different message from those of the scribes and the Rabbi were there to catch him in order to ask the traditional interpreters of the laws questions or to raise their suspicion of this new preacher to the scribes. They went there not for interest in the message but to catch him out. But frequently the message of Jesus overpowered some of them and they became converts. But firm devotees of Jesus were Africans. His number one enemies were imperial Romans. He was a dangerous radical that had to be watched. To the Jews Jesus did not meet their aspirations for a Messiah and if the Romans they equally despised dealt with Jesus it would not raise many eyebrows. That remained the situation until that fateful feast of Passover in the temple at Jerusalem. The Romans were eager to deal with Jesus. They found that the Jews would offer no opposition or resistance.

Hence they got him. They might have given the Priests and members of the Sanhedrin the Supreme Council of the Jews a chance to interview him on his views on the Jewish Laws. This was not the trial. The trial was before Pontius Pilate, the Roman governor the legal representative of the imperial order. He found him guilty by crook and trick. He delivered him to the Roman soldiers to carry out the sentence. Pilate might have sought a little favour from the Priests by asking whom they wanted to get rid off. He was sure the Priests had no love for Jesus. He was totally dispensable to them. It is false that it was the Jews that were guilty of the death of Jesus.

The Romans killed him. Their soldiers were involved in every act of the death of Jesus. They were in charge of crucifying him on the cross.

They gave permission for his burial. After his death, the Romans hunted down and arrested most of his followers and punished them. By the time of Emperor Nero it was cleansing the Empire of this sect. They were slaughtered in every possible ways that pleased Nero. It was only during the reign of Constantine that the Empire embraced the Christian faith. We are bound to ask who kept the flag flying until Constantine gave the Christians a breath of freedom. It was mostly the unfortunate Africans whose role in the early Church is not made prominent. But the significant role of St Augustine of Hippo is beyond doubt in bringing Christianity to most parts of Europe. This is emphasized by the fact that neither the Jews nor the Romans were keen in this new sect.

It was mostly displaced Africans not very welcome in the Synagogues as they were Gentiles. The new sect embraced everybody and this warmed to Africans and remnants of the genocide in Carthage in Africa. Already the role of the Queen of Sheba in Solomon's court had made Judaism catch the fancy of the Royal court in Ethiopia. Recall Solomon had very liberal attitude in Judaism. Recall his prayer at the opening of the new Temple? He prayed for the foreigners. The Jews loved Solomon but felt he made the worship of Yahweh profane by bringing in the Gentiles. By the time of Christ Orthodoxy was very strict and frequently formed the basis of condemning Jesus for acting freely with the Gentiles. Jesus observed strict Jewish Orthodoxy but he seemed to have had Gentile Relatives. He was well disposed to the Gentiles and had no hesitation speaking to them. He taught them and patiently explained Orthodoxy to them without forcing them to adopt the ways of the Scribes and the Pharisees.

The imperial tradition was to make all roads go Rome. The success of any empire is to possess supermen citizens and to pioneer and be in charge of every good thing. The imperial provinces and people had Barbarians that the imperial officials had to civilize at great risks to themselves. The alien inhabitants of the provinces were mentioned only in adverse conditions to discredit them and justify the imperial action in colonising them. Africa had a fair share of imperial overlords for long over five thousand years. This is why it is scarcely mentioned in good light beyond the wonders in ancient Egypt and a bit in Carthage. Even the Carthaginians were portrayed as colonisers to justify the action of the Romans in eliminating them by gruesome genocide. This had gone on for years in ultra-conservative Straussite European xenophobic right permanently tarnished by wrong ideas and actions and cruelties against humanity and tyranny of greed. It is wrong as we have seen in weapons of mass destruction in Iraq recently. Carthage and Africa suffered the plight of Iraq, today. Iraq is lucky because high Technology does not allow the criminals to hide their crimes. Three thousand years ago, 146 BC the European minority hardened xenophobic criminals were able to destroy Carthage by genocide and ravaged Africa.

We must prepare for war if they dare to repeat this feat in this century and millennium. The world does not hate Europe or the West. If the West continues with their bad manners during the last millennium they must not expect the world to remain dormant and docile. Everybody in the world must disregard all our differences, and be prepared for war. The West has no culture. Technical and Scientific skills are not civilisation. They are advanced skills. Civilisation on the other hand is the feeling of humanity. It is ability to share the world that we did not make with other races of people and tolerate cultures. We must not grab land and resources from other people under the guise of superior firepower. The superior killing power of military machine must be matched against the ability of the whole world to resist Western propaganda of isolating individual foreign leaders to demonise to justify their war of loot. They use bribery and corruption using criminal renegade power-hungry traitors from the countries and people they want to seize their wealth by looting.

Aggressive fanatical extremist Strausite Conservative rights minority Western leaders must defend their actions in War Crimes Trials to justify their Aggression and Wars. They may know what we do not know. They claim to be fighting for the free world that is not free but imprisoned by them. They fumble about the world use corruption and crime to destabilise the world. They go for cheap capital and cheap labour. They mob up capital and gather it into private pockets. Anglo-American leaders must suffer the fate of Nuremburg victims of Second World War for starting unnecessary violence and war. They are not immune to punishment for what they did in Korea, Vietnam, South East Asia and South America in the last millennium. Education is free for all. The world must recognise Science and Technology. Let us die in learning these skills instead of dying in war we cannot defend ourselves adequately. Those who lead in Science and Technology and possess both the number and good fighting machines will overcome the tyrants of xenophobic greed. The Arabs are free to worship their Allah but they must learn to live in peace with non-believers. Everybody is a believer in something. That is freedom itself. The world must fight on the side of righteous justice and freedom that God offered free to everything it created. We must share the earth together. Democracy as practised in the West is a ruse. It is not democracy. It is fraud.

It is worth noting that the ancient fathers, African leaders, the Pharaohs, the Carthage, Barca, Hamilcar, Hannibal and the brood of African lions, the Barcine brothers and finally Queen Cleopatra sold this idea to Julius Caesar and his successor, Marcus Antonio and they accepted it. The Greek ancient fathers including Alexander, son and heir of Philip of Macedonia accepted this principle. Cleopatra was a descendant of Ptolemy that we Africans accepted in that belief that we must learn to co-exist together in the world. Julius Caesar had a son from Cleopatra to confirm this concept of co-existence. Caesar introduced this legitimate son at the age of ten to the Roman Senate as his legitimate heir. Octavius and his group sabotaged all his efforts. They proceeded to murder Caesar, Marcus Antonio and Caesar's heir by Cleopatra, African European fit for the true West made of Africa and Europe. The powerful faction of xenophobic terror gang led by Octavius had their way. The Roman Empire died under the weight of their oppressive policy. Today the West after several fratricidal wars may also suffer the fate of the Roman Empire. The nuclear weapons are around. Everybody should get this bomb in their well-disciplined group not for harassing anybody but to ensure that anybody who creates Hiroshima and Nagasaki in this millennium will equally have the weapon in his home to feel the effect of their terror.

The original model of Democracy that the Africans practised and Aristotle saw in Carthage and sold to the Greek Constitutional

Conference was by peaceful negotiation and persuasion and not by war and violence. The Western model just as their religion in the colonial territories in the last millennium is a fraud. The UN must give a definition to Democracy and human rights. We have seen that the West has no sense of human rights in their behaviour in Iraq. The US is yet to recognise the right of Africans they stole from Africa to enslave. They are yet to recognise the right of the corpses of our ancestors the Arabs stole and sold to them and the ones they stole to lie in peace in their graves. These are a few violations of human right by the West. The environmental damage they inflict in several places on earth is abuse of the right of other people to live in a clean environment. Their wars of loot are violation of the right of others to life. They violate the right of their victims to live. They violate their peaceful existence. They steal their means of livelihood. Conflict Resolution guarantees individual freedom. It treats individuals with respect and excludes arrogance and harassment. It avoids conflicts. It has to avoid false promises and provocation and intrigues. Democracy is the freedom and security of the people to choose their leaders without rigging and electoral foul play and have a constitution free from violation and the rule of law is maintained. It respects the right of man.

It is worth noting that the conservative Straussite xenophobic rights are in a minority. They are, however, overpoweringly influential and very cunning. They deliberately make their victims people to blame for their plight. They make their people live in fear for their lives by creating permanent conditions of siege mentality. There are always imaginary enemies lurching at the door to attack them and destroy their so-called civilisation. Hence they have to be battle-ready always. This enables them to exercise firm control of their people. This is very important for the survival of all generations of this minority criminal group. They had crashed several generations of civilisation. These crashes are always attended by upheaval. The people made permanent underdogs by the rise and fall of the reign of each series of generations of the conservative Straussite rights like the Africans are progressively made worse than before. The collapse of the "holy" but appropriately unholy Roman Empire led to Arabs filling the gap left in Palestine and North Africa to create a permanently feuding Palestine and North Africa the home of macho Arabs with perpetually feuding against each other and their neighbours. They abuse Muslim Islam religion to justify their actions. The weapons of mass desolation, destitution, deception had been constituted into weapons of mass destruction of Africa. Africa has been dying a slow death from the actions a single weapon of mass damage of its leaders, infectious corruption. Corruption has humiliated and damaged Africa. Corruption has dehumanised Africa and all black people on earth. There is one hope left to a chaotic world.

That hope was bequeathed to us by our ancestors and the leaders of the ancient world. God, the creator of this world and the universe deliberately divided and kept different people within their groups and defined borders. He united them as members of humanity, languages, proximity and rich and generous resources. Our forefathers in Africa saw very early the importance of making friendly alliances and building the world into friendly zones. The Western Atlantic made of Africa and Europe and developing at par was accepted by African leaders, European leaders, the Greeks, Alexander, the Greek scholars, the palpable products of ancient African civilisation and advanced Education, the genuine Roman leaders, Julius Caesar and Marcus Antonio all persuaded by Queen Cleopatra. It was the tiny negligible fraction that Octavius led that used violence to disrupt this vision of the world. They believed in subjugating, enslaving and looting Africa. The Arabs filled the empty space when the Roman totalitarian authority collapsed. They drove the original black African indigenes out of the homes and their land across the desert.

They closed the door to Africa and locked up the black people within the forest cut off from the rest of the world. The recent European colonisation came and went. Today, the Arabs had started land grabbing war and violence under the influence of Muslim Islamic religion. They had started slave gathering again. Our hope and that of the world lies on what happens in Africa as the first step friend of Europe and a viable member of the Western Atlantic Alliance bonded in viable Education in Science and Technology with citizens who can do things for themselves. They must be productive. They must not be poor and hungry consumers without the knowledge and skills to produce what they consume. The West must wean African leaders off pandemic corruption and ignorance. Africa in permanent depression will eventually result in the current West falling victim to that depression. The West has got to use all its numbers and lands and these include Africa as a major and significant part of the West.

The progress in the West has always obtained its oxygen from Africa. Its fault has always been the use of black Africans as slave labour but excluding them from the benefits and results of this hard labour. The West cannot continue to exclude black people and Africa from its prosperity and hope to win the competition in trade and development with the East. It will lose that competition. Therefore, we are at the cross road of choosing between the old choice and vision of the ancient fathers and that of the ultra-conservative Straussite rights. Their vision feeds war and violence. The world is exhausted with war and violence. This has taken over three millenniums. Today it has failed and left the world in pandemonium now christened "Terrorism". We must abandon the ultra-conservative right faulty vision of the world. We must destroy weapons of mass destitution and desolation, poverty and corruption.

It is not beyond our reach to make everybody who needs to enjoy the fruits of Science and Technological advances acquire the knowledge and skills to be able to do things for themselves. This is vital to produce people with means to produce their needs. It is wrong to assume that these people would continue to remain as admirers and consumers of the products of the knowledge of Science and Technology but have no clue about how to acquire this knowledge and use it to improve their productivity. The white people in the West must desert the ultra-conservative rights and go back to embrace the vision of our ancient fathers and Julius Caesar and Marcus Antonio of the West that includes Africa and all the black people. This West will compete peacefully with the East. We need a world of equality and not a world of the masters, servants and slaves or "have" and not "have." The West needs even development. This involves the spread of knowledge and skills. It is not distribution of money or investments. It is offering the people the knowledge and skills to empower them to work to produce what they consume.

Muslim Islam, religion of the Quran and the sword was born in African Sahara and Arabian Desert. It was off-shoot of Christianity that Mohammed, a caravan trader that became its Prophet after receiving message from Allah. Allah is great. Allah is good. The Arabs sold it to Africans with the sword. They harvested slaves from slave hunting in African interior. They equally sent in imam and mullahs that grabbed African lands and made themselves imam, sultans and emirs in Africa. They made religion into law and government. This has been the difficulty of Muslim Islam in embracing change. It is totally stupid for people to leave their homelands to alien countries to escape from hardships but to turn around to demand that the citizens should change their ways of life to allow them to observe their lifestyles. It is totally unacceptable to waste time to listen to students requiring to change the School uniform and curriculum to allow their religious lifestyles. The answer to me is simple. If you want education accept established Academic discipline. Wear the chosen official uniform. Attend Assembly of worship at the School regardless of religion. We are a School with long traditions. If you choose to join us accept our laid down rules and traditions. If any student is in a Muslim Islamic country he has to observe the rules and traditions. If you want to be educated accept the discipline. The School is no place for the right of man or practice of religious faith; it is a place for learning and strict discipline. The people who go on the bandwagon to defend young Muslim girls subverting, violating and breaking the School discipline must shot up and advice the students to keep the School discipline if they want to attend School. The UK has made a mistake by bending its centuries of habits to accommodate strange religious faith in its Institutions.

This is what the Academic discipline is all about. We in Africa must not bend the rules to accommodate religion. Religion must learn to keep the discipline and the rule of law. Jesus said, “Give unto Caesar what is Caesar’s.” He did not say give only to God. Any religion that does it otherwise is corrupt and counterfeit. Religion accepts rulers and their laws. No religion says that it is only God’s or Allah’s laws that believers must accept. If it does so; it is wrong. God accepts earthly authority and power. The believers must communicate with God in their thoughts. They must express him in their services. It is wrong to hide under the name of God or Allah to violate the law and ignore the rule of law. Religion is a personal matter. It concerns the individual and his maker, God. It has nothing to do to restrain individual freedom and violate the rule of secular law. No religion has right to impose its rules on the people. Theocracy and religious laws are unacceptable as means of maintaining law and order. It forms a nanny state and violates the freedom of non-believers. Religious faith is strictly voluntary. It is unacceptable social molestation and bullying to force innocent non-believers to accept the faith or its rules. Attempting to gag people, the Media and authors from discussing religious issues and History of religion by irrational mob actions such as rioting, destruction of property, threatening people with death and disturbing public order in the name of defending the faith and burning books is downright criminal act and breaking the law. Genuine founders of religion and faith were not military commanders. They would not order in their crack troops to disturb public order when people criticise their messages.

Equally the believers are not to police religious message or the religion. If the faith is genuine and the message from the deity, it would endure all criticisms. Gagging the public to defend or protect religion or faith degrades or devalues the faith and creates doubts and uncertainties in people's mind as true and genuine message and faith stand out on their own. It is unacceptable and stands condemned. Regardless of what religious myths the adherents may use to deify the sages and founders of religion and faiths, they were born as human beings and had human weaknesses. As a matter of fact it was their experience of human weaknesses that made them preach to them on what God, the deity desired of human beings. The message may be sacred but not above human criticism. Good and genuine religion and faith are not cult societies. They have nothing to hide. Finally regardless of your emotion and the way you feel about your faith, you have no right to attack people without the same sensibilities as you.

We must not forget that this is the way Arabs dumped Muslim Islam faith on innocent Africans fourteen hundred years ago. The Roman Empire that the ultra-conservative Octavian rights developed and used to plunder the world collapsed, the Arabs rushed in to fill the vacuum. They went on the rampage of land grabbing jihad. They drove out the indigenous Africans from their lands and homes in North Africa. They seized Palestine from its original owners, the Jews. The black African ran across the desert to settle in the rain forest of the sub-Saharan region. Therefore, each time the Western ultra right embarks on its exploit; the black people become innocent victims. The slave trade and slavery dehumanised us. Colonisation fragmented and disorganised the whole continent of Africa. It left Africa in the current chaos after the dissolution of the European Western Empire. The nominal independence abandoned Africa in crisis and chaos. It is unfortunate that the ultra-conservative minority right used their powerful influence, intrigues and violence to impose their vision of the world on the reluctant world. They rejected the majority vision of the world. Now it is this old vision of a West that integrates Africa as a vital part of it. The demand of this vision, today, is frightful. It demands a lot in money and physical labour. Yet these will be good investment and provide jobs for our people for a long time. It will stabilise the world and maintain the peace. Magnanimity is compassionate and generous. An integrated Western Atlantic and Southern Western Atlantic may stop bubble Economy of boom and burst and stabilise capitalism.

The world can no longer tolerate "haves" and "haves not". Grinding poverty is no longer acceptable way of life. We must remove obstacles to prosperity. We must live within the rule of law. Democracy is not the right of greater fire-power. Democracy was originally designed and adopted to abolish violence and cheating in the transfer of power. Democracy is incompatible with war, violence and corruption. The level of global poverty, today, is justified only by gross injustice and a false sense of fairness. We must be living in a different world by believing that we can use greater firepower to force the world to accept current lopsided wealth distribution under duress. The world will have to learn to share global wealth. Let everybody have easy access to Education and genuine productive skills. Every person must work and produce much of what he or she wants. Let nobody be encouraged to live on charity. The generosity of the donors is helping the recipients of aids to be idle and indolent. It works against nature and the creator.

Nature made every living thing labour for its living and survival. We human beings must not bend the rule by letting our generosity condemn some of our fellow human beings to live on permanent charity. We must make our aids and charity offer education and skills to teach people the way to work for what they need. This is the help the third world needs. Avoidable indefinite division of people into groups based on religion or ethnicity is deliberate indulgence on avoidable duplications and waste of scarce resources. Binding constitution and secular laws that ensure that everybody observes the rule of law in the community unites different people to conserve the scarce resources and promote prosperity. Observance of the rule of secular law is freedom and democracy. Criminal intrigues and corruption cause divisions, agitation, disputes, war, violence and poverty.

It is a shame that all European Empires from the Romans down to the most recent ones started with brutal genocide in Africa. The preparation for the holocaust by the Nazi started with the second Reich Genocide in South West Africa by Kaiser. Dr Fischer the voo doo German Doctor and scientist decimated and violated the African dead in the name of false Science and Megele violated the Jewish dead in the name of false Science. After all the Jews are one of the most intelligent human races on earth. Yet this voo doo Science occurred to them. The Germans have accepted their crimes against humanity but they must pay up. The British are yet to apologise and pay up otherwise they will remain cursed for ever by the righteous God and their island nation would be put to sword and destroyed by genocide. The black African must act with one voice and condemn these atrocities. Time does not wipe off our sorrows nor the brutalities our innocent ancestors went through in the hands of these people who claim to be civilised but are the most Barbaric and brutal of all human race. The black race must bunch together to fight their corner for justice from the people who committed these crimes against their fellow human beings. Cursed be they till the end of creation for their bestial and mean cruelties to satisfy their greed. Those who did these things finally died and left the world and their loots behind.

Those who continue to indulge in armed robbery and plundering of the world will finally kiss the cold hand of death and leave this world without their loot. The so called treaties and agreements purported to have been contracted between African tribal chiefs and white colonisers were broad daylight fraud. How can you explain agreements contracted by people under duress without any understanding of what they signed for in language or in writing? White people have no value for any agreement they can violate by force of arms. We saw it between the Carthaginians and the

Romans. We also see it in recent cold war armistice agreements. They all are in tatters waiting to explode in brutal armed conflicts. It is extremely stupid to talk of non-proliferation while the most Barbaric people in world History have the nuclear weapons and are improving on them. They had already detonated two in Japan for whatever reasons they had to do it. They can do it again. All those who can build the bomb should do it. The next adventure should take us all off this planet with our insatiable greed and unfathomed cruelties.

If we decide to do away with the bomb with simple variable means of detection of violation with stiff sanctions and penalties for the defaulters and culprits we should all do it together? I am neither a racist nor advocate of doom or preacher of hate. It is a challenge to the conscience of those whose ancestors committed all these atrocities against completely innocent people in their homelands in the name of insatiable greed and wealth. The descendants still continue to do it today as they see nothing wrong with the actions of their ancestors. They continue to lie to their conscience in the pretence of being civilised or clever. It is vain arrogance of madness of power. Power can slip and the proud falls. The tyranny of greed is still enslaving the world despite all the talks on democracy." Impera et divide" or divide and rule, hatred and disunity favour the bully but not the people lured by greed to adopt it in the name of democracy. Democracy wants safe environment, sharing, spreading true knowledge and education and skills training and fair genuine liberty and equality and peace and not war and violence. We all are human beings on earth. Just as in the human fingers we have diverse forms and functions. What the Western white Europeans did in the past in the name of ruthless wealth and resource acquisition was deplorable and atrociously criminal.

Capitalism has given a very ugly face to free enterprise. It has exploited money and consumer materialism to design perfect all life slavery state with illusion of freedom and possessions. In the Western Capitalist system you borrow money to acquire all your life needs. But you work all your life to repay the loans and debts. The owners of the money own you as a work horse. The money and property owners are the leisure people who work less but enjoy enormous wealth from the labour of their slaves. The African debt burden is typical example of this open slave labour farm. The corrupt and ignorant African leaders sold their nominal freedom and that of their future generations to the property and money owners. They also sold their mineral rights to these heartless wealth grabbers. The tendency of these traders persistently hiking their profits every year is the scandal of capitalism. The inflationary increase continues devalues the currency. It is a bad system. We should struggle to maintain the value of the currency.

Prices of goods and services should fit into stable currency stable value. We should have inbuilt stable currency value the prices of goods and services should be subject to without the currency losing value every year. We must remember that money value was initially measured by gold weight. This was the origin of Archimedes Principle. It was to ensure that the weight was from pure gold. The specific gravity was instant response to prevent cheats and fraud. Capitalism needs human face and sympathy. The incentive to work hard is one advantage of free enterprise. Unfortunately free enterprise must have some measure of freedom. Hiking up the price of money borrowed by rate of inflation is bad and fraudulent. The worst thing in capitalism is its attendant crimes and corruption. Capitalism must respect and recognise Integrity and virtue. It must reject violence and wars. It must avoid willy nilly deals. The community and society should be empowered to place a limit to the amount one person should have. Equally there should be a limit to the number of shares one person should hold. Sharing must form a major part of the human society and community.

The Romans introduced racial xenophobia into international relations to intimidate the world and make Roman citizenship an honour and reward. The Romans executed the first well-documented war of genocide in Carthage in 146 BC. It is no secret in history that the Romans abused friendship of Carthage and Africans. My impression of the Romans is that they were power drunk lawless people. Compare the ancient Greeks to the Romans you will draw this same conclusion.

They tore off all the agreements they made with Carthage once they knew that they were strong enough to defeat her. They betrayed the traitor, Massinissa of ancient Libya. We cannot talk of our fate on earth, today, in Africa without remembering that twelve million innocent Africans were brutally uprooted from their homeland and ferried across the wild seas and the Atlantic to be enslaved in the US and other distant lands. Two million innocent black Africans died in this hazardous exploit. Today, the descendants of the remnants of this man's inhumanity to man, are one hundred and fifty million of depersonalised, dehumanised and completely humiliated people scattered all over the world. Majority of them live, permanently below poverty line. Their bullies continue unabatedly to bully and abuse them. They continue to be victims of mean racial xenophobia. In the US democratic freedom may flow along the roads but the poor and deprived African Negro continues to be a victim of the law in Tulia in Texas and other cities.

Of course democracy is by power of persuasion and not by barrel of the gun. Violence has nothing to contribute to democracy. Democracy is by mutual respect and trust built up by gradual persuasion and credibility. The current iron fist violates religion and human rights. It destroys democracy. Unfortunately it takes a long time to develop mutual trust to create the fertile soil for growth of democracy. Perhaps we have violated democratic rights of the democrats to create the law of the jungle. The Greeks brought democracy from Africa to Europe to abolish the law of the jungle. Violence and the concept that power belongs to the most violent strong man are not democratic. The theory that the man with the most powerful divisions, rules is anathema to democracy. Unfortunately we are slowly marching back to that iron and Stone Age of Tyranny.

Wise counselling is not cowardice, disloyalty, treachery, or betrayal. It is not the white liver of Walter Mitty. It is the ingenuity of a curious mind that sees the hurt in the culprit as well as in the victim. The resolution of conflict is when the culprit recognises that he is hurting the victim and the victim recognises that the culprit may have reason for his cause. Wisdom recognises that both parties feeling hurt may be erroneously chasing justice while none of them has justice to offer and both of them may be wrong. The powerful God is compassionate. He who has the rod of power to wheel must also be compassionate. He has to be compassionate and capaciously magnanimous. The folly of killing for God is a huge joke. It is a revelation of the hollowness of the martyr understanding of God that has power of life and death over man and all living things.

Muslim accepts that God gives life and He takes life. The Christians accept that God said, "Vengeance is mine". Therefore, the last thing in this equation of carnage and slaughter is God. It is painful to suffer death and humiliation. It is equally hurting to allow evil to thrive and let the culprit go unpunished. One thing is true. The murderer will die one day regardless of how long he may live. Equally God has no reward for those who destroy lives in His name. God does not require human beings to destroy lives in His name. God gives and takes away life. Yes a wild bear or lion feeding on human lives and farm animals can be put down. This does not apply to human conflict. It needs conflict resolution. Conflict resolution requires compassion, magnanimity and compromise. The current military campaign against terrorists is returning to, "an eye for an eye" and ignores one cardinal advice to be patient and allow vengeance to belong to God.

I feel that the war against terrorists has gone too far. It has threatened our humanity and civilisation. The Western militarism is over five thousand years old. It is part of the Western culture. My knowledge of this institution dates back to the Greeks and the Spartans but crystallized into a perfect war machine in the hands of Alexander son of Philip of Macedonia. He made militarism into a global institution. The Romans perfected it into a crack machine of global conquest and authority. Yes there is virtue in gallantry but we are at the doorstep of global village made real by high Technology. Enormous changes had occurred both in military Technology, rules of engagement and global power balance and old military valour and gallantry are no longer the only way to serve your people. Economic magic is perhaps better regarded than war nowadays. Therefore resorting to costly war and massive destruction it entails to be a war President is a big joke. This is self-illusion and not service to the people you kill and destroy their lives and properties. They are not making sacrifice to the nation but to your vain search for honour. Can you imagine a father making sacrifice to the nation by killing his erring little child?

It is good to read History but we must recognise that time has changed a great deal. War and violence may not necessarily yield the results they are expected to achieve. Now is the time to look for and use a third way to maintain world peace and harmony among human beings for prosperity. It is no longer easy to hide and enjoy wealth and prosperity from those you are doing business with. High Technology should now provide the means of providing education and creative skills training to all global youths to enable them to work their lands to earn a comfortable standard of living from where they live. The tragedy is to superimpose the concept of Hitler and the second global war. This is not the early forties when European Empires had to be defended.

War and violence and martyrdom of suicide bombers should not be allowed to fuel the machine of tit for tat killings. We are now at the threshold of being challenged to define who really is the terrorist when killing has been made so easy? Brutal and gruesome murders are described as fire fight and corpses are displayed for public viewing as means of convincing the citizens. We seem to be powerless in arresting and arraigning criminals before the law. When the world is unable to settle issues involving single individuals and their families without going to war to kill innocent people and destroy their properties we are moving to a chaotic world of lawlessness and anarchy.

Rather we hunt down people and kill them without giving them any chances to defend themselves before the law. We declare those we hate, "criminals" and convict them to death penalty by mob condemnation without any recourse to the law. It is strange that a person should be allowed to have power of life and death over people he does not know except what he claims is intelligence information. We can no longer define crimes as reprehensive acts against the law. We are in lawlessness and anarchy. Lovers of the rule of law and freedom must allow wisdom and courage to prevail and denounce this gentle drift to lawlessness and anarchy. The elderly must be losing their minds by allowing the ultra conservative right Strausites to run away freewheel from the law. Determined leaders have ears to hear those they lead and the groans in agony of the people they hurt. Listening to themselves alone is tyranny. They must be brought under control and the rule of law. Spreading fear that people who condemn unjust war are unpatriotic and put soldiers' lives at stake is baloney. It is avoidable war that kills innocent soldiers. It is the leaders who declare unjust wars and order soldiers to fight that put soldiers' lives at stake and great risks.

The shock expressed by George W Bush when he visited the slave shipping Island in Senegal in Africa, this year, 2003 and his expression that it was the greatest human mass movement and dehumanising human cruelties of the last millennium sums up the feelings of all black people on earth. Africans who passed through that gate of no return are still living below poverty line without hope in several parts of the world. This evil trade is still scarring Africa and black people all over the world, today. This was the greatest act of man's inhumanity to man and violation of human right in history. Yet we continue to live with empty promises and false promissory notes. False declaration and promises constituting merely hot air seem to form part of the politics of the rich world. This was done by civilised people with great value for human freedom and the dignity of man. The Ancient World revered Africa from Egyptian to Carthaginian era. The people who live in this great continent and land pioneered human curiosity, learning, education and creative skills training among human beings on earth. The creator has a role for all the things He made. Each thing made has a function. At times in Science and Biology we just do not know the function.

In certain situations we attribute these structures that we do not know the function as redundant organs. A clear case is the clitoris. It has specific functions in the female. Its erectile property promotes sexual stimulation in the female. This ensures the self replication through sex. The pleasure from the act is genuine natural incentive to be involved but the major objective is nature's secure and guaranteed method that human creation would continue. This is further made secure by endocrines releasing hormones that stimulate the function and action of this tiny organ. What a shame that some human communities in total arrogance of ignorance carry out female circumcision to acquire their vain selfish desire to stop sexual desire. Unfortunately the all knowing nature, God had made the endocrines that release the hormones that still perform this nature's predetermined function. Of course human beings in arrogance of ignorance still perform genital mutilation and now gloriously in assured bluff of ignorance, justify the practice by taking cover under culture. This is what happens when we neglect natural intention for our right to exist.

Africa is uniquely placed to practise good education, training in skills, Technical expertise and sound apprenticeship and diffuse them to all parts of the world. The reward for this function is the rich natural resources God gave Africa for this function. It appears along the line Africa took to pleasure of enjoying the reward and the tools it had for its function without performing the function. It neglected its vital function and reason for its creation and existence. It is equally good to observe that nature then took this function of disseminating knowledge aware from Africa. We then descended from the heights of the pyramids, great temples and fantastic tombs into paupers' graves, poverty, diseases and ignorance. We must now in our lowest estate shake off the shame of living in the dark in the midst of enormous light from the golden sun and go in great humility in search of knowledge, understanding and intelligence to regain our original function of concentrating on education and skills training to recover our unique position and function in the world. We neglected the world we were supposed to enlighten with knowledge.

The world gained knowledge and wealth but still lacks that fine tuning and sobering of power and influence that Africa had on human affairs. I always say that the Biblical History of the exodus of the Jews from Egypt is symbolic of Africa in the Ancient world. Pharaoh, perhaps the powerful Ramses the Second had several encounters with Moses. He never settled it with sword. He continued with conflict resolution. Today, the dogs of war would have settled this issue with smart bombs and genocide. Today the power and influence of the Jews is a testimony of the fact that we had great value for life. There are religious myths dimension to this story. Recall that Moses was adopted son of Royal family. They never punished him for the betrayal. African adoption tradition recognised and associated the adopted child with his Biological parents and family group. Africa never toyed with your family background.

The family influence was supreme and respected. The ten commandments of the Bible now constituting both secular and religious laws of world are African basic natural laws. That is the way all Africans and Priests of religion prayed. In our prayer of Justification, we always plead our case with God by saying that because we have not broken or violated all these laws, Oh God listen to our petitions. It is prayer of justification and vindication. This is the way we pleaded our way to God with the guards of the underworld when we died. The same plea of prayer was offered before the court of God on the day of the final judgement for us to qualify to join the members of the place of rest from work on earth. We were then justified to join Amon ore, Osiris, Melkart, Baal and Astarte, the great residents of the underworld in God's presence. We do not need the intercession of a third party to persuade God to accept us. Our religion teaches us that we are directly accountable to Him. We are not job conscious. We are service conscious. The law of God directs us to be duty conscious and law abiding. This is the difference between African traditional religion and concept of God. We know that he is all loving. This placed great restriction on the influence of the power of the rulers. They were God-fearing. Today leaders of the rich powerful nations of the world had replaced God with their powerful offices. They have no fear. They say, "The bug stops here." Africa must return to the Priestly duty of searching for true knowledge and disseminating the message of the fear of God and civilised human relations.

It cannot therefore be said that Alexander son of Philip of Macedonia did not know the people and the land he was raping and plundering. The Romans knew the people they were killing and the cities they were sacking and destroying. They knew the values of the treasures they stole from us. They also know the enormous damage and destruction they inflicted on our wild life and forest in North Africa. This is perhaps they said very little about their influence in Africa. It was all tragic catastrophes for the people who were more civilised than the Romans when the Romans arrived in Africa to destroy them by genocide to establish their influence and authority. The slave traders and masters knew the people they were dehumanising and humiliating. They knew the people they depersonalised and abused. They even used the beautiful young ones for sexual pleasure and comfort. The strange thing with these people is their sexual perversion and incest. Fathers had sex with daughters to breed more slaves. They sold them to make more money. Money is god of the West. We have to write down these things for civilisation and record in history. Recent limited genetic survey of descendants of slaves showed white paternity in most cases.

This confirms my story. Unfortunately in the West they do very daring bad things but they do not take kindly to people like me who write about these their evil ways and exploits. The West must now know that if they do not want bad Press they should avoid actions that create bad Press. I am only researcher, scholar and African keenly interested in the way civilised West behaves away from their homeland and the way they treat people of other races different from them. I am particularly interested in their role in the demise of Africa. Africa may have to be weaned off dependency on the West. It is hard to comprehend or understand why the West continues to live in the past when it comes to dealing with Africa. The Western Technology is out of place with the way the West deals with Africa. All matters of vital interest in helping Africa are reduced to mere talking shop making false promises. The very corrupt and ignorant mediocre African leaders are gullible. They swallow the empty promises and distribute false promissory notes to their citizens.

Africa is in a different environment from that of the West. The eco-cultures of the two are worlds apart. Africa and the West must recognise this. At the moment nuclear weapons are awash in West. Non proliferation is a good policy but the West has a duty to tell the world why it has so many nuclear warheads? Are they preparing for war with extra terrestrial hostile forces? For genuine peace on earth the West must embark on credible disarmament with the world for the safety of all of us. There is grave danger in allowing one group of people to produce and keep these lethal weapons. There is equally great temptation to deploy and use them at war if one group has the weapons. It is this risk that justifies all or none regulation concerning nuclear weapons. Nobody should produce and possess it or everybody should possess and own it. The only rule and regulations should deal with safe keeping and disposal of nuclear wastes. Anybody who uses it in conflict should sustain stiff penalty. If the whole world finally recognises the danger of these weapons it will then sue for genuine disarmament. This should be our objective.

The Western leaders have not given us a firm promise on the use of these weapons. US dropped these bombs on Japan in the 2nd WW. Most the global institutions are Western global quangos. They are ineffective in dealing with the global problems. Western democracy did not prevent the West from seizing the Americas, Australasia with attendant genocide in the past millennium. Western democracy did not prevent the mass trafficking and trade in human beings, slavery and brutal colonisation and looting of wealth in Africa and other parts of the world in the last millennium. The clumsy way the US is attempting to democratise Iraq and the Middle is scandalous. You cannot sell democracy to any people by throwing lethal missiles at them. You cannot persuade them by collaborating with conmen and power-hungry tricksters to dehumanise and humiliate them as we saw in Abu Ghraib Prison. Civility demands humane and compassionate treatment of the weak and ignorant. Arrogance of racial superiority is dangerous as a vehicle for delivering democracy and civilisation to alien lands and people with different cultures and religion.

THE MISMATCH OF FORCES IN THE WAR IN IRAQ HAS MADE A MOCKERY OF OUR CIVILISATION. WE HAD RETURNED TO THE STONE AGE OF RULE BY TERROR.

Before our time our ancestors had strict rules and regulations on the conduct of war. The protection of non-combatants, children, women, disabled persons and people neutral at war is ancient rule of engagement at war. The Geneva rule is just an enforcement of this ancient rule. Unfortunately the US with all its tantrums and trumpeting of democracy violates it at will. The leaders secretly give the notion that they have no qualms over its violation as long as its fighters can get away with it. They flatly deny any knowledge when caught red handed. It is astonishing that the world allows the US to have an exemption from prosecution for this serious war crime. Even in sports we take care to match the contestants. American war against terrorists has violated all the rules of war and civilisation. There is tremendous mismatch of forces. There is no protection for non-combatant vulnerable people. The Iraqi child victims of this war are clear examples of the callousness of killing and maiming in this war. This war is like a combat between flesh eaters and bull elephant. We do not witness it in nature in the wild. The uranium tipped missiles and other Technological smart weapons involved in this war make this war a total mismatch. In the ancient conducts of war, combats were organised in space and time. Armies had visible leaders in the battle field. Killing was restricted to battlefield during fighting had. It is speculated that US and UK Private Security Companies fight three quarters of the War in Iraq. Britain and the US had privatised war and means of killing. George Walker Bush had privatised. Capitalism had privatised wars and means of killing as Private Business. Capitalism has already privatised Reproduction Means with GM Foods and IVF. We are facing Danger from CAPITALISM and this is Privatisation means of Production to Private Individuals and Capitals to own as Investment Shares. It is time we rein in Liberal and free for all Capitalism. We must control and regulate the Capital and Private Ownership. It is now eminent threat to our Freedom. We must now mix the Economic Models. Ownership must involve Socio-political Public shares and Private Capital Investment Shares. Employers and Employees must own Shares and be involved in Managing and Running the Business.

The war zone was not a wholesale killing field. Tit for tat killings are very dangerous for peace after war. The US leadership must understand that might is not always right. The September 11 New York twin towers assault was deplorable. The month of Sept seems to be eventful period in world History today. The US response to this has destabilised the world. It has triggered off imminent violence that may be beyond the ability of US or the world to control. It may take us back to the Stone Age. It is time for the world to summon the US and the "terrorists" to discuss their grievances. We share this world with them. We have the right to appeal to them to cease fire and talk peace in the interest of survival of mankind on this earth. Human pride and personal injuries are involved in this unequal warfare. Healing is needed for peace to return. The world cannot sacrifice the so many people in the West, Iraq and Afghanistan to the three thousand and the damaged twin towers. It is time we count our losses, nurse our wounds and hurt and control our anger and emotions. The leaders must stop this war. They are all rational people. Winning and victory would not restore our losses. The people who suggest continuation of the war are doing so for their self pride but not in the national interest.

Conflict resolution needs a third party outside the US and the terrorists' zones. Stop the killings now. We know that you can kill but each of you wants life and not death. The hawks in the right conservative America are still hounding for a pound of flesh from the rugged mountains, valleys and caves in Afghanistan. The security of American people lies in the streets of America. The people who knocked down the twin towers lived and acquired all their needs in America and not in Afghan villages. Get back the troops to the American homeland and streets. Talk over mutual security with the Afghans. They can be prevented from visiting or living in American homeland if they fail to guarantee and provide securities for Americans. Sadly the UN Secretary, Banki Moon is a compromised partisan. He is unfit for conflict resolution. President Barack Obama is a very respectable and trusted world leader. The Afghans and all the combatants in these conflict would trust him if he offers to negotiate quietly out of the Media long lenses and pressure from the conservative hawks. People's talents are different and diverse; some people are arrogantly and thoughtlessly violent while others are thoughtfully peacemakers. The wreckers of peace are not heroes. They are mischievously, recklessly and ignorantly placing the nation in avoidable danger. Mighty America may have problems with some people in Afghanistan but it has no genuine reason to waste both American lives and resources in the place. It can persuasively provide peaceful aids to effect change in the place. The calm, quiet leader and thoughtful hesitant leaders is a hero. He knows where to pick up a fight. He does not start a fight in all provocative situations as a political tout and thug. He avoids risking scarce public resources, precious lives and funds in irritating trivial but provocative situations. This is the difference between the leader who reads History but neither understands nor knows History and the leader who reads, understands and knows History. Afghanistan has been the grave and waterloo of several great Armies from Alexander, the son of Philip, the second of Macedon till now. This one is stuck with Ahmed Karzai as the only Afghan friend and route for escape after eight years; is it not in shambles already? The election was a revelation of sham, fake and counterfeit democracy it has on offer. It was a disgrace to Democracy and the free world.

All the so called United Nation Institutions appear to be the Quangos of the powerful Western ruling machine and instruments of Western power. They are ominously silent. The animals in the wild have their rules to maintain the peace and prevent the tragedy of self-destruction and extinction. The gross mismatch of forces and gradual carnage developing in this crusade against terrorists is a very serious threat not only to human civilization but also to the very existence of human beings on earth. The killings have made murders cheap and human lives worthless. The rate of slaughter in Iraq should shame the US.

At this rate Saddam Hussein would have gold and platinum medals for massacre during his years in office. Let us be honest death from US is as bad as death from Saddam. Both destroy one thing, innocent sacred life. US and its citizens reject this. US and Iraqi citizens value their lives. Anyone of them losing his or her life is dead and no more. Let us now see this folly as human beings. The world and the UN must ask US to leave Iraq as it has no treaty with the Iraqis to be there. No UN article authorises it. Any after thought UN action to offer legitimacy to this day light robbery is fraud.

Any Iraqi group that the US forms to exercise authority over Iraq is illegal and unacceptable. I am not pro Saddam or pro anybody. I am a Christian. Christ would not accept what has happened. He taught us to give Caesar what is Caesar's even though he did not approve of the Roman rule. US abused the blood thirty idiot, Saddam Hussein to devastate Iran for nearly a decade and found nothing wrong with him. Now this tyrant is old and US is doing everything to replace him with another tyrant and puppet of the US. US can use its wealth and influence to do things to spread prosperity in the world.

It authorises lawlessness in the world. The US is too precious to the world to be involved in this mess. At the same time it is wrong for the golden boy of the family to commit murder and be bailed out because he is too precious to the family. US is seizing power from God. No nation should stage a coup d'état against God. This is what the US has done. The US spent the last millennium raising up dictators and slaughtering people in South America its backyard. We had the Iraq-Iran gate and the Sandinista rebels in Niguaragua.

All those bloody dictators had bloody US finger on the trigger. US has failed to tell the world if it has to use this century to do the same in the Middle East? US has notoriety in South East Asia, Vietnam, Laos, Cambodia, Korea and other places. It left these places in ruins. Can the US now a lone superpower offer the world something better than violence and bloody tyrants defending the US interest? US requires a major review of its foreign policy aimed at making the world a better place for all humanity. US Intelligence experts and Army had always been known to be involved in abuse of human rights in South America and all the areas the US had been involved in covert warfare.

The slaughter at My Lai in Vietnam and recently in Iraq and Afghanistan all had the characteristic signature of the US Intelligence and the Army. Yes this is democracy according to civilised US. Secret murder squads stand to be condemned. Despite frequent denials the US under Republican right governments had always been accused of being covertly involved in atrocities. Is it a coincidence that US alone refused to sign and sponsor the International Court of human rights at The Hague in Netherlands? The US seems to have a lot to hide in abuse of human rights and violation of human rights and the rule of law. It is always rogue minority involved. Unfortunately this minority had failed to disappear over the years and several generations. Is this not an inherent culture instead of the action of rogue minority?

Since we come into this world by only one way and leave this world by only one way and so far regardless of what Science can offer the Technology of fertility we still require female human womb to support the human embryo to grow until birth we should recognise that we have one thing, life in common. We all die and leave this world regardless of what Technology offers to prolong life and our life achievements. We have a duty to treasure and respect this one thing we have in common "life." The terrorists and the US must learn to respect each others' security of lives. They owe it to humanity and their God to give value and respect to life. We all have this in common in this world. We all should appreciate investment in the safety and security of life.

Peace is a priceless investment for the safety and security of life. We came alone and should go alone. Suicide bombers and war fighters are not wise. They may achieve mass death but each person embraces one thing death. Even if we blow up the world we live in each person will face one thing, death. Death is our inevitable end and way out of this world regardless of the way, when and how it comes. The man who administers death to others will finally die. Nobody can escape it no matter how he or she loves life. This is why most of our past heroes are not around. They had kissed death. Abraham Lincoln and other great men and women could not escape death. Why do we not embrace wisdom and invest in peace and each other's security of life and property knowing that one day we will die and leave this world in our own time?

There is no UN article that makes it a war council for the US or NATO. The world would like the UN Secretary Kofi Annan to publish such article for everybody to read and know if there is one. The US has no authority or right to invade Iraq even if the Iraqi dissidents hired it with oil as mercenary. The dissidents can hire the UN to hold fair and free elections. The dissidents are subverting democratic principles. The US is an accomplice in this destruction of real opportunity for democracy. Let us not be fooled. A strong man doing US bidding will finally emerge in Iraq. This is not democracy. It will be another bloody dictatorship protected by Western Press and Media that will cover up its crimes.

It appears the arm-chair military strategists and intelligence specialists had hijacked the war against terrorists to impose their ideology and vision of the world on humanity to promote their global business and dominate the transnational corporate business. They seem to aspire for the return of the ancient Roman Empire. This is a very dangerous strategy capable of incinerating the world. These people are not mavericks. They have their strategy. Unfortunately they cannot control events if they get out of control. This is why the world should not stand by to watch events unfold.

We are being led to our doom by minority ambitious few. This minority lack clear vision and understanding of the implications of their actions. Let the wise world intervene and settle the differences they use to achieve their selfish and very narrow ambitions. We should not let the distress of American people and the so-called terrorists and their differences and misunderstanding to be hijacked to upset the balance of world peace. We must rise up with courage to offer a just settlement. We must offer justice, comfort and hope to the afflicted and security to all.

It is a shame that several people in this ignorant minority want to be like people of yesterday, George Washington or Julius Caesar. Unfortunately yesterday had passed. It will never return. Their idols and role models had lived in their times. They had died like all mortal beings. It is time for these hero worshippers to know that the times had changed. Change is inevitable and unavoidable in the lifetime of all generations. This is why we have this formidable war machine. It is change in militarism. What was acceptable in Washington's time or in Caesar's time may not be acceptable today. "Tempus fugit non redit". Time flies and does not return. The mini Caesars and Washingtons must know that they are neither Caesar nor George Washington.

There are a lot of beautiful things and excellent achievements of the ancient for the benefits of the world, today. They deserve praise for these. The world in their lifetimes allowed their activities. The world in our time has changed. Western Europeans seized the Americas by genocide and transformed them into prosperous and affluent homelands for themselves in the last millennium. Today, a world dominated by rich and affluent West frowns at genocide. It is unacceptable crime against humanity. No sane hero worshippers should fancy the repeat of the feat of their idols and role models.

We all should aspire to change the world by using high Technology to offer valuable and focused education and skills to every citizen all over the world to enable everybody to work their lands and make a comfortable living out of their places of abode. This will stop illegal immigrations and mass population movements to destabilise the world with asylum seekers and refugees. It is a way of reducing international crimes, prostitution, drugs, sexual perversion, human trafficking, and slave trade, money laundering and global corruption by transnational corporate business. This should be our aspiration now but not empire building. The world is not in mood to acquiesce to the bloody business of empire building. Citizens of the world should have adequate focused problem-solving education and skills training to take care of themselves in their homelands. Africa has enough resources for its citizens to develop for their prosperity.

The US is in a unique position with the leaders of other Western countries to dismantle the postcolonial borders of unviable rogue banana states in Africa. They are not fit to be nation states. They are costly to maintain. They are wasteful in resources. They are unviable economically. They cause instability in Africa and threaten world peace by frequent total breakdown of law and order that makes them havens for religious fanatics and international criminal fraternity. They are failed nation states because they were not up to nation state status in the first place. They have caused intolerable human sufferings and insecurity. They have devalued human life. They had encouraged the development of savages. They had advanced child abuse to intolerable level by developing child soldiers, killers and criminals. They promote drugs, money laundering, human trafficking and prostitution and spread of diseases.

They are open to people with criminal money. Their limited resources are used in funding international crimes. This has threatened international peace. They have become fiefdoms for people with ability to kill people for reasons they cannot justify. The citizens of these failed nation-states must understand that their vital life needs and security take priority over citizenship of rogue banana republics and fiefdoms of brutal and criminal illiterate tyrants without any sense of the rule of law and sanctity of lives and properties of the citizens. They will embrace knowledge and good life when they see the way to them and the results.

The US should encourage the development of African Union with a binding constitution that respects the rule of law. African Union should be a model of modern nation state committed to law and order with responsible leadership with sense of civic duties and integrity. The US searchlight of focused education targeted to solve the environmental, social, cultural and economic problems in Africa should take over the current strength and energy to destroy things and use it to train people who can build things. It is the US that truly knows the potentials of Africans and what they can do if properly motivated. The African Negroes must equally know that they have a duty to use their latent potential to motivate the world to give them opportunities to embark on genuine and adequate education and effective skills, trade and apprenticeship training to promote orderly and sustainable development. This is our way out of poverty and its misery.

We must take responsibility and go for what we want. The African Negroes are peculiar people. They have the potential of being deceived and duped several times by the same people that had meddled with their affairs to destroy their progress. The African should never fail to notice and recall the deleterious effect of the West meddlesome actions that used the illiterate Armies they trained and left behind after independence to destabilise and topple the postcolonial independent regimes in Africa. The blight of Africa today is the aftermath of the rampant subversion by the West of most of the African postcolonial governments. The amazing and astonishing thing is that the very colonial officers that never respected the basic fundamental human rights and their welfare were keen to indoctrinate the poor illiterate Africans to demand these and democracy from their leaders. Unfortunately, they never taught these poor and illiterate people the meaning of these ideal throughout half to one millennium contact they had with these people. Till, today, the Africans are unsure what Western democracy means. They have been manipulated to perceive democracy as the end to their poverty, misery and ignorance. They are made to think that their mediocre and ignorant leaders should provide them with all they lack without their working for them. May I tell Africans bluntly that they and their leaders must know that their wealth and prosperity lie on the good education and skills and their genuine work, blood and sweat? We are cheating ourselves by being corrupt and morally decadent. We gain nothing from fraudulent and criminal behaviour. Our soft and cheap money from embezzlement of public funds denies us the opportunity to exercise our body, our brains and our manual skills. It takes away our concentration on the duty of leadership. It makes us negligent of our responsibilities. The slogan, “Everybody does it, why should I not do it?” is gaining moment in the community. The cheaters, the poor, the vulnerable and the whole community suffer when the system collapses from bad behaviour and dishonesty of a few.

They are corrupt and purposeless in life. Politics has become commodity for making money and wealth. Africa needs economically viable few nation states or United States of Africa able to concentrate on focused education targeted to solve several of its development problems. We need fewer leaders but a lot more skills. We need very skilled and well trained manpower. The skilled manpower we need should be proportional to the task we have to accomplish in Africa to feed its people and stop violence and crises. The US can do this. It will also help the US solve the problem of resettling ex-slave descendants in the US and all over the world. So far this has not been satisfactory. The beauty of seeing the US soldiers side by side with Nigerian soldiers in Liberia must not be lost. Perhaps we can do more together provided we have a common objective for all our actions. The US and the West have moral obligation to help Africa. Africa collapsed under their tutelage. They abused and violated all norms in stealing and plundering the continent. Good planning is essential for the Economy. The manpower development must be proportional to areas of need. It is no use people entering Institutions of Higher Learning to major in Islamic and religious studies while graduates in Agriculture, Civil Engineering, several other parts of Engineering, Science and Mathematics, Health, Banking, Insurance, Commerce and Education are lacking.

It should be turned into determined crusade to deliver focused problem-solving education and skills training to the Africans. Targeted educational programmes should tackle the problems of housing, road communications, food production and health in this vast continent, the origin of human beings on earth. We have shared the US together and we can share Africa together. Today is that time for us to look at the world in this light. It has not been easy in the US but we seem to be settling down to things that matter to all human beings. The US can apply this to Africa now to unlock its enormous human potentials to develop the continent to be a true second home to the US. The "House of Elders" should sit selected distinguished retired virtuous Africans from all over the world. Africa by tradition had been led by its elders. They control the youths. The concept of the "House of Elders" is good. This would provide retired excellent leaders avenue to remain in contact with events in politics of the African Community as well as in the Diaspora.

We are not talking about strategic significance of Africa but real true second home for the US as we have seen that we can co-exist together. The US has already proved this. It was not without some difficulties. But it is my sincere belief that a rich and affluent Africa will advance the US cause on earth and ease things. You may note that I do not spare to criticise the past behaviours. If I pass from bitter criticism to offer friendship to ease the problems inherent in the current relationship and solve the intractable problems in Africa, you may appreciate the vision of this proposal as any harm to the US is harm to Africa by the virtue of the accident of slave trade and slavery that had brought Americans and Africans together. We had shared many trenches together and suffered the humiliation of death together. Now let us share the challenge of developing Africa and its resources together for our comforts in our short lives on earth.

The Barack Obama Charm:

This is new event. It may be a way out for the world. It can copy the US and give every citizen a chance. Some white males still remain anxious. They are campaigning surreptitiously for failure of this experiment. A section of the white male dominated Western Media is involved in this. They know that George Walker Bush damaged the Economy by conducting two wars simultaneously. He squandered the money. They equally know that Afghanistan fought three wars by 1919. It damaged the USSR fragile Economy. Today George W. Bush is wearing a cowboy hat and riding horses in his Texan Ranch. The white male press is not speaking to him. Yet this press would go to soup kitchen in Chicago to interview poor black people if they are satisfied that Obama has not made them rich after less than hundred days in office. This is astonishingly mischievous incitement of poor black people against their own President. This white male press knows that black poverty had remained an issue as old as the US. It is not an issue for Obama to settle. It needs resources and time. Obama has neither.

The war against terrorists and the doctrine of pre-emptive strike are a great threat to world peace and human progress on earth. It would lead to global conflagration that will destroy much of the world as we know it now and our civilization as we know it, today. The hawks have reason to note this. The war against terrorists and the doctrine of pre-emptive strike have no genuine basis to burn up the world with fire and smart uranium tipped bunker breaking bombs. Do what is feasible in your generation, in your own lifetime because time has changed. Change is real even to patriotic historians. Everybody still has the unique opportunity to join the greats in History provided he or she takes up what is feasible in his or her generation and lifetime. Nobody at the moment can define who is a terrorist but we know who the killers of fellow human beings are. At the moment they are US and its ally soldiers and the resistant fighters the US and the West would like to call terrorists. They are neither terrorists nor insurgents. They are patriotic resistant fighters fighting to liberate their country from foreign occupiers. Each of them has got reason to fight and die but we, fellow human beings on earth have the duty to ask them to stop killing each other in the interest peace on earth and humanity. It is a sad day that the US is riding on the back of traitors and the UN to seize Iraq.

We are devaluing our lives by tolerating this slaughter. How did we suddenly come to this point of settling issues by summarily execution without giving the victims any opportunity for self defence? There is justified public and leadership anger but wise counselling prevails upon those provoked to anger not to destroy and damage everything in their anger for we have a common destiny. It is our destiny as human being that is involved in this Barbarism. We are displaying corpses on television screens and internet spaces for our children to watch. What are we teaching them? Are we telling them that life is so cheap that they must not spare the lives of those who offend them? We claim to be civilized but History will not forgive us for being so wild and primitive in this issue.

I wrote a small piece a few years ago on compassion. The Western politicians promptly picked it up and incorporated it into their political slogan. "Compassionate conservatism", the slogan says that it maintains values and tradition of sympathy for the people living below the poverty line and the down trodden." Compassionate conservatism" they say works for the people. There is political dimension in every proposition. Compassion means that a superpower that can destroy its opponents several times over should assume that passion of God that can destroy the world at the blinking of the eye but He does not do that because He pities our folly. He tolerates us. He is merciful towards us sinners. He is capacious, accommodative and He pities us. He does not want to be provoked to destroy the world because of our irresponsible acts and behaviours. In short God does not want to be irresponsible because we are irresponsible. God is always compassionate on us. We mortal and fallible human beings in our blind arrogance ignore God.

Now that the world has the US as the only superpower, the US has the responsibility to recognise that it can kill several times over in anger and be compassionate, magnanimous, capacious, generous, pitiful, merciful, and inhibitive and slow to anger and provocation into irrational action. Compassion means having pity on the weak, poor and ignorant including those that provoke you to anger. Unfortunately, the US has turned its overwhelming power into an instrument of terror, dehumanising torture, menace, atrocities, inhuman cruelties and genocide.

I love America but America should use the resources it uses in destroying the world to build a world where everybody would have viable education and skills to work his land of birth to sustain him or her. Construction and not destruction is what the world wants. I may not live in the real world to think this way but the founding fathers of the US risked everything to found a home free for them to build and worship God with liberty. USA is prosperous enough to accomplish this. The US can use internet to reach vast areas of the world to spread education and skills training to return the world to work and prevent indolence.

The US must know that brute force cannot make big lies true. It cannot deliver Democracy from the barrel of the gun. Subduing the weak to control their resources is abuse of power and crude bullying. Sending your soldiers into battle under false pretences to slaughter the innocent is double crime against humanity. It is a crime against the soldiers whose profession is abused to terrorise the innocent people and against their innocent victims they slaughter in their illegal duty. The blood of slain soldiers and that of the innocent people they slaughter soaks and wets your hands. The leaders owe responsibilities to God and the human beings they damage by their actions. They lie to God but God knows the truth. He judges us according to what He knows about us and not what we tell Him. We cannot lie to God.

America has the resources to build and not to destroy. America equally has the resources and the freedom to destroy. The choice is America's: a broader vision of the world or a narrow vision of the world? American leaders have a choice between military destructive gallantry and peaceful reconstructive heroism, compassion and gallantry. There are very many genuine Americans willing to do this but the powerful corporate America sees the world as a market where money can be made. This may be good for business but the human needs of the world demands that every human being should have genuine means of livelihood to work for his or her living. Today, this requires adequate Education and appropriate skills acquired through approved good apprenticeship. Science and Technology are in the heart of change of human life on earth and everybody should know this. Education in Science and Technology should be mandatory to give human beings a good bearing of the world around us. Africa has no choice but to acquire Technology and mass Technical education. Our lives now rely solely on products of Technology.

The price tag of peace is lower than that of violence, war and destruction. There is no religion, culture or tradition that accepts what is going on now in the world. The current level of violence may bring lucrative and bustling business to the armament industry but it is leading us to catastrophe. Equally insistence on the control of weapons of mass destruction that allows the West and friends of the West to keep them is not the best way of controlling these weapons. Whoever designed this philosophy for the International Atomic Agency must return to the drawing board and design a viable atomic safety and security for all. We must hold leaders who authorise the deployment and use of these weapons in war or in any situation accountable even in the face of victory. If the Agency is conscious of the effect of nuclear emissions on the environment, it should have the mandate to tell the keepers of nuclear materials to rectify the safety laws. It should have the power to seize materials for safe destruction. It should have the resources to dispose of nuclear waste. It is counterproductive to use the Agency as an organ of molestation by the West. So far many of the UN quangos had become weapons of molestation by the West.

What does the West intend to do with these weapons? Do they keep them as we keep insecticides to kill insects that we dislike? Do they keep them to get rid of people that disapprove of their views of the world or to fight aliens that may invade the world? The truth is that as people who value life we all must see ourselves as equals in the discussion of weapons of mass destruction. We must discuss the way the world can eliminate them and ensure that nobody produces and keeps them any more. It is totally inhuman and irrational to accept some people to keep such lethal weapons while preventing others from having them. The world must decide if we all have to do away with these deadly weapons or keep them. If one country has it for its defence others should join hands together and manufacture theirs to defend their freedom and democracy. The world nuclear vision should be all or nothing. We either eradicate all nuclear weapons or we keep them. Now the affluent nations are engaged in armament of the space. We on earth should get earthly weapons including nuclear for self defence. It is just common sense.

You would wonder why an article on AAAD should dwell on what the US does in the world. Several millions of Africans live in the US. America has strong role in African Renaissance. It is African tradition to use terse words to advise the family in a critical situation. America is an important member of the global family. It is equally an important member of the African family by accident of slave trade and slavery. A substantial fraction of the population of African Negroes is American citizens. We have a duty to be concerned with what hurts America and its people.

America must play a peaceful and unifying role in the world. Dividing the world into the bad and good groups or friends and enemies of the US to promote the US armament manufacture and sales is not a viable foreign policy for world peace and security of the US or the world. The US war in Iraq is a gladiatorial show with achondroplasiac dwarf riding an elephant. The dwarf is no match for the elephant. The American enterprise in the Middle East can be better managed than by avoidable and purposeless war and its destructions. It provokes hatred and hostilities.

The US could have rebuilt Iraq without the war. There is no moral justification of a war to kill many and destroy a lot of properties to overthrow a foreign government and replace one leader. It is waste of resources. Removal of one person from power is not worth a war by the US with its formidable war machine. Equally if the US had genuine reason to remove Saddam Hussein it could have done that legally without the use of violence. Human beings allow themselves to be deceived. We are gullible or we are downright timid and cowardly by failing to see injustice and complete violation of the rule of law in the US and its puppets invasion and occupation of Iraq. We have also watched with amazement the spinelessness of the UN. It is a misnomer to call that thing United Nations. We are not united. We could not unite to defend Iraq from tyranny of either Saddam or the US. We watched Iraqis being tortured by both in the same Prison.

Peace is essential for the AAAD take off as a vital part of the African family is in the US. We cannot stop the current spreading violence. We appeal to people of wisdom to search for an alternative way to peace without war. War kills terrorists and Americans. Let us not wait for victory. Let us search the path to peace. To the terrorists or whatever they may like to be known as, violence is not the way to heaven or to solve the multiple global problems.

Of course, Mr Meacher recently reminded the world of the events of Sept 11. The world sympathised with the US but the world was equally amazed that a group of boys seized the US airspace for almost two hours hijacking US planes with ordinary knives to cause mayhem in the US a superpower without any reaction by the most powerful superpower army in the world sending planes into the air to intercept the evil flights. No air force guns ordered to shoot them down. No leaders appearing in public to offer leadership.

The confusion was profound and the silence was cynical and ominous. The Caspian Sea and Middle East oil may genuinely break the silence on this level of negligence and failure of leadership in such a critical national emergency. The bullishness of the leadership when they re-appeared from their hideouts after those fateful two hours of mayhem could not match their meek response to the events of the two hours that took away the twin towers with several lives. Till now the leadership has not offered the great American people the reason for their inaction and where they were for two hours without offering leadership to the US in distress of hostile attack.

The aftermath reaction of the leadership has been damaging to world peace. In their efforts to impress Middle America and their friends they have behaved like big bulls in the China shop knocking down everything in their path and breaking and destroying innocent lives. This is ingenious cover up. The US President and its top leaders have a duty to explain what really happened during those vital two hours when boys without any weapons of mass destruction (WMD) bought kitchen knives and went on the rampage of the US air space with trail of destruction in lives and properties. It is easy to evoke emotions in this.

The administration might have been grossly negligent in its civic duties of offering security and protection to the US and its people or they were naïve over security of the US, the only remaining world superpower. The saddest events of the aftermath of this Sept 11 has been the costly and counterfeit security that the administration is offering to the US, its people, the West and the world. It has split and divided the world into limitless hostile fragments socially, economically, politically and religiously and created deep divisions and personal animosities. If anything it has failed to offer protection even to the soldiers involved in carrying out orders to secure the peace.

It is the President Bush's action against terrorists that seems to be re-enforcing and strengthening the terrorists and creating new fertile operational grounds for them. Mr George Bush may be President of the US but he is only one person. The rest of us in this world owe a duty to real Peace in it. Responsible wise people must stand up and act fast to restore peace by negotiation and persuasion. We feel the combatants are human beings. They have to listen to genuine neutral fellow human beings for the cause of peace in the world.

God is peaceful. He is not violent. After all the destructions by the forces of nature, peace and calm usually returns.

Denial of Meacher's allegation is inadequate to explain what happened during the crucial two hours of real mayhem in a country with the highest defence budget in the world. It has the most sophisticated equipment for detection of threat and communication of hostile incidents among the relevant officials. Yet nothing happened. The leadership should not adopt macho posture to escape blame. The macho attitude is damaging and offers no real security. Now the elections are coming. The people need answers to these questions and not bullying and accusations of the people who ask these questions in true democratic dispensation and the right of free speech of disloyalty or unpatriotic behaviour. Patriotism involves being at your post to perform your civic duties of defending the homeland from hostile forces as those of Sept 11. These people are very responsible patriotic citizens. We aliens involved are true friends of America as a bastion of democracy and freedom.

We want to know how prepared and responsible the custodians of our security and freedom in the face of national emergency such as the Sept 11 twin tower destruction were. Bullying those who ask genuine questions and accusing them of lack of patriotism have no place in this debate. We need genuine answers. We deserve the right to know where the President and the Commander in Chief, was and what he was doing and how he reacted. Where was his defence Secretary and what did he do? President George W George emerged late. He became bullish but where was he, during that crucial period of two hours? He seems to be a sheltered leader. The father or influence of the father sheltered him from going to Vietnam. Now he is the President. He is sheltered by secrecy of Intelligence and Security. He is the Commander who has never tasted life in the trenches of war. This is why George W Bush takes delight of declaring war. He has no knowledge of how to fight a war. He has no knowledge of what solution war can provide.

We do not want detailed answers to avoid security questions but we want convincing and persuasive answers to re-assure us that someone was in charge of security on Sept 11 but events were beyond every possible intervention to prevent at least part of the destruction. What did the administration know and when did they know it? What did they do to prevent it? Was it impossible to prevent it? It is not enough to use security and intelligence implications to cover up. The house was burgled. Where were the security men? Why were the alarms not on? Everybody at the moment is innocent until we have the real answers before the elections. The war against terrorists offers more deaths, hatred but no security. The war against terrorists cannot eliminate the weapons of mass destitution and desolation, criminal corruption of the wealthy multinational conglomerates and the way they do business in the third world and the poverty and misery they cause in these places. Is the US not ashamed that all the people they fight against were their partners in business? George W Bush should start to wonder why the US frequently has to fight its erstwhile friends. Is it a mother that consumes its young? The root to current violence and terrorism lies in the answer to this question? The brief period each of us has to exist in this world offers us equal ownership of this world. People fight and become violent if someone tempers with the right of that equal ownership. The destitution and desolation in Africa constitute a focus for explosion. Poverty, AIDS-HIV, ignorance and misery can destroy Africa.

Let responsible people of concern offer no more troops but delicate secret mediation to stop it. The parties involved must listen to reason and be patient to resolve their differences. God is Allah of peace. He wants us to stop this carnage. He wants us to love our neighbours. He wants us to forgive each other. The lives lost had gone. They cannot return. They do not justify adding more lives except if there is a sinister objective to the war different from saving lives from terrorism. We love our lives. The terrorists love their lives. Let us all genuinely call a halt to this senseless destruction of lives and properties. We have no choice but to share this world together. God is Allah that gave it to us. We have no authority in trying to eliminate each other. We cannot change what He has fixed.

There is the argument to make the US strong and impregnable for total safety and security of the American people. September 11 showed and demonstrated that there is no such thing as total safety and security of any section of the world we share with our fellow human beings and other living things. The war against terrorists has equally demonstrated and illustrated to every wise person and foolish person, the brave and courageous, the timid and cowardly the futility of this concept and philosophy. It just does not make sense to kill and destroy more in the name of trying to prevent further deaths and destructions. A foreign policy of bigotry, arrogance, bullying and intimidation is expression of insanity and terror. Changing one's style of walking to march like a leopard hunting for prey is not totally right.

It is a demonstration of fear. It is the step of a coward attempting to play up to courage, boldness, and a false attempt to be brave. David started fighting as a boy. He found marching in armour cumbersome. In his natural gait he slaughtered Goliath with only catapult, stone on a sling. Goliath marched with the gait of strong armour and a coward. Trumpeting strength as a sign of safety and security is a false assurance of national and global security. It is shared security that the world desires. We are our brothers' keepers. The risk to the safety of the weak is the danger to the security of the strong. It pays to be paranoid to gain power but it is dangerous to deceive the people with false sense of safety and security for this purpose.

Going out to make enemy of the world in the name of the security of my nation is not a good strategy for world peace or global safety. Sending troops and fighting forces to every nook and corner of the world is not a safe strategy for maintaining global peace. Provoking friends and recruiting new enemies to justify war and armament manufactures are not compatible with the sanity of peace. They are signs of loony militarism and war. It is worth weeping up emotions of Sept 11 but is it safe to burn up the world because of Sept 11? How many people will die and would the destruction be justified by only Sept 11? Is there an alternative way to resolve the events of Sept 11? Two wrongs cannot possibly be right? It is not the brave but the wise that will rule the world. Sheath your sword and talk peace. Peace, safety and security will come to the wise, the humble and the rational leader. Formidable war machine like Goliath's military attire is impressive but it just does not represent peace, the real need of the world for safety, security, wealth and prosperity.

Unfortunately, removal of one dictator and tyrant creates more dictators and tyrants. A friendly tyrant is a killer and a criminal just as a hostile dictator. It is time the world settles down to make laws that are binding and will prevent the emergence of future dictators. It is the rule of law that will prevent dictatorship and tyranny and not war and violence. I cannot understand why the West has quietly readjusted boundaries they created in Europe but they have failed to readjust the artificial borders they created and left behind in Africa in spite of the number of warring failed states now described as rogue states and banana republics. The West knows that these rogue states were never up to nation states in the first place. Why do the West, the United Nations and the African Union not embark on re-integration of Africa and genuine boundary readjustments to create viable nation states in Africa governed by the rule of law and respect for human rights? Is this not a concept that a democratic and free world should accept as practicable in the real world of the rule of law and law and order?

It is not the number of countries in Africa that will protect human right and observance of the rule of law. Prevention of massive official corruption and prudent use of the scarce resources are the ways to rescue Africa from its current dilemma and misery. It is ordinary common sense that the fewer the leaders the less would be the wastage of the scarce resources. The funds wasted on unproductive leadership should be invested in the development of Africa. The new trend should be to educate and train efficient and effective manpower for any project to be commissioned on the continent. Africa is too vast to be developed by imported labour and manpower.

ALL ITS PROGRAMMES AND PROJECTS SHOULD BE UNDERTAKEN BY INDIGENOUS LABOUR. This is easily achieved by first training the manpower and labour even for five to ten years before launching the projects for them to manage. The world has paid lip service to corruption in Africa for too long. It is equally embarrassing to observe that the West uses corruption to do business with the third world and Africa. The British Empire was built by conquest and giving bribes to local chieftains. The so-called NATO troops use bribery to buy local people co-operation in Iraq and Afghanistan. They use even food and second-hand clothes relief materials to bribe local people for support. Corruption is the spine of the conduct of Western Business in the world. Yet it is the West that complains the loudest against corruption in the third world and Africa. This is a complete ridicule and a contradiction to Western complaint against corruption in Africa and the third world.

Now that Africa is facing disaster, the world and the West should take a firm stand against this vice in Africa. Even NEPAD is inadequate to curb corruption in Africa. Naming and shaming may not be out place. Stiff penalty is necessary to deal with corrupt states and leaders. Serious disease needs radical cure. Corruption in Africa requires radical measures to curb it. The answer lies with the rich West. The way the rich nations of the West buy votes in the United Nations Security Council should not be overlooked or ignored. They may call it aids and investments but it is downright bribery. It stands to be deplored. The US aids and investments in Egypt may be genuine but they take the shape of bribery. They make the US policy in the Middle East bankrupt and ineffective. Let us base all our aids in this century and millennium on education and skilled manpower training to produce the people and the teams to manage the investments and be partly responsible to the donors in efficient and effective managements of the projects and also to the recipients for delivery of efficient and effective services to the targeted populations.

Africa needs positive education capable of solving its problems. Africa virtually shares the Americas with Europe by the accident of slave trade and slavery but the indolence and disarray in Africa had not allowed Africa to benefit from the privileges Europe has taken for granted in this enterprise. It is the brain and skills in the hands of Africa that will change the misery in Africa. Rapid growth of Science and Technology at the centre of focused Education targeted to solve the enormous problems confronting development and progress in Africa is what the AAAD should encourage as a top priority. The high Technology can do this now in Africa several times over. Now there are people trained to treat post traumatic syndrome in people who has passed through bad spell in their lives. The Africans had neither counselling nor any Psychological support after their trauma in brutal colonisation, slave trade and slavery. The Government compensated the slave owners but the slaves were given nothing. They were left to look after themselves where the community was racially xenophobic. The damage these events inflicted on black people and Africans still persists today. The successful Asians, today never had this bitter experience.

Africa has become escape route for global politicians in difficulties. They blow hot air and issue false promissory notes for aids to the continent. Failed scientists and specialist consultants claim their credits and authority from works in Africa. New diseases are quickly traced back to Africa and freelance specialists write several papers on them. Unproven data are lifted from one literature to the other. The authorities on them in World Health Organisation continue to grow. The funds spent on these continue to grow. What fails to change or grow is the state of Africa. The reason for this is not far from understanding or difficult to know. Unless the African themselves have the education, knowledge and the creative skills to do things for themselves and use the vast and enormous resources of this continent to build and develop their land by themselves no amount of foreign aids or investments would improve or change the current condition of Africa.

Academy of Africans in Africa and Africans in the Diaspora is autonomous and independent organisation of all Patriotic Africans of distinguished scholarship and intellectual distinction on earth to give them a forum to use their skills and expertise to make positive contribution to the way to solve the intractable problems of Africa. The African sons and daughters on earth, today, are capable of deciding on the way this continent should go about to solve over five millenniums continuous problems of Africa. AAAD or in short African Academy must help in designing and making sure that what the African child learns, the knowledge and skills the African acquires are adequately practical for use in solving the enormous problems of his vast miserable continent. Scholarship is the choice and a way out of our current malaise. Sound scholarship will allow citizens to branch out to various professional careers to tackle a great deal of problems of Africa. Education in Africa has sadly been planless. Africa must plan Education of its youths. It must fulfil the needs of manpower and employment. The funds must be adequate for sponsoring it. The current practice of people travelling abroad to obtain qualifications randomly without considering the needs of

Africa should be discouraged. All our funds should be invested on improving and equipping the Academic Institutions in Africa.

HOW WILL AAAD DO THIS?

Already, at present Africa has more Universities and Institutions of learning than the US but the continent is fragmented. Every one of these Institutions is very poorly equipped. Its institutions and resources are fragmented and not focused or purpose-orientated or targeted for solving particular problems. The intellectual concentration is dissipated and diluted and fails to penetrate our learning youths and the society at large. There is tremendous waste of our resources and talents. Before an African scholar completes his studies he is old and tired unable to contribute to advancement of learning and improvement of the community. The reason for this is that there is no biting centre of excellence to offer him a home early for his studies. This makes the funds available for developing these institutions and courses they teach limited. Avoidable duplications cause substantial wastage of resources. Clustering to politics and administrative non-productive jobs encourage indolence, corruption, poverty and ignorance. It leads to deliberate negligence of the vital jobs essential for maintenance of vital services in a viable developing community. Trade and Technical jobs and careers constitute over ninety eight per cent of the duties that sustain modern cosmopolitan cities and countries with complex administration and services. Science, Technology, Scholarship and Research constitute the basis of a growing community. It is regrettable that African youth study nothing about their continent and do no research. They run round the world in search of better and comfortable living and become frustrated and disappointed. Their leadership may wear the crown but they are still ignorant fools.

Without these things a modern community is a dying community. It lacks the ladder to climb up to the top. It lacks the fertilizers to support the growth of the plants. It lacks the foundation to support the massive building. There is the debate of lack of advances in Education in the Islamic culture. Africa has a double dose of this malaise. Islam is the opium of most people in Africa. Africa in recent times is guilty of indolence and criminal neglect of Education, skills training, Scholarship and Research. Africa is dead in learning, active Education, skills training and apprenticeship. The Arabs are still able to produce copper and brass ornaments but Africans cannot produce essential wooden tools we use daily. Where are we heading for, the stone age?

The isolationist and separatist nature of imperial impera et divide Bantu minirogue states with prestige projects beyond their budgets in most cases make focused education with targeted programmes difficult to achieve. The number of these minisovereign states increases the number of avoidable duplications and wastage. Regional shared facilities in Education, health and other projects would allow more funds to be available for growth and enable greater numbers of people to use them. Fewer well equipped Regional Institutions would serve the people well. In the past we were comfortable with the Universities of Ibadan and Fourah Bay because they were well equipped and well staffed. Distance did not discourage attendance. Quality of Education was good. The graduates were of high calibre.

The wastage is colossal in human and natural resources. The learning, knowledge and skills the citizens acquire are not targeted to problem solving in the continent. They aim at injecting more people to non-existent job market with valueless meal tickets. AAAD will assist in co-ordinating the activities of these institutions so that they pursue programmes that will offer Africans education, learning and skills training targeted at problem-solving and job creation and development in Africa. To do this the AAAD will generate and control funds or encourage Governments and Institutions to provide funds to develop problem-solving research programmes in universities and institutions to help Africa and Africans all over the world. Planning is essential for the Economy. It is important to know the vacancies available and areas needing staff. The areas requiring expansion must be known and manpower development and University attendance and Scholarships should use this planning and statistics to avoid wastage and frustration of students by unemployment. Attendance at Higher Institutions should approximately be equal to the manpower needs and areas needing staff.

AAAD will help institutions to specialise in particular areas. Chemistry teaching and research should be concentrated to special institutions. The same should go for other subjects such as Physics, Mathematics, Civil Engineering, Mechanical Engineering, Electrical Engineering, Electronics and Computer Engineering, Pharmacy and Material Chemistry, Aerospace and Aeronautical Engineering. Medicine should have Specialist Centres and research centres. Genetics and Biology should be concentrated to a centre and Agriculture and Food Processing should have priority in special centres. Civil Engineering Construction works are guessing at everybody visiting Africa. They can be accomplished only by African Civil Engineers. All courses must have actual industrial part. The industrial part must be on real projects in the community. It is better to keep students on the courses until they are qualified to work on and lead in the projects. We can no longer afford to have Agricultural specialists with malnourished children because their parents do not know how to farm. These are special areas that the AAAD should concentrate on to develop first class education for African youths instead of wasting them in unnecessary and avoidable and wasteful wars, violence and crimes and prisons.

We must avoid wasting our human beings. Economic empowerment means giving first class effective education and creative training to all our children and people to convert them to first class manpower and workforce. I define Economy as avoidance of wastage and to add to this careful planning. We had served as slaves to develop the West and make it prosperous. We must acquire Science and Technology to fashion our working tools to serve our employers effectively and efficiently. We must understand modern working tools to use them effectively and efficiently. Strict Educational planning and avoidance of wastage are essential for developing Africa. Targeted-problem solving programmes should be the rule and the norm. We produce goods we do not consume and consume goods we do not produce. Fragmentation and wasteful repetition of programmes are consistent with "impera et divide" of alien colonial government but unfit for a continent in a rush to cover five thousand years of neglect, plunder and looting.

To prevent avoidable duplications and wasteful repetitions of projects characteristic of colonial fragmentation and creation of rogue and failed Bantu states in Africa, we essentially must set on to re-integrate Africa to create economically viable nation-states capable of providing funds for running public institutions that will serve the people instead of wasting the scarce funds on multiple duplicated uncompleted or poorly run projects. Africa can never attain prosperity by this. The comment that all efforts develop Economy for Africa had been abortive because of corruption and its rugged terrain is not true. The efforts failed because the colonial masters failed to re-integrate Africa that dismembered before they left. Nobody conducted any scientifically proven Economic research to confirm if the current Bantu rogue states we are having would be economically viable. It is only re-integrated dismembered Africa that would be viable economically.

2. Africans were captured and taken to far away lands and the US to create the miracle of wealth in the West. The West plundered and looted the continent of Africa and subjected the continent to ruthless and brutal colonial rule for several centuries. Today all Africans on earth and all races on the continent and friends of Africa should rise up in unison to help Africans to rebuild their homeland. Africa has friends and sons in high places. We love and appreciate our adopted sons and daughters and almost adopted son and friend like Bill Clinton and his family.

It was Bill Clinton that first expressed his sympathy for Africa by posing the suggestion that for Africa to achieve rapid development its land and properties must be given equity values so that their owners can pledge them for funds from the financial markets for investment on vital projects on the continent. This is better than a few people from the United Kingdom are proposing to seize these lands free to employ Africans on peanut salaries to farm them for their selfish private benefits all in the name of investment and jobs. So far nobody has acted on this suggestion at least to open up the debate on the topic. People say he did nothing for Africa. Africa is rich enough. It does not require handout. It wants people to assist African children to acquire knowledge and skills targeted at using the rich resources in Africa and their energy to solve the problems of development on the continent. This is the only way a nation develops and escapes from poverty. Secondly Africa has been a long standing problem. Two term period of Presidency is too short to solve African problem. The resources needed to solve African problem is vast. It is important to retrace how Africa came to be here. Africa was dismembered by colonial masters to rule. It has to be re-integrated to be economically viable.

3. It is nonsense and expression of ignorance to talk of free trade as a way of escaping from poverty in a place where most people have zero skills and remain idle most of their lives and means of production is extremely primitive. They have neither goods nor services to exchange in the free market. They need the right education and creative skills training to produce the goods first before taking them to market to sell. Mineral resources are not goods the people produce. Dependence on mineral resources as the main stay of the economy is just African governments' acceptance of the total dependence on nature for everything, the food we eat, the houses we live in and the water we drink. It also confirms our total reluctance to use Science and Technology to assist nature in the way we earn our living and improve the growth and cultivation of the food we eat. It is precarious to rely completely on nature for the supply of our food and the products we sell for foreign exchange without using Science and Technology to improve our skills and productivity. Therefore, the AAAD is out to organise the people with the knowledge, skills and ability to effect this badly and urgently needed changes in our lifestyle.

4. The allegation that corruption is a major problem and cause of poverty in Africa is equally only partially true. The sponsors of corruption in Africa are the multinational conglomerates, the wealthy transnational. They abuse the egg-shell coconut empty headed African leaders they fool and dupe to gain favours to make maximum profits for their share holders in the West. These idiots are duped to sign papers that give them details of huge funds in their names in Western Banks. There has been no proposal to re-integration of Africa dismembered by recent European colonisers before independence. This is vital for Economic health of Africa. People would argue that the colonisers folded their blankets and left in some parts of Asia but those parts are doing well. The success depends on the culture of the people and the terrain involved. Africa is unique. Dismemberment and fragmentation are bad for both the African culture and its terrains. Re-integration is essential for the

Economic Health of Africa. Bush wars among Bantu rogue states in Africa sustain European armament industries and jobs but they decimate African Economy. Re-integration and not war is what dismembered Africa wants. To make Africa Economically viable money above the levels of what the European colonising masters gave their colonies, must be made available to support the Bantu rogue states created from dismemberment of Africa. Re-integration is cheaper and easy to run. It is economically viable.

These funds are in Switzerland and other Western Banks and not in Africa. Most of them never have access to the funds till they die or leave office. Therefore, the culprits of corruption in Africa are the people who encourage this practice and keep the money. They are Western transnational corporate conglomerates. They are the people who pay these funds into Banks on behalf of their clients, the African corrupt politicians.

Recently the British Government of Tony Blair failed to co-operate with Nigeria to repatriate such funds the tyrant, Sanni Abacha deposited in the British Banks. Unfortunately, pandemic corruption and disunity have encouraged Britain to keep these funds. We are still soft on corruption. We seem to be using corruption to fight corruption. My advice is that the tap of corruption should be plugged on both ends. This will convince the world that Africa at last is really serious in stopping corruption. However, I am not convinced that corruption synonymous with capitalism that the West uses to do business with the world is solely the cause of failure of Africa. Colonial dismembered Africa has to be re-integrated to work. At the moment Africa is like a vehicle dismantled in the mechanic workshop for repairs. It cannot work until it is re-assembled again.

I challenge the West to seize these funds and return them to Africa if they are really serious in helping Africa. There is no need for George W Bush to vote unapproved money to tackle HIV-AIDS in Africa and turn round to feud and wrangle with the Congress. Let him lead movement in the West to return this stolen African money corruptly stored in Western Banks, Off-shore Banks, tax havens and Switzerland. The corruption in Africa is a weapon of mass deception the Western con business men use to fool the African leaders to dump both African and aids money to Africa in Western Banks abandoning and neglecting Africa in abject poverty. The West has a precedent in seizing drug funds and terrorist funds. What prevents the West from doing the same with African stolen funds deposited in the Western Banks?

5. AAAD knows that development in Africa depends on effective knowledge and skills of its citizens. Success in this depends on prudent use of its limited resources to achieve this result. NGOs and donors to Africa must aim at getting Africans to have useful skills to do things for themselves. AFRICANS DO NOT NEED HANDOUTS. They need sound education, knowledge and creative skills to do things for themselves and produce the goods they consume and be able to purchase the goods they do not produce.

.

This is what Africa needs. The fast development of Western global NGOs is a risk and threat to Africa. They are fast filling the gaps left by religion and colonialism in Africa. The previous two had a role to play but left the continent in ruins. The NGOs are a stop gap that encourages Africa to be dependent. We must wean Africa off this new threat of dependence on outside help. Equally charity is fast developing into a lucrative profession for young Western graduates. It is dangerous to allow it to reach the level of British jobs that the politicians will have to defend. Aids and investments must involve the people who benefit from them. They must essentially help the people to free themselves from depending on aids handout. A re-integrated Africa with citizens confident with sound education, solid skills training and substantial apprenticeship in trades will definitely succeed. Africa composed of several Bantu rogue ministates as at present will continue to fail.

Once the AAAD has been established, its members will plan and execute its programmes. It will assist Africa to make maximum use of its existing facilities for these satisfactory results. Africa can rejoin the world when its citizens have the right knowledge and skills to develop their land and improve their standards of living and economic security. Africa must produce highly skilled manpower to attract global investments. Unfortunately, I have come to discover the white establishment in the West have come to view my writings as anti-West articles. This is not true. These are Historical facts that must not be ignored regardless of how sensitive they may be.

The West has its way of life to defend and protect. That way of life may be preying on poor innocent and needy black people without means of defending their lives, way of life, land and property. A way of life that destroys the livelihood of many cannot go unchallenged or be justified as worth being defended. My writing is not holding the West responsible for all the woes of Africa and the black race. Mass human trafficking and movement of slave trade and slavery and brutal colonisation of Africa completely ignored the interest of Africa and the victims of these evil practices. It is stating facts of history and asking the black race to get their acts together to confront the challenges of the future.

The success of a people depends on critical review of the past, the present and plan for the future in the light of these facts. This is the way the human thought is used to build for a better future. How can the West defend their past actions in Africa and among black people as taking their way of life and interest into account when they did all these things? How can they deny that these activities did not damage Africa to the extent we see, today? The colonial borders created the rogue states, banana republics and failed states of today. It is the West that gains from the African jungle bush resource wars. They also complain loudest.

The West should not think that we Africans or the black people have no way of life to defend. We all have the God-given right to be in this world with other races of human beings. We equally have the right to enjoy the labour to build a happy life from the resources of our land for our people. We also have the freedom to express our feelings when others hurt us and our interest. The West should no longer take our silence for our approval of their sadistic acts against us and our interest. The worst form of provocation is demonstration of bliss of arrogance of ignorance of the self-esteem of the black people due to past racial xenophobic abuses and degrading of black people by the white brutal colonisers of the African continent and slave traders and slave owners. These tyrants of greed do not want us to forget the past. They are continuously reminding us to remember how vicious and cruel they had been and can be if we dare to disapprove their evil and barbaric treatment of our people. Such arrogant attitude is reprehensible. We have full democratic right to reject past alien colonial masters seizing our fertile lands for a few colonial remnants with flag of convenience to farm using our poor and miserable people for cheap labour in the name of employment.

If Africa and the black people are to make headway over their current insurmountable problems, the white past alien colonial masters must change their attitudes towards us. They must see us as human beings with essential needs. They must accept equality of all human beings and opportunities and desires. The African leaders must equally behave responsibly. They must stop being stupid and mean. They must respect themselves, their people, land and the people they have do business with. How can they expect to attract respect for our people and Africa, if they are seen to be very corrupt and continue to launder embezzled money in foreign Banks and safe banking havens while soliciting for debt pardon from the G8 group? How many white male would give white land to black farmers under the conditions the Zimbabwean white male farmers are demanding from senescent Robert Mugabe? None! Stop bullying and abusing Mugabe. He is doing a great thing for Africa. Job seeker African Zimbabweans must go elsewhere to earn living.

It was my little Italian fruit seller girl that said “Everybody steals from Africa”. This was a casual joke but it is true in all its context and dimensions. The West feels Africa is its Garden of Eden full of all bounties. Africans should discourage massive stealing and looting of the continent by making just laws and punishments for the thieves within and without. Stiff penalties should now be set for corruption. Foreigners steal from Africa. Africans steal from Africa. Several people from the black race betray Africa and steal from Africa. This is the plight of Africa in the world even in the hands of the Africans.

Those who base their business in Africa on corruption should have their asset and investment forfeited in the continent if they are found guilty of corruption. Those who demand and receive bribes and those who give them should have stiff jail terms in the continent. Our great ancestors were not corrupt. Corruption sells out the land and its people. African Union should make the fight against corruption its major target. We must be prepared to lose long standing friendship and business in this crusade but we will gain if we eradicate corruption.

AAAD exists to enable black people to think of themselves as a race of human beings capable of making maximum use of their energy and resources to change their lives for better. AAAD believes in well focused co-ordinated targeted programmes to make maximum use of limited resources for the benefit of many to make maximum impact on development for progress and change in the standard of living and lives of our people. AAAD LOATHES AVOIDABLE DUPLICATIONAND WASTAGE OF RESOURCES. This is one of the major causes of poverty in Africa. There are too many "Presidents" and ministers in the continent and too many governments. We have to think seriously if this is more important than food and drinking water that we need and everybody is desperate to get them.

A few well funded and equipped institutions can produce the type of manpower we need. The same is true for well equipped and funded Hospitals. Duplication follows the pattern of the rogue states the Western colonial masters created and left behind in Africa. The enormous funds wasted on these substandard duplicated projects accrue to the Western global transnational corporate conglomerates in big contracts with highly inflated values. Duplication is the disastrous catastrophe of brutal Western colonialism. It wastes our resources on substandard poorly managed projects and uncompleted in most cases.

This is the way NEPAD should be thinking. Equally fewer "Presidents", ministers of government and fewer effective governments and less bureaucracy in exchange for improvements in the lives of all our people enjoying a higher standard of living and the security of a wealthy first class nation would be definitely better than what we have at the moment. Why do we not sacrifice the current ineffective system for something better in African Union instead of wasting our resources in fruitless bush wars that benefit weapon manufacturers and gun runners and make us worse than before?

If we accept the ability and Authority of the United Nations to solve our problems what is our justification in rejecting the ability of African Union made up of our people that know our problems first hand in doing the same? Putting it in other words, if we know our problems first hand and ideal solutions to them, why do we not devise methods and transform ourselves to achieve these objectives? Why do we subject ourselves to wars and destruction while waiting for the international community to come and bail us out? Why do we allow the warlords to hold us to ransom? Are they more powerful and more relevant than all of us, their victims?

This is the role that AAAD will strive to fulfil in our lives. Change is part of life. Yet change is difficult to take in. We have seen great changes taking place in Asia. The Technological advances in Japan, Taipei, South Korea, Malaysia, and Singapore and now in India and China are phenomenal. Even North Korea is technologically making headway despite its enormous problems. Africa has to make up its mind to improve its Educational facilities. We may not take the European or Western strategy. Equally our environment is different from that of Asia. We have some similarities but our ecology is different. Africa is the richest continent in raw materials or natural resources. Our population is smaller. We have two massive deserts.

Pandemic diseases are threatening our population and they can indent our population. We are overwhelmed by bush wars beyond our control. The US fought and obtained independence from the UK. Hard work and Education have made the US the world's number nation, today. On the contrary, Nigeria was ahead of former British Malaya. After independence, indolence and poor and disorganised education have made Nigeria backward and far below Singapore and Malaysia that evolved from former British Malaya.

Our recent Western European colonisers left us unmanageable borders and overblown numbers of rogue states. This has placed the control of our borders and resources beyond our authority. The Western transnational corporate conglomerates are still able to foment trouble in Africa by sponsoring crisis and civil unrest. Much of our resources and energy had been wasted on politics and crisis management because of the unworkable political and administrative structures the former Western colonial masters left behind. These are failed states that Africa inherited from its colonisers. These are redundant colonies. Local and alien conmen run them now as private estates for fortunes. They fail because they were not up to state or nation in the first place. Let Africa and the world not beguile themselves. These failed states are not up to statehood. They should be merged into new nation states. Africa can no longer dock the issue of a complete overhaul of the nation states in Africa in the light of the current long lists of failed states. The burden of failed states has crippled Africa.

It is making Africa a failed continent. The failed states are now dubbed rogue states. Africa and the world can no longer afford to bear the problems of failed and rogue states. Africa requires very urgent re-integration of its dismembered parts. Africans should reject Independence and opt for remaining colonial dependent territories of its former colonial masters if it cannot manage re-integration of its dismembered parts. Africans are suffering too much from a failed postcolonial Africa. The world is tired of chaos in postcolonial Africa. Return of sea piracy to African shores and frequent bush wars is obstructing world trade. Totally failed state like Somalia is making life hell for the world. The world has no option but to demand re-integration of dismembered Africa. The African Union has no resources to cope with problems of these states. The people who created them just shrug them off. They call Africa a chaotic continent. They fail to accept the role they played in making this continent a chaotic continent and land of failed states. The blame for the disaster of Africa lies squarely on the shoulders of imperial colonialists. These failed states were created without consulting the diverse people in them.

Africa needs fewer viable nation states protected by democratic constitutions and laws that protect individual citizens. AU has the cardinal duty to undertake comprehensive readjustment of postcolonial borders and re-integration of these mini-colonies now constituting themselves into nuisance of failed and rogue states in Africa. Most of the imperial colonial created states are failing because they were not up to nation states in the first place. We have to remind the world that the population of Africa is small compared to that of Asia. Its land mass is the second largest on earth. It is the richest in mineral and natural resources. We can use these encouraging statistics to transform the continent into environmentally friendly, wealthy and prosperous land. The Africans do not need miracle of religion to do this. They need just the right type of Education and skills training to achieve this. They can use their existing facilities to achieve this but they have to change their current lifestyle of profligacy and colossal waste of scarce resources. They must concentrate on their homeland to make it work better for them than at the moment.

They were properties of the former colonial masters. They ran them as integral parts of their various countries covering external trade, defence and security. They also took up a lot of the responsibilities of the nation state such as external affairs and defence. It is expensive and wasteful to maintain the failed states. It is equally futile to attempt to rescue them. Recolonisation is a major threat to survival and freedom of Africa and the black race. It may be the beginning of genocide. The HIV-AIDS pandemic is frightful new disease. Is there any secret motive behind this? The problems of Africa, today, are direct results of the recent brutal colonisation of the continent by the West. Those who suggest recolonisation of Africa are out of their mind. We cannot solve the massive problems left behind by the former why then think of new with all its problems?

AU and the UN have urgent duty to plan well and conduct mass continental referendum to create viable non-rogue and failed nation states in Africa. We can no longer pretend that the problem will solve itself if we sit over them. They are direct results of colonialism and its desolation. The former colonisers have no moral right to propose recolonisation as a solution just as former slave masters would not suggest further slavery as a solution to problems of freed slaves. Revision of postcolonial borders and creation of real nation states in Africa is urgent duty and honest responsibility of the AU and the world. Re-integration of dismembered Africa requires urgent action. Dismemberment is not good for postcolonial independent Africa. It has to be re-integrated.

They continue to use these unworkable structures as conduits to foment further troubles in Africa by promoting Resource wars. We have essentially to look for a viable third way to educate Africans and give all our children creative skills training to make Science and Technology as part of our culture. African Union will essentially have to make hard choices. We may have to choose between retaining unviable rogue states and poverty and lack of security and doing away with rogue states and poverty and their attendant frequent crises insecurity and chaos. The African and black children must learn the importance of team work. You are a single piece of wood in the bundle. A single piece of wood cannot provide enough heat for the energy needed to run our machines of our orderly and sustainable development for progress, wealth and prosperity.

Merger for strength must be the message for all Africans and the black people the world over. Leadership must be for a trusted few. The Western journalists and leaders must be off their mind in Africa. I have been thirty years in the West. Secret military installations are no go areas. Loose talk can make you lose your job. In Africa they fool our people that free speech means seeing nothing good in government and leadership. This is colonial interpretation of democracy and freedom. Yet they never tolerated any of these things as alien colonial governments in Africa. Why do they want to see what they never allowed and tolerated in our land when they were ruling over us? It is deception to cause trouble. The United States of America is strong because they are united, pool their resources together, work hard and choose their priorities correctly. Now the European Union is slowly gathering momentum.

They are gaining momentum and making progress. Those who want to sit at the corridors to jump on the bandwagon of success are squatters. If the enterprise fails, they would disappear before people rush out of the sinking boat. The success of the white people is not because they are white but because they know the value of united efforts and the sacrifice that unity entails. They know the value of working for the team and team work. They recognise the distinction between team and group efforts. We black people tend to take everything home away from the team for ourselves as individuals and deny the team the incentives for unity and team work. We black people must recognise the place of unity and team work. We must remember we black people had our viable system of government which could have matured into something modern and fit for our people. This was abruptly arrested and replaced with brutal suppressive colonial foreign government that worked for the interest of the imperial colonial foreign countries that regarded us as overseas territories and possessions unknown to their ordinary citizens.

Unfortunately we continued to run this sort of alien institution as government after independence. It is neither responsible to our people and land nor to any reliable alien government as imperial master. Now we have a group of scroungers both local and alien running the continent of Africa as their private estate and business at a great cost to the people and the world. Sadly there is no genuine social stratification to distinguish the value of hard work and merits from wealth and affluence from crime and corruption. This has produced the dramatic result of replacing talents with mediocrity. What we are doing looks like attempting to reach the top of the sky scrapper still standing firmly on the first step of the ladder. We block the ladder and the way for good climbers to reach the top of the sky scrapper. This is the waterloo and the dilemma of Africa at the moment. We must allow the social centrifuge to function. Hard work must be rewarded. Merit must count. Talents must be distinguished from mediocrity. Education and skills must take priority over truancy and malingering. Ethnic loyalty or origin must not overrule talents, merits, suitability and ability to perform the tasks correctly, efficiently, properly and adequately. The success of hard work is incentive to others to work hard to succeed. This creates role models for others to follow. This is how modern culture is established and traditions created. Hard work may root out corruption and culture of indolence. The African concept of the community is the pyramid.

We may have to make our constitution represent true democracy in the way our founding fathers invented and practised it before the Greeks saw it and adopted it. Aristotle a Greek philosopher saw Democracy in Africa. He recommended it to the Greek constitutional conference for adoption. Today, the West claims monopoly of this civilised way of ruling the human society. Foreign intrusions, colonialism, and influences of alien religions had distorted and damaged African pioneering spirit and views of our world.

Today, we have been the victims of our self neglect, treachery and betrayal of the community by disgruntled elements. Traitors and corrupt individuals are criminals who collaborate with greedy foreigners envious of the resources of our land. Traitors and corrupt individuals sell our land and resources cheaply to aliens and tyrants of greed. The West does not spare its citizens involved in treachery and corruption that damage their common interest. They exert maximum penalties on their national traitors. The West kills its spies. Africa must start to kill proven spies and very corrupt citizens to deter this crime. You cannot be a loyal citizen and a foreign asset. We must start to respect our secrets.

True democracy must protect the individuals and the community. No individual citizen should collaborate with foreigners under the pretext of restoring democracy to the people. Democracy cannot be delivered from the barrels of the gun. Democracy cannot be delivered by alien powers regardless of how friendly they may be. Democracy evolves from the sense of justice and total well-being of the community. Democracy is the practical application of "do unto others what you expect them to do unto you". It is simply applying the rule of law that you will accept as true and genuine justice when you are confronting the law. It is the culture of a civilised society of accepting that individual freedom depends on the universal freedom of the whole community. The relativity of freedom and justice and decent treatment of human beings in a community is what democracy is all about. Africa of our forefathers was very conscious of civic education. Democracy is by persuasion not by fraud or rigging of elections. It is by popular choice. The so-called heralded Western Democracy is stained by Western interest which deploys all foul and criminal methods if the results do not go their way. This can be pre-election rioting from spinning and inciting and false propaganda and murder. Finally they can recklessly rig the election for their supporters. The same goes for the advocated Western democracy. It allows the Western traders to escape with their loots from foreign countries.

Education was based on civic order, leadership in the community and adequate skills in trade by approved tenure of apprenticeship. The prosperity of the community depends on the skills of the citizens. This is the value of industry in the community. Food may be abundant in a place. To prevent hunger and starvation the people must know how to convert it into edible and consumerable form. This is what education, learning, knowledge and creative skills training provide for the citizens. We must produce what we consume as a major part of our occupation. We have to produce what we do not consume only after producing what we consume in abundance. We must stop depending on external aids as investment. Reliance on NGOs is dangerous and risky. Africa must unlock the door to prosperity by making the knowledge of Science and Technology a permanent culture of its citizens.

What type of education is best for Africa? The curriculum of studies must give the African child a lot more in knowledge and skills than his or her counterparts in other parts of the world. They must have practical skills to help them get on in the community. African Institutions must start to distinguish themselves by offering their students the Diploma of Bachelor, Master and Doctor in their various disciplines to emphasize the practical and technical aspects of their training. Our studies must be based on practical and problem solving rather than on theories. Knowledge has no value if it cannot solve problems in the community. Possessing food when you do not know how to cook it or have means of processing it into consumable food and make it edible does not stop hunger and starvation in the community. Africa is rich in resources. Africans need the skills to convert them into consumable products, valuable assets for prosperity. This is what employment is all about. AAAD is a forum for African scholars to discuss their problems. Africa needs practical applicable Education with multiple skills training to broaden the scope for work after Education. Education must not be viewed as a way to easy money without labour and work. It is the wrong concept of education as a means of escaping from work and manual labour and making easy money without working for it that is the cause of massive corruption in Africa. Education should not be for meal certificate but to enlighten the mind and provide skills and enhance civic thinking. It must, however, train the student for practical skills.

The student must stay on Education as long as it is needed for the student gain some skills. The student must have trained on what he or she is good at. The type of Education an African child requires at this time must be linked to work and Industry so that Africa can cover much of what needs to done and students can develop work culture. Students must respect the dignity of labour. At the moment the African student sees Education as a way to escape manual labour. The Chinese and most Asian students see Education as a gate to skills and work. Equally the African students seem satisfied with sham Education and poor knowledge. They have tendency to neglect their duty of learning and cheat at Examinations. In Nigeria moral decadence among the illiterate ex-soldier politicians and leaders has affected student leaders. They are cult leaders used by their parents as political thugs to bully and intimidate fellow students and teachers to suppress opposition from the Academic Institutions. These leaders do not care what national assets they destroy to keep themselves in power. Therefore a global community interested in rescuing Nigeria and Africa from its misery must combat these things that affect its Education and Psyche.

Many Africans regard education as a way to escape manual labour and swabbing manual labour for office work in air-conditioned offices. It is licensed malingering with authority and rich rewards.

"BURN OUT SYNDROME" BY PRESSURE AND STRESS AFTER SEVEN TO TEN YEARS IN LEADERSHIP POSITION IN PUBLIC SERVICE.

This syndrome takes a toll of mental, physical and health of the leaders who perpetuate themselves in office for seven to ten years. They run out of bright ideas. They become exhausted mentally, physically and deteriorate in health and show signs of mental strain and Psychiatric illness. Unfortunately, they may use their influence and position to cover up their deficiencies. They may degenerate into brutal dictatorship. They may rely on falsehood fabrications, and stern denial of true events and incidents. They may resort to war and violence to cover up their personal defects and deficiencies in office. Burn out syndrome is a serious impairment of judgement in leaders who stay too long in office.

Unfortunately Nigeria and most African countries do not realise and recognise that after seven or ten years of service in public office as the leader of Government a person suffers from burnt out ideas resulting from pressure and stress of office. A recent BBC programme actually illustrated and demonstrated this clearly in a number of their past very active and effective leaders who later lost control and ran freewill as a result of pressure and stress of office not only on their judgements but also on their health and physical wellbeing. It catalogued, Sir Winston Churchill, Anthony Eden, Sir Harold Wilson, Sir Harold Macmillan, Lady Thatcher and currently Tony Blair. These were active and effective leaders that time, pressure and stress of office affected their final performance and health in office. I can add to this list that the one Party rule in postcolonial Africa, which perhaps, destroyed the continent with "burn out syndrome in office."

The leaders ran out of both good health and bright ideas. They became loony dictators and destroyers of their people and Africa. I can add a few names to this British list. Kwame Nkrumah, Yomo Kenyatta, Malawi's Hastings Banda, Dr Nelson Obote, Yakubu Gowon, Ibrahim Gbadamose Babangida and now Olusegun Obasanjo. These people all suffered from" burn out syndrome" from overstay in office. Even return to office after a spell outside is no cure to this syndrome. We have seen this in the cases of Dr Nelson Obote and the old man, President Obasanjo. Another case in question is Mr Mugabe of Zimbabwe. The list is long all over the world. In Indonesia Surkano and his successor, Suharto are obvious examples. The Soviet system crashed under the pressure and stress of "burn out syndrome" in sit tight in office leaders who lost all senses of direction in office but rather took to the bottles and made themselves friends of the Vodka and perfect dictators. This staying too long in a stressful job until one is exhausted and loses all initiatives in decision making. Loss of new initiatives leads to irritability, exhaustion, wrong decisions and tyrannical behaviours. It had corrupted most leaders and ruined many countries.

Recently we saw Bill Clinton, one of the most active and effective US leaders in last century. He was nearly damaged by the "burn out syndrome" pressure and stress in office. It is extremely risky to see people like Babangida preparing to recycle themselves to the office of leadership. Nigerians deserve to know of the existence of this syndrome. They can see what it has done to them and several other countries. This is why "House of Elders "is ideal for a few leaders with past excellent records. Return to office is not ideal for the health of these people or that of our nation, Africa and the black race. A veteran statesman like Lord Dennis Healey acknowledged the existence of this syndrome. He advised against staying too long or hanging unto public office or leadership for too long. The democratic constitution should allow a leader a specific period. It should share responsibilities equally to all cabinet members. They must be answerable to the leader and special committees of the House of Representatives and the Senate. In Africa, the "House of Elders" made up of talented Africans of good repute and global standing should be the final court of appeal for good governance and redress of wrongs and conflict and feud resolution. Africa must weed out leaders with moral decadence. Moral decadence among the Senators damaged the Roman Empire. It led to its collapse 476 AD.

We can even add that mighty and powerful empires had frequently collapsed with leaders that suffered from "burn out syndrome". Stress and pressure of office affected their mental, physical wellbeing and health. They frequently became paranoid and lost power of sound reasoning and judgement. They became irritable and impatient. The state apparatus became shaky and unstable. Frustration replaced optimism. Pessimism prevailed over optimism. Doubts took over from certainty. Defeatism became the rule instead of exception. This is what leaders staying too long in power could cost their various nations and people. It is therefore mandatory that leaders should not be allowed to take their nations and people down with them by overstaying in office. The "African House of Elders" should be a refuge for excellent past leaders to take them off the chimney of state stress and pressure of office at the hot end of leadership of Governments. The tenure of office should be five to seven years for one person to stay in office without any repeat.

We propose that the AU should open the "House of Elders" to accommodate our respectable past leaders for co-ordinated advice to our current leaders. We are losing the rare privilege of having Nelson Mandela, Kenneth Kaunda, and getting our leaders of substance to retire with dignity and honour and hand over the baton to the young ones in time to guarantee continuity and smooth running of the continent. Africa needs the "House of Elders" urgently. It is only our high calibre past leaders with proven record of leadership and good characters that can go to the “House of Elders”. It will be the Authority and collective voice of Africa in world affairs. Khedafi should be in the “House of Elders by now. Ben Bella if he is still fit should be in the “House of Elders”. Robert Mugabe regardless of the opinion of the Western white male media should now be in the House of Elders. We hope the West will learn not to be meddlesome in African affairs? The way they behaved in Zimbabwe had been very disgraceful and an unsolicited open and deliberate interference in that country’s affairs. The UK and its white male dominated Media must know that Zimbabwe is no longer a territory the UK. They find it hard to accept the fact that Zimbabwe is free and no longer their colonial territory.

They failed to intervene to stop Ian Smith and his white hordes slaughtering several African Negroes for asking for the simple freedom to take control over their land. Now these people are openly intervening to let a few white people to seize our fertile lands permanently. They claim to be speaking for African Negroes in Zimbabwe. Where were they when Ian Smith and minority whites were slaughtering us for this land? Where was Western democracy? Where was Western democratic basic fundamental human right? Now they remember South Africa. What do they want South Africa to do? Where were they when the African Negro children in Sharpsville were mowed down in front of the camera? I am not resuscitating the past to call for vengeance. It is always helpful to appeal to Western civilized culture of democratic freedom. We just shine the searchlight on the past in order to justify the present and the future. It is the past that controls the future. Assuming that black lack the faculty to analse events is false. Black people feel that actions white people hurt our sensibilities. We understand what the whites do but we have no means to deter them. We are equally not forgiving but we have no antidote to deter them. We leave everything to their moral conscience.

The House of Elders should have the authority to adjudicate in African conflicts and acquire global assistance to quell crisis in the continent. It will help NEPAD in its par counselling among African leaders. The “House of Elders” should be able to investigate some cases of corruption and economic crimes in Africa and speak to some of the transnational corporate conglomerates doing business in Africa. These people who overstay in office at times causing some nuisance and mischief would play constructive role in the "African House of Elders" in their retirement just as the British House of Lords does in the UK. The House of Elders will fulfil African traditional respect for its elders and taking their opinions and advice seriously. We badly need this input in the governance on the continent. It is time this continent speaks with one voice. Only distinguished African sons and daughters will go to the "House of Elders."

Not all past Heads of State will go to the House of Elders. It is not a dumping ground for former Heads of State. It is a House of Honour, Respect and Distinction. Nelson Mandela and Bill Clinton as Honorary visitor and other prominent Africans and friends of Africa cannot afford sharing platform with people of doubtful integrity, refriars and non-leaders and touts. Distinguished people with bright ideas to promote genuine democratic and progressive leadership in Africa and among all black people from all walks of life will constitute membership of the House of Elders. They will be the men in grey suits who can whisper to any leader to step down and go quietly. They will be the supreme power to act in African affairs in the world on advisory capacity. But their advice will carry weight. It will be confidential but legally binding. Anybody or group ignoring the advice of the elders is challenging Africa and Africa can no longer afford to stand idle in the face of individual or group challenge. The House of Elders will be just and fair but it will expect genuine discipline, self-esteem and integrity in African leaders. They essentially have to be people who know what they are talking. The African House of Elders will exist to bring order into the chaos that is Africa, today. Africa needs orderly and sustainable development for wealth creation and prosperity.

It is insult for the West to refer to our leaders as people who say one thing in the public and another thing in private. This has been the tragedy of the Arab league. The Arabs are reaping the results of their leaders saying one thing in the public for public consumption and another thing in secret to betray their unity to the very people subverting that unity. The black people are very successful as individuals. Now is time for them to chase success as a group. Group success provides security for all individuals in the group. Group success allows more individual success and increases prosperity in the community. This is why merger strengthens corporate business. AAAD is voluntary African body dealing with Africans in Africa and in the Diaspora as a group to improve their education and skills training. AAAD will generate group consciousness for success.

The "House of Elders" should have provision to accept Africans in the Diaspora as its members. It is purely advisory but passively active and input from our sons and daughters in the Diaspora will broaden its outlook. The "African House of Elders" is urgently needed to give the world African Voice in this chaotic world. We have to express our feelings in times of crises. Nelson Mandela spoke on our behalf but nobody listened. The heart of Africa is in America because of the accident of slave trade and slavery. We cannot allow the US to be hurt. We equally would not allow the US to behave stupidly in panic or unnecessarily harshly in self-defence. We can say that the US has delivered its message in anger. Now is the time for the US to sit down and listen to the world before it is too late and things are out of hand. Wisdom is the harness to power. Now is time for Wisdom to prevail over anger and emotion. The US as a superpower will essentially have to co-habilitate with all human beings living in the so-called rogue states and protect their lives and properties without sacrificing its core values for freedom and democracy. The US requires its wisest leaders now.

I have seen Communism collapse. I have observed the tremendous achievements of Western capitalism and its bubble Economy. This has a tendency of boom and burst cycles. They cause recessions massive unemployment. I also know the enormous price the world has paid for that progress and achievements in human beings and materials. Equally I know the price Africa paid for those achievements. I have equally seen the victims of the two systems. The plight of Africa is partly due to them. Africa is a victim of these systems that suffocated the African system. None of them can take over African system by politics, religion or ideology. In the light of this knowledge and the real facts on the ground in Africa, all Africans should rise up with courage to revive our system.

The fact that Africa trained a prospective Pharaoh for several years before the person was given the staff of office to lead in ancient Egypt seems to have escaped us all. Today, every Tom and Dick can be the “President” even when he cannot lead his family of wife and son. With due respect to the West, their brand of “democracy” fails to recognise Democracy. It is not only free elections and law courts where people buy justice according to their means. It is right to choose the leaders and everybody being equal before the law just as they are before God their Maker. The Western leaders have immunity from the law while in Office. The election expences in US and Western elections is democracy for the highest bidder. The brand of democracy in where the corrupt rich and criminals buy votes and assume office through electoral malpractices is counterfeit and fraudulent. True and real democracy is by persuasion and free choice by the people of the leaders they have faith in their ability to lead them. Unfortunately mercenary democracy denies freedom to the people to choose their leaders. It encourages crimes and violence as the mercenary leaders corruptly encourage crimes and violence to get more funds to buy elections. Definitely, this is not democracy. It is commercial democracy and the merchandise is corrupt political office. It erodes the basis for democracy. It consolidates corruption and tyranny.

Yet this is when power corrupts man. Any leader having a brush with the law should leave power and sort out his problems with the law until he is cleared from any guilt. Therefore there must be a neutral body always ready to step in and take over the administration until the leader having some issues with the law is free from guilt. There should be provisions for the common people to challenge wrong policy of the government and leaders before the law provided there are genuine reasons for the action. Legal action must be cheap and accessible to all the citizens. Access to justice must be open to all. The African expects justice to be just and fair. The African has great revulsion to injustice and corruption. This is why Africa has collapsed. The House of Elders is ideal for the newly formed AU to establish to play this vital role. It will fulfil this role in African politics. This may be an example of how to supervise modern politics and democracy to make it work. The leaders must be subject to the people and the continent of Africa. Africa is not their private estate and the citizens their tenants.

Africa is our home and any part of it burning is our home burning as we had seen in the past. What the West is doing in Afghanistan and Iraq is running away from opportunity for genuine democracy but continuously shouting, "Democracy, democracy". This confuses all the onlookers. They do not know if democracy is frightening the people off. This instantly makes the word, "Democracy" instil fear into the people. The Democracy the West uses to confuse their victims and deceive the world is toxic Democracy. It is fraud and not Democracy. Democracy, today, should be freedom to choose your elected politicians and leaders free from interference and intrusion from all interest groups and freedom to criticise your elected representatives without repercussion. Democracy is incorporated into right of citizens. Its supreme charter is the Constitution. Its guardian is a free and independent Judiciary appointed by the Judiciary Commission. Nobody should be above these Institutions. Everybody must be subject to these Institutions of Democracy and the rule of law.

I can conclude this Academic proposal by pointing out the fact that slave trade, slavery, brutal and plundering colonialism and current method the West uses in doing business in Africa and racial xenophobia all lack democracy. Running around like mouse in the house shouting "democracy" would not change the current plight of Africa. It is focused education and training targeted to solve local problems that will help Africa. Foreigners cannot solve African problems. The solution to the problems in Africa lies with the Africans themselves. They must make their own efforts to solve them. Total reliance on outside help to bail them out of their current chaotic situation amounts to molestation and blackmail of those people they need help from. The Africans must convince the world that they are ready for business. They must be ready to pull the Economy and Africa out of the pit. They cannot achieve this without first creating the Africa they want to develop and the world to help. It is obvious that this is Africa re-integrated from past colonial dismemberment and fragmentation. Nobody can cure African Economic woes without re-integration of the dismembered colonial parts. These dismembered fragments are what the Western colonial masters left behind for the African leaders to take charge of. Unfortunately most of them are too small to be economically viable. The leaders had been timid to declare their failure to work openly especially as we accuse them of being corrupt. Equally most of them do not want to lose their privileged positions. It is now left to them to choose between a strong re-integrated Africa economically strong to support all citizens and the leaders or weak Bantustans scarcely able to support the leaders we accuse of corruption.

Education is the food for the soul of human being and the nation to place both in healthy spiritual understanding of the nature, God and the creation. We can no longer continue to abandon the feeding of such a vital organ of our existence and spiritual welfare to total aliens. We should no longer starve the soul of Africa, the black race on earth and our understanding of the world around us of education. We should neither feed it with the wrong type of education nor with information that we least understand. We must have basic understanding of what we teach our children. Such information must be focused to lead our spirit to God and resolve our crises here on earth. Well planned educational programmes targeted to solve our enormous problems are what we need. We must not abandon this to the mercy of funding constraints of the politicians or religious leaders. AAAD must be run with funds from its members, donations and fundraising activities by its members and the African masses. This is the way we should plan to tackle our current problems. At the moment the current African leaders give the world and the African people the impression that they do not know what they are doing or are talking. Why on earth do they go for jamboree and luxurious dinners with the leaders of the G8 to ask for debt pardon while several of them have vast amounts in foreign Banks and are still laundering vast amounts in secure Western Banks and off-shore banking havens? Who is stupid, they or G8 Leaders?

We do not need titular Education. It is fraud to have Engr Sholagun around when all our Engineering problems cannot be solved and need foreign engineers on big contracts to solve them. Wherever we find Africans performing under the supervision of aliens either within Africa or outside Africa they seem to be doing very well. They are the spice and seasoning salt or sugar of success in such groups. Now is the time for us in AAAD to find out why we fail to maintain this rhythm of success when we are left on our own? Equally the AAAD must have active genetic typing and matching of Africans the world over to help us to determine how far Africans have mixed with the rest of the world. We have to rebuild Africa from the scratch from people dehumanised and excluded from the centres of human activities for millions of generations and for over five millenniums. Our cardinal mistake had always been fighting for our individual interest and neglecting communal public group interest. Our leaders from ancient Egypt made the same mistake. They pretended to ally with Ammon ore and to represent Him on Earth and neglected the duty of uniting the people and expanding our territory. They broke up allied territory due to frequent personality crash. They wasted their time defending their offices instead of the State and the Community. They failed to be uniting leaders. A number of European leaders and Asian leaders expanded their territories and united their people and the community. Today, African leaders are still guilty of using State resources in protecting their positions in office and neglecting State and Public interest. It is even worst now when they are in charge of unviable Bantustans that cannot be made economically viable. It is obvious that they should sacrifice their personal interest and positions and allow re-integration of colonial dismembered Africa.

We essentially have to rebuild our nobility as Africa is a continent that virtually depends on its elders for leadership. More so is our reliance on the nobility. Oligarchy has no meaning to the Africans. Integrity, virtue and nobility are what Africans need in their leaders. Wealth has no place in African leadership. Wisdom and integrity are the virtues we respect in our leaders. This is what made Africa take to their Pharaohs. This is why Africans showered their Pharaohs and leaders with gifts that made them richer than others in the community. Africans never accepted wealth acquisition by their leaders by appropriation and extortion as most alien leaders did. We are not job conscious people. We are service conscious people. Our first priority is to render good service. We look forwards to rewards after rendering satisfactory service. We, however, must take public interest in our leadership seriously. Self-sacrifice and honesty are in high demand in African leadership.

This trust was destroyed by aliens who seized that position from trusted African sons and daughters. These alien “Pharaohs” assumed the office because of its grandeur and prestige. They did not know the responsibilities, conduct and public expectations of the people from their Pharaohs that created the bond and trust between the Pharaohs and their subjects. The European and Arab cultures were totally unfit for the office of the Pharaohs. All of them rule from the top and exercise power of office to take their subjects as issues secondary to the needs of their office. Ancient Africa had leaders that were primarily integral part of the community and their first priority was the welfare of the community. Macho behaviour was not essential. The leader was to be wise, humane, compassionate and of exemplarily honest character and a person of great integrity. No alien really understands how to administer a foreign land and what type of Government is best for foreign people with cultures different from their own.

The current "tit for tat" war against terrorism requires a peace maker. This is the wise man bold and brave enough to confront the combatants with the absurdity of the situation and their positions. What value will they give to their victories and humanity? True wisdom would demand peaceful resolution of this feud. The Africans at the centre of this feud have a duty to explore the feasibility of genuine peace as an alternative to war and worthless victory. The war against terrorism is attrition and self-mutilation of a bleeding world. Where are the wise people in the world to plan and execute the path of peace?

Neither the terrorists nor the people against terrorists have life to offer to human beings. Both have death and misery to offer to the world. Both of them lack peace and security to offer to their victims. Both of them are violating God's Law, "Thou shalt not kill." "Christ admonished Roman soldiers to do violence to no man." Therefore, neither terrorists nor the executors of war against terrorists are in God's service. They cannot expect reward from God they are not serving and whose law they are violating with impunity. Let the wise mediators confront the combatants with these facts and seek genuine compromise to restore peace and security to the combatants and the world. Let us not allow anger and emotions to erode our core values for fundamental human rights, freedom and democracy. The bravado emotional outburst of violence and hostilities is not the way out of our current dilemma. Wise and rational decisions are important for action to stop the carnage. We desire genuine peace, safety and security and not victory. We deserve real peace. Continuous war and violence for victory are destroying the channels to genuine peace.

The expression "war against terrorists" seems to be infectious. The invading occupation Army is fast becoming terrorists terrorising the populations in their homelands. Military occupation was frankly rejected in the Second World War in Europe. It is obnoxious and unacceptable today regardless of whatever spin and propaganda the invaders use to justify their action. Uninvited alien boots in the streets of any land are abomination to the people and will always meet resistance from people with civic pride and duties to their land of birth. Negotiated peace in this situation is better than forthright hollow victory. Such victory will be a breeding ground for future blood thirsty dictators who would have to kill to stay in power. This is not what democracy wants. It is no business of the Anglo-American invaders and occupiers to dictate to the Talibans what Religion they should practise. But we have the right to use the UN to isolate them if they fail to comply with civilised standards. If they fail to observe the right of man we should not fall into the trap of abusing human right ourselves, we should isolate them and throw them out of International Institutions. There must be basic International Standards for the UN to recognise a Government. The conduct of the Government must be compatible with a secular Constitution and not a Theocratic Constitution. The UN should not accept any Theocratic Constitution and laws. We must not go out to deal with fanatic extremists physically. We must deal with them through the UN and International Institutions. It is time these Institutions have clearly stated the requirements for admission into them. Any country that does not meet these requirements must be rejected.

The terrorists have the right of audience to give reasons for their action and justify them. They equally have to offer what they want as a solution to their grievances. The victims of terrorism have equally to tell the terrorists what they want. No religion should have monopoly of any global land. The world must have the courage to legislate on religion. It must be free and voluntary. Religion must never have veto or political power to influence the lives of human beings. Religion must be a matter of individual conviction. It must be purely voluntary. Religion must stay out of politics and the Economy. The settlement of any quarrel involves getting the parties to talk.

The world can no longer tolerate people going about to impose their beliefs on unwilling and reluctant people in the name of religion.

Freedom of religion must now have voluntary acceptability attached to it. People uninterested in the faith must be free to be left alone. God-soldiers who kill in the name of religion must know that they are committing criminal murders. God objects to murders in His name. Genuine religion should abhor violence. God has power to kill if He wants. He does not give that power to the murderers now going about killing in God's name. They are lying against God. They are deceiving their followers. They are destroying lives that God values and sustains. The believers must tolerate non-believers the same way they accept believers. Mutual respect for each other is what the believers and non-believers must have. Differences in faith and belief and religions should never justify the basis for conflict, violence and war. We claim to worship God. God is love. He loves all human beings, peace and harmony.

This is my fear of current drive towards Western democracy and pax Americana. No foreigner can deliver political and religious cultures to foreign lands. Cultural borrowing is voluntary assimilation of useful alien cultures to enrich local cultures. Democracy is by persuasion and friendship. Intrigues, double dealing, past History of the role of Western influence in the world, violence and aggression make the West unfit to sell democracy to the world. The West colonised most parts of the world. Colonial rule was famous for its brutality, violation of basic fundamental human rights, abuse of freedom and democratic rights of colonised people and plundering and looting of colonised lands and territories. It was notorious for arrogance and racial segregation. The African Negroes were dehumanised, taken to the market and sold as slaves. They rendered slave service for over two centuries and a number of generations lived under slavery and human degradation. I was born poor. I worked hard and acquired first class education. But even now institutional racial xenophobia had prevented me from using my skills to continue to help the community and work to earn a living because I write about some of the activities of the civilised and affluent West in poor, miserable and wretched Africa. Unfortunately, I have to write these things down for posterity.

Yet I have to use the privileges I had through education to offer my beloved homeland and people that unique hope that sound education and skills training are the door out of their poverty and ignorance.

I have faith in the ability of Africans to make high achievements once they are set on the correct path to opportunities. AAAD is out to embark on mass effective and focused education targeted to solve multiple problems in their homelands. This is my personal opinion. It does not represent public view of what is happening now in the world. A world that remains silent is cowardly. It allows fear to take precedence over sensible and wise judgement, (common sense) in these vital issues. I owe no apology to anybody for taking this stand exercising my right to free speech and expression. The West has right to look back to its colonial past with pride. We the victims of that glorious past equally have the right to express our feelings freely and unhindered by fear and intimidation. It is not the expression of our experiences that hurts. It is the punitive and brutal tendency of the colonial alien administration that denied our people all opportunities for growth and development and abused and violated our basic fundamental human rights that hurt.

Those who disapprove of free speech and expression are at the peril of being embarrassed by what they fail to hear from other people on their behaviours and actions. I am one of the survivors of over five thousand years of white European abuses of the fundamental human rights and freedom of the black persons in Africa and on earth by racial abuses, discrimination and segregation, intrigues, lynching, murders and genocide, slave trade and slavery, direct wars and proxy wars, brutal colonialism, plundering and looting of the African continent and now by debt burden and uneven and unfair trading regulations. Yet we are still here as black and courageous people. This is not the time to dwell on hostilities. The white people should not be embarrassed by what their ancestors did. They treat their past with pride and seem to continue with new hostilities. Keeping accurate record of events and what people do to others is not expression of hostilities and hate. Equally silence does not mean ignorance of what is just and acceptable.

This is the time for every black person to use that ability that made us good slaves to work for the European prosperity and survived all the abuses and ill-treatment to acquire practical problem-solving education and practical proactive creative skills to work hard for our own prosperity and security here on earth. It is not African culture to lie our way to crimes and deny our crimes or harass people who mention our crimes in their discussions. If we are brave enough to commit crimes we must be bold enough to accept the analysis and records of our crimes. Criminality, violence and war are trademarks of History of the European white men. Events are associated with particular wars and national heroes are created in wars and slaughtering of fellow human beings. The European culture seems to create enemies always to justify their militaristic and aggressive wild culture of heroism. Wars create national heroes. But these heroes had killed their fellow human beings. They had been made savages and perfect killers for their nations and people. Wars kill people and destroy lands and properties to create national heroes and win victories. What victories celebrate by getting dead victims, massive destructions in lives and properties and ruins of vast land mass? The war heroes are very strange people indeed.

It is the Europeans who must review their culture to justify their behaviours towards their fellow human beings particularly with other human races. The black people must accept that Science and Technology are here to stay. We must rapidly adopt the knowledge and skills they offer to apply them to the way we work. We must improve our work culture. Wealth is not in hard currency or in faraway foreign lands. Mineral and natural resources are not wealth. They are wealth if we have the knowledge and skills to convert them into what we consume. Wealth is in our homeland, Africa and prosperity is in the practical problem-solving knowledge and proactive creative skills we have. Wealth and prosperity are in the lands of your birth but you must make them user-friendly. Good Education, knowledge and skills properly managed with hard work generate wealth and prosperity. Wealth and prosperity of the nation are the type of education and skills training its youths and people have. It is not natural and mineral resources. Educated resourceful and skilful citizens constitute the wealth and prosperity of the nation. Wealth is the Education, total skills and apprenticeship the citizens have in a viable community. Wealth is the culture of people who know the value of persistent hard work and treat their responsibilities seriously. A healthy community treats its civic duties seriously.

The owner of the weapons we use in killing ourselves in bush wars is the only one making fortunes out of our misery and death. Africa does not manufacture these weapons. We cannot improve our standards of living by killing each other. This is what we did in slave trade. Yet we are worse, today, and more miserable than before. Armament manufacture and sales are very lucrative job generating venture. Unfortunately arms are for war. War kills people and destroys properties. Yes armament manufactures and sales may provide the jobs but arms kill people. Several other forms of manufactures for peaceful purposes equally provide money and jobs. They also promote trade and peace. There can be very bustling business between nations without arms trade. Africa just does not need arms. It needs a lot of equipment for its enormous constructions now needing to be done. We just do not have money for arms or fighting wars.

SECTION TWO: AFRICA, WHAT CAUSES ITS STAGNATION RETOGRESSION, POVERTY, IGNORANCE AND MISERY?

Having sojourned for almost thirty years in the West and visiting Africa my beloved birthplace on earth, I cannot help to observe that Africa and the black race lack sense of orderly and sustainable development and management of their resources, human and material. They are woefully ignorant of the knowledge of money economy. They do not know that money is meant to pay for goods and services. A healthy economy is the balance between goods and services and money in circulation. When excess money is in circulation compared to the goods and services the money can buy it is inflationary economy. Fine tuning of the economy means production of valuable consumable goods and services that the community needs. This is in turn dependent on the availability of highly trained manpower. Education and skills training come into play again here. How do we make Africa conscious of the role of effective education and skills training?

High standard of education and practical skills training based on modern Science and Technology are essentially important to achieve these objectives. It cannot be overemphasized that, today, much of Africa consumes what it does not produce and produces what it does not consume. The leadership tragically is made up of mediocrity while the talents and intelligent elites are kept out.

Gross mismanagement of all the resources, massive corruption compounded by gross imbecility and absolute ignorance of the leadership of the responsibilities of government in handling public funds to fund public utilities and pay for goods and services the government needs for running the community further complicates the problems.

NIGERIA is a typical example of what destroys African prosperity and the prospects of emancipation of the black race from slavery and chaos. This is a relatively prosperous country saddled with leadership that is neck deep in mediocrity and corruption that is totally ignorant of the existence of talents, value of practical education and focused and problem-solving skills training for the youths. The leadership specialises in job destruction and disorderly and unsustainable development. They pride themselves in destroying everything and institutions that enhanced the progress of the community. They destroy education, institutions of learning and the fabrics of practical and applied education and purpose-orientated and problem solving education, health services and health care institutions, communications, railways, shipping and air travels. They fly abroad to have treatment when they are sick. They specialise in affluent lifestyles without any feasible means of supporting it but supported by massive embezzlement of public funds direct from the treasury. The treasury and its holdings are the private property of the politicians and the administrative officials. They squander public funds on themselves and their relatives and friends.

They send their children abroad for education. They are illiterates and have no knowledge that the value of effective education is that targeted to solve problems in the community in their environment. Little do they know that Education in the West aims at tackling problems in various countries in the West, Europe and America and that the environment and problems Africa faces are different and require education designed and targeted to solve the problems in the African environment, culture and traditions. While the West is struggling to conserve energy and obtain better heating during winter cold Africa needs means of using its energy to keep cold in the hot humid weather heat and provide water to combat drought and encroachment of the desert in its habitation and recovery of land from the desert. Yet no African cares about these things.

Nigeria is famous for unnecessary duplications and enormous wastage of scarce funds and resources. There is unbridled rivalry without means for very lavish lifestyles. This has resulted in everybody rushing to politics for the tremendous rewards in bribery and corruption and kick backs from it. The struggle for political appointments is life and death. It is fraught with all manners of crimes including murders. The instability resulting from this deadly struggle destroys the economy and potential for recovery in Africa. Africans are yet to overcome their individuality and selfishness that frequently strangles their civic duties to their homeland and fatherland. They are poor because they do not know team work. They are yet to treat their continent with affection and loyalty. They have to respect life and property of each of their citizens. The land cannot be kind to them when they are very cruel to it. The African will never gain respect in the world as long as he specialises and indulges in abuses of his kind, fellow citizens and children, be it in slave trade or in political hostilities and violence. He dehumanises himself by abusing his fellow countrymen.

Carrying truck loads of the scarce money we make from sales of our mineral and natural resources to launder in the off-shore banking havens and invest in luxury properties in the West will never solve our problems of poverty, misery and ignorance. Permanent stagnation and retrogression in development in a fast progressing and developing world of high Technology have transformed us into Stone Age nation. We are a failed nation state the West now christens as rogue state or banana republic. The tragedy is that our illiterate and mediocre leaders unknown to talents, self-esteem and patriotism just do not care. We can drift to hell. They just do not care. Worst still they do not understand that broad smile of flattery is not indication approval of success. It may be mockery of failure due to stupidity and mediocrity in the face of all facilities for success.

Travelling across Nigeria, it is not difficult to see why poverty, ignorance and misery reign supreme in the rule of mediocrity. There is no single viable educational institution but yet more and more of these are established with giant signboards every day. There is no single viable health care institution but yet more and more mushroom teaching Hospitals with giant signboards are established everywhere. There are no roads but contracts are awarded for road construction every day. There is no railway but yet there is a railway board. Similarly there are boards for shipping and airways but yet there are no ships or planes. Huge allocations are made in the budgets each year for these items. Yet nothing materialises except huge signboards representing nothing but phantom new projects the funds for which the officials cart away into their private coffers. This can be described as budgetary embezzlement of scarce public funds by officials.

MILITARY COUP d'état.

It is incredible to contemplate coup d'état in Nigeria after a long time of fruitless turbulent and very corrupt military rule. But yet recently the soldiers had been plotting coups and risked the dangers of death penalty. The reward for successful coup d'état is worth the risk. The coup leaders gain access to the exchequer and control of the treasury. The past military administrators are fabulously rich. They have money to buy Nigeria several times over. They buy elections and gain control of the civil governments. Yet they still prefer the autocratic and corrupt military government and its lawlessness. The past military officers are so rich that even those of them in detention in prison have enough money to take over the prison to run it and gain freedom to manage their affairs outside including enough resources to plot military coups. Muslim Islamic influence and ethnic loyalty in the face of grinding poverty and failing indolent civilian government paralysed by feuds and corruption are making fertile soil for future crisis. The past military officers and officials are much richer several times than Nigeria itself. Nigeria cannot pay its civil servants and pensioners. The government is incapable of getting these people to return the money they looted from the treasury. They are using this money to frustrate the government itself. Corruption is still rife. Officials still abuse their positions of responsibilities and squander public funds on their private projects. Embezzlement of public funds is still very common among the politicians and officials. The government seems to be incapable of looking after public institutions and utilities. The truth is that the so-called civilian government are the criminal corrupt soldiers in muftis and civilian clothes. They have enough money to buy Nigeria to rule in the midst of abject poverty, ignorance misery and a failed state. This is Nigeria ruled by Olusegun Obasanjo, an ex-military leader frequently found at the fire side of the President of US in the White House perhaps to show his democratic credentials to the American people. He has never been able to return a penny out of the money the soldiers looted from the treasury to the exchequer. He has not arrested any soldier to set him as an example in his fight against corruption. He is a paper tiger in this fight. His Nigeria always occupies top position as one of the most the most global corrupt countries in the Transparency International neutral grading. This oil rich Nigeria that taught all African leaders corruption. The Nigerian Army taught African Armies military coup d'état as means of acquiring power to loot the treasury. Nigeria has a sham democracy led by very corrupt criminals. It cannot progress with these ignorant corrupt criminal leaders who steal public funds in excess of their monetary need. The Nigerian Democracy is called Ballot Box stuffing Democracy promoted by thuggery, open corruption, bribery and violence.

Normal people work hard to achieve satisfactory results in Education and skills training to improve productivity and their living standards. Unfortunately Nigerian soldiers backed by their religious chieftains want to seize and retain power to stop any development while collecting oil revenues to squander on their wasteful luxury lifestyles. They sponsor stagnation and retrogression. These people had been in charge for almost half a century. The leadership has been very corrupt and totally irresponsible destroying all basic infrastructures. They neglected roads, the railways, shipping and airways in state of disrepair. They neglected Education and Health care and left them in a deplorable state. They frequently closed down Schools and Universities and completely ignored the plights of students and their studies. They destroyed discipline at Schools and ruined Academic discipline and invaded Institutions with cults. Nobody cares about high standards, excellence and talents. Mediocrity is the rule. There is no discipline. Chaos reigns supreme. Cult leaders, children of the corrupt politicians rule the campuses. The Academic Staff are under their rule. They execute fellow students in the classrooms in front of other students who run for cover with their lecturers. They release live bullets from their firearms in the Examination hall while the examiners and the candidates run for cover in the chaos and panic that prevail. They intimidate the lecturers to pass them. Poor lecturers have to comply for their lives at risk in the hands of these violent people. Passing them to get rid of them is an unattractive option but a necessary safety net in the hands of the lecturers and security of the Campuses. They walk into jobs. Jobs depend on who you know and not what you know. Their parents are the government. Some of them are Party thugs and stalwarts. This is Nigeria, the giant of Africa.

They completely wrecked national discipline and ran a lawless, criminal and very corrupt society where skills and talents had no role. Success in society depended not on ability and positive achievements but on contacts and the people in high positions that the individual knew or could bribe for favours and lucrative positions. While modern progressive leaders pride themselves in job creation they specialised in job destruction. These are people angling to return to power by coup d'état to continue to destroy the country instead of rebuilding it. The choice is that of Nigerians'. It is their country, their destiny and the future of their children or these people out to destroy everything for their selfish ends. Yes President Obasanjo may be a failure due to these very people who do not want him or anybody outside their criminal fraternity to succeed in rescuing this country from their grip. They left a very unwieldy constitution damaging to the country and the rule of law in place to allow them to bend the rules in every aspect of lives in the country. We are yet to summons enough courage to call a National Independent Conference to hold frank discussions by the stakeholders in this country on its future and draw up a working constitution, viable binding secular laws and codes of discipline to run this country properly.

Decimation of public utilities to infinitesimal point where nothing is viable, visible and, functional except representation by signboards and fake budgetary manoeuvres, seems to be the case everywhere. Even professional qualifications are not represented by skills but by certificate signboards. The Engineer is recognised not by practical work but by title, "Engr sun or moon." The Architect is recognised not by their famous Architectural works but by title that allows them to give or acquire lucrative contracts at inflated values or join politics with high yields in pandemic corruption. Sir Christopher

Wren is synonymous with great buildings like St Paul's Cathedral and several famous buildings in London. Brunel and Stevenson are famous in the world for their pioneering Engineering inventions and collaboration to build things instead of title. Nigerians have craving for titles. Their mushroom Universities offer more honorary degrees to mediocre and total idiots without any value for education, knowledge or any skills. Titles rather than genuine education and practical productive skills are means to social recognition, politics and criminal wealth by extreme corrupt means. We must educate and train professionals that will work and do things with their hands instead of craving for titles. The professional bodies must abandon the cravings for titles. They must now develop means of encouraging skills and practical work. How come that people frequently people who do not know that I am a Medical easily recognise that I am a Doctor even when I deny that I am not one. They still insist that I looked like one. Of course, I am. As a barber Surgeon I go by the Title "Mr". This makes me believe that there must be certain Professional characteristics the public recognise to identify true Professionals.

People without any ideas of what is involved in contract jobs win lucrative contracts at inflated prices from governments just to sell them to firms that would execute the jobs poorly at exorbitant prices. These are well-placed people in the society. Mediocre and illiterate elites without any scruples for the rule of law, or fear for corruption and crimes dominate public life. The Mafiosu Cosa Nostra Nigeriana is in full control of the country. They make very comfortable living by crimes and corruption. They rule the country by raw terror. They hold phantom elections. They ignore the popular votes. They pay their thugs and criminals to stuff the ballot boxes with voting papers marked with candidates of their choice. This gives them indefinite control of the country. This is naked stealing of elections by rigging. The officials have no scruples for the rule of law or integrity. They seize power by coup or rigging of elections for power is worth more in corruption and embezzlement of public funds than the risk of acquiring it by violence and criminal means.

They may choose to run away with the money without executing any contracts or execute them very poorly. The experts to approve the jobs are nominally titled specialists without any practical knowledge of the jobs they are to approve. Most of them are interested in sharing in the loots. Even when they know what is required and would like to insist on quality jobs pressure from corrupt officials who share the loots render them ineffective. Nigeria is a total disaster and a curse to the black race and Africa. It is the scourge of Africa. I sincerely pray that God should one day have mercy on the suffering souls of the black race and dissolve this citadel of sin, abomination, corruption, moral decadence and crimes against humanity.

DECIMATION: INFECTIVE AND COLOSSAL WASTE OF RESOURCES AND FUNDS.

This is a new political terminology of corrupt and bankrupt nation state. It is unlimited and infinitesimal division of the country into mini and unviable Bantu states and each state into infinitesimal and unlimited counties and districts and proliferation of political and public offices. It is reckless and unlimited and endless expansion of facilities until they lose values and serve no purpose. It is a con way of driving corruption in the society and the community. The limited funds and resources are divided ad infinitum until the tiny fragments disappear in the pockets of very corrupt officials strange to productive labour but very well talented in crimes and graft. The profligacy of politicians and government officials and pandemic mismanagement of all resources and funds is infectious.

There is wild and unregulated rivalry without any regard to means. The politicians and public servants indulge in overdressing. Each wears clothing materials that can do for ten people. They appear in floats of flowing gowns. They change their clothes as in a fashion show or beauty contest. The women are overdressed. There is wild and unregulated competition not justified by any visible means except corruption and crimes. There is no public accountability from top to bottom. The government is fond of slogans. Words but no action seems to be the rule and no exception. Total paralysis of action against corruption and crimes is the rule and not exception. The judiciary and the judges openly receive bribes to pervert the cause of justice. Unimpressive feeble official warning and suspension occasionally follow isolated few cases and incidents of these cases. Religious riots sponsored by advanced party of

Arabs on mission to arabinise Africa South of the Sahara by ethnic cleansing and genocide continues unhindered. This party seems to have stranglehold on the leadership of most postcolonial countries in Africa in West Africa. Arab Muslim sponsored Mahadrasah students start riots after Friday Prayers led by fanatical extremist Imam and Mullahs. They burn properties and kill.

Any efforts to dislodge these Arabs that trace their ancestry to Mohamed in Saudi Arabia from the leadership in democratic dispensation, usually lead to massive blood shed by wars and violence. The massive destruction, gruesome atrocities, ethnic cleansing and genocide in Darfur and other parts of the homelands of the ethnic African Negroes in Sudan are parts of this long term plan of the Arabs in Africa. They want to control all the major oil producing lands in the world. Kano in Nigeria is the hotbed of this Muslim Islam religious mix of Arab nationalism. This was a major cause of religious wars and seizures and selling of Africans into slavery. The Arabs castrated our male folks and used them as eunuchs to guard our women in captivity in their harems. We are not advocating for revenge. The Arabs should know that while we deplore the US for attacking them, they have no licence to abuse religion to seize and deprive the African Negroes of their homeland. Israel is strong enough to evict them from their land they seized several years ago.

The government specialises in proliferating phantom projects. It claims lands and destroys its vegetation and trees. It starts laying foundations for buildings just to disappear with the funds to abandon these places in environmental destruction with erosion and rendering the land unusable. Signboards are monuments to these dot and dodgy development programmes of very corrupt governments. The economic significance of this type of corruption and profligacy is the fact that lands, properties and funds are tied down in multiplicity of uncompleted projects. The wastage is colossal. The result is that all public institutions are represented by prominent signboards but no activities or services. Substandard services are the rule and no exception.

The resources and energy are dissipated infinitesimally until they are all ineffective and serve no purpose. Health care institutions offer no health care. Schools and academic institutions offer no education and training. Unlimited and unregulated proliferations of these mushroom institutions result in complete lack of staff and equipment. They exist only in name and big signboards. The services they offer have no value. The certificates offered to students in institutions of learning have doubtful value. They fail to represent what students are said to have known. There is no orderly and sustainable development (OSD). Illiterates and idiots enjoy the pegs of corruption in high places and public service.

Is it not time that those who had held this country to ransom from 1966 recognised that they had failed and that it is time to release this land from their imprisonment to look after its exhausted citizens? I speak to the senior retired military officers, tribal groups and octogenarian geriatric professional politicians. We all are in transit through this world. Let us not damage and destroy everything along our path. You have embarked on tragically catastrophic self mutilation and indescribable self-destruction in complete ignorance of wealth acquisition.

All of you admire and like the West and Europe. The difference between Africa and the West and Europe is that the West indulges in increasing and expanding the prosperity of their land while the Africans indulge in stealing from their land to increase and expand individual and private wealth. Public wealth and affluent land can generate and sustain individual wealth but individual and private wealth cannot generate and sustain public wealth. An impoverished land cannot generate and sustain wealth and prosperity. It is the contribution and sacrifice of each citizen that builds a rich and prosperous land and community. It is not the sacrifice of the land and the community to enrich private individuals that builds a rich and prosperous land. The real wealth of the citizens of any land is their genuine focused, problem-solving and practical education and well-targeted productive skills capable of solving the problems the community faces and producing what the community needs. Stealing oil money to parade oneself about as millionaire or billionaire destroys this real concept of wealthy citizenry. Fiddling with figures of government expenditures is not wealth but criminal corruption. Nigeria has many criminal thieves and robbers but no rich citizens.

Nigeria can create very rich citizens by investing its enormous oil wealth in pioneering a type of education that offers its citizens discipline, respect for the rule of law, honesty, integrity, self-respect, virtue, respect for honour and not ill-gotten wealth and self-esteem. The interethnic scramble for oil money has wrecked and destroyed work culture in Nigeria. It has ruined discipline among youths in Nigeria. It has caused permanent interethnic friction in the community. It has caused permanent breakdown of social order. Education must offer knowledge applicable to life and solving life-problems. Education must offer skills training targeted to solve problems, do things that need to be done to improve the environment and our living standards and produce and manufacture the things and goods we need for our living and comfort. Any knowledge and skills must be able to sustain the citizens in work to make a living from genuine labour but not from con and fraud. Education must create things. We may call it creative education. Education is not how to read and write and speak English. It is the total body of information, discipline, and manual dexterity and skills the individual has acquired to enable him or her to function in the community and earn a decent living within the rule of law in a free society. It must initiate the citizen into the community to lead independent life free from crimes and corruption. Education is a failure if the certificate the student carries lies about what the student knows. It is fraud and criminal negligence if the authorities fail to offer the citizens satisfactory and adequate Education to see them through life in this Scientific and high Tech age.

It must offer the citizens skills and means of working for their living by either intellectual exploit or appropriate skills and manual dexterity and work. Education must liberate the citizen from intrigues and corruption. Education must be all embracing including the dignity of labour, manual work, art and craft and intellectual knowledge of the highest calibre. No citizen should leave School without excelling in one of these skills and acquiring genuine and feasible means of the livelihood. Education must be genuine induction of the child into the community and should involve knowledge and skills and carry the child through life on earth. Well equipped Trade and Technical Schools should offer Vocational Education in various trades. The training must be formalised and standardised to offer high levels of skills. This will improve the quality of our maintenance culture currently grossly lacking in all its forms. We must move all apprenticeships from road side shacks to formal Trade Schools. The apprentices must undergo formal training. They must be familiar with modern tools and acquire very high level of proficiency for trade certificate or Diploma. This will improve the quality of services they render to the public and maintenance too. We need integrated Vocational, Trade, and Technical Grammar Schools. This ensures that a child achieves something before leaving School. It will also improve the quality and standard of our public services. Apprenticeship will have uniform professional standards.

Ancient Egypt and Carthage in Africa taught the world the concept of Education. Europe adopted it and later used it to dominate the world. The black race pioneered Education and in this wilderness of the dark ages in Africa and among the black race, we have no choice but to return to the light of real Education in the classics, Science, Mathematics and Technology. The black race will regain its influence in the world by accepting the value of genuine truth and sincerity in the pursuit of religion and real Education. We must invest much of our lives and resources in Education. Knowledge, understanding and skills are the key to wealth and prosperity. Counterfeiting Education and vital skills training as we have done in the last thirty years is not a quick way to catch up in development. It destroys us physically and spiritually. It destroys our confidence in the competition to win in the economic emancipation of Africa and the black race. Education is not European. Africa proudly invented all forms of writing the West had used and is using, today. They copied them from us. Unfortunately Africa gets no credit for this.

There is no Academy to catalogue not only our past achievements but the present and plans for the future. We have mostly illiterate and mediocre leaders who have no value for education and skills training. They just cannot understand the value of genuine and effective education and good skills training. They are swindlers and anything goes. They came into national prominence not through educational achievements but through swindling, crimes, rigging of elections and participating in several military coups. Most of them were street touts and thugs and have no sense for respectability and honour. This is why most African leaders are content with the deplorable situation in their various countries. They had never had it better than what they see. They just have no clue how to make things better than what they have because where they find themselves is a great improvement from where they came to occupy high positions in government. This is why they devote all their times working out how to remain indefinitely in office. They embezzle all public funds across their way to launder abroad to ensure that they would never be poor again. Of course little does it occur to them that they should find out why they are poor? They understand poverty as not being in government and do everything to be in it.

We in Africa invented all forms of writing the West uses, today. We invented Mathematics, Trigonometry, Chemistry and Engineering. The Engineering and Mathematical feats of the great tombs, temples and pyramids are living witnesses of our educational skill and the Chemistry of embalming of the dead in Egypt is not Arab or Europeans. The Chemistry of purple dye and the Royal purple manufacture in Carthage in Africa are well documented in the classical History. The advanced manufacture of fabrics, linen etc in Egypt is equally well documented. These people are new comers. They came to see these things left by our own ancestors. We will recover from this African social degeneration, regression and degradation of the black race by genuine and totally determined effort to return to fully satisfying education and religion that faces God in truth and sincerity. We must not forget that the Arabs came here between 642-698 AD. Alexander son of Philip of Macedonia saw the Arabs during his march only in Gaza where he confronted and defeated them. He never saw or confronted them in Egypt. Hence they were not in Africa then.

He entered Egypt not by fighting and military conquest. He was received into the city after the Persian rule in Egypt had crumbled after Alexander had routed them in the battle field. Alexander came to see our temples, tombs and pyramids in place. These structures were already in place several thousand years before Alexander arrived in Egypt. It is not true that Alexander and the Greeks brought civilisation to Egypt. We were far more advanced than the Greeks. The Greek invaders refused to return to their less civilised and less affluent homeland and chose to settle in more civilised and more affluent Africa. Ptolemy, Alexander's General who succeeded him as Alexander died without an heir. Ptolemy actually defiled our heritage, kingdom, and civilisation until his offspring, Cleopatra and children were destroyed by traditional European rivalry and aggressive militarism by the Romans. The Greeks destroyed our civilisation and stole our heritage. The Romans betrayed our friendship and destroyed Carthage by subversion and sabotage. They moved in to plunder and loot our continent through traditional European tyranny of greed and aggression in 146 BC, which are still plaguing Africa and the world, today.

Unfortunately Middle Eastern upheavals always involve Africa. The Muslim Islamic religious revolution and march across the world caused enormous upheaval in Africa. It is still causing a lot of confusion and chaos in the continent, today. Today, Muslim Islam is fighting for its survival. This is not African survival struggle. Muslim Islam had caused Africa a lot of aggravations and distress. Muslim Arabs started slave trade across the Sahara in Africa. The Muslim Arabs took Africans across the desert. Muslim Arabs destroyed our religious culture and traditions. They exploited our religious faith and loyalty to God and monotheism handed over to us by Akhenaton and Queen Nefertiti. They replaced our God with Allah. They planted Arab macho culture with Muslim Islamic teachings. In the event of the third world war Africa must be neutral. African-Americans must ensure that Africa is neutral. We have no issues at stake. Our land must not be used by the West as launching pad for their offensive. African co-operation with the West must be for peaceful co-existence. No inch of African soil must again be used for prosecuting Anglo-American Western war of conquest for plunder and loots and world domination any more. We are not for war and violence. Unfortunately mediocre and corrupt leadership can mortgage Africa and betray our land to be used as battle field for alien war that we have nothing to do with.

Infectious epidemic of megalomania and pandemic kleptomania are the rule rather than exception. Those who cannot afford a one bed room property go for multiple room two stories properties. People with funds to build moderate bungalows go for two stories mansions. The towns are littered with uncompleted buildings covered by bushes, pests and wild life. These tie down funds and lands that would be used otherwise to support the economy. Huge mansions erected with embezzled funds straddle posh reservation areas. Most of these are derelict and human beings share them with pests, rats and cockroaches. The catalogues of wastage are long and limitless. It can go on forever. It is responsible for poverty, misery and massive corruption and crimes. Nobody seems to be in charge. Anarchy reigns supreme. Even sacred religion has been turned into money minting institution where people lie to God and insult the Holy One. Is African disaster total? I can proffer a few suggestions and advice in addition to immediate and total assault on practical education for problem-solving applied knowledge in Science and Technology and massive targeted skills training aimed at solving our enormous and protracted problems.

ORDERLY AND SUSTAINABLE DEVELOPMENT (OSD):

NEPAD had been proffered as a solution to the chaos in Africa. I add OSD to this. It is better to have a single well-staffed and well equipped Hospital to serve millions in the population than to have one million non-functioning Hospitals that exist only in big signboards. Equally it is better to have a few well-staffed and well-equipped educational institutions than to have several millions of poorly equipped and poorly staffed ones represented in names and signboards only. A few well-staffed and well equipped institutions would provide high standards of service and generate high calibre manpower that can be used in expansion and provision of more viable institutions without compromising the standards and quality of services. Quality of services is more important than the quantity of the institutions to render the services. It is unwise to train doctors that will help to create more iatrogenic diseases. Talents and ability must be the hallmark for staffing our institutions of learning. Staffing our institutions with half-baked mediocre staff is a serious blow to learning. Poorly trained manpower constitutes more unemployment problems than well trained manpower. Poor Education is a terrible deterrent to progress. Poor Education retards progress and causes stagnation. It is a disaster in the face of rapid advances in Science and Technology. Poor Education is permanent life handicap to the Student and a scourge to the Economy.

It is wise to dress moderately and save money for other important life projects. It pays to live in moderate well-completed building than to live in uncompleted mansion. Each person should have one building for himself and the family to avoid massive corruption and crimes. The government must complete one project before embarking on others. Any uncompleted building or poorly maintained property should be taken over by the government and local authorities to complete and rent to the public to provide adequate housing for the people. People who build oversized properties would know that they are at risk of losing their investments. For individuals cannot control the limit to what they can own in the community, the community have the right to place a limit and restrict what a single individual can legitimately own? Even in Britain the public frowns and objects to one person having several holiday homes to leave scarce properties unoccupied.

This is not advocating for communist socialism. Capitalism has limit to unlimited demands in the face of limited resources and funds and pandemic corruption and crimes. We must not allow our bad habits to tie down the funds that we should invest in profitable projects to support the economy. Economy means being economical in our lifestyles. Lavish lifestyles are incompatible with economic prudence. Economic prudence is cardinal for orderly and sustainable development and prosperity. How can you combat corruption and crimes when most officials of government and public officers are openly corrupt and display their loots by lavish lifestyles? Babangida now campaigning hard to return to ASO Rock, the castle of his estate, Nigeria christened bribery and corruption as settlement and made it into a national culture. I cannot judge the right or wrong of this action. It damaged everything that Nigeria stood for. Most of our infrastructures, dignity, self-esteem and virtue died under Babangida. Our confidence as a proud nation died with his toothy smiles and terror. Can we afford the return of Babangida reign of toothy smile and terror again? He had a habit of compromising individuals in his honest habits of honesty and integrity. Short of this he send in his murder squad to deal with the opponent. Vatsa could not escape his network. Bisalla and Dimka and Golmwalk fell to his axe and intrigues.

I feel sad to see a nation that fails to prepare its youths for continuity of life after its octogenarian geriatric leaders should have gone. Unfortunately the previous military leaders who survived death from intrigues and violence in the Army who had now replaced military uniforms with flowing gowns do no longer believe in death. They feel they had come to live to plunder and loot this land forever. They had established a club of mediocre elites to plunder and loot this country. I wish them luck but the French nobility never thought that tyranny of greed could deny them of power. The misery and frustration written on the faces of our hungry youths can be transformed into nastier violence than armed robbery and insecurity of lives and property. Our leaders seem to have extra lives. They never think of death and leaving this world.

Life supported from the national treasury is too sweet to them for them to think that life has an end. Unfortunately life is a relay. We have to run our course and pass over the baton. Nigerian leaders seem to run one man relay. They fail to understand that relay is run by a team that has got to be prepared. Our leaders destroy every preparatory ground in our country and resort to sending their children abroad for education to prepare them for returning to take over when they die. This is not hereditary office. The Army has betrayed Nigeria. It has squandered our trust in its ability to rescue our land and our pride. Nigeria is too sophisticated to be led by illiterate and ignorant octogenarian morally decadent retired military officers in the year 2004 or in the year 2007.

Nigeria has worn these coats before. It is now thirty eight years since these very people took over this country to demolish it. Unfortunately they had not made their mark in any positive way. They had failed in every way. If they had any respect for this land, its people, Africa and the black race they would have disappeared from our public view. If they were patriotic and had any self-esteem with honour they would have disappeared from the public scene. They are hanging about to cover their back for the crimes they had committed against this land and its people. Abacha paid dearly for this exercise. His family has kept part of the loots as a reward.

They had not protected her from the hostile weather and misery. Nigeria does not deserve to wear these worn out military coats again.

It is sad that these people are openly displaying their looted wealth to use to buy Nigeria again to abuse in their corrupt and criminal ways. Nigeria has talents most of them had been compromised to live with mediocrity. It is time our talents take over the administration of this land to manage it as a state in modern world where global village competition based on education in Science and Technology and focused and targeted problem-solving skills training is the key to progress. It is not money laundering and acquisition of properties abroad in the West that constitute wealth. Wealth is the high standard of education and productive skills of the citizens.

I am ashamed that children of poor people brought into the community by sacrifice of people who sacrificed a lot to help them to come into positions of serving the nation have seized the nation and held it to ransom as hostage to feed their lavish lifestyles without recognising that they are damaging the nation. People claim that they came into public life by Sir Ahmadu Bello and Sir Abubakar but fail to acknowledge that neither Ahmadu Bello nor Abubakar did what they are doing to our country. If they did that these people would not be where they are. What moral justification sanctions the senior officers of the Nigerian Army on very generous pensions and fringe benefits now swabbing their military uniforms with oversized flowing fanciful gowns to play the role of politicians in a democratic dispensation to earn all their money and entitlements while disabled and retired privates of the same Army are not paid their meagre pensions?

They are subjected to endless screening to route out ghost pensioners. Several of them have neither the funds nor the means for the long and tedious journeys to the screening points. These people and their families live with hunger and starvation and diseases. Several had died from hunger and starvation while waiting for the pensions owed to them to be paid. These are the very soldiers who fought the civil war with these very corrupt retired senior officers. Civilian pensioners and their families do not fare better. They are owed their pensions year in and year out. The politicians and public officials are busy flaunting their stolen wealth. It is equally unfortunate that the very senior officials screening these poor folks to route out ghost pensioners are themselves the beneficiaries from these ghost names on the pension lists. The payments from these frauds accrue to them. Why then ask them and their agents to screen for these fictitious names?

It is no surprise that key Nigerians benefiting from life of fraud, embezzlement and corruption would do everything to prevent national identity card. They do not want to be identified as fraudsters in their crimes against this land. Year after year we bury them with national flag of shame and disgrace. We shower praises on them in obituaries and funeral orations. May I say what we should rightly be saying, "Go, and cursed be you for you lived a life of curse to this land and to your fellow citizens. Go and justify your actions before God, your maker."

Recently the President Obasanjo held national award day and gave Ibrahim Gbadamosi Babangida the most controversial military officer and multiple coup plotter and coup-installed military leader and president who killed more military officers than any other and damaged both the Army and the nation the highest national award. Was it for the role he played in the Dimka coup and the killing of Dimka, Bissala and Gomwalk? Was it reward for the treacherous circumstances of killing Mama Vatsa? Perhaps it was a reward for Orka massacre and the destruction of this country by protracted post Abiola election crisis that Babangida presided over that finally abandoned Nigeria in the hands of the psychopath and tyrant, Abacha? Maybe it was reward for Babangida action that finally offered Olusegun Obasanjo a second chance after the Dimka incident? Whatever prompted this action made a mockery of National Award. It queried Obasanjo's integrity and sense of judgment.

Are we being ruled by intrigues of a relay of conmen in uniforms without any qualm over what clothes they wear to take charge of the treasury in this country to continue with their lavish lifestyles at the expense of this nation and its core values, respectability and dignity? The Army officers responsible for the demise of this nation to feed their filthy, criminal and lavish lifestyles should be ashamed of themselves. Babangida took Nigeria into OIC without any consent by Nigerians. Now Muslim Islam is involved in quasi-religious war and conflict. He will be a very dangerous leader for us to have. Equally Nigerians have to appreciate changes in the world and time. There is absolutely no reason to reinstate Ibrahim Gbadamosi

Babangida in power in this country of over one hundred and twenty million people. He started religious feuds in Nigeria. He was one of the Islamic fundamental fanatics as soldiers in the Nigerian Army that mounted very bloody counter coup after January 1966 when the soldiers ran amuck and went on the rampage murdering Easterners in a gruesome Pogrom and ethnic selection. He was actively involved in the bloody civil war that wasted the scarce resources in Nigeria. He was involved in the series of coups that bedevilled Nigeria when intrigues and betrayal took over in the Nigerian Army. He is an evil genius and a survivor. The criminal corrupt fraternity want him back in power because he usually opens the treasury to them to loot while he helps himself to Head of State's share of the loots. They think retrogressively. He had agents in posh Swiss Mountain resorts with hot line to the ASO Rock. This is the man that criminals want to hand Nigeria over to, to rule as President.

We must allow younger people the opportunity of the challenges of leadership. Babangida monopoly of the country's leadership is totally absurd. Yes Obasanjo got away with it. We have seen the results. Babangida has never been able to render good accounts of the way he spent public funds during his time. He spent billions of dollars in planning handing over. He never did it. He never justified why he squandered the scarce national funds the way he did. What type of frustration and disappoint would take us back to surrender our destiny to this man who contributed a great deal to our ruins? If Babangida loves this country more than himself let him out of that patriotic affection stay out of the race to be head of this country again. Patriotism can be expressed in this way. He can still help the country from outside the leadership away from ASO Rock.

Let one of them come out and challenge me and confirm that this is the nation they took over by seizing power in a bloody coup that was followed by a series of blood letting murderous violence and extreme intrigues from the civilian leaders in 1966. We know all of them have extra lives except their victims who are always victims of the supreme terminators. If the senior officers now gallivanting this country as victors cannot challenge me that this is the country they took over from the civilian administration when our educational institutions offered excellent education, health care institutions were second to none, our railway was working, our roads were good, our infrastructures were all working, they should hold their heads in shame and retire from public life.

They are a disgrace to military discipline and gentleman's decorum. It is difficult to understand why people who bear arms in the name of this nation, the black race and Africa should behave this way. Hannibal an African General and patriot was acclaimed by all his enemies as being the best behaved officer, gentleman and a military genius and leader. Why should we allow a tiny group of senior military officers to seize our country to rule by massive corruption and crimes? The current well-trumpeted nascent democracy is a continuation of criminal corrupt military dictatorship in coalition with their corrupt civilian collaborators. It is not my duty to talk down my country but these people had been talking down this country for too long.

It is worth letting these idiots know that I am a first class surgeon, today, because the civilian government that they replaced gave me the opportunity. They all had the same opportunity. They had embarked in destroying these opportunities for subsequent generations. They had embarked on plundering and looting our wealth and laundering our money abroad and acquiring exotic properties in faraway lands. This is unmitigated self-destruction and destruction of our nation and the black race. I do not know if these people have any self-pride or vision of the future? Have they heard of racial xenophobia and subtle institutional racism? Why do you talk of investments while you are busy carting away our scarce funds to launder abroad and invest in luxury properties? Charity starts from home. Why not invest the funds you take out of the country to launder abroad in foreign Banks here at home, if you all are seriously interested in investments here at home?

WHAT THEN IS ORDERLY AND SUSTAINABLE DEVELOPMENT, (OSD)?

It is basically taking up one project and completing it before embarking on a new project. It is having few completed quality functional and well-maintained and well-managed institutions and infrastructures instead of having large quantities of unfinished and poorly maintained and poorly managed ones rendering no services or unsatisfactory services. It is avoidance of unsustainable rivalry. It is building and completing a family house that your pocket can sustain. Responsible and patriotic citizens should own what their legitimate earnings can buy and sustain. How do they explain how each public servant owns wealth far in excess of his or her legitimate life earnings apart from the fact that such a public servant is neck deep in corruption? Nigeria is homogeneously corrupt. It is Nigeria that stood with the UK and France to oppose re-integration of dismembered Africa that torpedoed our Independence from the word "Go".

This impedes its progress as its citizens do not have to work for what they own. They just have to pilfer from the public coffer. The current moves against corruption in Nigeria tantamount to commissioning and sending corrupt individuals to investigate and arrest other corrupt persons. Otherwise, it looks like an attempt to deceive the community and the world that action is taking place against corruption by sending a criminal to arrest an accomplice or another criminal. The society stinks with corruption and the stench is nauseating. The leaders pay lip service to honesty and integrity when they are criminally corrupt. They lie to God. They lie to their fellow human beings. They lie to themselves and live under the false illusion of being great leaders because they had managed to hang unto power by rigging and fraudulent methods. They have no leadership quality or character. They live by intrigues and subterfuge. They are devious and vindictive. They do not know the duties of leadership and the meaning of integrity, honour and honesty. To them leadership means opportunity to embezzle public funds and strip the assets. They walk pompously and present bloated and overblown ego in their flowing and several times oversized gowns in the Public. Africa and Nigeria are wholly leaderless. These people are opportunistic rogues and thieves and not leaders.

The whole nation is littered with millions of uncompleted projects. These tie down the scarce funds for orderly and sustainable development. They blight the environment and render arable lands unusable for farming and other developments. They encourage erosion, growth of wild weeds and pests. This blights the economy and makes the people poorer and miserable. It is further compounded by the fact that these multiplicity and duplications of redundant projects provide safe outlets for various generations of administrations and their officials to embezzle public funds. If this is not how to destroy the economy of the nation the leaders and senior public officials would have to tell us what ruins the economy and condemns the nation and its citizens to a life of misery and poverty? We must take up one item or a small number of items and complete them well before embarking on other projects and programmes. We must resist the temptation of taking on several projects beyond our means at the same time or projects too expensive for our means and resources. Corruption and criminal money made from phantom projects are principally responsible for the wastes uncompleted projects cost. The other reason is to help politicians score political credit for bringing development projects to their areas even when they are phantom projects. Most parts of Africa are littered with abandoned and uncompleted projects.

Long time ago the musicians admonished Nigerians, “Cut your coat according to your size.” Today this advice has fallen on deaf ears and Nigeria is dying a slow death as a failed nation state. The oversized flowing gowns of the politicians and public officials are definitely not according to their sizes but far beyond their sizes and their means. We have failed to make our land prosperous. We have resorted to impoverish the land, the environment and our communities in attempt to enrich ourselves. A poor overall environment and atmosphere are depressingly miserable and hostile and destructive to wealth creation. The damage we inflict on the economy by corrupt practices and kleptomania generates poverty and gives us false illusion of wealth and affluence in ghettos and slums. The society and the environment we create are depressingly hostile to wealth creation and prosperity. We get our money tied up in uncompleted phantom projects. This is self-inflicted poverty trap. The funds invested in these uncompleted projects are sheer waste of scarce resources and money that should be used in profitable projects for jobs. Multiple uncompleted projects in Nigeria is evidence of how large the fraud is in that country as people just launch the projects to lift money from the treasury and run away.

Corruption causes indolence and inflation. It stifles production and causes imbalance of goods and services and money in circulation.

This is poverty and not wealth. It generates paper and base metal money awash in circulation but without goods to buy. Politicians and public officials just fiddle with figures and ignore productivity in the economy.

Finally merger to provide viable and functional orderly and sustainable effective services is better than spreading out and expanding the facilities endlessly until they become overstretched and make no impression or impact on the needs of the community. Centralising essential infrastructures to concentrate equipment and manpower to serve larger population is more effective in Education and health care delivery than current tendency to disperse them to form clusters of mushroom institutions without values or impact on the community. Attempting to use a loaf of bread to feed millions instead of just one or two does not make impact on hunger in the community. A prosperous and affluent community and environment constitute the basis for wealth creation and prosperity. A society of pick pockets as represented by homogeneously corrupt Nigeria is grinding machine of poverty with citizens without any initiatives for wealth creation or means of generating prosperity. The Nigerian ostentatious lifestyle creates and supports poverty.

Wealth distribution is essentially important for participatory democracy. Wealth distribution is not endless state and local government area creation to share the money among corrupt officials alien to work for their living but remaining as social parasites and criminals depending on criminal patronage and contacts. This is a society thriving on cronyism and not on genuine achievements. Genuine life achievements derived from personal efforts in Education and skills and effective management of these assets and talents is incentive for development. It is not hiding behind military tanks to seize power by military coup de'tats to loot the treasury to acquire money and means to buy power by naked corruption. The ex-military coup promoted officers owe a duty to tell this nation how much they were worth before 1966 and how much they were worth before they were propelled by coups to control the treasuries and the oil money. It is sad that these people are congratulating themselves for destroying this country and the opportunities for the citizens and youths of this country to offer themselves chances of acquiring ill-gotten wealth. Today they are richer than our country that cannot pay its workers and pensioners.

THE WRITER'S BRIEF CV:

Born to Grace David AKPAN-ESSIEN and David AKPAN-ESSIEN hard working peasant farmers with very high sense of duty, dignity and virtue, 21 March, 1946 I was taught the dignity of genuine labour. My parents believed sincerely in genuine progress and encouraging their children to achieve more than what they achieved in life. For me heaven was the limit provided I had the talent to shine. To them Education was a gem. They encouraged me to reach to the heights. My elder brother saved his daily meal allowance to reach the target of ten pounds to enable me to go and start Secondary School. They supported me until I completed my Postgraduate Training in Surgery in the UK and acquired the coveted FRCS of the Royal College of Surgeons of England. They hated mediocrity. Their motto was, "Be the best of what you want to be." My parents dreaded corrupt life of dishonesty and crimes. They disdained politics of extortion and graft. I started Secondary School with £10 only. This took my brother a year to save from his meal allowance working free on a truck lorry. The ten pounds created a flood of scholarships that sponsored my Education till the end. It is prudence in using investments and scarce resources. I can confirm that my excellent clinical skills and brilliant work of my colleagues in the NHS had helped to prolong my life with metastatic cancer of the Prostate. When the Doctors are at the end of the road, I have to design intensive treatment for my disease as a competent clinician. Usually it works and when I attend the OPD for review the colleagues always marvel what I do to keep long. Excellent Medical clinical skills, good Research and manual dexterity in treating myself competently all help to prolong my life in this disease. Ability to administer treatment to myself without waiting for District Nurses makes my treatment easy and prompt. A good Doctor is confident in what he knows without being told by others who may be biased and jealous.

The bridge that I had to cross to be here had been damaged by the joint destructive efforts of the very people in my generation with poorer and mediocre talents than mine and their alien collaborators.

These were people without means to escape from poverty except through crimes and corruption. It is sad because they were able to get to the bridge with the help of people who had great vision for our land. They abused their positions to destroy this vital bridge for the poor to escape from poverty and ignorance, because they cheated their way to that bridge that they and their foreign collaborators, the multinational conglomerate corporate global business that lives on crimes, corruption, poverty, misery and ignorance of our people had now destroyed. They had destroyed the sound Educational and skills training facilities and replaced them with counterfeit and fake structures represented by big signboards without rendering any Education or skills training. The Schools in my youth offered genuine and effective Education and learning opportunities. The rules and regulations were binding for both the teachers and students. Education is life-long process. It is not a way of escaping from poverty. It understands what life means and demands. It knows the way to do things here on earth and live happily.

Medicine.

Medicine deals with maintenance of a perfect machine made by nature (You may call it God). It is full of knowledge of the ways to deal with a fellow human being anxious to solve problems affecting his life and health. This relates to the patient's family, relatives and the community. It extends its anxiety to the team looking after the patient having all the problems affecting his life and health. Permit me to say that health is a state of well-being and normal life. The Doctor is charged with listening to the story that only the patient has. The other part of the story may come from a close witness or the person that the patient first told the story of abnormal changes in his health and life. The parents observe these changes in their children and approach the Doctor for help. Unfortunately the writer suffered the fate other vocal black African talents social exclusion despite their enormous talents and skills. A few examples of these unfortunate talents included Prof WEB Dubois, Robeson and a large number of talented Musicians including Billie Holiday and Artists. We had been damaged by silent exclusion. We hope that racist white Europeans would abandon social exclusion of vocal black people. We ask for tolerance and accommodation of our opinion.

We are not dangerous people but long standing victims of racial prejudice and bias.

We cannot progress under these conditions. The policy of social exclusion had deprived most black males of jobs and means of looking after their families. This has destroyed the African family background essential for community discipline. Our women are abandoned in doles as single parents totally incompatible with our culture. This has damaged us and even the white community that practise it. I am not bitter because I know the excellent skills that I have regardless of what those who hate me may ignore. GMC cannot create a good Doctor. A clever man comes of naturally regardless what those hate him may say and do to him. Public supervisory bodies are good as long as they are neutral and are not biased or prejudiced and offer themselves to be used for witch hunting and slander. The UK GMC is part of establishment, the Intelligence and the Judiciary that the white male dominated community use to punish any black person they deem is disrespectful to them. They expect all black people to be submissive.

The beauty of Medicine is the fact that the Doctor is challenged with listening to the stories patiently. He has a system of analysing these stories. He asks collaborative relevant questions. This is called systemic review. This is based on the Doctors knowledge and the pool of information the Doctor mandatorily had learnt to be accredited as Medical Practitioner. It is the duty of the Doctor to use this professionalism at first encounter to equip himself for what to look for when he examines the patient. We have seen that the stories of what is wrong lie with the patient. It is the duty of the Doctor to use his professional skills to get them. The Doctor uses the stories, his professional knowledge and skills and the information he has acquired from the common pool of information and knowledge in Medicine to examine the patient to have a broad view of what has gone wrong with the patient's body. In a good Doctor Medicine is a reflex that switches on once in contact with patient.

He proceeds to use this knowledge to ask for relevant tests to confirm his suspicion. The next step is to initiate some treatment and allay the anxieties in the patient and the relatives and offer clear advice and information on how he is going to proceed to solve the patient's problems. The Doctor then assembles all the information he has collected on the patient's ill-health and determines on the treatment and the solution. We could see that the whole process relies on collective information and a number of important sources that the Doctor must handle with professional dexterity. The patient and sources of information on the patient's problems must be respected. The pool of information on Medical knowledge that the Doctor had studied and the Doctor as the analyst and interpreter and user of the information to solve the patient's problems are the different important players in the chase for solution to the patient's problems.

How does this process compare with life on earth? Our individual life depends on others that we must handle with respect. We must not rely on our knowledge alone to get it right. We equally must have the patience to listen to others and use our cumulative knowledge to analyse the information we obtain. It is useful in learning. It is useful in business and human relations. It avoids imposing solutions to other people's problems relying on our knowledge alone. Unfortunately, top Medical Practitioners had ruined the lives of people they are supposed to protect by use of dogmas and reliance on their knowledge as the sole authority. It is betrayal of knowledge and expert skills. There is no dogma in Medicine or Science. There is a system of order and sustenance that must not be violated. Procedures may be helpful but they are not rigid laws. There had been enormous problems of recent in Medical Practice because the Doctors flout the rules of the Profession. They rely on their knowledge and skills alone to solve the problems.

They ignore the tradition of building up the total information for solution to the problems. It is painful to observe that a lot of people, today, are behaving like magicians and palmists. They seem to know what is wrong with you before you tell them. The Doctors use the magic of their knowledge and skills to harass and menace their innocent clients. The leaders use the magic of democracy to bully and terrorise their victims without regarding the human factors as important as their authority and power to determine the solutions to human problems. The scientists abuse the achievements and advances in scientific knowledge and technological achievements to dupe the people and strip them of their assets by transforming nature's free assets into money minting enterprises. Munchausen's syndrome by proxy may have traces of truth in communities under the pressures of life in modern society, but it is tyrannical concept in expertise and skills. The MMR vaccine publication and allegation of causing autism in vaccinated children reached the public through wrong route for publishing Scientific and Medical Research findings information, through the tabloid media. Such information should have gone through specialist Journals. They are properly screened and the Authors advised on further investigations before re-submitting it for evaluation for publication or rejection. The way the information reached the public is still raising doubts in parents. Is there any subgroup of children at risk of this complication? No-one knows.

Experience in the British National Health Service, (NHS).

NHS is the greatest asset the UK has. It is the best common institution Britain has. Perhaps, it is the best way to practise Medicine. It allows the Doctor to do the best for the patients. It is a very vast and extensive establishment. The Doctors, nurses and other workers in NHS complain of extra workload on top of their clinical commitments. Unfortunately, NHS has too many non-medical administrative staff. They sap into huge expences on the NHS. They constitute a source of distraction from clinical work. They waste a lot on stationery and too many publications. The supporting non-medical staff is helpful but there are too many of them now. With good organisation, the NHS can manage with half the number they have now. More money should be spent on clinical care for patients than on administration.

The intrigues in NHS.

Many Hospitals run properly. A few Hospitals are very poorly run. They hurt their patients and gang up and lie. They go on the offensive to damage their victims by slandering them. They use smear whispering campaign. They spread false rumours that they suffer from diseases that they do not have. The call this risk management and damage limitation. When I developed cancer of the Prostate, the Consultant I was working under advised me to do half time. My illness then was not so serious as to affect my clinical work. The Consultant then embarked on harassing me in my miserable state of just being diagnosed with cancer. I was virtually forced out. The Authorities then went on the offensive to damage me. They started whispering campaign to slander me to prevent my winning at industrial tribunal. They sent me to the Hospital Doctor in occupational therapy. The Doctor reported that there was nothing affecting me apart from the recently diagnosed cancer that they knew. They wrote a secret letter to the General Medical Council (GMC) that I was suffering from Psychiatric illness. I continued to work as a Locum Consultant in the NHS unaware that the GMC had this whispering malicious slandering campaign on its record.

I took up Locum Consultant in selection interview in a Hospital in the Midland. I had three middle grade Indian Doctors working with me. Unfortunately, they had failed to impress me as confident clinicians in their grade. There was one in Dept of Surgery in the Hospital where I worked as Locum Consultant in Scotland. A young man of 29, a petty drug dealer and IV drug abuser with groin stab wounds was admitted in haemorrhagic shock. He was pulseless. We resuscitated him. He came over. Hemodynamic returned and he started bleeding again. We padded the wound firmly. The Indian surgical registrar was in attendance. Such patient needed immediate treatment in the theatre with facilities to explore the wound. I politely asked him when he was taking the rebleeding patient to theatre- He gave me the wrong answer; he said when the patient was stable. How would such a patient be stable without exploring the wound in the theatre to stop the bleeding? They left the patient without exploring the wound in the theatre. He died of hypotension and haemorrhagic shock. They claimed that he died of DVT and pulmonary embolism. Even if this was true failure to stop the bleeding in the theatre and rehydrate him properly contributed to it.

Again in the Hospital in the Midland one of the middle grade Indian Doctors was on duty. I was the Consultant covering him. He attended to a patient in severe acute asthmatic attack. The patient was so short of breath that he could not complete a sentence when the Doctor attempted to take History from him. Such patient was for mandatory admission. The Doctor gave him a shot of nebuliser and discharged him home without informing me. Shortly, after the patient returned in a poorer state than before; the Doctor again failed to inform me. He called up the Anaesthetist. They vented the patient; they inserted a wide bur needle into his chest. They continued venting him without inserting a chest drain. They created iatrogenic tension pneumothorax and killed him. One f the Indians had FRCS from Glasgow and I had one from RCS, London. He was wooing the Authority for my job. He told me that he was fighting for his right. The circumstances of the asthmatic death were so upsetting that no Doctor mindful of the patients would fail to be moved by sympathy. The patient was salvageable if the Doctor knew what to do for him. Postmortem confirmed iatrogenic tension pneumothorax. There was a lady Personnel Officer. She told me to adopt risk management and damage limitation. I refused. I opted to forgo my job. The Indian Doctors in NHS gathered their in their ranks to defend the defaulting Doctor. The job hungry Indian Doctor led the flay. They teamed up with the Hospital Authorities. They got the GMC involved. GMC then got this job hungry Indian Doctor that was working under me to write confidential reports on me. GMC then invited me to "Fit to practice" session chaired by an Indian Consultant. The GMC personnel arranging the meeting was an Indian lady. Unfortunately, metastatic cancer had broken my spine. I was paralysed and had to go in for surgery. I informed the GMC to obtain the reports from the UK Hospital Doctors treating me. The Senior Doctors wrote to the GMC but the GMC ignored their reports. Again, the Hospital was to damage me so that I would not be treated favourably in any industrial tribunal. Nevertheless, I was too ill to do this or to work.

Indian Doctors form the lifeline of NHS Doctors. They appear to be chasing away African Doctors. Even the little daughter of my friend, a very brilliant Doctor with FRCS, MSc and MD at very young age had complained of Indian Doctor Intrigues. Her Consultant had to rescue her. She is a very brilliant and respectable Doctor and scholar unused to politics and intrigues in the NHS. Indian Doctors would continue to dominate the NHS as they now constitute about fifty per cent of Medical School intake in the UK now. Clinical Practice is not safe when Doctors are not fully committed to patients in their care. My job is to represent my patient in life or in death.

The decay of the family structure by artificial lifestyles of the so-called modern society is fast eroding the human soul, spirit, mind and intellect. Style has become more important than the nature's unchanging orderly and sustainable developments. Even changes all obey this law. It is the lifestyle of the modern society that ignores and violates it at its peril. The whole world has been based on a ladder case orderly and sustainable system. Those of us trying to dismantle it under the pretext of modernism are not wise. We lack the means to achieve our objectives. Interventional Medicine and Science can work only if we do not allow style to interfere with nature. Nature offers a lot of things free and with a purpose. We offer it for money and style.

We should not depart too far from nature by being lured with money and style. The family to me is still the basis of orderly and sustainable development. Reliance on one another is the bundle that makes up the community. Isolationist and individualistic life may be attractive to the arrogance of life achievements but yet it is the community that will recognise, praise and reward the success. Yes, I may be wonderful but yet I learnt all I know from others. It will always continue this way in life. I owe a lot of gratitude and thanks to all the people I learnt from. Let us not prescribe our selfish solutions to other people's problems without patiently listening to them and seeing where the problems are arising from. We must learn to recognise that we are a tiny part of the bundle that forms the community even if we are leaders of very powerful countries or specialists with marvellous skills and knowledge.

Those who admire and praise our achievements are as important as those who criticise us as well as those who fail to achieve as much as we do. We must always think like human beings. We must temper our knowledge and skills with human feelings. Parents will not normally hurt their off springs. If they do we must not pass sharp judgement; rather we must find out why they do it. The truth behind the search for abnormal occurrence may surprise us with the real answer. What we claim to know very well may be false. This is the summit of expert skill. At the end of enormous knowledge and skills we still find that we have a lot of things we are yet to know and understand. Yet life has no time for us to know all we do not know. King Solomon found out this several thousand years ago.

Even when we are about to depart, we still find that there is a lot of things that we do not know. Sadly we should all recognise that life has not enough time to learn everything. This would be compatible with eternity. Ours is not eternal but mortal and fallible.

Wisdom has no replacement in wealth, achievements and knowledge. This is where humility finally bows before nature. At the end all we had acquired and gained in life become empty before wisdom and nature. Yet nature allows changes to occur in orderly and sustainable development. When we ignore this we become rowdy rabbles, chaotic and disorderly and totally confused.

AAAD is a clarion call to all black people, Africans and all our friends in the world to help us to repair the damage inflicted on Education, spread of knowledge and skills training in Africa. The African child, today, essentially needs appropriate Education, excellent knowledge and understanding of the world around him or her and efficient and effective skills to work his or her land. We do not need relief handouts or trade in the open and free market where we have no skills to produce the goods and services to sell in it. We need the knowledge and skills to produce the goods and services that the free and open market requires. It is fraud and no use rushing to the free and open market without good quality of goods and services or good understanding of the way the market works. Previous advice from these UN quangos to Africa had led us to failure and disaster. We first need good Education, knowledge, understanding and sound skills to handle this new concept of free market before we embrace it. It is not a safe concept or philosophy in our current situation. We have no means to derive good results from it. Our Education and skills are poor. Five to ten years of concentration on Education and skills training in Africa will be adequate.

I am an African of Ibibio extraction, perhaps originated from Carthage from that fateful journey of Admiral Hanno, (Eno) who sailed from Carthage with thirty thousand people to establish a new settlement in West Africa based in the city of Cerne around the Cross River. This gives us the claim to Canaan as the Phoenicians originally lived in Canaan in Tyre, Sidon, Akka and Byblos. Ancient pronunciations are definitely different from the modern. The same goes for languages and colour of skin of people. These change with environments and dominant cultures. Hence the Jews are white, today, and the African slaves speak English, Creole and several European languages. We were great sailors. Long ago Admiral Himilco, (Imaikop) made several trips to the Isles of Cassiterite, the tin islands, the British Isles to carry tin from the mines of Cornwall. He gave a vivid description of the inhabitants of Britain then. They were primitive by his estimation at the time. This shows that various people and places on earth had gone through enormous changes. The African Negroes and Africa are not immune to changes. We have to change or perish with time. Effective Education, learning, knowledge and skills are knocking at our door. The world is dynamic and changes all the time. Those who want to make it static do so at their peril of being left behind. India used to suffer from starvation. Today India can feed itself and export rice. The morally decadent corrupt African leaders cannot feed their people but they eat American long grain rice.

We speak out our mind on the truth and justice. Would the Americans or the British accept the Iraqis or the Arabs to invade their countries to execute massive destruction of the country and slaughter of its citizens for whatever acceptable or unacceptable reasons? Would they accept occupation of their country even with the offer of establishing democracy and reconstructing the country? If any British or Americans would accept this then it is alright for them to justify their actions. If they honestly would object to such an invasion no matter how genuine the reason for it may be then they just have no moral justification for their action. The West colonised most parts of the world. It failed to make the world better. It left most parts of the world with poverty and current chaos. What moral justification has the West to return to occupy these places again claiming to establish Democracy? Why did they not do it before they left in the first place?

What moral justification has the West to march its Army back to these places claiming to return to put things right? It could not rectify things in these places in five hundred years. Why then does the West claim it can do what it could not do in five hundred years in a few years in a world that had changed immensely since their empires collapsed? Are they fooling themselves or the world? How democratic were the Western colonial territories in Africa? Did they show any respect for fundamental human rights by brutal colonial rule, slave trade and slavery? How democratic were the expeditionary forces and the trails of their destructions? What respect for basic fundamental human rights and observance of the rule of law did the Western colonial masters show in racial segregation and various wars against the indigenes that requested for freedom and independence? If the West is serious in joining the third world in repairing the damage the enslavement of colonialism inflicted on Africa and the third world let it do so without slogans and ideologies for guidance for good governance. Already if Saddam Hussein in all his years slaughtered the Iraqis at the rate the West is now doing he would get gold or platinum medal for mass murders. There is no publicity because the Anglo-American coalition is killing to install democracy for the dead and their survivors. Death is death whether from Saddam Hussein or from the Anglo-American coalition of willing murderers. Anglo-American atrocities are atrocities. George Walker Bush is a Texan. Oil is Texan Business. Saddam Hussein engineered the establishment of OPEC. The Bush would never pardon him for this single act. Nobody has asked the Bush what shadow deal and Business they had with the Osama bin Nadin family; it is rumoured that late senior brother of Osama had some Business deal with the Bush. It is important the Bush openly dispel all these gossips to justify taking the US Army into war. The gossips of a chain of events led to Sept 11 and the current military are strong. It will rest our minds if the Bush offered a firm rebuttal of the rumour. It is not fair that the Bush caused global upheaval and vanished into silence at their Texan Ranch to behave as nothing happened. Equally the US hired the Mujahidin to fight a proxy war against former Soviet Union to expel them from Afghanistan. What were the terms of contract for their mercenary role? Mercenary not happy with the way their clients execute their contracts frequently turn round to fight their clients. Carthage frequently fought against their mercenary forces to expel them from Carthage.

AFRICA AND THE JEWS:

It important to mention that the Jews were intimately involved in the classical History of Africa represented in the Holy Bible but buried in religious myth. My view is that black Africans from ancient Egypt under the rule of the Pharaohs particularly the Powerful Ramses' the Second migrated into Palestine and Lebanon to do business. They brought back cedar wood for the great construction works in Egypt at the time. They spread across as far as Syria. Initially the Carthaginians the Phoenicians, Canaanites that migrated to Africa were involved but the lucrative trade attracted the entrepreneurial Jews who joined them in the enterprise. The relationship between these two groups was very cordial during the reigns of both David and Solomon. Hiram was a friend of both David and Solomon. He helped David in the building of his palace and Solomon in the building of the Temple. He provided both the materials and the Architect, Hiram. Solomon paid Hiram with land that Hiram did not like very much. Africa had been home to the Jews for a long time. Mary and Joseph took Jesus to Egypt when his life was in danger. Africans do this in dangerous times. They run to their relatives; it is strongly speculative that Mary and Joseph ran with their baby son to relative in Egypt. This shows the intimacy of relationship between the Jews and Africans. Weakness and poverty loosen and destroy bond of relationship. This happened to Africans and the Jews.

I read the prayer of Solomon's dedication of the Temple with tears falling from eyes. This great wise leader prayed to God to listen to the prayer of any foreigner who came to the house of God to pray and request God for help. He never gave any conditions. His solicitation to God to help the foreigner who comes to pray in the house of God was completely unconditional. This is a great lesson to the Jews, today. This is a great lesson to the Christian West. This is a great lesson to everybody in the world, today. The wisest and the most successful Jewish King took it upon himself to pray to God to help foreigners, immigrants, refugees and economic migrants. He never gave them conditions. He never proposed induction ceremony. He never defined the language they should use to offer their prayers. He simply asked God to listen to their prayers and requests and to help them. How beautiful is it that the wisest and greatest and wealthiest King on earth was not afraid of losing his wealth and kingdom to foreigners but he prayed for them? The exclusiveness of Orthodox Judaism, perhaps, should learn from King Solomon. Any religious faith excluding non-believers or attempting to recruit and convert non-believers by bullying or by exclusion and denial of privileges is guilty of molestation and religious intolerance.

He never prayed for protection against foreigners coming to defile the Temple with profanity but he sincerely asked God to answer their prayers and provide their needs. The current generation of the Jews must loosen up and be free with foreigners. The Arabs have right to protest as victims now. They equally have the right to know that they made several people victims and landless in the past. Those victims never called for elimination of the Arabs. They should settle for safe and secure peaceful co-existence with Israel and all their past victims. The Arabs are not innocent victims of circumstances. They brutally evicted people to get their lands. They are still fighting for land conquest in Sudan in Africa right now. The Ethiopia Eritrean conflict is smouldering embers of Arab incursion into Africa for land conquest. The Arabs have right to settle for what they have before their past explodes on them. Accept Israel and sue for friendship before your past finds you out.

It is not enough to use religion and Muslim brotherhood to cover up the crimes of land grabbing. It is sad the Arabs are currently engaged in scourge earth policy, ethnic cleansing and genocide in collaboration with Arab Sudanese government in Darfur in Sudan in Africa. We do not condemn injustice in the right hand while justifying the same in the left hand. Those who need justice must look behind, in front, right and left to make sure of their certainty in calling for justice. In matters of sharing this earth together with other people we must essentially prepare to compromise because where we find ourselves living, today, might have been the homeland of other people. Equally we may not know the circumstances and the way we came to live where we are and to own the land.

This type of hostility towards African Negroes is intolerable. Can we trust the Arabs as fellow Africans? The Arabs must convince us that they are our friends and not here to displace us from our land.

It is very unfortunate that all foreigners who want to share Africa with the African Negroes, the original owners of this continent, all look down on the black people. They bully and abuse them. They dehumanise them and want to use them as beasts of burden in their homeland all in the name of employment and open market. The Arabs for a long time had this ambiguous attitude. Sadly for a long time African countries severed relations with Israel in protest against Israeli occupation of Palestinian land. Unfortunately, the very Arabs they made that sacrifice for have no respect for African Negroes. They call them slaves in their African homeland. We actually had no business in Arab-Palestinian conflict. Our sympathy should lie with the Jews who like us are victims of Arab macho arrogance, intrigues, corruption, crimes and cruelty. We accept the Arabs, to this land of Africa. The Arabs must accept Africa as their home and be willing to integrate to build up Africa and receive fellow Africans with loyalty and love. Africa loathes extreme religious fanaticism. Nobody should attempt to impose religious faith on the community. The Sharia Law is too old for modern age; while it remains as moral law for the soul, it should be condemned to the Archives. Secular Laws keeping pace with dynamic changes in the community should be the rule.

Their attitude in Sudan is a revelation of their real attitude towards black people in Africa. It is a record of their intention in Africa. They do not respect the right to life of African Muslims in the Sudan. The black Muslims are victims of ethnic cleansing and genocide by Arab Muslims in Sudan. The whites in Zimbabwe want to be landlords and commercial farmers employing Africans as farm labourers by cheap labour in the free market. It is left to future Africans to decide their attitude towards the ambiguous behaviours of the core Arab establishment and the white European-Africans. Are they ready to accept equality of humanity and opportunities? We still deplore ill-treatment of the Arabs by all the people guilty of this atrocious and vicious crime. At the same time we deplore vindictive and devious attitude of our Arab neighbours. The Arabs are very astute business and enterprising people. They had always been in the desert caravan trade. The Prophet as teenager accompanied his businessman uncle to Syria. He met the Hermit Monk, Beheras there in Syria. But the problem with Islam, one of the fastest growing religions, with a quarter of world population as believers and followers of the faith is its mixture and blending of force, psychological brain washing, devious and subtle intolerance, social seclusion of members and traditional Arab entrepreneurial culture all together. The Arab macho Patriarchal culture is suffocating women. Traditionally, Africa had never denied women franchise. Muslim Islam had imposed denial of franchise to women on African converts to the faith. There is nothing wrong with Muslim Islam but it must change with Allah's dynamically changing times. Allah is not rigid and the message of His Prophet should be flexible as long as it does not compromise the core teaching of the faith.

Since three quarters of world population are non-Muslims the Muslims have a duty to live by example to court their friendship. They should not threaten them with covert or open conversion to Islam by imposition of the Sharia Law. Reciprocal respect for the faiths and beliefs of all people should be the hallmark of good relationship. Acceptance of any religious faith should be voluntary. This is not isolation of Muslim Islam for criticism. It equally applies to all religions with isolationist tendency. Secular socialisation is essential for the spread of education and skills. Everybody in the world, today, men and women, Muslims and non-Muslims uses electronic equipment, mobile phones, computers, internet etc. Allah does not prevent their use. Hence Allah does not prevent boys and girls learning how to make them. Therefore, let us hope that the allegation of Taliban destroying Schools is mere war propaganda as Communism atheism which, today, turns out to have been a lie. The Communists had their Orthodox Religion. They resisted the West using Religion as a back door to subvert their system and spread their Propaganda. Education is a universal Language and Taliban should not exclude itself. After all they are fighting sophisticated electronic warfare. They use electronic equipment both men and women. They find nothing wrong in using them; they must adopt a liberal policy towards modern Education for their boys and girls after this war. This will help them in life after this war. This is not Western Education. It is global pool of knowledge regardless of religion and faiths. It is essentially for boys and girls as knowledge is not exclusive. Girls given opportunity can do better than boys; hence, it is important to educate both boys and girls. Tradition changes. Failure to change destroys any people. It renders them irrelevant and obsolete.

THE ARABS AND AFRICA:

Africa and the black race had been innocent but cowardly victims of European ultra-right fanaticism and racism. The Straussite ultra-conservative white male European right seemed to have started from events in Rome. Africans led by Barcine Carthage had strived in vain to civilize the rustic farmers in Europe that founded the city on the Tiber. At the beginning we felt in our generous and magnanimous spirit bore no hostility towards this new European city to rival Athens. We even signed defence treaty to defend them in case of attack by hostile forces. A number of times we had to fight against the Greeks in defence of Rome. But when Rome was able to stand on its feet, Africa became its utmost desire to defeat and loot its wealth. In 146 BC aided by the traitor and a Royal outcast Rome destroyed Carthage by ruthless barbaric war of genocide. All roads go to Rome but I may also add, "All good things in the world were looted by violence and taken to Rome." Today, this Policy has continued. Every wealth in the world is looted and taken to the West. Before this time the Roman European ultra right had rejected all overtures of friendship and peaceful co-existence from Carthage in Africa.

They sacrificed Julius Caesar and Marcus Antonio in bloody revolt for daring to suggest peaceful coexistence with Africa. They seized all our investments in Europe. We were earning over a million pounds sterling from mining alone before 146 BC. Barcelona is named after Barca, a famous African noble and courageous general, the grandfather of the Right Noble Lord General Hannibal Hamilcar Barcar, the true symbol of what leadership meant to Africa not polluted by European corruption and violence. The Spanish City of Barcelona is named after Barcar. Even Spanish may not be told this. The city is the African footprint in Spain. This demonstrates the African influence in Europe where we did business for over five hundred years, half millennium before we were thrown out and our wealth confiscated by Rome. Octavius descended on Africa and made the whole of North Africa, the African Province of the Holy Roman Empire. Octavius made himself Caesar Augustus and presided over this unruly and unholy empire. Note it was the Roman Gen. Scipio Cornelius Publius that flushed African Carthaginians out of Spain. Nevertheless he resisted subjugation and humiliating

Carthage. The evil and unholy Roman Empire ceased to exist in 476 AD

This evil man, Octavius and self-styled Caesar, Augustus made Africa his playground. He destroyed the forest. He made fortunes from its rich fauna and felled its rich hard wood trees for enormous constructions in Rome. He embarked on endless constructions of amphitheatres for staging gladiatorial shows with captured African wild animals from its rich fauna. Octavia's deforested North Africa and caused expansion of the Sahara Desert. The Romans thus slaughtered all living things in Africa, human beings, animals and plants. They carried out scorched earth policy in Africa. Octavius and the Roman Empire like all mortal things eventually died and disappeared. They left a vacuum in Africa. The Arabs fanned out from their home in Gaza and other hideouts to seize the whole of Palestine and Africa. They made their violent land grabbing scorched earth policy and ethnic cleansing into a religious mission. This happened only fourteen hundred years ago. The Arabs talk of Muslim Islam as a religion of peace and friendship among the nations. They are yet to bring some truth into this declaration. The Wahabis preach fundamental fanaticism and violence. They practise violent slave gathering and land grabbing. Arabs are fun-loving macho people. Their name seems to come from the language of the Koran. They love cheap wealth and use everything in their path to make money. They are spineless fanatical extremists. These days they use energy wealth to hire Western Europeans to meddle in their local power politics and fight their feuding wars. The West had been fighting the Gulf wars partly from these mercenary contracts and partly from its energy interest in oil and gas from the Middle East.

The Jews have right to recover their land from these violent people. It is they who should sue for peace and apologise. Time does not obliterate crimes. Africa should stop being timid. It should ask the Arabs on its soil to behave and stop hostilities to African natives and women or be thrown out as the Jews our distant cousins had done. The Jews have greater right to settle near their cousins than these macho wild men. We should ask for assistance from Israel to help us overcome Arab religious menace, their hostilities and desertisation of much of Africa. The Muslim religious fanatics are retrogressive group that fail to accept any change. The world has changed. They use all modern Technological gadgets but fail to accept changes. The House of Saud may be the face of stability to their friends but they are absurdity to this millennium. If they want us to co-exist they have to change. The Wahadis had used their vast resources to spread propaganda and cause several crises in Africa especially in Nigeria.

It is important to inform the ignorant that there had never been an age in Africa that denied franchise to women. Recall the known ones Queen of Sheba and Cleopatra. It had never been our culture to deny franchise to women until the Arabs brought their anti-women religion Islam to Africa. We must not forget that intermarriages allows easy spread of dominant culture especially when supported by religion and enforced by violence and death penalty as in Muslim Islam. Recently there was sham show in Channel Four one of the British TV stations trying to credit Gaelic with song leader and response by the audience in Negro Spirituals and Gospel Music. It is worth informing the world that this is a feature of all African songs in all forms. One person leads while the rest respond. We seem to talk of culture in complete isolation and fail to note that human beings are travelling and community animals. Cultural exchange is one of the rewards of travel in addition to improved aspect of feeding. The Africans were in Southern Europe for over five hundred years. They were particularly welcome by the Celtics and I would assume the Celts are close to the Gaels. Music is very easily exchanged. Hence it is no surprise the Gaels sing with leader leading the response of the congregation. We must also note that when we speak of Africans we are talking about one of the oldest human race on earth. The Gaelic Celtic people had always friendly and receptive to strangers and accommodative to new cultures. There have been attempts by some ignorant and arrogant Western Europeans to claim every good thing on earth. I have always reminded my readers and audience that Admiral Himilco saw very rudimentally civilised shepherds in the Isles of Cassiterite, Britannia.

They were by all intent regarded as primitive by the African sailors from Carthage much used to civilisation. Before the Romans could mount invasion of Africa to destroy Carthage in 146 BC they had to steal one of the African Carthaginian boats to dismantle to study and learn boat building to mass produce boats. They, however, ingeniously improvised and added the hooking planks as they did not know maritime warfare by boat ramming that the Carthaginians were experts. This gave them their first maritime victory. Hence the arrogant racially biased people must learn that Europe took a lot from Africa. The string instruments that the Roman nobles played while watching gladiatorial fights in the amphitheatres built by Africans with African materials was invented in Egypt. It is the source of organ and Piano, today. We must equally note that the early followers of Jesus were Africans. The Romans were slaughtering them in great numbers to prevent rebellion. It was Constantine who courted their support that adopted Christianity. We equally see in Ethiopia the oldest Orthodox worship. We also recall the scene in the Roman Senate when Marcus Cato displayed African wealth the Roman spies brought back from the continent. They were richer than what the Romans had and knew. Hence, Marcus Cato declared, "These are the wealth of Carthage in Africa. A land that has these is worthy of every Roman noble. The land that has these is only three days' journey from this place." Invasion of Africa was led by the nobles as they could not trust the commoners to bring back to them all the treasures. Africa was far more advanced than Europe. It was equally richer.

Even by the time of recent European invasion and colonisation of the continent they were still scouting for the gold the Carthaginians paid people in West Africa to establish the city of "Cerne" with over thirty thousand people. This population expanded after the destruction of Carthage. But two things prevented progress in Africa in the new Carthaginian home. We were blocked and cut off from the rest of the world. The Romans looted all our Academic, Technological and industrial foundations. They killed and took back to Europe a great number of our Academicians and skilled people to work for them. This in addition to what the Greeks had gathered from us over several years was the origin of the so-called European civilisation. In West Africa we have remnants of Carthaginians spreading along the coastline while the locals occupied the hinterland. They kept their food, way of worship, singing and dancing. There is even a song in Calabar, "Canaan, and Canaan Calabar .....Oh ndifreke fi etc. It preceded the arrival of the European fortune seekers. It is similar to the Jewish song about Jerusalem. "If I forget thee........ etc."

Muslim Islam was abused in violent Arab land grabbing crusade. Today it is still a religion of violence. It is the Arabs that have got to redeem their religion from land grabbing violence. So far they had failed to do so in Palestine and Africa. Islam is a bloody religion in Sudan. Where the Arabs are successful they call the natives slaves. Where they fail as in Israel they play the victims. The world is sick and tired of this Arab game. The Arabs looted Africa of treasures and human beings and sold them cheaply for weapons of war. They robbed the dead and the living. They stole living human beings and dead bodies from their graves and sold them for money. The Arabs made tomb robbery into very lucrative business. They developed trade in mummies into lucrative business. The Arabs plundered the artefacts of ancient African civilization. This was never Arab civilisation. Time is overdue for them to stop deceiving themselves and the world that they had civilisation in Egypt. Arabs arrived in Africa too late to claim that older civilisation (Arab Conquest: AD 635, 639-717, and 642).

The Wahabi Arab fanatical macho religion must disabuse their minds of thinking that Africa is land of Muslim Islam. Africa is strictly religious moral continent. Africa actually embraced and accepted the three religions in the West, Judaism, Christianity and lately Muslim Islam. We actually provided safe homes for these religions. The Romans were all out to destroy Judaism and Christianity. They survived in the minds and homes of Africans. Muslim Islam riding on camels arrived with the Koran in the left hand and sword in the right on land grabbing mission. Let us make it clear to the Arabs.

We are prepared to tolerate them in Africa regardless of the way they arrived here. They must accept that they are Africans and live by the rule of secular civilised law and abandon macho self-protecting tyrannical Sharia laws. This is obsolete and behind the enormous changes that had taken place in the world. It is already dangerous to allow religions walk our streets to rake havoc on the people and the community. Religion must be confined to the places of worship. It should not have any role in politics, government or commerce. The geographic constitution and the distribution of land, deserts, savannah, forests, water and the oceans strongly emphasize the importance of uniting the whole continent into United States of Africa under civilised constitution under the rule of secular law to allow free movements of the people in the continent. Religion must be free but confined to the places of worships and the mind of the believers. The community must be free from the constraints of religion. Religion must not interfere with people's lives. The West has the power and means in co-operation with others to confine religion to the believers and stop it being used to molest innocent people. It should be offered to new converts by persuasion. Members should be free to leave as in all other things in life including marriage. Children are free to choose other religions and marry out of it. This must be incorporated into new charter on human right. Freedom of choice of way of worship that must be lawful and does not interfere with other people's freedom and choice of worship and religion must be included in the human rights to settle age-old confusion in this matter. Freedom of religion is a blank cheque. It allows people to hide under it to rake havoc on innocent people.

All black people have a lot to disapprove of the atrocious behaviours of the Arabs. The Africans in the Diaspora would find it obnoxious to discover that the Arabs are still indulging in selling African children into slavery and grabbing their lands. We may have to tighten our belts to confront these macho cowards even with their walking human bombs. We just have to live as brothers and sisters. Short of this the Arabs should leave Africa with their antic macho aggressive behaviours. Meanwhile, we appeal to Israel that they must stand firm. They must revive our brotherhood and assist Africa to develop rapidly to generate our traditional brotherhood and friendship. All of us welcome the Arabs provided the Arabs accept to live in genuine peace with others under the rule civilised secular of law. Exclusiveness is not in the interest of the Arabs. They must learn to share. It is not sensible to brandish the two state policy in such a small place. It will lead to arm build up and frequent violence. Rather the Arabs should demonstrate their readiness to share the place with Israel and transform it into a virile prosperous land. This will confirm their genuine intention to live in peace. They had made the little opportunity they had into intifada violence. The two state policy will convert the place into permanent war camps always at war or preparing for war. The future for peace is bleak with the two state policy. It will be freedom to prepare for war and victory. It will be inducement and encouragement for preparing for land grabbing.

Their past treatment of African Negroes in their homeland, Africa was deplorable. They seized them and enslaved them. They castrated their menfolks as eunuchs to take charge of their African Negro female slaves in their harems. Definitely we will not tolerate this type of behaviour in the future. If they want to share this land with us they would have to behave and avoid macho and cruel brutalities against our people. Already they have Israel to settle with and learn to live in peace with them. If they continue to provoke us black people in this land they would not have where to go to if we throw them out of our land in North Africa. Do they feel that we do not know that they are living in our homeland seized by Arab Muslim religious war in Muslim Islamic Arab Conquest of Palestine and North Africa? We all want peace and justice. Let peace and justice not be the monopoly of the victims alone. Let the victims acknowledge the agony of the oppressors who may have no option but to correct the past injustice to get peace. Israel must get back its secure home for the Arabs to have justice and peace not by right of absolute possession of the land of Palestine but from humanitarian concept of compassion. King Solomon acknowledged the existence of foreigners and their desires.

How justified is the current Arab-Israeli intractable conflict in the face of this prayer by one of the most important founders of the State of Israel? Let us not ignore the way the ancient fathers viewed our world. Let us not ignore the way David and Solomon behaved towards foreigners. They recognised their friendship. They did business with them and trusted them. They were at peace with them. David recognised that his hands were bloody. He knew that Solomon's reign was to be peaceful. Solomon knew the way of peace. He respected and made friends with foreigners. Hiram was a staunch ally, friend and confidant of both David and Solomon. Solomon never advocated for restriction of foreigners. He seemed to have welcomed them. He asked God to grant their requests when they heard of the fame of the Temple of God and came there to pray.

Unfortunately, the cordial relation soured during the reign of Ahab who married Jezebel from the Canaanites. Jezebel was unpopular with the Jewish populace. Ahab was a bad king. The Jews blamed Jezebel and her god Baal for this. From this point there is a lot of mix up between religious myth and the truth. By the time of Jesus of Nazareth the Roman rule was on the accent. They were the master of their known world having wrested power from the Carthaginians in Africa in 146 BC by genocide after protracted wars. The Romans nearly lost power to Hannibal. They were very suspicious of any person that pulled the crowds as Hannibal did. They also were superstitious of return of Hannibal by reincarnation. With this type of ruthlessness and suspicion Jesus never stood any chance with the Roman authorities. Collaborators always do the nasty job of betrayal for the imperial power. Caiaphas and the Jews played this role well for the Romans. They apprehended Jesus and executed him on the cross. It was a neat Roman job. The plight of the Africans suddenly disappeared from the story and Jewish religious myth took over. Christ was a victim of Roman imperial power. Romans killed Jesus with collaboration from the Jews. They were the only imperial authority with power to sanction death penalty in Palestine at the time.

We were very hard working people with very high sense of integrity and virtue. We were God-fearing and respectable. Unfortunately the recent Nigeria disaster had blighted our self-confidence, moral culture and pride in honesty. Our sense of values had been destroyed. Our institutions had been corrupted. They no longer have the values they used to have or offer the type of quality services they used to give. In spite of these things we are still very uneasy with the current plight of Nigeria. We are used to modest life of self-respect and integrity. We are not warriors but when we have to fight in anger we fight and die in honour. I would not be surprised to read about the great General Hannibal if my observation is true. Even in modern warfare it is hard to see a true Ibibio fighter that runs away from battle. We are a very small ethnic national. Yet we sincerely believe that war should be the last resort from extreme provocation after all means of peaceful resolution of conflicts had been exhausted. Eruption of violence of war gives human beings no time to think rationally. The concept of triumph and victory becomes overriding in war.

Integration is not a bad idea but those good qualities and values of a people deserve to be preserved in the face of being swarmed by alien cultures. Equally cultural borrowing must avoid cultural virus of corruption and vice. I am a very proud Ibibio son and a very patriotic African and a black man. I believe that we can take the world by storm if we work hard. Problem-solving and purpose-orientated Education and focused and targeted skills training to offer every black child visible and reliable means of independent living and earning a living are the key to African emancipation and black Renaissance. Our work must be durable, orderly and sustainable to give us independent life. The word employment is English word that betrays the concept of work. We must always aim at working either independently or in employment. The African concept of employment hinges on salary and paid job. There may not be enough work or satisfaction. It is the salary that matters. This has destroyed our concept and understanding of work and productivity. The French President Chirac could not be far from right in describing the free market as the Communism of our time. Diversity is the soul of creation itself. Uniformity is the tower of Babel that will surely collapse. Diversity in creation is the soul and heart of creation. This is why we have human races. Animal are diverse in their own creation. Trees are different the way we do things. One of the most stupid things of the so-called Western civilisation is the advocacy in trade, Economic method and culture. Nature, eco-environment and natural life diversity do not support it. It is only the violent tyranny of greed of the Western culture that supports it. Even the natural spirit of the West that derives from natural diversity fails to support it. The world leaders in our time sheepishly support it out of ignorance, fear, timidity or lack of understanding of natural diversity. We need diverse Economic methods without the vices and corruption we have in the capitalist free market which is free only for crimes and corruption. It is the people who operate any Economic method that give it a bad name and failure. It is not the method that is faulty. The West must accept competition without sabotage. It must stop using corruption and intrigues to sabotage rival methods.

I am a simple professional surgeon too proud to condescend to cronyism or politics of graft. I find it extremely embarrassing to own wealth that I never genuinely worked for and explain how I came by it. Sound education and practical skills are wealth but rich mineral and natural resources are not wealth. They constitute nest of indolence, graft and poverty. I am not a politician. I believe that the key to eradication of poverty in Africa is eradication of dependence on the West and our past colonial masters. Africa has essentially to abolish artificial colonial borders and re-integrate the whole continent and all black people in the Diaspora displaced from this continent by accident of slave trade and slavery. We have to bring all our resources together to develop our lands and homes. There is absolutely no such thing as superior race of human beings. There is superiority of hard work and efficient management of resources. There is superiority of education and skills.

The key to super race is in first class Education and skills of its citizens. There must be perseverance, persistence and continuity. I am yet to be beaten in any competition I study hard, work hard, master the rules and go out to compete as a black man among other races of mankind. I always win with other races. Hence there is no superior race. What is superior is excellent knowledge and consistent hard work to achieve results. It has worked for me. It can work for you. It can work for Africa and the black race on earth. As long as the world continues, there will always be competitions. The success in any competition lies on good preparation and the willingness to go out to compete and give it your best and ignore all sorts of intimidations, be it from affluence or from race of humanity. The African man must respect freedom more than life as a slave. Recently an East African Indian writer summed up the wretchedness of the timid African man. The white man lives on the hill breathing clean air and guarded by dog. Next up the hill lived the Asian guarded. The dogs prevent native Africans and timid men living down in the valley from going up the hill. This is the social stratification of the African in his homeland. He has got Independence but does not know what to do with freedom. Hence he is nominally free but yet the white foreigners and Asians still dominate his homeland. The African male is a pathetic case.

He is a coward ready to show his heels instead of standing to fight to defend his home. The black man must be willing to fight and die in defence of his land, wife and children. He must not run away or be a slave or informer to the enemy. This sort of behaviour makes the black man a slave in his home. The wife of the Carthaginian

General who surrendered to the Romans was so upset by this man her husband kneeling to kiss the toe of a Roman dirty Barbarian in a burning city that she denounced him and she and her three children resplendent in Royal purple committed suicide. She threw the children into the fire and jumped into it herself. She told him he was a coward. He could not be her husband and father of her children. The male Africans are worse today. They are stupid. They have no shame for being slaves on their homeland. HIV-AIDS is devastating us. We have no Education, no skills and no Research facilities and Programmes to launch counter Research and adequate surveillance to defend ourselves. Look at Darfur and the Arabs. The black man is a disaster to Africa when only Israel can tame the Arabs. The whole AU has no means of teaching the Sudanese Arabs a lesson. Violence begets violence.

Today, the white man is swarmed by refugees and immigrants. Yet Africa tolerates white criminals coming in and out of our homeland at will. Africa not sold out to aliens. Without the corruption AU should band aliens that do not want from visiting Africa even for business. We should ban homosexuals from Africa as this white man's lifestyle is un-African and unacceptable to us. We have the right and freedom to protect ourselves from this queer lifestyle. Fowl smelling men smeared with rectal faeces are objectionable to our simple clean life style. Equally whatever the white people would like the world to believe HIV-AIDS came from homosexual. Even the new resistant strain is created by homosexual men. Unfortunately the white people seem to think that any harm done to black people is not criminal. Hence HIV positive white people are totally unscrupulous over giving it to as many black people as they can. They had been reports of cases. The Southern African cases are suspect of some white mischievous people with the virus who would not mind distributing it to as many black people as possible by paying prostitutes and even decent ladies a lot more money than they would get to distribute their bug in Africa. They would even do it to people in their homeland. But there is inborn racial xenophobia and hatred of black people by most of the white people regardless of denial of their existence that they would not care a jot if they are hurt. The original hatred Rome showed in 146 BC still exists and is worse with rich and affluent Europe. I do not advocate for hatred but let us be frank with each other. We must either hate each other until the black man recovers his honour in the 146 BC return match battle field or we sue for genuine peace or adopt the line of mutual respect without the current exchange of vague courtesy. The profession of friendship that lacks mutual trust and respect is deceit and betrayal. Such utterances do not pass the lips of the false friends and hidden enemies.

Now my life has been spent. Advanced cancer has taken toll of my body. I am in pains twenty four hours but my zeal for emancipation and Renaissance of Africa and the black race on earth is unyielding and has not dimininished. My desire, wish and ambition are true liberation of Africa and the black race on earth from Western European bondage and domination. These are people who have no genuine interest in us but yet they would not leave us alone. We have no grudge against our white masters. They hate us but we have no cause to hate them. They are out to provoke us but we have no cause to be provoked by tyrants of greed whose main objective is to seize our land as they did in America through genocide. We are good competitors. We want to be free to compete fairly with others in this highly competitive world. The West cries and moans whenever they are confronted with loss of lives of its citizens. Unfortunately the West lives by war and violence. War and violence destroy lives and properties. The victims of Western five thousand years of persistent aggressive and active military campaigns value their lives and properties, ways of life and lands just as the West do. The citizens in the West are very fond of reminding the world what harm terrorists had done to them. They fail to tell the world that those the West feel are evil people also have genuine grudges against the West. Western hostile actions harm their victims just as damage the terrorists inflict on the West hurts its citizens. There is no justification for any form of hostilities.

But let us all emphasize the sacredness of lives and how we all value our properties. The poor values his hut and life the same way the billionaire values his life and mansion. We do not condone any form of violence or tit for tat killings. Let us denounce all forms of violence and pray for all victims of violence. A succinct observation is the fact that most of the people the West is fighting against were friends of the West. They were brought together and taught violence and guerrilla warfare by the West. The West used them to fight their proxy wars. What has happened that they are now number one enemy of the West? How are we sure that in the quest for victory in this war the West is not training another generation of people that will confront the West in future? This is why we strongly advocate for peaceful settlement of this conflict to avoid the West overtly training more people that will challenge the West in future and cause more trouble. The West is unfortunately an accomplice in the evolution of this conflict. Please settle it peacefully.

The world rejoices that Khedafi has decided to resolve the differences between the West and Libya. Wisdom demands that peaceful co-existence is better than open hostilities. Khedafi lost his daughter to that conflict. That girl was as dear to him as other victims of that conflict and feud. The price tag of violence is high and wasteful while that of peace is cheap and profitable. The West is not a saint. Brutal colonisation was not without a price. It had its victims at all levels. Equally it is extreme dishonesty for a few ignorant people in the West to claim that they know best what is best for people in foreign lands far away from their homelands. They do not know where these people live and what they eat but yet they claim to know what is best for them. The nonsense about establishing democracy for others to operate in their countries is a slogan that lacks all credibility. We do not have to serve apprenticeship for democracy or go to School to study it. Democracy is a convenient way of participatory governance allowing individual freedom.

Democracy evolves as a necessity for participatory good governance and people's free choice. People choose their government out of volition. Unfortunately electoral expenses had made free choice the prize for the highest bidder. This has evolved into institutional endemic corruption in Africa and most parts of the third world. The devil does not live in Africa alone. They equally live in the West too. Let innocent citizens not be made victims of the actions of their leaders. The leaders must know that it is criminal to rush in and slaughter innocent citizens because the actions of a few disgruntled people. The greatest danger to settlement of disputes is adoption of victorious posture. It is mischievous to rake up all previous grudges and grievances that people were willing to forgive and forget. Settlement of disputes and conflict resolution demand that people should embrace the concept of peace without old prejudices, bias and grievances. Bearing old grudges and grievances is reluctance to let go the causes of conflicts and disputes. It is an expression of willingness to continue with conflicts and disputes instead of accepting settlement of disputes and resolution of conflicts. Resolving conflicts means forgiving and forgetting old grudges and grievances. It is not name-calling and abuses. It is final settlement and not endless demand for compensation in a powerful capitalist consumer-materialistic community.

The problem of the current crisis is failure of the West to accept that it is actually harming and hurting other people. It claims total innocence and righteousness despite its notorious past History that is the cause of the current global crisis. The West has retracted to lying to deceive its youths into feeling that that they are innocent people being persecuted for their enormous success. It forgets about its brutal colonisation of the world, the plundering and looting of several lands in the world, its slave trade and slavery of the African Negroes and its intrigues and subversion and unbridled aggression. The damage to the world Economy by its unfair trading and massive corruption in global business cannot be overstated. The West spent of the last millennium supporting dictators and tyrants. We have to be frank to understand the way each of us feels. This, however, does not justify the current tit for tat killing. It is no solution to the problem. What we have to understand is that our different lifestyles are damaging our human relationship. We have to modify our lifestyles in consumer-materialism and religion to prevent them damaging us individually. The current conflict does not need further killings or victory but conflict resolution and settlement of disputes. We must abandon old grudges and grievances and that air of innocence and self-righteousness. We must regain our humanity. We have no right to hate each other. None of us will live for ever in this world. We should not spend our time killing each other. After all each of us will die one day regardless of the way that death comes to us.

THE ANGLO-AMERICAN AXIS, AFRICA AND THE WORLD.

The West has no business to continue to molest and intimidate us. Their greatest weapon of mass destruction is their insatiable greed.

They had used this to lay waste most parts of the world. If our white male tormentors have any human conscience they should notice that they had damaged the black race on earth several times over in the history of humanity on earth. All the catastrophes confronting the black race on earth had come from the white race. Their racial xenophobia against the black race has been unabated. It has no end. It has taken several forms. Today, it has been christened institutional racism. It is subtle. It is manifested in all forms of our dealings with the white people. The white people have right and freedom to practise racial xenophobia provided they leave us and Africa alone. The white race is yet to tell us what we had done to them to warrant the type of hostility they have shown to us. It is true a few white people are fed up with institutional racial xenophobia but it is a weapon of control the white establishment cannot do without. It is a psychological weapon of intimidation, bullying and blackmail.

I have always remarked that this establishment believes in rationed democracy and restricted freedom for African Negroes and people outside their group. The recent collapse of the case of breach of official act against GCHQ employee, Anne Gunn in London has confirmed this observation. Could you imagine the Anglo-American establishment authorising its spooks to spy on six members of the UN and the Secretary of the United Nations, Kofi Annan for wavering over illegal aggression, occupation and violence against Iraqi people? This is Anglo-American establishment that talks of Democracy, freedom and fundamental human rights? The former British Commonwealth Minister, Claire Shore actually confirmed on the air that she saw a transcript of conversation of Kofi Annan. She was afraid that her discussions with the UN Secretary might be circulating within the American establishment. Former members of the GCHQ came out to confirm that the practice was common place in the UN. They said their Governments pay them to do the illegal things while the Government uses legalistic arguments to protect them as criminals and perverts of international peace and breakers of the law. It is now obvious that George W Bush and Tony Blair lied to the world and their people to invade and occupy Iraq illegally. The credibility of these leaders is in total doubt. Their actions are shrouded with their obsession with Iraq. Where then is the position of the UN as custodian of world peace? Is it fast becoming Anglo-

American war council? It is being used to slam punitive sanctions on their foes. The UN is Anglo-American Quango. It needs thorough Review to be converted into a Global Body but each time the West would employ delaying tactics to block review.

The Anglo-American establishment has been taking the world for a ride. Here are people who talk of Democracy, freedom and fundamental human rights but yet they are notorious for being guilty of all the crimes against humanity in the world. They had established a formidable aggressive war machine that had committed atrocities against all human races on earth. They were guilty of genocide in several parts of the world. They were guilty of slave trade and enslaving the Negro race. They were guilty of decimating the population of Africa by genocide and forced human trafficking, murders and slavery and forced and slave labour and enriching themselves by selling African Negroes into slavery and exploitation. They had been guilty of declaring and fighting illegal wars for territorial expansion, plunder and loots. They are famous for breach of fundamental human rights and abuse of freedom. Their concept of Democracy must be different from that of other people. The West ruled most parts of the world for over five hundred years.

They were very brutal and practised racial xenophobia and tyranny of greed but never Democracy or human rights. They degraded and dehumanised whomever they liked. They were total outlaws. They violated every rule in the Books of fundamental human rights. Where then is this Afterthought on Democracy and human rights several years after the dissolution of the Western Empire and colonies? Are they new coverts to Democracy and human rights that they never practised in their vast Empires and colonies? Rule of law was the last thing to cross the mind of the imperial colonial overlords. Where, then is this new concept of the proselytes and crusaders of Democracy and fundamental human rights coming from? These are people that took great delight in obtaining photos of their people butchering and lynching the Native Americans and Australian indigenes in a gruesome genocide in the last millennium. Recent events in Afghanistan and Iraq had just revealed that the tiger does not change its habits. They believe in wars and violence of aggression to bully and intimidate innocent people in their homelands for loots. The West must change the conduct of its civilisation that allows its citizens to brutalise other races of human beings. They must convincingly renounce racial xenophobia as their culture. Vague exchange of courtesies and pleasantries is not racial tolerance. It is ambiguous.

The postcolonial corruption, tyranny, wars and violence are direct aftermath of what the indigenous local leaders learnt from their former colonial masters. The colonial masters trained the Army and the Police. They also trained the senior government officials and continued to play this role in the postcolonial era. These officers were abused to promote corrupt practices and armament sales. Multiple jungle wars were actively encouraged not to establish law and order but to advance the ideals of Western victory in the cold war and dismantling Communism in Europe and the West. Today, we are watching the rebound of these policies. The tragedy of this is that we fail to see what is happening as the results of our past practices and habits. Rather we perceive them as new threats, new enemies and new dangers that must be dealt with. Perhaps it will be helpful if we review our past policies, practices and habits and correct flaws that led to our current problems. We will start from ourselves and correct our past mistakes in the light of what we know and others know too. We Africans have a lot to answer for what is happening to us. It is from this background that we will make progress in self-development and human relations. Human relations involve more than one person. Everybody has the responsibility to make it work. Continuous and persistent lying, deceits and intrigues do not support trust and reliable friendship.

WORDS OF ADVICE TO THESE NEW APOSTLES OF DEMOCRACY:

We have every reason to ask these people that whatever the reason for their action, they have right to ask us how we live our lives? Do they know where we live, what we eat, the water we drink, and the environment in which we live? Understanding these things is important for the growth of Democracy, fundamental human rights and the rule of law. The fertile soil for the growth of Democracy, fundamental human rights and the rule of law essentially requires appropriate Education, effective knowledge and practical skills. The people must understand any new philosophy or ideology that the West is trying to sell to them. The people must essentially have viable and sustainable means of living for safety and security. The truth is that we live in abject poverty, misery, and ignorance most of our lives. The proselytes of this new Democracy and fundamental human rights do not just know what we go through daily in life. They do not know our culture and traditions. They prey on our needs and suffering. They exploit our naivety, gullibility, poverty and ignorance.

The gospel of capitalist free trade and free market may be plausible to the apostles of free enterprise. Yet the fertile soil for growth of any crop must be right for the crop the farmers want to cultivate. The right crop in the wrong soil fails to grow. The soil must be suitable for the crops the farmer grows on it. Not all crops would grow on all types of soil. Similarly not all types of soil would support the growth of all crops. Nature has got inbuilt variety and diversity in everything it created on earth. There are tropical and temperate plants and animals, why? Perhaps what we should be doing is to encourage Democracy based on the culture of the people concerned. Uniformity or unanimity is not natural. One of the reasons that the West succeeded in discrediting communism was highlighting the unnatural nature of the decisions and the statistics the communists published from time to time. The demise of Western capitalism is this craze to repeat the Biblical tower of Babel, uniformity and unanimity for safety and security. It is fraud for the United Nations Security Council always to vote unanimously on almost all issues. This is another dogma coming from capitalist platform. Capitalism is free choice and diversity. Western capitalism is fast becoming intolerant of diversity. It is becoming irritable over diversity and free choice.

The practices of the International Monetary Funds, IMF, the World Bank, and World Trade Organisation, WTO had successfully blighted the Economies of African countries and the third world by advancing false utopia of uniformity and unanimity. Have you ever seen a Doctor that uses one drug to cure all diseases he comes across in various and diverse patients? There is no single drug in Medicine that cures all diseases. Equally the prescriptions the UN quangos offer Africa and the third world to cure the ills in their Economies had been ineffective. They had blighted these Economies. The free market and privatisation are old medicines in new bottles. They are just no starter. Stop prescribing conditions and regulations. The United Nations should reflect diversity of humanity in various parts and regions of the earth.

We have to be honest and sincere in acceptance of diversity, in religion, culture and way of life in various and diverse parts and regions of the world. Diversity and way of life must not support conflicts among various people in the world. We must appreciate diversity the same way we appreciate the different colours and scents of flowers in our gardens, the way we admire various animals in nature and various plants in the forests. It is totally out of fashion and unnatural thinking to assume that everybody should do things the same way. Capitalism is fast becoming a dogma laying down the rules for the way human beings on earth should do things. Capitalism prides itself on diversity and freedom of choice of individual initiative in doing things.

Yet capitalism survives on caprices and pranks of crimes and corruption. We must now start to accept the fact that the success of capitalism does not lie on all the reasons it offers for it. It is the result of persistent fraud and cheating. It is the result of crime and corruption inherent in the system. Capitalist attempt to regulate the third world economy had failed because it is based on fraud and deception but not on facts. Capitalism has no magic wand to cure the ills of African collapsing Economy. The sociocultural background supporting the African Economy is different from that of the West. Hence the West just has no idea how to revive the collapsing Economy. It will be helpful if the West can plug the waste pipes, money laundering, debt burden and massive corruption through which African money flows to the West, thus damaging the Economy. It is the Africans themselves that will learn how to correct the flaws in their Economy and lifestyles.

Other systems suffer from insincerity and flirting with capitalist habits while professing to loathe them. Ideological dogmas are not the key to success. Appropriate Education and practical skills are the most essential features of success in development. Effective work culture and good management of the resources are the powerhouse of wealth and prosperity. This has been the key to the American success. The Americans work for their wealth and prosperity. Tyranny of greed and intrigues of unhealthy rivalry seems to be taking over from this spirit of hard work. The cosmopolitan immigrant expansion of the US perhaps has eroded the core culture of the melting pot of the American tradition. The US seems to missing the real features that made America, America, and appreciating diversity of culture. Perhaps before we attempt to sell the concept of Democracy and human rights to any people we must first learn to understand their way of life. Tolerance of different ways of doing things is the concept of capitalism and private business. This tolerates mixture of publicly owned utilities, heavily subsidised utilities and privately owned corporate businesses. Good Education and skills and efficient management form the core of success of the mixed business.

The Dr Shallabys and the Iraqi national congress, of this world may not necessarily be good Democrats even though they might have lived and prospered in the West. Several of us live in the West for several years and enjoy the way of life but when we return home we take to the worst form of dictatorship. Dr Hastings Banda of Malawi was a good example. Our challenge at the moment should be to give the people appropriate Education and skills and help the people we want to help to manage their lives and resources under the rule of law. Religion should not leave the mind of the believer and the holy places of worship to take over from the community to dictate the way they should live their lives. Secular laws and not religious laws should watch over the observance of the rule of law in the community. There is nobody who can honestly confess that he or she had direct instructions from God on how mortal people on earth should live their lives. God gave us the freewill and diversity to enjoy on earth. God has no laws binding on the secular society. Religious laws have no place on the secular society. Secular laws develop with social changes in the society to regulate the society under the rule of law while protecting individual rights and freedom.

We know that the Arabs feel their petrodollar can buy them anything including Democracy. I may promptly remind the Iraqi National Congress and Dr Chalabi that you cannot buy Democracy to install yourself as a dictator and a tyrant protected by an alien mercenary Army. Democracy comes from the heart and liberal culture open to new ideas. It is acceptance of the rule of law and the principle of equality for both male and female. Is the Arab religion-supported macho culture ready for Democracy and an open society? This is the question the Arabs themselves and not the Iraqi Congress or Dr Shallabi have to answer. You cannot hire an alien Army to come and install Democracy in your land. Any citizen that hires a foreign Government to overthrow the government in their homeland is a traitor. The West frowns at traitors. They kill them. Seizing power in your homeland with foreign assistance is criminal act of treachery. It is treason. Allawi is a king without a crown. He is a mask the Americans wear to commit heinous monstrosities and barbaric murders in Iraq. He is a traitor. He is not an Iraqi leader but another Mobutu in the sixties the Americans used to destabilise Africa gain access and control of the rich resources in this part of Africa. Till now the wound on the Congo has not healed. Africa is bleeding as a failing continent.

The Western European cousins always move together to attack anybody the clan disagrees with. It is astonishing that the world has always allowed their disagreement to become global quarrel and their fight global conflict. We cannot fail to observe that the countries that mobilised to fight in most Western conflicts are the ones that evolved from the Western European crimes against humanity in the last millennium. We equally should not fail to observe the pressure they apply on innocent standby to joint them in their hostilities against their foes. We always see the US, Canada, the UK, Australia and all satellite European nations usually rush out like swarms of bees to sting sense out of their enemies. The West has the severest punishment for traitors and collaborators. Yes most of our leaders are corrupt tyrants. Those who replace them are corrupt.

Yet the West treats foreign traitors and collaborators with red carpet for helping them to subvert and sabotage alien hostile governments. It exploits human rights organisations to protect them. Is it not yet time for the West to tell people discontent with the type of politics in their homelands to have a body like the "Council of Elders" made up of respectable decent and neutral people from their community for the sole purpose of conflict resolution and arbitration in disputes? Local people know the issues involved better than the so-called international community. The UN will do better acting through such bodies instead of through political agitators, activists and appointees. Activists are tyrants in the making. They are frequently more corrupt than their predecessors. This has been long African experience. Council of Elders will rectify this menace.

Is it not ordinary common sense that if the West does not tolerate its citizens to collaborate with its potential enemies, foreigners from countries the West has dispute with are traitors who have no moral right to be doing the dirty job of caricaturing their homeland and leaders for the West. It is equally shameful that the leaders become paranoid, murderous tyrants and persecutors of their people. They turn leopards feeding on their people, the very people they are supposed to protect. Why should the world rest on its oars while the European cousins mobilise to isolate and destroy its enemies? People the West has grudges and grievances with may not necessarily have disaffection with the United Nations and the world. Therefore, hijacking the UN to apply sanctions on such countries is wrong. UN sanctioning doubtful and dubious military actions against such countries is equally wrong and criminal. It is manifestation of corruption and complicity in crimes of the UN.

The attempt to suborn collaborators to get the United Nations Security Council to approve attacks on Iraq is still reverberating in all corners of the world. What justification have the Western European cousins and satellites got in joining forces to vanquish anybody who disagrees with any of them? We should not take sides in disputes. Now we have the West worried about immigration, refugees and asylum seekers. The West must know that other people have no moral right to accept the influx of immigrants from the West any longer.

History is not on the side of this Western European family war machine. They are the people guilty of slave trade, slavery, brutal colonisation, genocide, massive crimes against humanity and multiple land seizures in the last millennium. The evils we are now fighting against are direct results of the lawlessness of the Western colonisers in the world during the last millennium. Rational people strongly deplore the destruction of innocent lives and properties in the name of fighting injustice. The innocent people deserve to be protected from the hard-line attitudes of the Western right establishment and the desperate and reckless actions of suicide and city bombers. They destroy innocent people. They strike terror into innocent people and expose them to terror and death. God does not need martyrs. Equally we are not in this world to fight for victory. We are here to seek for peace. The Council of Elders is a club of equals free to speak their mind. It has no hierarchy. Africa essentially requires such an institution to regulate what the politicians do.

We cannot take sides in this quarrel. We advocate for peaceful settlement of all disputes. We will not escape from poverty by being involved in this sort of carnage. Urban terrorism will not give us safety and security. Without safety and security we cannot achieve the peace to work and create wealth and prosperity to escape from poverty. The resources we commit to war and violence are the funds we should invest in wealth generation. Our only hope is that genuine people will rally together and sue for peace from all people of war and violence. Time is overdue for the black cousins to come together not in a war council but in a peace council. We have a common objective. We have to acquire appropriate Education, right type of knowledge and skills to work and earn decent living standards for self-esteem and respectability. We essentially have to be our brothers' keepers.

Gangster action of mass hysteria is incompatible with the culture of all black people. We should never advocate for such. We advocate for re-integration of Africa, our homeland from colonial dismemberment and fragmentation, merger and team work to liberate us from the crutches of abject poverty and ignorance. Regular rioting and crises cannot rescue us from poverty. Haiti had been free for a long time. It keeps on starting from the drawing board. The same is true of the homelands of most black people. Slogans are not the same as good Education, knowledge and right skills to work and produce satisfactory results. The African Negroes had been made slaves for a long time now. They seem to find it difficult to be free to work for themselves. Majority of them hang about always looking for new masters and jobs under new masters. They need independent initiative and the drive to work for themselves free from supervisory influence of the slave and the master.

THE ARGUMENT NOW RAGING ON THE RE-ORGANISATION OF THE UN AND DEALING WITH FAILED NATION STATE ROGUE STATES OR BANANA REPUBLICS.

Yes there are several of these, all over the world, today, in Africa, Asia and Europe. They are usually associated with crimes, corruption, militant and aggressive religious fanaticism, wars and violence and extreme ethnic national violence, ethnic cleansing and genocide. Unfortunately, these weaknesses are often exploited by a number of interest groups. The rich West ranks first in seizing opportunity, to sell arms in exchange for rich resources in these places. They also collaborate with the criminal and corrupt tyrants and the dictators, the African warlords who lead these mayhems. The international criminal fraternities equally cash into these trouble spots to turn them into crime havens aided by the local warlords. They deal with dirty money from all manners of crimes including drugs, arms and human trafficking. The West can help Africa by preventing money laundering. It will also prevent crimes. Most of the criminal organisations prevail with money laundered from crimes.

We cannot talk of failed nation states and rogue states without examining the causes of failures of these nation states. Several of these nation states are artificial colonial creations left behind after the previous colonial powers left. All of them were created by dictatorial colonial powers without any consultation with the people who lived in these places. Neither the people nor their leaders were consulted properly in a democratic way to establish these nation-states. They were created by fiat of the colonial powers that seized these lands as their colonial overseas territories and properties. Little did it occur to them that the inhabitants of these lands had their like and dislikes just as the people in Europe, the English, the French, the Germans and the Russians do? Even though, they are all white they have their different ways of life. We are all black African Negroes but we have our diversities and different ways of life and culture that cement our bonding. The white males are notorious for abusing black people this way and walking away pompously. After slavery they collected compensation from European white male and walked away from liberated slaves who were paid nothing. When the Western white male Empire collapsed they never thought of putting things right for the people whose life they had disrupted for several years but just walked away. Re-integration of dismembered Africa was vital for success of postcolonial Africa but the good Western European white males just walked away. Today, they have given reason and blame us for failure of Africa to succeed but fail to mention their role in this failure.

A second thing is the fact that most of these places were far from reaching the qualifications for nation state status. Yet the former colonial powers left them with nation state status. Of course we should not be surprised over poor performance when we recruit unqualified people and leave them with important responsibilities and duties to execute. This is exactly the position and situation with these failed nation states or the rogue states.

The other problems we seem to overlook are the fact that these failed nation states have the tendency to recycle leadership that had failed in every aspect to offer good leadership. These seem to specialise in crimes and corruption. They rely on their cronies and hangings on to hang unto power. These people are prepared to flout every rule in the book and commit all manners of crimes to stay in power. A few examples can be found in Africa. We have seen the stagnation in Nigeria. Obasanjo has not made any impact. Now Babangida is busy warming up and sparring to return to the ring. This is a man involved in all the tragedies and catastrophes that had happened to Nigeria. One cannot fail to have the impression that Nigeria specialises in choosing utterly redundant and hopeless leaders that specialise in damaging the country. A country that allows the mob, the Mafioso Cosa Nostra Nigeriana to seize power and recycle it among its members is a failed nation state. The way Arap Moi ruled in Kenya was another case in question. Robert Mugabe is already becoming antique furniture in Zimbabwe. The Zimbabwean case is understandable. Robert Mugabe is a clever and understanding patriotic African. He does want to make the same mistake our leaders made over re-integration of colonial dismembered Africa after the nominal independence, in land case in Zimbabwe. He deserves sympathy from all patriotic Africans and reasonable global leaders and people. Equally even the much heralded democratic dispensation had not been able to produce leaders free from crimes and corruption. Zambia was a recent example. Haiti is another disaster of black homeland and failures.

The list is long. We cannot catalogue everything wrong with the failed nation states. But the suggestion that the UN should be re-organised to sanction seizure of failed nation states to put things right is a very wrong idea indeed. The former Western European colonial masters had up to five hundred years to achieve this but they failed to do so. What then is the guarantee that they can do it now under the cover of the UN? Is this not a ploy for these people to return to these places to plunder and loot them under the cover of the UN? They had been doing these throughout the postcolonial era using active collaboration of the tyrants and dictators they are now denouncing. Now they want to change colour like chameleon. They want to wear the UN coat shouting “Democracy, Democracy and Democracy and go back to do what they are used to doing, plunder and loot these lands. Colonisation by the West through the agency of the UN is not the answer.

If the UN is to succeed and the West is really serious to restore these failed nation rogue states to the rule of law and Democracy, they essentially have to reconstitute these lands and people into viable nation states. The people themselves must be involved. They must be made aware of the realities of life. They essentially have to live together with all their neighbours under the rule of law and Democratic Constitution. The nation has to be viable and everybody must be equal before the law. Africa must have a neutral” Council of Elders” that must have people of good characters not only from Africa but also from all over the world for conflict resolution. Regional conflict resolution bodies are very important to assist the UN. Democracy is not solution to the coalition torture cells in Iraq. The solution here lies in the answer to the question why should the Anglo-American alliance that went to Iraq to liberate the people from Saddam Hussein torture cells quickly become tormentors of the very people and use the same cells for torture?

People who live in the region are better placed to resolve conflicts provided they are not partisan to the conflict. The international UN force is no starter. It brings back the sad memory of brutal colonialism and racial xenophobia and arrogance of the Western European white males. All world leaders must be accountable for their actions and decisions. Control of the weapons of mass destruction is good but the leaders using these weapons must be held accountable for their decisions and actions. This is a better way of holding the leaders responsible for their decisions and actions. Fear of West's brutality is greater than weapon of mass destruction. Why is the West afraid of weapons of mass destruction in the hands of other people than theirs? They must have ulterior motive to use them to bully and cow others. Now oil supply seems to be the answer and not the WMD.

The West has its problems. Its economy relies on exploiting and cheating the third world. It also practises racial xenophobia. It is arrogant and nannies the nations of the third world about by bullying and intimidation. They all know that they cannot rescue a drowning man by this arrogant and non-committal aloof attitude. The solution to the problems of the third world failed nation states lies with the people of the third world. They must be involved in solving these problems. They must have the right type of Education to understand their problems. They need the right type of skills to tackle these problems. Most importantly the West must stop its patronising attitude. It has to tackle its domestic problems without giving its citizens the impression that their problems are from an external enemy or the third world and they must make the sacrifice for them to defeat the third world to improve on the quality of lives in their homelands. The Western leaders of George W Bush political orientation are very mischievous. They start foreign wars offering false reason all to maintain peace at home. This is what Bush in Iraq and Afghanistan. He calculated that he could use Iraqi oil to sponsor the war without American taxpayers' money. He is simplistic and cannot imagine any obstacles on his way.

The practice of always having an external enemy to focus the attention of citizens in the West and justify their sacrifice in confronting a common foe may be good for Western leaders but it demonises other world leaders and exposes innocent citizens of their countries to suspicion and hatred. This habit threatens world peace. The West can exist without having the baddies. The West has no real enemies except those they had made into enemies to help their leaders to point to them to justify their actions in militarization and armament manufacture for combat readiness. Army needs potential enemies to justify its existence and expenses. This is a dangerous brand of Western politics. Armament Industry provides jobs and trade is lucrative. There must be justification for arms manufacture; war.

The West seems to have an enemy each time to concentrate the attention of its citizens on the real danger. Over exaggeration of threat is always involved. The former Soviet Union was demonised into being imminent threat to the way of lives of people in the West. They were all atheists and anti-Christ. Recently it became the Axis of evil Iraq, Iran and North Korea and now Al-Qaida. It seems to be fast evolving to the third world failed nation states and pre-emptive strike. This is a ploy to build American empire under the false label from the UN. This is dangerous. The world is not ready for the costly business of empire building. The world is yearning for ecologically friendly, orderly and sustainable development. It is not ready for brutal atrocities of occupation Armies and bloody empire building. The ultra conservative rights in the West always have the ultimate goal of empire building. The sun never sets on British Empire. The commonwealth is a loose string on the empire. It is time Africa forgets about that empire and start to look for our way out of its misery, disasters, tragedies and catastrophes it left behind in Africa.

I owe no bias or prejudice to anyone; I owe wisdom to all decent people in the world. Simplistic theories are obsolete and dangerous. The planners must know that they are taking us into a third world war. We cannot solve all human problems but we can help human beings to overcome their difficulties and solve their problems. You do not pull the gun to shoot your child for failing an examination. You help your child by finding out the weaknesses that caused the failure. You find safe and friendly ways to put things right. Pre-emptive strike and occupation are not the way to deal with failed rogue nation states.

It is very obvious that the West is attempting to use the very tactics they used to damage Africa in the past to bring Africa to its knees. African people are continuously recycling the people, the dead woods that destroyed and damaged every opportunity Africa had in rectifying things that went wrong. Can you imagine Doctors using the same drugs that kill their patients for treating all the patients that come to them for cure? This is what the Western authorities and Africans themselves are doing. Brutal colonialism, slave trade and slavery and intractable racial xenophobia and social exclusion damaged Africa immensely. The African themselves lack the ability and initiative to choose leaders that can appreciate their problems and find ways to tackle and solve them.

They seem to tolerate any people in power that have the knack and ability to damage them and their land and destroy their opportunities. They are famous and notorious in recycling good-for- nothing dead-wood leaders without any initiatives or ideas of the responsibilities of leadership in office to continue to inflict long-term damage to their land and its opportunities. This is self-inflicted injury and damage. This is the way Africans tolerated slave trade, slavery and brutal colonisation, plundering and looting of their land by Western imperial colonisers. They just seem to have no sense of good governance and what is good for their welfare. They also lack self-esteem and affection for their land of birth. The Africans must now know that their lives are very dependent on their land.

They have to take care of that land. It is their civic duty and responsibility to protect their land and people from local and foreign predatory and irresponsible leadership. The Africans must know that a determined population has power over any individual out to hijack power from them to lead their land and place them under bondage. They must not accept to be voluntary slaves to any group bent on subduing them to irresponsible, callous, corrupt and criminal leadership. The African must appreciate the sensibilities of collective responsibilities of looking after their own interest in Education, skills training and good and responsible leadership. The leadership must not be allowed to be above the rule of law. He must not be allowed to damage the economic opportunities of the people and the land by reckless, expensive, corrupt, criminal and irresponsible lifestyle. The African leaders are all outlaws. They must appreciate the place of law and order for the society and must act within the rule of law. The Africans must take responsibility for the conduct of their own affairs in politics, economy, care of their land and their total welfare.

POLLSTERS AND THEIR RESULTS IN CURRENT THIRD WORLD CRISES:

It is difficult to understand why the West uses anarchy and undemocratic wheelbarrow to cart democracy and the rule of law to the third world. A recent opinion poll conducted by an Oxford organisation in the occupied battlefield of Iraq is a case in question. This is an occupied land controlled by American allied troops armed to the teeth. They all live in fear of their lives. They would be foolish to offer answers to questions that would portray them as having Anti-American feelings. They are all American war prisoners. How on earth can such pollsters persuade intelligent people in the world except their own people to accept the results of such opinion polls as valid documents? They are thrash and not statements of truth. Can such results from Guantanamo Bay inmates be given any credit for credence of truth? No it is only puerile Western propaganda. It may serve the purpose for consumption of Western media but not the interest of the victims of Western war machine. It is bogus to talk of opinion polls in the battlefield.

Access to the real victims of Western action is restricted by language, culture, fear and the enormous difficulties the US military action has placed on their way. The con and tricks of pollsters should not replace the free choice of the people. Even the Western style of elections is unsuitable for most parts of the third world. Why should the world not leave the choice of leaders and the methods of selections to individual people but guarantee that the choice is free from fraud and intimidation and the people chosen are not corrupt criminals? Accountability is more important than the choice and its conduct. The leaders must be held accountable for their actions in office. They must have stiff penalties for all wrong doings while in office. The people must have free means of bringing bad leaders to justice. Regional Councils of non partisan Elders and the UN should act along this line and ensure that such leaders are brought to book. The powerful Western influence should not protect such leaders from probity. If the leaders know that they would be punished for misdoings and poor performance they would obey the rules.

Conducting con polls in the name of acceptability of war and occupation is fraud and deceit. Access to war weary and intimidated people is difficult and not free and true representation of the people's choice. Therefore, whoever conducted that poll in Iraq must know that his findings were not valid results. We seem to have broken all the rules of lying and propaganda in the war in Iraq and war against terrorists. There is absolutely no law against lying. But is offence in lying to insult the intelligence and good judgement of your audience. The former colonial masters lied to their colonial subjects in religion, good conduct and behaviours, probity in office and lifestyles. Now we all know that they lied to us. They deceived us. Neither were they just, fair nor honest in their dealings with us. Therefore, wherewithal is this new move towards democracy and fundamental human rights? Is it an afterthought, con or ploy to fool the UN to return to wreck more havoc on the third world and Africa? Now the world knows that George W Bush and Tony Blair lied and used fabricated intelligence to invade a sovereign country and UN member Iraq. It is sad the world allowed Bush and Tony Blair to slaughter Saddam Hussein by sham trial by their collaborators and cronies. They murdered callously his two sons. It is difficult to believe that these events were real and not dream. George W Bush is a simpleton but what of Tony Blair who is both a Christian and a lawyer? It is good to leave all to his conscience. Even politics has conscience.

The best way to deal with the problems of Africa is to correct a lot of the flaws of past colonial rules and their artificial creations. We must correct the borders they created. We must ensure that true and viable nation states under the rule of law and binding democratic constitutions are created to replace the nonviable rogue states in Africa. We must prevent the recurrence of wars, violence and genocide. The democratic constitution must prevent ethnic and religious feuds, conflicts and riots. There must be ways of settling conflicts without resort to wars and violence. Citizens must acquire the discipline of living within their means. The government must live within its means and balance the budgets. The budgets must be modest and within means without borrowing beyond means of paying back. The donors and investors must know this.

Acting beyond the scope of this disciplined Economic prudence must leave the donor or investor to suffer from his or her folly of being liberal with the funds given out above what the debtor can pay back. Therefore, correcting the flaws that cause the failures of nation state of rogue states does not need UN sanctioned wars and violence and occupation. The rich and affluent Western nations must correct their past bad practices. The third world leaders must stop their lives of crimes, corruption and tyranny. The third world citizens must learn the value of good education and skills training, hard work and living within their means. Africa must stop recycling poor and bad leaders. The way most African countries choose and select their leaders is astonishing. It gives you the impression that they deliberately open their storehouses of treasures to well known notorious armed robbers to plunder and loot them. Why do reselect corrupt and criminal leaders to lead?

It is difficult to understand the motive behind this their persistent behaviours. Ethnicity and religious faith and loyalty cannot justify the folly of victims of corrupt and criminal leadership to continue to aid and abate their tormentors to continue in office to inflict more damage and destruction on their land, the economy and their lives. If the West is serious in establishing effective world order under the rule of law, it may not be out of place for the UN to lay down the rules for qualifications for membership of the UN and its Agencies. This must include the integrity and calibre of leadership that will promote the rule of law, economic prudence, freedom and democracy. Crime syndicates, the mob and the Mafiosi of various nations and their international connections are grabbing and consolidating power in democratic dispensation to convert these countries into their operation bases and havens for crimes and corruption.

The West and the UN have to take this observation very seriously. Criminals are cashing into Democracy to continue with their lives of crimes as usual. The local and international election committee must have effective means of rigid vetting of potential leaders to weed out corrupt criminals who use their stolen wealth to buy offices and official positions to continue with their lives of corruption and crimes. It may not be enough to claim that a well-known criminal and corrupt boss is the best choice of the people. The interest of neighbours and the world community must also count in order to avoid military intervention to kill and destroy innocent people as we have seen in recent times. It is easy to prevent bad people from getting to positions where they may become dangerous to safety and security of their people, their neighbours and the international community. It is amazing to hear of the Anglo-American invaders talking of people fit to lead in Iraq. What do they know about Iraq? Can the Iraqis claim to know who should lead in the US or the UK? Of course, I can predict that their action has set up a chain reaction.

Leaders must have short terms of service. They must be accountable and must be held responsible for their decisions and actions while in office. They must always be brought back to answer for whatever went wrong while they were in office. It is intolerable to have the Mobutus enjoying their wealth while the countries they ruled remained bankrupt and insolvent. Africa is riddled with these types of billionaires. Nigeria is a typical example. The West knows this. This is the way to help the third world and Africa. It is not by war and occupation.

Attempting to use bogus pollsters to justify illegal and criminal actions is fraud. People may be gullible to accept such pollsters but they must know that the people assumed to be involved in the bogus exercise just do not understand what they stand for. Sitting in the comforts of West to analyse the results of pollsters in Iraq or any foreign land for that matter is distortion of democracy. It is falsification of public opinion and corruption of democracy to justify criminal fraud. It is fabrication and deception replacing democracy with tyranny. This is the description; the dictator gives to democracy to justify his grip on power. He claims that his dictatorial power is authority from the people for him to rule with his gang of cronies. We are damaging democracy with lies and fraud.

The American Establishment is yet to respect the fundamental rights of the African-Americans and people that they abuse, intimidate and massacre in their illegal wars. It is insult to our common sense for the criminal American establishment to issue statement on fundamental human rights claiming that Iraq and Afghanistan under them are democratic and free and observing human rights in the blood bath of their war of illegal occupation to steal their oil. What on earth in credibility would make the US establishment issue this type of statement and insulting respectable nations such as China and the rest who do not go out to enrich themselves with illegal wars of loots? They are battling with the problems of overpopulation and scarce resources.

It is either they do not understand the meaning of democracy or fundamental human rights or they abuse these terms to bully their victims into defensive position so that they do not question their gross abuse and violation of human rights of their citizens. The Anglo-American establishment is no custodian of human rights and democracy. Use of dirty tricks against their citizens and opponents is very rampant in the Anglo-American establishment. I have been a victim of this filthy abuse of power and freedom. The world itself is a victim of this nasty habit. The leaders of the nations they prey upon are caricatures of their dirty tricks. They bribe and hire criminal collaborators to use in blackmailing and damaging innocent nations struggling with their national problems. The Anglo-American establishment uses dirty tricks and blackmail to justify using legalistic bureaucracy to punish and exclude people who speak out against official injustice.

The world cannot be a safe place if the Anglo-American establishment continues with this type of behaviour. The circumstances of the quarrel between the Mujahadins in Afghanistan and Saddam Hussein in Iraq should not be left as past events. These are the very people the Anglo-American establishment trained and armed to fight their proxy wars against the former Soviet Union and Iran and described them as freedom fighters and defenders of democracy. What went wrong in this cosy and cordial relationship? Why does the Anglo-American establishment bully innocent people with dirty tricks campaign to join them to fight against these people they trained and armed to do their dirty jobs in the world for them? The world is timid and Anglo-American establishment bullies, cow them to keep silent while they are rampaging the world with illegal actions and wars threatening the world peace. At the same time there are very many genuine Americans enthusiastic in helping the less well-to-do parts of the world. They may even be treading on the toes of those they want to help out of zeal and enthusiasm without knowing that they are hurting them and their feelings. Mutual understanding of each others' intentions will cool the current tensions. It is wrong to claim that all Americans are involved in these horrendous acts. The US is still lecturing people on human rights that it is number one abuser and violator of human right. US is the only nation in the History of man to have dropped the nuclear bomb on its enemies. What is the US right and credibility to tell others not to do these things? No the US has no moral right to tell others not do them.

HISTORY OF PARTNERSHIP BETWEEN SUBSAHARAN AFRICA AND EUROPE.

George W Bush had just told us to study History. Tony Blair also advised the world not to ignore History. History can be inaccurate or what the Historians like to make it. But the genuine truth that evolves from History, at times, can be shocking and revealing. There is no record in History of success of partnership between the white race and the black race. The ancient Greeks admired the spread of knowledge in Africa and frequently Greek students studied at the feet of African masters but yet even such loyal students ended up getting the best from Africa for the good of Greece. Then came the era of Alexander, the son of Philip of Macedonia, and later that of Ptolemy, his General, who took over after Alexander's death. The partnership between the European Greco-Roman and Africans frequently ended up in failure. Even the skills, the beauty, romance and diplomatic skills of Cleopatra ended up in failure, war and violence. The relationship between the Romans and Carthage in Africa ended up in genocide and total destruction of Carthage in 146 BC. Few people know that the Romans had Province of Africa.

Trade between early Europeans, the Portuguese and the Spanish started the European slave trade and slavery of the African Negroes. It led to racial segregation, xenophobia and social exclusion of the African Negroes from all social activities and several deaths by rough justice and lynching. It resulted eventually in pillaging brutal colonisation and looting of the African continent. It is all a catalogue of failures of partnership. Even after several centuries of partnership between the colonies and the colonial masters it eventually ended up in failure. The postcolonial partnership in trade and aids piled up debts now described as debt burden and equally resulted in failure that is currently causing anxiety in the West and the world. The relationship between black and white had always been based on deceit and falsehood christened diplomacy. This is polite lying and barefaced fraud and deception. The relationship between Europe and Africa had always been based on inequality. The white people always treat us it in an atmosphere of superiority. Let us now inform thee white people with crude immature culture propped up with high Technology that their culture is the most immature culture among the human race. High Technology has provided method for easy ways of doing things. It has not changed the immaturity of the European Western culture that does not know the difference between human value and material wealth and it has frequently destroyed human lives for consumer materials, land and material wealth not belonging to them. It kills for pleasure.

The right of the mortal royalty that destroys innocent, harmless and vulnerable young women to enjoy the pleasure of old goats and Geriatric society ladies is trampling on the rights of common citizens. Henry V111 did this and got away with it. Charles and Diana, the Princes of Wales presented modern example of the royal prerogative. That poor girl kept on telling the world, in her life time, that she was engaged in a sham marriage as Prince Charles the heir to the English Throne was practically married to Camilla who was married with grown up children to Parker Bowles. She was advised to consult the Psychiatrist for paranoia. What do we see, today, Charles is wedding Camilla. The European Western culture allows this and homosexual sex despite the fact that it is associated not only with HIV-AIDS and several other diseases because of the fact that the anus is the dirtiest human orifice that virtually makes the perineum the most contaminated part of the human body. The real black culture and most black people in the world, a great majority of black people for that matter object to this primitive dirty habits. Our true culture abhors destruction of human life. It is so precious that in our culture insisted on exchange of live human being for murder and the exchange was not harmed but used to replace the lost human being murdered. Moses learnt his law in Egypt in Africa. He wrote the Ten Commandments based on black African basic moral laws. This is based on principles of social and community harmony. Aristotle saw Democracy in Carthage in Africa and described it to the Greek constitutional conference. The Greeks adopted it. They gave it the name "Demos Cras", people's authority or rule. This Africa that the Western European consumer-materialists are destroying was bacon of human civilised standards.

The finest in all successful human beings comes out at his darkest period in life. This is the finest period for all genuine black leaders on the globe to rally together for the cause of their fatherland and heritage on earth, Africa. We do not make any differences between black people on the globe from any part on earth. This is a call to duty to all black people. We all had been victims of the Western European consumer-materialists and their middlemen the corrupt and illiterate African leaders. We must form a global movement to oppose abuse of real freedom and democracy and slave trade and slavery. These are the evils of Arab Muslim controlled fringes of the Sahara Desert in Africa South of the Sahara Desert.

The world was amused to find how empty African leaders are. A number of them came to London and Europe to talk trade and investments during this deep European recession. They are totally ignorant of the global Economy. They came to Europe for shopping. They lack the initiative to investigate what is happening. They have no common sense of leadership to plan what Africa can do in this situation. Perhaps some of them came over here to find out if their laundered money in safe havens is secure. While all European and Asian countries are doing everything to find solution to the current meltdown in global Economy, African leaders are asking the West being crushed under Economic collapse to come and rescue their non-existent Economy. When will African illiterate leaders put down their begging bowl and plan their Economic growth? The behaviours of those African leaders clearly demonstrate that African leaders cannot think for themselves or plan for their continent. It is risky to take them seriously. Africa has no future with these leaders. Any global youths seriously concerned with the future of Africa must look for a way to rescue Africa from the folly of these leaders. They fumble about while the world burns. They go on pleasure trips while their continent is bleeding. The African leaders should find out what has happened to global Economy. They should find out if Africa can help. They should commission African study group to study what everybody is doing to rectify and remedy the faltering Economy. This is the time for us to study what can go wrong with the Economy. This is time for us to study what people do to tackle Economic collapse. African leaders must know how global Economy works. They must know how globalisation works.

We have no choice but to make all sacrifices to link the whole of Africa by road and rail networks from the Cape of Storms to the whole of North Africa to gain access to all parts of this neglected and tormented continent. See how powerless we were in Darfur in Sudan? Our women alone would drive nomadic Arabs out of our land but our castrated men and eunuchs could not do it. The world controlled by racial xenophobic Western European consumer-materialists and their puppet agents and cronies now styling as African leaders showed no interest in stopping genocide and ethnic cleansing in Sudan by alien Arab nomadic invading Muslims and slave-gathering and land grabbers. Are we black people so timid that we are totally defenceless in the face of exterminating forces, HIV-AIDS, extreme poverty and raw exploitation threatening our extinction?

Late Sir Abubakar Tafawa Balewa, first Prime Minister of Nigeria once went out of his courteous behaviour to describe this habitual lying and pretence as “exchange of vague courtesies, pleasantries and loathing over genuine friendship. It is not recorded and recognised that in the annals of classical History African Negroes had been top Generals and leaders in European Armies, Bishops in European churches and leaders of business and communities but where did all these achievements end? I would say in the dustbin of history of failure of partnership between white and black race. If we want to make this one succeed let us not pay false lip service to partnership because we feel guilty over the plight of Africa that is desperate for help.

Let us not use new lies and deception to defraud. It is only ignorance of History that will make people deny the need for apology for what Europe did to ruin Africa to this extent. Recall Alexander, son of Philip of Macedonia arrived in Egypt with his hordes and did his worst to destabilise our institutions of state. He was not as dangerous as the Romans that invaded Africa in 146 BC. They destroyed Carthage by genocide and looted materials and intellectual stores from Africa. The Romans took the Carthaginian alphabets; they captured some

African Carthaginian citizens. They took them to Rome to teach them and their children how to read and write. This is the story what the European Romans did in 146 BC. They also took home our educators, scholars, Scientists, Engineers, boat builders and expert seamen and mariners. They seized and took back to Rome our Agriculturists and farmers. These Africans were enslaved to teach the Romans farming. They taught them grape growing and wine and raisin making. This is the same way African Bantu Negro slaves taught the European Aryan Caucasians how to cultivate tropical crops, maize, rice, sugar, bananas and pine apple in United States of America. The educated slave masters took down line by line notes on the methods they observed from their slaves. They produced written texts on the way to cultivate these crops. They followed up with continuous studies and Research. Today, most of the rich sources of information on Agriculture and farming come from this source. The African from the Egyptians to the Carthaginians wrote books on Agriculture. The Romans even seized one of the volumes of these books to translate to give as directives to their citizens for farming and cropping. These generations of Africans had been particularly idle, inactive and lazy. Africans are harming and destroying Africa.

THE ROMANS AND AFRICA:

St Augustine of Hippo made tremendous contributions to the spread of Roman Catholicism and survival of the Christian Church. In the East we had the able assistant to Peter, the Great, Abraham Petrovich, the Moor of Petersburg, Gannibal made great contributions to the growth and development of Russia. Abraham Petrovich was the Great Grandfather of the Father of Russian Literature, Alexander Pushkin who prided himself an Ethiopian and derivative from ancestral Africa. Abraham Petrovich was an Engineer and an expert in building Military Ramparts and weapons. He helped Peter the Great in developing the Russian Army and building up the Russian State.

The Romans and generations of Europeans who did business with us indulged in bullying. They called us savages. Sadly we failed to object to bullying but meekly tolerated it until it grew into racial segregation. It also grew into a complex in us. This affected our development adversely. There is one single fault in black people. This the Europeans observed and capitalised on it. The black people are proud and strong in victory but very humble in defeat. Once defeated the black people are humble. They lack the potential to reorganise and continue the struggle. This culture is manifest in black people in all their life struggles. It affects their attitude in all enterprises: education, skills training, apprenticeship training, study of Mathematics, Science, Technology, Engineering, Industrialisation, Agriculture, Medicine, Commerce, Business and Economics and all manners of crucial life commitments essential for improving their living standards. The Europeans on the contrary regard defeat as an incentive to persevere and continue till they succeed. The black people abandon their life objectives. Rather they become degenerate and take to much undignified practices such as corruption, crimes and anarchy.

The Romans first demonised the black people in Africa. They blacked out their nationality names and dumped them all into the nigger slave group later to be replaced with Spanish-Portuguese word, “Negroes”. Blacking out name and replacing it with derogatory name calling are both insulting and depersonalising dehumanisation. Yet the Romans created the Roman Province of Africa. They proceeded to plunder and loot Africa dry. They created the first environmental destruction by destroying the African Forest in North Africa. They turned the whole of North Africa into a desert that easily allowed the Sahara Desert to expand into much of North Africa despite the Mediterranean Sea, the Atlantic and Indian Ocean. They looted Africa to build Rome and the foundation for European Renaissance. Ever since, each generation of European children had followed in their ancestors’ footsteps. They had been born to prey upon each generation of African children. They had persistently plundered and looted Africa while neglecting the development of both the land and its people. Now Africa is crumbling under the weight of this continuous European looting of its wealth. The worst thing is that the African middlemen, the rogue state leaders are now members of the looting club. They are the African money launderers in the West and off-shore islands.

Unfortunately the Western Press rules the waves. They report only what they like to report. The current craving for partnership with the West is yet to work and succeed. Even the partnership between the Negro slaves that offered several centuries of slave labour to their white masters never resulted in success. The free descendants of African Negro slaves in the US, the African-Americans' partnership with the whites in the US is yet to produce success. The partnership in shared free citizenship is yet to yield equality of opportunities and justice. This catalogue of failed partnership between the white race in the West and the black race in Africa and the world is not denunciation of this relationship but a statement of Historical fact between such partnership. It compels us to make it work. The best way to proceed in this new phase of co-operation and rescue of Africa Europeans and ignorant criminally minded corrupt Africans jointly destroyed is to embark on genuine Education and skills training to all our youths, launch genuine construction projects and get Africans to work for themselves. We must abandon racial xenophobia and create genuine equal opportunity and partnership.

THE WEST MUST APOLOGISE TO AFRICA AND CORRUPT AFRICAN LEADERS MUST BEHAVE TO EARN RESPECTABILITY FROM THE WEST.

The Europeans must apologise for what they had done in Africa, multiple genocides, cruelties and atrocities and the damage to Africa. No European action in Africa was beneficial to this land. It was all Churchill and Monty big eternal empire among the savages. Any brave and intelligent descendants of the African slaves would not shy away from demanding for an apology just as Europeans in our position would do and had been doing all over History. Any person that denies or rules it out is just stupid or insulting our intelligence.

Even relationship between children born into mixed relationship between black and white had become victims of failures of these partnerships. This book has highlighted these failures to bring into our attention that the persistent failures of relationships between black people and white people, black countries and white countries and black homelands and white homelands must be tackled realistically in any future partnership to prevent it degenerating into mere talking shop blowing hot air as in the past. There seems to be lack of will and sincerity. We seem to be content in lying to each other in approved diplomatic deception. The black race seems to be content with the description of being polite, moderate, agreeable and congenial. No citizen should be moderate in the defence of his fatherland. The flame of your burning zeal should burn off hostile aliens and ills affecting the progress of your land of birth. Your continent is your home. You are in charge. You have the right to swagger about in it. You gain nothing by playing uncharacteristic humility. You do not need any compromise in discussing the affairs of Africa with aliens. The only compromise in such discussion is what is acceptable for the benefit of the continent and the African people. It is embarrassing to be asked to bring more goods to the market to lower the prices. That is not the way to trade in the open and free market.

THE WORLD TRADE ORGANISATION (WTO):

Thanks to God the current collapse of Banking, meltdown of the Economy and deep recession had opened our eyes to the weakness of the free Market. WTO does neither look attractive nor appear as the final Court of Appeal. WTO has never been attractive to the developing Economy of developing world. It will blast it out of existence and replace it with produce from developed well-supported farms of developed countries. The EU and the US should help the poor sub-Saharan Africa to develop and stabilise their Agriculture before joining the WTO.

The white people seem to be content with black people that live in fear and are timid to ask for the truth or tell the truth. Unfortunately, success in partnership must be based on frankness and the truth. It is better not to attempt to build up any partnership if we cannot be frank and honest to each other and tell the truth about the partnership as we find it. We owe it to success in partnership between the West and Africa to base our relationship on sincere sharing of Education, knowledge and skills to produce people who understand each other to make the partnership work and succeed.

The black race, Africans, white and black must note this long list of catalogues of failures of white and black partnership is to emphasize that the black race has the duty and responsibility to take charge of their priorities in any partnership and not to be sheepishly trusting or ruin it with their criminal habits, corruption and individual idiosyncrasies and clumsy culture and traditions. Rather trust in any partnership must be based on the genuine value of that relationship to us. NEPAD or current Committee on partnership between the West and Africa cannot yield positive results unless the Africans themselves understand that past partnerships failed. What made them fail? This is left to speculation beyond our real comprehension.

It confirmed that we had never really been serious with partnership. The partnership had never really been built on mutual trust. It has always been that of slave and the master or servant and master beyond the reach of equality and mutual trust. The African leaders are described as moderate and not people with leadership potential and vision for their people and their homelands and their place in the world at large. They do not exist to please the West. They exist to lead their people in the world with complex economic, political, religious and social problems that affect their welfare. Partnership is for genuine mutual help in Education, learning, exchange of useful knowledge and skills training to create people who can work for themselves. It is not to help in toppling the government of a neighbouring country the West has grudges and grievances against as at the moment in Zimbabwe where the white people in the West blame South Africa and Khedafi. Partnership is not the platform to betray your neighbour to his enemies. Providing military bases for covert warfare and espionage is partnership in crimes. Before getting involved in new partnerships we must give analysis of past partnerships.

Partnership must have its objectives and targets. It is not exchange of vague courtesy and pleasantries. This is a real challenge to both white and black to make their partnership start to work. It must give the black race and Africans the equal opportunities for justice, Education, knowledge and skills to make them do things for themselves and be truly independent. They must have the initiative and management skills to take care of their resources. The success of partnership depends on all the partners. We must show self-esteem and initiative in all partnerships. Partnership is not sycophantic dependence. Occasional flattery in relationship is healthy. Partnership must be inclusive and not exclusive for genuine exchange of ideas on how to do things better than before.

But partnership based on permanent flattery and platitudes is fake and counterfeit. So far it appears the partnership between the West, the whole black race and Africa had been based on flattery, platitudes and spineless civility. This type of partnership lacks initiatives, objectives and sense of direction. For the partnership to work equality of opportunities is very important. The partners must accept responsibilities. They must not abuse the opportunity of freedom to work genuinely. Each partner must play his or her part in working hard to produce what they consume and what consolidates partnership. Equality of opportunity also means equality of privilege to work independently with initiative to do things well. It involves using the opportunity to render genuine labour to produce satisfactory results. Partnership must yield fruits of hard work of all members.

It does not depend on patronage of chronic cronyism. It is partnership actively doing things that Africa needs. It is patronising to be told that individuals are acting from conviction of conscience. The West has never treated Africa with any conviction or good conscience. If this new partnership is to succeed let it be based on necessity and needs but not on conviction and conscience. This is real and genuine effort to express the silent opinion of majority of the cross section of all reasonable black people and Africans in the world. We are entitled to this opinion judged from our long History of failure of partnership between the Western white people, the black people and Africa. We should allow emotion to overwhelm us. We must realise that should go wrong has already gone wrong. We can neither repair such damage nor use apology to brush it aside. But sincerity and trust require some sense of remorse and apology.

Yet we are undaunted. We need genuine partnership and help. Equally we must go into partnership not to subjugate our freedom but to earn it and our self-esteem. We must acquire the confidence to be independent and free. We must have the appropriate Education, knowledge and skills to work for ourselves, self-improvement and our land, Africa. This must be the vision of successful partnership. The black cousins must unite as the Western white cousins. We have reason to unite and re-integrate. It was not our choice to be separated in the first place. We were forcefully separated by slave trade, illegal human trafficking and slavery. They also used illegal drugs to damage us and make money. We black people have a duty not to depend on the West to bail us out. We have to work for our own salvation. We also must have a way of extracting the best from friendship. The tragedy and catastrophe in Iraq have taught the world no foreigner can rescue your country from its problems. There is no room for gullibility. We have to face the realities and facts of life. Each of the nations of the world that had abused and bullied Africa at different times in different generations had unique opportunity to help this continent but yet none of them did so. Africa is still a victim of foreign bullying and abuses. What of Africans themselves and where are the people who claim to own this continent? They must decide the way to resolve the problems the continent is facing.

Human beings behave like human beings. The sergeant in American marines resigned because he felt the weight of genocidal killing in Iraq. His superiors bore no qualms when he took up his and the concerns of the ordinary young soldiers with them. He had no choice but to tell them that they were engaged in a genocide mission. The impression I gathered was that the American marines are animalised into rabid dogs to bite everything in their path. They are trained as perfect killing machine. They were deceived to believe that everybody they saw in the place was enemy. They soon became tired of killing children but the leaders responsible for this carnage are denying. They rather accuse the messengers instead of the owners of the message the US leaders of the war.

How long will America and Britain fool the world over democracy and basic fundamental human rights? The Anglo-American past world record on democracy is basically worse than that of Milosevic of Yugoslavia and Saddam Hussein of Iraq. The only difference is that they have regular change of leaders. Individual leaders at times modify the hard line policies of others but beyond that the core policy of predators and exploiters of weak nations remains constant. A country that trains its youths to kill this way cannot lay its dirty bloody hands on decency, civilisation and democracy regardless of its wealth and prosperity. After all there are rich and prosperous criminals all over the world. The discouraging thing is that these very people are on record in history as being the cruellest racial tyrants the world had ever known. They have record of being guilty of genocide in most parts of the world. We would hope they had lived out of this habit now that they are wealthy. But we had been deceived. They can still kill for wealth, resources and money. The problem is that they cover their crimes with slogans and lies.

Fragmentation of Africa forcefully tore us apart. We have every reason to come together. We have now seen that alien religion and its laws are not the way out for us. The Arabs that professed vague brotherhood in faith to us and abused us in the past cannot get their acts together. They seem to have betrayed us and Africa. We have no choice but to regroup and merge together to face the world and take responsibilities for our lives and our land Africa. This is our land and we are not passive partners. We owe it as our civic duties and loyalty to defend it. It does not belong to any religion. We African Negro race do not have to argue the ownership of this land with anybody. Wherever the black people are on this globe, Africa is their undisputed homeland. They need effective practical education in Science and Technology and good training in productive skills to become masters in their homeland. The men must be men ready to die for this land and not run away. They must not allow themselves to be intimidated. We have one common currency in life. We will die one day no matter how careful we may be. Therefore the enemy should not intimidate us. If we confront him he will die from our blows from fighting back.

A HISTORICAL REVIEW OF WESTERN EUROPEAN WHITE MANIPULATION OF THE BLACK PEOPLE IN THIS WORLD TO ACCEPT THEIR FATE AND PLIGHT AS PAST ACTS, FOR WHICH THE CURRENT GENERATIONS CANNOT BE HELD RESPONSIBLE. OUR PARTNERSHIP SO FAR HAD BEEN A DISASTER. THE CURRENT GENERATION SEEM TO BE WORSE THAN THEIR ANCESTORS.

During my childhood in the colonial days in Africa, the black child was taught that the worse anti-Christ and Satan on earth was Communism. We were taught to hate the Communists and Communism. We were taught to pray for people under the Communist rule. It was criminal for any African leader to speak to a Communist leader or accept aids from Communist countries. The African leaderships were fooled to commit their resources to the fight against Communism. Even after the Independence any leader that had Economic dealings with Eastern European countries was branded Marxist Communist and hounded and hunted out of power. Any political leaders that had Communication with anybody in Eastern Europe were given the same treatment. The corrupt and ware ward African leaders took a queue from this and branded all their genuine opponents as Marxist Communists. This helped them to attract sympathy and support to suppress opposition and keep them out of action to gain the freedom to continue with their criminal corruption, misrule and tyranny. The West supported criminals like Mobutu and Jonas Sivimbi in power. The very West punishes severely all their traitors. They encourage our people to be traitors and their spies. We should also have the same severe punishment for our traitors. We should kill them all.

It also isolated us out for abuses by our postcolonial masters who branded all our differences with them as Marxist Communist opposition to Democracy and tendency towards dictatorship and tyranny. Unfortunately the leaders and victims of these dirty tricks campaigns and blackmail from the West had any response to them because neither they nor their friends in the East knew the proper reaction to this propaganda. The Communist hierarchy had over bloated ideas of their success in penetrating the newly independent states in Africa. The Africans equally had misconception of diplomatic relations. The great Western propaganda machine had a field day in military, economic, political and religious campaigns. At the same time these people that successfully painted evil picture of Marxist Communism and sold it to Africa and the black race was busy making contacts with their cousins in the East to persuade them to dismantle Communism. The black people and Africa were busy floating about in ignorance advancing Western ideas. Today the West is busy rebuilding and resettling Eastern Europe and not Africa they exploited its resources to fight and dismantle Communism.

Now Marxist Communism, a European ideology has disintegrated. What has happened? The West and their European cousins are fast resettling, rehabilitating and re-integrating their cousins in the East at the expense of the black people and Africa. Language, culture, traditions and differences in Education has been pushed to the sidelines. What matters is that the individual has essentially to be a white European to qualify for any position. You may be a well-qualified black person but the white Western cousins would invariably prefer their white cousins from the East to you. There is no envy or jealousy in this practice. It is something the black race and Africa should learn from. The West is vigorously pursuing re-integration of Europe while ensuring that the black race is kept divided and Africa remains divided, feuding in war, violence crises and chaos. We remain cap in hand shouting for aids and investments. They offer us arms in exchange for our resources. We are stupid to be fooled to acquire guns to destroy our homes and places.

We lack both the means and resources for re-integrating the black people on the globe. We have every reason to strive and re-integrate the global black people. We all went through the same scourge for over five thousand years on earth. We suffered under the European cousins. We endured their military and racial xenophobic abuses together regardless of where we were on the surface of this earth. Our qualification for this torture was the fact that we were black. This single genetic marker and qualification should equally qualify us to strive to re-integrate in spite of all the odds and obstacles. The machinery of black re-integration is very slim but they are there in the age of global village of information Technology. The black people have a duty to come together in their own interest. It is not worth an honour eating from the table where your people are forbidden to gather the crumbs because they are upsettingly poor, miserably dirty and woefully ignorant.

We must know that the West has the difficulties of diversity in languages, culture and traditions in their Eastern cousins just as we do with our global black cousins. We also have poverty and ignorance in greater amount than the West. Even this can be turned into our advantage. We have advantage of speaking several foreign European languages. We can use these in Education, spread of knowledge and skills. This will help in communication with one another. Our communication potential now is better than that of the West and Europe. We had no choice but to acquire these alien languages. We can apply them to our advantage in embarking on massive Education now on the cheap. We can also use it in building the basis for genuine relationship between the other nations and Africa. The unique advantage we have in communication, today, can be used in Education and skills training of the black people on earth. The crusade on black Education must be led by the black people themselves. They must make the sacrifices needed in this crusade. The global black youths must have sound education and useful skills training.

We had remained indifferent while the European cousins divided us, intimidated, dehumanised, enslaved and abused us while using our rich resources to build up their formidable Educational and skills training basis. Can we also wait and remain without any initiative or action while they are busy re-integrating their Eastern white cousins using our resources and even labour? The West is, today, having good co-operation with their erstwhile enemies in the world. Rush across the world from East to West, from the North to the South, the West is busy co-operating in matters of Technology and trade with nations like Japan, China, Korea and Taiwan and several other people. The black cousins re-integration does not mean failing to co-operate, or befriending the West in matters of mutual interest in the world we share with them but ensuring that we maintain our internal genetic cohesion for strength and self-esteem, dignity and virtue while we do things together. We must all respect equality of opportunities in Education, skills training trade and commerce and justice. This is the hallmark of the herald of trumpet for re-integration of global black cousins to spread Education, learning and training in skills.

We must not allow isolation of clusters of disadvantaged black people as militant agitators and good for nothing people. It is our duty to take over such people and educate them that Education, knowledge and good skills are the way to true freedom and not agitation, crises and violence. Feuding gives the enemies advantage to organise and divide you into clusters of aimless agitators to abuse. We have no choice but to embark on massive Education even while we are deprived, poor and disadvantaged. It is the sacrifice that we make that will offer us true freedom, wealth and prosperity. That type of resolute determination and sacrifice has made the writing of this book possible. Read it with faith, determination and optimism in your ability to be focused to confront your hardships to win. We must ignore distraction and false promises of democracy. The Iraqi people are leaking the wounds of their gullibility and vulnerability to lies and deceits. All the angels of democracy and freedom have each got a secret agenda for their war action and violence. Learning from experience is the best way to learn. We are not new to democracy. We invented and pioneered it. Our brand of democracy must be suitable for our cause. It must not seize initiative from us. It must not divide us for the enemy to rule us. It must support our loyalty to this land Africa. It must support our culture and prevent the enemy from subverting us.

I am sick and tired being told that that it cannot be done. No it can be done. We have to be focused and determined to reach our target. The united black cousins must assume responsibilities over the day to day problems they confront in life. The English have it rightly so, "there is no such thing as a free meal." Let no black person remain indolent any longer expecting a free meal. There is no such thing as a free meal. There is no obstacle beyond the ability of delegated human being to overcome. We black people can overcome all our problems if we confront them with delegation and determination to overcome them.

We have all gone through the burrows in the rock of torture, humiliation and suffering together. Let us in the name and the heart of our freedom equally go through the labyrinthine journey into re-integration of the black race now that the white cousins are doing the same. It is not our business what the West is experiencing in the hands of their enemies. They are equally entitled to call their enemies names. We have no business calling anybody names as we do not quarrel with anybody. The Arabs abused us. The white cousins abused us. Why then should we take sides if the West and the Arabs quarrel? We should be neutral and peace makers. We stand to gain nothing from their feud. The West in its character will finally settle its differences with the Arabs. We just have no excuse in the name of religion to be involved. God has children. He has no enemies. Africa has other people and lands to share this world with. We have no obligation to create enemies. We have no enemies as we have a duty to make friends with the world and even those who hate us. Lack of appropriate Education, good knowledge and skills are greatest enemy at the moment. This is what we should tackle. We cannot tackle it in isolation or in the midst of imaginary enemies. This is avoidable diversion from the truth.

Let us not take over the differences the European cousins may have with other people or races of humanity. They have their ways of dealing with their problems. We essentially must devise our independent way of dealing with others. I cannot fail to admire Madiba Nelson Mandela. After over half of his active life had been spent in the dungeon of racial xenophobic hate and Apartheid, he came out to befriend everybody in the world. He visited Mamuar Kaddafi of Libya and Fidel Castro of Cuba. There is no better example for future black and African leaders than this. We must be independent and not gullible to be told what is good and what is bad. A free mind is free from imaginary good and evil. The black cousins must concentrate on what is good for them, their various homelands on earth and Africa. We must learn not to take sides in quarrels. We must be neutral peace makers in conflicts. Our Economy and status in the world now cannot support conflicts but friendship with all. Revenge and retaliation are not our option. As human beings we expect nothing short of apology from those who abused us and brought us to this dead end. The accident of our destiny and fate had spread us all over the earth. We cannot therefore take sides in any quarrel as we have our brothers and sisters all over the world. Wherever we go to fight it will be brother facing brother in mortal combat not of our making but purely for alien interest. In modern age of commerce and wealth creation require peace and not war and violence.

We need urgently, "The Council of Elders of the black cousins to co-ordinate our activities to prevent our being overtly subverted to do the dirty jobs of the white cousins in the world under the guise of the United Nations resolutions. Our needs may not necessarily be the same as that of the United Nations. Our judgement may not also be the same as that of the UN. The UN is bulky but lopsided supported the demands of the white cousins in the World. Why do we not make it be the melting point of the caucuses of the various continents, regions, religions, social, political and economic groups in the world instead of playing the role of inert dictator frequently hijacked to advance the causes of the European and Western white cousins?

It is not the status or might of the organisation that is its power. It is its rules and regulations, and the rule of law and the way the members great and small observe them. The UN is weak and lopsided because the US and its allies are virtual outlaws. They break the UN resolutions at will. This is not life under the rule of law. Arrogance of power and excellence does not bond with unity of purpose. It is intimidation and bullying. This is neither freedom nor democracy. Radical re-organisation of the UN to make its rules and regulations binding on all members great and small is essential for world peace. Coalition of the willing is divisive, exclusive and not inclusive.

Re-allocation of the of the United Nations Security permanent members' seats and veto powers is not the solution to the current chaos. Radical solution for the current chaos is ensuring that everybody is equal before the rules and regulations of the UN. The first world order collapsed when the Romans picked and chose what they would observe and what they flouted without any penalty. Today, the new world order is collapsing because the US and its allies pick and choose what they would observe and what they would reject and flout the rules and regulations. Look at the so-called world court on human rights, the US and its allies are exempt. The same US is busy sending people to be tried there. The US before the eyes of the world watching snob the rules and regulations of the UN world Court established the Guantanamo Bay dungeon to violate every rule and regulation on human rights. The US lecturing everybody on human rights is torturing and killing innocent people in their own countries and homelands in Afghanistan and Iraq. Death sentence is still in vogue in the US. The poor and deprived Negroes stand to be imprisoned and be executed falsely in the US, today. Yet US lectures everybody on human rights. This is hypocrisy and raw intimidation. US has the right to hold its head in shame and stop talking about justice, rule of law, democracy and human rights that it violates every day without any qualms.

What is wrong with our world? It is fear of the rich and powerful and the worship of consumer materialism. It is acceptance of crimes, corruption, lawlessness and violation of the rule of law by the rich and powerful. Equality before the law is the heart of all civilisations. There is no civilisation in the presence of exemptions from the rule of law. There are lot of very sincere and genuine people out there, who can halt this drift into medieval anarchy in name of fighting terrorists. The great Technological advances are too sophisticated to support such anarchy. Peaceful co-existence under the rule of law is the answer to current chaos and insecurity to lives and properties. It will be near impossible to tell the US citizens to tune down their arrogance. You cannot be the number one law beaker of the rules and laws you want others to keep. This is what the US is doing. It is nonsense to talk of persuading the US. The US should lead by setting example. It is not doing so. It is ready to yap others for not doing the right thing. Yet the US does it wrong all over. Its craving for wealth belies the History of its creation. The US has to do better.

The current demonstrations and war against terrorists are gambling with lives. Equally the people of violence must accept that they are hurting the innocent and inflicting wounds on the innocent to give ambitious and violent people aspiring to world domination an excuse to pursue their life ambition. This is no solution to global problems. It cannot be clearer to the warring parties than this, that their actions are aiding each other towards their goals but the end-point will be total chaos in the world. This is not the heritage each of them would like to leave behind in the world; neither in the name of religion nor in the name of national pride and power.

Where then is our hope? Our hope is in real quiet diplomacy and peaceful negotiation and settlement of the current feud by all wise people of goodwill and vision of the future of our world. The victory we need in this war against terrorists is victory of the world and not military victory with national flare. It is victory of the world statesmen and national statesmen and heroes. Such quiet diplomacy must negotiate strict adherence to secular binding rules and regulations that each of us is able to understand without the ambiguities and taboos of religion. We all in our diverse ways and sensitivities have no choice but to share this world together. The only choice we have is to make binding rules and regulations to make this global family governed by the rule of law while allowing individual and group freedom and fundamental human rights to thrive and not to make them victims of the war against terrorists or religion.

Creating martyrs is not the way. Constituting a group of people into religious militant fanatical fundamentalist martyrs is not the way. The way is to constitute different communities into friends and working partners involved in promotion of genuine and adequate Education, appropriate skills training to work effectively and efficiently. Partnership based on hard work to improve the living standards and welfare of all citizens is what the nations, today, want. Partnership based on freedom and independent initiatives is what we all want. Any aids must help us to know the ways to do things for ourselves.

The behaviour of Anglo-American establishment is the major threat to world peace now. Their current crusade against weapons of mass destruction is an attempt by the enemy to disarm the opponents before the real fighting starts. The real campaign should be for the Anglo-American establishment to change their ways and chronic militarism. They cannot whitewash their criminal ways with preaching democracy and fundamental human rights. The Anglo-American establishment behaviours violate all tenets of fundamental human rights, democracy, freedom and world peace. We share this world with them. They must change their old habits.

You may ask why a proposal on the establishment of African Academy in Africa and the Diaspora should concern itself with what is happening in the world. Africa needs Education and skills. We cannot succeed if the Anglo-American establishment does not change their imperial habits and culture. They view Africa as their playing field for imperialist exploitation and means to sponsor covert and proxy wars. The success of this policy relies on chronic poverty and mass ignorance in Africa. This policy overtly opposes Education and spread of good skills in Africa. A number of white people used to openly lament why African Negroes were allowed access to Education. They gave the vague excuse that this destroyed the culture of the people. There is neither human culture that survives in isolation nor needs sanitisation to be pure. Every culture needs cross pollination to grow and expand. The black African is able to live everywhere on Earth. He is open to all cultures and GENE exchange.

Europe acquired Education from Africa through the Graeco-Roman axis but they never regretted that it damaged their culture. It is important that world peace is not disrupted by power drunk imperialists. Education must broaden the mind to see the difference between good and evil and right and wrong. The behaviours of the Anglo-American establishment must acknowledge and accept change in all living things and human relationship. They must equally accept that the world has changed. The world has no bone to grind with the Anglo-American establishment but they must acknowledge that we all have right to be here in this world. We share this world with them. They are part of this world. They are not the world. They share this world with us. They must recognise that we have a stake in this world. We are not tenants on their estate and they have no right to bully us to take part in or approve of illegal wars and criminal practices in American super-power dominated world. It is criminal to lie to justify war and violence. Deceit is insulting to us.

There is something beautiful in some Anglo-American citizens. They had resisted some of the excesses of the Anglo-American establishment. They had registered their disapproval of some the criminal acts. This is why some of these crimes explode and come to the common knowledge of the population. The world applauds their courage in speaking out against the rise of this new Anglo-American right. Responsible citizens have spoken out against their lies and belligerent activities. Why should people who shout democracy at breakfast, lunch and supper go around the world to commit crimes and buy collaborators with bribes, corruption, blackmail and dirty tricks? How democratic is smear-campaign? We have to educate the world on the behaviours of the people who abuse democracy as a pass word to dupe the world. Democracy is by persuasion.

The Anglo-American establishment has false credentials for democracy. Three cheers to their courageous citizens who had exposed the fallacy of this false claim to democracy, freedom and fundamental human rights. Now the world is fully aware of the aims and objectives of the Anglo-American right establishment when George W Bush was catapulted to power from a very undemocratic election settled in a partisan law court without genuine respect for the rule of law except by casting a single vote of doubtful integrity in a similar fashion to the judgement of Pontius Pilate. The Iraq war was illegal. We all knew it then but now the whole world knows it. America has to pay the Iraqis handsome indemnities for the damages they inflicted on the Iraqi people and their land in an unjust war. This is the observance of the fundamental human rights, democracy, freedom and respect for the rule of law. The Anglo-American right imperialist colonial abuses are responsible for global poverty. It is a major threat to democracy and world peace. Now they have left Iraq in a mess. They went into that country with blatant lies and false pretences. They occupied the country. They criminally divided the country by raising up old grievances among the different interest and religious sects groups by European traditional divide and rule fashion. They armed some groups to use to bully, terrorise, intimidate and slaughter the patriotic few that oppose the wild undemocratic and illegal Anglo-American actions. The Anglo-American soldiers are still occupying Iraq despite the pretence that they had left. They periodically round up patriotic Iraqi and silently torture and murder them in the name of phantom Iraqi Army of people on their pay vouchers.

It is not African way to ask for retaliation. It is my duty to ask the white racists to leave us alone. I equally implore the black race not to be distracted by white hostilities but to go all out to acquire Education in all its forms and make applied skills training the hallmark of our lives and culture on earth. We have the resources. We can succeed in the competition to make Science and Technology the anchor pin of our culture, development and progress. This is what has transformed the West from poor warring feudal autocratic overlords trampling over the rights of their rivalries and peasants into affluent militaristic aggressive affluent society.

A BRIEF HISTORY OF EUROPEAN MAGNIFICENT MILITARISM:

Our recollection of formalisation of this formidable war machine dates back to the Spartans. Herodotus gave narrative of the battle of Thermopile between the Greeks led by King Leonidas of Sparta and the Persians led by King Xerxes close to the straits of Hellespont. The Spartans were the first European city state that trained for war, lived to fight wars and actually relished in wars. It brought up all males to be fit and able men of war. They were fit warriors through and through. Even females were inducted in the art of war. The Spartans never retreated from battle. They were brave and courageous men of war. They were heroic to the core. They had both the Technology and fighting skills. Under Leonidas, the King of Sparta, in August, 480 BC, they gave the Persians what it took to face the Spartans in war.

Even though the Persians bribed their way to gain the upper hand in the battle to rout the Spartans, they were mortally wounded. This made them vulnerable to future defeat by the Greeks that finally sent the Persians under Xerxes packing permanently from Greece and Europe. The tragedy is that the Persian Army was multinational Army made up of troops from all corners of the Persian Empire. The Persian Navy was made up of people from Tyre and Siddon, Akka and Byblos- ancient Phoenicians in Canaan and later African Carthaginians with maritime dexterity. The Spartans were the first European whose culture and way of life conditions were totally committed to European militarism. Death is better than slavery and freedom is not without a price. There is some uncanny resemblance of some village names to those of Phoenicia. Our people are Ibibio (Byblos). There is Aka Village. There is Calabar (Cerne Canaan) Note the Phoenician pronunciation might have been different from what we use today. The Phoenician-Carthaginian alphabets had no vowels. Equally the colonial dismemberment of Africa has also confused the situation a bit. It is certain that thirty thousand Carthaginians came to establish the city of Cerne, the true location of which the Europeans could not locate accurately. But a lot of us believe that these people spread along the coastal and Delta areas of West Africa. The mountain in the script and narrative is surely the Cameroonian Mountain, the only one in West Africa. The site seems more of Calabar than Senegal alluded to by the European script and suggestion.

This Spartan Male Military culture, perhaps, encouraged homosexual culture in the Greeks and later the whole Europe to keep males away from women to make them effective fighting machines. Recently, I was appalled by the ease the Greeks accepted homosexual relations as normal and not the behaviours of sexual perverts. It has now dawned on me that it was developed as part of their military survival and tradition and never as genetic Scientific trait as they are fraudulently trying to fool the world and some of the Senior Bishops to accept as natural way of life. However, the fact that some of them have to undergo a barrage of plastic reconstructive surgery and hormonal manipulation therapy to develop feminine traits cannot fool normal people except those who fail to notice these practices or are too gullible to believe what people say in the name of Science. The homosexual practice is a lifestyle and not a genetic trait. Therefore the homosexual fraternity does not qualify for minority rights. If they do other strange lifestyle fraternities should qualify too. Homosexual practice is now a significant European culture. It is equally clear that Europeans are ignorant and confused about the sexes. They would rather speak about sexuality. Sexuality spells the way the Europeans approach sexual issues. There are a load of Paedophiles and all sorts of sexual perverts in all social classes. They seem to be quick in killing their women and children.

This will erode the rule of law. It will corrupt nature and threaten the very foundation of the existence of human beings on earth especially in the face of genetic engineering and current efforts to clone babies from body cells. Surprisingly Africa frequently hired Spartan mercenary Generals to fight wars. Yet we never adopted their pure militaristic culture and queer practices. We did not object to their behaviours either. They had the liberty to do things their own way while we also had the right to observe our culture and ways of life. Homosexual practice had never been African way of life. It is degradation of male respectability and character. It corrupts nature with human lifestyle and pleasure. We have to deplore this lifestyle of perverts as abnormal that it is. We deserve the right to preserve our way of life including our observance of the sensibility of natural differences between male and female. We have no right to use modernism to subvert nature. Nature knows the difference between male and female. He labelled the male with XY chromosomes and the female with XX chromosomes. Why then do we lie to both Science-Biology and nature? We even lie over obvious differences of the characteristics of male and female.

The culture of persistent war and violence in the name of security has got something to hide. People die in wars. War destroys properties and disrupts communities. The West has right to accept that the way they reject aggression is just the same as the way their victims disapprove of their wars and violence against them. The West is well armed but the fight for life surpasses arms. The West has fantastic stories of over five thousand years of magnificent military campaigns and wars. Yes gallantry is great but do they realise that victories in wars come from killing people and destroying properties and disrupting lives in the communities? Yes there had been heroes but what about the dead? The West has been killing people for over five thousand years. When will it stop? The West now has perfect killing machine. What is the future of our planet? The current chase for victory and the temptation towards empire building are very dangerous indeed. The world is not in mood for this type of behaviour and attitude. Nobody hates the West. Nobody is envious and jealous of the West. We admire the achievements of the West. But let the West not sacrifice us or the world to these achievements. It can go very wrong here. The West must now recognise that crude militarism is splendid but war settles nothing. Winning and victory do not make the west secure and safe.

The world is sick and tired of Western militarism. The West has no licence to go about the world killing people and destroying property. The West is ever preparing for war, fighting war either directly or by proxy. The world also has interest different from that of the West.

The UN must declare if it is Western military council and Quango. The UN Secretary has a duty to tell the World that he is working for the West or a world body. Nobody threatens Western security. The West created the Taliban and Al-Qaida. If you have a lethal scorpion as a pet do not fret it stings you. After eight years of wasteful war the West has only Ahmed Karzai to show as the only friend it has in Afghanistan. Pakistan is burning fighting a proxy civil war to please the West. The conscience of Western leaders should now worry them; they should think if they are doing the right thing. If they feel they are right, their sense of right must be different from that of most of their citizens and most people in the world. The Western white male and all their cousins rush like a swarm of bees against people in Iraq and Afghanistan. This is not right. The world should not stand idle and observe this without telling the West that this is not the way to behave. The people they are fighting against are global citizens. Equally the Muslim must dismount their horses and sheath their swords and stop the jihad. Some Muslims are denying their militaristic behaviour but they had not officially declared the jihad. Denials or bullying and molesting those who want Muslim Islamic disarmament are not the way of silencing or intimidating world. The right thing to do is for Muslim Islam to declare an end to jihad started about 200-228 AD by the Prophet and his faithful followers and believers. War takes at least two groups to fight. This book has researched for thirty years a period of over five millenniums of global History. It has found these two groups as pugilists. What are they doing now; is it another crusade? In the name of which God are they doing this? No God wants you to fight on earth in his name?

THERE IS NO JUSTIFICATION FOR GENETIC SCIENTISTS TO CLAIM PATENCY RIGHTS. THE GENES BELONG TO THE CREATOR. THE GENETIC SCIENTISTS FOUND THEM WHERE THEY WERE.

This section is not out to condemn consumer materialism, capitalism, money or Science. It essentially highlights the danger and great risks of capitalism conniving with Science to justify monetisation of the free society, life and the free gifts of nature. Genetic-manipulation of means of natural production of human beings, animals and plants and food may be a subtle attempt by capitalist consumer materialism to take over these means of production to control them to justify charging money for them and abuse of these means to support the consumer-materialists' lifestyles. Come off it. Nature has populated our planet with people, animals and plants and all manners of living things including our very selves ever since the beginning of times. Science and Technology had enriched life on earth. Technology has led us beyond the borders of limitations that previously restricted us to being content with limitations of nature. Does this then justify our attempt in corrupting Science and Technology to justify our monetisation of nature? The IVF uses sperms and ova and uterus (womb) from nature without paying for them. Why should it charge for the procedure? The Public should pay for the cost of equipment and Staff. The individuals concerned in the process should not charge fees. Charging fees the parents the impression of buying the child as a slave. It is a form of slave deal. Parents should feel happy and thank nature for giving them children at last without feeling some financial strain.

Communal control of the air breathe, the water that we drink and free choice of the food that we eat is more aligned to nature than privatisation of these items in the open free market. This is eroding the power of nature. It would be genuine if the process completely excluded the power and the force of nature. No rather what we had succeeded in doing had been to use our powerful optical equipment to take out body cell, use powerful pipettes in extracting its contents, take out natural female ovum and pipette out its contents to inoculate them into empty shell of somatic cell from the body or we just inoculate the contents of the somatic cell into empty ovum cell shell. We also use cells and DNAs of various organisms to cheat and corrupt other organisms to produce things different from themselves and their progenies.

On the surface, these are great achievements. But do we have to con and challenge nature this way to justify our Scientific and Technological prudence? Why are we fast changing natural ways of production into consumer materialistic way of monetisation and human control? Life has been here for several million years. Science and Technology have improved life on earth. They had equally damaged much of the earth. The destruction we had inflicted on earth's vegetation, ecology and water reserves is yet to be repaired. Can we use the resources we are now using to mimic nature inaccurately in the name of Science and Technology to re-forestate the earth to rescue fast dwindling drinking water reserves on earth? Is it safe to privatise water into private companies that pollute the same and turn round to sell bottled water to us in the name of safe portable water? Where are we heading for in capitalism and consumer materialistic world? Capitalism and the Market seem to be seeking means of privatising natural means of breeding and production and charging money for them. This form of Research and discovery should be public funded. The services they offer should be free; the Public should fund any expences involved if they accept this human intervention in natural free events in reproduction. The argument remains that the sperm, the ovum and the female womb involved are natural creator's property and not those of the genetic engineering interventionists.

It is not out of place to describe what gene Technology and genetic manipulation skills had succeeded to do so far. They just intervene at certain points of natural processes of reproduction in nature vitally essential for continuity of life on earth to achieve their objectives. They rely heavily on nature that they are attempting to correct its flaws. They need the female womb, (uterus) to grow their test tube babies. They need human bodies to pursue their trade. Yes we have successfully broken the gene and now the gene sequences are at our finger tips but we are yet to understand the bondings and helices that transform lifeless molecules into living organisms. This is nature's key to life. The more we achieve in Science and Technology the more perplexed we become over God and nature. The less we know about the true nature of the creation. The big bang created the particles and the atoms but who created them. The more the scientists deep into these matters the more complex they become. Nature is, however, kind in one thing. He always allows the curious mind access to some simple ideas. As surgeons we use our skills to do very complex operations. Nature heals the wounds and trauma we inflict on the patients. We get the credit. Yet it is nature that heals the wounds we leave behind.

Natural creation is spontaneous but Science and Technology are manipulative subject to human errors too. Natural processes are self-duplicating that had sustained the earth for millions of years. We are mortal human beings but nature is continuous. It will be here when we all are gone. We lack the continuity of nature. We may even finally unfold more secrets of nature in Science and Technology but we just do not know what nature plans for the world including our very existence here on earth. The question then knocks on the door. Are we directing Science and Technology in the right way to unfold more of nature to make life easy for man on earth without rivalling and competing with nature to take over from God? Science and Technology are yet to unraffle the mystery of nature and God. Is this not a subtle attempt to bring reproduction and nature under the free market of consumer materialism and monetary control?

We cannot deny that Science and Technology had improved lives on earth immensely. We cannot also deny that the advantages of Science and Technology had created fifty per cent of the problems confronting us on earth, today. Therefore we are that point when fifty per cent of our energy and resources should be devoted to further advances in Science and Technology while the remaining fifty should be invested in repairs of damages they had inflicted on earth and the environment. It is wonderful the rate we can cover space on earth through Science and Technology. They had improved our quality of life beyond belief and recognition. At the same time they damaged our environment and natural ecology to a point to cause us great anxiety. Science and Technology still have a lot to learn from nature. All Scientists should now learn the immediate and long term effect each discovery and invention have on nature and ecology. The euphoria and hilarity of eureka should not dampen their search for the safety of the new discovery and inventions.

Science and Technology are very rational concepts in human development in fabricating new tools. It is rational concept in Education and apprenticeship. AAAD is at the cross road where Africa without widespread appropriate and intensive Education and good skills for its development continuously lags behind the vast progressive Education and efficient and effective skills in Science and Technology that had been made in the West, Europe and parts of Asia. The very rapid way of developing Very high quality education among all global black people to make our youths appreciate and use our rich natural resources to unfold the complex processes of nature through Science and Technology is beckoning to us. Africa needs intensive Education, Mathematics, Science, Modern Engineering Skills, Technology and a lot more skills to evolve citizens who will work for their living and development. We need these at the time the results of massive progress in information Technology can be deployed to prolific effect in teaching and supporting teaching. We can learn a lot from the mistakes of past Scientific and Technological researches. The black people have tremendous energy reserve they are unaware of. We need a body as the AAAD to awaken this latent dormant energy in black people for a better cause. Part of this energy is wasted in crimes and destructive activities damaging to our interest. Corruption sells us and our secret decisions to complete strangers daily. The wild bush wars kill our youths, destroy our very modest properties, reduce our population and make us poorer as long as they last.

Consumer-materialism is slowly eroding the credibility of Science and Technology. Monetarism seems to be scarring quality researches. Wrong products are rushed to the market to damage people and the environment. Publications are fast becoming eroded by plagiarism. Ideas had been lifted from literature to literature until pieces of information with doubtful veracity and authority stay at the fringes of the truth. These are the floaters of the truth in research in Science and Technology. They are fast blurring the demarcation between the mathematical concept of Science and the debates and logic of Arts. We have to be cautious that we do not allow Science and Technology to fall victim to capitalist consumer-materialism and monetarism and the free market. This is a danger to liberal Education. It is risky to use artificial means of Science and Technology to commercialise natural means of production and reproduction to sell it for money.

Rushing to the press with raw and unchecked information damages the credibility of Science. Recent scare of gastrointestinal complications and autism of mumps measles and rubella vaccine, (MMR) was an example of the consumer-materialism and monetarism pressure on research. It took research out into political debate. It appears non-scientists and even scientists are lying in the name of Science. This has eroded the credibility of Science. We are gradually getting to know that scientific theories are observations of facts but not statements of truth. Facts are frequently subjected to the scrutiny of probing for the truth. They can be modified in accordance with the revelations of further facts. This is Science. Research like Munchausen by Proxy degrades Science. Controversial Epidemiological Statistics masquerading as Scientific Research adding further stress to mothers in distress and sorrows for losing their precious children should be avoided. They are Pseudoscience. Statistical Computer Model research is dangerous for Biological and Medical Research. Old fashion very large real human population collection before Computer statistical analysis is still very important these aspects of research. Publications should first go to Specialist scientific journals for thorough scrutiny before reaching the media.

We do not say that capitalist consumer-materialism is bad. We do not condemn it as being bad. The free market is not a bad thing. Our observation is that excess of anything is bad. Obsession with anything is bad. Variety is the spice of life. Diversity is not deviation from the truth. Communist socialism we now know was not human disaster but the tragedy was the failure of the people who managed it to recognise variety and diversity in human behaviours and ways of life. Consumer-materialism, monetarism and the free market are fast becoming victims of militant fanatics who are out as suicide squad soldiers ready to defend their beliefs and ways of life without showing any respect to religious sensibilities and ways of life of other people. The creator made the world beautiful by use of varieties and diversity as a good artist uses colours to blend the beauty of his drawing and painting. We must tolerate differences in religion and culture. We have no right to force people to abandon their faith to accept our own faiths, religious laws that cannot define modern world of Science, IT and high Technology. Imposition of religious laws in any form is forced conversion and violation of the right of man (human rights).

Uniformity is a disaster in Economic planning. What is good in one place may not be good in other places. We must acknowledge the sensibility of religious beliefs and ways of life of other people. We may have the military might, power and wealth to take over any place we want but we must always recognise that people own those places. People live in those places. The poor man's hut is as important as the palace to the princes and the princesses. There is king because he has subjects to take care of. The existence of one depends on that of the others. We have not exhausted all the arguments but the argument is strong that we should be tolerant of each other. Intractable warfare, violence and senseless destruction of lives and properties are not compatible with heroism as we know it, today. People living in the past must recognise the dawn of day and the changes in times and ages. Let us invest our resources for war and violence in the cause of peace. We can still be great nations without fighting wars. The argument of fighting wars to bring about peace no longer holds the truth except for people of violence and crimes. This book has been long in writing and publishing. The recent address in Ghana of President Barack Obama was totally in consonance with its concept about Africa and global black people. It is time for them to choose what they have to do to escape from poverty. Surprisingly the Nobel Prize winner for Economics this year equally has been working on the theme of this book. I am not an Economist. Common sense teaches me that the Community that works, consumes and its livelihood depends on what private business, corporations and the capitalist free market do can trump all of them. I have proposed the concept of community appointed housekeepers in all businesses and in the governance of all nations. I have equally proposed the concept of double auditing to avoid one taking advantage of the other to corrupt the system.

The housekeepers should be on fixed salaries to avoid bonus culture. In the corporations they should play the role of advisers, In the Government they should replace the politicians in taking charge of the treasury and handling Public funds. They should approve funds for Government programmes But must tell the Government of funds in the coffer. They must resist excessive budget deficit and over bloated national debts. Their duty is to guide the Government in spending moderation to avoid saddling the people bloated over spending. They are not Government. They are the community housekeepers of their money to sponsor the programmes of Government in power. The politicians come and go but these Community housekeepers stay as an arm of the civil service. In the corrupt third world they can report the G20, the IMF and World Bank.

Any attempt by the military to interfere with politics and Government should empower them to freeze national funds and transfer the assets to IMF and World Bank. The G20 should look into a statute like this to discourage frequent destabilisation of the third world flimsy Economy. This is legitimate as these upheavals call on the affluent world to take over looking over their civilian victims through charitable organisation like UNHCR and the NGOs.

Economic prudence, avoidance of corruption, profligacy and wastage in grandeurs and recognising priorities are the backbone of good economic management. Command economy ignores varieties and diversity. The guidelines of World Bank, IMF and WTO are all elements of command economy in monetarist consumer-materialism, open and free market. This is why most of them had failed to work. Privatisation again is central command economy. It fails to recognise the collapse and failures of several private businesses. This can bring the economy to its heels. Mixed economy is not out of place. Economic prudence and good management are the key to success of any Economy but not dogmas. The West fails to tell the world the whole truth. The massive subsidies they offer to their businesses are the life-line of public funds to keep them afloat. The subsidies actually make these businesses public and privatised only in name.

Unfortunately the European white people and the West have made wedging wars for loots into a lucrative business. For over three thousand years now they had been wedging wars initially among themselves and now against the whole world. They use any new inventions to find their killing potentials and values at war first before commissioning them for civil and commercial use. They test them first for military use before adopting them for civil and commercial use. They had tested everything on earth for military use and killing potentials. They had developed microbial and chemical warfare into lethal weapons of war. They had used physical forces to kill. They are ever increasing the potentials of their weapons of mass destruction while threatening the people they plunder and loot their wealth not to develop means to protect their lands and themselves. What are the Western objectives in these issues? It seems their desire is not the prevention of the spread of these weapons of mass destruction but gaining absolute monopoly of these weapons. We essentially have to ask the hawks in the West who are the likely targets of their WMDs? What is worrying is the fact that the white people because of the background of extreme suffering and poverty they came from and used gun powder to intimidate the whole world to plunder their wealth and steal from them are always anxious to maintain that past global supremacy. In Africa I always say, the greedy white people stole from the living and from the dead. Stealing from the dead was massive tomb robbery. They stole live human beings and corpses, the mummies. They also specialised in brutalities and lying efficiently and absolutely. They are efficient lying machines. This has been grafted into their culture. They called it initially as inaccuracies, later "being economical with the truth. Now it is called spin.

Today, the arrogance of the new rich and powerful in the West is gradually making them unable to acknowledge and accept change. It is a credit to the whites that they had released change to life beyond their control. It is now a real challenge to the whites to make up their mind over change. Change is inevitable in evolution. Any living thing that failed to change and adapt became obsolete. It suffered from disaster and extinction. The type of change I am advocating is simple. It is the change that exists between a child and the parents. When I was an infant my parents treated me as such. When I grew up and became a man I observed a total change in the relationship between me and parents. They became my loving friends. Issues were discussed on the basis mature adults and friendship. The West must stop name calling and using derogatory terms to describe Africa: underdeveloped world, developing world and now third world. What is the difference between Malaysia and Africa? Nigerians accepted independence as a long national holiday and opportunity for mediocrity. Chinua Achebe's "Things fall apart and the centre cannot hold" and "This is our chance" are all in place in the Nigerian situation.

Dr Mahathias is well-educated leader and Nigeria had the misfortune of having illiterate and rogue ignorant leaders each doing his best to empty the treasury to launder in Banks abroad. They are neither respectable nor acceptable. Most of them were criminal old colonial soldiers. They had indulgence in conducting coups and overthrowing governments to rule by tyranny and open anarchy.

They destabilise the governments. Today Nigeria is under social disorder and anarchy. Corruption has replaced law and order. The rule of law has gone to the dogs. The leaders are corrupt and law-breakers. Nigeria had been unfortunate to be leaderless from the onset while its assumed leaders did their own things. The leaders are wholly ignorant. They cannot differentiate religion and ethnicity from politics. This has caused a great deal of confusion. This is mainly a feature of the Bantu people in Africa. The Africans should now know that they gain more from unity than from division and individualism. Ethnic and religious tolerance is very important for progress. Africans must accept that not all religious and ethnic groups would have equivalent talents at all times. The talents are national assets regardless of their origin. The nation should use them according to their merits. The rest must accept leadership from the talents and distinguished fellow citizens. Nothing should hinder our loyalty and pride in our nation and its able leaders. We must love and trust our fellow citizens regardless of their ethnicity and religious inclination; we must not pick and choose who should be an African and who should lead us as long as he or she is fit and able.

It is equally curious to ask the West their real intention of having this absolute monopoly of WMD? Do they not think that this is bullying and intimidating the whole world with threats of war? Can the world accept to crouch to a corner at the thunder of Western white European WMD? May I suggest that the international atomic agency must be matched against the international agency against exploitation, corruption, plunder and looting of foreign lands to protect the third world from exploitation by the West that lives by exploitation of the third world in the name of trade and commerce? This will enhance the credibility of the West in support for peace.

The insistence of the West on prevention of weapons of mass destruction in the hands of people the US disapproves of while keeping them and allowing them in the hands of their friends is dangerous and very suspicious and has sinister motives. It is a major threat to world peace. This has to be sorted out. The world cannot be safe and secure with WMD in the hands of the West and their friends. It is a very dangerous world out there. Silence over this is mischievous and dangerous to global peace. The West has right to pick up any issues to justify its war. The world cannot remain spineless cowing away from bullying from a few people from the Western right hawk philosophy and vision of the world and Western way of life and its influence. We have to make it clear that freedom must be free from suspicion of hidden ambitions, domination, and abuse.

Genetic engineering had enhanced their microbial warfare potentials. The West has to explain the regular appearances of strange microbial disease pandemics. They must tell the world that these are not from their genetic manipulation microbial warfare laboratories. The truth commission in South Africa alluded to the existence of such facilities in the West. They were investigating for killer bug that would kill black people while sparing the white. This has increased my anxiety over the devastation of AIDS-HIV in Africa. The world was silent because the powerful West suppressed that information. The curious way Apartheid South Africa developed nuclear bombs and kept them until the end of Apartheid is still a mystery. The West developed the nuclear and hydrogen bombs. They dropped nuclear bombs on Hiroshima and Nagasaki in Japan.

They have stacks of these lethal weapons and have no qualms in dropping them on people who challenge their world domination. The Jews are our distant cousins but it is hard to imagine that Israel has nuclear programme and weapons while the Arabs should never. I equally deplore these weapons in the hands of loony dictators. Use of nuclear weapons in war is genocide and crimes against humanity. But what right have the Anglo-American right ultra conservatives to keep these weapons while others do not? They have no qualms lobbing these weapons on any of their opponents. Today, they fool a lot of us that they had to drop them on the Japanese to save their lives but not those of the Japanese. Today they can still drop them on others without the means to retaliate. Their behaviours in Iraq have taught us that the leopard does not change its skin.

I believe in the rule of just law and law and order to guide human activities on earth. The best thing that the new world order can do to avoid war and violence is to make just laws binding on all, great and small, rich and poor to control not only the possession but also the use of weapons of mass destruction, WMD. This will form the basis of punitive measures against anybody violating these laws. It is no use exploiting lopsided conventions to chase potential enemies of the West and their allies. True justice is not on the side of this type of execution of justice. This is not charade against the Anglo-American power axis or the West. It is the observation of wisdom for the world I may soon not be around to play any part in its events. May God give people the courage and wisdom to support the cause of justice in the world?

Aggression is the way of life of the West. Events and places are named after wars and battles that took place. Times are fixed by wars that took place. What does the West think about wars? Do they think that they have a licence to go out and kill others? Do they think that those they kill do not value their lives as much as they do with theirs? This world has right to prepare for a third world war. The world does not hate the West. America and Britain have no licence to go about rampaging innocent people in the world and littering carnage and destruction along their paths. Enough is enough. We who share this world with them have no choice but to prepare for war and be ready to fight and die until the Anglo-American war machine and terror are destroyed to set human beings on earth free from the threat from this monster. They had taken on the world for too long without effective collective response from the world. Let religious or regional loyalty or economic interest not condemn the whole world to slavery under Anglo-American economic and military machine. No right minded and sane person advocates for war and violence but if we cannot escape from war and violence forced on us we have no alternative but to stand and fight until the enemy recognises that nobody has the magic wand of death by war and violence to offer to others. We have two things in common life and death. Over these two we have no victory.

They love their freedom. We love our freedom. If they compel us to fight for our freedom we have no choice but to do so. This time the whole world must make sure that we use our total number and resources to crush the threat of Anglo-American war machine of relentless aggression for over three millenniums. This war machine must be brought to rest by one way or the other. I am not an enemy of the Anglo-American way of life but they have right to recognise that the rest of the world also have a way of life and interest different from theirs in this world we share with them. The Iraq incident is an eye opener. Their policy in the Middle East is deplorable. They create the tyrants and use them as a pretext to execute their aggression and obnoxious policy in the region. They had taken the world for granted for over three thousand years. The arrogance of Anglo-American right establishment in over-ruling the whole world to go into war on total false pretences is a clear signal that they are ready to take on the world. They treat the world with spite. It is strange that the UN and the Security Council are now called upon to pick up the pieces.

The world has no choice but to rise up in unison to stop the menace of this Anglo-American aggression claimed to be a continuation of the Roman Empire in our time. They are doing it by cunning and Machiavellian principle. It is foolhardy to attack innocent Anglo-American citizens in their homelands but it is unacceptable for their leaders to rush out as a swarm of bees to attack and slaughter harmless citizens of a poor and defenceless country claiming to be fighting terrorists and bringing democracy to the people. Poverty, hunger and starvation are enough burdens for these desperate people. War is the last straw for them to endure especially when the same Anglo-American power axis created the tyrants they are now chasing. Their war and violence is a double edged sword. They went into Iraq and Afghanistan to scatter the people. A few of the people that could afford to flee to the West had been continuously refused refugee status and entry into the West. Where do they want these people to go as they had invaded and occupied their homeland?

It is a challenge to the whole world and humanity. This is subversion of the whole world and the human race on earth. If they expect the world to treat them kindly with respect and dignity they have to treat the rest in this world with respect and dignity. So far they have not done so. I always say the blood of people slaughtered by them constitutes another and new ocean in this world. The world can no longer hide away from this naked and unprovoked persistent aggression and unruly Anglo-American culture. We have to put our progress and development on hold and confront this monster terrorising the world. We must give Anglo-American warlords ultimatum to stop its victory march and aggression. They have to settle their conflicts with their clients by negotiations and peace talk.

The smash and grab war machine must be halted and crushed. This is not a call to arms or support for the so called enemies of the Anglo-American interest. But that interest must not trample upon the freedom and right to life of majority in the world.

We ask the world for equality of opportunity to compete fairly in purpose-orientated Education and problem-solving and focused skills training targeted to solve our enormous problems left behind by white slave trade, slavery, human and drug trafficking and brutal colonisation, plundering and looting of Africa. We have been made scapegoats of Western corruption and crimes because of our abject poverty and deprivation made into catastrophe by covert bush wars for the West to sell their merchandise of death, arms in exchange for our rich mineral and natural resources. Unfair trading conditions had damaged Africa and made our lives into hell. The Western UN Quangos, the IMF, World Bank and the WTO had blighted the world Economy. Their unfair trade, corruption, crimes and trade malpractices have damaged world trade and impoverished the nations. They have a life to live in this world and we equally have a life to live too. There is one thing both the Western colonisers and their victims have in common. The lawless Western behaviours had damaged both their victims and the West. The West has the resources to fight lawlessness but Africa just has no resources to combat societal lawlessness. The West should now use its UN quangos to fight global lawlessness. There must be stiff penalties and permanent sanctions against law breakers. Parental control and influence over their children must be restored. Youth discipline must be maintained. People just feel they can do anything and get away including murders. The society must fight back and regain power and authority over people in it. Nobody should be above the rule of law in the community. The heavy hand of law must descend on all law breakers regardless of their social status in the community.

We must base our development on applied practical and problem-solving education and focused targeted skills training capable of yielding essential manpower for us to compete favourably with other people. Every African and black child should be able to solve his or her environmental problems by use of scientific and

Technological knowledge and skills to earn a decent living from his or her place of birth. Our dignity of labour should fashion modern tools for work. We must embrace the responsibility of being on this earth. If we have to fight for our lives we should fight and die like men? The West talks a lot about the way the Greeks and Romans wrested leadership of this world from the East and Africa. We must retrieve leadership and control of our lives, homelands and wealth from all aliens. Co-operation must not be equivalent to subjugation. Freedom is sweet. I welcome all lovers of genuine freedom for equality of opportunities for fair competition and hard work to join me to place Africa once again on the world map. It is no use advocating improvement, development and progress in Africa while rejecting equality of opportunities for solid and sound education and skills training for Africans. We do not need handouts of food and drug parcels. We want education and skills to produce them for ourselves. The African Bantus must wake up and join the rest in the world to work very hard in learning and physical labour to provide for their families and homelands. Engaging in endless bush wars and relying on handouts from Western NGOs to feed their population, the African Bantus neither do justice to themselves nor the Western NGOs. They are menacing and molesting the West. The warlords must take their fighters out of the trenches and out of the bushes and return to farm to cultivate the land. The warlords must be tried at The Hague for crimes against humanity. The West seems to feel that this is African problem. There is no such thing as African problem; it is global problem. The world must confront it with all sincerity. Anarchy and lawlessness are global problem today. The world has to tackle it with all vigour. The UN, EU and AU must set up a commission for re-integration of dismembered Africa. The Berlin Conference 15th Sept, 1884 consulted no African Bantus or held referendum to dismember Africa in the scramble for Africa. Therefore, there is no need for a referendum to re-integrate Africa. Any funds should be given to the new countries from re-integration for a kick start. The secular constitutions for the new countries must be brief and clear. It must separate the exchequer from the control of the politicians. The national financial management board (NFMB), top financial specialists appointed by the civil service takes charge of the finances. It finances statutory approved variable projects of government and government Departments: Health, Education, Security, (Police and Army), Works, Constructions, and Agriculture etc. Government auditors supervise the NFMB and NFMB auditors supervise each government Department. Government Inspectors examine the projects to guarantee high standards and completion.

AFRICA:

It is speculated that life started in Africa three to four million years ago around today's Ethiopia. The spread of human beings around the world had been investigated with Archaeological Palaeontology and Genetics. It is, however, sensible to speculate that the various forms of Homo erectus might have first spread around Africa. They might have metamorphosed into perfect homo hominis before crossing into Eurasia and other lands because of massive body of water and the cold climate. On the other hand there might have been a form of Homo erectus that was able to exist in water as well as on land. The most recent Chinese discovery of metamorphosing flying animal might have been a form that could cross the oceans to cover the world. On the other hand their world might have been completely different from ours. The land mass might have been the same before different ice ages divided it into the continents and the Oceans, The animal and rain forest in South America and Africa are similar. Of course, this is mere speculation. Maybe one day Genetic studies and accurate carbon dating can provide some clues.

We are good competitors. We can take on the best in the world and win. We have so far failed to take on modern Education in Science, Technology and focused, problem-solving and targeted skills training to equip our youths with knowledge and skills to take them along life with means to use the rich resources of our land to earn decent lives. We can compete and win in the Education, Science, Technology and useful and applicable skills training arena. We must develop the culture of patient investigation and search for solution and answer to our problems. Good discipline and efficient management of resources are the key to success in these fields. Endurance of disappointment, failures, and being patient until satisfactory results are obtained are good attributes of a good Scientist and researcher. We have to work patiently for good and satisfactory results. Today's Africans all want all results in their life time. They do not invest for posterity. There must be a generation of Africans that would be ready to make all the sacrifices to work and invest for the future and posterity. It is such investment that will take Africa out of the slums and ghettos. No matter what the West may say about Mao Tsedung he took China along the path of progress even with the mistakes he made. He created the basis for Progress. He is the father of Modern China. Yes people will die when any nation or people embark on progress. Transcontinental road and railway network building in Africa would take a few lives in the Sahara Desert and rough African terrains. There is nothing without a price and sacrifice. But that is not a deterrent to human progress. The same goes for industrialisation. Yet it is stupid to cross legs and sit for manna to come from heaven. It would not happen.

He must have the eye and ability to detect the answer and solution when he has them. Archimedes, the Syracusan genius a Sicilian and Scientist had African masters. The Romans beheaded him because of his loyalty to his African masters and native Syracuse. He stood shoulder to shoulder with Africans and used his Scientific and engineering ingenuity to fight off Roman Western European endemic unprovoked and naked aggression for power and world domination. Ever since the Western aggression against the rest of the world had continued unabated to feed their lavish lifestyles with filthy lucre of loots from their victims. The West is very conscious of their freedom and way of life. We wish they would recognise that others also have interests and ways of life. They have used destabilising naked aggression, violence and unprovoked wars to pillage, plunder and loot the world. They talk of civilised standards. What civilisation is there in this type of conduct and behaviour? The conduct of persistent military campaigns has no justification for security. Using intrigues and intimidation to establish foreign military bases is unacceptable occupation of foreign lands. Forming defence cordon around friendly autocratic rulers is hostility.

There has been a lot of talking about winning the race to lead the world and stay at the front. Europe stands to be and applauded for doing and achieving this. It has consolidated this as the reign of terror and domination of the world by aggression and conquest. It wrested the power from the East. Cyrus of Persia, and his descendants, Xerxes and Darius had wrested power from African leaders because of indolence, disunity and lack of vision of the future, self-esteem and patriotism for our land, mother Africa. In Egypt Cyrus had taken control of the African continent and the march of African civilisation. The awe and respectability of Africa in the world arena was no more. Complacency in matters of unity, consciousness in the defence of their homeland from alien invaders and lack of cohesion and strategy to merge together and co-ordinate popular efforts at warding off enemy offensive still plagues and paralyses Africa, today. The black men are always ready to fight and die as slaves of the very people who seize their lands and colonise them. They are always ready to fight and die in other people's wars even if they are fought to their disadvantage. They have been doing the nastiest things of the European wars of conquest. When they are not fighting for causes unknown to them they turn against each other in fratricidal bush wars. They pledge African rich mineral resources on the cheap, in exchange for European armament. This continues to worry the world about majority of indigenous people living on the African continent if they have the knack to think for themselves. Why can't they concentrate on developing their land? Why are they globe-trotting to see things in other lands and return to their desolate land without taking any steps to improve it? They must be lacking capability to develop the land. Gen Montgomery suggested that the South African Boers and Europeans should eradicate the savages as he called them by genocide and let Europeans with capability to develop the land take over. He was an Irish not highly rated in the European circles then. Yet I do not blame him for the suggestion. The black people are always ready to attend the feast but they are not capable to stage one for others. It is time they get their acts together in their interest. In the global world none can sit and cross his legs expecting help from others. Recent financial meltdown was an eye opener for those who cared to notice that it affected all parts of the world. Everybody had to devise means to rebuild the Economy. Did Africa see it? What is Africa doing to seize this opportunity to escape from poverty? Rather some African leaders were so stupid and thoughtlessly came London to ask for alms; yet Britain is one of the worse affected countries. Can these leaders plan a strategy to deal with global emergency such as this? It is in their interest they do. Europe is not their brains; their brains are in their skulls.

The Persians went on the world rampage and gobbled up the city states and municipalities of Greece. They took on Europe contesting with the Greeks and gambled away the freedom of our continent in lavish and reckless lifestyles. Their autocratic rule was in complete contrast to the Greek liberal views and freedom. The Greeks fought back. Unfortunately, today, the autocratic and cruel rule of the Anglo-American establishment is irritating the world into violence they describe as terrorism. The terrorism of Anglo-American rule is igniting the fuse of violence that will finally lead to conflagration and incineration of our world. Restriction of weapons of mass destruction is not the answer. The answer lies in the curtailing of Anglo-American ambition to take the world by storm. The Anglo-American establishment must stop exploiting poverty, misery, ignorance and religion to their advantage by using them to create tyrannical rulers and dictators. Someone told the Anglo-American alliance sometime ago that their action was the recruiting sergeant for Al-Qaida and Taliban but it is difficult to prove if they took this seriously. There were neither terrorists nor rampant plots to blow up things and places until they invaded Iraq and Afghanistan. If there were few incidents, they were containable but now it is burning like wild fire sprayed with petrol or gasoline. Where are we heading for, another global conflagration?

The Greeks that used to treat Africa with respect and most of their scholars studied at the feet of African masters suddenly found Africa vulnerable and as people without courage to defend their freedom and not revered intellectual giants they used to know. The Persian profligacy and exorbitantly expensive lifestyles and heavy taxation and levies made the Greeks restless. These habits forced the Greeks to harness their efforts to resist and expel the Persians from their homeland to regain their freedom. The Athenians and the Spartans fought back the Persians to regain their freedom and liberal ideas. Africans remain disunited and submissive. They failed to unite and fight off alien invasion. This was self destruction. Alien invasion should always call for united offensive and defence. Individual and group differences exploited by alien enemies should never sacrifice your land. The Africans must know that individual or group differences have no place in national emergency, war or foreign invasion of our land. No foreigner has the same value for your land as you, the indigenous groups on that land. Any intruder comes to subjugate you and take your land. The foreign invaders always use false Machiavellian friendship to divide and rule.

Unfortunately little do they know that the Greeks learnt their liberal views from their African masters? They adopted Democracy from Carthage in Africa. It was Aristotle that offered his observations of the practices in government that he saw in several city states of the time including those in Sparta and Carthage in Africa. He recommended the practice in Carthage in Africa. This was popular consultation of the population by leaders over difficult decisions. They took the contributions the population made to modify their final decision in the Assembly of leaders. The Committee of hundred was the equivalent of the Senate in Carthage. The actual number was one hundred and two. The Priest and his attendant were the extra two. They were not members and had no votes.

The Western classical historians did not know why it was called "committee of hundred when it was actually one hundred and two members. As an African I do not find this difficult. The extra two people were the Priest and his attendant. They were not official members but religious people to bless the sessions and attend to the needs of the members. They also attended to both spiritual and health needs of the members. There is something beautiful about the Greeks. They love the growth of knowledge in Africa and went all the way out to acquire it for Greece. They promptly took on board the idea Aristotle sold to them and adopted it. They christened their newly adopted idea as "Demos Cras". This had since become the European Greek "Democracy".

Unfortunately, the Europeans had grown confident over the years. They fail to give Africa credit for what they take from our continent. Historians like Herodotus though father of lies and Greek and Roman propaganda from time to time gave accurate analysis of information and history of events. This has become the European Greek democracy sponsored by Greek love of freedom and liberal views. African dimension is never mentioned. Unfortunately the Anglo-American colonising and smash and grab culture and tendency have watered down Democracy to suit their tantrums and corrupt society. The writings of Carthaginian Admirals like Himilco or Hanno recorded by ancient historians like Herodotus and others did not see it or reported on it in their extensive seafaring and travels. Rather they gave the opposite stories. They had no boats that could cross the Atlantic in the ancient times. It is extremely doubtful if they ever visited any place beyond Europe. On the other hand the Africans went several places. They left their foot print by the black people they left behind. The African maritime explorers always left some people behind in places they visited to organise trade. The Native Americans were extremely hostile to visitors. The Anglo-Americans succeeded with gunpowder and powerful guns and a culture ready to tolerate genocide. African religious culture in the ancient times would strongly frown at genocide. We never used wars to destroy stock but just to suppress revolt. Our respect for human life is enduring and emotional attachment to ethnic group existence is inclusive and never exclusive nor as to rule out our sympathy for their surviving war. Our Philosophy of war accepts our opponents as people with grievances they are ready to fight against. We fight wars as supreme sacrifice and our opponents are equally making supreme sacrifice. They have reason to go to war.

I love to substantiate my wild claims in African classical History with proven incidents that people tend to ignore. The story of the lost civilisation in the lost land of Atlantis is very well known. It is a popular myth in ancient Greek stories. Plato wrote on this elaborately. Socrates taught Plato. The Greeks executed Socrates for teaching strange ideas and corrupting their social thinking. Socrates had some influence from Sola who had contact with Egyptian seat of learning. Sola heard the story of Atlantis from the Priest in Egypt. The Egyptian School taught that Atlantis was beyond the Pillars of Hercules (about the Straits of Gibraltar). The Greeks picked this myth from Africa. Plato wrote extensively on the Atlantis. The concept spread all over Europe. It waxed and waned with all generations. The miracle of pyramids and embalmment in South America still remains a myth. I strongly suggest that ancient Egyptian maritime power crossed the Atlantic to America. The Archaeological artefacts are scattered everywhere. The Anglo-Americans are desperate to locate the Vikings in the Americas. It is the day dream of neo-power to create European equivalent of Egypt. This generation of Europeans had acquired a lot by military conquest and scientific inventiveness. They just do not have a glorious past equivalent to Egypt.

Writing similar to that of Egypt was associated with this too. Were they two simultaneous spontaneous developments on the two continents? Was there any hidden link between the two? I hazard a guess that there must have been a hidden link by maritime travel across the Atlantic. Of course such contact was not regular due to the vastness of the Ocean and poor means of making the risky journeys. The emphasis here is the fact that even a popular European concept such as Atlantis originated from Egypt in Africa. The past glory of Africa will return with adequate Education and appropriate skills training and devoted apprenticeship. Orderly and sustainable Education, skills and approved apprenticeship in Trade and Technical Institutions must form the basis of recovery in Africa. Sound Academic and Educational basis must form the basis of Africa rejoining the world. All other routes are unsure channels. They would collapse if not based on sound and excellent Education and skills. Making adequate Education and appropriate skills the foundation of our future development will ensure that we have the means to sustain all future further developments we may undertake to embark on. We will be sure footed.

By the time the Greeks pushed back the autocratic Eastern Persian yoke and rule, Africa was already under Persian tutelage. Defeating the Persians offered Africa on a platter of gold to the Greeks. By the time Alexander, son of Philip of Macedonia attacked and defeated the Persians under Ahasuerus Egypt in Africa became a priced jewel in the Greek crown of his massive victories. I deliberately offer this observation in the classical History of the ancient world over three thousand years ago to inform the world that Europe never seized Africa by conquest in the battlefield. Africa never had any direct military confrontation with Europe. The Carthaginians were content to live and trade in Spain, and Southern Europe. They brought them prosperity and security. But the Romans were equally determined to drive the Carthaginians out of Europe. The Romans were dubious and unreliable. They were equally liars. They fought a number of wars against the Carthaginians, most prominent of which were the three Punic Wars. These were rightly Roman African wars. The Romans used them to halt African influence in the world. The Romans were vindictive, devious and very deceitful. The warrior king family of Carthaginian Generals, Barca, Hamilcar, Hannibal, Hasdrubal, Hanno and Mago fought the Romans like brave lions. They were called brood of African Lions. Hannibal was a very distinguished leader and a brave soldier. He offered the Roman Generals the products of his Military skills and ingenuity.

We had no reason to act as we are not a colonising power by nature. The Carthaginians were in Southern Europe for over five hundred years with headquarters in Catalonia in Spain. Yet it never crossed our mind to colonise that land. We believe in equality of all people and freedom for people to choose their way of life. We were not a colonising power. We did our business peacefully. We never terrorised the people. We never used intrigues and corruption to tear them apart. We never used “impera et divide” (divide and rule) to tear them apart for us to exploit them. We never denied them the opportunity to learn from us. We never made suggestions such as George W Bush recently proposed embargo on nuclear Education. Education, learning and acquiring skills should be free. The limit should be individual ability and not legislative restriction on racial grounds. FREEDOM of learning must be inalienable right of man. But scholars must never go to acquire knowledge and skills to use it to hurt and damage their enemies. Scholars should never target their enemies. No Science, Technology and knowledge should be targeted to war.

It is extremely silly and makes nonsense of Democracy and freedom to learn that some aspects of liberal Education are to be curtailed because of security in the West. I wonder if George W Bush still remembers that the Anglo-American scientists stole this knowledge from the Germans through German European Jewish feud of the Second World War. Does he know that the US dropped this bomb on Japan because Japan did not have one? George W Bush has no right to tell us what knowledge we ought to have. He cannot tell any free and sovereign nation what it should have and not have as long as it has the means. Madame Curie a French citizen actually worked on Uranium and plutonium. George W Bush suggestion actually makes the world curious over the Anglo-American intention in the world? We must have equal opportunity to compete. It is time for the whole world to review its policy towards the flow of knowledge. Anybody or nation with knowledge and skills including the food that we eat, today, must know that all came from a common global pool and not from their patch of stolen land. There is enormous cultural borrowing in the world. The global population is very dynamic.

Even George W Bush would be surprised to know that the global population is continuously mixing ever since human being started to exist on earth. People move from one region on earth to the other while they return from the same region back to where they originally moved from. The Europeans moved to America and transformed it to the US. They attracted other races to the place and created the great melting pot of rainbow nations and cultures.

The best peace of mind the US can give the world of its intention is to allow free flow of knowledge, skills and sound apprenticeship. It is to the benefit of the world and the US as clever people are not restricted to the US and any knowledge is a global asset. We should not regulate the flow of education and knowledge. Rather the world should regulate the use of nuclear weapons in conflicts. Abuse of the weapons to damage and bully others should be forbidden by global laws. Eventually the world should denuclearise by mutual consent. Total destruction of weapons sounds exciting but you cannot eliminate knowledge and skills especially in these days of sophisticated recording skills. Hence, strict regulations are what we want to control the nuclear weapons. I have been taken on a journey round the world and the past because of writing this book to see how the world was at various ages and generations. It has become obvious that the world requires good and stable Economy and good leadership. Spread of sustainable wealth and prosperity and investment in jobs and works, constructions and not destructions and wars would provide funds and resources to develop the world. People spread and expand and start conflicts because they want to acquire some property and wealth for their security. They want better life in imaginary far away places seen in satellite televisions and the internet. The world, today, has a duty to give practical education and skills to every young person and youth to create better life for himself or herself in the homeland. In Africa farming, construction basic manufacture based Economy would sustain the people in jobs until the next century. This would open the continent up for proper trade and business. It would prevent the flood of refugees to the West.

Of course, our age is very advanced in sophisticated Science and high Technology and we are very wealthy. We just have to regulate the distribution of wealth. We must stop Economic crimes;

corruption, fraud and excessive greed and we must reach out to the underprivileged and try to understand the way they feel. We must try to know why they had resorted to religious fanatical extremity. We all are members of Nature the creator's family. Even animals have their families. They look after their young and feed them. The carnivores hunt and catch their kills but they share the space. Even dominant alfa males territorial demarcation groups maintain their marked territories but share the space with other animals. Human beings are just a species of animals regardless of their physical features. We are duty bound to share the earth space. When we rush to eliminate savages and terrorists we finally become terrorists ourselves. Our sophisticated civilisation should make us settle conflicts by talking and resolution. Investments in wars and violence are a waste of resources. They would help human beings to work on the land to improve their plight. The war against ignorance has been ignored but it is what threatens the very existence of Homo sapiens. What we should fear most is fear itself. Fear makes us live in uncertainty and anxiety. This is Psychological illness. Psychological illness has a violent part: war and violence. Those who brand a rational peaceful and polite leader and President as naïve are not only naïve but very ignorant of the world.

They are ignorant of Science in this Scientific Age of Darwinism of Natural Selection. They may be misinterpreting Darwin for he covers the dynamism of evolution. This involves space sharing by genes. The internal body constitution make-up and the Ecology are in equilibrium. Even some sick genes survive in the equilibrium. This is why we have congenital and familial diseases. The space tolerates all types of genes and several genes survive the space. We just have to share the global space and tolerate each other. Recently some youths took to molest a congenitally disabled child and her mother. This led to the mother losing her cool. She burnt the child and herself in a locked vehicle to death. These bullies failed to understand that neither the child nor her mother was responsible for the deformity. The creator selected the faulty gene. This caused birth of a disabled child. People and bullying children should tolerate and help the disabled and disadvantaged people compassionately. There is a place for compassion in the world. It is not cowardice to have some sympathy for the suffering and unfortunate people on earth.

We all must do everything to get nuclear know how. We concede the right to campaign for re-election to George W Bush. Academic knowledge is not the right of loyal citizens. The Jews had contributed a lot to modern scientific knowledge. Can you imagine what the world would miss if someone had succeeded in restricting what they could study and learn? The brightest brain can come from any group of human beings. America has benefited from this more than any other nation in the world. Therefore, it will be a very sad day indeed to restrict students from certain parts of the world from studying certain subjects. It is wrong to deny some students the privilege of studying certain subjects. This proposal is wrong. It will damage the spread of knowledge. It is direct attack on human rights and equality of opportunities. It damaged Africa and the black race in the past. We are still struggling to repair the damage and escape from inequalities. It will damage education and destroy learning. Africa should merge together and unite to control its resources including all its mineral resources. The uranium deposit mining should be banned. We have no means to monitor the safety. Careless mining can cause a lot of illnesses and cancer. Several global scientists rushed to help during Chernovile Nuclear Accident. As clever people are not restricted to one part of the world or one type of people we must make every type of knowledge free; one clever scholar may one day discover safe antidote against nuclear weapons and nuclear toxicity just as one person discovered its existence. Free flow of knowledge and skills is very important for human existence on earth. We must avoid interfering with it.

But we are extremely anxious when George W Bush describes his war as that of civilisation against those he deems uncivilised and primitive. In the past, this concept promoted and justified brutal genocide and crimes against humanity and seizure of the lands in Americas, Australia, New Zealand, slave trade and slavery of African Negroes, brutal colonisation, plunder and looting of the African continent by the white people from the West. This new doctrine of civilisation against uncivilised people causes much of right thinking people in the third world a great deal of anxiety and distress as superior fire power, war and extreme violence seem to be confused with the concept of civilisation and savages. This type of attitude in the leadership is dangerous and irresponsible. It may encourage extremist citizens to embark on the destruction of the inferior and uncivilised enemies of the state. Already some people had been placed on confinement for purpose of state security.

This legalises and justifies the current atrocities as it did in the past in the last millennium with serious consequences for several races of humanity in several regions of the world. In the name of peace, let conflict, war and violence not be made a crash of civilisation against the uncivilised people. This will justify the destruction and elimination the wild and primitive people threatening civilisation. There is civilisation in every human community. Conflict resolution should exploit this quality in all human beings and most living things. They are all civilised in their own ways. There is absolutely nobody out to destroy civilisation in the world, today. Everybody is enjoying the products of Science and Technology. They do not hate them.

The only real military encounter with the Romans was the Punic war. We just hated the smash and grab militaristic culture of the rustic and wild Romans. We love individual freedom and freedom of the ethnic nationalities to pursue their own ways of life and cultures. We are not a colonising power. Today, power of wealth is abused to crush the poor nations and make them poorer than before. This is undemocratic and unjust. Injustice breeds violence and wars. Hence led by Carthage as African flag bearer at the time we fought three wars against the rustic Barbarians from Rome to defend our way of life and those of our European allies in Spain and Gaul. This is a city we originally protected from destruction by the Greeks but times had changed. They were attacking us ferociously. They broke all the international treaties we had with them. The West has not really disarmed and stopped fighting wars ever since the Romans started conventional Army. They had improved on the quality and quantity of conventional standing Army. They had improved on the quality of lethal weapons. They had never stopped fighting. They fight among themselves but now they are taking wars outside their lands to weak third world countries to create a new sort of empire in the guise of advancing democracy. When will the West stop fighting? They always manufacture reasons for fighting; colonial wars were fought against savages. Ideological wars were fought to defend human civilisation and Western way of life and interest. They indulged in spinning, propaganda and lies to justify the wars. The West has cunningly maintained a state of war against some of its components, its neighbours and the whole world; why? Will the West denounce war and pledge to use the world resources it has wasted on wars to mass global development? We should open up the world peacefully. The world should involve itself in mass construction using the resources and funds we use for wars. Yes it is fine to give reason for war and justify its conduct but is war the only way to resolve conflict? How many more thousands would die because of Sept 11 and twin towers damage? Let us stop the slaughter and talk. The Muslims must know that nobody should impose religion or its laws on reluctant people. The only way to peace is religious tolerance. It is time to confine religion to the minds of the believers and faithful.

AFRICA AND THE MIDDLE EAST:

Africa has never believed in militarism, aggression and conquest. We are astute travellers. We are not a colonising power. We travel and live in faraway places among the natives on friendly and equal terms. Yes we fought a few wars in classical History but they were based on the defence of our principles of freedom. We never had a standing Army. Our wars were fought by levies and combatants returned to their families and communities after. Unfortunately Africa is always unlucky to be prone to having fellow Africans as traitors ready to sell our freedom to strangers in exchange for exotic foreign goods of their fancy even when they do not understand their real values. They receive bribes from complete strangers and aliens to betray our homeland to the enemy. They even take on board the promise of power from the colonising foreign invaders who are fighting for the same power they promise to the traitors. Alexander of Macedonia saw the Arabs in Gaza and not in Africa.

Hence they were not in Africa at that time. They started to arabinise Africa about 648 AD. This continued till 698 AD as Muslim Islamic conquest and crusade. There are two events that turned the plight of human beings on earth and changed the global history; the destruction and sacking of Carthage in Africa by Rome in 146 BC and the Arab Islamic conquest of Palestine and North Africa in the seventh century AD. The Arab conquest of North Africa and Palestine is just fourteen hundred years old. It is not several millennial event.

Therefore, the leaders involved in the resolution of Arab Israeli conflict must not fail to observe this in their deliberations.

The Roman chased power but when they collapsed they left a vacuum to be filled with Arab Islamic conquest. The Arab Philosophy is a dangerous cocktail of power politics, fun loving entrepreneurial wealth chasing without any morals, Macho man, religious fanatical extremism, cruelty and ability to hate in the name of Allah. They are exclusive monotheists and intolerant of other faiths and their neighbours. Mixture of socioculture and ignorance in understanding and tolerating other religions had maintained chronic global conflicts and engender hatred among human beings. The Arabs should strive to know their neighbours close to them here on earth that they see and know rather than rely on and kill in the name of their faith. We can make peace with Allah only when we have lived in peace with our fellow human beings. The same advice applies to adherents of other religions and faiths. If you cannot live peacefully with your neighbours that you see and know here on earth, how are you sure that you would fit into the crowd and residents in Paradise?

It was the Quran or the sword. Of course it was a terrible religious deception to seize our land by conflict. It is sad this Arab dirty habit of ethnic cleansing, genocide and conquest and arabinisation of Africa is still continuing in Darfur in Sudan. Right now the Arabs are destroying Darfur by brutal ethnic cleansing and genocide under the nose of the whole world. African Union is still blowing hot air and no action. As an Africa, may I suggest that if the Arab government of Sudan has money for war it should equally have money to feed its displaced citizens? Sudan must be asked to produce money to feed all its displaced citizens. There is no need asking donors for money. A country that has money for ethnic cleansing and genocide should have funds to feed its citizens. Even if kind donors feed these people, they should send the bill to Sudan later. If it fails to settle it the world should impound all its external assets. Islamic conquest of India initially relied on slaughter and slave taking until when it met with stiff resistance that it modified its tactics.

Hence Islam had depended on violence and force for its spread. It is time that Islam should accept the right of man and become religion; chase the human soul and not be confused with politics and Macho culture of hate and cruelty. Secular Laws are compatible with human community. They are amenable to social changes. They are reviewed according to human needs at the time and changes in the community. The Asian Muslims in the UK want changes in the Blasphemy Law but they would not accept change of their concept on Koran and the Prophet. They accepted division of India into India proper and Pakistan but bluntly refused and rejected the division of Palestine into Arab Palestine and Israel. This is immoral and irreligious. It fails to love its neighbours. The Arabs should learn to move along with global changes and forget the painful past, monopolistic monotheistic religion and recognise and accept their neighbours and the world. This and only this will give them peace. RPGs and rockets, wars, violence, suicide bombers and kidnapping and murders will not give them victory and peace. Nevertheless, the behaviour of neo-Israel is atrocious. It lacks the friendly, sharing and welcoming behaviours of David and Solomon. Israel must show sympathy and compassion in their relationship with the Palestinians and Arabs. They are paranoid and emotional towards security and no one would blame them but it is inhuman for them to live in affluence and look down on Arabs and their children in abject poverty in open Prison here on earth. The world must abandon the two state theory and adopt integration and one state to prevent any future conflicts over water and fertile land. Let all the aids and weapons money be used to sink more wells, irrigations and improving living standards for deprived Palestinians and poor Israelis. Let the leaders on both sides speak to their people to bury the hatchet and abandon emotions and embrace the new dispensation and start to look to the future. They should confine the past and all its mistakes to the History books.

Any group causing mass movement of citizens must be held responsible for feeding the displaced citizens. This doctrine is a deterrent to ethnic cleansing and genocide. It is simple if you have money for war you should have money to cater for your citizens displaced by war. How can the Arabs expect our sympathy when we Africans know that they are ruthless and brutal land grabbers? They want Africa to control all world oil reserves. The African Negroes must alert the world of this Arab ambition. Africa is not property of Arab Muslim Islam. The world Muslim Council must note that Africa is too poor to be involved in this religious intrigue. It is brutal to fight brutal ethnic cleansing war under the guise of religion. The Muslims have a duty to separate religion from politics even when that religion is a way of life. Surprisingly the people in Darfur are Muslims but African Negroes the Arabs want to seize their oil bearing land. We are always prepared to accommodate the Arabs but they have to stop their provocation and war. You are an African on this continent or you return to Gaza. It may not be nice to say this but persistent provocation is equally nasty. It is inimical and injurious to good neighbourliness. It is costly business to grab land under the pretext of having religious converts. Arab deceit has been exposed in Darfur.

Our travels took us to spread throughout the Middle East, Palestine, Lebanon where we went for cedar wood and later papyrus reeds for paper. We spread as faraway as Syria. Unfortunately incessant Middle East crises in politics and religion had damaged Africa irreversibly. Most of the business we had done with the Middle East had always been poisoned with damaging macho and autocratic culture of the Middle East rulers. The advent of the Muslim Islamic religion had damaged Africa a great deal. This religion is a mixture of politics and psychological brainwashing. It teaches submission to Allah and his Prophet. Unfortunately the leaders and the mullahs seem to assume the role of Allah and the Prophet. We fought off the Hittites, Turks and defended Africa. Our ancestors were conscious of the price of freedom. It is the sacrifice of our life and blood. We in this generation are castrated in the brain. We think freedom is for the West to offer us. Freedom is the labour and sweat we invest to catch up with others in life competitions. Freedom is the daily conscientious work and labour to improve the living standards of your people. It is neither politics nor victory at war. It is the success of hard work that makes the community prosperous and wealthy. It is freedom from poverty and misery.

They constitute themselves into nanny states and use religion to regiment the communities. They seem to encourage indolence and spread of ignorance in their subjects. They discourage individual freedom. They tend to encourage violence in the name of religion. Unfortunately, Allah does not need people to kill in his name. Allah has power of life and death over all human beings. He does not need an Army of martyrs and suicide bombers. The West seems to adopt the same policy of tolerating religious fanaticism as long as it does not affect its business. Now that religious freedom, zeal and fanaticism are causing massive global upheaval it is time to review this policy. It is affecting Western interest. We deplore the destruction of lives and properties in the name of god. God is a loving Deity. God needs no Army. He does not destroy things.

We deplore the concept of nanny state and nanny world led by the Anglo-American power axis. The current nuclear policy of George W Bush is a declaration of nanny world. His war in Afghanistan and Iraq is action of nanny world masters and overlords. It takes the shine out of Western democracy and free society. Equally we deplore killing innocent people because of frustration with actions of some world leaders. It is wrong to punish the citizenry for the wrongs and mistakes of the leaders. I strongly implore the wise and courageous people in this world to rise up and challenge this bankrupt policy of condemnation of innocent people to death for the actions of their leaders in the world. Nobody should die for the mistakes of the leaders. War is a struggle between life and death and survival of a nation and its citizens. But luxury war of show of power, intimidation and racial arrogance and bullying is self-inflicted injury. Leaders leading their nations into wars of aggression are no better than Adolf Hitler. They deserve the same punishment as Hitler and leaders of the third Reich. The world is guilty to acquiesce to this type of conduct. The world is guilty by acquiescing to war and violence. It is and accomplice to war crimes. Why should the UN be a repository for repairing the damages of these criminal wars?

WHAT SHOULD AFRICA DO TO ESCAPE FROM POVERTY AND LACK OF DEVELOPMENT AND PROGRESS?

Africa has no business to do with aggression and militarism. Today, it is the battle of intellect. We must return to the search for knowledge and modern skills in research in Science and Technology. Education suitable for our culture and environment and skills training fit for production of modern tools for our work are not beyond our reach and means. Violence is no solution to our multiple problems poverty, hunger, starvation and diseases. We must acquire knowledge and skills the way the Greeks acquired it from us. They took it from Africa and spread it in Europe. Problem-solving practical Education is the key and the way out of our current social, political and economic problems. We must acquire the skills and teach our youths how to make modern tools. We must change our concept on money economy, work, culture and habits. Mineral and natural resources are not wealth. The wealth of the nation is the high standard of focused problem-solving Education, knowledge, well-targeted skills and hard work of the citizens.

Japan and Korea are good examples to confirm this observation. They just do not have the resources. They have very high standard of effective Education and skills. In addition Africa must abolish bribery and corruption by death penalty to force people to abandon this nasty habit. All other forms of punishment are not effective deterrent against bribery and corruption. Bribery and corruption had killed more people in Africa than wars and diseases. They cause wars and diseases starvation and hunger. Our rich natural and mineral resources are too attractive to alien predators who would not hesitate to use bribery and corruption to buy their way into them. Weapons and military power are not what we need. Former Soviet Union had more of it but it did sustain it or give it stability. No knowledge should pass us by and no useful skills available should escape us. We must spend longer periods studying. Every child should go through Education and apprenticeship. Our maintenance culture essentially has to improve. We must engage our talents and send our mediocre to the training School to acquire useful skills to work for themselves. Serious work and hard labour engage citizens. They take their minds away from planning evil and mischief. They increase productivity and wealth. They constitute sinews and outlet for getting rid of surplus energy. Hard work makes people think positively and plan their days and future. People must acquire the culture of going about their business without being jealous and envious of those who are successful in what they are doing. The must adopt the team culture and work in teams.

Our friendship with the world out there should be based on exchange of useful knowledge and skills. Ideology and religion should never involve us in dispute or conflict. The West has no right to restrict where we acquire knowledge and skills from. It is harassment and insult to nanny us along this path. It is uninvited interference in our private affairs. Friendship is no excuse for restricting whom we can befriend. It is not marriage. Even marriage does not restrict friendship. Equally we should have no restriction or limit to the knowledge and skills we can afford to acquire. We are in a hurry to catch up in Education, knowledge and skills to produce modern tools. We are mature enough to choose what we need. Western religious indoctrination never prevented us from worshipping the way we like it. As a matter of fact we have successfully got the West to adopt the way we worship; we use musical instruments and songs and dance. We go into a bit of frenzy in worship. Majority of us obstinately refuse to accept same sex co-habitation and tolerance of sexual perversion.

Go into modern aeroplane and see the cockpit and the sophistication of the interior. Compare it to what the Wright brothers constructed in 1902. You would realise that we have been going backwards or we have been sleep walking in Africa. The sophistication of the modern planes is evidence of the rapid advances European and Western Science, Technology and inventiveness. It is not magic but hard work and concentration. Reliance on natural and mineral resources, corruption and crimes had abandoned our people in the hands of viciously gripping poverty, misery and ignorance. This is the tragic catastrophe of Africa. Can we learn? The Western leaders these days do not take kindly to leaders and people who advocate that their people should abandon bad habits that deter their progress. Africa has no choice but to take on the West in healthy competition in the search for knowledge and skills in effective Educational programme designed to solve their problems. Education and effective skills training through adequate apprenticeship for all our youths are the only way we can escape poverty and misery, hunger, starvation and diseases. The nonsense over trade is rubbish. Get the knowledge and skills to produce the goods to sell in the free market. Do not be fooled into the market where you have no goods and services to sell or the money to buy. The free market is a fraud. It is not the solution to African problems. The solution to African problems is the right type of education and skills to make Africans do things for themselves to develop their land. The free market cannot help us. The so-called cash crops are not produce for the free market. They rely on the needs of the consumers who may not replace them with synthetic materials. They may not need them any more or may reduce their consumption to minimal. Cash crops need extensive labour and land but yet their demands and prices are erratic and unreliable. Agriculture and food production are more reliable than cash crops. Cash crops damage the environment. Cash crops are ecologically hostile and economically unreliable.

I can still recall Ronald Reagan still showing early signs and symptoms of Alzheimer's cerebral atrophy abusing Mamuar Khedafi and addressing him as mad Khedafi. Unfortunately I have been abused and blackmailed because I decided to take on racial xenophobic intimidation, victimisation and harassment by mediocre white doctors without genuine knowledge or better skills than mine except flashing their skin colour and rolling their tongues in speaking English their native language. This does not deter me from telling the black race not to be intimidated but to ignore inferiority complex and take on the white in a fair and equal competition in Education. Dirty tricks campaigns should not deter you from demanding equality of opportunity for fair competition in Education and skills. I sincerely believe in equality of opportunity for open competition in Education and useful skills training and satisfactory apprenticeship. I also do believe that the white people have not a lot to offer us because of their attitude towards us. We essentially have to develop our own home made programme to use in our environment in Africa. We equally have to make our own efforts before requesting for help from other people. Anybody willing to help Africa must offer our youths genuine education and sound skills training and patience in acquiring good apprenticeship. Africa must have maintenance culture for regular repairs of their infrastructures and constructions. The youths must learn to work in teams. The Igbos were very prosperous when they worked in teams. Now they seem to take to individualism. They are less successful; they must return to "ka ndi Igbo and nwanyi". It was good team culture but it must learn to make and accommodate friends for survival in a global world.

The West has a duty to pay Africa and the black race reparations for the crimes, cruel and brutal slave trade, slavery and plundering and looting colonisation and brutalities. My reason is that at the abolition of slave trade and slavery the slave owners were paid compensations while the slaves received nothing. The brutal colonisation plundered and looted Africa and dehumanised and impoverished and deprived the global black people of their wealth and skills. The West received damages and war indemnities from Germany for world wars. It received the same from Japan. Korea received damages from Japan. The Western POWs received payments for the work they did as prisoners of war under Japan. What then is wrong why the long suffering Africans and the black race should not receive reparation for the crimes against humanity that the West had committed against them? The plight of Africa and the black race on earth should affect the conscience of white people in the West if they are human beings. The current deep recession has made me retract a bit from this. It is true that the action of the West has damaged the African Bantus extensively. It also damaged the whites. Their criminals place very little value on life. The West has the resources to deal with the social consequences of their actions. Africa has no resources to deal them. To rehabilitate people and deal with the social consequences of the Western action, the West should help black people to restore discipline among their youth. Good education and planning for jobs in their homelands will rescue a disintegrating Africa. Social discipline is important. The Economy must support rebirth of strong families.

We must base our development on applied and practical Education and skills training capable of solving our problems. We do not need food parcels or investments with doubtful values. Education must offer the African child the means of earning independent living. We must have skills to make decent living standards from our land of birth. The African child must know that wealth and prosperity are in our land of birth and not in faraway places. Friendship and co-operation must not be subjugation, humiliation and slavery. We must retrieve our self-esteem. It is shameful to be refugees or asylum seeker economic migrants to clean streets and toilets in faraway lands where we are not wanted. This is not tirade against the West or any religion. We all have right to be here on earth with all the other races of human beings. We have the freedom to plan for our future. We also have the right to define dangers as we see them. Might is not right.

It is not extremist view. It is not fanatical agitation in politics or religion. It is not racial xenophobic hate. It is not incitement to violence or terrorism. It is just ordinary common sense that Africa and the black race should get their acts together and merge together for their common interest to have that critical mass of talented people to run their own affairs as the West has done. They must not compromise on issues of their land. "I was born here" is not a licence to take over the land. The land belongs to everybody in Africa and the black race. We have no right to compromise over this issue. The West has no compromise over this. Africa should not be a soft touch over this vital issue. A person in the West has several places to go to, all over Europe, the Americas, Australia and New Zealand. The black African has nowhere to go. The black person is rejected for his skin colour as economic migrant and criminal. Why then should we give our lands in Zimbabwe, South Africa and Kenya to the white migrants? Where shall we go to? Where shall we live? Is it not unfair that the West should demand this from Africa by bullying Robert Mugabe and destroying Zimbabwean Economy by subversion and economic sabotage? What is democratic and just about this naked aggression and bullying by the West led by Anglo-America?

We must pull our resources together and use them to feed Africans and hungry black people on earth. The white people are driving us to extinction by destabilising us all over the world to have monopoly over our rich resources. This is slow genocide. We have to speak out while we can stem the tide of persistent latent hostilities driving us to extinction while the white leaders proffer to be our friends. What type of friendship is this punctuated by institutional racial xenophobia and latent lethal hostilities? Auschwitz resulted from racial xenophobia and arrogance. Authorities overtly preside over racial hatred by being passive and pretending that they do not know that it exists. The looming hatred may be ignited by stress of war to trigger off Auschwitz and holocaust.

We cannot succeed without burying our difference as the West and Europe had done. Africa has no reason to hate anybody. We have a duty to work to improve our lot in this world. Let all of us, black, white, red, green and blue, of every religious, ideological, economic political and cultural persuasions, who had chosen this land to make it our home, join hands together to make it work for us as the Americans had done in their homeland. We do not have to be emotional and fanatical under the pretext of patriotism. Regardless of the colours of our skins, languages, races, political persuasions and levels of civilisation, having chosen Africa as our home in the year 2004, we are duty bound to owe our loyalty to our homeland, Africa and make it work as people on other continents, Americas, North and South, Europe, Asia and Australasia had done. The mere choice of this continent as our homeland compels all of us to bury our differences and work as a team under genuine rule of law that will not allow the perpetuation of recent alien colonial brutal injustice to persist as in the unfair and uneven land distribution as in Zimbabwe, South Africa and Kenya. The African culture and tradition accepts land as property of the community. Any reforms that snatch land from the community are wholly unacceptable. It is stated that human beings spread from Africa to cover the whole world. Look at Africa; it was all inhabited by black people. Today the Arabs had grabbed the North by conquest in the seventh century AD. The whites from the West are planted in South Africa, Zimbabwe and Kenya. We have no objections to these but these whites have refused to integrate. The Arabs look to Arabs in Arabia and Asia Minor and the whites want to establish small Europe in Africa. Can we all unite and develop Africa as our safe and secure homeland? The colour of our skin is not a permanent distinction from nature; it is the way we breed. If we indulge in cross breeding one colour will finally dominate. Therefore it is foolish to hang unto the colour of our skin.

Equally our culture and traditions do not accept homosexual relationship as natural regardless of how many Africans may be misled to this strange and queer and weird culture. Modernism must not trample upon our core culture. Africa will not go about hunting homosexual people as long as they do not use their lifestyles to molest people and upset the community. It is not the tradition of Africa to concern itself with harmless consenting lifestyles as long it does not become a menace to the society and the community. Attempting to corrupt our sacred religious beliefs on basis of discrimination is subversion of the rule of law in our homeland to cause confusion as grave as slave trade, slavery and brutal colonisation of our continent. We have right to protect ourselves with laws to prevent this sort of confusion. We have right to our way of life that rejects all forms of sexual perversions including homosexual and lesbian lifestyles. They are artificial corrupt lifestyles. They are queer and strange. They are unnatural and affront to natural processes. The homosexual lobby is very powerful and evil bullying. Can the Western leaders and politicians tell us who made laws to make male; man, female; woman to protect them and make them perform different functions in the creation and breeding? There is no such legislative body. Nature created them so and simple method of reproduction will continue to be so even in Science.

Ours is a very religious community. We cannot afford to allow licentious lifestyles of the West to corrupt us. The West is an open Society up to certain limits. It has its own ways of life and interests. It disallows strangers to violate these sacred ways. The West has freedom to follow their queer way of life. They have no right to force us to accept what we disapprove of in lifestyles. This is definitely not discrimination or social exclusion. It is natural of decency. We do not have to accept all lifestyles the West adopts and practises. Homosexual Practice is primitive, weird, strange and queer. It is dirty and unacceptable to genuine black African people and their culture.

The nonsense being peddled by certain interest groups that homosexual practice is natural to some people is unproven neither in nature nor in Science. This is neither a cultural, Anthropological nor Sociological debate. It must be Anatomical as clear as the differences between a man and a woman. Hormonal manipulations, extensive plastic Surgery and use of gamut of sex tools are symbols of affluent lifestyles and not the bend of nature and creation. The word transvestite is irritating and provocative. Women marrying each other are obnoxious and objectionable. There is no reason why two women should cohabitate as wife and husband. Each sex has a purpose in life. The most important thing in a woman's life is to have a child if it is possible. Even very highly educated career women still take enormous pride in their children. My daughter, Ekaete's mum told me she did not want a child but she seized my daughter from me once she was born. Now I cannot see my daughter because she took possession of her as her property.

THE CURRENT GLOBAL COMMISSION FOR AIDS TO AFRICA:

This is a great idea. It will soon degenerate into a talking shop just as previous genuine intentions to help Africa. They all eventually became political slogans. Africa rejoices because this attempt has come at the time I was writing this book and lamenting over the failure of Africa to base their development on Education and skills training. The Education must offer effective knowledge to make the Africans know that they have the responsibility to look after themselves and their land. They must have appropriate and efficient skills to do this. They must know the value of self-esteem. They must know that crime and corruption destroy their opportunities in life and their land. They must know that dissipating their limited resources and funds to provide facilities beyond their means is wasteful and ineffective. They can produce maximum results and effects by using their limited funds to build few well equipped centres to offer the type of Education and skills training they need for their development. Africa must avoid colossal wastage of resources. Without re-integration development in Africa will always fail. Economic development will continue to be a nightmare and frustration. We must re-integrate Africa, stop corruption and crimes and give Education (including civic education), good practical skills training and restore value to apprenticeship training before we invest resources to develop Africa. This is mere common sense to all in this hectic and challenging exercise. The Ecology of the place requires integration of the desert, savannah, and rain forest. Free movement and communication of people and goods will develop sustainable trade for healthy Economy and wealth. The par group of African leaders must discuss very seriously the re-integration of colonial dismembered Africa.

Orderly and sustainable development based on adequate and effective Education and skills training are what Africa needs. Any such scheme must be led by Africans themselves. The continent is vast. No aliens would be able to produce enough manpower to do this and sustain it for Africa and Africans. The Africans themselves must be able to do things for themselves. They must acknowledge their talents and give them the opportunity to move things forwards. The mediocre must equally recognise the real talents. They must no longer hold down the continent by ignoring the talents. Equally the talents must operate within the remit of the rule of law and good discipline. The services must expand in accordance with the resources and funds generated from successful and profitable previous investments. The expansion must be orderly and sustainable. Africa must avoid wasteful, unsustainable and disorderly expansion of its services and development. This had been the main feature of development in postcolonial Africa. It is the major cause of current chaos in the continent. It has sustained poverty, corruption and crimes.

The first action of the new Commission should be to take census of uncompleted and abandoned projects in most countries in Africa. This must be classified under the headings public and private. This will give some ideas on the colossal wastage in the system. Wastage in money and resources are rampant. It will also give clear ideas on the vastness of planlessness endemic in the length and breadth of the Society, in Government, public and private businesses. Any efforts to help Africa must start from this drawing board. Nigeria is an example of this popular spectacle in Africa. Environmental damage by this terrible habit is enormous. It may require some investment to repair the damage. It is not far from revealing why we are poor. We waste our resources. How can we prosper without completing any of the projects we had embarked upon to do? We had failed to complete all the projects we had started in the past twenty or more years. The politicians use these dodgy projects to strip our assets and deceive the voters. The energy and funds sunk into these uncompleted projects are enormous and colossal wastes. They could have produced much needed food for the population.

How should we then go about to help Africa? We may have to scrap a lot of these redundant projects and recover recoverable resources to use in developing few viable essential projects. We may also have to merge a number of projects to develop effective serviceable and sustainable projects capable of generating growth in the Economy and development in Africa. We essentially have to avoid wastage, corruption and crime in this continent to avoid its imminent disaster and catastrophe. Equally it may be necessary to help in completing key essential projects and trim them to sizes that are serviceable and sustainable. We must avoid duplication, oversize, needless expansion and wastage. These are major features of Africa that had damaged its orderly and sustainable development. Centralisation and locating projects at accessible locations to many regardless of the powerful influences of politicians and officials to site them in their villages without access to the bulk of the population must be adopted with vigour to avoid wastage. Complete privatisation is not the way. Africa has not got adequate managerial skills for total privatisation. The privatised utilities would collapse just as public ones.

It is cardinally essential that the Africans must have effective Education and skills training to give them the discipline of maintenance culture. Africa is not a manufacturing continent as Europe, Asia and America. Yet these manufacturing countries maintain their old infrastructures while Africa neglects them to decay until they need replacement with new ones. No nation can afford this type of wasteful lifestyle. The African can be helped only if he learns to use his or her limited funds and resources with prudence. They must essentially learn to develop projects consistent with available funds and resources. They must avoid over bloated projects and white elephants. Africa must remove politics from vital projects providing essential services: health, education, constructions and important engineering works.

The new Commission must learn to watch and supervise Africans working to help themselves. It must not lead them. Rather it must observe from the side line just as the driving instructor teaching a pupil driver to drive a vehicle. The mistake of spoon feeding Africans must be avoided at all costs. Let Africans learn to solve their problems. Get them fully involved. Remove from the scene their corrupt ignorant and mediocre Governments and their officials. NEPAD or no NEPAD these groups cannot change or be changed. The old Missionary practice of involving the communities in their development projects should be used as the basis of involving the people directly. The government should give grants to the projects if they have the means. The Commission should develop effective inspectorate system to ensure that any projects they are involved are not subject to abuses and mismanagement that make Africa not work. The communities must have control and be in charge of their projects, maintain and manage them. The Africans are hard working. They always help others to develop their homeland but fail to develop their homeland. They must now resolve to labour to create a living for themselves. They must develop their homeland, Africa.

Privatisation in Africa is no starter. It allows corrupt politicians and officials to seize public utilities to damage them. The mediocre leadership has no ideas about shares and share holders. It allows the Lebanese mafia and other international criminal fraternities to steal these public assets and properties to dispense of them and disappear with the funds. Tiny Rowland and his group successfully did this to postcolonial Africa. Africa and this new Commission have a lesson to learn from this. We do not have to wait for another fifty years to learn from our past. I have been very blunt. I have been deliberately provocative. I do not have long to live to preach my message in diplomatic terms. This does not justify any suicide missions or cold blooded murder of innocent people. We are all victims of the policies of the establishments that believe erroneously that it is acting in our interest. Unfortunately what the right establishment in the West fail to understand is that we are living in a challenging world. They have to accept that time changes and change is real. The cardinal and fatal mistake of the Western right establishment is its failure to accept that change is real and universal. They had witnessed the enormous change in the West. Change is inevitable in our relationship as the world itself has changed. The old status is obsolete.

They gained a lot from this change in Science and Technology. It has changed their lives and standards of living beyond belief. Equally the world has changed a lot. Sadly the Western right establishment believes that it can control and regulate the change beyond their borders in the world. They are ready to flex their military muscle and tremendous wealth and influence to achieve this. They bully the United Nations to achieve this end. Unfortunately the Western right establishment cannot have its way without war and violence. Democracy is by persuasion and free choice. Freedom is free for the West and the world. It does not need guidance from the West. The West is a good colonial imperial power but never a midwife for Democracy. There is no single past colonial territory where the West left behind the principles of Democracy. It left behind, violence, wars, divisions, corruption and feuding. From Africa to Asia its path had been riddled with postcolonial crises, chaos, wars and violence. Gross economic mismanagement is always the rule rather than the exception. We have no excuse to cross our legs and sit down expecting changes in our fortunes while we continue to indulge in these old bad habits. Human instincts dictate that we should do something. Appropriate Education, adequate knowledge and skills are the starting point. We must have viable Educational and skills training projects and programmes. Every year the Chairman of African Union (AU) should address the UN and UN Economic Committee what African leaders are doing to develop the continent and improve the lot of its citizens. This is a new Consultation method to allow the world to join the Africans in attacking challenging development in this continent. We have covered space on the ground, in the air, on the water and under the seas and we have taken the Science of Astronomy far advanced to understand our galaxy and the universe. Africa still remains a daunting challenge, the heart of darkness that has refused to open up and yield its secret to the world. Global effort is needed to open up Africa. Africans themselves must resolve on what they want. Do they want to retain their ethnic and religious loyalty with attendant abject poverty? Do they accept to abandon old loyalties and accept re-integration and secular union and true Democracy with integrity, virtue and honesty?

The major cause of African economic failure is enormous wastage of funds and resources. There are very many unnecessary duplications and wasting of funds and resources in every field of development. There is senseless planlessness. They fail to plan building of their infrastructures. They duplicate them and ignore economic necessities in preference to politics. This causes failure of several projects and wastage of funds and resources. At individual and family levels there are catalogues of vast choices and wastage of funds and resources. Wrong choices litter everywhere. These squander the scarce funds and limited resources. They do not know how to save their money. They waste money on irrelevant things that they scarcely need.

There is thoughtless and irrational competition without means. Everybody wants to own expensive things. This is why corruption, fraud, embezzlement of public funds, crimes and stealing are rife. We have to wean the Africans off unequal vast appetites in acquiring possessions and wastage of funds and resources. A lot of people talk of poverty in Africa but fail to give genuine reasons for the poverty. They keep on talking about trade and open market. The World Bank and the IMF keep on coming up with voodoo economic theories like structural adjustment programme. The Africans must learn not to duplicate projects and waste funds and resources. They must stop wasting funds and resource on avoidable and costly lifestyles. They must learn to safe money. The UN quangos fail to learn why African Economy is resistant to all efforts to put it right. They prescribe the same treatment for all its ills. Of course none of them works. The diagnosis has not been made. Re-integration of dismembered Africa to form proper countries is first step.

NEW EDUCATION POLICY IS ESSENTIAL FOR GENUINE AIDS TO AFRICA.

If the West is really serious and honest over helping Africa, it must first of all develop the derelict Educational Institutions on the continent and equip them adequately to train the Africans to offer them adequate and effective knowledge and equip them with efficient skills to enable them to do things for themselves and take charge of their lives. There is no room for subordinate economy. The enormous flow of capital from Africa to the West calculated in several trillions of dollars to sponsor African students in Western Institutions can be used to do this in Africa. The colossal wastes in this loose pipeline can be plugged. The investment can be well targeted and regulated. The students can be well monitored. The projects involved in the studies will also be targeted to solve African problems. This will allow planning for jobs and development.

This will also check the flow of economic migrants, refugees, and asylum seekers to the West. It is a way of controlling illegal immigrants to the West. It is utmost essential that Africa should have effective control of the Education and training in skills of its citizens. Nigeria alone spends several trillions of dollars on Education of Nigerians in the West but the results from this investment are minimal. This money can be used in improving Educational and skills training facilities in the country. Only genuine Academic Aids should take students out to study few items unavailable for studies in the local Institutions. This must be with the proviso of developing such studies locally. It pays to import teachers to teach in local Institutions. They would teach more students for the funds invested. It will also allow Education and skills training to be planned locally. The investment on Education and skills training must not be diverted for other things. It must increase annually. It must be a little above inflation. Equally Education and training must be developed to earn some income by helping in some essential community projects.

There is one thing about capitalism. It is not very honest about the sources of capital accruing to it. It is very confidential about sources of revenues. It defends such sources with all its resources including war and violence. Dirty tricks and propaganda are very effective tools in the armamentarium of capitalism to defend the sources of its income. The Western citizens always hear of how much the West gives to the third world and Africa. May I suggest that the West should please publish the flow of capital from the third world and Africa to the West? This will help the West to know well how to help the third world and Africa. The data and the statistics should be published regularly to help the world to know what is really happening. It will also prevent violence as the youths would know what is going on. This will prevent them from being brainwashed by unscrupulous people with hidden interest.

Equally it will allow the West to decide on how to help Africa if it is genuinely interested in doing so. Equally it will check money laundering to some extent. It will allow the West to decide on what sacrifices it has to make to rescue Africa from its current demise and enormous problems. The West will essentially have to sacrifice part of the money accruing to it from Africa to help this miserable continent. Equally citizens in the West will have sympathy towards Western aids to Africa if they know the exact amount of money the West makes from the African continent. It will be gratifying to understand that it is not a one way traffic relationship. It is beneficial to both.

The events of Sept 11 were tragic. At the same it had very profound lesson to teach the world that we depend on each other for safety and security. Before then individuals outside the sophisticated affluent West would look at the sophisticated jet planes with curiosity. It would never occur to him that ordinary normal human being could go near its cockpit let alone hijacking it to use as instrument of destruction and murder. We do not know what type of instructions the Afghan Mujahadins had on guerrilla warfare during the fight against the Soviets. The ingenuity of hijacking jet planes and crashing them into buildings to cause mayhem, destruction and death is very strange to most people. We are still wondering what may again come out of the current war against terrorists. It is wise to caution that leaders should learn from their past mistakes and be careful. How can we be sure that the current anti-Western terrorists who were Western allies in the Mujahidin Fight against the Soviets in Afghanistan did not learn their tactics from the West?

It is not very wise to expand the Army and Intelligence to combat this threat. After all the suicide bombers of Sept 11 never used conventional equipment, Army nor sophisticated Intelligence. Even the Iraqi Congress turned out to be fraudulent self-seeking lot capable of offering very false Intelligence information. It will be extremely risky to involve this sort of people to offer Intelligence for our security. Expansion of Intelligence is not a good investment for security. Safe security is to expand the spread of wealth and prosperity and make every part of the world have what to live for. When most parts of the world have what to defend as the West has, it will be difficult for them to start destruction of lives and property as we had seen in the recent past. Human beings are protective over their possessions. We cannot justify aggression and offensive war on flimsy pretext and false premises. What justification, have we, to add more innocent lives and destruction of more properties to Sept 11? Life is precious. We should not sacrifice more human lives for this cause. Continuing these wars in search and expectation of victory is madness. The Western security is in the West and not in Iraq, Afghanistan and Pakistan. The Western leaders are afraid of their shadows for starting these futile wars and violence. They are afraid to sue for peace. The West is a Democracy and not a dictatorship. They leaders should stop lying to and hectoring citizens. They must be courageous and go into quiet negotiations for withdrawal and peace. The long road to organise Security and government for these places is further waste of resources and lives. Let the people resettle themselves in their own. Pay them some compensation and return home. Human beings are fallible. They can make mistakes.

This is our world. Any good things and actions of the people who lead us are for our own advantage. Several decent people in the West had left their very lucrative positions in protest against the wrong doings of faulty leadership. They had risked their personal securities to expose criminal behaviours in the leadership. Africa and the third world must be very grateful to them. These are very courageous people indeed. Loyalty to the world and world order is now challenging loyalty to individual nations. The new world order is now challenging clandestine criminal national loyalty of the past. Good conscience and integrity are now challenging breach of confidentiality and national security in questionable and criminal actions of Governments that allowed slave trade, slavery and brutal colonisation in the past. The rule of law is now questioning the concept of just war and violence. We are living in interesting and exciting times. New Economic order is challenging the old Economic order. The real results of the old order are now threatening world peace and challenging the wealth and affluence of the past lopsided development that allowed one part of the world to plunder and loot other parts of the world.

The Economy of the affluent world cannot continue to parasitize on the rich natural and mineral resources of the poor and needy world. It is obvious that the person who accepted to be a suicide bomber has been driven to despair to find no value in life. It is the duty of the leaders of the rich and affluent parts of the world to put value back to the lives of these desperate young people. It is not the whole truth to accuse religion and psychological brainwashing. We have a duty to put back value into the lives of these young desperate people. War and violence are not the answer. Making their lives have value is better than war against terrorists, death and condemnation to the dungeon in Guantanamo Bay. It is ordinary common sense that treatment of patients with suicidal tendency is not murder but protecting such persons from harming and killing themselves. Treating suicide bombers from this background and negotiating settlements of disputes would produce better results than war and violence. I am not a pacifist. But the war against terrorists has no front and any victory from it will not have value in safety and security. Make the terrorists love life and have value for their lives. The US and their allies are the aggressors in Iraq. The Iraqis in the US camp are traitors and collaborators. The Iraqi resistance is in defence of their homeland. Of course no responsible and patriotic persons would tolerate alien aggression and invasion of their country.

We must just decide to liberalise education and skills training to give everybody the knowledge to work and use our God-given energy, our land and all its resources to make this land work for us. We all must share the joy of equal opportunity to inherit this land in this twenty first century to work hard and actively make it prosperous. Poverty shares hostility and ignorance. Let all genuine and decent human beings in this world who love humanity join me in salvaging humanity from imminent disaster and catastrophe. We all are in transit in this world regardless of how secure or insecure we may be. We are in this world not to take it over from God to turn it over to our own racial group. May God bless you all always to speak out and fight for peace, justice and fair play among all human beings. We are all human beings regardless of our colour or culture or way of life. Life is what we share together let us not destroy it. We all will finally die and leave this world, why do we have to hurry it for others? May God's wisdom temper our blind ambitions so that we do not damage this world out of our ignorance? May God bless all human beings that love truth and justice? At the end of all our Science and Technology, God is real and not a myth. The end of my sojourn on earth was sealed the day I was born. My positive role in earthly community is to help my family and the community climb more steps of the ladder towards the top and to be at peace with my neighbours. The colour of our skin depends on the way we breed. If we breed along the white axis the community finally becomes white and if we breed along the black axis the community finally becomes predominantly black. The language the community speaks takes the same preference. English is fast becoming global language. Therefore most of our natural features are not permanent. We acquire them by natural selection and environmental selection.

The environment and the community play a major role in human evolution.

Sharing, honesty, integrity, respect for human rights, persuasion, not coercion, bullying, intimidation and violence are the embodiment of democracy, freedom and civilisation. Aggression and violence cannot bring peace or democracy. War is not the safe way of acquiring security. War creates permanent social wounds and malignant scars. Great leaders are not necessarily war leaders. The price tag of war is destruction. The price tag of peace is prosperity and security. Why do we then glory in aggression, war, violence, destruction and chaos to hide our ignorance and personal deficiencies? Indulgence in war and violence is deliberate efforts to hide the truth. The Economic direction of war is the armament industry. Gun running is a lucrative business. The destruction of war is enormous and cancels out all its gains. Victory is suppression by pacification. It creates permanent scar of animosity and suppressed hatred. War may discourage people from resorting to violence to achieve their objectives but it never changed the culture of hard work in the Germans and Japanese. Equally conflict resolution achieves peace without the destruction of war.

Truth is buried in chaos and confusion. Reliance on intelligence is direct admission that we have a lot to hide. Our world is not better by expansion of this evil machine of lying and propaganda. Intelligence gathering is a hostile act. Expansion of intelligence is direct expansion of hostilities. Investment in war and violence is not insurance for peace and prosperity the world badly needs now. We appeal to all gallant and brave people of good will not to allow violent people to take over the world. The world needs friendship, safety and security more than ever at this moment. The safety and security of one group should not be at the expense of the safety and security of other groups. This is why it is difficult to accept what is going on in the world at the moment. This is why the moral of negotiated settlement of the current war of attrition has a strong appeal.

Our forefathers over five thousand years ago used mortar and bricks to immortalise their achievements. The magnificent great tombs, the temples and the pyramids had baffled the changes in times and events. Several people had cashed in to own these artefacts that do not belong to them despite the fact that our land had changed hands several times. Strange people without any understanding of these great creations of antiquities of remembrance and adoration to our God claimed falsely that their ancestors made these great Architectural and Civil Engineering feats of great magnificence and beauty. The only false witness that they have is the fact that they are now living there but time and History deny them the real credit. Their ancestors came there only fourteen hundred years ago with religion and god very unfamiliar to the Lord Ammon-Ore Osiris, Melkart, Baal, Astarte, mother of God and the guardian of our fertility and beauty. We still name our children after these great deities of antiquities. How many of their children are named after the great acts of these great deities? To my knowledge, there is none at all. The Arabs seized North Africa and Palestine from indigenous Jewish and African owners and inhabitants in the Arab conquest, 642-698 AD. The period is long enough to confine to the History Books provided they quietly integrate and make friends with the indigenes. They must denounce the fanatical extremist policy of eliminating Israel. They must tell their children how they came to be there; people spread out and look for new homes due to overcrowding in the old. This is what happened in Arab conquest. Now Israel is strong enough to reclaim the land but the world has changed. Both should swallow their pride in the name of peace and compassion and learn to live together in peace.

The Sun the giver of life presided over all at the peak of the pyramid where life merged with the Gods and fertility came direct from God. Today the Aramaic word, “Amen” may represent the Echo, “Ammon”. Equally, regardless of what everybody worships, today, the symbol of the sun is gloriously represented in the crown and wings of the angel and even the kings and queens respected this unique symbol of power in the design of their crowns. The rays of the sun are still represented in them. The mitre and the masks still represent the pyramid, the melting point with the sun and the gods. The African has several pet names for God. Even with Akhenaton and Nefertiti and monotheism, the African still prayed to God with several words of praises of His mighty power and generosity. We are unique in this culture of showering God with praises by using several names for the same God to express its mighty power and our appreciation of it. The Jews to some extent have similar habit. They have Yahweh and Jehovah. Therefore some of what people refer to as Polytheism might have been a form of Monotheism where the worshippers use different names of praise and adulation to address the same God. Usually such an address refers to the quality and characteristics of the deity. In our language we use Baal, Grace, Love, Mighty----Mfon, Ima, Ibom, Okposong Abasi. But the cardinal Observation in the Ancient History is the fact that regions that practised Polytheism and had liberal policy towards religion were progressive in trade. In Asia, India, Japan and China are clear examples; the Muslims are attempting to damage the open door policy of polytheism and religious tolerance in India and China. The West attempted to sell and stimulate religious contention in Tibet to destabilise China. However, they could not succeed because the Lala llama is experienced leader and familiar with Western politics. Buddhism is religious philosophy alien to hurting any living thing, war and violence. The West and the Muslims must disarm. They are still armed and fighting. They have no licence as terminators of human lives on earth.

It is therefore, hardly creditable that people attempt to claim cultures completely alien to them because that culture has some credit and gives them some air of respectability. Unfortunately History and time that frequently give out the truth may not respect their false claim. Even the Bishops' staff of office seems to have been copied from the staff of the office of the Priest of the sun god. The world would be surprised to learn that the black ring of the Muslim Islamic turbine seems to have derived from the garment of the African sun god priest "Okpono Idiong." We had very advanced civilisation. Even the so-called rule of law and observance of law and order by the Romans was copied from the African-Carthaginian Phoenician strict observance of the rule of law.

The first Court of Law in the Roman Empire was established by the Africans in Palestine to try law breakers and give them justice as opposed to the summarily execution of perceived trouble shooters on the cross as practised by the Romans without giving them any platform for audience. This court ran for over a hundred years before the Romans that barely tolerated its existence as long as it did not interfere with their authority recognised it and transferred it to Rome. This gave the Romans the credit for observing the rule of law and observance of law and order. The Africans that pioneered their long practice of giving the accused audience and defence were cast to the dustbin of History. The conqueror writes the History which always favours the winner. The catalogue of African invention to civilisation is long but after five thousand years of loss of freedom Africa just has neither the records nor anything to show as its contributions to civilisation. There is something curious about all faiths on earth. Each of them seems to have something related to the sun and light just as the Egyptian sun god. It seems nations copied their sentiments of the deity from Egypt. This does not mean that the Egyptians discovered the deity but it can be something to confirm that human beings travelled out of Africa to populate the world. Recall the world is dynamic. People travel to and fro places. Some stay back in places while travellers return to join them. This human habit does not confine pioneering ingenuity to one group or region. Ideas flow about with human mobility.

Recent events in History have borne us witness. Eastern Germany could scarcely come out of the cold war as the real Industrial heartland of the German inventions and manufactures during the last war only after forty years under the Communist rule. Similarly some industrial heartlands of the former Soviet Union can hardly bear witness to these roles they played in the Soviet era. Therefore, it is expression of ignorance of the role human continuous uninterrupted activities play in continuity of Education, skills and industry. Alien victorious rulers always ban all aspects of social activities they consider advantageous to their victims and defeated people. Usually Education, skills and industry are the first victims of this policy. Looting, vandalism and neglect take toll of Education, skills training and industry. These all explain why Africa has nothing to show for its past achievements in modern industry after over five thousand years.

Unfortunately no human marker of achievements in History is as enduring as God's marker, the gene. The IT computer, today, may be God-given key to enable human being to unlock the gene padlock. We would be silly to rely on the past beyond our control to show for our worth. We would equally be stupid to hang to the past that changes and time had rendered redundant. We need modern effective Education, practical knowledge and skills. Time changes and all living things must change with the time to survive. This is what Charles Darwin described as "Evolution". Africa, the black race and Africans essentially have to change. African leaders must equally appreciate the significance of change. They must allow change in the leadership during their life time. They have to retire to avoid becoming redundant while in office.

THE IMPORTANCE OF CHANGE OF LEADERSHIP TO AVOID STRESS AND PRESSURE.

The pressure and stress of office and leadership soon render the leaders thick and irrational. They become victims of succumbing to tyranny and dictatorial tendencies and irrational judgement under the guise of acting by conviction. Conviction yields very little to good leadership. Understanding the human needs of the people you lead and how long your role as the leader is beneficial to them is essential. The menace of modern leadership is failure to know what the people need and how long the leader can be useful in staying in office. The leader must know what the people need and how long he or she is useful as a leader without being taken in by adulation of his or her cronies. Cronyism and sycophancy are real dangers to good leadership. They encourage dictatorship and tyranny in return for favours from the leadership.

This is corruption and corruption corrupts the leadership and damages it irretrievably and permanently. One thing that affects our modern world is failure of the community to harness the leadership. The community lacks means to control the leaders. The so-called impeachment of the President or the leader of Government is ineffective. It is a proven major offence that justifies its use. But the daily conduct of the leader is unregulated. The control of his access to public funds is atrocious especially in Africa. The way the leaders spend public funds must be regulated. The community must control the leadership by writing in the constitution the conduct and responsibilities of the leader. His social conduct must give respect to the office. Moral decadence and undignified behaviour should carry mild warning. No leader should be allowed access to public funds. He should spend public funds through "Finance Management Board" that has to approve what he spends. The Board should have power to reject the spending and see what has been done with the money. The leader should have no access to Security Money. The Board should control all the spending of public money including the voted Security funds. It must be sensitive to reject dubious Security projects. The Board is Budget Regulator. It is preferred that the Board is composed of nonpartisan. It should be made of experts and specialist financial managers and administrators. It should be part of the Civil Service. It is the eye of the community on the public money and its Authority is from the public. It should sit with various Government Committees to hear the spenders in Government argue their cases.

It is this pressure and stress that force some lunatic leaders into dictatorship and paranoia. They talk of conviction. Leadership is not by conviction but by persuasion and popular consensus. Conviction can be wrong and may become the instrument and property of oppression by a tyrant. Conviction is not dignity or integrity. It can even be a manifestation of thick decisions expressed by lack of fresh initiatives but poorly thought out plans to impress the audience that the burnt out leader still has what it takes to lead. The claim to conviction may be the first sign and symptom that the leader has lost sense of rational decisions. The leadership and the people they lead must accept change in all living things. The best feature of nature in change is that we are all mortal human beings and must accept the principle of relay. The leadership must always have reliable relay team and must hand over the baton in time to allow genuine continuity and smooth running of the relay team. One man's show is tiresome and monotonous. It usually crashes. The Western democracy is limping on the path of change and observance of the rule of relay run but yet it is not perfect. Human ambitions frequently interfere with orderly and sustainable development in the leadership.

Democracy respects public opinion. Conviction is the fanaticism of religion responsible for part of the violence in the world, today. Even religious conviction can be erroneous. There must be recognition that one's way of life may not necessarily be acceptable to other people's ways of life and culture. This is what the rich, prosperous and affluent West must now recognise. Militarism is not essentially acceptable culture and way of life to us Africans. The black race and Africans must stand up to express this aspect of our culture to the world and the merchants of death, armament manufacturers and dealers. People dominated upon for over five thousand years are poor and totally stranded in culture and ways of life. The bug stops with the master. The West and Europe had been master of the expanding world for over several thousand years. Africa, Africans and the black race are ready to accept every genuine person that had accepted this continent as his or her homeland as long as he or she is willing to share this land with us and be loyal to this land and its prosperity. Squatters on our lands as successful alien commercial farmers with flags of convenience are not welcome. They have their loyalty elsewhere and not in Africa and its people.

As human beings we have the unique ability of communication and suing for peace in the middle of violence. It is not an act of cowardice to take the path of peace even in the midst of extreme provocation, aggression, war and violence. Victory in a war is not as great as victory in the ability of the world leaders to expand prosperity to feed the hungry masses whose frustration can be exploited to make the world unsafe and insecure for both the rich and poor. We need victory over abject poverty, hunger, starvation, malnutrition, diseases, misery and death. We need victory to overcome lack of proper and effective Education and skills currently responsible for worldwide poverty and ignorance. Ignorance of the ability of human beings to fend for themselves and the reason why one group has success over the others is reason for the current violence. We cannot correct this by war but by gentle persuasion, good and effective Education and skills training to provide the knowledge lacking and causing gross misunderstanding among humanity.

Aggressive military posture is counterproductive. Negotiation and gentle persuasion are the way to settlement of the current feud. We gain nothing from violence. Blessed are the peace makers for they shall inherit the earth. God bless you all who listen. God bless you all who believe in the truth and justice. I have been very candid. This is no expression of militancy or fanaticism or hate for our fellow human beings. We have a duty to share this world with each other regardless of the way we feel. It is not the duty of the leadership to tell us how we have to do this. It is the creator alone that determined this. We must receive this message in good faith. Human beings need peace to acquire Education, learning, knowledge and skills to work his land and die and depart when he or she has served his or her time here on earth. War and violence can terminate life in death. Natural aging and senescence do the same. Why do we devote all our time then to training to kill in war and violence? The message of wisdom can sound very foolish. Capitalism lives on jobs. Capitalism equally appreciates alternatives. There are several alternatives to armament manufacture and sales to protect employments. Have we explored and tried them in democracy?

AAAD INVITES ALL AFRICAN SCHOLARS TO JOIN HANDS TO CHALLENGE OURSELVES AND THE WORLD OVER THE PLIGHT OF AFRICA.

Afric**ans in Africa and Diaspora have to it by DIY. I was returning from the Hospice Day Centre in London when the pupils and students were just dispersing and returning home. I could decipher that the whites attended different Schools from the black by the different uniforms each group wore. The ages of the whites were young. They were smart and orderly even in the streets. The black were noisy, disorganised diversely dressed including girls in burkha. The girls' hairdos were too elaborate for serious and academically minded students. Many of them were teenagers. These are the lots AAAD would target to convert them into hard working Academic machines. The Asians are doing it; why are we not doing it? The future of Africa depends on these but we abandon them to roam the streets aimlessly. AAAD volunteers should be able to organise and give these students some extra tuition and some Academic discipline. They should learn to concentrate and be serious in what they do. They should teach them how to cultivate Academic culture and discipline.**

Most of these students have single parents. Their parents do two or more menial jobs to support the family. Generating ambitions and objectives in life in these students is important. Africa invites all its scholars to launch and run the AAAD as my life is far spent but my spirit will always be with you. Success attends to those who have defined goals in life and implant success in their brains. Every African complains that we are disunited; who will unite us? Africans are leaderless. Recall what Doctor Martin Luther King Junior did in a short time of his life? We need leaders in Europe; our Scholars can provide that leadership. Rise up on your two feet and provide that leadership. It is a challenge and a difficult job fraught with all sorts of frustrations. It requires enormous tolerance and patience. The African leaders in Europe must bring all willing and volunteering Africans of all colours from the four corners of the globe together and encourage them to work in teams with objectives to get Africa to rejoin the world from exclusion. Every African University must have AAAD Research Programme. We must avoid duplications. Institutional integration to avoid wastage is important for good equipment and quality staffing and high teaching standards. Regional or national teaching curricula and common degree examination in each discipline would maintain high standards and prevent cheating and examination mal-practice.

With the AAAD the Chief Examiners in each discipline could be any part of the world. He calls and collects questions from all the lecturers teaching the discipline. From the submissions he selects questions; he can merge questions from various Institutions to draw up the final questions. The examination in each discipline should be in three parts, MCQs, Essay of 5 questions with answers limited to 2 pages each in 3 hours------36 minutes per question and finally viva and practical work. Technical, Engineering and Technology candidates attend vivas on the projects they did while working in real on going jobs in their field of studies e.g. an Architect would present the drawing of a building he or she took part in producing the physical structure from it; Agric student would show the farm and live-stock developed at least in 2 of the years spent in the discipline and civil Engr the building, road or bridge he or

she actively participated in building or maintaining. Etc. Even the Arts would equally have 3 examinations including a viva. Fifty per cent of our University work should be practical. Any Education should be applied to real life.

I owe tremendous gratitude to various sources and the BBC and the British Museum for the sources of the valuable information in this book. Most of the information is derived from Books from Second hand Bookshops. Unfortunately, these books were stolen in the Republique de Benois, Afrique. I have to thank my late excellent Headmaster, Chief Evans Udong for his enormous academic ability that transformed several of us from poor and deprived peasant families into very optimistic sound academic machines capable of competing with the best and finest in the business. Before this time all that School and Education meant for us was to become village Primary School teachers. As a result of his encouragement most of us proceeded to study further. He was a role model for teachers to emulate. The teacher must aim at producing better pupils in life than himself or herself. Mr Etim Akpan Enang one of our senior teachers was a philanthropist and a disciplinarian. He helped to transform our Primary School to high grade performing School. He actually paid School fees for some of the children from poor families with his meagre salary.

I also have to remember my young men's company and friends. They were a joy to me even though I was Ibibio and I had just completed my A 'Levels and they were Igbo and already graduates we got on very well. They protected me and kept good company with me and so were the Nwachukwus, husband and wife. I felt at home with all of them. They encouraged me to live in hope to survive the brutal Nigerian civil war to return to University to continue my studies. They were all thrilled with joy by my success, graduating and completing my PG. They were my role models. Olu Joe an Itsekiri, lately the Principal of a Grammar School in their area, was another friend. Fred Enaholo an Ishan boy and Adewumi, a Yoruba boy were all with me at the UCH, doing Medical Laboratory Technology. We were young and the Medical students were smart and attractive. We decided to abandon Techniques to pursue Higher Education. Fred and I are Doctors and Adewumi is a Biochemist. Akpan Simon Robert (Nda) was my favourite Primary School friend.

I have to thank Mr Ukoye and his late wife Nenaya. These people gave me lift to and from work to protect me from molestation and being hijacked to the war front to be shot by unruly and ruthless and vandalistic wild Nigerian Army. I still cry for my niece Inyang Anthony Eshiet executed by marauding rogue Nigerian Army while trying to plead that they should spare the life of her uncle, a rich merchant, Jimmy Eshiet. They murdered the uncle and my niece in my village, Ikot Eyo, Ubium. The Army came in Nigeria Army jip to ask for money. Nobody asked Gowon the Head of State and Commander in Chief to pay some compensation as my niece was the only child of the mother. It is not too late that Nigeria Army paid my aunt, Affiong Eshiet.

I mention them to emphasize Nigeria youths were more united before the civil war that ruined our country than it is today under Mafiosi Cosa Nostra Nigeriana rogue leaders. We were content with friendly competition and support for each other to progress regardless of ethnic origin. The civil war was a disastrous catastrophe. It destroyed our sound Educational foundation and jobs. It replaced the rising middle class and students with wild illiterate soldiers and destroyed all our young Institutions and opportunities. It killed civilization and civility in Nigeria. The Army introduced murders, corruption and crimes to Nigeria and Africa at large.

We equally knew that becoming Primary School teacher was not the end of Education. He gave us both Academic and moral encouragement to aspire to the heights. I equally thank my great supporters in those days of total despair when ability was without means. I thank Chief Okon Walter, late Mr Edelduok, and Secretary of the Ubium District Council. Finally, I owe a lot of gratitude to my late parents, Chief David Akpan-Essien and Grace David Akpan-Essien and my brother Akpan David Akpan-Essien for his sacrifice and unflinching support and faith in my ability to succeed in the face of all obstacles. He gave me the ten pounds, needed to pay for my fees, tuition and boarding to start Secondary School. The finest soul of success is endurance and perseverance. Subservience is not humility. Ruthless efficiency and genuine chase for excellence is not arrogance or vain pride. A sense of civic duties and social responsibilities justify all these.

The black race must show the world that submission to slavery is neither humility nor stooping to conquer for survival. It is the lowest ebb of humiliating dehumanisation. It makes beast of the slave owner and imbecile of the submissive slave. Life is freedom. Freedom is initiative. The West offers the black very limited opportunities. The meagre opportunities cannot liberate the black race from the crutches of abject poverty and ignorance. Even the highly trumpeted democracy is equally highly selective and the freedom for the black is strictly rationed. Justice to the black is haphazard and proportional to means. This book cannot remedy what is wrong with our world. But it can highlight what is wrong with our world and what we can do to help people to help themselves. The cost of freedom is hard work to acquire the right education, the right knowledge and the right skills to work to support life and freedom. I prefer freedom and self-esteem to wealth. I leave behind for the black race the search for right type of Education, knowledge and skills to lead Africa and the world in matters of intellectual competitions and originality of thought.

WHY HAVE I MADE INFORMATION ON AAAD INTO A CATALOGUE OF GLOBAL EVENTS?

It is cardinally important to remind every reader that Africa had always been here in this world. The black people had always equally been around for a very long time indeed. The black people constituted the first travellers and explorers in the world. They travelled and built boats and sailed across the seas and oceans to distant lands even when other human races did not venture to travel out. We were not the creation of the West. We existed before the West ever ventured out to distant lands. We equally interacted with other people. We may, perhaps, have the longest records of doing business with Europe and the West. Unfortunately, this had been made into partnership between slave and master due to Western militarism aggression and conquest and the willingness of the black people to tolerate this unacceptable state of affairs. The role of Arabs in Africa and their religion Islam equally played significant part in the demise of Africa. The Arab occupation of the African Mediterranean Sea Board and northern fringes of Africa cut the black people from access to the world. We became confined to the forest south of the great Desert, the Sahara. Therefore, it is important to catalogue the roles black people had played in the world of human activities to lay the foundation for the AAAD and the vision of the future. Living in the past and weeping up past emotions is living in the tomb. We are living in changing modern time. We should do things the way others do at this time. We must copy the social conduct of modern time in using intensive Education in Science and Technology. Modern citizen values learning and knowledge.

The richness of the tropical forest made us self-satisfied. There was no incentive to go out on long distance expeditions for supplies as the forest provided all our needs. Indolence set in as external contest is great incentive to combat and competition readiness. The black race became cut off from the world and hemmed in by the Arabs. Unfortunately by the time we were re-exposed to the world again our culture, traditions, education, skills and tools were obsolete to compete with those of others. Progress needs continuous stimulation for combat and competition readiness. Continuous Education has no replacement in tackling problems facing Africa. We have to share this world with other races of human beings.

We must assume the responsibilities for our living in this world. We must do what others do to derive maximum benefits from their lands. We should adopt and copy skills that we may be lacking. All living things learn this way. Hence we should invest all our scarce resources in Education and training. Our best asset is appropriate Education and good skills. The knowledge and skills to do things are more certain than the begging bowls asking people for handouts or reliance on a free market that has no value for our goods and services. Genuine aids must help the beggar to have the appropriate Education, adequate knowledge and skills to work and escape from begging. Any alms that feed the beggar to remain a fit and healthy beggar all his life fail to achieve the objective of making the beggar overcome a bad point in life to regain confidence to lead normal life again. Any successful group on earth is that group that is able to make a full living out of the land they live in. The successful group makes a living out of the land they occupy.

This is not written to make the black race, Africans and Africa or any readers feel that Africa is a victim of circumstances. It is written to inform the world the way Africa and the black race came to be here. It is also to advise the black race, Africans and Africa that they have a safe way out of the pit provided they abandon indolence and despair. It is equally written to advise the world and genuine African friends that they have a way of helping Africa out of its current demise. The black race, Africans and Africa must have the incentive to work for their progress through appropriate Education and adequate knowledge and skills training. They must adopt integrated Education. They must formalise and surmise their apprenticeship. They must integrate all their roadside shack apprenticeship into integrated formal Trade and Technical Schools to ensure that the training is made formal and systematic and no African child will ever again fail to have Education to carry him or her through life. Basic skills to sustain the child through the entire life must form the basis of curriculum of studies. We are not victims. The Africans themselves are the tragedy destroying their fortunes. They conspired and collaborated with Arab and white slave traders and depopulated Africa of able bodied people and got in return gun powder and Scots Whisky. The African slave hunter suddenly had the job of selling his children to strangers. Today the African has another job in crime. It is called corruption. He steals African money to launder abroad. What a disastrous person is the African always ready to swallow crime and indulge in tragic catastrophe leading to self destruction. Are we human beings capable of recognising self-interest? We are the first people to dehumanise our fellow citizens, brothers and sisters for the foreigners.

We seem not to know or recognise self interest. I frequently these days hear some Europeans expressing better genuine concerns about the backwardness of Africa and the plight of the black people on earth while the black people themselves Majority of Africans and their leaders just do not care. The young people bother about perfect skills in crimes and travelling to Europe to plug money from trees. There is no new international crime that we fail to see a Nigerian involved. It is self destruction. Most of the young Africans I see in London study finance and management; no Science or Technology. Engineering and the rest make no impression on them. Finance and management offer contracts to aliens for their constructions and repair works at grossly inflated prices with fifty percent commission. We just have to use our five senses and do what others do to live with hope in this world. Education means genuine reading and job training means modern jobs like all types of Engineering. We must reward genuine knowledge and skills. Politics for the Africans must return to the slums to where it belongs. Until politics returns to the gutters it belongs we will be nowhere. Elevating it to respectable position is promoting crimes. Crimes and corruption destroy Africa. We had our ancient ways of selecting leaders. They were people of genuine integrity. Corrupt criminals set bad example. They are the people that damaged politics.

We are people who have to get our acts right. This is our way out of this mess. I am gradually coming to the conclusion that the animals we share this continent with observed in the "Wild Life Programmes" on the television seem to be better organised for life on this continent than ourselves, human beings living here. We owe it a duty to learn from them in order to succeed living on this land. We have over-stretched nature with our demands without modifying our lifestyles to cope with the stresses of nature. We now have to use Education and skills training to aid nature to produce what we consume from the natural and mineral resources of this land.

The blunt, straight talking and harsh way this message has been delivered may betray it as a repudiation of some groups to demonise and blame them for what has gone wrong. This is very tempting misconception. This message has no room to apportion blame. It is out to make accurate observations on the way we all have been behaving to find ourselves in the current difficulties. We equally believe that the time we spend squabbling with each other and exchanging violence in war with all the resources we devote to these can be used for adequate and effective exchanges in Education, skills training and formal apprenticeship to work to produce the wealth and prosperity each of us wants. There are still very many genuine white people in the West who reject unprovoked aggressive militarism to create war leaders in the West and they speak out against this policy. They are equally a lot of white people in the West eager to see a change in the old policy. They genuinely want to help Africa and the third world. We owe a lot of gratitude to them.

The world has a lot to offer us. Each of us must work hard to achieve good results to improve our standards of living. We extend the hand of friendship to all. It is our fault if we fail. It is our joy if we succeed. The enormous success in the West is success of all humanity. It is our duty to advance the frontiers of these human achievements. The West must be generous to assist the rest to acquire good Education and skills training to work for themselves without depending on food and drugs handouts to survive. We welcome all peace lovers in the world and thank the great role models in the West who stand tall and talk in defence of peace and good world order. In these difficult times we need people with wisdom and courage to argue in defence of peace. The safety and security of one is the safety and security of all. The life of one person is as valuable and precious as the lives of all. The loss by death of one is as distressing as the loss of many. We all share this world together. Let us all learn to share Education, knowledge, skills and labour. We equally have to share the responsibilities for the safety and security of all in the world.

The West has made tremendous progress in advancing the frontiers of knowledge and skills. The world owes a great deal of gratitude to the West for these achievements. Several other people had contributed a lot to advancement of Education and learning. The world equally owes them a lot of gratitude. The West left a lot of scars on people from several parts of the world because of slave trade and slavery of African Negroes and brutal colonisation and land seizures in several parts of the world. We cannot continue to live in the past. Time has changed not only for the rest of the world but also for the West. Let us embrace the changing times. Let us use the opportunities presenting to us to sow world peace and advance further the frontiers of Education, learning, knowledge and training in skills to make the world a better place for all. The rich and affluent should treat the poor with compassion. The mighty and powerful must resist the temptation of being provoked to extreme violence as to threaten our civilisation. Let the poor and the weak not resort to violence as to damage the opportunities for development and progress. Orderly and sustainable development can take place only in peace and security of life and properties. Let us all in all wisdom embrace peace and respect the sanctity of life and humanity.

There is real threat to world peace and security of lives and properties if we yield to the temptation of dividing the world into rich and poor along religious lines, faith and beliefs based on civilisations. To emphasise those things that make us different is a risk to global peace and security. This will brutalise and hurt our world immensely. Conflict resolution will be plagued by suspicion and settlements of disputes will be difficult. We need wisdom to deal with our current problems. There is also the risk of dividing the community into people spying on each other. This will cause confusion and chaos as people will settle personal feuds and grudges by making false reports on their enemies to incriminate them. Equally financial rewards may tempt unscrupulous people to incriminate innocent people to obtain money. I would strongly admonish that the best way to settle this crisis is by quiet level-headed negotiation between the combatants. This will avoid sowing seeds of long and protracted discord. We have to abandon emotions, old grudges, grievances, bias and prejudices. We must search for genuine settlement of grievances and grudges. In our current situation no religion supports hatred, war and violence. Peaceful co-existence wisely supports peaceful resolution of conflicts.

The black cousins had had raw deals from several people all along History. We do not call for hell and brimstone on our abusers, bullies and tormentors. We extend the hands of friendship to all. Aggressive militarism may be the path of valour and gallantry. Victory is sweet and very tempting in conflict but in this situation do we consider the loss of lives and destruction of properties worth the cost of victory? Are there other alternatives to war and violence? This is not a war involving professional soldiers. Innocent civilians, children, women and the sick take the toll. The white cousins getting together, does not affect their loyalty to their various countries and homelands. The black cousins getting together should not affect their citizenship of their various countries and homelands. It should not affect their allegiance and loyalty to their various countries and homelands. The great advantages, the West derives from the white cousins getting together helps the West. The black cousins coming together will definitely yield us some benefits in several spheres. Western Democracy accepts freedom of expression and association as basic fundamental human right. This is History, for Education not incitement or provocation.

Recent events have shown and confirmed our suspicion and fears that the Western white cousins would not hesitate to use genocide under the guise of slogans of fighting terrorists, religious extremists, bringing democracy to execute genocide again in this century as they did in the last century to seize the Americas. Yes it is nice to emphasise religion, colour of our skin, ethnic nationality, and several factors that divide us and make us prone to assaults from freelance land grabbing resource snatchers led by the Anglo-American establishment using the terror of superior fire power and military machine. The inhuman ruthlessness of assault on innocent inhabitants of Fajuya and other Iraqi cities has confirmed the inhuman nature of this real threat to humanity. The UN is spineless and totally hopeless. This mob Army claims that it is executing UN order. The Anglo-American male white must decide if they would accept change of relationship with the rest of the world. They would have to accept the common humanity of the rest of the world. They would not load their war machines and rush against other people in their homes to gun them down as animals and burn down their houses. The Arabs must abandon the habit of involving the Anglo-American white males in their feuds. They must stop living in the past with its emotions and embrace the future. They should stop Arab militarism and accept that there would not be another Arab conquest in Palestine and the Middle East. They must learn how to live in peace with their neighbours.

UN up to date has failed to issue any articles of its charter to deny or confirm this Anglo-American claim. It has not had the courage to protest against the brutal bombing and lofting missiles into cities full of innocent civilian population. I wonder what the West and USA would say if any other people did this. The Anglo-American democracy is now openly in shambles. It had always been a charade and criminal deception to defraud the world and bully others but now the truth is common knowledge to most people in the world. The people who seized USA, Australia, New Zealand and most other parts of the world by gruesome genocide, traded in and kept African Negro slaves and ruled the world by brutal colonisation and practised the most lethal racial discrimination and exclusion cannot overnight turn true converts of democracy. It is a mockery and con deceit. The Anglo-American imperial colonial war machine would not fail to seize any opportunity to execute maximum atrocities and cruelties to seize lands for loots under all guises.

The Anglo-American authorities are busy mass producing battlefield nuclear weapons without telling the world who their main enemies are. They are busy campaigning against non-proliferation of nuclear weapons. Whom are they fooling? They seem to be preparing to take on the world to control global resources. This is pure naked greed that lacks security and safety for the whole world. It lacks any consideration for humanity. Africa and the black race had always been at the bottom of the ladder prone to abuses. We are not victims guilty of self-neglect. We are not willing to pay the price for freedom. We are a confused mob lacking initiative on basic rules of self-preservation. Self-preservation to us means capitulation and acceptance of slavery and loss of freedom. Unity is a necessity in confronting a common enemy and threat. Unity is strength. We lose nothing in uniting to challenge a common enemy. We now have the NATO and the EU. They all may represent good causes for their members but what is their significance to a world that is not at war with any of them? It is difficult to comprehend.

The attitude of the US that claims to be a model of Democracy, basic fundamental human rights and civilized standards of behaviours falls so short of expectations that we cannot fail to conclude that all its claims are mere charade to camouflage its real intentions in the world. Its real intention is to seize the world by terror of its military might. The US is yet to offer genuine reasons for its presence in Iraq. It has lied to God, the world, its friends and its citizens so far. It now owes its integrity and credibility to offer its true reason for invading Iraq. If it was for Saddam Hussein, they now have him. They should leave the place. Iraq is not part of US. The Iraqis will rebuild their homeland. They do not need the US for this. The US should pay the Iraqis indemnities for the destruction of the place. They should get out of the place to set good example of civilized standards of behaviours. Unfortunately these are people that genocide and gruesome atrocities to other human races had not touched their consciences for several generations. Each generation struggles to excel the past in executing perfect genocide. They hide their crimes with lies and fabrications. The shocking stories from participating US soldiers should shame their leaders who sanctioned these brutal atrocities but are now denying leaving innocent young soldiers to blame.

All Africans and the black race must now learn that the differences between their common interest as Africans and black people and the owners of the continent of Africa as their global heritage and homeland and their individual petty national interests are insignificant in the face of the threat facing Africa and all Africans and the black race on earth, today. Africa belongs to all of us. It is our duty to protect and defend it from all predators. We should never allow our individual petty national or private interest to place Africa at risk. This happens when we allow feuding to affect our unity in working together to solve the problems of educational and skills backwardness responsible for our current poverty and misery. We have to sacrifice our individual petty national interests for the common cause of our security and safety in the African continent, our homeland.

Just a decade ago, Africa and the black race watched helplessly genocide in Rwanda in front of the world. The Hutus became savages and destroyed their Tutsi neighbours for no just cause or reasons. Even if they had any genuine reasons, the slaughter of their neighbours, the Tutsis completely forfeited such reasons. Our ancestors had rules and regulations that strictly outlawed genocide as crimes against humanity. It was an offence that carried very severe punishment. There were rules of engagement in war. Women and children were never to be hurt. The West that fragmented Africa to rule in brutal colonisation quietly abandoned the people to be massacred in the frenzy of tribal feud they created by using “divide and rule” to weaken their resistance. They sold the arms for the African bush wars. The owners of these arms are savages. They have the heart of darkness and evil. They all disappeared into silhouette. The people of Rwanda were abandoned to endure painful deaths in a gruesome genocide in Africa since the Romans destroyed Carthage by Barbaric genocide in 146 BC.

Africa and the black race have a lot to learn from the past and recent events. We have nothing to lose in unity of all our people and people who live here on this continent for the sake of our continent, Africa now facing extinction from poverty, ignorance and HIV-AIDS.

We are also facing veiled threat from current wave of resource wars. African Union is not a far-fetched idea or choice. It is very mischievous for the West or Europe to say that it is the brainchild of individual to take over the continent. The West has several united corporate bodies. Human beings led moves to establish them. Human beings lead them without the fear of taking over. Most African leaders are old. The risk of them taking over the continent to dominate is very minimal by reason of their ages. The colonial fragmentation of the African continent has resulted in the creation of several rogue and failed states. We Africans have the brains to recognise the failure. We had the courage to get rid of the colonial powers by acquiring the nominal independence. We should have the eyes to see that it does not work with so many unviable rogue and failed states. We equally have the intelligence to perceive that we have to do something if we have to sustain our independence.

Re-integration of colonial dismembered Africa is no longer a theory or topic for political debate. It is now an urgent action that must be taken to tame Africa to prevent it going down the drain. Whatever we do some people will be affected more than others. Some people would have to make greater than the rest. But Africa and the world cannot be held to ransom because some people will lose their positions and privileges. This is the obstacle to African Unity.

After all when the colonial masters dismembered and fragmented Africa without consultation with local people and Africans, some people were affected more than others. Several leaders lost their positions and social privileges. They endured this even though it benefited not from it. But re-integrated Africa will definitely benefit. It will not benefit our past colonial masters. This is why they have been campaigning against it since we had our independence. The frustration is the fact that past colonial master uses very dirty tactics in campaigning against re-integration of disremembered Africa and African Unity. The French foment trouble as a pretext for sending in the French foreign legion. They also station some French Military Units in some of them. They also promise them aids. They brainwash them to be more French than the French. This is a form of Psychological warfare and brainwashing. The British are master Imperial colonisers on the cheap. They use bribery as aids. They use subversion and Economic sabotage. They sponsor crises and petty wars between neighbours.

Now the EU has joined frail to keep Africa divided and disunited. They do these things because they know that African leaders are ignorant of what is good for Africa and its people. The leaders cater for their personal interest. They are gullible and take in fear the past colonial masters warn them what would happen if Africa is re-integrated. The intellectually weak leaders in Africa should ignore the past colonial masters' tales of woes of what would happen if Africa is re-integrated and take a firm decision to re-integrate Africa. I am one of you. I would not deceive you. Re-integration of colonial dismembered Africa has greater benefits for all of us than retaining the present dismembered nonviable ministates.

We essentially have to sink our differences and take some courage to evolve viable nations. We must also develop continental union to take charge of central and global issues affecting Africa. We all live in a house. That house is Africa. It is our duty to keep it in order. We have to bring our talents and resources together to build Africa fit for the world in our time. We cannot do this if each of us continues to be corrupt and have national scarce funds in our pockets to run away with them to launder in foreign banks. We can do this only if we are ready to make the necessary sacrifice and co-operate with each other to work for progress. We must have a common objective for Africa. That objective must be based on Education and skills training to make our people do things for themselves. We must accept the challenge of working for ourselves. The concept of employment must mean the ability for us to work for ourselves. Our Education and skills training must aim at making us work our land and other resources to sustain our lives without looking for paid employments. Paid employment is a colonial concept that is fast waning and disappearing. It is a concept of capitalism, private enterprise and market bubble Economy with regular boom and burst, recession and mass unemployment. There is inbuilt defect in Capitalism that we have not been able to locate. There is powerful and influential group that is campaigning for capitalism, private entrepreneur and free market. People who raise doubt over Capitalism seem to have made mistake or committed an offence. Nobody should feel guilty by doubting the full benefits of Capitalism.

The capitalist lobbyists make doubters of Capitalism doubt their Democratic credentials. Capitalism, private enterprise and the free Market are not the same thing as Democracy. Democrats can be non-capitalists, non-free marketers and non-private entrepreneur. Therefore, do not be intimidated by capitalist lobbyists by expressing your doubts of the of irreplaceable benefits of Capitalism. The global Economy, today, needs a system of business that will involve everybody in working to earn a living in active employment or private entrepreneur without suffering from redundancy. It must be a system that leaves nobody wasting away in redundancy. Life has no break from eating. It should have no break from working to earn a living and food to eat. Such a system must be regulated by all it provides jobs for. It should not be controlled by bureaucrats or politicians or ideologists. It must be regulated to prevent legalistic criminal practices common in Capitalism. The new system of managing finances, funds, trade, commerce and the Economy must prevent fraud but guarantee continuous employment. It must be stable not having frequent collapse. It may not have enormous capital floating in it but it should have surplus funds in it. It should be able to generate guaranteed profits not in excess to overheat the Economy and cause boom and burst. We may call this system "DEMOCRATIC ECONOMY". It consists of well regulated free market, private entrepreneur, and private capital and tax payers' capital. The Regulators have authority to visit any of these Businesses and examine their Computers and Books for the health status of the Businesses the Conduct of their Managers and Administrators. The Regulators should be a mix of specialists and experts in the Civil Service and experienced honest and respectable leaders in the community who must understand the regulations. There must be regulations covering the core Business of the Economy: trade, commerce, Banking, Insurance and all financial and fund management. Democratic Economy must allow Business freedom but prevent overloaded unstable growth of the Economy, collapse and recession.

The Financial Management Board (FMB) should top financial experts and experts in Government business recruited by the Civil Service with fixed salaries. Their duty is to keep the money and give it out to Government Departments and functionaries only when they are convinced that the spending is genuine. They equally have to send their experts to examine the projects to ensure that they are well done. Government auditors regularly check their books. Their auditors regularly check Government Departmental Accounts. This is to keep the politicians away from the treasury and concentrate on the duty of governing.

The fact that the past European colonizers divided the continent of Africa like salami into unviable Bantustans that still exist today as rogue states and banana republics and failed states and no African leaders had taken any steps to query or change the statuesque is a scandal, today. It is the manifestation of African leaders' ineptitude and the white man's abuse and cruelty to the black race by deliberately abandoning him in the arid desert to degrade the environment and die of drought and deprivation. It equally shows white man's total disregard for the environment and ignorance and selfishness in the pursuit of his selfish interest, consumer materialism by not realizing that human beings left like that would degrade the environment up to destroying it. It is equally a scandal on the intelligence of the black people for not knowing that the existence of such Bantustans is detrimental to their interest. When late Kwame Nkrumah, Sekou Toure and Marcus Carvey advocated for a UNITED AFRICA the corrupt and criminal white people mounted a counter propaganda and used their agents to counter and neutralise them. Unfortunately, these leaders presented their case as a political issue. This is not a political issue. It concerns human life and its essential necessities for staying alive.

The Western European colonisers failed to recognise the fact that as colonial appendages and colonial suppression of the people's needs their so-called overseas territories worked with heavy colonial support. They just cannot work as independent states. Most of them are patches of dry desert land and lack reliable source of water.

It is a surprise that protecting their continuous interest in their former colonies the European white males failed to recognise that a UNITED AFRICA would also serve their interest too. Look at the current drought, locust invasion, famine and malnutrition in Niger such disasters and catastrophes can be avoided only in a UNITED AFRICA. Human and animal habitats need access to water and fertile lands. European colonisation totally ignored these essential needs in salamising Africa into arid desert and savannah European colonial Bantustans. There are no words to express this action other than the fact that it was banishment to the desert. If the black people are human beings they will stand up and ignore all their differences to re-integrate colonial dismembered Africa to dismantle these borders. They should see the suffering of their kindred abandoned in the arid desert to die in drought and famine. They should take prompt action to rescue them by giving them access to water and grazing land. The permanent solution to this is not appeal to the NGOs for aids but re-integration of colonial dismembered Africa to form proper countries to allow everybody access to water, grazing land and reliable farmland.

They are too costly to maintain socially, culturally, economically, religiously, commercially and politically. There would be initial problems in dismantling them. We have seen it in Germany an affluent country but our poverty and lack of sophistication and affluence are to our advantage in this exercise. This is after all re-integration of colonial dismembered Africa, the past colonial masters could have put back as they saw it just as people do washing up after eating. Walking away without washing up is regarded as bad manners. The white males often swagger away after damaging Africa and Africans. People deliberately mischievously make re-integration of colonial dismembered Africa a political argument. This is not political argument. It is genuine Economic argument. It is a social argument. It is human right argument. Dismembering Africa was a gross abuse of the right of man. It indirectly prevented freedom of association, movement and access to their common utilities like springs and farmland. It also caused Economic quagmire. Today Africa is trapped in this snare because its corrupt leaders and former colonial masters benefit from it. Some people actually divided at Independence. Malaysia and Singapore are a success. Pakistan and India were disasters from the start. The African rugged terrain needed re-integration. It is wrong to dab genuine non-political argument with politics. The question remains: (Do we divide African countries according to people and their ethnicities or according to the nature of land distributions and Economic viability?). The word "Bantu" means people of several languages. This means a parcel of land would accommodate several diverse ethnic groups. Hence division must be based on land that provides basic human needs for Economic development. It is a binding secular constitution and a non-corrupt Judiciary that should provide security to the citizens.

The difference would not be too great but we would face language and communications problems. Yet we pulled through them in alien European colonisation that gave us nothing in the form of benefits. Rather they left us to be exploited and these problems we are facing. The benefits of the current situation still flow to the former colonial masters and their multinational corporations that specialise in criminal and corrupt activities in Africa. They sponsor bush wars and gun running and money launderings. They deny us freedom of movement essential for our Economy in Africa. The methods of movement are too costly for a healthy Economy. Goods movements are tortuous and costly. We urgently need transcontinental networks of roads and rails. The West is currently glutted with Economic migrants. If they help us to sort out the mess they had made of our Economy that we had also helped them to destroy by our warping corrupt habits and wasteful spending on economically unviable projects and thoughtless borrowing we may have no need to abandon opportunities at home to hang about in the West. This will relieve them of African Economic migrants. The West also has to stop meddlesome attitude in Africa.

We can prosper only if we control our borders and develop continental Economy. We have to get credible Banking system and trade freely at the world stock exchanges. Our land must be a viable equity. We must sell our produce and receive payments in our currency that should by right be supported by a lot of precious metals we have in abundance both in our soil and in our reserves. The disaster of trade in human beings and slavery had linked us permanently to the Pacific lands. We must develop our homes in the Pacific to enjoy the wealth in the motherland. The nonsense the IMF, WTO and the World Bank are talking about trading nothing to get our way out of poverty is irrational and empty talk. Agricultural Economy alone cannot do the trick. Mixed Economy is the ideal. We have a lot of raw materials and energy to produce our basic industrial needs. Today recycling is important. We must have well-developed recycling industries to cater for wastes of our consumption. We should start building Africa from within. Several people did it that way. When outsiders see our efforts they will rush to help us. We

Africans are stupid and gullible. We are lazy and refuse to think and learn. Today the West would talk of Mao Tzedung's red storm troops and Tiananmen Square. We would swallow the thrash and forget that in all races of human beings there are always people like Chairman Mao. British Henry the V111 and his storm troopers devastated and plundered the ancient churches and Cathedrals, great national heritage to annoy the Catholic Church for refusing to let him have his way in marriages. Therefore, vandalism is not confined to one race of human beings. Equally Henry V111 is not the only person that we can accuse of covetousness and infatuation with women of his choice but in this age we can point accusing finger at Prince Charles, the Prince of Wales.

He was married with two children to late Princess Diana Spencer, the Princess of Wales but still wanted Camilla Parker Bowles. Therefore, even though times had changed people's behaviour and choice still sits on the floor to manifest itself. The vision of wisdom is the acceptance of the fact that life is short and we cannot have all we want on earth. We also have to be content with what we have.

Our ancestors lived on this land. They trod the length and breadth of this land. They communicated with each other through their elders and leaders. This is why the "House of Elders" is crucial to take charge of law and order. The advantage of the House of Elders made up of respectable past African leaders of good characters is enormous. It will make leaders behave as though they have a future. It will allow them to retire from front line politics in time. It will take them away from mischief. It will also offer them some constructive role after frontline politics. It will essentially create a responsible African group to moderate events on the continent. We badly need people with authority to intervene in disputes on the continent of Africa. This is a continent that had these mediation facilities long before several parts of the world thought about them. The "House of Elders" will unite global black people and reduce conflicts in Africa. It will also open channels for Economic co-operation among all Africans in Africa and the Diaspora. It will facilitate Economic planning. Projects will be sited at suitable places and not at inaccessible backyards of influential and powerful politicians.

Effective conflict resolution group of non-partisan honest and respectable Elders with mandate and authority from creditable Africans must be constituted to play this role. We cannot rely on foreigners without any understanding of our problems or genuine sympathy for our plight to resolve our conflicts. Without ethnic" entente cordiale" and peaceful co-existence it is impossible to establish participatory democracy. Ethnic tolerance is important for choice of effective and competent leaders. Competent leaders are important for economic development and growth. Accepting re-integration of colonial dismembered Africa and Union guided by written secular constitution and strict adherence to the rule of law and not relying on ethnic patronage and senseless zoning of the leadership and exclusion of some ethnic groups allows choice of talents for the leadership of the nations in Africa. Exclusion and marginalisation destroys both the victims and the people who practise this. The Nigerian Igbos should immediately be accepted for leadership of that country. The Hausas must now realise that the Yorubas are using them to exclude the Igbos for them to use their intrigues to damage Nigeria the more. Every Nigerian should be eligible to be President provided they are fit to lead the nation. Ethnic and political party rigging of elections must stop. We may use the Primary to select delegate to Electoral College. Secret sample voting at the constituencies on final election day by people unknown to candidates and contestants to compare the ballot of the electoral college all add up to success of choice.

The Union will allow the resources of our continent to be pooled together for even development of the continent. It will also allow good management of the resources to benefit Africa and Africans and stop foreigners siphoning away these resources to use in developing their lands. Balkanisation and division of Africa into ineffective non-viable failing nation states allow foreign exploitation of our continent to the detriment of our people. This exposes us to poverty, feuding and conflicts. The West fuels the conflicts by selling arms to the combatants in exchange for our rich resources. The easiest and cheapest thing for us to do is for us to have the common sense to resolve all our conflicts and stop wasting our money on arms that we scarcely need.

We need construction and not destruction. It is easy to be lured into conflicts in the presence of poverty and ignorance. There are so many freelance phantom white European experts who specialise as pack packers roaming about in Africa to deceive and fool a lot of our people. The truth is that no foreigners know how to improve the lots of Africans and the black race. They colonised us for almost over five hundred years. They administered our land over all that period. They just did not know how to improve our land or our lots in life. What is the motivation for this new move to change our lot? How genuine are they? No foreigner knows better what is the best way to settle the problems of economic failure and underdevelopment in Africa than the Africans themselves? The Western European colonisers divided Africa into patches of land by drawing lines on in a very poorly drawn map on a horseshoe designed table. None of them knew any of the places on that map. Leopold the second of Belgium did not attend but sent his operative. The operative was an ex-workhouse resident that left Europe to travel the length and breadth of Africa. It was this man that helped the European leaders that assembled in Berlin on that evil day, 15th Sept 1884 to share Africa among themselves. He drew the straight lines on the map for them. No native African was present.

At independence the colonisers swaggered away after failing to subdue the native Africans to abandon the concept of independence. Unfortunately, the post-independence African leaders were in the main Primary School teachers without any knowledge of international affairs or leadership. They were excited to move into the houses previously occupied by colonial administrators. They moved from their villages where in most cases had no tap water or flush toilets to the headquarters as they used to be called in those days. None of them had any idea of how Africa was before 15th Sept 1884. Hence it never occurred to them that Africa needed to be re-integrated for independence to work. The problem was confounded by the fact that each of them spoke different colonial language and scarcely could communicate with each other. Each of them also liked being the head even if where they lived was arid desert or savannah. Also the phone or telegraph they used passed through the capitals of nations in Europe that previously had the colonies. The Any foreign assistance that fails to recognise this fact is ignoring the cardinal rule of aiding the people to improve their living standards. The Africans themselves must know that they have to do most things for themselves. No foreigner regardless of how benevolent he or she may be would sacrifice all the time to do the things that the Africans should do for themselves if they are genuinely interested in improving their lots in life. Self-help and not outside help is important.

The people live with their difficulties all their lives. They know what would make their lives better. They may not know or have the means of achieving it. This is where foreign assistance comes in. The people must have appropriate Education and skills training to know the means and how to use the resources provided by the foreign aids to work and solve their problems. It is totally out of place for foreigners to preach the gospel of democracy to completely alien land. The people to use the democracy are the ones living in the place. It is not foreign apostles of democracy. The people know their needs. It is their needs that they will adopt and use at the end. This is very clear the way black churches worship, today. They all have reversed to their traditional ways of worship. They do not use the traditional Roman Catholic or Anglican mode of worship any longer. Now they worship in traditional African way. They decorate the churches with African arts. Therefore, importation of alien culture without expressed consent of the people is totally unrewarding exercise of delusion of power. The people finally settle for what they know best. This is why any alien aids must involve the people as the lead executors of the schemes.

Union or re-integration of Africa is cardinal for Africa to evolve economically viable and stable nation states. This must be bound by the rule of secular law binding in a constitution written and approved by the people. Ethnic national tolerance must be fundamental to co-existence. The "impera et divide" (divide and rule) of imperial colonialism must be overcome. This is illustrated clearly in the Iraqi conflict. The emphasis on the differences between the Sunni and Shia Muslims has suddenly become so pronounced that one is forced to think that they are not Muslims and belong to the same religion Islam. This is convenient for the Anglo-American invaders and occupiers of Iraq. This is what imperialist colonisers feed on "Divide and rule." They always see vast divisions and differences among citizens of a country. They fan up trouble to create factions and divisions.

Africa must find means of pooling its enormous resources and wealth together to generate revenues and funds to use in developing the continent. The wildlife management in the continent should be centralised. Management of forest resources should be centralised for adequate control and to generate adequate revenues and funds for care of the forest resources and reclamation of the desert. African mineral resources should be jointly managed to prevent abuses by Trans-global multinational conglomerates as at the moment. There is fear of dictatorship. Union of African states must guarantee collective leadership and not dominant individual. It is a Union of equals. Equality of life and opportunities must be the hallmark of African Union. This is why the "House of Elders" has a significant role in the type of secular constitution that African Union should have. We are aware of the fact that former European colonisers would rake up morbid fear in several Africans. We must not fail to recall that the European ethnic nationals had had deeper animosity and antipathy for each other than the Africans. They had fought more wars with each other than the Africans. Yet they had decided to put away their differences to unite. Why then should we who did not have such rifts and conflicts until the European imperialist colonisers came to create these artificial barriers and divisions not come together in a Union?

Africa can afford trans-continental rail and road network. This will provide employment for many. It will unite the continent. It will also improve and unite our economy. It will improve communication on the continent. Joint projects on the continent will definitely improve the economy and the continent at large. This is what should be engaging most of us Africans and black people all over the world at the moment. We cannot as individual countries now fast becoming failed nation states, succeed in coping with the problems confronting us. We have to think seriously what is good for us. Not all Africans and black people are in a position to comprehend the whole picture of our continent. Several of us are even unaware of the tremendous problems our people are going through. The massive deaths of young people from HIV-AIDS are not adequately reported in several parts of the continent. Unfortunately, the level of ignorance is so great that victims of HIV-AIDS are assumed to have been killed by witches and wizards and evil juju people. This has generated enormous conflicts and fear among the population as deaths from this infection seem to affect most sexual partners involved. There was a very pathetic case of a poor father being accused of killing his graduate son and the wife who contracted HIV-AIDS and died from the infection. The child knew that he was suffering from the disease but failed to tell the poor father.

This is why mass Education and skills training should take priority over all other things in Africa at the moment. The Africans must undertake self-help. No matter what amount of aids the world may offer Africa, the continent cannot develop until the Africans themselves have proper Education and skills training and undertake economic development of their continent it will all be in vain. The continent is vast and the Africans acclimatised to living there should lead in the projects to develop their continent. This will need total commitment by talented African leaders. Self-less sacrifice is what is needed from devoted leaders. The people who make such sacrifice to develop Africa may not live to reap the fruit from their sacrifice and labour but future generation will benefit. Africa will be set free from chronic poverty. There are examples all over the world. Chairman Mao Tsedung took China with enormous difficulties out of feudal aristocracy and Western colonial intrigues and sabotage to create modern China. Several people in the West would do everything to refute this statement as they would like to discredit every nationalist struggle for emancipation. There is nothing wrong with inspired genuine national emancipation as long as it has genuine objectives. It is always in conflict with colonial aspirations. They always do everything to sabotage the efforts to make them fail. We must beware of colonial intrigues and sabotage. Our leaders and each of us must learn to trust each other for the sake of unity of our continent. We gain nothing from disunity and preserving individual self interest ignoring Africa.

It is insulting and provocative for foreigners to dictate the type of the relationship that should exist between our diverse nationalities. We had white past colonisers of Nigeria in Northern Nigeria constituting themselves into a shadowy group called "Friends of the North". They instigated the Muslims and ethnic nationals in the North to attack

Easterners. How can past colonial masters be friendlier with former colonial subjects they used to call savages (Gen.Mongomery) and fellow black brothers and sisters than their fellow Africans? Such friendship is suspicious and mischievous. It led to the civil war and its devastating effect on Nigeria. It took Nigeria several years behind. Those friends of the North had since disappeared. They are not around to help the North now. Nigeria is facing tremendous problems. They succeeded in sabotaging and destroying the zeal and enthusiasm in people after the independence. The basic truth is that imperialist colonisers do not want to see any change for good in their so-called areas of interest. It is equally embarrassing that neither the West nor any Western country has had the temerity to define their interest. What we have seen and known about this interest has been plunder, loots, fraud, crimes and corruption to the utter destruction of the affected countries. Why should their interest be so damaging to these countries? It must be curious interest indeed.

It is wrong to assume that my impression is holding these former colonisers responsible for failure of their former colonies. Rather my impression is that these former colonies were not constituted to succeed. They also took no steps to correct the in-built flaws that impair their success. They seem to be content with living with permanent failure. Most of them are so gullible and stupid that they believe they will always have someone to bail them out of trouble. That is why they swallow and absorb to their detriments all the diatribes and rubbish that the World Bank and IMF feed to their system as economic advice and directives. Confronted with HIV-AIDS they rely on WHO for help. They just lack the ability to organise themselves to tackle problems confronting them. The more they fail to organise themselves to tackle their common problems the more these problems and new ones pile up and the scantier and weaker is their response. Now we seem to be overwhelmed. The leadership concerns itself on safe laundering of the money they embezzle.

We need courageous and talented leaders. They must have initiative in finding solutions to problems. Running around the globe looking for investments is not a bad initiative but is not a solution to our current economic problems. We must tackle those problems, we ourselves can solve before looking for help to tackle others.

Evolution of African Union and establishing institutions to regulate and supervise management of a number of projects are all the things we can do without any external help. Planning and improving Education and skills training are not beyond our capability. Repair and maintaining our roads are our responsibility. It is when we have successfully completed these basic projects that we should call for outside help. Most countries now attracting aids had developed high standards of Education and skills training to generate high calibre manpower that foreign investors need. Poor Educational standards and lack of skills fail to attract foreign investors. Most countries in Asia attract investment because they have highly trained manpower, high standard of education and skills training. Their students are eager to learn and invest in their future. African children want it easy. They cheat in examinations and fail to learn and study seriously. Corruption and bribery are solution to all deficiencies.

WHAT ARE THE MAJOR OBSTACLES TO ECONOMIC DEVELOPMENT IN AFRICA?

It is worth considering these in the sequential order of their importance as major obstacles to Economic development and progress in Africa.

Slavish attitude of dependence on authority to do things for the community is a major hindrance to personal initiative and pioneering, inventive and creative spirit. This affects individuals and the community as a whole. Nobody really knows the origin of this culture of self-neglect in the black people in Africa. But it is obvious that Africa lost its freedom and was a dependency of the Persians for a long time. Cyrus defeated Egypt and subjugated Africa to Persian rule. Unlike the Greeks that combined Sparta and Athens to fight and evict the Persians from their homeland, the Africans seemed content to remain as subjects of the Persian Kings. By the time Alexander, son of Philip of Macedonia drove the Persians out of Europe and their global dominions, Africa was one of those Persian territories he seized. The Greeks took Egypt and established the Ptolemaic dynasty.

The Africans were content to be under the Greek tutelage. Even by the time the Romans entered Africa in 146 BC Africa had no response. It was content to remain under Roman domination. For almost over five thousand years several generations had been content to live as tenants on their land depending on alien rulers as their landlords responsible for getting things done. The Arab conquest of Palestine and North Africa redrew the map of the region. Later the Ottoman Turks invasion and subjugation of Africa by military terror and religious brainwashing took over. The Africans again had no positive response but they conformed. We had developed a culture of dependency on alien leaders resort to brutalising their people and massive corruption. They establish action cells of murder squads to terrorise and murder their opponents. They are very corrupt tyrants without respect for talents and public opinion. They are very corrupt mediocre relishing in ignorance and exercising tyrannical punitive power detrimental to economic growth, development and progress in Africa. Africa cannot make progress without getting rid of this sort of leaders. They are the problems and not the solution to the difficulties Africa has in its development.

This shows that Africa lost self-esteem several thousand years ago. Many generations born seemed not to appreciate the significance of freedom, self-esteem and individual and community initiative for self-advancement. Then came the era of slave trade and slavery when Africans were content to sell their children into slavery and black people were content to live as slaves in alien lands or in their homeland under foreign rule. This traces the background of chronic dependency state of most Africans and the black race. We seem to be overwhelmed by fear. We seem to succumb easily to subjugation. We seem to lack genuine initiative for freedom and independent life. We seem to depend on others and God to do things for us. The Africans are afraid to speak out against injustice and violation of their freedom for fear of losing their petty privileges from the authorities. Africans are content with mere existence and empty life even if it relies on others to feed it with rubbish.

Another factor is ethnic loyalty and rivalry. On the surface this should encourage community spirit. Unfortunately it has constituted a major hindrance to nation building in Africa. It has destroyed loyalty to the land of Africa and its defence from foreign enemies and invaders of the continent from the ancient times till today. In 146 BC Massinissa of ancient Libya conspired with the Romans under Cornelius Publius Scipio and sold out Carthage to the Romans. Traitors of Africa to foreign enemies and invaders had always escaped punishment. Therefore, ethnic loyalty, feud and individual selfish ambitions had always betrayed and harmed Africa affecting its unity and economic development. There had been attitude and tendency to plunder and loot the continent by rival ethnic groups. There is popular neglect of the interest and economic development of the continent. Ethnic loyalty had affected social discipline and the rule of law as well as administration of law and order in the continent. This had affected economic development in Africa.

The colonising Europeans of Africa either through ignorance or deliberately failed to acknowledge that just as in Europe and unlike in Asia, Africa is unique and similar to Europe in population distribution. The fact that Africa has black people just as Europe has white people they have different nationalities not tribes or clans. Europe has France, Russia, Germany, Italy, Albania, Spain, Britain and Portugal. It would be suicidal to fragment them and integrate them some as appendages to form countries different from their indigenous and natural countries. The scramble for Africa and divide and rule, "impera et divide" did this in Africa and inflicted permanent damage to the continent. The Berlin Conference on 15th Sept, 1884 subverted corruptly by Leopold 11, the white butcher of Africans in the Congo who was not an attendant in the Conference itself is a revelation of what really happened then. No African was in attendance in this Conference that was to divide Africa like salami and share it among these land rogue land snatchers to constitute into colonial Bantustans. The US was in attendance as an observer. It is said that on a large horseshoe table there was a poorly drawn African map with the whole centre empty. None of the attendants knew what was at the centre. It was only an ex-workhouse pack packer that had travelled much of Africa, an agent of Belgian Leopold 11 that helped them to pencil in straight lines representing colonial Bantustan borders. We cannot leave History. George Bush said, "Read History." We cannot make any Progress without History. We have to undo this damage and create "Magna Africa" as an umbrella body to collect the funds from its resources to invest on its construction projects to engage its people and youths and share it fairly among its components.

4. The other factor affecting economic development is the divisive tendency of religion. Muslim Islam seems to discourage the believers from joining non-believers in development of a united nation state. Equally the black Africans have a dependency culture that believes that God will do everything for them even when they make no efforts to help themselves. Muslim Islam suits this cultural concept of God. The Muslims believe that Allah will provide all their needs. Again this weakens loyalty to the homeland and patriotic spirit to work for economic development of Africa. Muslim Islam attributes public funds to gifts from Allah. This culture does not treat embezzlement of public funds as a crime. This encourages corruption, abuse and wasting of public funds. This hampers economic development of Africa.

The attitude of African leaders and public servants towards public funds and property in their custody is to embezzle them and waste in expensive lifestyles. There is enormous avoidable duplication and wastage of resources. The duplicated facilities disperse the manpower thin and are very poorly managed. As a result none of the facilities are viable. Thoughtless wastage of funds and resources is a cancerous debilitating and crippling scar on the Economy, development and progress of Africa. This has caused stagnation difficult to overcome. Any attempt to rescue Africa from poverty and misery must tackle unnecessary wastage of funds and resources and its resultant corruption. We cannot fill this tank if we do not plug tight all waste pipes.

In the presence of these inhibiting factors, does Africa have any grounds to evolve economically viable nation states or union to advance its economic development? Of course there is no continent or region of the world without its own problems. These are no impediments to their economic development. Self-interest and survival meditate against allowing these problems to obstruct means of escaping poverty and misery. Therefore, Africa should ignore old prejudices, bias, grudges and grievances and embrace genuine unity with binding secular democratic constitution adhering to the rule of law to promote its economic development for the welfare of all its citizens now facing extinction from abject poverty and diseases.

Nations do not exist because they do not have differences, diversities and problems. They exist because they have mutual interest to work for and defend. They use diversities to strengthen their existence. Ancient Africa and parts of Europe used cross ethnic marriages to promote mutual trust, promote peace and friendship. They exist because they recognise the fact that they all in their diversities share a common landmass and peaceful co-existence instead of feuding and war is better for their common interest. They develop and promote rules and regulations to govern the society. The necessity of common interest and group action promotes the development and growth of the nation. At times nations develop after several years of war and hostilities. People simply grow tired of war and violence. They finally find common sense in peaceful co-existence. The nation then grows to defend its common interest. They build up the economy to acquire means of looking after themselves and providing safety and security.

The situation in Africa is a matter of grave concern to all intelligent Africans and the wider world. We are challenged with demonstrating to the world that we can lift ourselves out of all our troubles and decide on means to develop our economy to provide security for all our citizens. This means that we are ready to make the essential sacrifices to build a viable union with authority to manage our resources for the purpose of orderly and sustainable economic development of our land. Shrewd management of our resources for the common good of our land is what we need now. Dictatorship no matter how benevolent is not the answer to our current problem. It is the collective will of our people to make such sacrifices essential to evolve this land into a powerful nation by appropriate education and effective practical skills training that will take us out of the pit.

We must ignore all our differences and come together merge together and form viable union or economic body that will control and manage our scarce resources and funds to use them to develop every part of this great continent. This is the greatest honour we can give to Africa, its long suffering people and the future generation. The temptation to embezzle public funds to launder abroad in foreign banks is great but when we die we leave Africa in its misery and poverty. Which generation of us will vow that we will leave this land better than we saw it in our life time? I appeal to all concerned Africans to show loyalty to our beloved continent now facing enormous difficulties in a changing world to rise up as courageous and patriotic citizens and bury all their differences and move in unity and firm determination and put their heads together and develop salvage plan to rescue Africa. Criminal and corrupt wealth is not sustainable wealth.

We can do it but we must be ready to make the sacrifice. It is only ourselves that can positively salvage Africa from its current plight. We have to be united and have control over all our resources and the funds they generate to use in funding development and construction projects. This requires efficient fund management. This is why African Union and the House of Elders are required to bring the whole continent together for decisions to be made centrally. We may be suspicious of African Union but we cannot change the plight of Africa without trusting each other and achieving unity for the whole continent to get everybody involved in its development. Since we all live here and endure the hardship confronting Africa now it is our duty to join hands together to do something to remedy the situation. Unity is important for us to achieve our goal. We have to agree on the means we can unite to get things done. We need selfless leaders with wisdom willing to listen to each other and the people they lead. They have to thrash out all ambiguities and avoid unsubstantiated suspicion. Binding rules and regulations are better than suspicion. We Africans are major part of our current problems. If we resolve to remove this obstacle we will set Africa on the route to recovery. The secular constitution and a non-corrupt Judiciary must deal with Economic crime. Control of funds must be taken away from the politicians.

They should be fearless and not afraid to bring any pressing issues before the committees. This is the way to resolve conflicts and avoid confusion and misunderstanding. This is the land that has sustained us on earth let us not abandon you when you need us most. Land of our birth, you are worthy of our adoration. Our ancestors defended and protected you from our entire foes including the Hittites (the Turks) from Anatolia. The achievements of our ancestors are still attracting global and our admiration even at this time today. What do we give you in return for your generosity? You deserve our love, sweat and our blood. Land of our fathers, give us courage and wisdom to live in security. Give us the courage to denounce evil and speak out against the evil of crimes and corruption. Dispel our fears of the mighty and strong. Give us the courage to defend the truth even if it means laying down our lives. All African Negroes must know that crime and fraud do not generate true wealth and happiness.

Bad reputation cannot generate trust. Lack of trust is stagnation in poverty, ignorance and misery. How did Nigeria, one the world's rich nations, manage to become the number one fraudulent nation on earth full of fraudsters? Nigeria can never thrive with crimes, frauds and corruption. We must regain self-esteem, virtue, integrity and honesty. We have to be trusted to succeed in global business. We must regain initiative in honesty and integrity. The use of private murder squads is despicable. It stands to be condemned. It is left to the conscience of the people who hire these killers and the killers themselves to confront their God for these cold-blooded murders. This land and its people do not deserve this level of destruction by the tyranny of greed of a few individual greedy people that hold it to ransom and destruction. The ex-colonial Army officers initially drawn from criminal fraternity with culture not different from Idi Amin are spokes in the wheel of progress in Nigeria. They had seized politics in Nigeria to cause crime and corruption pandemic. A harsh infectious disease requires a harsh treatment. Patriotic youths in Nigeria do not be intimidated by the murder squads of these criminals. Plug your courage and take them and their supporters by storm to recover your land and freedom from them. Make Justice summons them to give accounts of their stewardship. They feel they can scare us away but where are we to run to?

MERGER AND UNION: RE-INTEGRATION OF COLONIAL DISMEMBERED AFRICA.

We had already alluded to split personality of the African Negroes. They have the spirits, the souls, hearts and minds that admire the world and its riches. We have bodies reluctant to go with the dictates of our psyche. We had relegated active and continuous genuine Education, creative skills training and patient apprenticeship to acquire skills to the dust bin. We fail to unite and merge our bodies with the psyche that love wealth and prosperity to acquire that critical psychosomatic mass to labour and toil with sweat to achieve what we desire even though Africa is the land of milk and honey full of all our needs provided we are ready to work for them. Merger and unity require tolerance and understanding. We have to discard individual and group arrogance and posture of xenophobic discrimination, superiority and domination. We must share what we consider as valuable attributes of the union and adopt them to promote the growth of the merger.

We must have sympathetic understanding of the weaknesses of individuals, groups and components of the union and make genuine efforts to resolve these issues amicably. Evolution of successful merger and union requires patience, persistence and sacrifice. A successful union must recognise talents and merits. It must respect the cultures, traditions and the characters of the groups in the union as long as these are not destructive and detrimental to the union. Divisive tendency must be excluded as any union must be inclusive and not exclusive or dominated by individuals or cliques of syndicates. Equality before the law and opportunities forms the basis and spine of reliable and successful union. Merger and union are a necessity to gain that critical mass and strength to act in the defence of common interest and promote sustainable development.

When we had allowed our bodies and the psyche to unite and merge to form a viable psychosomatic mass then we will essentially have to merge and unite in our families, streets, villages, clans, ethnic national groups, races of human beings, countries, cities, and continents of the world and as human beings to place ourselves in a good position to share this world together and help each other to overcome the travails and perils of life. Merger is not surrender or defeat but the way nature has created the world to stop bickering, jealousy, conflicts, wars, violence and murders. Merger is acceptable attempt by human beings to form that critical mass to work and produce rapid results consistent with lifespan on earth. This is why Africa must forget the atrocities of the past and unite and merge together to confront the challenges we all face in living on the African continent. We face tragedies from our fellow human beings both local and foreign and catastrophes from poverty, ignorance and diseases. We face the hostilities of the environment, droughts and expanding deserts. We face the challenge of pulling our resources together to have the funds and the resources to tackle most of these problems. In frustration and absolute ignorance we find short cuts in violence and murders, secret elimination of our opponents. We waste the manpower we should use in spreading Education and skills training to work this vast and great land. We still grow old and die. We leave the world to continue without us and our atrocities, disasters and catastrophes.

The amazing thing and the pathetic situation is that after five millenniums, five millenniums Africa continues along the path of decline. We seem to have lost the sense of taking care of ourselves and interest. We had really not appreciated the responsibilities of free and independent existence right from the time the Greeks under the command of Alexander son of Philip of Macedonia evicted the Persians from Egypt and took over Egypt to rule. We seem to be waiting for any new alien rulers to take over our land to rule. We seem to be relieved by the arrival of such foreign rulers on our doorstep even when we do not know what they would to us and how they would treat us. The truth is that we lack good leaders. Our leaders are selfish and full of themselves. They just lack vision and self-esteem and sense of civic duties. They have no clue of loyalty to their people and their land. They do not understand the call to public duties. They take up leadership not for what they can offer the people and the land but for what they can corruptly gain from their respectable positions. They are totally ignorant of the responsibilities of the leadership. This is the current problem of Africa.

Foreigners seem to take up the initiative to express their concern over the plight of Africa. No African leaders seem to be genuinely concerned with the plight of Africa. They, it is that are responsible for the current demise of Africa. They are corrupt. They embezzle the scarce public funds to launder for themselves in private accounts in foreign lands. They recruit and train murder squads to murder and silence their opponents. They destroy opportunities and jobs.

They neglect all infrastructures including Educational institutions, vital communications networks, roads and railway. They leave them to rot and decay. Even when complete foreigners express their concerns for the plight of Africa, the African leaders have no positive contribution to make. They help to reduce such efforts to mere talking shop. They blow hot and fail to produce any action. They lack the initiative. They relish in empty slogans. They seem to relish in -ity and –ism for expansion of their English vocabulary. Recent commission for Africa in London is the most current. We should stop divisiveness created by colonial rule in Africa. The Africans should be helped to develop viable merger and union. They must develop responsible and accountable leadership.

They run their various countries as private estates. They treat their opponents as trespassers on their estates. They are very divisive and are afraid of any merger or union as this would diminish their influence and domination of the lands they are in control. It is their individual interests that matter but not the common good. This is the tragedy of Africa. We have leaders who must be listened to but they just do not listen to anyone. In the TV wildlife programmes, African animals in the wild seem to have better organisation and listening capacity than most of the African leaders. Most African leaders lack the ability to listen to genuine advice and criticism. They cannot read and do not understand most written accounts in History. Leadership to them is fun time and every female in the domain belongs to the leader. Little wonder that he leader does not know all his children. The reckless and uncontrolled breeding saddles the leaders with family expenditures beyond their means. Hence the widespread corruption and stealing of public funds is the rule and not an exception. Decadence is rife in African leadership. The leaders give themselves no room to think, plan and consult. They engage all their time in fun and corruption. They plan mischief and ways to silence their opponents and pacify the people by fear and terror.

We have no choice but to offer Africans appropriate Education and practical Technical skills training and quality apprenticeship to make them do things for themselves without waiting for others to come and bail them out. This is the way the world must show Africans the way to wealth and prosperity. They have to make the journey by themselves. The world should equip them for the journey by giving them practical good Education and effective practical skills training. The Africans have a duty to take responsibilities over their existence in this world. The Africans must learn to take charge of their responsibilities.

The African leaders are the only people who continually fail to perform well in the job but keep on bungling about in the job without producing any results. Yet they are allowed to continue in the job. This is the root cause of the failure of Africa. The leadership seems to be free for all. Each of them just seizes the opportunity to go in and swindle as much as he can. Unfortunately nobody seems to care in spite of the deteriorating condition of the continent. We badly need a "House of Elders" of honest and virtuous Africans from all walks of life charged with responsibility of holding African leaders to account for their actions. The continent is starving and suffering from HIV-AIDS and other diseases. Yet there are African leaders investing the little money they have in arms and fighting senseless bush wars. Others keep murder squads and private armies to terrorise and intimidate the people under their rule. The colonial masters took charge of these things in the past. Now there must be African body to take charge of these things. The leaders must be held accountable. The Council of Elders should take charge of these things. Bad and criminal leaders should stand open trial their crimes. Even posthumous trials can be done to disgrace bad criminal leaders. They must punished by stripping them of all the honours they used their intimidating influence to gain. This would exclude their children and hangers on from positions of responsibilities to the public. The neutral House of Elders must be empowered with authority to do this. This would be a deterrent to future smart opportunists that may attempt to seize power to swindle the community and rule by tyrannical repression.

It is unfortunate but we have to be firm. Africans must take responsibility for what has happened to their continent since the European colonisers packed their luggage and left the continent. It is no use grumbling without speaking out in no uncertain terms that Africans owe the world good explanation to what has become of their continent. They have one of two choices. They must accept the responsibilities of freedom and independence. They must labour and toil to create wealth and prosperity. They must act responsibly. Their chosen leaders must show that they can lead. Alternatively, they can surrender their freedom and independence and accept to be dependencies of countries that will look after their affairs. Independence and freedom do not mean fighting to control the treasury to collect mineral royalties from multinational corporate conglomerates to spend lifelong holiday without working and living in state house.

If we cannot produce the goods we need for consumption we must allow those who can do so to take over. We are talking here about taking charge of responsibilities of independent and free existence. The world is no longer in mood to tolerate sections of this earth to decline, decay and be run down by tyrants and despots to abandon them in a mess to challenge world conscience. The African problems are intractable and unyielding. The Africans must embark on crash and rapid genuine Education and practical skills training to return the continent to work. There is so much to do in this vast continent that there is work everywhere. The challenge is for the African leaders to get their priorities right and take the initiative to embark on construction work to rebuild the continent. It is their duty and not that of the so-called world community whose efforts their bad habits will drown if they throw down the rescue net without committing the leaders.

The major catastrophe of Africa at the moment is leadership. Most of them are self-conceited, full of themselves and foolish. They are ignorant of the responsibilities of leadership. They spend most their time on having fun and planning the safety of their corrupt and tyrannically despotic regime. They are vindictive and devious. They dubiously claim that they are security conscious. The so-called security is selfish protection of their official positions. It is elimination and killing machine to get rid of the opponents and critics of their regimes that they concentrate on. The leaders have no programmes for sustainable development of their land and improvement in public services. The reason is that each of them has individual private programmes. It is these private individual programmes that they know and understand. They have no clue about initiating programmes on improvement of public services. Our leaders are middlemen for the European mafia of the corporate business. They lack the idea of what the people want and what should be done to improve their lot. They destroy jobs instead of creating them.

Africa has neither the money nor wealth to offer its citizens and inhabitants. We can afford project-orientated and targeted Education and effective creative skills training to offer every citizen and inhabitant the means to work and use the vast resources of Africa to improve his or her quality of life. When we have adequate education and appropriate skills to work we would have means to occupy our time and stop being engaged in mischief. Africa must have a sense of its direction. We must embark on sustainable development. We must give each citizen and inhabitant the tools to work to produce what we consume on this continent. The tools are appropriate and right type of Education and skills training. It is the duty of each citizen to run and clear the hurdles. The African Negro is able and capable of overcoming inferiority complex and mediocrity in education and skills training. We must consciously consider how we came to be here.

It is exciting to observe wildlife programmes on the audiovisual media. The wild animal uses its senses to survey the environment and plan its living. It uses its vision to see. It uses its sense of smell to smell what it sees. It touches and feels and uses its mouth to taste and predators use their ears to hear and nose to smell and again the mouth to taste. Learning is the interaction between the senses of vision, smelling, hearing, tasting and touching all co-ordinated by the brain to interpret and make it into knowledge and skills. Repeated alien incursion and intrusion into Africa had destroyed, distorted and damaged the environment so much that it no longer constitutes a good platform to stimulate the senses to react to activate the brain to store knowledge and skills. Restrictions and exclusions of alien rule based on arrogant racial xenophobia and suppression of indigenous talents and free learning, liberal education and skills training had inflicted fatal blow on indigenous apprenticeship. It had damaged and stifled liberal and appropriate education and skills training. Several thousand years and billions of generations were born and passed away without that vital environmental stimulation for learning and role model to follow. This is the major reason why we are lagging behind in genuine education and targeted skills training. Today Science and Technology and good Technical education cannot be replaced with politics and antiquated religious dogmas. Africa in unison must embark on educating its youths in high standards of project-related education.

The African Negro is able and capable to learn and catch up with others in the world. Good education and genuine skills training are costly. They need genuine and adequate investments in time and money. The youths must be committed to learning. They must be enthusiastic and willing to learn. The politicians must make money available to provide adequate facilities and equipment for effective studies. Corruption, examination malpractices and poor discipline must have definite sanctions and stiff penalties. Misbehaviour should deny opportunity for education and skills training to the culprit. Such people must be severely punished. Good discipline is the key to success in education. It is not only the students that must observe the rules and regulations but also the teachers. The teachers must know how to teach and the students must know how to learn. The teacher must encourage and not discourage students. Racial xenophobia intimidates and discourages students. Social exclusion damages people. Education must be all-inclusive. The African child can be impulsive. He or she would frequently show raised hand to answer questions. White European teachers feel that this is disruption. No please; it is African culture. The child may offer wrong answer when allowed to speak. The best way is to give such a child a few minutes to speak and encourage him or her. Telling the child you had had your turn let others try is not bad and makes the African child feel ashamed, diffident and timid to raise up hand to answer questions next time. This may distract his or her attention and make the teacher not pay attention to the pupil or student. Some experienced teachers rotate the questions round the class until they get the right answer. They then ask the class to listen and ask the correct student to repeat the answer or they may amend the right response and simplify it for the students. This is good tactics as each student remains quiet preparing for his or her turn.

The white Europeans should have sufficient honour and courage to tell themselves and the world how long African Negroes were socially excluded from vital activities of genuine education and skills training by the conduct of discriminatory racial practice of Western European colonisation of Africa, slave trade and slavery? This is the root cause of lack of progress and confusion in Africa, today. Racial xenophobic social exclusion is the worst form of genocide. Is it strange that most of the activities where African Negroes excel today, they were socioracially excluded for several centuries just a few years ago? Who takes the blame for this? Learning involves environmental stimulation. The racists European colonisers and oppressors of the African Negroes and global Negro race destroyed our environment. They made it depressive and damaging to incentive to learn.

They destroyed all our role models and replaced them with arrogant mediocre white skin. They transformed learning and the anxiety and curiosity to learn and know into exclusive talent of white skin and no more. Therefore, attempting to learn and know without having white skin was attempting the impossible. Total idiots and mediocre white people bore the air of superior knowledge when they knew nothing. Their duty was to confuse, intimidate and frustrate black people. They set them non-visible and non-existent goal and target. They condemned them to learning throughout life without applying the knowledge and skills to tangible development and progress. This is one of the reasons why Africa is not making progress. We are not building. We do not plan or start to build or plan positively.

Of course the knowledge and skills are parcelled in a confused and disorderly way so that the student would always lack the means to apply them. They are not sustainable. It is worth looking at the so-called manufacturing and industrial projects the white people set up at very high costs in Africa. They are all white elephants and empty shells. They just do not work. The spare parts are scarce. The maintenance is poor. They were all set up not to work. Where any of them works it is sabotaged. Equally any successful black celebrity is damaged by white Press and Media blackmail, gossips and whispering campaign. There is no exception to this. It is obvious that the white colonial and imperial propaganda is to damage the black race and Africa. They had damaged both the role models and the healthy environments as incentives to learning. They pretend to wish us well. The African Negroes and the black race have a duty not to be taken in by white pretence and persuasive lies. They must develop alternative plans and strategies for orderly and sustainable developments, progress, effective education and skills in Africa. They must know that knowledge is dynamic and equilibrium of forces, information and new ideas bombarding your senses. It is your desire to learn and assimilate the new information. Applied knowledge must be practised.

It was necessary to look into most aspects of the relationships between white and black people, Europe and Africa and Africa and other places on earth, for several millenniums before writing this book. Its objective is not to denounce or blame any group for the demise ofAfrica. It is to be very candid over these relationships. It is to make Africans and African Negro race aware of their responsibilities in this world and to warn them that those responsibilities had had nose dive in the past. The realities of that accident and its long neglect are telling on Africa, today. The times had changed. We must appreciate changes. We must appreciate and recognise our independent existence. This is associated with responsibilities. Africa may be the first region in the world to define democracy the way Plato vaguely wanted to define who should be leaders? Some people are best being led to allow the leaders to lead. Every job has descriptions except the jobs for political leaders. Africa may determine job descriptions for its leaders. The Pharaohs had stringent descriptions and qualifications. We may essentially return to selecting our leaders from people with specific qualifications and not with bogus flattering manifestoes.

There are specific training programmes and qualifications for every job except in politics. There is even training for leadership responsibilities. Politicians are involved in offering leadership to the people and the nation but they have no training. This is why politicians are confused over their responsibilities. In recent times the Western conservative right politicians feel that their duties are to wage wars and build empires and colonies for their nations. Hence we frequently hear them bragging of being war leaders. They seem not to know who voted them into power. Instead we frequently hear leaders like George W Bush and Tony Blair speak positively on the choice of Iraqi people several thousand miles away from their homelands. They just have no clue about the people they claim to know their choice. These people do not know them.

They never voted for them. These leaders abandon the people who voted for them. They go about lying over complete alien lands they just do not know the people living there. They wage illegal wars and occupy these lands against the wishes of the people. They criminally proceed to call genuine resistance fighters terrorists. They the foreign criminal occupiers of these people's homeland are the terrorists. They are guilty of genocide. They do not deserve immunity from prosecution. If they feel they are right in their actions, they should defend them in the court of law. If they win then they should sue for slander. I challenge them to accept standing trial instead of cowering behind manipulated immunity and perversion of the course of justice.

These criminals talk of democracy while soliciting for immunity for themselves and their troops for exemption from litigation for their atrocities, abuses and dehumanising innocent Iraqi people. It is insult to democracy for these criminal liars to talk of democracy. The records of their past genocides fail to accredit them with democratic practices. The UN is guilty of being an accomplice in the crimes of breaking and violating international laws by sheltering these criminals. Before the attack and occupation of Iraq these people argued that their top world class lawyers supported them. Why are they afraid of bringing these lawyers to defend them in the law courts? Unless the world and the UN bring these people to a neutral world court to defend and justify their actions all talks about democracy and the rule of law are mere hot hair. What right have we to try Milosevic and Saddam Hussein if we fail to try George W Bush and Tony Blair? Nobody or nation should be above the law if democracy and the rule of law are to work. It is total nonsense if some criminals obtain immunity from prosecution and escape from the law and punishment. We make a complete mockery of justice. The world is nowhere with this sort of conduct of its affairs. We may have to forget about justice if we cannot administer it.

The level of ignorance among our leaders also destroys our chances. I do not hold anybody responsible for our failure in Africa. It is multifactorial. Therefore my writing is not expression of hatred for the white people or repudiation of black people. It is a statement of facts with candour. Some people come in for heavy criticism in this but far be it; I have no reason to hate anybody. I have my self-pride and academic mind to say it the way it should be expressed without prejudice or rancour. The objective is to make people learn from their past. It may be success and achievements or failure but we still have to learn. The current global crisis has taught me that no parts of the world are exempt from crisis and chaos. The well-fed die of overfeeding and obesity. The malnourished die from starvation and vulnerability to diseases. The common disease of Africa is poverty of leadership. The presence of very corrupt and ignorant people on the leadership chairs had hurt Africa and Africans. Re-integration of the whole continent advocated by Colonel Abdel Nasser and Kwameh Nkrumah but sabotaged through semiliterate leaders in Northern Nigeria and the French axis by the West and its powerful Intelligence has turned out to be common sense. It could have avoided wastage by avoidable duplication. Let us not continue to be stupid and suffer. Let African Union appoint a Committee of wise people in Africa, the Diaspora and the West that was responsible for creating the unviable and failed state Bantustans sit down and examine aspects of re-integration of Africa to make Economic sense and avoid the complications of dividing Africa into salami slice Bantustans. It has made African earnings from mineral and natural resource wealth disappear into private hands. Nobody can develop Africa without collecting these funds in a common pool. Europe developed because each of their countries collected much of these funds into a common pool for their development.

A lot of Africans do not know that these funds were used in building Rome and ever since they have always been available for building Europe and the West. The West is rich and beautiful. African resource funds and live human labour helped to build the edifices. If the Africans are serious and ready to rebuild Africa, strengthen AU and give it control over the funds and embark on sensible planning and use their youths to do the job they must not take re-integration of colonial dismembered Africa lightly. Stop corruption and crimes. Embark on genuine applied Education for knowledge and not for meal ticket and massive practical skills training. These things become experience after a number of years. Experience is present when people do things by reflex. Education must become the culture.

The underfed die of malnutrition and associated diseases. The rich frequently suffers from crisis of arrogant actions. The poor is a victim of weakness and in-affordability of poverty. Yet without the rich the poor would not know that he is poor and without the poor the rich would not know that he is rich. This emphasizes the fact that each of us has a role to play in this world. Each person has the right to be here. That right is from God our creator. It is equally important for every person to appreciate changes in life. Each person has inherent energy to change from poor to rich or vice versa. Therefore, it is wrong to resign our fate to God. God admonished us to toil for our living. If we love God and do his will why do we not obey his admonition? We just have to obey God and do what he told us to do on earth. The study of Science and Technology is the way God reveals Himself to us. Africa must integrate the study of Science and Technology into our religious studies. We have a lot to accomplish with the knowledge and skills of Science and Technology. Neman was to bathe in the River Jordan. He did it and became whole even though the Tigris and Euphrates were there..

Africa is to adopt genuine education and effective skills training and sound apprenticeship for each citizen to have visible and reliable occupation and means of living. The continent has a lot of construction jobs for several generations for its development, wealth and prosperity. It is left for leaders with foresight and civic responsibilities to start them and get them to work. The resources to use for these are there. We should not hinge such efforts on funds and money. Once we start thinking of money, we are giving excuses why we should not work to achieve our aims and goals. It also opens the flood gates for intruders to intervene to discourage us. A lot of intruders always know what we should do and should not do. They tell us what we need to succeed. At investigation of world investments in the nineties it was found that African leaders had almost fifty billion ponds sterling but none of them invested in Africa. All the funds were invested abroad. The new G-20 and the EU and the UN should use their influences to return a large portion of African funds to a re-integrated Africa for reconstruction of the continent. The world must open up Africa for both internal and external movement of goods and people. Those that claim to know what Africa needs neither know Africa nor what it needs to overcome its problems. Of course they just do not know what we need to do to succeed. The truth is that our success worries them sick. There are a lot of timid and cowardly African Negroes afraid of their shadows in the presence of the white people. This is what encouraged and made the white people make fortunes from selling African Negroes in slave trade and kept African Negro slaves. Slavish and fearful behaviour and silence in the face of mortal danger are not the attributes of good manners or temperate behaviour. It is bogus timidity and intemperance. It fails to promote friendship and mutual understanding. It fails to sponsor trust and reliability. It fails to stimulate respect and knowledge of what friendship and relationship desire. It causes mistrust, anger and feud and finally open hostilities.

It creates boring tolerance. It generates favourable grounds for abuses and atrocities. Such behaviour is humiliatingly dehumanising and self-destructing. God gave us all our senses complete and ability to phonate to express our likes and dislikes, acceptance and rejection. He also equipped us with ability to show our disapproval with anger and to fight if need be. What a disaster it is that only the timid African Negroes had failed to use these good gifts of nature appropriately for self defence? The African Negroes displays inhuman tolerance of unacceptable dehumanising torture and punishment. The illiterate, Geriatric, ignorant, decadent, dishonest and corrupt African leaders should listen to lamentation and suppressed rage in Blues of true African daughter, Billie Holiday over the tortures, floggings, demonstration public executions by shootings, lynching and hanging from tall trees of black people in the USA as late as 1956 when Billie Holiday sang that song. The inhuman behaviours of some black leaders are all to blame. Their individual selfishness and greed are all to blame for the suffering of black people on earth. A person like Olusegui Obasanjo was more interested in photo sessions with George Walker Bush and other Western leaders and building up his financial empire than taking his duty of leadership and governing seriously. Most African leaders despite their bad reputation, poor leadership and tyrannical cruelties still want to immortalise themselves by naming everything after themselves.

They just have no limit to what takes life out of existence. They sign up for just existence and not life. Existence alone without life is not worth having. This is why human beings accept death in preference to existence without life. Living in permanent dehumanising humiliation is existence without life. Slave trade and slavery are existence without life. Any human race that undertakes such barbaric and inhuman practice deserves to be treated with contempt. The African Negroes have a duty to defend what is precious unto them, life or mere existence. The choice is theirs. They must start from themselves to treat one another with mutual respect. They must have value for life and respect it. They must know that we exist here to be alive and live life with great responsibilities. Life is worth defending in emergency, war and illness. This means that every living human being has life that we must treat with respect and preserve in all situations. Corruptless and honest life with integrity is defining character and virtue free from existence. Greed and individual selfishness are exhibits of superficial and hollow life consistent with existence. Real life must make its mark by being considerate, compassionate and sympathetic towards the welfare of fellow human beings.

Any human race that abuses life and clings to mere existence deserves to lose both. This is the African Negro. The African Negroes must now know that existence is not life. Life is freedom to work and create wealth and prosperity for yourself and participate freely in human activities and endeavours. Existence is wretched survival. It dumps you in permanent poverty. You exist to be abused and bullied as a work horse. Death is better than existence. We must avoid abandoning human beings in mere existence to avoid hostilities and war. People who feel that some people are happy with existence are wrong. They do not know human nature. Express anger is not as dangerous as hidden anger. Hidden anger erupts into open hostilities and war. It engenders hatred and violence.

This means that if we have justifiable reason to fight and die to defend our lives from being subjected to mere existence in our homelands we should never look back. It is worth time to go rather than being condemned to mere existence in our homeland. Aggression and imperial colonisation are acts of reducing and subjecting human beings to mere existence and degrading lives to dehumanising humiliation and make them valueless. Mere existence is empty and voice of life. Even Christ said that he came so that we may have life and life more abundantly. Existence is not life. It is eternal torture. This is what the African Negroes had accepted and tolerated for several years.

The current attempt to spread existence to cover greater part of the world should be resisted. It is here that all human beings with wisdom and deep intelligence and thought should seek for the answer to the suicide bomber. He or she has flatly refused existence. Those who feel that they can enforce existence on humanity with powerful and dreadful weaponry must stop and think. We may end up with a world where human beings exist with powerful and dreadful weaponry without genuine life. We must accept and learn to share life on earth as fellow human beings. Each person must have adequate education and skills to work for his living and not existence. The cowards must know that it is time to talk and defend decency in human beings. Every human being knows what is decent to support life in every existence. Why do we then pretend that we can enforce mere existence without life in some racial and religious groups? It is totally bogus thought to reduce my wise thoughts of admonition to racial or religious vituperations. If you have no brains for wisdom and profound thought on the human activities on earth, you may dismiss my words of advice as an article for racial and religious disharmony and diatribe.

The wise will think very seriously how they had encouraged the growth and spread of mere existence and not life among African Negroes for several millenniums. The African Negroes are equally as guilty as those who made them replace existence with life. Their lifestyles tolerated existence in place of life. The people who replaced their lives with existence had no human response and resistance. This meant quiet approval and acceptance. Existence soon became a culture after several millenniums and generations. Any habits, voluntary or involuntary existing for several generations and several millenniums soon become a culture. Culture is very difficult to eradicate. It is tolerated by both protagonists and agonists. On the other hand it is acceptable to argue that if the slave accepted his role why should the master bother? The golden rule of do unto others as you expect them to do unto you still applies to human relationship. We also argue for what obtains in the real world where survival of the fittest prevails. Both arguments have strong roots.

I would say that every human being exists to life. Life is a fierce competition.

Fortunately, each of us is equipped for this fierce competition. It is our duty to keep our gunpowder dry for this human endeavour. It is our civic duty to discharge our responsibilities in executing this cardinal role in this life competition for victory of our group. It is essentially group struggle. It is group game. The African Negroes just lack the sense of group game. This is why they had lost out in the competition for several generations and millenniums. You are not fighting for yourself. You are fighting for the group. All my life I have fought for honour not for myself but for the group. A respectable group has enough honour to share among each member of the winning group. Respectful decorum means that you fight your corner for the success of the group.

The victory of the group is the banner of honour for each member. It will be stupid to chide the aggressor. It is equally deplorable to abuse and criminalise the defendant. The level of war and violence no longer has morality. It is totally inappropriate to call a patriot in the defence of his or her homeland a terrorist. In the words of the greatest general the world had ever seen, General Hannibal Hamilcar Barca, the African patriot, applauded the Romans for fighting him to defend their homeland and honoured dead Roman officers. He praised each of them for discharging his civic duties to his homeland. A good sportsman recognises that the crown of honour is not his alone to take. He has to compete for it. Africa has enough for. Let us all make Africa work for all of us as a group.

Neither, gold, platinum nor diamond would make me serve as a mute donkey a brutal and cruel master that fails to recognise that I have life to live in my existence. When he leaves the brutal idiot would neither go with gold, platinum nor diamond when his time is due. This is why we have several gallant men of valour that had kissed mortality as normal human beings. Therefore, it may be our civic duty to fight for life in our existence is true valour. Existence without life is death. It is worst than hell. Hell is a place of serving a sentence but existence is a stage that we have all means to bring life into it provided we recognise that it is a team or group game. The African Negroes must realise this aspect of being here on earth. Let no fool rush to read this book to apportion blame or provoke racial or religious discord to justify violence or war. White and black all have places to defend to death. Our life struggle to prevent mere existence here on earth is to acquire adequate education and skills to work satisfactorily to live life in our existence here on earth.

A good General must know the skills and tactics of his opponents. He must read the battlefield and the mind of his enemies. He must know how to control his resources in this battlefield to fight the enemies effectively. Surrounded by death we must know that we must offer death to advance and move forwards or receive death and be out of trouble. This is the strife we face in the world. Nobody in his right mind should accept existence and spectator role as the African Negroes. We are all actors and participants. The black people will have to return to the drawing board of basics of life on earth. Work as a team. Be ready to compete with others. There should be less internal rivalry but you must always be ready to get your team to compete in good and adequate education and skills development and productivity on your land. Avoid waste of resources. Stamp out corruption and graft. Food production is very basic skills in all living things. We must do everything to produce the food we eat. We must live in peace in our group and with our neighbours but if we have very genuine reason to fight we must be fully committed and maintain our domestic unity. Aggression courts defeat but defence endears victory.

It is important for African Negroes to give themselves a new image. The image we bear today is chaotic in everything. Our body hygiene and language all bear the air of chaos. We must think seriously of presenting a new uniform image. There are number of things we do well but we have to project ourselves. The white people must be given some credit. The way some of them receive and warm up to Madiba Nelson Mandela deserve some applause and credit. African Negroes should learn from this. Equally the way they live with one another despite their past bitter wars is an example for us to imitate. The white race had the worst conditions of living on earth. Their weather and environment were completely hostile. Their class set up was hierarchical. The strongmen held the rein. The lesser folks fought with the strong men and for the strong men to hold the rein.

Despite all these inhospitable conditions they finally fought their way to good education and adequate skills to contain both the elements and the tyranny of their leaders. They worked hard to achieve wealth and prosperity. They had improved Science and Technology to catch world attention. They had improved the lot of mankind. They stand to gain credit for all these. The African Negro must note that they cannot continue to remain indifferent and block the way to progress to create wealth and prosperity. Handing out food and medicine parcels to the African Negroes is not the solution. It is stupid and incomprehensible for a black ex-soldier to admit that he does not know how to clear the bush to plant maize for his family. He is a typical example of what is wrong with the Negroes in Africa. This man had been addicted to laziness, and easy pay packet and having his needs provided for by others that he had lost the initiative to work and provide for himself. This is a great difference from what happens in the West. Top executive returns to land to farm and do it with praiseworthy dexterity. They confess that they found it difficult and hard initially but soon caught up with the farmer's way of life. A typical African child went through all aspects of farming in his or her area before completing School. I had the same training from my parents before proceeding to train as a Medical Practitioner. The child must be brought up to be a human being before completing his or her education. In today's concept the Africans must integrate sound and good education in Mathematics, Science, Technology, adequate skills and satisfactory apprenticeship to equip their youths with versatile means to live and work to provide for their needs.

Anybody interested in helping the African Negroes must ignore emotions and confront the realities of life. They must teach the African Negroes to redouble their efforts in good and practical well integrated education in Science, Technology, adequate skills training and apprenticeship. They must study the environment and effective use of their land. They must learn how to avoid wasting their scarce resources. They must avoid enjoying easy and comfortable life without working. They must prevent corruption and all elements and factors of their cultures and life that encourage corruption. They must avoid malingering and fraudulent living. They must not live by crime, illusion of wealth and empty satisfaction of day dreams. They must appreciate the importance of unity. Uniting the continent into larger units and integrating common services and infrastructures would avoid unnecessary duplications and waste of the scarce resources. They must tolerate one another. They must avoid bogus rivalry. They must be involved in healthy competition for excellence. They must appreciate the place of genuine role models for social success. Merit must count at all levels. Recognition of talents must form the core of achievements and leadership. Mediocrity must not be allowed to survive by intrigues to hold genuine talents and achievements to ransom. This frustrates and holds down the continent in stagnation, retrogression and permanent retardation of progress.

The African Negroes and all Africans must know that dismantling colonial borders would allow free movement of citizens, trade and progress. Africa will become a big and vast attractive market. They must essentially invest fifty to sixty per cent of their budget on education to equip the citizens, with (good practical education,) reliable skills training, civic discipline, knowledge and skills. Genuine self-esteem and confidence to work and reach excellence in your labour is essential for success. We must accept and love our land of birth as the greatest gift nature has given us. We must cultivate the land and rear the right livestock on it. The food and wealth we need are here in our homeland. We must realise that everyday is a working day and no status in life exempts us from work. We have to work hard at home as we do at other places. We must make our land productive and our land will be prosperous and we will be wealthy. Prosperity and wealth do not come from foreign land. It is sad to observe that the people taking us out of current European global recession are two powerful Asian countries, Japan and China.

They have neither natural resources nor cash crops but they have good Education, good skills and sustain the richness of their skills with excellent apprenticeship. Why then are black people prosperous? We are divisive and lack political system that should bring us together to regulate the way should work and improve our land and Economy. We cannot live in isolation. We must change with the changing times and with other people. We must learn from them. The changes we observe in time and in other peoples are changes in nature. We have to change. We should be neither arrogant nor indifferent. The black man must abandon his indifference and arrogance to be humble to learn from others. Why do we have top class leaders in all human generations, St Augustine of Hippo in the Catholic Church, the Great Barcine warrior Generals: Hannibal, Abram Petrovich, Nelson Mandela and today President Obama while our leadership below this level is either non-existent or very poor? Africa requires committed and delegated leaders from the village to all levels in the community. All our children require civic Education and any youth crimes deserve stiff penalty. We have no choice but to toughen up our youth on how to live in this world. Some Africans had developed the artificial Party Culture and stealing from Public Funds and living beyond their means. Our civic Education must include Money Economy and respect for Public Funds as well as living within their means. They must learn to be their best in whatever they do and must learn to work in teams.

Our Dignity must be restored through adequate education and good skills training. We had higher income per capita than most countries in South Asia by 1960 when most of us became independent. Today, our income per capita is at the level with Bangladesh that does not have the resources we have. Our leaders should answer the question, "What happened and where are the funds?" Unfortunately, ignorance and lying are common place in Africa, today. There will not be any satisfactory and convincing answer to this question. We foolishly squandered the funds in crimes, stupid bush wars and rubbish arms and corruption. Africa failed to correct the flaws of colonial borders. It retained them at great costs, duplications of common services, infrastructures and wastage of scarce resources. The selfish interests and ambitions of a few made our mediocre leaders ignore most of these things. We must start from ourselves and our leaders to revive Africa.

They like to see us fail for them to exploit. If they knew we would not be where we are at the moment. Today, it is time for us to do what we want to do quietly and ignore the meddlesome intruders. The African Union has already said what we expect it to do but will they sincerely do what they say? They talk of resources and facilities. We have to improvise. Necessity is the mother of invention. We have to slowly build up our own. We have to make them. Initially they may not work but later they will. The West did it that way. We do not need sophisticated Western made completed equipment. They hinder us. They stop us from looking for our own solutions. We must accept our sacred duty to work and live life and prevent mere existence. I refused to exist to dishonour my race, family and all those I loved in life. Life is a relay race. We must run our bit and hand over the baton. Africa had been destroyed by those who fail to understand this basic principle of life on earth. May we all have the understanding that we are not here to stay forever? We all are mortal beings. My choice is knowledge and skills and not paper and metal money.

It is sad that frank discussion of the flaws that damaged Africa would necessarily sound like diatribe and incitement against some people. Unfortunately, this is not the case. The truth is that the damage to Africa is made of multiple factors and involved several people and black and white races. We cannot ignore them. It is not worth discussing the damage to Africa and to advise on steps to repair the damage if we cannot talk of the role of each player in this drama. We Africans are not sacred cows in our demise. We bear the blunt of the blame for what has happened to our continent because we have been stupid, docile and totally oblivious of our civic duties to our land and people. We lacked vision of the future. We remained blind to the enormous growth in progress, wealth and prosperity around us. We remained indifferent to changes. Nature imposes changes on people who refuse to accept changes. This is what is happening to Africa.

The Africans have themselves to blame. They continued to lie and pay lip service to changes. The OAU existed for several decades as a talking shop. Now we have the African Union and NEPAC. Will they be another talking shop without action? They complain of lack of resources. Who will provide the resources? If the Africans cannot devise means of getting the resources they need to make these things work they should pack up and forget about them. They must not establish bodies and organisations and expect white people to fund and run them for them to benefit. Are they begging bodies? The Africans must learn to take up responsibilities for their orderly and sustainable development. Our leaders always sit and cross legs expecting the West to bail them out.

The patronising attitude of the white people in the West encourages indolence in Africans. The West is not duty-bound to give aids to Africa. African leaders must take up their responsibilities. The West must stop intrusive behaviours in African affairs. They must not give our leaders the impression that they are working for them. We know that some leaders are agents to foreign Intelligence organisations. The plight of Africa should genuinely be a scar on the conscience of these leaders and the organisations that employ them. It is now an open secret that the CIA engages most of these leaders. We saw in Mobutu and Jonas Sivimbi. Recently we have also seen in Iraq. Of course these leaders should have the conscience to ask themselves how many patriotic Americans in responsible positions would accept to be agents. The meddlesome and deleterious attitudes of these foreign governments are neither helpful to them nor to us. The treacherous leaders irresponsibly abandon their duties to the people they claim to lead. These leaders neglected their duties to the people and Africa. It is they who now expect the West to pick up both the bills and rubbish left behind by the negligent and irresponsible attitudes of these leaders. The cost of the West doing business with them is enormous and expensive to both the people in the West and in Africa. The nanny state is neither beneficial to the West nor to Africa.

We all are embarrassed by daily deterioration of the state of affairs in Africa, today. Events are deteriorating daily. The news is always discouraging. The Press is poor and each day poorer and worse than the day before. Little did we know that the Sudanese Arabs would choose this time to start land grabbing and slave gathering jihad again in Africa. The African remnants in the continent demonstrate insensitivity incompatible with self-esteem and survival in the face of grinding poverty, HIV-AIDS pandemic and resurgence of all the infectious diseases that were nearly eliminated or brought under control such as tuberculosis and typhoid. Malaria is raging and drug resistant parasites are fast developing. Newer viral diseases are creating havoc among our teenagers, the cream of our investment in the future. They damage children yet unborn in the womb. They damage the elderly, the frail and the infirm. Malnutrition is rife and endemic. Life has become the cheapest thing to dispose of or be ignored. Slave trade has resurfaced. Trafficking in children and young women are common. Crime and corruption are fast becoming our way of life. Our leaders have forgotten that people get old and die.

The Arabs have a choice. They must join all genuine and honest people in the world to condemn ethnic cleansing and genocide against black African Muslims in Darfur in Sudan if they want to live in this our continent, Africa, with us. They can return to Gaza to continue fighting a futile war that they had never won. They came out of Gaza to confront General Alexander who routed them before he entered Egypt where he encountered no futile confrontation. Are they trying to confirm what Israel has been telling the world that they cannot live peacefully with other races and ethnic groups in the world? If they continue with violence, war and land grabbing massacres, ethnic cleansing, genocide, slave gathering jihad and slave trade, we may have no choice in future but to drive them out. They came here by war violence and conquest buttressed by religious deceit and intrigues, only fourteen hundred years ago. Ever since, we have tolerated their rude macho and insulting behaviour. Our shame and hurt in Darfur may be wiped off only by driving out the Arabs from our land. Let us hope it will not come to this.

They had used a doubtful faith Islam, to destroy our land and civilisation. Islam is a doubtful faith because of the way Arab Muslims use it for war and violence. They are forever fighting jihads, why? They had used Islam to hold us back and cause permanent stagnation in Africa. Now secret Arabinisation of Africa is in the open. The people in Darfur are Islamic Muslims but they are not Arabs. They are black Africans and wrong type of Muslims. They are slaves to the nomadic and landless Arabs. Their women and men are sexual pleasure tools to Arab deviants and perverts. They sell our girls into sexual bondage and slavery. Western Christian organisations have been paying ransom money to redeem our girls from sexual bondage for several years of conflict between the Arabs and black Africans in Southern Sudan. The world must tell the Arabs that this is not the time to tolerate slavery and slave trade. The world has been silent until now. Right now some people are still having a double tongue over Arab atrocities in Africa.

The Arab atrocities had taken a toll of children and adults in Israel and Africa. Now they had descended on the West. The world must tell the Arabs that they are no more innocent victims by taking on the lions and tigers. Protracted and fratricidal bush wars persistently destroy lives and properties in Africa. The Arabs are no fools. They had sponsored these wars over the years to gain absolute control of oil and other resources in Africa and other parts of the world by spreading Islam. The Wahabi School in Saudi Arabia was used in spreading this message. The cold war and Saudi cash sponsorship supporting Western armament production and sales concealed this ambition for years. They had wreaked havoc on the people and the continent of Africa. Refugees and internally displaced people are scattered everywhere. Arabs and Muslim radical fanatics run amok with suicide bombers. Religious and ethnic riots and crisis are the rule. The tragic catastrophe of Nigeria is typical example of Muslim Islamic havoc on the community. The warlords had taken over. They deeply embedded in Government.

They had hijacked our fragile efforts at democratic rule to continue their rule of terror. They had tainted participatory democracy with the Sharia law. The women are condemned to permanent male macho domination confined to life in the backyard under male authority. They are physically present in whatever uniform is suitable for the time for their tyrannical rule. They make a mockery of elections by rigging and fixing them. Corruption is rife. Its pandemic chaos is infectious like the flu. The flu of corruption in Nigeria has affected even long- standing trans-national and multinational corporate conglomerate like the Shell Company. It has distorted its image. It has degraded and destroyed Africa. The hope of Africa and the black race lies on urgent rescue. That mission needs all Africans of concern all over the world. In this hard and difficult time, Africa owes gratitude to Ms Condoleezza Rice for her role in selling rescue of Liberia to Americans. She is like Ester that loved the king but did not forget her people in bondage. Colin Powell braved the wild and hostile depressing situation in the Sudan to deliver the sharp message to leaders. I greet the courage of these African-Americans. The sad thing is that they always fight alone, while the fat cats in Africa, know how kill each other but cannot ward off naked attack of this type. Quiet diplomacy is nonsense when total strangers terrorise and slaughter your people in gruesome ethnic cleansing and naked genocide. That expression, "civilised standards", has a meaning when your house is not on fire. Rescue operation is what a burning house needs and a community facing war and violence of extinction has no choice but to fight back till the enemy appreciates peace. It is appalling that African leaders are tyrannically daring in killing their people. They are timidly cowardly in leading the fight against outside invaders. They are forever taking refuge to hide from enemies. Small Israel knows how to confront the Arabs.

The only hope lies on a few privileged displaced people in the Diaspora. All over History of African liberation and emancipation of the black race from bondage the Africans in the Diaspora had always pioneered the struggle for freedom. The castrated men on the continent had always preferred to be carried in chains into bondage to serve strangers as slaves. It is therefore no surprise that a few nomadic Arabs in Sudan had held Africa to ransom. The African Armies are waiting for logistic help from the West and America. They want them to come and do the fighting for them. What a shame to have men who are more hopeless than women in the face of danger? The cowardice, corruption, intrigues, crimes, tyranny and treachery of our so-called leaders betray and harm Africa. They destroy our chances. These are the people damaging Africa and Africans in the world.

Africans in the Diaspora are better placed to know the destructive and detrimental role of the so-called leaders and the warlords play in the plight of Africa today. Every human being and all living things have two vital points to run the short transient race of life. A viable child is born into this world. Right there he or she starts this race. The outcome of the race depends on the level of understanding of the race. The African leaders and the warlords have no knowledge of the content of the race. They do not know its starting point and the end point. The success in this race depends on what the contestants can do for the community. Unfortunately, the African leaders rely on what the can do for themselves as individuals but not what they can do for the community. They lack the understanding of the community. They equally lack the knowledge of time and changes.

In the past, Hanani brought the type of news I am now giving you to Nehemiah son of Hachaliah in captivity in Shushan about Jerusalem. He wept and prayed. God gave favour with the king and got the opportunity of returning to rebuild the Temple in Jerusalem.

Today, information Technology and the Media are awash with news about the homeland. In the midst of these disasters, tragedies and catastrophes, the so-called corrupt and cowardly African leaders are planless. They are guilty of being selfishly content with dismemberment of the African continent into nonviable fragments to serve them as their fiefdoms. They are guilty of totally avoidable duplications and unnecessary massive wastage of the scarce resources. They compete with each other as in a beauty contest. They wear oversized gowns over ten times their sizes while most of their people go naked in the streets. I fail to comprehend or understand why the Arab government of the tyrant, Bashir in Sudan is looking for extra time to complete Arabinisation in Sudan after over a quarter of a century of bloody and brutal war in the Sudan and fourteen hundred years of brutal slave-gathering and land-grabbing wars and violence.

I do not think Obasanjo's presence in the Sudan would change anything. It is not his business being there at this time even though he is the current chairman of African Union. He should ensure that Bashir does not use him as a delaying tactic. He should not make any move until he has firm word and promise from Bashir that he would put a visible firm halt to the activities of his militia and troops. Obasanjo's visit may be counter productive. It may water down the positive and effective message our firstborn son Colin Powell delivered on behalf of the US, the world and Africa to this tyrant. It seems so far I have been proved right. Bashir is playing for time. He has so far enlisted China for support using oil, Pakistan using religious loyalty and emotions, Algeria using joint regional and ethnic interest. Now he has enlisted the tacit support of Britain.

The British Foreign Minister, Shaw went there and made very vague statement. He shook the hands of this tyrant. The British Prime Minister went there and shook hands with the tyrant. He again ended up with spin and more hot air and vague statement tacitly condemning the black people in the Sudan to the authority and tyranny of Bashir. They had tacitly sealed the fate of Darfur black Muslims by telling Bashir that he has authority over their plight. This is Britain in Africa. They play games with us. Obasanjo heads a government dominated by fanatical and radical very corrupt Muslims. Obasanjo is yet to win the struggle against pandemic corruption in

Nigeria. Nigeria is still very corrupt. Obasanjo has gone to Darfur to gain some respect after Colin Powell had done much of the ground work. But what influence has he got with the fox tyrant, Bashir? If he returns empty-handed he would succeed in watering down the powerful message that Colin Powell delivered to Bashir. This would not be helpful. Now we have seen that Bashir has succeeded in watering and diluting down the message. Obasanjo took Bashir's lieutenants and the victims in Darfur to Abuja. He accommodated and banqueted them under the pretence of mediation. This is an example of how not to use diplomacy. The brutal atrocities of Bashir's tyranny and its ruthlessness do not demand meek and fragile efforts at negotiation. The issues involved are a mixture of brutal cocktail of religion, racial xenophobia, ethnic feud, traditional Arab intrigues, politics and Economy of resources punctuated with long-standing brutal war and violence.

Do I trust Obasanjo to tell Bashir that Africa is not in any compromising mood to tolerate Arabs abusing black Africans any longer in this century and millennium? Obasanjo's record in conflict resolution at home, in Nigeria is poor. We just do not want him to water down our message to Bashir and the Arabs. Nigeria is yet to overcome corruption and crimes. He is not the UN. He cannot alter the world ultimatum to Bashir. He is a self-confident individual. He was one of the contestants for the post of UN Secretary when Kofi Annan was appointed. Attraction to be involved in UN negotiation is tempting but is Bashir the person to do business with? It is always worth telling my brothers and sisters wherever our misfortunes and fortunes had placed us in the world that the vision our ancestors had of the world, had not changed. Right from the Pharaohs genuine indigenous Africans had never believed in land grabbing and resource wars. We seemed to have accepted the concept of integrating Africa and Europe as centre of power and March of civilisation from the West.

The Pharaohs accepted this Queen Cleopatra in her encounter with Julius Caesar sold this concept and vision to Caesar. Julius Caesar accepted this persuasive vision and philosophy. He became friendly with Queen Cleopatra. They had a son together. Caesar introduced this son dressed in imperial robes at the age of ten as his legitimate heir to the Roman Senate in Rome. The ultra-conservative rights in the imperial politics at Rome led by Octavia flatly rejected the proposal. They plotted and assassinated Julius Caesar. Marcus Antonio took over. He was determined to protect Caesar's legitimate heir and Cleopatra. He wanted to execute Julius Caesar's will. The plotters again conspired and started a civil war. They finally executed Marcus Antonio. They destroyed Cleopatra's family. They rejected partnership. Their vision was total conquest and subjugation foreign nations. They were subjected to Roman imperial tyranny and treated as slaves. They were incorporated into the Provinces of Rome. They initiated crude racial xenophobic discrimination. They insulted our leader, Queen Cleopatra and called her, a "whore."

Before this time the Carthaginians accepted the concept of partnership. Barca lived and fought in defence of the dignity of Africa and the freedom of Africans. He resisted the concept of imperial expansion in all its forms. Hamilcar his loyal son lived in Europe and fought for independence and freedom of Africa and Africans. He took Hannibal his son at the age of nine to Europe. He lived there and fought several wars in defence of human freedom, integrity of Africa and the African people. He supported the natives to maintain the rule of law and their freedom. He cultivated the concept that the freedom of various ethnic nationals in Europe was bound to the freedom of Africa and its people. He admonished them to resist any hostile forces threatening this balance and freedom. The story has it that when a European king died two of his children were traditionally fighting for the crown for succession. Hannibal in characteristic way of African respectability for seniority presided over the case and after thorough search for the truth and justice; he decided to offer the crown to Brancus the elder child and settled the case without bloodshed. Hannibal and that brood of African lions lived and fought against the Romans who persistently showed their intention to subjugate Africa and make slaves of Africans to loot our land and destroy our civilisation. Cornellius Publius Scipio vanquished and drove out Africans from Southern Europe and their base in Spain. They confiscated our properties. At this time Africa was making, over one million pounds sterling, annually from its investments in Europe. Could you imagine what a nation that was making such amount at that time would be, today, if the Romans did not destroy our efforts and stole our wealth? Despite this Scipio advised the Romans against destroying Carthage a very advanced and wealthy civilisation in Africa. But Marcus Cato and his group were totally committed to looting African wealth.

He was voraciously eating the finest raisons and showing enormous African wealth brought back by Roman spies. Cato commented, "A land that has this is worthy of the blood of every Roman noble." In 146 BC the Roman ultra-conservative right destroyed Carthage by a war of genocide. Scipio was so upset that he denied himself the honour of State funeral by denying them access to his body at death. This was the level of respect and admiration that the ancient warriors had for themselves and the sport, war that is lacking today. George Walker Bush, a man alien to soldiering and war, Dick Chenne, and Rumsfeld all not experienced in war and soldierly gallantry and conduct at war had brought undeclared courtesy at war into shame. They conducted warfare as a game hunting for wild boar meat by gatherers. They were out to kill for huge contracts to share the State funds. A good team of Professionals planning a war knows rules of engagement and protecting POWs and civilians. They have to recognise that they are fighting against fellow human beings who are defending their lands and interests and have reason to defend them to death as a mark of Patriotism and loyalty to their homeland. They have right to defend their homes. They have right to protect their lives and their citizens. Hence they deserve absolute courtesy in life as POWs and in death as casualties and martyrs of war. They are gallant people. These USA war-ignorant leaders robbed the USA of the opportunity of showing the world that it understands these Principles of war and that is a civilised country. Great Warrior African General Hannibal understood these in his struggles against the Romans. He treated them courteously. He understood their right to fight and that they were gallant men of honour. Unfortunately the Europeans including the Romans had always been Barbarians in war. The Romans beheaded Hasdrubal. They wrapped his head in wild green leaves and cast it into Hannibal's camp. This was very Barbaric and damaged Hannibal a great deal. He remarked, "This is African head severed off." Torturing victims of war is primitive act. It is an expression of ignorance of war. War is not hunting. European won and took control of the destiny of the world. It also set the world on the pathway to over two millenniums of crises and chaos. We see it in the Middle East, today. By 1919 Afghanistan had fought three wars. Recently it had fought the Russians. Now it is fighting the Bush soldiers of the willing. European global control had achieved Economic miracle through Science and Technology. Unfortunately, peace has eluded the world. The world at this level of wealth and prosperity requires free peace. We hope that the US citizens will give Barack Obama to make the US friend and one of the leaders of the world.

Today we can see that warfare involves bigger and more lethal weapons and human hatred for each other has no end. Dehumanising fellow human beings in hostilities is the norm and not a rarity. We are yet to see a lot of insular British people forgetting about the world wars and giving their German opposing Armies any credit. Since we have to share this world together and each of us victorious and the vanquished would finally die and leave the world to face his maker, God we have to be generous and magnanimous after any conflict. The Psalmist truly confines both Monty and Rommel to their homes in their graves and Churchill and Hitler to theirs. The world has a duty to get away from hatred.

The story of the tragedy of the victims of severe trauma stress syndrome as narrated by Mr Robert at forty shows how wars and violence had bred human beasts. They find it difficult to live without wars. Robert lived dangerously close to war zones. The problems these innocent European victims of wars had created in Africa as dogs of wars, mercenaries in African bush wars partly come from these lots who earn their living by violence and wars. Most of these people come from the notorious and infamous French Legion in Africa. Roman colonisation in Africa cost us the loss of Carthage to Roman genocide in Africa, the first well-documented genocide in human History and the loss of our Mediterranean Seaboard to Arab occupiers. Today, these occupiers and their at times chaotic religion had failed to give Africa peace. We hope the AU would persuade all of us to adopt secular constitution and live by the rule of secular law and not obsolete religious utopia totally incompatible with IT global world of high Technology. This takes us to the effect of colonisation in Africa.

We cannot fail to give credit to single minded British people like Morrell and his friend, Kessman who single handedly used their skills and resources and through expert pioneering journalism with Liverpool Guardian fought the powerful King Leopold 11 of Belgium and the bloody tyrant and butcher of Africans in the Congo to a standstill and prevented total genocide in the Congo just last century. We must replace Leopold in Africa with Morrell and Kessman. We must eradicate the memory of Belgium in Africa for hiding the crimes of their King, Leopold, the butcher of black people in the Congo from the world. William Wilberforce and his friends fought and made British Parliament see the evil of slave trade. The British occasional philanthropic spirit deserves praise and place in History. The era and unpredictable behaviour of Tony Blair has cast some doubts on this. But we still have the George Galloway and Tony Ben and recently late Ted Heath as legends of the British philanthropic spirit. History may be favourable to Blair if he sees his African project through and remembers to remind the Iraqis that the British Army is not a fortress to protect them from their tyrannical tendencies and hatred of themselves.

The US has had the opportunity to be philanthropic but it has allowed the ideological Straussite conservative rights frequently wrong in most of their ideas to squander their chances. The French are dubious, devious and vindictive and very unpredictable. King Leopold did not attend the Berlin Conference of 15 Sept 1884 that the German von and German leader summonsed. He must have been a cannibal enjoying human flesh meat from severed right hands of Africans perhaps out of superstitious Belgian rituals. If Leopold was not a cannibal the Belgians have the right to tell the world what he did with severed African right hands? The Europeans are infamous due to their tendency towards incest.

They have very immature sexual habits. Beautiful African children were slaves they used to satisfy their quest for paedophilic and incest sexual practice. These are not the trade marks of sophisticated and civilized people. The Europeans who colonized and plundered Africa for the most parts were very primitive people. He slaughtered ten million Africans. Germany had had its own fair share of punishment from the Creator and they have the opportunity to persuade Europe to dismantle the multiple Berlin walls they created in Africa. The Berlin wall condemned a section of Germany to poverty. Multiple Berlin walls in Africa had made Africa irreversibly and wholly poor. Belgium and France starting from Leopold 11, the tyrant butcher and

African right hand snatcher in the Congo who criminally asked for the destruction of incriminating evidence against him of his Barbaric cruelties in the Congo when Morrell exposed him to the world and Britain forced investigations into his activities used money to bribe Stanley, a criminal workhouse boy who spied and sold Congo to Leopold the butcher. Leopold started serious corruption in Africa. Surely such beasts as Leopold cast doubt on European claim to civilization. Racial discrimination and stigmatization of black people renders most of them primitive and ignorant before me. Homosexual practice demeans them. The word homophobia is wrong in syntax as homo hominis Latin word for human is not for man alone. The Greeks and Romans practised this queer and strange sex but they had no word for us Africans who disapproved of it because of our sensitivity to decency. The anal canal to us is equivalent to toilet bowl full of toilet effluents foul and smelly. Take no offence the Europeans have some dirty habits in their culture that we black people strongly disapprove of. We share the zeal for learning in common. They first learnt from us through the Greeks but today we have to relearn from them.

Today, most Africans are starving but Europe gets a little under half of its food from Africa. When they return pest-infested grains from what they and their animals cannot eat it forms big news for the Press and the Media. I do not hold them alone to blame also the illiterate and corrupt African leaders. Most of the French leaders living and dead are yet to tell the world and the French the details of their dealings and business with late "emperor" Bokassa of Central African Republic. It was a section of greedy Romans, Marcus Cato and Octavia, Caesar Augustus and his accomplishes of fellow tyrants of greed followed by the cruel and brutal slavers of Africans and colonizers that created this tragedy in Africa. The catastrophe and African blood would ever hunt them in hell. These were not human beings but beasts. Shame on them who lay false claim to humanity.

We can see from this story how popular the concept of partnership as opposed to total subjugation and enslavement was. The Greeks all wanted partnership. Alexander son of Philip of Macedonia adopted Egypt as his free home. Cleopatra was a descendant of Ptolemy that succeeded Alexander after his death. Ptolemy was a

Senior General of Alexander who had no heir at death. Carthage and Africans wanted partnership. The Barcines wanted partnership. Hannibal spared Rome because of our traditional humanity and his choice of partnership and not war and terror and violence. The Europeans adopted empire-building and pacification of alien lands for loots. They have stolen enough now to escape from poverty. But they had destroyed peace. They have no peace.

After over three millenniums, it is obvious that the concept of imperial expansion of the ultra conservatives in the European West has failed. Empire building is a failed concept and vision. Partnership is the only path to democracy and peace. The West, today, has to consider partnership with Africa. Practical education and active skills training for the Africans have no alternative. We have to rehabilitate Africa. Construction work in Africa will sustain the whole of Africa and the West in work and jobs for over a century. African resources alone can sponsor this if we stop corruption, stealing and unnecessary duplications. Everybody must essentially work. The rule of secular law must guard the peace and security. It is the true West made up of Africa and Europe, it is, that should compete with the East that is fast expanding technologically and in wealth and prosperity. Peaceful competition, today, needs a vast market, well-educated people and skilled workforce. Do you know that what you see in Egypt as relics of our surviving civilization is the onset of Architecture limited by the materials we had in the Nile valley. The Greek took a leaf from this and used the materials in their environment to build more for their Diana and other goddesses including |Athenian while the Romans benefited from cement that volcano manufactured free for them and succeeded in building more with slave labour? The march of civilization started here in Africa and the pioneering Africans were not Arabs. Let them not claim it. The little claim they may have is the fact that their conquest in Africa was associated with killing and castrating of Africans into eunuch to look after their wives to seize and stole from them in their harems. God is punishing the Arabs today. They have to change one hundred degrees from their traditional wickedness. The Quran has no power to save them. Allah can save them if they repent.

For over three thousand years, three millenniums, the argument of choice between integration of Africa into Western civilisation seized from Africa by Rome or empire building including Africa held as imperial overseas territory and defeated land and slaves. As I have illustrated above, majority of people opted for integration but powerful and vocal minority, hard ultra-hard conservative right group vetoed this majority opinion. They used terror, intrigues, capitalist criminal corruption and deliberate weeping up of non-existent fear and brute force to advance and force their unpopular decision on the population. Time changes everything. Even unpopular ideas finally become statuesque after several thousand years. The victims finally suffer in silence. Honest and just people find everything wrong with the practice but they fail to see real positive actions from the victims to alter the miserable conditions in which they find themselves. This has been the situation between Africa and Europe for over three thousand years. The major arguments, "integration" and empire-building are still raging in the West and Europe. The soldiers Leopold the butcher used were our fellow Africans. This is why the Europeans felt we were not human beings. People who did that to each other to please strangers were definitely lower than gorillas in their intellect. The elephants mourn their dead. The African wild people seem to slaughter and eat their kind. AU must ban such behaviours on pains of death. AU must now speak out in unambiguous terms against slave trade, slavery and child sacrifice and murders. Let me tell you fellow Africans. "You had been stupid and subhuman. Make yourselves assertively human beings. The world and Africa would open for you. Normal living things close ranks in danger to fight off foreign intruders. Africans male must learn to do this. It is wild to be aggressive if the situation calls for a fight. Fighting is part of nature. Any aliens coming to fight against us must from now face our human savagery. We must close ranks and fight. Everybody on this land is now African. You are accepted as pacifist but never as a traitor regardless of what your social grievances may be. Fighting or doing anything to hurt your people because of any grievances you may have against them is an act of treachery and betrayal of your land.

The demise of the Roman Empire offered opportunistic Arabs and their nomadic religion room to seize the whole of Palestine and North Africa by force in an unholy land-grabbing and slave-gathering jihad. They drove out the natives by massacre and terror. Today, Israel is back. The Arabs have a chance to talk peace and share the land. In

Africa they have to adopt integration and equality. Democracy based on the rule of secular law and equality of opportunities is the door to peace. Religious freedom is the heart of participatory democracy. They must accept and respect multi-religious faiths. The community must legislate against religious ghettos. Religious freedom means that citizens can accept and practise any faith without molestation or open or secret punishment. No religious riots should be acceptable. Religious riots and crises must carry severe penalty both for individuals and the sects as a group. Any religious intolerance must court abolition of the religion. The authorities must have power to suspend activities of any religion that disturbs the peace. The creator created everybody to share the world without the menace of any sect or religion. Religion must preach love and peace. Religious violence is direct appeal to the community to withdraw recognition and freedom from the violent group. There is no room for religious laws being imposed on the community. Adherence to religious laws should be strictly voluntary among the believers. Religious laws violate penal codes. They have no business to do with the society that must be governed by acceptable secular laws established by peaceful debates and agreements. The naivety and cowardice of Africans had blunted them to abuses by all races of human beings. The newer generations of Africans would have to be sharper and willing to fight and endure hardship until the enemies are defeated. There is history of genuine heroism and gallantry apart from that the Barcine Generals. We must learn to stand firm in the Battle field and fight our alien invaders and not our brothers or join alien enemies to fight and punish our brothers.

The two ideas, integration and empire building and degrading and pacification of Africa had been around for over three thousand years. The ultra-conservative Straussite rights with very wrong idea about civilisation, peace, spread of genuine practical Education, skills training and growth of global prosperity had hijacked all the credits of advances in the West from ruthless colonisation and plundering of foreign lands and claimed success for their tactics of terror and smash and grab. They had used fear of imaginary enemies and continuous wars and violence to control and win support of their people. A review of world history reveals that the West led by these criminals would always have some enemy to fight. They successfully made a monster of the Soviet Union to justify their armament manufacture and sales for over forty years. The demise of the Soviet Union meant that they were out to find a new enemy or manufacture one. It is a fight against terrorism a non-visible enemy. Afghanistan and Iraq are now war fronts.

A starving Iraq suddenly had enough weapons of mass destruction to destroy the world including the US. This has now become weapon of mass deceit. Capitalism is now famous and synonymous with criminal corruption. The cheating and rigging of the so-called democratic free elections render democracy unattractive. Capitalism and free market are fast becoming counterfeit theories disseminated to rob the world of its wealth. Nothing justifies less than one percent of the world population and landmass controlling over ninety percent of global wealth. The world is tired of wars and violence. The audio-horn growing inflexible debating leaders must notice that time and events do not stand still. They and all living things change. Therefore, any person that lays claim to the mantle of leadership must accept continuous changes in the world. The ultra-conservative right group must accept the law of flexibility and changes consistent with evolution. The world is tired of empire-building and pacification to plunder and loot their wealth. The world is not in mood to tolerate empire-building and imperial wars in this century or millennium.

This is the century and millennium of truth and righteous justice. Credibility will no longer be the casualty of war. Leaders who swallow credibility and regurgitate lies and deception to the public will get into the record book of ignobility. The world is no longer in mood to tolerate gun-boat diplomacy and intimidation to disseminate false history. The US wanted Saddam Hussein. They have got him for a year but their war to dislodge Saddam is still raging. Iraq is today a killing field. We must be stupid to listen to the collision of the willing now qualifying for a coalition of the weird liars. The UN has a choice. Offer Iraq and its oil and gas on a gold plate to the US and give us peace or ask the US to go home and leave Iraq. They must pay indemnities to Iraq quietly for the destruction of the country. This will convince everybody that the world is not in mood to tolerate direct or proxy wars in this century. Integration is the choice full of hope.

Empire building and military pacification of foreign lands, by war and violence for plundering and looting of wealth are out of fashion. The West has a duty to repair the damage they did to Africa in their interest. Africa now needs construction and not destruction. Construction will provide jobs and open up the continent. The commission for Africa must give Africa a reliable productive education and good skills training. If this commission is serious open up transcontinental road and rail networks to join the continent and open it to the outside world. It will provide jobs for a long term for both Africans and the West. Reclaiming land from the desert or dedesertification of the continent is a challenging but very profitable task. We have to attack the lack of infrastructures vital for orderly and sustainable development. Touch and go approach to Africa does not scratch the surface of the problems in Africa. Debt pardon would provide more money for the corrupt politicians to loot and bank abroad and in off-shore havens. Feeding hungry Africans is a non-starter. There must be a solid permanent frame built to support the economy. The Africans themselves must build these structures. They must have things that will sustain the community in permanent employments and provide essential services to the community. This is lacking in Africa.

THE COMMISSION FOR AFRICA AND FAILURE OF LEADERSHIP IN AFRICA:

The last African leaders that made every effort at collective defence and Security were the Barcines over four thousand years, four millenniums ago. Barca stood up to help the people ward off the enemies of Africa. Hamilcar followed in his footsteps. Hamilcar actually sacrificed his family to the defence of Africa. He made Gen Hannibal see and know who the real enemies of Africa, its global status, wealth and civilisation, were, viz. the wild ultra-conservative rights in Rome, from the age of nine years. His brood of African lions, Hasdrubal, Hanno and Mago were enlisted in this struggle. The other leader that cared for the welfare of Africa was Queen Cleopatra. Apart from these few most African leaders were always self-preserving people. They were damn-right selfish. Survival of the nation meant their personal survival. YOU SCARCELY HEAR OF Africans who took a firm stand to confront the enemies of our land. The leaders seem to be the first to run away to hide in the forest once the enemies struck at our home.

Yet these were the leaders notorious for killing their citizens and people. Our people and the leaders seem to indulge in the habit of themselves into traitors to betray their lands to the enemies. They specialize in treachery and take delight in collaborating with the enemies of our land under the guise of punishing their brothers and sisters they have intra-family row. We must overcome this habit to work for the common good of our land. We have to act as one person in times of Emergency and national disasters. Until we learn to do this we should forget about being a nation. A nation moves in one direction in times of Emergency and danger. The resolve to survive must not have any question mark. Successful and victorious nations have citizens that unite to confront their problems including facing the enemies as one person. They forget about all their differences. Every nation has people with differences but the successful nations are those their citizens ignore all their individual differences and stand together to confront the enemies of their nations. The Africans seem to choose the periods of national Emergencies, threats and disasters to exaggerate their differences and offer these as excuse for abandoning their nations in danger. The African seems to feel that national disaster is time of recompense for the people he or she disagrees with in the community and the nation. We fail to know that deserting your community in times of danger is self-neglect.

Over four millenniums ago Africans abandoned Africa initially to the Europeans and accepted the Romans converting their land into a playing field. When the Roman Empire collapsed, they tolerated the Arabs to move into the vacuum to seize the whole of North Africa. The Africans abandoned and deserted almost all their islands to Europeans. Their faulty sense of self-preservation made them ideal slaves. One drunkard was able to keep two hundred or more Africans as slaves. This happened because each of the slaves had very different comprehension of survival independent of the rest. The African fails to understand that individual survival is synonymous with the survival of the group. The group united to achieve survival is stronger than any surviving individual. The African is selfish and wants it alone. Their leaders take their cue for their conduct from this individualistic behaviour. They are exceptionally selfish.

Nothing stands on their way to individual survival. Oppositions are ruthlessly crushed. They are corrupt and siphon the scarce money they earn from the sales of their natural resources abroad to bank for themselves. Again this is prompted by the strife at individual survival at the expence of all, the community and the nation. If they lose power they want to survive in comfort all be it in a foreign land. Deposed African leaders are content living abroad without power. To them this is survival. They overstay in power and exercise selfish individual survival. Even though they control national finances, any funds voted for public services are stolen and converted into individual purse. They would rather invest the funds in their private lives of luxury rather than use them to do things for the public. This is why they had completely neglected the activities of the government for the past half a century.

THE GEOGRAPHY AND LAND MASS OF AFRICA: THE DESERTS AND THE ARID SAVANNAH, SCARCITY OF WATER ESSENTIALLY DEMAND THAT THE COLONIAL BORDERS AS THEY STAND VIRTUALLY CONDEMN SEVERAL COUNTRIES TO BANISHMENT TO THE DESERT. THEY ARE CONDEMNED TO LIVE IN PERMANENT POVERTY IN THE ARID DESERT AND SAVANNAH AND NO HELP WOULD RESCUE THEM EXCEPT RE-INTEGRATION TO ALLOW FREE MOVEMENTS OF GOODS AND SERVICES. THE CURRENT IMF/WB LOANS TO FINANCIALLY STRICKEN COUNTRIES IS AT RISK BEING DISBURSED TO THESE ARID POOR MINI-COUNTRIES. RE-INTEGRATED VIABLE COUNTRIES WOULD FORM UNITS THAT CAN BORROW FROM GLOBAL FINANCIAL INSTITUTIONS. THIS WILL AVOID DUPLICATIONS AND WASTAGE. IT WILL EQUALLY PROVIDE LAND AND RESOURCES FOR ECONOMIC GROWTH AND EXPANSION. AFRICANS MUST CHOOSE IF INDIVIDUAL OR GROUP INTEREST IN CURRENT ABJECT POVERTY OVERRIDES THE SACRIFICE TO RE-INTEGRATE TO HAVE GENUINE BASIS FOR ECONOMIC GROWTH AND EXPANSION. TODAY WE LIVE IN A GLOBAL VILLAGE AND THE CONCEPT OF A COUNTRY LARGE OR SMALL UNDER TYRANNY MAY STRIKE FEAR IN THE IGNORANT BUT IT IS FAR FETCHED.

WHY THEN DO WE REQUIRE RE-INTEGRATION IN AFRICA? WE NEED IT FOR REGULATORY LAW AND ORDER. WE NEED IT FOR LANDS, WATER RESOURCES TO PREVENT SOME AFRICANS AND THEIR ANIMALS BEING BANISHED TO AND ISOLATED IN ARID DESERT AND SAVANNAH AS UNVIABLE ROGUECOUNTRY,FORECONOMICGROWTHANDEXPANSION. RE-INTEGRATED COLONIAL DISMEMBERED AFRICA HAS DEFINITIVE AND CONTROLLABLE BORDERS. A United Africa would take charge of its land and resources. It would collect the revenues from its resources to use in developing the whole Africa. The Berlin Conference on 15th September 1884 that divided Africa like salami into these sterile and arid desert and savannah to condemn majority of Africans to live in banishment to dry desert in permanent poverty. Therefore, re-integration of these unviable colonial Bantustans into a united Africa and viable units that would allow free movements of people, goods and animals is essentially a top priority for a healthy Economy in Africa. Therefore, the greatest obstacles to development in Africa are the colonial Bantustans many of which are in the arid desert and savannah and very poor corrupt leadership.

It is no surprise that after twenty years of my single man's campaign for re-integration of the African Bantustans Niger and its surrounding Bantustans had exploded in front of the world. Permanent solution still demands re-integration of African colonial Bantustans to create proper nation states. Binding constitutions with strict observance of the rule of law to induce integrity in the leadership and the citizens are what Africa needs. The African landmass, its Geography and environment demand this. The humiliation of Africans having to live in Bantustans not of their creation like prisoners and slaves is difficult to understand except for the ignorance and selfishness of its corrupt leaders that find them as their private estates and fiefdoms. The world cannot continue to pick up the pieces of colonial misplaced interest and corrupt and poor leadership in Africa while majority of the vulnerable people and children in Africa pay with their lives. African life is cheap but the suffering of the dead is an eyesore on our television screens. In the IT high Technology global village these things can no longer be hidden from the world. Why do we then continue to evade a permanent solution? The world must act to re-integrate Bantustans. A United Re-Integrated Africa is solution crying to the whole world to adopt it to solve African Problems.

One of my problems with the white Western European Democracy is its ability to tell perfect lies and deceive the world with empty knowledge that they have no clue about. They defrauded us with religion they knew nothing about and used it as the opium to brainwash and sedate the world. Having violated religion to valueless scrap they had taken this pseudo voo doo Democracy. It is empty talk. If anybody can be democratic the corrupt armed robbers from Europe guilty of several genocides and telling perfect lies about their victims to their people, cannot be truly democratic. The Greeks adopted this practice from African Carthaginians. I can now tell the world we in West Africa Coastal areas are Carthaginian remnants. Our gene memory has better record of Democracy than this counterfeit democracy. Our problems had been poor and corrupt leadership corruptly imposed on us indirectly by Western European white cunning and crafty businesses and establishment. The mischief of modern British so-called perfect-lying diplomacy has recently been revealed in its sales of nuclear Technology to Israel. The morality of the sales is not my concern but the corrupt and criminal perfect lying way they were done is of great concern to trust of these islanders with innocent face of world greatest moral conscience. Why go around the world to captivate people trust with perfect lies and deception? It is difficult to understand the mindset of these islanders strange to integrity and ability to tell the truth. It is phoney trust such people with annals of corruption and criminality. The world has changed immensely but these conservative islanders are very slow to change.

The world should move on and ignore the multiple personalities of these islanders. It is extremely difficult to understand people who had sometimes had people who stood up uncompromisingly for human rights, and fought very bravely against man's inhumanity to man and human cruelties against their fellow human beings being equally guilty of criminal wars and atrocities and multiple genocidal actions against innocent harmless peoples in the world. Can it be due to the fear of the outside world coming to overwhelm their insular security and culture? I would strongly advise my adopted country the UK that the global village of IT high Technology world offers us adequate security without sheepishly being appendage of the US. The UK is in a strong position of being a moderating force to prevent some of the ultra-conservative actions and behaviours of the US. We have to choose between being part of that vocal world that condemn excessive and destructive Hitlerite patriotism. Such patriotism is militarism and aggression. It is no use at a time that we should take care of the environment and spread Technology to protect the eco-environment. Radicalism and fanaticism can be religious, ethnic, racial or wrong concept of power, force and patriotism. The poverty of leadership in Africa is a tragedy not only to Africa and the global black race on earth but also to the world. The true African character and culture was portrayed by our best and excellent leader that Africa ever produced Rt Noble General Hannibal Hamilcar Barca. We speak out our mind without fear or favour. Democracy and freedom of speech do not approve of silencing the citizens as students in the class room. This will be another animal farm. Shakespeare observed in one of his books that the enemy tells the truth about you.

Silencing people you do not approve of what they say is the fault of dictatorship that denies them the privilege of gaining from balanced argument and hearing what their potential enemies think about them. Silencing critics, however, nasty they may be or how you hate to hear them hinders free speech, individual freedom and democracy. It denies the leadership and the community of the opportunity of listening to opposing views of the various people in the community. The enemy you know is better than the friend you are not very sure of and do not know his true views. Christ compared this situation to weeds growing with the crops. The truth will always triumph over fallacy. The time may make mistakes and wrong actions look as the right thing to do but the truth distinguishes itself with time. There is no real nation to defend and die for in the global village. Hence the resources invested in international wars are wasted.

I cannot belabour the importance of tolerance of different points of views as the cardinal principle of freedom of speech and democratic practice. But let us not muddle up the law with free speech and criminal actions. Attrition war of aggression for no genuine acceptable and convincing purpose resulting in the deaths of soldiers and innocent civilians is a crime of murder. The people responsible for such military action are guilty of total disregard for lives and property and crimes against humanity. Equality of life and the needs for comforts of life is important for democracy. The Rt Noble African General Hannibal Hamilcar Barca represented African democratic credentials and military principles by justifying the facts that the Romans had a just cause to fight against us while he led our triumphant campaigns against the Roman war monger Senate in Rome even though it was this notorious Senate that challenged Carthage to military action. We always recognise that the owner of any land under military attack have the right to fight back to ward off such an attack. Therefore, it is irrational thought to use abuse derogatory abusive words or bogus counterfeit democracy as an afterthought to justify unjust military action. Warriors and soldiers were gentlemen before the Roman storm troopers went round the world plundering every land. The Western military machine is a copycat of Roman plundering and looting machine. A timid world led by corrupt Geriatric poor and corrupt leaders is spineless and ominously silent while the world is burning. I do not fail to talk of the events that my life stressed by a failing health had witnessed in this world. The West and the US went and brought Osama bin Laden and his radical Muslim entourage from all over the world to Afghanistan to fight and expel the former Soviet Union from that land. Mission accomplished these erstwhile friends and comrades in arms and effective fighting machine are now pitted against each other in a bitter military struggle. The same West and the US equipped Saddam Hussein Iraq to attack Iran and punish that country for what it did against the US under Ayatollah Homeni but unfortunately now the same people are talking about the evil of Saddam. I have always said that the West is taking the world for a ride with its wealth and affluence. They are now training the Iraqis that will fight against them in the future. They are grooming Iraqi leaders that will oppose them in the future to maintain the momentum of wars of the future. This is very destabilising influence in the world.

Most people would object to be ruled by obsolete religious laws that were made for horses, donkeys and bullocks for tilling the land and wars with swords, bows and arrows to be used in ruling modern world of IT high Technology global village. Again the US and its satellites are ambiguous and ambivalent over this. Their allies in Iraq seem to be agitating for Sharia law Theocracy. Civilised secular laws essential for multiethnic communities, democracy and business seem to be ignored. Yet this is what is likely to cause trouble in future. It is worrying to find that religious extremism and fanaticism friendly to US fails to gain the same accent of rejection from the US as that from groups opposed to the US. Excessive religious zeal is dangerous to God and man. Moses was asked to strike the stone once but he with zeal struck it more than once and displeased God. Hence we here on earth stand to condemn misplaced religious. God does not commission any of us to be his mouthpiece or policemen here on earth. The religious founders were definitely good people who felt our fear and respect for God would make us be fair to our fellow human beings. Unfortunately we have failed woefully to understand the making of the minds and will of these Prophets of God let alone knowing what God wants of us. We deliberately make our desires supersede both those of the Prophets and God. Our desire to destroy each other is contrary to God's desire. Yet it is overwhelming. The Barbaric way we dropped the nuclear bombs on Nagasaki and Hiroshima and continue to produce more powerful killing weapons shows that we are blood thirsty and do not know the purpose of our being here. Yet we have no antidote or response when death calls on us. We die like rat.

The thinning minds of nuclear regulators should not fail to recognise the beastly and perverted human minds and vanity and perverse concept and arrogance of victory. A world that is not lunatic with fear and cowardice should accept the fact that we cannot uncreate the nuclear weapon or limit its spread or prevent its deployment and use in bitter wars. We should allow those who can afford to manufacture and keep them safely so that they do not create health hazards to people, to own them. We should concentrate on its use in war. Anybody who explodes this horrible weapon in a foreign land to subdue its people should have its land and people destroyed. This is more effective control law. It will allow you to use it to destroy an alien intruder on your land and suffer the consequences but not to take to subdue people on their land and leave them to suffer from the aftermath of such an action. Strict regulations of confining nuclear destruction to the place of its manufacture for self defence if they choose would make people choose whether to use them in war or not. The punishment for breaking such law is destruction by combined world multiple nuclear weapons s the world should not sit to observe another Japan without punitive retaliation and severe punishment. Any country that allows its leaders to deploy the nuclear weapons in war would be sure it has voted for global destruction. The truth is that the amount of nuclear weapons we now have would destroy the world several times over and a mad leader can attempt to subdue its opponents with it to trigger off nuclear holocaust and Armageddon. The real deterrent is agreement to jointly and verifiably destroy all nuclear weapons on earth. This is the only credible solution as we all know no ideology or sophistication would stop human beings from beastly behaviour.

The current envisaged UN Security Council re-organisation should go deeper. It must ensure that the continental basis of permanent seat distribution must also include veto for all or replacement of veto with simple democratic non-corrupt or bribe-acquired aids-promise majority vote. Any vote acquired corruptly must be made null and void as in democratic elections. The UN must stamp out corruption.

The UN must start acting on continental basis. Each continent must now organise itself to have continental council of security, economy education and skills training. The continent should now take up the responsibility for maintaining the peace. It should also have facilities for economic co-operation and development. It must equally have responsibility over its environment and ecological preservation. Common replacement tree-planting is an activity that each continent can safely encourage. We are losing a lot of our water reserves because of the fast rate at which we are losing their tree shades. It is simple to replace a removed tree by planting another. Good forest maintenance is feasible and continental funds can be made available for this project. Education and skills training for youths are items the continental council can deal with. The continental council must have a role in mineral and natural resource development on the continent as part of its environmental control programme and means of collecting continental funds for continental pool projects. Continental projects will prevent avoidable duplications and wastage in the face of limited means and unlimited demands. It will also produce more skilled people and jobs and create another level of transnational but close level of organisation and co-operation and re-enforce the UN authority.

Issues like the nuclear weapons control should be viewed on continental basis. The continental council led by nuclear possessing nations should have some control over the nuclear weapons and facilities on the continent. The UN should deal with the continental councils in resolving conflicts involved in these matters. The truth is that nobody in his right mind would use these weapons in war. Miniaturization and incorporation of nuclear materials into conventional weapons to increase their destructive powers are disturbing practices at the moment. The US bunker puncturing bombs are associated with cancer and teratogenity. We have the right to tell the US to protect the unborn child and the innocent civilian suffering from cancer from radiation poisoning. It is no use stating that a powerful the powerful nation like the US should abandon its security to the continental council but it should accept that the residents of its continent have the right to contribute to the way the US uses this very powerful weapon. The same applies to other continents. The concept of continental frontiers is new but it may develop to be a very useful tool of administration in IT high Technology global village.

We cannot overemphasize the importance of using the wealth and the enormous advances in knowledge, education and skills training to advance the frontiers of development, progress and prosperity and avoiding crises, violence, aggression and wars. It is equally right to accuse me of looking for utopia. Yet we claim human power to be dominant over all other creations in the world. This claim is incompatible with our inability to resolve our difference to exercise and organise our habitation to be under the rule of law. Law and order and strict self-discipline and our ability to obey the rules should help us to organise the human community along the line that nature planned our environments. One of the most important hallmarks of civilisation is tolerance. We must tolerate each other and even those we hate. The rule of law should make it clear those things the community disapproves by law. Disobeying the rules or violating the law carries penalties. Secular Laws sanctioned by popularly approved constitution are articles for maintenance of the peace and order in the community. They are instruments of preventing offence. Secular laws are neutral laws that apply to all in the community. They avoid making the law protect any particular interest groups in the community. In these days of religious zealots and special interest groups hijacking the law to deal with their opponents it is important that the law must be secular and neutral to be just. The leadership must accept that it is for all in the community. It is for both supporters and opponents and all religious faiths. Religion must now come under legislative administration not from discriminatory rash action but under general laws covering the conduct and practice of religion and faith. No religion should be discriminatory or has the right of exclusion or harm to non-members. No religion should practise obscenity or violence to anybody. The African sects with child sacrifice and punishment of children for witchcraft must bear some penalties for breaking the law.

Time is overdue for all religions to inform the community of their core message. And what their sacred books really teach as core message. It is not only important for peace of the community but for the cause of History when we all had left this world. It is a record that future generations would appreciate. It is also important for education and information that we all should have information on core teaching of their various religions. Religions are not cult societies or secret organisations. Hence they should not have any difficulties in declaring their core message to the authorities and the public. This will go some distance to dispel any confusion that may exist in the quality of the message the preachers preach. Ware saddened by the sudden death of Robin Cook. This is a great man that had confirmed teaching of Jesus that Man shall not live by bread alone. This is a man who stood by his conscience and self-sacrifice. He was not selfish but was ready to sacrifice his personal interest for the common good of humanity. He opposed the war in Iraq as a matter of principle with reverberating echoes of man of integrity and clear conscience abandoning all his privileges to defend good conduct in global affairs. His sharp wit and intelligence had proved him right and won respect from friends and foes. I cannot mortgage my integrity, dignity and conscience for pieces of paper and metals in the name of money or for food and hold unto a job against my virtue and decency. I love my job and the excellent skills I have in doing things. But offering my skills to the community is not at sacrifice of decency and virtue.

There had been a lot of debate on civilisation and the quality and superiority of civilisation. This book has been written not to criticise or incite but to educate. There is no such thing as our way of life and superior civilisation. The African civilisation like most things African is senescent and confused. It has polluted by various alien invasions and occupiers starting from the Romans to the events of slave trade and slavery down to the brutal colonisation of Africa. Alien religious intervention and very poor quality of leadership had not helped either. But yet our Matriarchal system offered franchise to women long before the rest of the world ever did this. Hence the female in the Pharaoh families were very powerful indeed. We had the Queen of Sheba and Cleopatra. The Western Media and Press are prone to ascribe these to fables but the truth is that African women had franchise long before others ever contemplated on doing so. African leadership, however, degenerated to very poor quality a very long time ago. The major cause of this seems to arise from the fact that we tend to place allegiance to family and personal security above community safety. This tends to breed cowards, timid and corrupt leaders without any knowledge of communal leadership abandoning and deserting the community in times of danger to chaos and confusion at the very moment it needs very strong and determined leadership. At such times Africa had always been leaderless. Potential alien invaders and occupiers of Africa had not lost sense and knowledge of this cardinal weakness in African leadership. Today African leadership is still very poor, selfish and corrupt and ignorant. They lack the essential embracing and all inclusive character that leadership requires. The lack resolve, determination and courage. Yet these qualities are needed in crises. We can therefore conclude that there is no such thing as superior civilisation or way of life. IT and high Technology or superior education and excellent skills training are not traits of superior civilisation or way of life.

Rather civilisation and superior way of life are the way we organise our community, families and maintain that tie binding children and youths to the family discipline and respect for life. One of the problems of the world has been the loose tie in the families. This has led to semi-lawless people spreading all over the world to cause mayhem. This is why the continental councils would have to establish code of conduct for the way people behave in alien lands away from homelands. This where the UN human rights would come in to regulate how we should treat aliens and the way aliens should treat the natives. The two to five millenniums had been a catalogue of abuses and bullying. Bullying, brutalities, cruelties and deliberate maltreatment of aliens on their homelands had been the norm. It is not only free trade or foreign aids that the world needs but also the way aliens behave and conduct their businesses in alien lands is important. Plundering, exploiting and looting distant lands away from your homelands because the natives are ignorant are not expression of superior way of life and civilisation. It is stealing or robbery. These are criminal and unacceptable.

Environmental degradation may be far away from homeland but global destruction of the environment affects us all on earth. We all always failed to note one thing the whole world is proud and appreciates the IT high Technology. In the current conflict people are talking about hatred. Yet both sides are using the products of IT and high Technology with equanimity. Why on earth should anybody hate people who had made life more comfortable for all of us? Added to this high Technology is a world heritage. The world stands not to hate any section for its riches and affluence. We equally owe a duty to peace to tune down our arrogance and disregard for the feelings and sensitivity of others. Equally religious arrogance and insensitivity have no place in cosmopolitan multiracial and multinational communities. Nobody has the right to impose his religious thinking on others. Conversion must be voluntary. The hidden laws of members of families of religious sects being punished for conversion or marrying to other faiths must now be outlawed and incorporated into human rights law as a serious breach of human rights and interference with individual freedom of choice. I cannot apologise for repeating and emphasizing the urgent need for all people in Africa to make the sacrifice to produce the money and pay to alien construction firms to build transcontinental rail and road networks to improve communications on the continent for free movements of goods, services and people. This will link Africa to the outside world by land. It will also help the programme of land reclamation from the desert (dedesertification) and improve water supply to desert travellers. It will constitute the nerve line of African Economy. These can be run as toll travel networks for the investors until they recover their investments. The construction will provide long term jobs for the whole world. We all stand to benefit from both short term and long term. Traditions and habits die hard but it is time for all of us to think of our world as our home and improving it is home improvement. The philosophy of colonisation is to subdue and make the most of the resources of subdued land by asset stripping but in the IT high Technology village we are not very wise in damaging one part of the world our village to enrich the other. This makes colonisation frivolous and daft. We stand to benefit from high quality and high intensity practical education and skills training.

I am neither an agitator, a fanatic nor a radical. The type of education I had does not make a politician. I have a sharp mind that quickly sees through events and draws its conclusion. It is mere common sense that for whatever reasons the past White Western colonisers might have established their Bantustans in Africa without any consultation with native Africans; these Bantustans have turned to be a major obstacle in the wheel of economic progress in Africa. They are costly to keep. They cause wars and violence. They generate feuds among the ethnic groups. Some of them are people abandoned on hostile arid lands desert and savannah. The Geography and Ecology make economic progress impossible. Re-integration of these Bantustans into the whole Africa and dividing Africa into tolerable and viable units will help to eradicate some of the economic obstacles. It makes sense to re-integrate colonial dismembered Africa. This is no more political slogan but socioeconomic necessity to open up Africa for internal and external Business. This is essential to develop African Economy that has been refractory to all global efforts to improve it.

Good practical thought-stimulating education and sound skills training are the vast gaps in the life of an African child. The greatest challenge of our time is to fill these gaps in the lives of African children. There is no apology for suggesting that the first have of any life should be spent on formal education and skills training. This is to prepare the individual for productive life ahead. Unproductive life results in poverty. A productive life full of initiatives creates wealth and prosperity. It also reduces crimes. People actively engaged in their business scarcely have time to plan criminal activities. Any good human organisations and establishments frequently take full accounts of the annual returns to calculate the profits. Any losses or fall in profits are examined critically to find out the causes. This is the method we should approach the African problems. The Bantustans had failed. The leadership has failed. The whole continent has failed to make any progress. We have to revisit all the three failing components to correct the mistakes inherent in them. Africa cannot be in good health without correcting these mistakes. The embarrassment is that Africans do not care. Are they working people or indolent truants loitering about without the will to work?

The Cross and the burden of persuading Africans to look across, very poor leadership, timidity and cowardice, selfishness, corruption, self-inflicted sufferings in this world and embrace the sacrifices required by unity and collective action to embrace sound practical education and practical skills training, true freedom and see the great advantages of unity and rapid re-integration of our great continent into a viable global powerful economic entity have been heavier than my short life on earth. Why people who would do anything in the name of religion to go to heaven at the end of their short lives would be resistant to do things that would improve their lives here on earth is strange to me. Why do they not do something to improve on what they know before aiming big for what they are not sure of? Why do we accept to live in our shadows and reject realities of life? The false and poor leaders are our false prophets.

They take sacrifices from the people in the name of improving their lots and feed themselves fat. They preach the message of separation and divisiveness to preserve their sterile Bantustans and fiefdoms. They pay false lip service to unity of mother Africa. The world has one message to Africans and Africa: “Unite and survive, remain divided and disunited and perish.” The choice is yours. It is you alone that have solution to your enormous problems in this world. Look around you and see what other people have been able to achieve and do for themselves and their land. Ask yourself why are we failing? The shame is now ours alone. We have nobody to blame. Religion can never rescue us if we are so deceptive to God or Allah we profess to worship. God the creator is virtuous, sincere and honest. Our corrupt and deceptive life is repugnant to Him. The leaders of sub-Saharan African Bantu rogue states must each know that their fiefdoms are not what our Ancient leaders ruled over. They ruled over Africa that re-integrated dismembered Africa may look like. Can we think for ourselves beyond what we plunder from the state? If we did we would realise that the type of Africa we have does not work. We would challenge ourselves why our Africa has failed. It would be obvious to us that what we have had been fragmented by past colonial masters to be viable. Washing up follows a good meal. The colonial masters have one bad master. They do not wash up their mess after a good meal. They swagger away arrogantly. They never wanted postcolonial Africa to work. They would have re-integrated colonial dismembered Africa before handing over but rather they fragmented the territories more before handing over. The African rugged terrains make a non-reintegrated Africa not work.

The black Africans are the only human race that would tolerate all types and forms of dehumanising ill treatments and humiliations and many of them even feel proud to own punishing remnants of these vicious cruelties and atrocities as though they were created by them. They are very proud to retain the vicious and barbaric atrocities of the wild Romans over four millenniums in Africa. The Romans executed genocide on the only Africans, the Carthaginians that were knowledgeable of what they were up to in the world of their days. Massinissa of ancient Libya which meant the homeland of African natives enjoyed the role of treachery and betrayal of Africa to the Romans through the agency of Scipio Cornelius Publius the Roman Commander and General that drove the African Carthaginians out of Spain and seized millions of pounds of African assets and investments. The Romans proceeded to invade Africa and looted and plundered our Mediterranean Land with acquiescence of the docile and stupid Africans. The Romans undertook scourge earth policy in Africa and created the first recorded but unspoken environmental disaster and global warming that extended the Sahara Desert to what it is today. The criminal Octavius, the Caesar Augustus that was around by the time Jesus was born. This idiot cut down the trees and took them by badges across the Mediterranean to build his amphitheatres. He captured the animals for gladiatorial shows and some of the games to feed his greedy Roman nobles and Senators. The Europeans pack packers arrived at our door step and hoisted rags on poles seizing our lands as extensions of their wild and primitive kings and queens territories. Disunited and divisive Africans could not offer any effective resistance. It is even worst in Bantustan Africa, today. The AU troops in Darfur sit down there feeding fat and enjoying some fun with their beautiful tall women. They want the West to come and do the business for them. They want them to supply them with logistics and arms. They want them to lead the fight for them. Yet some of them are informers to Sudanese Arab Bashir.

In Berlin sitting around a horseshoe table with a badly and poorly drawn African map empty in the middle as the European leaders in the Berlin Conference 15th Sept 1884 had no clue over who was living in the African hinterland. Without any African present or consultation with the Africans they made straight pencil lines across the empty space to create the unviable Bantustans that are the rogue and failed states in Africa today. Despite the passage of time and the claim that Africans are a bit civilised and the apparent failure of the Bantustans no African has the initiative to change the statusquo even though neither them nor their ancestors had any role in creating them. Slave trade came and went but no African seems to bother. It is calculated that the total reparation that British Economy owes the African slaves alone is 7.5 trillion pounds sterling and apology for the damage and their evil fortune making and wealth creation. The businesses that created wealth African blood money are up and wealthy. They have to pay up to clear their conscience and blood from their hands. Nemesis catches up with evil traders. They may one day face holocaust and poverty if they fail to do one right thing: pay up and apologise for their crimes. The money the West spent to rescue the Economy in recent Banking Collapse shows that the West can pay damages. But we are not money-minded people. Offer of excellent sustained Education, skills training and perfect apprenticeship and honest integration into Western Economy and funds and labour to open up Africa to allow internal and external free movement would do for compensation for our hurt by what the European white male did to us and our land in the last millennium.

The African docility is stupidity and intolerable cowardice and imbecility. The world is not inhabited by Africans alone. They are other tigers that can eat up the descendants of the abusers of Africans. The best thing that the West can do is to stop futile argument but rather proceed to set good example by apologising and paying up even by token measures to establish precedence for the future rulers of the world to follow. We Africans have a role to play by letting our past abusers and bullies know that we do not have to plant bombs in their cities to make them know that we feel the hurt. They are human beings like us.

They see evidence of the injustice. The debate that there was no law against what they did is totally futile because we are not debating the law here. We are challenging their human conscience but not the law. There would be no need for law if they knew what they did was not violation of law that needed to be made to prevent their brutality and cruelty. Equally can they prove that that they had no law in their land that forbade what they did to us? Their laws were to protect us. Violating and breaking their laws to abuse us was criminal. After all here we are blaming Japanese cruelties and atrocities. We went there to kill them in war but they overpowered us and punished us. Yet we blame them for inhuman cruelties. Germany and Japan had paid up and western citizens received the payments. It is your human conscience that should pay up to defend your humanity. Africans have also got to exercise their human conscience and act as human beings conscious of the power of the community and unity. The Africans are timid and cowardly. The corrupt illiterate leaders are afraid to raise our case. They fear to lose their privileged positions for requesting for compensation for our torture and labour and what the European white male looted from our land.

The sacredness and sanctity of individualism and isolationist attitude encrusted in a nutshell of selfishness that has become self-destruction to all black Africans and the whole black race on earth must now challenge itself and blame itself for the demise of Africa and the black race on earth. It must now embrace acting in concert for group action to rescue Africa from self-ruin and destruction. Unity, sharing and tolerance are not beyond our reach. It will allow us to live in peace on this land. It will prevent alien and hostile intruders fermenting and fomenting trouble to dump redundant lethal weapons in exchange for our rich mineral and natural resources. Logging and diamond cutting had continued in the DEMOCRATIC REPUBLIC OF CONGO (DRG) throughout its years of misery, wars and violence. This has been the features of all African bush wars. Streams of refugees feeding from NGO's kitchens and receiving medicines from them but who gets the money from these exploited African resources? The answer lies on the bush wars.

I am body and soul a Westerner by Geographical position of Africa, the way we have been doing business for several millenniums and interbreeding with all the peoples in the West. We Africans and the Europeans cannot escape this sad episode of human beings exploiting fellow human beings. It may be frequent gene interchange or the nature of the Europeans that creates that unique club to which I belong. It is exemplary. We are in a minority but highly intelligent from all walks of life. We frequently stand up and speak in the defence of the truth. This is the club of truth. The Straussite loony conservative right do not like what we say. Unfortunately they cannot deface the truth. The face of truth stands out from the muddy jumbles of lies and tissue of lies. It is strange and funny that people who are frequently wrong call themselves right. Their conduct is wrong. Their utterances are wrong, divisive, incisive and provocative and discriminatory against black people.

Africa is not a top priority to the West. The West is confused because they had damaged this continent irretrievably for over two millenniums. Whatever they can get out of Africa is now in their pocket. They had devised and stabilised this very large slave farm to work for them economically. They had raped it of leadership. They had planted permanent seed of dependency on it. They had conditioned them to believe in fables. They had donated permanent poverty to them as an inheritance. They had spread corruption and crimes to them as religion. The people totally ignorant of leadership and poor in leadership qualities launder huge amounts of their earnings in the Western Banks. Hence Africa is the lowest priority in the Western list of world domination. It is the first step of the ladder too close to the ground that can be over-stepped and ignored. It does not need replacement if it is broken. Hence genocide in Rwanda and Darfur is not of concern to the West. These events do not prevent them from taking home their loots from Africa. It is not my place to blame the West for the plight of Africa. The Africans and the black people themselves are to blame. They it is that are in the dock. They are to tell the world what they had done as human beings to save themselves from disasters.

It is equally wrong to prescribe solutions. All Africans are aware that their lives are far from being comfortable. They all know that there is something not right. Nobody has the courage to stand up to put things right. They are all timid and cowardly. They are drowning without any rescuer in sight. They have to learn how to swim fast to mount their home-made salvage and rescue. Religion and its massive brainwashing did not work. Democracy is a charade. The West is definitely not democratic. It runs a chamber of military tortures and death. It is a hidden cell of bullying and intimidation. It has conditioned its citizens to live the way the leaders want them. The Western wealth and affluence are like sweets available to offer to its citizens in times of stress. People complain of Africa being in the lowest priority to the West. Have you ever seen a hunter worrying to rekill a dead animal in his hunting sack? Africa is such meat in the Western sack. They have no business to rekill the animal for meat. I have never seen very stupid people as the black Africans. How stupid are they by not spending some time of their lives to study the white people in the West? We must know and understand the Western white people, our next door neighbours as one of the cardinal things to do to understand our environment.

It is not what they write and talk about themselves that we should know and understand. It is the live persons that we must study and understand his emotions, life ambitions and psychology, human sympathy and understanding of wealth, crime and corruption. These are the things that we must know and understand about them. Democracy and religion are charade to the gullible. They challenge you to understand the way the white Westerners had used them. They challenge you to know their understanding of these terminologies and the places they take in their lives, communities and societies. Unless you know and understand these things you would not know what the genuine truth is. The black Africans have three things to use to redeem themselves, knowledge, steady and loud voice expressing their approval and disapproval and genuine skills to do things for themselves.

They must build up their critical mass to develop the market for commerce in a world dominated by free enterprise. You do not join that market as individuals but as Africa. This is where re-integration is significant. Rwanda and Darfur had taught us that nobody will accept to fight and die for you. You have to do your fight alone. As a surgeon I know that black people have brains. I have dissected them and operated on them. They essentially have to use their brains. Individual wealth collections make no impression. They frequently disappear with death. Group collections make significant impressions. Community wealth has sustainable continuity. This is what has created wealth and affluence in the West. Above all they last and transform the society. What you collect as individuals in life does not generate social wealth but group collections generate social and community wealth and affluence. It is no use to preach re-integration of Africa to black Africans. Fifty years of existence as independent Bantustans in Africa have failed. It now makes sense to re-integrate Africa. Failing to take action is our fault and nobody else. Listen to me O' Africa, I cannot betray you or hide the truth from you. I am a child of your womb, your belly. My gene is yours. Let each of us work hard to collect wealth not for ourselves but Africa Magna. It is group wealth collection that creates wealthy, affluent and prosperous land. Once death comes our wealth we and our individual wealth, affluence, and prosperity fail to exist. But the community and the group that we supported in our lives would continue to exist as long as the succeeding generations continue to work hard and maintain the health of wealth, affluence and prosperity.

Africa cannot unite to form a strong union because the leaders are selfish and each wants it alone for himself. None of them wants to make sacrifices for the interest of the public and the nation. At a glance of the map of Africa, it is obvious that much of it is arid land. The little fertile land is at the fringes of the Oceans. The deserts and the savannah occupy much of the land. For human beings to survive in progress and prosperity there must be free movement of people, integration of all the resources to raise the capital to invest in orderly and sustainable development of this land to avoid wasteful and unnecessary duplications of public utilities and infrastructures. The strength of the whole land is more effective and powerful than that of individuals and individual units or regions. We can achieve this unique condition if we Africans place the interest of our land as a nation above all other and individual interest. We must separate our individual interest from the interest of the nation. It is therefore important that we must consider seriously complete reification of our leadership. At the moment they are above our land and people. Our land and people must essentially be supreme and above all our leaders and people. This land must have the power of life and death over all its citizens to control them. The contract between citizens and state, demands loyalty above what individual selfish interest demands. The safety and security of the state is paramount. Abuse of public office by corrupt practices demands the severest of punishment.

The concern expressed in certain quarters about the plight of Africa, today, may be genuine and encouraging. But how many real Africans true victims of the collapse of the African system take active part in this debate? How many of them express the real African concern over their plight? How do the Africans the victims of the collapse of their Economy and their system tell the world what they really want? How many of them tell the world has gone wrong and what should be done to put things right? It is a folly that the foreigners talk about trade, and increase in aids. But what have the Africans themselves have to do to help themselves? Economic empowerment demands that the Africans themselves have to rebuild their continent from the ruins of repeated invasions, destructions, plunders and loots. The destruction inflicted on the continent by slave trade and slavery and brutal colonization and ruthless plundering and looting of the continent. In the last century alone the European colonisers plundered African wealth to fight two European tribal wars for global domination. They falsely called them world wars. The world had never had any reason to fight a war. It is the Western European tyranny of greed, cruelties and naked atrocities that had subjected the world and Africa to current deprivation. It is mere common sense that Africa has the responsibilities to embark on massive building and reconstruction work. It is construction work that will provide jobs, education and skills training for mass of African unemployed youths. Africa needs road and rail from the Cape to Algiers, Tripoli, Cairo, Tunis and Rabat. This construction will open up the continent and provide new Economic opportunities. We have to reduce the number of countries in Africa. We must equally remove two important groups that constitute economic impairment to Africa. These are ubiquitous European transnational multinational European corporate global business using corrupt African leaders to plunder Africa for their share holders in Europe and the West. We must remove the corrupt and ignorant geriatric leaders. They have no clue about the responsibilities of leadership facing collapse from diseases and abject and miserable poverty in a vast advancing world. They do not know whose interest they are representing. They seem to be ruling in the interest of the Western leaders and not of their people who are dying off. Once the Western leaders talk of new aids they rush and collect the money without asking for conditions to use the funds.

This had been the situation from the slave trade, colonization, cold war and now Africa facing catastrophe. These "leaders" have to go. Those who want to help Africa must eliminate these obstacles to their aspirations to help Africa. They must embark on getting Africans to do things for themselves. Education and skills training must lead economic empowerment. Economic empowerment in Africa must mean I can do it. We can do it. Africans can do it. We black people can do it now. We have the means to do it. Our Education and skills are adequate for us to do it. We are ready for equal competition in the world. This is the way to help Africa. Meddlesome economic aid has no place in economic empowerment of Africa. Africa does not need Tiny Rowland and his group of three or the likes of Mark Thatcher, today. The Western Press and Media has no moral right to deride Robert Mugabe for recovering our land from rogue colonial farmers. Let the British farmers return to Britain to farm in their country and homeland. Africa does not need white farmers or land owners. We cannot tolerate white land lords at the time Europe and the West is paranoid about immigration. We should not be a soft touch on immigration and land ownership. Genuine assistance to Africa does not need recolonization of the continent. The West must apologise to Africa for past cruelties, atrocities several genocidal acts. The West is a shameless liar. It knows why it has to apologise to Africa. Nothing the West did on this continent that benefited Africa. There are still mines of the first and second world wars in Africa that the West pretends they are not there. They have moral duty to clear these mines from our desert. The West cannot rescue Africa as long as it continues to consider its relationship with Africa as that between master and servant. The HIV-AIDS pandemic is a case in question. The West has not come clean. Is this virus from its germ warfare laboratory? We need to know the truth. Our mutual trust had reached the lowest ebb in Apartheid. It is plausible to praise some Westerners in the role they played to remove Apartheid but the white core establishment was serious over victory in Apartheid. The West has to remove the suspicion. Let it also be a lesson. We are human beings sharing this world. The things that damage the black man will also damage the white man.

This is important for the safety and security of our land and people. The traitor must die for his acts of treachery. We should not allow selfish individuals to sell out our land and people. If they cannot join us to save our land from disaster they have no reason to be alive to be supported by this land. The relationship is that you support the land and the land supports you. You desert the land in disaster, the land deserts you. You should not betray this land to its enemies and stay back to reap the reward from your costly treachery. Traitors and corrupt leaders must die. We must devise real African participatory democracy. The West is too corrupt and greedy for tyranny of greed to allow it to practise democracy. Alexander and the Greeks felt uncomfortable to accept obeisance because it was in contrast and incompatible with the Greek sense of freedom, equality and democratic practice. They refuse to Graecise citizens of conquered lands. Rather they were willing to learn alien cultures. Alexander and one thousand of his officers each took Asian wife. Alexander, himself presided over the wedding ceremony in Asian culture in one day. This action of Alexander confirms beyond doubt Alexander's belief and Greek acceptance of integration and equality. The aggressive military conquest and empire building are incompatible with democratic practice and equality of opportunities. The ancient fathers actually knew the significance of integration and partnership even after military conquest. We Africans started and adopted this policy with the ethnic nationalities of Southern Europe. Carthage was doing business, trading and mining in Southern Europe for over five hundred years with headquarters based in Catalonia in Spain. They respected and treated their leaders as acceptable equals. The city of Barcelona is named after Barca the father of Hamilcar and grandfather of warrior General Hannibal.

Today, the Europeans had been in Africa for over four thousand years. Led by the Roman ultra-conservative leaders, they had adopted the policy of smash and grab military conquest and Empire building. This depended on demonising the leaders of conquered territories, degrading them and total destruction of the traditional leadership of these places and replacing them with their stooges and cronies answerable to the imperial authorities and frequently hated by their people they rule over on behalf of the alien colonising power. The imperial authority is based on exploitation and plundering of wealth from the colonies to support their home governments and people. The colonies are open slave farms working to provide for the needs of imperial authorities and people. Today they are clientele states dependent on the orders of the imperial power and its directives. Empire-building and colonisation of foreign lands amount to economic castration of these lands. They become imperial clientele states and colonies. Integration and partnership allow the development of the structures and communities that would support economic growth, orderly and sustainable development.

Two centuries ago, there was very strong argument in support of continuation of slave trade and slavery. The argument was based on the vital role of these practices played in the Economy and jobs. The victims of these vices did not count in the argument. The supporters of these practices completely failed to consider the suffering of their fellow human beings. They failed to see the damage this evil trade was doing to Africa. They were content with the wealth the inhuman practices were yielding. This argument dominated the British politics of the time. Candidates in support of slave trade and slavery won elections. It took a lot of time to persuade and convince the people to change their mind over the economic benefits of slave trade and slavery. It still took some time to convince them that there were other ways of supporting the economy and protecting jobs. The reluctance to change and protracted debates prolonged the suffering of African victims of these evil practices and continued to damage Africa. The African slave dealers just like current corrupt ignorant Geriatric money laundering leaders and illegal dealers in African minerals felt that they had acquired sustainable business. They were indifferent and wanted the trade to continue for what the earned from it.

Today, African raw materials, oil and gas, platinum, gold, uranium and diamond and very rich tropical forest resources are, regarded as indispensable core component of the Western Economy. Oil and gas are at the heart of current Western high Technology Economy and very high living standards. Again Africa is held prisoner with other parts of the third world of this enormously advanced and successful prosperous Economy. Unfortunately Africa has come out the worst from this economic structure. The first Western economic progress and prosperity were built on the corpses of millions of Africans and the ruins of the damage they inflicted on the continent. This second phase of Western economic lift has been achieved from total collapse of Africa from unfair trading practices and HIV-AIDS pandemic and its associated practices. It has been made worse by poverty, ignorance and corruption. The use of African resources to develop, sustain and support this Western economic progress and prosperity while Africans had been excluded from them for several centuries is immoral. The vital role African resources play in Western wealth justifies integration of Africa into the West as partner. It is not an easy task. It is a difficult proposition. Yes African resources support Western wealth and prosperity, but the miserable state of Africa now makes it worse than a Greek gift.

Yet the current plight of Africa is a bleeding wound in Western and world conscience. We have no choice. We have to take courage. We must stand up and challenge the factors damaging Africa. We must whole-heartedly confront corruption, crimes and money laundering abroad and off-shore banking havens. We must tackle the collapsing social system including education and skills training of the youths. The infrastructures must be rebuilt. The Geriatric leaders must be replaced with young modern entrepreneurial and honest technocrats. Education and skills training for the youths must take top priority. The Africans must learn how to plan the management of their Economy. They must avoid unnecessary duplications and wastage of scarce funds and resources. They must be ready to dismantle colonial borders and re-organise the continent to include all the citizens in viable units allowing free movements of the citizens to enhance economic growth.

The Geographical structures of the African landmass and the distribution of arid lands, desert and water essentially need even distribution of the land so that every citizen has equal access to all available lands. This will allow pooling together the funds and resources available for development of the continent. Unviable colonial borders' rogue states must give room to economically viable nation states capable of development. The African commission must not be shy of suggesting essential vital reforms necessary to take Africa out the current slum and prepare it for orderly and sustainable economic growth. The Africans must be ready to make essential sacrifices to create wealth and build up their prosperity. Africa integrated into the Western Economy to which it is the powerhouse, must learn new discipline and be ready to observe the rule of law. They must learn fiscal discipline. It is nonsense to suggest re-colonisation of Africa. Who wants to own a dead race horse? Everybody wants to own a live successful winning race horse.

For Africa to escape from this wilderness of despair and desolation and the current Commission for Africa to make any dent on the current poverty, misery and ignorance in Africa, it must first build the infrastructures to support orderly and sustainable development. There must be road and rail networks to link all parts of the continent and the North and South. This will integrate Africa with Europe, the West and the world. There must be road to your house if you want people to locate where you live to do business with you. This is the greatest problem of Africa at the moment. It has very poor and obsolete communication network and accessibility. Easy access is important for movement of goods and commerce. Trade depends on easy communication network. Practical Education and good skills training are essential for repairs and maintenance. Maintenance culture is absent in Africa. Modern infrastructures require skilled workers for regular maintenance and repairs. These will provide sustainable long term jobs and services to the community. It is only common sense that in times of recession, construction, and building of essential infrastructure provide jobs, skills and the needs of the society.

A sympathetic Englishman recently commented that most of the colonial infrastructures in Africa had collapsed but even the few that survive most of them are not linking Africa but lead to the ports and outlets for goods leaving Africa to foreign countries. He admonished undertaking massive construction works to link Africa first internally for movement of goods in the continent. I have been advocating for transcontinental rail network from the Cape to North Africa and roads for several years. Here again I affirm that there is Technology for the construction and there are funds for the work provided sub-Saharan Bantu Africans tighten their belts and release the funds and stop stealing the funds for their personal use.

Provision of immediate needs is less important than getting the people to acquire skills for production of their needs. The world has seen what running the wealthy, prosperous affluent Western European Economy on the resources taken from Africa as its mainstay but excluding the people living in the continent and Africans all over the world had done to the continent and global black people and even other Africans. An Economy that relies on the resources of the African continent must now take steps to integrate the continent and its entire people. It must not continue to exclude the continent and its people. It must become inclusive and not exclusive. This is important to produce virile people to revamp and refurbish the land. Well educated people with efficient skills training in ancient Egypt in Africa pioneered Western civilisation over five millenniums ago. The genocide and ethnic cleansing that altered the population of the people in this land and replaced them with the current people living there, today, perhaps had damaged the places and Africa greatly.

The new inhabitants had not made its mark after fourteen hundred years. The continent of Africa is crying for help from the West where it rightly belongs and the world where it has always been the focus of attention. The Arabs from Asia must know that finding a new home by ancient land grabbing conquest masquerading as religious movement does not make new converts slaves. They might have been conned to accept the new religious faith from their traditional religious culture and belief in God but this does not make them slaves on their land. God or Arab Allah has no slaves.

Now that we know that that the ancient Greeks, Africans, prominent Romans accepted integration and partnership except a tiny but powerful and influential minority in Rome that favoured exclusion and subjugation under a global empire that they lacked the foresight to know it was not going to last forever, we must summons courage and embrace integration and rehabilitation of Africa into the West by rebuilding and rehabilitating African education and skills training based productive productivity and independence. This is a major flank of Western defences. We do not need only the land but the original people God placed on this land and we must make them strong and virile again for secure defences of the Western flank. We are not talking of joining ideological camp, NATO or EU but autonomous Economic unit capable of supporting itself and contributing the Economic growth in commerce, trade, Banking and Insurance.

The new comers to African land had not been able to recreate that magic in ancient Egypt that brought light to the West passing through Greece and Southern Europe including Rome. We had wasted one hundred and fourteen years arguing over imaginary beliefs, impractical obsolete Arab traditional macho laws that seem not to believe in changes. They fail to note that time changes. Generations live and die. They are replaced by new generations with new changes in their own time. Time and life do not stand still. Sharia law may have something to offer the changing times but it has to be modified to suit the changes in our times that had changed beyond belief. The world each traditional religion knew at its inception, is today, very different from our world today. Therefore, attempting to use the religious faith and its obsolete laws to control people and events is a non-starter. It does not work. It is only secular laws that can adequately control different people in different parts of the rapidly changing world transformed into a global village by high Technology.

The earth has started to visit the space. The concept of the universe is fast becoming real, Human being had visited and walked on the moon, heavenly structure at the centre of the mystery of the heavens, in the Islamic faith. We do not know what the prophet Mohammed should have advised the US astronauts that landed on the moon if he were alive at the time of that event. Perhaps he would have given some advice to them. While we regard every religion and their pioneers as sages that had been a source of inspiration to all generations, we must now accept that they dealt with the problems of their time even though they had enormous inside knowledge of human weakness and the perfect ideas of what are acceptable to God in human relationship. Our problems today are different. Secular Constitution and laws to offer the united community security and protect Democracy and right of man are more important than fragmentary autonomy. The type of thing the

West is using now to warm itself back to its former colonial position can be described as selective Democracy and rationed freedom. It attempted to use fire power and ruthless bombing as at first when it used cannon fire to terrorise people to subdue them. This has not worked; hence this belated ramshackle and shambolic Democracy is an emergency package to buy time to justify their continuous occupation of alien lands.

AFRICANS THEMSELVES MUST LEARN HOW TO RESCUE THEMSELVES FROM POVERTY. NOBODY CAN DO IT FOR THEM DESPITE ALL THE GOOD WILL.

Even our current secular laws find it difficult to catch up with the rapid changes in time, fast speed of coverage of land, water and space. September 11th had been an eye opener. Sadly the thoughtlessness of the interest groups of geopolitics had denied wise thinkers to take stalk of the real events and changes in our time. I have said this before in this book. A group of well-educated young men went into the corner shop to buy knives that could have been acquired by them for peeling oranges. They used them to hijack four US planes before the only superpower with the strongest Army, Navy and Air force in the world to knock down the twin towers in the middle of New York and proceeded to Washington to inflict damages. We all must have the courage to think that the world has changed. The population movements and changes are real. The new comers must accept the new homes and the indigenous people and spread their love of the changes in their lives to the new lands and their people. High Technology had brought the world closer and made the concept of the universe real. Human beings must change with time. We must not stand still. Changes in the world are real. Religion must now respond to these changes. It cannot stand static with obsolete and utopian ideas. The creator, God made the world and everything in it for us human beings to share. We have to share them and our ideas. This is fundamental to peace for peace.

George Walker Bush and Tony Blair failed to contemplate on the significance of this event in their watch. The audacity and the success of these boys should have baffled and bothered them. Yes

Osama bin Ladin might have given the money for the operation but if the boys had neither conviction nor the skills the operation could have failed. The satellite Television and internet exposes the way people lead their lives and the luxury they enjoy to everybody in the world today. They cannot hide these things any longer. Worst still the assumption and arrogance of underrating and ignoring the intelligence and skills of other people are at the demise of the West. If Bush and Blair were leaders with ability to think before action, there should have been no war. They could have spent time and used all friendly and peaceful methods to find out what instigated the boys to take such drastic, severe and risky action. This could have benefitted the West and the world. Their rash action has failed to yield their expected results. More lives had been lost. Today Bush and family are hiding in their ranch in Texas. Blair shamelessly claims a role in Christian Missionary crusade and Middle East peace mission. This is scandalous but this is a cruel world. A lot of people suffer from results of poor leadership.

The old method of colonisation and raw materials must now yield ground to sharing production and all its benefits. Every human being wants the best in his short time on earth. We all have to eat good food and enjoy the type of standard of living in our time. These suicide pilots must enjoy the fun of flying to enjoy life and wealth on earth in their own time. Inclusion and not exclusion is the solution. Exclusion neglects danger to be appreciated and hijacked to be used by obsolete religion that we ignore that it can be dangerous. Are we then doing everything to bring all human activities including religion to enjoy the enormous lift that high Technology has given to our age? I should here mention two important global events that had brought enormous changes in the world. The Arabian and Middle East oil had brought prosperity to the area. The Saudi Arabian authorities had been able to develop the infrastructures to support the regular annual pilgrimages to Mecca and Medina. The development in the air traffic had greatly eased the making of the pilgrimages to Saudi Arabia to bring the believers and the faithful together regularly every year. The Soviet invasion of Afghanistan angered the Muslim world. The Americans saw an outlet to release the global Muslim anger on the Soviets. They flew the Muslim fighters from the four corners of the world to drive the Soviets out of Afghanistan. They equipped them with the best but simple easily understandable and easy to use American Technology. They gave them training in sabotage and terrorist tactics. This like any other war opened the eyes of the Muslims. These two meeting points of the Muslims had changed their views of the world.

WE MUST ADMIRE CHANGE AND WORK FOR CHANGE.

This is a challenge to us. Do we go for total destruction and war and violence? Do we adopt the wisdom of change? We accept the risk and danger this change makes of people abandoned outside human advances and progress in our arrogance of taking bliss in our civilisation and rush after them with guns? It is our challenge to search and find these changes to use in constructing and not in destroying by excluding them from the civilisation and its changes. Let it not be known that in our age with all these tremendous advances in human activities, we lacked people of sound wisdom to manage what may be wrong in the Muslim faith currently crying out for changes to embrace them into the age of Science and Technology and rapid advances in skills training. Note the competence and originality with which they used the high Technology products and ordinary knives to cause so much damage. We are at risk by excluding them and ignoring the grievances.

We must convert hostilities to friendship. We must use destructive power to build constructive power. We must offer the humanity the love of the short life on earth and genuine hope in the life after. No religion should advocate undertaking destruction of life on earth to escape to enjoy the life after. The creator, God or Allah has the life both here and after. The choice is not ours or that of religion. We have the duty of protecting life here on earth in hope for the life after. If the creator had any assignment for us here on earth, it is to preserve it. God or Allah does not preserve us on earth or reward us in Paradise because we do things religious leaders, the imams, mullahs and the caliphs want us to do. God does not bribe believers in religious faiths to destroy non-believers. God accepts the adulation every religion offers him. Religion intolerance has no place in human community. Religion is the gate for individual believer to communicate with God or Allah.

It is a shame that after the fiasco of the three African Roman wars, Rome survived because of the distinct different ways we Africans and the Europeans view the world. To us it is a common home of mankind, man and woman. To the Europeans and the West it is the home and property of the brave and courageous. "Who dares wins?" This is not the place to discuss the life philosophy of different races on earth. The pyramid is one of the great wonders of the world. To us Africans, it distinguishes us from the way other human beings see the world. It is God or the creator's transient home for human beings. The Africans are very religious people. They regard the world as a place to stay to honour God. The pyramids were places symbolising the structure of the human society piling up praises from their different total integrated positions in the social strata to the sun-god that they worshipped at their time. Human praises to God were equal before God regardless of their position in the social pyramids. Just as each brick block contributed to the over-all height and the magnificence of the pyramids, the whole humanity constitutes the earthly human community. Africa believes in integration of the humanity and not on segregation and racial xenophobic discrimination and separation of the races. We do not believe or accept empire building. We believe in the sanctity of human freedom and life. We fare poorly when we ignore the community culture. It appears our ancestors knew the Science of gene interchange for producing healthy offspring. They practised intermarriage. There was no restriction of cross racial sexual relationship. Any attempt to institute restriction of inter-racial sexual relations had always been ignored.

This is why we Africans and the Europeans are the most integrated human race by intermarriages and breeding. Our time in Europe created the Moors. Because of the artificial barriers the ultra-conservative Roman rights created between the races to demonise the Africans they fought against their descendants, the Moors who embraced Islam to the wrath of the dominant Roman Catholicism. This culminated into racial xenophobia that has continued to plague the human society till today. The Moors were driven back to Africa. A combination of Moors and the Arabs were helped to drive out the original native Africans from their Mediterranean homeland to seal off the European homeland from African invasion. Yes because of the bullying European frequent aggressive militarism in our original

Mediterranean homeland we had to fight back regularly. Several millenniums had cut off Africa from these affrays until recent European colonisation of Africa when we made contact with Europe that had made enormous improvements on the Technology they seized from us when they finally overpowered us in 146 BC. We were no longer a match to the Europeans who had acquired gun powder from China and developed the canon gun fire, and lead ball guns. We were overpowered and colonised. In the face of the challenges of this time Africa has to be rehabilitated very quickly in viable Education and skills training to give effective cover to the Western Southern flanks. The frontiers had changed enormously. Note this, Africa is flanged by the Atlantic and Indian Oceans and open into the vast and expansive Pacific Ocean. We are capable of spreading knowledge all over the world and prepare our world for interplanetary exploration to search for other forms of life and civilisations.

WE MUST ABHOR VIOLENCE AND SENSELESS WAR.

Wasting our resources on more armaments and wars is avoidable waste. Let us allow wisdom to prevail over arrogance and pride. Jaw, jaw and not war, war will overcome all human tragedy. Let us not be provoked into the row of the tower of Babel. Let us talk to each other. I am a Christian and love my God and creator the way I was brought up to trust in him. In the global village I find that everybody believes in a higher being out there watching over us earthly people and each of us loves him dearly. Each person gives him a name in his own language and a place in his own culture. This is no excuse why we should in total ignorance start killing each other. In the name of the higher being each of us believes in and worships him in our own way and culture, let us talk and stop fighting over what we know very little about. Victory may be sweet but Lord Nelson and Napoleon each kissed death in his own time. Hitler and Churchill and President Roosevelt did the same. Hannibal, the greatest global and African General and Scipio are no longer here. Alexander, the son of Philip of Macedonia and a Great global general and the Persian King Ahasuerus are not here. This does not mean that we should fold our hands and wait for our end. We have to learn from the past to build the future. Great

Julius Caesar that actually created the Roman Empire is not here. History gives them all credit for what they did in their own time. This is why we hear about their names. Times had changed and we are living in a different age. Rehabilitation of Africa and preserving the environment together with the exploration of the space for routes to other planets may constitute challenges much as exciting as the great deeds of the ancient fathers in military exploits and killing each other. A lot of people in our world are still starving and lacking minimum comforts other parts of the world take for granted. We are yet to offer them the type of Education and skills training to enable them look after themselves.

It is not food and Medicine parcels that the world needs. They need the Education, and the skills training that had helped the West to do things for themselves. Israel and Arabs in the Palestinian desert offer the world the differences good Education and skills training combined with effective work culture would fill the gaps we witness, today. Self-destruction by war is not the solution. What I watch on the television from Iraq gives us no credit for civilisation. It is self-mutilation. It makes our Technological advancement valueless. It gives us the impression that we are struggling to find means to return the world to the dark ages. We have made life cheap and worthless. We do not see this in wild life. Let the people of wisdom and conscience speak out against the brainless macho guys. We do not need more victories of wars of destruction. We need war to conquer and control our world to provide for the living. We must respect human life and the environment.

We must respect order and the rule of law. War denies the culprit the opportunity to bear his shame. Why do we sacrifice innocent lives to the departures of voluntary suicides in the name of nation, gallantry and elusive victory? The victims of suicides drink the cup of death. Let wisdom prevail over human quarrels and differences. Human beings can mediate and settle differences evolving from religious beliefs. Piety does not remove our ignorance of the mysterious way God the creator works. Science and Technology do not make us wiser. If anything we are still farther away from understanding what the creator requires of us. We must love him by loving our fellow human beings we see and know. Let envy not drive us to senseless wars and violence. You do have to out at anybody you feel has offended you. You have a duty to analyse any provocation and plan appropriate response. You may expose your powerlessness or become embroiled in a protracted conflict. War does not settle disputes. It can damage and destroy things. It is not effective antidote. The fact that in eight years with massive losses in resources and lives the West (NATO) could come out only with unreliable single friend, Ahmed Karzai, is a confirmation that we cannot continue to waste our resources on one person only to avoid defeat. The West must leave the Afghan people to look after their affairs.

There is a new observation involving the ultra-right Straussite conservative in the West and their philosophy on the world and empire-building now. This is what is called colonisation by proxy or remote colonialism. The proxy colonial masters rule these colonies through indigenous traitors under pay. These traitors owe no loyalty or commitment to their people they had sold out to proxy colonial masters. All talks about Democracy are mere hot air and empty balloon. The events in the world now have shown that one tyrant is as dangerous as the executors of the tyranny of greed under the guise of supporting Democracy. Both of them are killers. In the first the unholy angels of democracy do not care about genocide and ethnic cleansing in places like Rwanda and Darfur in Sudan. The victims are black people and any resources the unholy democrats target are under the people who allow them easy and cheap access to them even if they are the criminal killers. They can get away with murder. For several years the West befriended Saddam Hussein and gave him all means of killing. They used him to punish Iran for throwing out the US from their country. They even used delaying tactics to punish Iran longer by supplying the two sides with weapons. This was known as Iran gate.

It prolonged the war and the suffering of the Iranian people. But everything turned sour when Saddam needed money for reconstruction after the war. He wanted more money from oil. He moved to seize Kuwait and placed Saudi client State in danger. The West knew that Saddam was instrumental to actions that caused the oil crisis and recession in the West and brought about the birth of OPEC in the seventies. They would never pardon him for that disaster. Hence the first Gulf War was a warning shot. Now after several years of sanctions, ruthless bombings and lies on WMD the world became uneasy with the damage sanctions inflicted on children. The cry to lift sanctions became louder. Saddam sensed victory around the corner. He started choosing his friends by offering generous contracts excluding the US and the UK that bombed his country ruthlessly. This was unpardonable Saddam's mistake. The US and UK got the Chalabis and Alawi proxy insider reliable informers on WMD. They gave them free passage, access and seats in Pentagon and Capitol Hill even to the discomfort of the Western Intelligence world.

The Bush administration was then ready to teach Saddam a lesson. They were to seize the oil and offer the contracts to themselves. Saddam had shaky seat as his tyrannical behaviour had estranged him to the Kurds and the Shiite Muslims. He was virtually standing on one leg. He stood no chance with the US and the UK using silk suit, silk tie and silk pocket handkerchief with Rolex watch-wearing Iraqi refugees circulating at the background like shadows. His age and several years of suffering by the proud Iraqi people stood him very little chance if any. Now we have seen what opportunism can do to world peace. Iraq had been demolished and democratic West had slaughtered several times the number of Iraqi people that Saddam took several years and wars to kill. Western emotional propaganda exposing trenches should remember that the Iraqis the West slaughtered in two wars, regular bombing sanctions for several years had trenches as mass burial grounds. As a true African democrat, I challenge the West to come out with true and genuine figures the number people their scramble for oil had killed in Iraq. This is important because wars kill people. Victory in war kills more people and destroys more things. We must not remain cowardly and allow the Western ultra-conservative Strausite rights to sanitise their wars. The spin machine of war propaganda demonises the war leader of their opponents and weeps up emotions to make their casualties of war victims of the monster. This is immoral. The war in Iraq is illegal colonial war in 2004. It is a criminal war. The people behind it must search their consciences if they have any and make sure that they had committed a crime of multiple murders.

Truth is like a bitter pill but it is still the truth. Let the victor or the victim not write the History of this war. As a matter of fact if I wanted to strangle the truth I would write in total support of the Western resource-control seeking strike force. The Arabs had damaged Africa more than any other ethnic group. It is easy to say this is your turn. Moral justice and African conscience of true justice disallows what has taken place under the umbrella of civilisation and democracy. It is wildly Barbaric. The Western combatants and their opponents were competing for the gold medal in tortures of prisoners and barbaric killing and cruelties to expose the beastly nature of human beings. For a long time Africans had not written about the true conduct of the people and races of human beings that inhabit this world. We have always written sanitised History praising human achievements. I write and praise all these achievements. I do not lose sight of the cruelties and atrocities involved in those achievements. In the last millennium the West engaged in land and resource grabbing genocide of several races of human beings. It is not right that the West should do it again in this century. Millions of Hollywood entertainment films would not sanitize cruelties and man's dehumanising inhumanity to man.

We are still the most destructive beasts that God created in spite of our achievements. We even seem to use our Scientific and Technological advances to improve the viciousness of our beastly behaviours. People of great wisdom must sit down and think of what is right as opposed to what is wrong. Wisdom transcends partisanship and loyalty or patriotism. It is an ally of the unadulterated-by-spin truth. It is no secret, that it has long been the ambition of Muslim Islam to islamise the whole Africa to allow Islam control the resources of this rich continent. This had led to massive long suffering and deaths of several indigenous Africans and the destruction of Africa. The static and retrogressive macho culture of Islam had caused stagnation of progress in Africa. Today, the once actively progressive and forward-looking prosperous continent on earth lies in ruins paralysed by failure and desolation. While religious piety enriches the faithful, it paralyses progress when it attempts to make human beings live by a set of macho laws claimed to come from Allah. Attempt to make them statutory laws challenges changes in time and life important for rapid progress. Such statutory laws stifle progress and condemn several people to live beyond changes and progress. How do you make statutory laws made a little less than two millenniums ago conform to the rigors of demands of rapidly changing modern society and Scientific and Technological advances?

Every religion and the world authorities and people must wake up from the slumber and give religion a decent place in the human society. We must demarcate religion from the statutory laws, rule of secular law, rules and regulations to promote orderly and sustainable developments in the human rapidly changing society. The religious laws are advice and instructions to guide the believers and the faithful in their individual life conduct on earth to be in conformity with their maker and creator and fellow human beings. They are not meant to be used in settling disputes or maintain law and order. The United Nations has a duty to explain this to all countries that want to be recognised as a nation. The human communities in true Democracy must be governed by the rule of secular law, rules and regulations, laws of their making so that any citizen brought before the law understands clearly what he or she had done wrong in contravention with the law. Introduction of Sharia Law is induction or absorption of non-believing citizens into Islam without their consent.

Use of religious laws like the Sharia is indirect seizure of power by religious authorities to control the community and the public without presenting themselves to be elected or chosen by the people. It is a violation of the right of man and a breach of social secular law. It is dangerous because it intimidates and bullies non-believers to adopt the faith and denies them the freedom of choice and it touches the individual soul regarding faith. It allows the religious authorities to supplant the authority of the government and political leaders. The Sharia has different treatments for the believers and non-believers. Non-believers have no audience in Sharia court. Everybody and every nation must not be above the secular laws freely made to govern the community concerned. These are rules and regulations that the community accepts as the law and order to guide the citizens and members in the community for maintenance of the peace. It is important to prevent breeches, exclusions and exemptions. They must be binding on all. This particularly concerns nations particularly the US. If the US wants to lead it must do so from the front by being law-abiding nation and not an outlaw nation by virtue of its fire-power. US as a world leader essentially have to use these laws to settle disputes. How can it justify using them to convict the guilty when it breaks the same laws everyday. It is strange, embarrassing and odd that the US goes around the world urging nations to send culprits to the war-crime Court in The Hague but it is exempted from the jurisdiction of that Court. Yet the US is a suitable candidate for that Court because of its action and behaviour in Iraq. This is where justice diminishes itself.

It is criminal for a father and head of the family to deliberately leave out some members of the family because he does not care about them. Such a father is partial and guilty of negligence of part of his responsibilities. Integration but not disintegration and inclusion but not exclusion is what a functional family wants. I challenge the US to behave as a leader of the whole and not as a partial leader of its camp if it wants to take up the difficult task of leading the whole world. It was extremely short sighted vision for George Bush to talk of a coalition of the willing. Iraq is a Nuremburg punishable crime. Hitler occupied Poland. Britain joined the war. Germany was defeated and its leaders perished at Nuremburg on the gallows. It is made simplistic but it is to emphasize the fact that occupation is totally unacceptable. It is more complicated and complex when honest people examine the past History of the US relationship with the people the US caricatures and demonises as its number one enemies, today. They were all best friends of the US. The US bloomed them for the role they are now playing. The US cannot eat its cake and have it in hand. That is not on. The real enemy of the US is its foreign policy. This has to be critically examined. The US must learn to accept failures and losses while jubilating and rejoicing over victories and triumph. The bogus policy of "you are either with me or against me" does not work with a vision of leading the world of diverse people. The US foreign Policy is the weapon of mass destitution of the world and Africa in particular. The weapon of mass deception to start resource war and violence does not give any credit the contractor politicians ready to burn up the world to get massive oil and energy contracts and support the US armament manufacture and lucrative arms sales.

An inclusive and not exclusive world and an integrated and not a disintegrated world must be tolerant of all types of people in the world. The bench mark must be the rule of secular law popularly accepted by majority of people to regulate the conducts of people in the society and community. This does not mean being integrated into the US society as the bench mark community but into the world community where the weak relies on the strong for strength and the strong encourages the weak to take courage and be strong. The rich should have compassion on the poor and the poor must learn the ways of escaping from crippling poverty. Exchange in the ways to overcome debilities in life should not be beyond human beings to offer to each other.

It is in this breath that I have repeatedly campaigned for applied Education and effective skills training to encourage and enable people in every region of the world to make a living from the resources of their lands. The Africans are offensive to the world and decent Africans because of their selfish attitude to changes in various regions of the world. The indifference of their leaders to enormous achievements in Asia and the ominous silence of the African populace are embarrassment to the world. Can they see what the Asians are achieving from first class effective Education, effective skills training and rewarding apprenticeship training? They are succeeding in teaching their youths Mathematics, Basic Sciences, Applied Sciences, Agriculture, Engineering, Technology and Information Technology (IT). Their success is a result of long term planning and investment of their limited resources in the projects. Neither the African leaders nor the indolent African populace seem to notice. Are we sending silent message to the world that we Africans lack the ability to organise ourselves and youths to achieve as much as the Asians because we do not have light skins and comb backwards. Can we abandon embezzling and stealing public money and use it to invest in active Science and Mathematics, Biology, Agriculture, Engineering, Technology and IT active Education to help us to develop our basic manufacturing basis? It is something the AU can do as it needs a continental centre. We just need a token centre.

They should have the Education and skills to deal with the problems of their environments. It is no secret that in a world where people blame all their problems on lack of money to fund projects, it is lack of the right type of Education and skills that actually causes the indolence and stagnation. Lack of funds is a lame excuse to justify latent indolence and reliance on money to escape the hard work involved in creating wealth and prosperity. We can provide our needs and solve the problems we have in all our homelands provided we have the right applied Education and skills to tackle the problems. We must be focused. We need the right tools to tackle our problems. It is then that we would be able to use the help people offer us to tackle these problems. We would equally be able to ask people for the right assistance. Throwing aids, Medicine and food parcels and money at problems of Africa and the third world would not solve the problems. It is good and right applied Education and skills that we need for solving our problems. Any help the Commission for Africa plans for Africa must involve the people in reliable applied Education and skills training to enable them to do things for themselves. I have already suggested the impossible as a challenge. All the road side apprenticeship must now be integrated into the main Educational system. This will give formal Education to our youths and regulate the standards.

They must be formalised and standardised to a high standard of service to offer trade to the students. This will improve the maintenance skills of the citizens which is lacking now. People and the communities will always look for these services. The owners of these skills would offer them to earn a comfortable living. It will save money and prevent avoidable wastage currently endemic in the system. I have already argued for every citizen to spend one third of life time in Education and skills training ---20years of each time. Necessity justifies this. We must compare ourselves to developed rich countries. We must use our own way and try to catch up. We may have to work ten times the developed countries now. Our Education and skills training must emphasize reading and numeracy as much as practical skills. Success in Examinations must be the passage for progress. Education must mean real discipline. The student must acquire discipline for orderly and sustainable development of this country. National Examination is the ladder of progress. This is important for uniformity of standards and orderly climbing of the national ladder without prejudice and cheating. We must eradicate corruption and grab.

Africa must develop into a United States of Africa under the rule of secular law as the free and democratic Constitution. Strong regional governments of compatible people to remove the bottlenecks of colonial incompatibilities deliberately built in by alien imperial powers to weaken us to make it easy for them to subvert and rule us in the divide and rule doctrine of "Impera et divide". Any responsible African serious over our overcoming our current handicaps must appreciate that for us to succeed we must resolve these nagging problem of colonial borders. The European who created this mess for us had returned to correct their borders to incorporate their people into the European Union. What are we waiting for? Are we waiting for the Europeans to get their acts together to return to cause confusion in Africa in the name of saving us from ourselves?

If EU is expanded to include post Communist Eastern Europe are we waiting for God or Allah to come and resolve our border problems by simply Re-integrating already well known previous territories that the colonial masters artificially created on 15th Sept, 1884 in Berlin? It is better to re-state how it all happened; the imperial colonisers sat round a horse shoe table on which there was a copy of poorly drawn empty map of Africa as none of them knew what should contain in the map. Leopold11 the tyrant of Belgium though he did not attend, had planted his informer, a white pack bagger in Africa among them. When they drank alcohol and argued mocking about on the empty map Leopold's informer and pack bagger who was just hanging about perhaps as interpreter, volunteered to help them insert places in the poorly drawn map. He got up and drew the straight lines now representing borders of the Bantustans African leaders use child soldiers to kill for monopolising and retaining power. Shame on you, traitors of Africa, because you love power more than your land of birth. Re-integration of colonial dismembered Africa with the consent of African leaders and African people will take away your power and oil and gas, gold, platinum and other minerals; hence you flatly refuse to discuss re-integration of dismembered Africa by a passer-by pack-bagger. Re-integration of Africa is to your advantage. It will restore old borders and allow free movement, create larger funds, cut waste and duplication of infrastructures and improve the quality of service. More people will be brought in to share the resources now being wasted by a few and hanging-on from previous colonial masters. There will be initial difficulties but this will soon disappear. If we endured the pack bagger borders for so long we should be able to endure re-integration of Africa that would bring all of us benefits. We would just need patience.

The second point in support of a United States of Africa is the African terrain of massive deserts, savannah and rain forest at the fringes of the oceans. This condemns some Africans to live in infertile desert and savannah with enormous resources that can be properly developed for environmental preservation and wealth creation and prosperity in Africa by integration and pulling all the resources together and allowing freedom of movement among the Africans.

The Africans in the Diaspora must now become members of greater African family. Planning must include all these Africans. Trade must be within before going external. We must rehabilitate all Africans in the Diaspora. I am very happy that The AU has sat up to remember that we have black people being slowly killed off in Australia and several parts of the world. It is not our business to state how black people came to be there. But this world has a duty to remember that Africa conquered the Oceans first with their tenuous crafts. They carted the margins of these vast expanses of water. They dropped boatmen at strategic locations as trade posts and positions to cater for their interest on their return. Equally sea routes and expeditions were very confidential matters in those days. The political situations were rather volatile. The volatile situation and change of situations could affect the trade route leading to abandoning the boat boys in distant seaport trading posts. I feel the Australian black natives came from this group. Equally, surviving ship wreck in the middle of nowhere could have created the native Australians. We must tell the Australian white that we would not accept their extinction by slow genocide. The land is rich enough to cater for their small negligible number. They deserve to be integrated into the system. Equally global Africans do not accept shambolic cosmetic pretence that the system has incorporated them while they are still outside being killed off by toxic alcohol etc. Let integration be visibly genuine at least even superficially as in the USA.

At seasons of quiet seas they sailed out to farther places across the seas and Oceans. Unfortunately there were two possibilities. They left the boat boys and could not return to recover them due to long distance or they lack the means to return. They could be swept accidentally to isolated long distant island like Australia where they had no means of return. The native Australians are such people. Their food is similar to ours. Their native Medicine Practice is African. They dance like us and enjoy rhythm similar to ours. The Pacific Ocean Islands were actually shared between Polynesians and African hybrids perhaps by cross breeding. The white race and black people are at the forefront of cross-breeding. Hence Africans in the Diaspora have a wide catchment area. Africa will slowly return to her children and bring them back to the fold. Ignore colour and language or habits. The African gene is African. Africa must plan to make room for these our children. The white family includes their cousins in Australasia, Canada and US. Why should the black family not include our remote and distant cousins? We must feel uneasy when these distant cousins are abused and ill-treated. Jesus said when you did these things to your fellow human beings on earth you did them to me.

The way people treat these cousins is the way they regard us. Apparently even limited gene survey had revealed that despite the display of skin colour most black people screened had white ancestors. People had always interbred. A lot of young female slaves were for interbreeding as light skin coloured slaves yielded more money or men just wanted fun and pleasure. Even at the height of Apartheid in South Africa we still had mixed blood children that I used to tease the Boers for. In Southern Europe, Spain the women preferred Africans who were affluent in Business and authority then and also soldiers. The Africans were in Southern Europe for five hundred years or more. Hence the Negroid features in Southern Europeans. Therefore the much trumpeted colour differences should not divide us. We are related in one way or the other. We may quarrel and fear each other because of the way the madness of power in colonialism abused Africans but cleaning up Africa and full integration of Africa as a strong Economy in Southern Western Atlantic as part of Western Economy still makes sense. Integration not subjugation is what our relationship wants. African resources had always been the heart of Western capital and Economy which excludes Africans themselves but in this collapse and recession the planning of recovery should bring in tidied up Africans and Africa itself for jobs in genuine construction to open up this heart of darkness to prevent people hijacking it to turn into criminal haven. The pirates had already started making it a hiding place.

I have been harsh to some naughty aliens in our midst. Africa is rich and spacious enough to accommodate all of us and we sincerely believe in non-discriminatory policy and culture on the proviso that the aliens in our midst do not use discriminatory xenophobia to grab our land and resources. We must equally be harsh and ruthless over crime and corruption. Stealing African Platinum, diamond, gold, gem and uranium and other rich resources and asset-stripping of Africa by taking fake African nationality deserve maximum punishment. Aliens feel this land is where to make easy wealth by corruption. If you love Africa and believe in its prosperous future, and offer it your loyalty you are genuinely African as your other compatriots. Let Darfur never rear its ugly head again. No body should insult a free African on this soil of Africa by calling him slave, not even Sudanese Arab desert nomads. I find it difficult to see humanity in these desert beasts more primitive than the camels that carry them around the desert. They have the right to know fourteen hundred years do not offer this land to them in preference to us who had been here for over five thousand years. The Arabs must know that they have not yet made roots in this land. They have to behave if they want to be here. We are ready to share this land with all genuine people who accept this land and respect its people. Any attempts at land grabbing or bogus religious fanaticism and murderous radicalism should send any strangers including Arab nomads packing back to Gaza. The African Union must have oath of allegiance to Africa. All prospective Africans must swear the oath.

Africa calls you everybody living in this beautiful land, you with ancestral right to this great land of human origin and civilisation now living in several parts of the world by our tradition of spreading to cover the earth, all black people on earth to join hands together and grasp our freedom in the world and rescue Africa from total collapse and progressive downhill daily increasing desolation. Africa has adopted you all. It does not adopt you to plunder her to enrich yourself to live in comfort and affluent lifestyle abroad in developed and advanced countries. You are all challenged to acquire practical and applied Education and functional skills and use them to rebuild this land on the equator and centre of the world to make it attractive and the envy of the world. Everybody here is an African. By the co-incidence of History of man Africa is the home of all mankind and human beings. We have no reason to exclude anybody from this land. But anybody who wants to live here must avoid lawlessness and corruption. Africa is the integrating point of all mankind and human beings. It does not accept racial xenophobia and discrimination.

What then makes me an African? I have to follow the tradition of my ancestors. I have to be exceptionally honest and courageous. I should never cheat or lie my way to success and victory. I should always respect life and give honour to God, the creator. I must see this world as a place to share with my fellow human beings. I should not live by cunning to enrich myself forgetting that no matter how much wealth I amass in this world my comfortable life on earth will always be three scores or four scores beyond which life is a misery and not worth living. Medicine, Science and civilisation or even extreme wealth cannot alter this. Even if we succeed to give strength to excess life in future, the Psychological factor of monotony would still make the extra prolonged life uncomfortable. It is pleasant to be called billionaire but are we not guilty of hoarding what we do not need? Giving to charity is plausible but what about giving each person the means to work for his or her living by giving him or her, the tools, Education and adequate skills? The gift of knowledge, understanding manual dexterity and skills builds a full loyal global citizen.

Please help Africa to release Africans from the prison of bogus religions and the restrictions they place on its progress. Africa wants to re-enjoy the free air of Democracy and the light of the sun unrestricted by the cold simmering moon at night. The restrictions of colonial customs borders are detrimental to progress in Africa. They restrict movement of wealth, trade, human beings, progress and prosperity. Could you imagine a land where the foreigners are freer to move about and do business than the citizens; while the citizens are confined to blind holes made for them by past colonial masters? Is keeping these blind holes and confining citizens to them for loyalty to past colonial masters for the great things they never did for the poor and miserable African citizens in them? Is it total ignorance of their homeland and reluctance to remove the obstacles to freedom and prosperity because the corrupt chieftains are afraid to lose power and their fiefdoms and their fringe benefits that stop Africans from dismantling these redundant colonial borders to allow Africans free movements on their land to promote business, trade and prosperity?

Do the Africans and their leaders understand that no matter what the world does to help Africa without removing the restrictions placed by these colonial customs borders to freedom of movement of the citizens? The movement of trade and business and pooling together all the resources of this land to allow planning to develop is essential for our Economic growth. The tropical rain forest, the savannah and the massive deserts currently hinder all attempts to open up Africa. But failure to re-integrate colonial dismembered Africa abandons it with several nonviable rogue Bantustans. Each Bantustan is a country that must have infrastructures of a country. This results in unnecessary duplications and wastage of resources in these infrastructures. We would never be able to rescue Africa from poverty without re-integration of dismembered Africa. Re-integrated dismembered Africa would form larger and economically viable countries than what we have at the moment. It would avoid duplication of infrastructures and save money. But the infrastructures would be of superior quality and adequate quantity. African development is based on relativity of the state of various terrains. In drought livestock farmers and nomads would have room to move their stock to safety for grazing and water.

The desert depends on the savannah and the rain forest for its rescue while the savannah and the rain forest depend on the rich mineral resources of the desert for their development. The Sarawa phosphorus is used by the West to manufacture incendiary bombs and fertilizer. Our rich uranium yields them the atom bombs. The United Africa must control our rich mineral resources not only to generate the funds to develop Africa and improve the living standards of all Africans in Africa and the Diaspora but also to enable Africa to contribute to world peace and security. If you drop incendiary bombs on children in a war Africa will stop supply of phosphorus to such wicked power. The control of the mineral resources and the funds generated from them are today in the private pockets of corrupt local politicians and their foreign collaborators, the so-called alien investors that exploit corruption, chaos, wars and conflicts in Africa to acquire mineral resources on the cheap. All these things happen when Africa is abandoned in underdevelopment and Africans in grinding poverty. Even the funds stolen by the local politicians are invested abroad outside Africa. This has made Africa the poorest of the poor in the world.

We may ban mining of uranium in Africa unless we obtain assurance that it is for non-military use. It is not African tradition to throw its weight about. We stand for justice first. We respect human life. Wealth and industrial Technological advancement should not make beasts of human beings. Civilisation, wealth and prosperity should produce human beings able to understand the wisdom of compassion and act compassionately. Fear of poverty due to rising prices of commodities should never drive rational civilised and compassionate human beings to destructive speculative war.

This is what Africa of our great ancestors stood for. Barbarian incursion into our land and ruthless colonisation poisoned and killed our culture. We Africans do not fear poverty as to indulge in criminal behaviours to prevent poverty or escape from poverty. The rich West in the last millennium committed the crime of genocide in several foreign lands to escape from poverty. The rich West must stop using bribery and corruption to persuade the world in the grip of poverty to sanction military actions against people who deny them access to their resources. This is abuse of democracy and freedom of the poor to control the little that they have. If civilisation violates the right of ownership and possession of the poor to the few things they have, it is not civilisation. The West has flatly refused to apologize for the destruction of Africa in Genocide in Carthage, the holocaust of slave trade and slavery and brutal colonisation and pillaging of the resources of our land. The West damaged Africa.

The West can help genuine Africans on the continent and the Diaspora to repair the damage done to Africa. This is not only in the interest of Africa but it is also in the interest of the West. The West is bragging about wealth. The challenge of our time is not how the West shares the wealth on earth but how it is prepared to genuinely share the earthly resources with other people on earth. Let the West not continue to fool itself by pretending that it can cater for everybody on earth. Let the West share knowledge and skills with everybody on every land to make all productive and able to look after themselves on their land. The world cannot hold the West to ransom because it works hard to have what it has. The West has already shared its Education and skills with Asians who are currently at the frontiers of crack Technology. The sub-Saharan Bantu Africans are refractory to good Western Education, skills training and sustained apprenticeship and their applications. They seem to snob and flout the world telling everybody that they do not want Western Education. Rather they want to replace it with counterfeit Education where the teaching is substandard, examinations leak and are rigged. They cheat in examinations freely. The certificates are fake. How can we be integrated into the Western Economic system with this sort of bandit conduct? We would weed out corrupt leaders and carry out radical re-organisation of our Education system to get rid of rotten apples. The current criminal behaviours of some Africans that seemed to have originally evolved from the Nigerian civil war is African self-inflicted injury. The Nigerian civil war allowed wild illiterate near savage people to seize power from educated Nigerians. Through series of coup d'état they finally seized the leadership of the country. They took turns to be the Head of state. As semi-literate Heads of Governments they lacked social polite finesse and the inhibitions acquired from polished higher education.

They could not read the rules and regulations in the Hotels they slept when on tour abroad. They depended on their officials travelling with them on foreign trips. The worst thing was that a number of them were criminals before they joined the colonial Army. They concentrated on promoting their ranks to very senior positions in the Army. Very few educated people joined the Army in those days. From the State House these people introduced complete indiscipline to the culture of the nation. They communicated in Pidgin English. Today every Nigerian including University students speak in Pidgin English. They made corruption a national character. One of them called bribery "settlement". He introduced 419 to Nigeria. Conmen had access to Government letter heads and facilities to dupe greedy foreign gullible people of their money by offering them attractive oil bunkering contracts.

Corruption and bribery became rife. Nigerians went about the world flaunting their ill-gotten wealth. One of the military heads of state even boasted that money was no problem but how to spend it. The coup culture quickly caught up in the whole of West Africa. Every African politician adopted corruption and bribery as a way of life. This brought Africa to where it is now. The truth is that Britain supported the Nigerian Civil War. Today Nigeria is under the grip of retired military officers' Mafioso Cosa Nostra Nigeriana; fraud is prevalent. Apparent criminal and corrupt culture is damaging Africa. All honest patriotic Nigerians and Africans sincerely assure the world that what they see is not true culture and behaviour of all our people. They should not lose faith in us. They should help us to re-integrate colonial dismembered Africa and choose honest, literate and responsible leaders. This is important for solving and overcoming the intractable and refractory problems of Africa.

Every living thing is a territorial animal or living thing. The African must note this. They have to stand and fight and defend their territory. From the time Alexander, son of King Philip of Macedonia entered Egypt Africans and their leaders had been running away from hostile invaders of their territory and homeland. They had been content in escaping to save their miserable lives as slaves of hostile enemies and invaders of their territories. The Africans must now learn from all other animals that they essentially have to defend their territories from hostile intruders and invaders. They must stand and fight and die. They must equally learn to eliminate all their dangerous traitors and citizens that collaborate with foreign enemies of our land to betray our land to the enemies of our people and homeland. We had run from our trading posts in Southern Europe and Palestine and returned to North Africa. We were driven out by the Romans. The Romans invaded Africa under Scipio. We accepted payment of crippling indemnity and living as slaves on our land to work and pay indemnities to the Romans. Later the Romans enthusiastic approval of senators like Marcus Cato moved into Africa and destroyed Carthage in 146 BC by genocide led by the traitor Massanissa of ancient Libya the typical trait and misfortune of Africa. There are always Africans ready to sell Africa to our foreign enemies for only trinkets. They, it is that must die first before they kill Africa in the hands of its alien hostile enemies. We must punish corruption and treachery or betrayal of our homeland to foreign hostile enemies of our people by maximum penalty, capital punishment. Africans must learn that they must have a secure territory before they can think of any possession including lives. All human races kill their traitors. Africa must kill all its traitors as other earthly people in various countries including Western Europe do. Africans do not need to be reminded or be persuaded to unite. Every African should now aware our continuous ownership of this land depends entirely on African Unity. Continuous isolation and individualism of each of the fifty three separate unviable countries are real imminent thread to our continuous possession of the land of Africa in the global world. Already some African countries are giving foreign countries land to farm. Do they know the significance of this?

We must accept to defend our territory and fight and die if need be. We have nowhere to run to any more. We have to stand and fight. We must stop the dirty habit of killing each other. Our weapons must now be trained against our real enemies. When the Roman Empire collapsed Arabs rushed in and took the whole of North Africa in Arab conquest of Palestine and North Africa. We still ran away. A lot of people accepted the alien Muslim Islamic faith to live like slaves in their home under Arab Muslim mullahs as Emirs and Sultans as their religious instructors. This was a very poor reaction in the defence of our territory. Today, the Arabs in Sudan are chasing us away from our homeland and calling us slaves on our land in Africa. What an insult is this? People praise heroes who sacrificed their lives to save the land from danger but we have names on empty monuments of great cowardly leaders.

Wake up all you, fools and let us unite and defend this land. Wake up all you cowards and let us rebuild Africa and defend all its territories. Africans have fifty per cent of the blame for the destruction of their continent. It is unmitigated self neglect. Today they are globe trotting looking for ready made countries for asylum. Small nomads in the desert in Sudan are conducting genocide against Africans in Darfur with total impunity. The victims are the long suffering black people. The nomadic Arabs are doing what the world likes "getting rid of the African Negroes". Our geriatric leaders are throwing about their flowing gowns. Unfortunately talking is not action. They talk about atrocities in Darfur but no more. This is Africa where we talk away everything. All the lip-professed friends of Africa can join hands and offer the African youths Education and skills. There is so much to be done in this land that we cannot finish our work in this millennium. There is no eternity in the world. The world is durable but mortal. Everything in it is mortal. We are mortal. Let us not hurry to war to destroy ourselves. Each one of us has a date with death. Why do we rush to war? While we are alive we must defend our people and our land. We should not run away if we are provoked to fight. We must stand and fight. The enemy also dies if he is hurt.

You are welcome to live here but you must be an African first. If you have no stomach for the fight to defend this land, our territory, Africa, you should not lay claims to being an African. If you can telescope time to see African leaders over five thousand years during crisis they all lack courage, fortitude and organisation to get their people to fight back and expel hostile invaders of their territories and homeland. Rather they voted with their feet. They always ran away. If they had Noble Gen Hannibal to confront the hostile intruders, they would resort to slander him and some of them would run to the enemy to declare their loyalty to him. They would tell the enemy that left to them they would welcome them but Noble Gen Hannibal was the obstacle. The Barcines fought for Africa but the cowards fought for their bellies and their wealth but they ended up losing both their property and the land. Unfortunately, today, our leaders are still lacking courage, initiatives, leadership, foresight and vision. They lack courage to lead men in danger. The African must from now on learn to be territorial animal. Get your territory.

We Africans do not accept homosexual practice as normal. It is criminal and violation of the rule of natural and social law. It is abuse and violation of the human person. HIV/AIDS came with this deplorable queer very strange human practice. There had been enormous efforts to dumb this human killer disease at the doorstep of Africa. Yet the strange things happening in the course of the development of HIV-AIDS came through homosexual practice. The violence and love of money of consumer-materialism are all evolution of the white culture we Africans should deplore and reject. It is exacerbation of racial hatred. Our culture deplores these attributes of a culture. The inner core of black culture rejects the attributes of tyranny of greed. The insult of slave trade and slavery, brutal colonisation and racial discrimination are unacceptable culture of the white man. These attributes of freedom had deprived millions in the world of their freedom and wealth and impoverished many. These aspects of white culture had made them wild and placed them in total disregard of the lives of their victims. The time had come for the whole world to stand up and challenge the bigotry and arrogance of some white people that bully the world to accept their lifestyle like homosexual practice as normal. No it is abnormal and deplorable to us black Africans. The continuous existence of colonial dismembered Africa with patches of land usurping the status of countries and masquerading as such only in names offers African resources on the cheap to past Western European colonial masters while Africa remains excluded from global Economy. The past colonial masters continue to own and benefit from African resources while Africa remains poor and undeveloped. Re-integration of dismembered Africa and ensuring that Africa has reliable and responsible leaders that will recover African resources to use in opening up Africa within and without to the whole world for trade and business is long overdue. Africa cannot develop while its vital resources are in the hands of past alien colonial masters.

Make it safe and secure and proceed to develop your territory by two methods only. Get good practical education and practical skills training and send your youths to work your land using education and skills as tools. Always be ready to die in the defence of your territory. Do not run away from invaders of your territory. Feel happy dying in the defence of your territory. Let that mutual trust of love, patriotism, possession in safety and security persuade you to stay in your territory. The best life you would ever have in the world is in your home land. It is not in the West in the UK or the US. The African resources must be pooled together as the products of the African Union and presented to the world market as African product. They must be sold from the African market. The money is then distributed to each region and part of it used for African common services. At the moment foreigners and Eton mercenary fighters live on them by promoting coups and civil strife and wars. There is absolutely no way Africa can resolve her current problems without first dismantling the former colonial borders, bringing their resources together, develop very high standard of Education that will give vast amount of knowledge to its youths to sharpen their inquisitive minds of research and very effective problem-solving skills training so that the African youths start to enjoy tackling problem challenging them.

It is by this method that we will be able to defend our territories and make our borders secure and safe. We will be able to grow the food we need to eat. The current colonial fragmentation of Africa can never produce the Africa of our dream. Most nations of the world are successful because they do not have the problems fragmentation and colonial and commercial interests placed on Africa. They have stifling, strangulating and retrogressive effect on the continent. We must teach our youths to work and stop cheating.

Nigeria under Obasanjo is a case in question. Nigeria was highly a respectable country but yet it suffers from neglect from the leadership. What then happens in the case of smaller desert patch land countries with extremely limited resources? It is mere common sense that we all Africans must make the sacrifice in dismantling the obstructive multiple colonial borders to create a territory easy to defend, maintain security and safety and to develop. A secure and safe developed central authority would be in a position to collect enough funds to disburse to the regions for their development. Equally Africa would have central development programmes and projects like road and rail network communications. There will also be central institutions that will stop the current unnecessary duplications and wastage. Sharing of these facilities would equally reduce the cost and increase their usage. Optimal usage of limited resources is both economic empowerment and enhancement. A strong centre with visible authority under the rule of law is very essential for investment and economic growth. The current structure in Africa is an empty shell containing nothing. Even the African illiterate corrupt leaders do not invest the funds they embezzle from the continent in Africa. They put them in foreign Banks and acquire huge foreign properties. This is not an incentive for investment, economic activity or planning. The market today relies on numbers, breadth and length, space for rapid movement of goods and services. The market requires that critical mass to be profitable. It is a great shame that all global continents have palpable defence force. Asia possesses nuclear force. Europe has nuclear force and America has nuclear force but Africa has neither a credible Army nor nuclear force. Yes denuclearisation would eventually take place but we should negotiate that with African credible nuclear force. It is a great scandal that in a continent with neither a credible effective Army nor nuclear force a country like Nigeria has more Generals and retired Generals on life full salaries and pecks. Yet Nigeria is a run down country where nothing works.

The African terrain and eco-environment essentially require removal of restrictive colonial borders and re-integration of the whole continent to constitute a viable market. To do this we have to persuade the college of African presidents sitting over empty shells of authority riddled with massive corruption and chaos beyond the reach of the rule of law. The miserable state of Africa now challenges them to choose either their vested personal individual interest or re-integration of colonial dismembered Africa and allow History to immortalise them for their vision and selfless sacrifice and action in creating modern united Africa. They would be credited as modern founding fathers of global Africa. Now Africa has neither good education nor effective skills training. Failure of re-integration of Africa and leaving it as dismembered colonial territories is crippling education and skills training in Africa and all its economic activities. This is essential to disperse populations stranded and frustrated in infertile arid savannah and desert countries created as possessions of former colonial masters to allow Africa to develop as an economic entity with authority under the rule of secular comprehensible law or the constitution. The constitution should include equality of opportunities and human right.

Western European colonisation abandoned Africa with several diverse people incubating empty shells of authority as "presidents" without any understanding of their responsibilities and the duties of their respective offices. This has exposed Africa to insurmountable ethnic, political and economic problems. Most of the "presidents" lack the ability to understand this situation. The only people benefiting from this chaos are the Western European multinational conglomerate corporations. They reap very rich harvests from rich African mineral and natural resources. Most African "presidents" lack both the understanding that they do not have the clout or instrument of authority to enforce the law or the constitution and the fact that they do not have genuine law or constitutions to enforce. Also both the poor eco-environment and physical poverty of the Bantustan cannot offer them alone the clout and resources to attract global attention. Rather people still view them as colonial countries. The only people who benefit from their existence are the former colonial masters and Western transnational corporate bodies and their shareholders in Western Europe. The local politicians get fringe benefits from these bodies while the masses of the population are left to irk out a living from arid infertile land.

They equally do not know what to do. They seem to listen to no comments made against their various countries. Most Western European countries that left them with these empty shells of authorities frequently accuse them of lacking legal system that can try criminals from the West ploughing on their rich resources or using their lands as bases for criminal activities. An example was the recent case of the son of former British Prime Minister, Lady Margaret Thatcher, her son, Mark Thatcher, who stayed in the comforts of his luxury home in South Africa to plot and sponsor coups and insurgency in mineral rich small countries in Africa. This shows that Africa must first establish authority over its whole territory to control all its rich resources to be in a position to ward off predators. This should have been done soon after the independence. But it is not too late now. The AU now knows the risk of not doing this. It is no longer the case of conflict between individual leaders, ethnic or religious groups. All patriotic Africans in commerce, business, Arts, Science, Academics, religion, politics in all parts of the world particularly in the Diaspora to stand firm behind Africa and develop genuine instrument of authority for Africa to use in recovery and control of all its territory and assets. The fortunes of Africa are closely linked to those of the Africans in the Diaspora cut off, isolated, tormented and abused over several years in dehumanising deprivation and racial xenophobic torture.

The problems confronting Africa is the fact that for almost three thousand years it has been unlucky to be inhabited and populated by degenerate Negro race contented to be barely alive, eat, drink and breathe free air. They could work like machines and beasts of burden. They seem to ignore the value of knowledge, education and skills training. They seem to place value on products of industry derived from education and skills training. Yet they ignore education, skills training and apprenticeship. They seem to have developed copious capacities for tolerating dehumanising abuses beyond elastic limit. The Europeans from the West and the Arabs trampled upon their right as human beings underfoot. Today, their misery in Africa and all over the world is challenging the human conscience. Unfortunately they still seem to be held back by leaders with impervious brains without the ability to see what is going on in the world around them.

These leaders have no vision of the future. They are content with the little they have. They are satisfied with the illusion of possessing things. Yet they have nothing and lack everything including minimum life comforts. The most precious wealth in this world is still defined by what King Solomon asked of God when God asked him to choose a request for favour from God. King Solomon chose wisdom. He needed wisdom to be able to rule over his people, Israel. I chose knowledge and good skills to be able to help my fellow human beings in distress. Africa and the Negro race have, today, very limited choice. They need two things only. One is very high standard of education that will give them mastery of their land, Africa to make it user-friendly. They need very high standard of skills training to acquire the skills to develop and use the resources in their land. They must be open to knowledge from all sources. They must know that each person has sixty to eighty years to live useful life here on earth with luck. None of them is here to live forever. They must contribute to the common pool of knowledge and skills as their wealth. They must avoid being made angels of consumer materialism, corruption and agents of tyranny of greed. They are corrupt because they like luxury goods and rivalry among their group and have children beyond the number they know.

It is not beyond sober conception that the continent of Africa must have African Development and Construction Corporation (ADCC) to take charge of planning development and construction works on the continent. It is this that will provide jobs and open up the continent. There must be a common pool of funds contributed by both citizens and all countries of Africa. The transnational and multinational corporations must contribute to this fund. The Diaspora may equally join. The funds should be used in development and first action must be the building of trans-continental African railways from thee Cape to Tripoli, Algiers, Tunis, Rabat and Cairo and must link much of the cities to open up Africa to the world. The current high speed rail would effectively facilitate travel and movement of goods around the continent. The resources of Africa can support this.

The Technology is there for successful completion of such a construction. It is a job and employment generating scheme. Construction is vital way of taking people out of depression and recession. Construction is the door to take Africa out of the current doldrums. Israel is one of the nations of the world with Desert Technology to offer Africa. Israeli citizens had been indulging in shady businesses in Africa but involvement in major construction works will open up African-Jewish enterprises and ventures. Australia also has viable and successful Desert skills, experience and Programme. Technology is there in Asia, USA and Europe especially the French know more about the Sahara than most of the Africans apart from the Bedouins. The French have the Sahara as the home of their Foreign Legion. We hope they would not sabotage this project. They owe Africa moral conscience to positively pioneer this project. It would be to their benefits as it would be a conduit for their goods from Marseilles to Africa. It would increase the volume of business passing through the Port of Marseilles from Africa and the whole of Europe and Italy would also benefit. EU would fear invasion by African Economic migrants but I can assure them that there would be so many jobs in Africa that very few would go Europe. Many Europeans would come to work in Africa. Now European oil and energy workers fly to do this but with this road and rail net works more of them would travel to work in Africa. Watching the television and seeing the desert routes illegal African Economic migrants from Libya take to reach Europe it is feasible to build road across the desert from sub-Saharan Africa to North Africa. It would take years to build because of sandstorms and difficulty in transferring materials particularly water but the trick is to build from residential areas from both North and South and use completed portions to transfer materials along towards the heart of the Desert to join both North and South. Combating sandstorms would need a special branch of Metrological forecasters. Equally special branch of Civil Engineering would be developed to design sandstorms protection shelters for the workers as well as for protecting the rail and the roads. Equally water pumped into some areas would be used to fight sandstorms. Huge rain water storage reservoirs would have to be built to store rain water in places with some rainfall to pump it along the line. Desalinated water would equally be used in some places using solar energy. Human skills develop with experience. Desert studies would become a specialty and create jobs.

Prominent Africans of unquestionable characters and reputable Banks should manage the ADCC funds. Multinational corporations doing business in Africa should contribute directly to such funds. Any nation with ruined Economy and massive unemployment usually embarks on massive construction work to provide the infrastructures lacking and employment for the citizens. Africa is no exception. African leaders are strangers to modern Economy and its concepts. Let all who pity the plight of this continent help Africa to embark on massive transcontinental construction work. Let the ten to twenty per or even twenty five per cent of the earnings from mineral resources be set aside for this project. Open up the continent of Africa by linking North and South across the desert. This is for jobs and communications. Note Education and skills are the two things Africa lacks. Africa also lacks youths who can work. Its youths are lazy and reluctant to work. Constructions to create jobs and open up Africa will be ideal for the concept of the market. Unfortunately those who want to help Africa speak with two mouths. What they say is true and convincing. What they do is total opposite of what they say. The whole thing becomes mere hot air and politics as time passes on. The only way to help Africa is to give them Education and skills and tell them to get on with it. Close the waste pipes of corruption and crimes. Tight supervision of tasks is important to ensure that there is no slacking back to indolence.

The slag has to be isolated and excluded from responsible positions. This is the way to whip Africa out of the slumber. They must join to have that critical mass in funds and power to do things together to move the continent out colonial poverty. We must resist the temptation of throwing money at African problems while the Africans are sleeping. Core Africans must be involved in rescuing themselves from poverty. It is wrong for foreigners to tell the Africans what they want. We can go industrial. If we are to join the free market, we should be able to feed ourselves and manufacture our basic industrial needs. We must be ready to compete. We should not ask for favours. Equally a prosperous Africa with cash is a promising prospective market as Africans consume a lot.

Is it a surprise that we got independence from the Western European colonisers but up to this time we do not know what to do with independent existence? We are timid to dismantle the restrictive colonial borders. We fail to re-integrate colonial dismembered Africa. We cannot organise and open viable Schools to teach our children and give them effective and adequate education and efficient skills. Why is it that we have perfected crimes and corruption? Foreigners are free to move about in Africa while Africans are confined to their restrictive colonial borders. They are not free to move freely about in their continent. The leaders fail to see any value in good Education and good skills training as means for encouraging Africans to work for themselves. They have no clue about trade and money. They do not understand how to preserve or create jobs. They destroy jobs, steal public funds and loot the treasury to launder the money abroad in off-shore banking havens. They destroy jobs. They are above the rule of law. Obasanjo, the Nigerian leader attended the Oputa Enquiry but his lieutenants, Ibrahim Gbadamosi Babangida, Mohamed Buhari and Abubakar all refused to appear before this tribunal. These three were part of the very corrupt military tyrants that ruled and ruined Nigeria. They demonstrated clearly that they can rule over Nigeria as corrupt military tyrants but they are above the rule of law. They are above the laws and constitution of Nigeria.

They dismantle all public utilities and steal the funds for maintaining them. They embezzle Government funds and launder the money abroad in free tax banking havens. They overthrow governments to gain access to the treasury and control it. These corrupt soldiers drafted and wrote Nigerian Constitution and imposed the same by military on Nigerians without any referendum. They made promotions and retirement in the Army very easy. The Army have more 4-star Generals than nations that had fought several wars. They have a fleet of retired Gens on full salaries and benefits and a platoon of state paid troops guarding and serving them. The state changes their vehicles every year. But the graduate youths are unemployed. There massive unemployment while retired Gens having fun 24 hours and corrupting our School girls by flouting the money they had illegally extorted from the tax payers by their phantom constitution and laws. They have private assassins to deal with people like me to silence them and frighten any future opposition. They have their agents in all public institutions; Universities, Trade Unions, religious gatherings and in communities. They establish and sponsor violent cults in Higher Institutions. They give them military training and arms to disrupt student and teacher activities. They pretend to be opposed to their activities but use them as thugs during election. They intimidate people in election campaigns and do stuffing of ballot boxes and delivery of stuffed ballot boxes.

Obasanjo is deluding himself or he is deceiving Nigerians. Nigeria has no authority to make all Nigerians equal before the rule of law. He claims to preside over participatory democratic government when he is powerless before this mafia triumvirate. Is it not time that Obasanjo stopped throwing tantrums over nonexistent Nigerian unity, and fooling the world and Nigerians and confronted the reality stirring at him in the face. Nigeria has no authority to control the military Mafiosi Cosa nostra Nigeriana triumvirate with their enormous fortunes built at various global banking havens from the enormous oil wealth they presided over in their times as rulers of Nigeria. If Obasanjo cannot probe these people for the disasters and catastrophes of Nigeria whom can he probe? Why does he talk of confronting corruption while the people who presided over corrupt regimes are above the law and the courts?

Obasanjo enjoys the title, “President of the Federal Republic of Nigeria”. This is neither Academic qualification nor traditional title. It is a role Nigerians voted you to play in their lives. Why do you deceive Nigerians? Nigeria has no binding constitution or reliable legal system. Is it above you Obasanjo to tell Nigerians the truth? He has no authority to use in exercising the duties of the Office of the “President.” He is reluctant to call a “National Conference of all stake holders in a virtually paralysed Nigeria to express their difficulties in the corporate existence of Nigeria and what should be done to correct the flaws. Does the world know that a Nigerian child born in Lokoja Nigeria whose father works and pays tax in Sokoto cannot attend School in Sokoto Nigeria because Sokoto is not his state of origin? Where is Nigerian Unity if Nigerian children are prevented from mixing at School? The military created the states by fiat to broaden the basis of sharing the oil and energy money among themselves to silence any opposition. Why do they talk of unity while they divide the country by restrictive, religious and ethnic steel pens? This is oil and gas money unity guarded with guns but not unity of human beings living in Nigeria.

Obasanjo, the world has observed, lacks the basic knack of the will to exercise the rule of law and get a viable binding constitution to use to exercise authority the Nigerians had vested on the Office of the President of the Federal Republic of Nigeria to apply his knack as a leader to exercise the rule of law and make every Nigerian subject to the law of the country. Obasanjo plays the role of a survival in Office. He gathers everything that will offer his regime peace for him to stay as the leader even when that means total paralysis of the functions of his Office. Oil has come to be a curse to Africa mainly because of the behaviour of Obasanjo. Under him oil wealth is for take by his loyal supporters such as Ibrahim Gbadamosi Babangida. He is above board despite his reputation as number one swindler of oil money because he is loyal supporter of Obasanjo and a member of the ruling clique and coup expert that can give Obasanjo some headache if he exercises the knack of applying the rule of law on which his Office is based as the executor of the constitution. All Nigerian rulers are experts in destroying jobs and not creating any jobs. Nigeria is a failure because almost all its postcolonial leaders were corrupt lawless criminals totally ignorant of leadership responsibilities. Equally Nigerians are cowards. They cannot stand up to speak for their country. They are afraid to die. They allow their criminal leaders to bully them.

Several oil producing emerging countries in Africa are praying God to spare them the curse of oil that had destroyed Nigeria under Obasanjo who pledged the oil to secure loans that Nigeria failed to pay back while his military boys were having a field day in global casinos rubbing shoulders with the world millionaires. Nigeria is in a limbo because it cannot qualify for debt pardon because of its enormous oil wealth and the billions the corrupt leaders had banked abroad that the creditors know. Obasanjo has been chasing Sanni Abacha money but Abacha family and the world monetary institutions that know several other oil money looters are unimpressed by his crusade against Abacha who is now harmless.

It is soon becoming a vendetta against Abacha for sending him to prison. There is absolutely nothing wrong in fighting crippling social crimes like corruption. President Obasanjo has no legal instrument for fighting it. The fight is half-hearted and selective. This is not the right type of action against a social evil like corruption in Nigeria. It is speculated and perhaps rightly so that corruption is now on the increase. Therefore, where is the fight against corruption taking place and what are the results of this fight? Obasanjo is old enough to know that he cannot continue to deceive us and fool himself. If he loves Nigeria so much he should gather genuine fellow Nigerians to create a secure and safe territory of Nigeria governed by the rule of popularly acceptable secular law, the constitution of Nigeria and instrument of charter for the President to use as a mandate to rule Nigeria and make Nigerians subject to the laws of Nigeria. Self-preserving President appearing alone before Oputa confirmed that under Obasanjo obeying Nigerian laws is optional. It is not a sign of humility. It is a sign of extreme weakness and lack of mechanism to enforce the law of the land. It may even be lack of the law of the land to enforce in fighting crimes including corruption.

Nigeria has no binding constitution. Come let us develop a viable and binding secular constitution that will constitute simple and easily understandable rule of secular law to bring all Nigerians under the rule of law as a first step. This is important so that Nigeria will have control over all its territory and citizens. It is important that all Nigerians must be under Nigerian simple and easily understood secular law. It is totally stupid to have a country defined by multi-faith. Religious freedom must be confined to the faith and the believers. It must not have any role in Government or politics. The world has seen enough of religious people who have no faith in their belief but exploit religion to fight wars and pursue violence. Obasanjo may accept to be powerless to be President but Nigeria is in danger to be powerless in controlling its citizens. National Constitutional Conference now deserves an urgent attention and essential place in the national debate. Mr "Do little President" not what Nigeria wants now. Obasanjo was totally helpless before the deaths and carnage of Sharia law declaration in Nigeria. He has always been helpless during ethnic riots and killings that took place from time to time. The world finds it difficult to understand why Nigeria that fought a bloody civil war with ethnic cleansing and pogrom all for national unity should be victim of regular religious riots; killings, burning and destruction of schools and churches and properties. They do this all in the Muslim Islamic Sharia Law. Nigeria under Christian Gowon leadership denied at that time that Nigeria was not a religious ghetto country. Today Nigeria is perhaps the only African country at the risky sharp end of fanatical Muslim Al-Qaida extremist brand of Islam. Nigeria is enjoys being second to Bangladesh in the transparency score in addition to being at the top of countries fraught with corruption and crimes. It lacks unity despite its past investment in blood of several of its citizens for unity. It is a country that its leadership had been hijacked by criminal military fraternity that its members continue to recycle themselves as head of governments while the country is in anarchy. They waste a lot of money organising sham elections that they steal the victory with violent ballot box stuffing. This is the sad story of Nigeria.

He has been helpless during indigenes' complaints against environmental degradation by oil exploration. How long will Nigeria remain in this state of flux in Obasanjo's hand as President of Nigeria? Obasanjo should never misunderstand my comment as hostility towards his rule or as a personal criticism. He must rather see it this way. He has the mandate to rule Nigeria. He seems to have faulty mechanism and charter to execute his rule effectively. He should enlist support from genuine Nigerians and well-wishers of Nigeria to produce genuine and binding charter to use in executing his mandate to maintain law and order. No Nigerian should be above the law of Nigeria. Obasanjo would have his name enshrined in gold if he succeeds in doing this in Nigeria.

It is Stone Age anarchy where the powerful and strong owned the few things available in the community. Every good thing belonged to the strong and the powerful. I would love to think that the ultra-conservative Western right would not seize American military might to conduct resource wars in the name of fighting invisible US enemy, terrorism, to promote armament manufacture and sales to offer big public contracts to themselves. Real genuine wisdom still demands dialogue and mediation for settlement of disputes. Victory on the corpses of the dead is primitive and a hollow triumph. Any affluent technologically advanced and prosperous community and society without respect for life and the environment are still very far away from civilisation. Civilisation has definite value for life and the environment. It respects the freedom of equality of opportunity, ownership and possession. Civilised wisdom understands that action calls for reaction, challenge calls for response. When people put their dirty hands of ignorance to claim civilisation but fail to understand this basic concept of life, they do not only lack wisdom but they also fail to know what civilisation means. The old people in the UK who were equated as children in 1939 during World War Two today advocate talking instead of bombing in conflicts. This is an advice the leaders, today, should not ignore.

The war in Iraq has betrayed our civilisation. Power belongs to the greatest firepower with greatest killing index and might is right to slaughter helpless women and their children. Equality of life is beyond the understanding of the man with several divisions with lethal firepower. He alone can dish out death and democracy at gunpoint. The world has no power over him but the world must do his will and biddings. The ambiguity of the UN in the grave situation makes it as worthless and helpless as the League of Nations. The UN gives the impression that if the rich and powerful is patient to hire allies it can use the UN as the war council to sanction war on the weak and poor. On the other hand Rwanda and Darfur in Sudan have shown that the weak and the poor stand no chance with the UN. The UN is not for the protection of the weak and poor.

The UN was established to protect Western interest after the Second World War. The Security Council has three permanent members from the West alone, two from tiny Western Europe, the UK and France and one from Eastern Europe Russia and only one China is from non-European stock. This is totally incomprehensible for a body that claims to represent the world. The world must seriously consider this gross incongruity and unacceptable state of affairs. Today, it is difficult to determine or predict what the hawks can use mighty and powerful US and its satellites to unleash on the rest of the world. Iraq has shown how helpless the world could be in such a situation. We urgently need regional bodies to replace the UN. It is these regional bodies that should constitute themselves into a new totally refashioned and remodelled UN. We cannot base the security of the world on the rich and powerful while we continue to talk of democracy.

If wealth and military might are weapons of mass destruction (WMD) medium military powers can rise up and seize some weak wealthy territories like Iraq to enhance their wealth potentials for more powers to be able to confront the increasing powers of the tyranny of greed of the rich and powerful. This would be a chaotic world. We are steadily approaching that time. The former Soviet Union can be reconstituted with new countries joining to constitute a counter force to the growing menace of US and its satellites led by the hawks. This would lead to a real world war. The shape of the world that would emerge after that conflict would be hard to predict. Regional bodies coming together to evolve a viable UN would prevent the impending disaster. It is criminal to make Democracy into a propaganda and ideology tool. The US and its satellites seem to relish in ideology to divide the world into camps but Iraq has shown that the US in the hands of the ultra-conservative Straussite rights are anything but democratic but abusers of human rights. US conduct so far has t been a sort of terrorist Army operating torture and rendition kidnapping camps.

The truth is what Saddam Hussein did in several years, the US and its satellites had done all of them in less than a year. They had murdered and slaughtered so many Iraqis that every Iraqi now fears the USA. He or she now lives in fear under stress of US terror. Raining bombs and shell fires and powerful artillery shells into crowded cities and towns in the name of bringing democracy or removing tyrannical rule is extremely Barbaric and totally uncouth and undemocratic. Sodomising Muslim men to degrade their persons, sensibilities and religion is wild exploit. Definitely this is not the act of people who know about civilised standards, respect for basic fundamental human rights, freedom or democracy.

It is extremely totally incomprehensible for the most armed nation on earth at this moment to use the wolf-pack scare-tactics to intimidate its people to generate fear to score votes and approval for it to gain freedom to seize resources from weak undefended nations to sponsor armament manufactures and wars of loot and plunder. It was sanction that weakened Iraq for the US to prey upon. Sanction should now be regarded as an act of war. The UN could not defend Iraq in its hour of need for defence from illegal aggressor. Therefore, the UN has no authority to introduce sanction to weaken vulnerable nations for the US to prey upon. This was a terrible act of betrayal. The UN must make sure that it does not happen again as it would make the UN an agent of the US and its satellites. Let the Iranians tell the world and the UN that because of this past observation any attempt to impose sanction on it would be a declaration of war.

Other nations in the same situation must ensure that the UN does not declare sanction to render weak nations vulnerable to imperial ambition of the US and its satellites and empire building brutal wars. The US and its satellites have no respect for UN directives. Why then should the rest be subject to the UN while the US and its satellites are independent of the UN? Yes the US contributes more to the UN to control unfortunate poor and weak people, for the US of the Ultra-conservative Straussite right hawks to gobble up into empire-building in front of the helpless UN standing as a toothless bull-dog. The Security Council as constituted now is a US War council. The veto makes it totally redundant. The veto and abstention cripple it in the face of threat to world peace. It is therefore essential that the nations do not surrender their security to the UN that has no means to protect them from the US ultra-conservative Straussite right hawks and wolves to prey upon and gobble up into their new empire of global military conquest now christened "precision Laser uranium-tipped bomb democracy". It is death to those who refuse US rule by proxy. UN sanction is siege and siege is war.

This is why it is essential to dismantle the UN as constituted now to allow natural change to take place. Each continent should get its acts together to take practical Education and skills training seriously. It should then embark on environmentally friendly development and organise trade so that it is truly exchange of goods and services for genuine needs towards development. The world should be ruled by the rule of genuine secular and democratic law and any form of dictatorship and totalitarian regime should be unacceptable. No nation should be allowed to hijack this to blackmail its opponents by branding them totalitarian to slander them and isolate them for exclusion and abuse. The rule of law should be interpreted by popularly approved Constitution as the people's charter for the leaders and the citizens as acceptable authority for their governance. The current apostles of war and violence in the name of democracy should be outlawed and made obsolete. The priority of forming regional bodies should be purely voluntary choice and action of people who would derive benefits from such groupings. Efforts by the rich and powerful and influential nations to prey on poor countries must be resisted. Friendship must be on continental basis to promote development and healthy competition. This is the way to spread development and prosperity all over the world. It will also curb the current waves of refugees and asylum seekers. The proposal to use Libya as a sorting ground for refugees will betray Mumuar Khedafi as a traitor and promoter of mass useful and selective human trafficking similar to slave trade to depopulate it of its top grade brains and fit workforce. Every continent should take charge of its people free travel not withstanding.

It is these regional groupings that should come together to constitute the new UN.

Every continent should have at least one permanent member of the Security Council that must be made democratic by simple majority without the current vote buying by promise of foreign aids. Each continent essentially casts its vote through its permanent representative with brief and precise reason for casting its vote that way. The Regional blocks should contribute permanent representatives to represent their regional interests but each representative should have one equal vote and decision must rely on democratic simple of majority without veto. However, the veto may be left in place to enable members protect their regional interest. There must however be mechanism for appeal against decision the victim of defeat regards as unfair.

A special committee of variable permanent representatives of the Security Council must review such cases and present the grounds for appeal to the General Assembly for popular simple majority democratic vote. The review committee is to prevent delaying tactics and throw out such appeals to stop delay to buy time. Justice must be just and upright. It must not be delayed. It must be free from doctoring and corruption. It must be free from the apron strings of the influence of the rich and powerful. This is what is causing the current war against terrorism. The Arabs and Muslims for right or wrong reason see themselves as victims of unequal justice in the Palestinian crisis. The Israelis are treated as sacred lawless cows.

Equal opportunity to justice is essential. The two-state solution to Palestinian crisis is a mirage. One state under the rule of democratic secular law and equality of justice is the answer. Religion must be free but must never have influence over the state. The State must work out programmes for religious observance and holidays but inciting and provocative religious symbols must be abolished. Equally folk tale religious stories and taboos must give place to a changing IT global village. Anybody challenging me must tell me how many cars or aeroplanes, telephones and televisions Jesus or Mohammed had. This is not insult to these great sages, holy prophets and servants of God. It is to emphasize the fact that we live in a different world from that of the times the prophets lived. Both came to preach the message of peace not of war, violence and hostilities. What right have we to live our whole lives fighting for the land we die and leave alone? Sharing is heavenly and the creator God. This is why he, it is that made each of us to share this world together. It is difficult to see how the two-state theory would not result in two warring camps with mutual assurance on annihilation of each other.

But if we resolve to settle their differences and work out plans for them to live in peace with one another and persuade them to take out war and violence from their midst, they may finally accept the responsibility of maintaining the peace. They are already living together but in ghettos blowing up each other with high explosives. It is cardinal that the best solution to Palestinian crisis is to create one home for them and offer each of them the responsibility to defend the home and maintain the peace. Each of them wants this place and if a suitable agreement acceptable to both camps of interests with firm warning that they have the duty of looking after the land and each other and keep to the rule of acceptable secular law as the Constitution administered by a government of their choice and equality of opportunities they would see the need to live in peace. The world cannot afford sitting by watching Palestinian children starving. Palestine is the home of the three major religions in the West and the world but the adherents and the faithful of these faiths cannot share the land and the few things in it. The temptation for each state to use proximity of two states to prepare for war from advantage position is attractive. But one state allows surveillance by the two.

Each one of them claims to be gathering the souls for the creator, Yahweh, God and Allah. If they cannot endure each other and share the land in their short lives here how on earth would they share Paradise or Heaven? The two-state-solution is theoretically acceptable but it has its inbuilt setbacks. It is an attempt to split the harem between two dominant sexually active male lions. Each is still eager to expel the other to take over the harem. Fortunately, human beings can be persuaded by reasoning. To stop several years of feuding between Israeli Jews and the Arab Muslims between whom pockets of Palestinian land had changed hands several times and there had been a lot of mixes of human beings separated only by hatred, why do we not work on removal of hatred and sharing of common facilities under the rule of reliable and binding secular law? The leaders of the two factions can adopt this and take leave of violence. If they genuinely want to expel hatred, fear and violence from their midst they must start to talk to each other. This is what they should look into thoroughly. Land is as important as safety and security. Any solution must achieve permanent peace, safety and security.

At the same time the Israelis are enjoying heaven on earth and slaughtering the Arabs. The tragedy of the UN is partisanship and criminal corruption of capitalism. A world body like the UN cannot afford to be seen to be a partisan of injustice. The powerful and rich nations buy votes by promising Economic aids and debt pardon. They equally use threats of penalty by defaulting in support and not giving support. Consumer materialism and sumptuous living have replaced the creator, God or Allah and the worshippers of wealth had forgotten that wealth and prosperity come from God and truth and justice count. Consumer materialism is vicious. It is the tyranny of greed. The Bush camp sees us the rest of the world as a pack of wolves ready to devour them. Therefore we have to be destroyed before we could harm them. This is puerile argument but in the US any silly reason can be advanced for the wrong action. Blatant lies are no longer held with suspicion. They have gained public acceptability and respect by a population slowly losing their power of reasoning to the computer and fear of the unknown and the future and change. The greatest danger to the world is that the US citizens at times deliberately choose people too ignorant to lead their immediate families let alone the US and the world, to lead them. Perhaps the recent financial meltdown was God sent to re-organise the world. It may bring to the fore-front people that take world peace seriously and not dethrone God from human affairs.

Leadership is a special responsibility. Utterances are very lethal and destructive. A responsible leader knows how to count his words and shut up instead of using faulty patriotism and ignorant acid tongue to ignite highly incendiary explosive situation. George Bush and his ultra-conservative right contractors owe us the right of fundamental principle of democratic freedom to be spared from being described as a pack of wolves ready to devour the mighty US. He may say he was referring to his nightmare enemies, terrorists. Fumbling into unnecessary war to seize resources of a foreign land to sponsor illegal war does not transform citizens and resistant fighters into terrorists. They are defending their home the way the US did against the Japanese or the UK or France did during the Second World War. Resistant fighters are heroes because they defend their homes from occupation aggressors from unequal position. Their shield of defence is spilling their blood to defend their homes. They are poorly armed. They fight from right and strong conviction. The world is very sad because at the very time the global knowledge, Science and Technology had grown to unite the world into a big village so that information is physically present, seen and heard by all at the same time in all parts of the world, a few ignorant people, Politicians with doubtful past scholarship achievements and questionable leadership potential had hijacked the tremendous Scientific and Technological achievements to do their bits to return to the age of the previous Roman Empire to play the role of Julius Caesar in Empire building and gaining victories and uniting the Empire. The people nursing the ambition of empire building must be crazy. Nobody is in mood of being part of American empire.

There are lot of Africans in the US still suffering under the crushing weight of slavery and racial xenophobic bigotry. We in Africa are ready to discuss serious partnership with the US to secure freedom for these tormented Africans and means of bringing friendship to Africans living in various Pacific locations. The Africans that toiled and laboured for Economic prosperity of the West should be rewarded with good Education and effective practical skills training to work and develop the motherland, Africa. We are ready to share

Africa with displaced Africans all over the world. We need skills and Education to recover our land from the deserts. USA and Israel have the Technology to teach us Africans to do this. The Africans should work non-stop to establish road and rail communication network on the continent. We should develop transport communications to link up with Africans in faraway lands to develop a common Economy. We eat the same food, wear the same clothes and have the same culture. Sub-Saharan African Bantu Negroes must develop sustained hard work culture and consciousness of responsibility. If we are farmers the weather should not disrupt our work. We should find means of continuing our work in bad weather. We must combine our work with some research so that we may develop alternative ways of doing things to increase our yields. If we have no interest in copying others in our professions, we should observe the European farmers. The potato farmers under rain and sun work on their crops in their farms. The livestock farmers have full care for the animals and skills that cover full care for the animals. Theirs is full time employment. Hence we essentially have to copy from others the work culture and ways of improving on our skills.

We must equally know that we are cropping on different terrains and different climates. Therefore we must crop in a way that is suitable for our climate and our soil. It is laughable to show how stupid some of us are; some military officers wanted to invest the funds they stole from the treasury on poultry farming. They did not know anything about poultry farming. They undertook European tour and returned after acquiring chickens from the European farmers. They built kiosks in every town to sell eggs. They wanted to apply what they saw in Europe to their farms without modifying their method to make it suitable for their climate and environment. They lost all their stock and their efforts ended there. Therefore we should copy the European work culture of research and patient sustained labour in all weather. We must essentially learn how we can modify what we acquire from others to make it suitable for our climate and soil and what we have to endure to succeed. Patience is important for success in whatever we have to do.

This is a great drawback to what Technology could do to the world in chaos and abject poverty in an environment facing a disaster in the midst of enormous wealth, effective education and skills that everybody can acquire at minimum cost to tackle these problems. It is strange that parents of a crying child failed to ask the child what was worrying him or her but rather took the whip and started to whip the child into silence. If this is not child abuse, what is child abuse then? War against terrorism is abuse of power. It is corrupting of authority to hide deficiency in leadership under a difficult situation. It is a display of incapacity to take wise decision under serious threat. Three thousand people and property perished in the twin tower. Now Iraq alone has lost over one hundred thousand minus the soldiers, and the property so far damaged. This fails to take into account Afghanistan, Pakistan and other foci of violence and death. Are the leaders who designed this solution to terrorism sure that this is proper response and it is the only way to tackle it and there are no other alternatives as this is costly in lives and expensive in money? How many innocent more people should die because of damage and slaughter at the twin tower on 11th September? It is all a folly to mount protracted military action to chase the people we hold responsible. It is a waste of the resources we should use in healing the wound of this unfortunate event. The leaders should call of the war to stop the violence and the killings and return home to plan security and vigilance better than what we had on 11th Sept. This may sound stupid but we cannot destroy all the ants that bite us. We may sometimes have to endure the painful bites without effective means to retaliate. Killing more people to add to those we had already lost does not make sense to me. Stopping the war will save lives and resources.

Sadly the creator of this world designed it for us to share. We definitely have no choice. We have to tolerate each other and have to be considerate. Our great ancestors recognised and accepted this principle. We have to set up the rules to maintain the peace. With great respect to the US and insular UK that accidentally forced itself into the world with Roman style smash and grab tactics to escape from poverty on their island we have to remind them that they have to return to the drawing board to learn the rules of sharing. The booming cannon guns and gunpowder opened the African rain forest and its rich natural resources to them. Their ruthless cruelties and slaughters and genocide yielded them the US, Canada, Australia and New Zealand. Racial xenophobia isolated them from retribution. Time and sheer luck offered the world to them to pillage, loot and plunder. Today, that degree of terror is totally unacceptable. Who are the terrorists in the world, today, is a question that integrity, virtue and honesty would not fail to accuse the military aggressors. They had flouted all civilised laws to invade foreign countries. This is lawlessness and terrorism. It is a crime of terrorism attacking a country that is not at war with you. It lacks compassion when you rain bombs from the air on densely populated towns and cities. Where is civilisation in this type of action? There is a proposal to finish off the Sunni Muslims by surrounding them and killing them off. This is genocide in speculation. The tyranny of greed is running mad. It is all in the name of energy, oil and gas.

It is interesting that John Forbes Kelly emphasized the fact that George W Bush abandoned the right target Al-Qaida-Taliban in the Mountains of Afghanistan to chase the oil and gas in Iraq and the big attractive and lucrative contracts they awarded to themselves in this dirty deal. This amounted to the Commander in Chief directing his Army to abandon their post to pursue the target rich in loots. The Western military exists mainly for looting. The Romans had three major divisions, the fighting, the looting and the occupation divisions. This is the tyranny of greed. Perhaps John Kelly lacked adequate clarity in communication. George W Bush is not a tenacious military man. He is a very incompetent Commander in Chief of the Army. He was totally hopeless in fast thinking for rapid action in an Emergency. For almost two hours during the fateful Sept 11, he was missing. His weakness as C-in-C was so obvious that even his nomadic fighter enemy was able to detect. His claim to steadfastness is sweet in the ears of his audience but the competence of a good leader is fast and rapid assessment of the situation to offer flexible safe and rapid response. Inefficient and inapt leader talks of inflexibility and steadfastness but human beings like all living things are biological entities and subject to evolution, changes and flexibilities essential for their survival in the changing environment in the world.

The good leader does not go blindly after victory alone. He goes for factors capable of procuring lasting peace and security to maintain an orderly society and peace. The Western ultra-conservative Straussite rights fail to realise that the leader leads all. The greatest mistake I have seen a leader make has been the conduct and utterances of recent leader of the mighty America, George Walker

Bush. He spoke as a no-leader. You are either with me or against me. No the leader leads all. He leads those who disagree with him. He leads those who agree with him. He leads left and right. You do not lead your religious conviction. You lead people with independent mind and diverse thinking. A good leader is a conciliator. He reconciles entrenched positions. He listens to the people he leads and takes their advice. Leadership means that you offer yourself to serve the people and not to serve yourself or to be served by the people. Far too often the leaders seem to lose touch with this concept of leadership and the duties of the leader. They seem to fumble along with their fixed and set ideas in total disregard of what the people want. The sound quality of the leader is to plot the graph of the views and ideas and calculate the mean and take it as his policy. He has to reconcile the entrenched views.

It is sad that Tony Blair we had great expectations from took to leading from the front losing us all at the back. This led to the tragedy of Iraq and his loss of credibility after making labour dominantly electable. He missed the adage of influence and power. You must win one to one argument before proceeding to sell it to the people you lead. You do not argue to win your people to sell to win favour and place in one to one argument. One to one argument is not confrontation but it is easier than confronting a group of people. The danger is that of being unwittingly swept off your feet to be hijacked for evil purpose. You should always be on your guard to stand your ground if you have any doubts and conviction to stand by. It is not disappointing an ally but having positive influence on the alliance. Alliance is not a gangland fraternity but mutual support for good purpose. The war in Iraq is foul fraud on alliance if anything menace and harassment to participate in a crime. It has turned out to be recruiting sergeant for terrorism and violence. Recently George Walker Bush stated that he had won homeland security for the US citizens. This is good news. The fortress US is a safe prison for its citizens but unfortunately all their needs including freedom of movement round the world lie outside this fortress. George Walker Bush has successfully made this unsafe for all unprotected US citizens. No country including the mighty US can provide every individual citizen outside his or her home country twenty four hour security cover. Therefore fortress US has turned out to be a safe prison for its citizens but outside this prison is very unsafe for the US citizens.

The citizens of fortress US would have to fight their way through the world to make contact with the free world for normal human intercourse essential for a great and prosperous nation like the US. George Walker Bush is ambiguous about the type of freedom he is bringing to the world. Is it the type of freedom to fix sham elections for US puppets, cronies and stooges in the name of the type of democratic freedom that allowed US citizens to offer dehumanising mean assault treatment to opponents of US domination of the world as we saw in Guantanamo Bay in Cuba, Kandahar International Airport in Afghanistan and Abu Ghraib Prison in Iraq? How can democratic freedom rain uranium tipped incendiary phosphorus bombs on high density populated cities like Fallujah?

George Walker Bush may be re-elected President of the US. He lacks clarity of mind and purpose. He is under the strain of ultra-right Straussite conservatives and he lacks that sense of the responsibilities of a leader of a great global nation in 2004. He wobbles under the weight of these great and demanding duties. George Walker Bush must wake up and create a free passage across the world for all Americans by waving the olive branch and talking peace with the world. It is a folly to ask the world to join him in the fight against terrorists in the war he seems not to know the real front. If the Commander in Chief lacks the idea where the front of this war really is how on earth does he expect us to join him and where do we join him in the battle? The USA George Walker Bush is fond of talking about should show decency and civilized behaviour. Yet this man had abused and dehumanised substantial African Americans and signed their death roll papers. He has presided over the greatest human rights abuse in this century and millennium in Iraq and Afghanistan. Is he not deluding himself and insulting the world by talking about human rights he had trampled under foot? George Walker Bush lives in a different world from our own. He is transforming the US presidential system into Bush Royalty. He feels that power to rule the world comes from the barrel of US guns and smart bombs. The US and its satellites alone should have the nuclear bomb. This is the world vision of a bent mind. All of us want to live and not to be blown of by the US n-bomb. The stability of Western Governments did not protect Japan from the n-bomb. The maturity of Western Governments did not stop the West burning

Dresden with phosphorus bombs. We all must make and keep this bomb in case anyone drops it on us.

If everybody feels that it is dangerous to manufacture and keep the n-bombs, then we discuss the terms of verification without cheating. We reveal all and surrender it to a very honest global body for safe keeping as disposal is costly. When the world is satisfied that nobody is cheating, it can start to get rid of it slowly. The Western lying machine may surrender redundant ones while fashioning new and sophisticated ones. If this happens any nuclear bombs surrendered to the common pool are returned to the owners. We do not need a lop-sided world with safety confined to a particular group while exposing others. The non-proliferation principle is bogus and irrational. Who wants to die? What do those who have and keep the bomb intend to do with it, fight alien invaders? If they answer this question convincingly satisfactorily, I will change my views on the n-bombs. The rest of the world cannot stand by while some people are manufacturing and keeping sophisticated powerful n-weapons and delivery systems. This would be suicide. The West has no right to select those that can manufacture and keep the n- bomb and those that should not keep it. The world leaders the West is persuading to accept this principle should be careful not to be hoodwinked. Yes everybody in the world wants disarmament but not propaganda. Some people keeping the n-bomb while others who can manufacture and keep it are prevented from keeping it is dangerous. It is neither a safe deterrent nor reassurance that those who keep it will not use it. This is not a loony left tirade. It is a statement of fact. Would the West invade Iraq if it had the n-bomb?

What would those who manufacture and keep these weapons do with them in a difficult war situation as it happened in Japan in the WW2? Dropping the bombs to prevent further loss of lives should never be accepted as a reason again. Retaliation for everybody to feel its effect is the only action that would make the world know that dropping the weapon on anybody; friend or foe is evil action. Total efficiently verifiable disarmament is a safe guarantee for security. The argument here is that in a global world where some people are allowed to do certain things while others are banned and prevented it is gross injustice and a restrictive and rationed freedom and selective democracy for some. Bullying and intimidation are hostile to peaceful co-existence. The way to maintain the peace is to be seen to be fair to all despite some outbursts in ignorance. Bogus noise making is less dangerous than fumbling into rash and irrational action from wrong signal. The nuclear issue has now proceeded beyond non-proliferation to designing a new treaty of non-use of the weapon in any form in any conflict. There should be no pre-emptive strike. Anybody violating this treaty and law must expect severe retaliatory action from other signatory nuclear nations. Violation is a snub of and insult to the rest of the world. This would make use of the weapon a risk and peril to nuclear nations. This weapon cannot be de-invented. The knowledge is there in the scientists. Therefore a binding treaty of non-use is the best antidote until nuclear nations see the futility and the danger of keeping it and sign a reliably verifiable total ban treaty of all forms of nuclear weapons and weapons of mass destruction.

It is tempting to dwell on emotion and national pride but wisdom demands prudence from a world leader that has to lead his people, mighty Army and terrorists of this world. He has to assume chameleonic skin colour camouflages in order to address each group in its home constituency. Yes it is tough talk to make it clear that we do not talk to terrorists. Yet the President of the US armed with wisdom and prudence can talk to all including terrorists. He has the right to tell everybody in the world that in order for peace to prevail we all must speak in the same language everyone understands. This is the language of the rule of law. The rule of law here means the rule of popularly acceptable secular law binding on all citizens discussed and approved by the people themselves as the article of their governance. It is neither obsolete religious, feudal law nor military decrees. These are unsuitable and not applicable to the complex world as we know it now. Today, the world can use only secular constitution all citizens approve in a free and fair referendum to guarantee the rule of law. The people's freedom and security can be guaranteed by laws applicable to and acceptable by all. Religion must always remain as valid method and means of communicating with our maker, God or Allah. Imposition of religion or killing in the name of Allah or God stands condemned by every human being and our great maker.

It is neither a culture nor a way of life. It is deliberate disruption of peace everybody badly desires for now. While the world strongly supports religion it is very important to keep religion out of politics and the governance. Religious laws may be acceptable in the regulation of the affairs and guidance of the faithful in matters of religion but they definitely are unsatisfactory for dealing with the day to day affairs of the people in the world, today. We are in a global village. Even within a religion, we have several sects. The Muslims have the Sunnis and the Shias. The Christians have several sects. It used to be Catholics and Protestants. Now it is the Evangelical against the rest of Protestants and Christians. Therefore anybody contemplating on the imposition of religious laws on the society and the people is unrealistic. Such person is manifesting total ignorance of the knowledge of modern society that has resulted from the power people including Osama bin Laden had derived from Information Technology and High Technology. Even the totally covered up Arab women and Arab girls carry up-to-date electronic cachets, mobile phones, cameras and walkman players. Therefore it is futile to attempt to keep them away from modern corrupting influences. The only thing to do is acceptable legislation using popularly acceptable secular laws that take cognisance of the interest of the manufacturers and users of these equipments. If the President of US cannot persuade the mullahs to see the ridiculous state of affairs and modify their tactics in order to join the world and be accepted into the community of nations he will not be to blame for ignoring them. It would then be obvious to all that they have totally different objectives and ambitions over the world that is totally not prepared to be tyrannized by obsolete religious laws. Religious laws are elements of social engineering unacceptable to democratic freedom. They are deplorable and objectionable and stand to be condemned.

I was forced to imagine myself as an American voter with my vote in my hand in the voting booth. I challenged myself how I should vote particularly when I had to vote for or against homosexual marriages and free-for-all genetic manipulation and embryo stem cell Research all in the name of Medical cure of obscure diseases of unpredictable nature. I virtually had no choice but to vote for George Walker Bush if he happened to support my views on these matters. I am not a religious fanatic but these are offensive to my human sensitivities. Animals in the wild do not do these things why should fellow human beings expect me to accept them doing them so that I would not be accused of being homophobic? This is deliberate blackmail to intimidate me to support their strange lifestyle of same-sex sex and marriages. I cannot bring myself to ignore my human sensitivities to accept this deliberate self-inflicted life scourge of strange lifestyle much beyond the comprehension of the Science of genetics, Human Biology and normal human behaviours. I love Science and Technology but Spin humiliates Science. It is not Science when it makes wild claims of curing obscure diseases. It upsets real Scientists when people advertise Science as solution to all human problems. I hate Science where discoveries are overblown and patented after the discoverers who just do part of nature's job. Campaign for Research Funds and sponsors had made Scientists go for the Media support. The Media does not know Scientific Language and has tendency to over blow the advantages of what is yet to be discovered and can be achieved if funds are available to carry out the Research. They fail to inform the Public that Research may take several years to produce positive results or may fail completely. It is wrong to build up false anticipation in victims of diseases. We may finally succeed in finding solutions to these but let us not pretend as though we had already solved the problems. The impression that only funds hold back the progress is wrong.

I therefore, vote against it and for any candidate that supports my view. It is, however, not too late for George Walker Bush to start to think like a statesman and not a gang leader or a political thug. George Walker Bush is the President of US and an important world leader. His choice of words in saying that he would embrace only people who accept his views is substandard. It ignores diversity of opinions and tolerance of diverse views that forms the spine of Democracy and free thinking in modern society for progress. Neither the Americans nor the world would have to think like George Walker Bush to be eligible to live under democratic freedom in this world. His perception is ideological dictatorship. This is a form of tyranny and nanny state social engineering. The world has not got to share his goals and vision of the world to be right. It is criminal to use war and violence to solve religious, political and commercial problems. It is not too late to settle the Middle East problems by peaceful secret negotiations and formal conflict resolution methods. The Arabs must recall that they came to Palestine by Arab conquest. They drove the Jews out of their land. They must therefore suppress emotions and behaving as though the Jews are attempting to drive them away from their original homes and embrace sharing Palestine with the Israelis. They need tolerance of their neighbours and other religious faiths. The Israelis must equally abandon building a Jewish state but accept sharing Palestine with the Arabs. Indefinite State of war is unacceptable to everybody.

Unfortunately the greatest danger to the world, today, has turned out to be not ideological differences between politicians and religious fanatics. Rather it is the level of ignorance of the US leaders with the enormous resources at their disposal to do the damage. Donald Rumsfeld is permanently on the negative side of the idiocy graph but he answers all questions affirmatively exuding with the confidence of ignorance and a fool. He has never visited several places in the world. He has had no information about oil bearing rocks he wants to own. He is sure dynamiting the rock would cost minimum collateral damage. How does he know? He knows because he is Donald Rumsfeld, the US Defence Secretary of State. He has precision weapons with inbuilt minimum civilian collateral damage in battles. Is this gullibility in the extreme? Yes perhaps this is the peacock fool on Mount Everest. This is the US that our world, today, has to deal with, a Paradise of idiots among the cleverest people in the world. Shame to the leadership and their followers. They lack wisdom in discharging their duties to their fellow human beings. They are neglecting the duty of care to the community that they were appointed to look after. The US is content using unscrupulous hired traitors like Alawi that would not be better than death if he were a perfidious and treacherous traitor and a US citizen. Corrupt criminals serve useful purpose for wealth-gathering by the rich, powerful and influential US. I know several Iraqis are honest self-respecting people. They are genuine resistance fighters defending their homeland from alien invaders seizing their land to pump petroleum oil.

They die in honour, today, in Fallujah. Their bones rest with their warrior ancient fathers in Babylon. Brave people, honour has medal and a place in heaven. Your sacrifice is not in vain. After all, all of us will go the same way after our time. No patriotic citizen folds his arms and crosses his legs to allow alien invaders of their land to roam about freely. He activates adrenaline and fights the intruding enemies. Definitely, the resistant fighters are not dissidents or insurgents. They are patriotic and heroic citizens. They are defending the only thing they have and know their land. They will repair their relationship with the USA after the war.

To die with honour and freedom is better than to live as slave with empty promises of sham-democracy. Rain hell fire from the air, tank shell bombs and heavy mortars and machine guns but these may be delivering democracy from gun-fire of egg-shell-brain leaders as it may be their brand of democracy. It is barbaric and primitive. It is American brand of democracy for Iraqi traitors and criminal murderers to feed to their people in exchange for US control of their oil. It is counterfeit democracy. Democracy is incompatible with murders and violence. The US war and violence in Iraq are totally illegal act of an outlaw nation. Tony Blair and George Walker Bush have to volunteer appearance at The Hague for war crimes. That Court has no legitimate legislative role if these two are not arraigned before this Court to answer for their crimes against humanity. The word equality before the rule of law or law and order is the spine of democracy. The US has treated its black citizens to sham democracy, inequality of opportunities in violation of their Constitution and the rule of law. It is daring to advance this bogus democracy to other parts of the world. If the US is ready to take on the rest of the world, the world should not shy away. It should take on the US and let us see who will blink first. The whole world must be greater than any part. No part should be greater than the whole world. The US has to learn to be part and not to be the whole. It is wrong for the US satellites like the UK to give the US the impression that it is too big to listen to us in this world. We all must listen to each other and stop being an outlaw. The world does not want a self-appointed policeman. Perhaps the world needs another genuine world war for us to really value peace and stop toying with freedom. The US democratic gift to the world is rationed democracy and limited freedom.

We all love good things. The US ought not to force its own brand of democracy down our throats. We will continue to spit it into its face.

But if democracy is good and acceptable we will go all the length to acquire it. After all it is true the US does not force us to strive to acquire its high Tech gadgets. We do everything to get them because we love them. Equally it does not mean that we have to accept the US brand of democracy because we use its high Tech gadgets. We pay for these things. The US is yet to understand democracy. It has to apologise for past misdemeanours. It has to be humble to learn and understand the basic democracy. It must accept free choice that does not interfere with free choice and freedom of others. US freedom and democracy must not rob others of their democracy and freedom. There is a sinister move by US to convert the world into a big slave farm where people live in sham freedom and democracy to work free for the US. The world would become the US dollar farm. Such a world may be of interest to the US but most people do not fancy it. Ideological monopoly is a dangerous trait of religious fanaticism. Capitalism and free market are as dangerous to humanity as the West viewed Communism in the past. Diversity in ideologies is stimulation to growth and progress. This is the way human beings learn. Monoculture is bad and fails to stimulate growth and progress. The US culture is immature monoculture. The US is in a unique position to appreciate polyculture. Unfortunately a few selfish people styling themselves as ultra right conservative had hijacked the US to make their dollars in the name of democracy and free market. They it is that give the US a bad name. They owned slaves. They are guilty of heinous violation of human rights. They have no respect for individual freedom. Their utterances do not pass beyond their lips. They just do not believe in what they say and preach. They are arrogant bullies. They abuse their victims.

The war against terrorists started with Sept 11 with the slogan we were attacked. The man Osama bin Laden gave the order for the attack. He takes shelter in Afghanistan. We would go for him. The Guantanamo Bay dungeon and US torture house came into the scene. Initially there was that sense of Euphoria that the Taliban and the evil Al Qaida had been overwhelmed. Then came the suggestion of assaulting Iraq for weapons of mass destruction. People became apprehensive and restive. Bare-faced fabrications and spin took over. Several people demonstrated in the streets but to no avail. Overwhelming lying propaganda took over. Weapons of mass destruction (WMDs) dominated the air. Finally in three days

George Walker held a victory Parade on board a sophisticated US warship. The two sons of Saddam Hussein were savagely murdered and dismembered. Their bodies had to be to be sutured again to be displayed on the Television. The war soon became one to overthrow Saddam Hussein and WMDs became quiescent and scarcely mentioned. Now it is a war to spread democracy in the Middle East. Displaying the bodies of Saddam's sons could only be done by George Walker Bush. It was Barbaric and beyond the comprehension of civilized people. It was the action of crude terrorists. The legitimacy of murdering them still demands justification from George Walker Bush and American justice under Bush. They were not combatants or soldiers. They were savagely murdered in cold blood because they were Saddam's children.

We start wondering which type of democracy, Kuklux Klan (KKK), Guantanamo Bay, Kandahar International Airport or Abu Ghraib Prison? We should stop lying to ourselves and our conscience. If we have any conscience at all it should challenge us over what we had done in the name of democracy in Iraq. No democracy calls for this type of action. It was in the early pages of this book that I suggested that if the US and the UK undertook invasion of Iraq their soldiers would soon become terrorists. Even the act of invading Iraq was a form of terrorist action. The atrocities Armies of the willing committed against the Iraqi people were all acts of terrorism. The military action in the Middle East is a futile adventure that should never have taken place in rational leadership. It is a shame that it took place in the presence of Geriatric leaders who should know better than their boys who behaved like teenagers. The elders behaved like people addicted to gambling. They had to try again as Gen Colin Powel might have not told them all the truth about driving the war to its illogical conclusion. We have now been a while in the battle field and it may take long.

I am yet to be proved wrong. They have done everything to lie to their conscience to suppress the atrocities committed by their troops in these places. There is brutal atrocity in this venture except democracy. Their local cronies if anything are hardened corrupt criminals. The Western business seems to be riding on the back of massive corruption to do business with its clients. Talking about democracy in those situations is frank dishonesty. Capitalism is synonymous with corruption and crime. Free enterprise is clever tactics to defraud. Justice is relative argument. It is logic of debate.

This is totally bogus and Africa does not need this type of civilisation. It is there to defend and protect the rich. A system that has no protection for the poor is tyrannical and oppressive. African legal system makes capital in the defence of the poor. Let us divide the baby and unconcerned attitude of the impostor yielded the correct answer. The baby was returned to the owner. The Western legal system is torn apart by prejudice and bias. It is staged as a play to protect the hierarchy and sham-feed democracy whose rules violate the law at will. It is shambolic and thrash. It is official instrument for oppressing the weak and poor to silence them. Its judgment is legalistic and unreal. People in jobs are expected not to comment on common issues affecting the community. Yet these are the cream of highly educated people who know what is wrong with the society. Their opinion is not toxic but corrective. The poor Microbiologist became one of the first victims of the Iraq war. He died a strange death described as suicide. Diana the Princess of Wales died in a car crash in the French tunnel. We have to roll back the power of the politicians. The Church is supine and prays for the leaders on Sundays. It collects money for collections. It cannot denounce sins because it is confused and just cannot differentiate right from wrong. This is the quality of our times. Christians lack courage to speak out for fear of losing its members. It has no message to its members and the degenerate community.

We cannot wait for the second coming of our Lord to execute justice. Justice stands out just and straightforward. We cannot pervert its cause. We lie to our conscience in attempting to pervert its cause. Born to two devout parents with eight other children, I grew up to appreciate what justice is all about. The truth cannot be suppressed by spin and being economical with it. You will not envy the man that God has blessed. Whatever your hand finds to do, do it well with all your might. My parents had no strong financial support for me but their moral support was impregnable. They also had very sharp wit in providing means of getting the funds at very critical period when everything seemed to be at dead end. They trusted fully in God. God provided for them and us. My late father, a poor peasant farmer would not compromise with perfection in all he did.

He expected us to be thorough and perfect in anything we did. He was anxious to know my practical skills in clinical practice after my graduation. From what most of my patients and the US Medical Missionary Nurses that I worked for told him he was happy and satisfied. He was very sick towards the end with Prostate cancer but the day he saw my final FRCS certificate from the Royal College of Surgeons of England he struggled and stood up. He grasped the certificate and kissed it. He embraced and kissed me. Two weeks after my father died. I miss him always that would always make sure that we did not starve. He gave me moral encouragement in all I did. He trusted my Academic ability absolutely. People used to ask him what food he gave me to make so bright at School. He was delighted as I always took the first position in the class. He never missed any parents' day. He always came to support me. He proudly attended my graduation and was very pleased to see me in my Academic gown.

Education and skills training are the only way someone like me would escape from abject poverty to appeal to moral conscience of a world that is buried in selfishness and arrogance of ignorance. We seem to delight in the misery of our fellow human beings. This book has been written to tell the world of unwritten History of Africa that the world does not know. We essentially have to know co-ordinated History of Africa. It is written by intuition and observation of the remnants of Africa culture still present in Africa, today. Also some facts are taken from books with remnants of African History. The problem is that this source of information is not very accurate due to the fact that most of the records had been destroyed by wars, neglect and looting and Europe now the master of the world was not substantially literate and most the alien religion regarded most artefacts of the culture as idolatry needing destruction by fire when most of the events took place. These things render accuracy of African History doubtful and of questionable veracity. Despite these doubts most of the highlights are true as this History travels fro mouth to mouth. Observing the way the native African do things today also help a great deal. Cultural dilutions also inoculate the History with uncertainties.

Artificial Bantustan colonial borders also fragment the History and reduce its accuracy. The other aspects of this book are the narration of factors that affect African Economy and relation between Africa and the rest of the world. The commercial transactions, frauds and corruption adversely affect Africa's ability to escape from poverty. Poor, corrupt and ignorant leadership is crippling progress and development in Africa. I do understand the meaning of moderate leaders. A good leader is not in moderation but in ability to lead in self-discipline and good foresight. African Union Research Institute devoted to Research and Strategic studies with adequate investments is overdue. Timbuktu and centres in Ethiopia existed before the dawn of white people on the African continent. Our ancestors appreciated the importance of this on the continent. We are a people castrated in the brain without this vital Research Institute. Science and Engineering Research on the continent of Africa are cardinal for our development. Our youths must have a well-funded Research Institute. Political influence, pressure and corruption had watered down the quality of education in Africa.

The African Union Research Institute would not compromise discipline and quality of its programme. Any student would be there purely on merit. It is a place for talents and developing talents. Whom you know in the hierarchy of government has no place in gaining admission to the African Union Research Institute. Collectivisation essentially must take precedence over individualism. Intellectual efforts must not have ethnic quota system without ability (Nigerians call it Federal character), religious faith quota, national borders and boundaries. This has helped the US stay in front in education and skills training and Technology. Africa must build this place and filter the whole continent and the Diaspora scouting for the best in talents. Incidentally the African Institute of Research is not a School. Graduates and Research workers do their work in local Institutions and Universities but they are directed, guided and accredited by the African Institute of Research. Our aim is to develop planning and sustained and permanent Research culture in our Higher Institutions.

Re-integration of Africa will cut cost of running the continent and release funds for vital projects such as this. Re-integration of colonial dismembered Africa was a critical part of preparation of Africa for Independence that was omitted because a lot of the leaders that the colonisers dealt with were old school masters afraid to talk to white male Europeans as equals and completely ignorant of what independent Africa was all about. They had totally different concept of the Economy. To them the Economy meant mineral resources in active mining or dormant. They also rated cash crops high. They made re-integration of Africa political argument instead of important Economic discussion. They failed to mention the role of our rugged terrains in our eco-environment and soil for farming potential as vital Economic necessity. Nobody bothered about the environment and Ecology in those days but we all knew that the colonisers salaminised Africa and it needed to be re-integrated. It was vital to the Economy. Without it we would never be able to develop our Economy. We need space with diverse soil types and climates. All efforts to develop our Economy had failed because Africa as constituted at present is economically non-viable.

I came to the UK in November 1977 to start my Postgraduate Training in Surgery. In 1983 I completed that mission by passing successfully the final Fellowship of the Royal College of Surgeons of England, a highly coveted position in our business. Before I came to the UK I was extremely lucky. I was a darling of most of my teachers and the nurses and as a Medical student did a lot more of clinical Practice than when I was a Postgraduate student here. A disgusting thing here is sycophancy and cronyism. Many mediocre do eye-service and maintain good public relations with the seniors and the nurses. They practice procedural Medicine. Beyond this they have no initiative. Medicine is a life long learning and gaining experience daily. Cronyism and eye-service dwarf the growth of knowledge and talent development.

Knowledge and skills are free like the air we breathe. I would compare it to walking in the forest foraging for new things. You pick as much as you walk. I feel strongly that Academic work is a competition. It is mean and no use creeping around the authorities for favours. It seems to work in the UK here. But I do not believe in it. The knowledge and skills I have must be indigenised to be part of me and give me absolute confidence in tackling problems. As clinical Medical student I spent most of my time with patients reading their notes to see what the Consultants and other Doctors were doing for them. I also learnt from Ward sisters and experienced nurses. It was my habit to attend all Post Mortems and the Pathology Laboratory to read the slides. Professor Wilson Onuigbo a rare pure Academician in Nigeria who had written several quality Pathology papers was my mentor. He developed very inquisitive mind in me. I always want to know what caused death in patients. Here some colleagues feel I do it to criticise them. Far be it; I just want to learn what caused death in patients. If it is avoidable omission it makes me remember next time I see such patients. I spend my free time to read and acquire new knowledge and understanding of the things I do not know. Wasting time on useless gossips and socialisation may be helpful to others but not to me. Life is just too short for us to assimilate all we would like to know here on earth. The Lord's Prayer specially calls for forgiveness for our neglecting those things we should do to deal with things we should not do. No earthly position is too important to abandon to protect your integrity and dignity and conscience. Clinging to a job for the purpose of salary and mortgage payment is not my way. My motto is "whatever thy hands findeth to do, do it well with all thy might." My happiness is not having the job but being on top of the job. Seeing a patient recover and regain his strength is a joy. Medical Practice is still humanitarian job; its success is derived from this concept.

Health is so important that its discussion should be outside politics. Everybody rich and poor wants to be fit and well to go about his or her own business. A number of diseases are infectious. They pass from one victim to fit and well persons. In this way they spread to cover the community. Curing one victim prevents them from spreading. Hence treating a victim is preventive in a way. Therefore, Public funding of Health Service makes sense. A healthy community is a good workforce. This is healthy for the Economy. Control of most viral diseases by vaccination needs Public funding. The Research to find the vaccine needs investments. Mass vaccine production is costly. Mass vaccination itself needs a lot of funds. The current swine flu Pandemic is a case in question. Investment of Public funds in its control has helped halting its rapid spread. The same is happening in the current trial of vaccine for two strains of human papilloma virus that causes female cervical cancer. The world is watching with interest the response of the American people to current efforts of the Democratic Party led by US President Obama to reform the US Health Service. Interest Groups led by Insurance Business and Republican conservative free marketers are attempting to make it a political argument. Health is everybody's concern. Everybody wants to be fit and well. The Public should fund it. Such funding is self-interest in a way.

The concept of Health Economics is worth developing as one of the subjects all Health workers must be taught. They have to study and know it. As Health consumes a lot of money its workers must know safe ways of avoiding wastage. They must avoid poly-Pharmacy. This is the practice of giving a patient several drugs especially analgesics of the same strength. Any valid potent drugs that patients do no longer need should be returned to the Pharmacy. This may need new ways of packing and dispensing drugs so that they may keep. More rapid bedside diagnostic methods should be found than now. This would reduce the volume of work in the Laboratory. The Laboratory should be central to avoid duplication and wastage. Health workers must make efforts to reduce treatment complications. This will reduce cost of treatment. The workers should not waste perishable and discardable materials by opening more than they require for treating a case. All these bits would save money.

The community must indulge in genuine competitive spirit. What I found in Nigeria just before the civil war was the concept that elimination of opponent to gain his position in offices and jobs was acceptable for justifying ethnic and religious hatred. People just failed to recognise the Industry in other Ethnic Groups. Hence this constituted the basis of loyalty and which side one took in that war. I found it impossible to desert my classmates and friends. Equally the simple Algebraic concept admonishes you to start from the known to unknown. In Biafra I knew the known but in Nigeria then I never knew the unknown. Hence I went with Biafra. I returned in rags after that war. Yes I had wasted time due to sensible calculation integrity and loyalty to friendship. But yet all those who sat down to benefit from Igbo positions did not achieve as much as the Igbo and they are all dead now. Little did they know that Igbo existence did not mean blocking the jobs that envied but it also meant having facilities that worked including the Health establishment that they would need in their middle life. They failed to understand that the Igbo succeeded because they have different work culture which most Nigerians including my own lack. I schooled with Igbo children. They were not superior intellectually. They have very high sense of duty. They are very industrious. They work very hard. Their students had very high sense of priority. They were always at their work twenty four hours. They never believed in cheating. They respected the rules. They believed in copying correctly. They would rather raise the standards instead of watering them down to take larger share of the so-called national cake. The Yoruba people are equally of similar academic ability but they like fun. They lack the Igbo working culture and industry. They supplement their efforts with cheating to make up for the time they waste in fun. But when working and having to compete with others where there is no room for fun and cheating, do not underrate the Yoruba students. They settle down to work hard as others and achieve excellent results. There is a cluster of people including the Ishans in the West Niger Delta area that are naturally clever and brilliant. They equally have the work culture and excellent choice of priorities. They are naturally industrious. The Hausas concentrate on Quranic education and fail to make their mark in Western education. They rely on very divisive quota system and federal character. They employ exhausted retired European Academics and Southerners in their newly sprouting mushroom Institutions. They give them firm instructions to water down standards and pass their boys for them to produce rapid manpower to fill their quotas in the Federal services. This drags down the standards grossly.

These were the very facilities the Nigerian Army vandalised and destroyed. Hence several of them had the jobs but succumbed to minor illnesses due to lack of Hospitals and good Health workers to look after them. Those who took the frontline to destroy these facilities go abroad to treat themselves when they are sick. They send their children abroad for education. They corruptly plunder the oil money from the treasuries. Unfortunately majority of our people cannot afford this luxury. Even if they could afford the system would clog up and fail to accommodate them. This is why all my age group had died out in my village. This will equally be the experience of many people from Africa. Public utilities including the local Hospitals are yours. It is your duty to keep them safe and well equipped. UCH, KCH GUY' and St Thomas' in London are no replacement for local cottage Hospital. The Village School is your friendly School and not £20,000 per session kindergarten in the suburbs of London. It is a pity several Africans would prefer having the Public funds in their individual private pockets rather than spending them on vital Public facilities and utilities like Hospitals and Schools. They choose to go abroad to Europe mainly the UK to use these things when they need them. The politicians and the military despite what they pillage from the Public are the highest paid people in Nigeria. The situation is worse than bonus sapping Bank workers in the West. The world would understand one of the reasons why Africa is permanently broke and undeveloped after the recent financial meltdown and collapse of the Economy and the current recession.

The Anglo-American-Western and their satellites War against Terrorism.

SUMMARY OF THIS HISTORY OF WORLD AFFAIRS:

It is no exaggeration to state that in all wars the victor writes the History. This is one sided and always exonerates the victor in all wars. I would refuse to accept that the vanquished opponents had no reason to fight and lay down their lives for something close to their heart, something dear to them and very precious for them to accept to lay down their lives to fight a war. I would even go further to suggest that at the end of any conflict let the world offer the defeated opponents a free platform to state their reason for accepting to fight a war. It is through this type of interaction the world would learn how to avoid all future conflicts and war. All conflicts involve more that one person, the victor. Satisfactory conflict resolution even after victory in war requires us to listen to all sides involved. The past practice of barbaric elimination of the defeated leaders is brutal blood hound chase. It fails to show our humanity as rational living things. Most reasonable people in the world had stopped capital punishment except in war. Can the globalised civilised world outlaw killing surviving defeated war leaders in genuine cross border international conflicts? On the other hand the criminal warlords as in Africa that are extended family of world criminal fraternity deserve the severest punishment as hardened and ruthless criminals.

I would even go further and suggest that the signing of Armistice must b the end of any war and conflict and war. Those who survive on both sides must live. They must not be killed. I challenge human beings not to be blood–thirsty. We must start to be human by giving value to every life on earth and by showing respect to human life. We have been very callous with human life. Perhaps this is one of the reasons that we see these walking parcel bombs, the suicide bombers. It is our impatience and impetuosity that makes us blood-thirsty. If we leave these people alone they would die in their own time. We seem to give undue credit to indoctrination. Indoctrination has no power over conviction.

It is conviction that does the damage. Our actions and body language tend to influence conviction more than indoctrination. The peace that we want in the world cannot be acquired by intimidation and bullying. War cannot settle global issues. War, today, is a very bloody business but it settles nothing. Human beings are gradually learning to accommodate the horror and shock of brutal war. They are learning to fight back hard even at the expense of their lives. Perhaps we should appreciate their courage and learn to respect them and stop demonising and abusing them. Insulting your opponents is not the right way to win a contest. We must always place ourselves in our enemies' position and evaluate how we would react to every action we take against them. Christ admonished: "Do unto others s you expect them to treat you." This is the simple social law we often fail to keep. It is wrong and insulting name calling to address the Iraqi Arab resistant fighters and the Afghan resistant fighters as insurgents. They are defending their land. This is the duty of every good citizen in emergency. At the same time war deserves to be denounced. It cannot settle any issues but if people cannot avoid war they have no alternative but should stand and fight. They should not show the enemies their heels. Cowards and bullies resort to war in settling conflicts.

AFRICA:

EGYPT: The lower Nile floods made it very fertile and Agriculture and Farming brought enormous wealth. This led to the rise of the first Pharaoh and birth of Egypt about 3100 BC. This lasted for 2000 years. Upper Nile was later annexed. Egypt became most prosperous and civilised in the Ancient World for three millenniums.

Egypt had its Religion, Political System, grand Engineering Building Constructions, Education and Apprenticeship system, Science and Medical Practice. Egypt developed boat building and Commercial Activities in the Mediterranean Sea and Southern Europe. The ancient Egypt expanded to cover Kush (modern Sudan). Pharaohs came from Egypt proper and from Kush at certain times. Egypt also extended to Syria and Palestine by annexation at times. Occasionally ancient Ethiopia and Libya seized the Pharaoic throne and ruled. The Egypt and Kush Federation frequently broke down and they went their separate ways but usually they returned to unite again.

Alexander the Great had commissioned Alexandria as important Commercial Centre 334 BC. This became rich and prosperous in the Region for several centuries. Prosperity in other parts of Africa was Regional sporadic and erratic in Ghana, Mali with trade routes to North to the Mediterranean and the Middle East.

Sub Saharan was cut off from the rest of the world for several years until the advent of the European colonisers. These adopted Laissez-faire Strategy, European Companies were content with what they looted from Africa. In the 70s Economic Forum pulled a population of Africans and found that it was 10% poor 1970. In 2000 the same population was pulled out. It was found to be 50% poorer. Africa had regressed to subsistence Farming poorly developed to sustain its population. South Africa has gold, diamond and copper but these belong to Commercial Companies and their shareholders. Belgian Congo has been victim of Multinational trading conglomerates who control its minerals and finances.

The Democratic Republic of Congo (DRC) is in sad situation. From Independence in the 60s it has been a slaughter house for its minerals. Initially the cold war opponents, USA and the USSR contested for the territory and promoted brutal and bloody civil war. Before the Independence, Leopold 11, the tyrant and butcher King of Belgian had tyrannised the people. Today after the Hutu led genocide in Rwanda, the Hutus ran to DRC. The Tutsis chased them into DRC which has become a battlefield ever since. The warlords are contesting for the rich minerals. They frequently change sides and alliances. DRG has the two important metals needed for the manufacture of mobile phones. While the war is raging Western transnational corporate bodies in league with the warlords forced the locals to mine these metals on the cheap for them.

Africa has a population of 922 x million. They live in 54 different states. In 2005 there were 175 poor countries, UN Human Report in 2003, 25 poorest countries were in Africa. Decolonisation in Africa was fraught with instability made worse by the Cold War. The Super Powers, USA and USSR recklessly offered military aids. Organisation for Economic Co-operation and Development (OECD) has also found the poorest in the world to live in Africa. Poverty in Africa has been intractable and resistant to every measure to abolish it. Attempts at building local industry had failed due to lack of Education and skills, apprenticeship, technology, energy, water, investments and paucity of local markets.

There is lack of resources for transport to transfer produce to foreign markets. This may be costly and unprofitable. It is South Africa and Egypt that have substantial role in the world Market. The rest relies on the sales of mineral produce through multinational corporations, they and their shareholders own and pay remunerations to the local authorities. Corruption, Bribery and crime make 30 sub-Saharan African countries the poorest in the world. It takes two people to sponsor and support bribery and corruption: the giver and the receiver of bribes. It is very obvious that Africa cannot make any progress without re-integration of colonial dismembered Africa. This is the heart of failure in Africa. The world shudders why re-integration of colonial dismembered Africa is not mentioned as the main cause of failure of Africa to develop. Yes bribery and corruption are serious vices in Africa.

CIVIL WARS AND INTERNATIONAL WARS:

At a certain time almost all sub-Saharan African countries was engaged in Civil Wars, Nigeria, Chad, Niger, Central African Republic, Liberia, Sierra Leone, Mozambique, Angola, Belgian Congo, Rwanda, Coitre Ivoire, Somalia, Guinea Bissau, Sudan and Internal wars in Ethiopia and Eritrea and Congo 1 and 11 wars.

EFFECTS OF WIDESPREAD POVERTY:

It is self-perpetuating. It causes diseases, starvation and malnutrition, and destroys lives and property and infrastructures. It spreads animosity, cold war and truancy in the leadership and breakdown of law and order. Corruption and misappropriation of scarce funds are common. War lowers Gross Domestic Products, (GDP). It lowers life expectation, raises infant mortality. It destroys the Right of man. It halts development, Economic growth, Education, skills training, and beneficial Apprenticeship Training. War is destructive and not constructive. Widespread poverty causes poor output, drought, famine and malnutrition, tragedy and catastrophes, Locust invasion due to breakdown of control and mass unemployment. Poverty causes illegal logging and poaching of the local fauna.

Destruction of Rain Forest causes desertification of sub-Saharan Africa. Stubborn and persistent failure of African Economy is important issue to Africa and the world. All attempts at reviving African Economy had seen very little success. At Independence because of rapid success of Soviet and Chinese Heavy Manufacture Industries of Command Economy the new countries even in the face of lack of Energy opted for this Model. The Super Powers USSR & USA ran round like headless Chickens to offer military Aids to destabilise sub-Saharan African countries. The aids soon dried up once the cold war stopped. Poor Africa again found itself again a victim of slave capture and sales, slavery, brutal imperial colonisation and themselves victim of the cold war.

There is total failure of leadership in Africa. There is total lack of attachment to the land, Counsel and loyalty to the Community. There is no wisdom or memory of History to advice for caution. Even at this time Africans fail to understand that world is in crises. It is now well known that neither capitalism nor socialism has reached the level to claim the banner of Economic Success. Human beings manage both. Perhaps Socialism is better than Capitalism because it has human element. It has community concept. It has two Party Interests in its Planning: employers and employees. It is not designed to abandon workers in the field to run away with Capital in times of hardships. We must recognise that Aids do not prevent drought and famine. It does not stop damages floods cause. Aids help victims to survive Natural Disasters to learn from past mistakes to correct them. Aids do not help people out of poverty. There should be positive Improvement in work culture and everybody should work conscientiously to achieve positive results. Labouring hard takes people out of poverty. Dependence on aids makes people poorer than before as people lack initiative. Good education and skills training and creativity help people to increase their productivity. Nothing replaces doing it with your hands yourself. Persistent conscientious continuous practice finally becomes a habit. It becomes a reflex. Initiative and work culture matures a nation. It gives the nation confidence. A re-integrated Africa with a strong popular secular Constitution with simple clear clauses spelling out penalties for corruption, poor leadership, any attempt at subverting the government including military coup, religious intolerance, religious interference with the government, religious riots, ethnic interference with the government and ethnic favouritism. The legal code should be written with clarity. The House of Elders should be absolutely neutral. It must consist of respectable people in the community. They must be honest and persons with great integrity and dignity. They should be honest, respectable, experienced people retired from diverse professional fields. They should essentially be drawn from African communities all over the world, Africa, Americas, Oceania, Caribbean Islands, Pacific Islands and isolated Ocean Islands to emphasize the oneness of Africans and African Unity to the world. This will also open up a channel of communications among global Africans. It will also offer Africans the opportunity to get to know themselves.

It is a Disaster if Aids create dependency on NGOs. There was an attempt to establish a false tomb stone to capitalism called "Washington Consensus." The Economy should be maintained by the Community. The bubble Capitalist Economy of boom and burst is not stable. It suffers from frequent failures. Everybody suffers in these Economic setbacks. Hence, both the Employers and Employees must be involved in managing Businesses. Shares are a good way of participation in Business trade by all participating Parties. Every shareholder should speak and vote on Policy decisions. Habits must be dynamic and not static but they must be changing and diversified to change with the changing Market and Technology. We must avoid overheating of the Economy.

Debt Relief sounds like a good but beneficiaries must have it clear in their mind what they have to do with the money they get? Have they earmarked the Projects to accomplish with the money they get? Debt Relief should generate income for investment in employment to provide growth. Getting Funds without planning how to use them is a disaster. It leads to stealing and wasting of the funds. It may open the floodgates to criminal money laundering. What did the borrowers do with this money? What did the lenders want the borrowers to do with the money they lent to them? What were the prospects that the borrowers had means to pay back the debts? Did the borrowers tell the lenders what they were going to do with the money and the lenders were convinced that the borrowers' projects would yield money for the refund of the debts?

What commissions did the boys who negotiated these loans with the borrowers take from the borrowers? The so-called third world loans and debts were one of the swindling of the ignorant, blind and illiterate poor people on earth in the last century and last millennium. It was fraud mounted by the Western capitalist to dupe the financial knowledge lacking and ignorant poor and corrupt third world leaders. It was a scam. Did the loans deserve refunds? Yes of course the leaders signed for them. It is admonished that the third world leaders must not have access to large sums of money as they are ignorant of money management and the financial market. They are equally corrupt and very dishonest. They are tyrannical. They should not have free wand over money in their countries. There was a time when the rich developed countries, lenders of money to African Bantustans found that most of the corrupt African leaders laundered the money they stole from Africa abroad in safe Banking havens and Switzerland. The amount money they found was enough to pay African debts three or four times over. What motivated them to lend money to such people? Why did they not advise them to take the African money back to invest in projects in Africa? They should have told them that they were willing to provide essential Technological skills and would charge them to the funds they found in the secret Banking havens and Switzerland. They could have earned more. Instead they continued to encourage them to encourage them to steal more of African money to launder in these Western Banking havens and Switzerland. Without clear borrowing conditions understood by the illiterate African leaders they lent money to them. It is a well known secret that much of the money lent never left the Banks involved. Most of the phantom projects the money was supposed to fund never took off at all.

The control of money should be by a small group of well trained experts who should vet projects before releasing money for them. This may cause less corruption and reckless wasting of money in the third world. Financial management must be by experts separate from government that should play the role of auditors of expenses by the Finance Board. The government should regulate on the conduct of the Financial Board. It should have experts to supervise and counterweight the activities of the Board to ensure that it runs properly and observes the regulations. The government acts on the reports and its expert supervisors and the free and untarnished Board Members discipline and replace guilty Board Members.

CORRUPTION AND CRIME are synonymous with Capitalism, Market and Private Capital and Business. Most of the Initial Private Capitals in the Western Hands in the USA, UK, WESTERN EUROPE, CARIBBEAN, CANADA AND LATIN AMERICA CAME FROM KIDNAPPING BLACK AFRICANS TO Sell FOR CAPITALS AND INVESTING THEM IN RUNNING SUGAR, TOBACCO AND COTTON PLANTATIONS THAT THE AFRICANS WERE ENSLAVED TO WORK IN. HENCE CAPITALISM NEEDS CHEAP CRIMINAL CAPITAL AND CHEAP FREE LABOUR TO DEVELOP. It is not a naturally spontaneous developing Business. Once the source of capital dries up the owners of Private Capitals declare Bankruptcy or Redundancy and run down their business. Industrial Revolution came in time with all its fruits and excitements to rescue the Capitalists from paying for their crimes and maltreatment of workers.

The Business owners failed to provide for the Welfare of workers. Workers were abandoned and ignored in hardships while Business owners withdrew to live well with their families. It is difficult to understand the behaviours of the financial and fund managers who pay themselves huge bonuses from the money they get from Governments to avoid Bankruptcy and collapse of their Business. These people responsible for safe management of funds from their depositors and investors virtually spend the funds on themselves.

They overpay themselves and make solid contracts to ensure that they are paid their contracted funds regardless of what happens to the Business they are hired to look after and manage.

It is sad that this had repeated itself without shame in Globalisation controlled by Bankers, Fund Managers and Politicians with rich Consultancy in Businesses with lucrative Bonuses. The Bonus culture of Speculation and swindling just liquidated the Capitals. This caused Economic meltdown and deep recession. The capital owners disappear abandoning the workers to lick their wounds again. The free Market ran away to hide. It has no solution to offer human folly. Regulation of Globalisation is urgent needed to control the capital. Globalisation involved rapid fund transfer. This must be regulated and controlled to prevent funds disappearing. There is everything good in Science and Technology but fallible human beings invent them and manage them. Social Factors in the human community and human Psychology demand that for effective control of the powerful tools that man has produced in Science and Technology have got to be regulated, supervised and controlled. Hence there is a strong case for regulation of Globalisation.

Our excitement and arrogance frequently make us forget the human element in any new inventions and Technology we make. We frequently forget and ignore making room for the new inventions and Technology to accommodate human needs in the Economy. We do this at the demise of the Economy. We must note from now that any new Technology we introduce is for improvement of human life on earth. We must make room for it to accommodate the human being. Let Credit Crunch not remind us that globalisation has got to make room for human beings. Human beings run and manage the free Market and Capitals. It is now time for the global community to regulate, globalisation, global free Market, global finance and funds. Banking and Fund Managers, Commerce and Business Leaders must have their work trimmed and their powers restricted and regulated. They must not have power to spend public money as their private finances.

AFRICAN ECONOMY:

African Economy has baffled every scholar and Economists of all degenerations in recent times when compared with that of East Asia. It has stubbornly remained refractory to all efforts to put it right. It has been speculated Africa has only 2% of global Economy. China, India, Malaysia, Singapore, Korea, Japan all have large fractions of the global Economy. Africa has the greatest hot Desert, the Sahara, and second largest tropical rainforest. Latin America seems to be doing well and is able to feed itself. In 2005 Africa had 887 million people scattered in 54 Bantustan failed states forming the poorest counties on earth. Capital flights and overseas money laundering had plagued African Economy for a long time. In the 1970s Africa's corrupt leaders had 187 billion dollars in the Swiss Bank. This was much in excess of all African debts at the time.

Road and Rail Communications are lacking. Air transport development lags behind Education, available skills or apprenticeship and maintenance. Agriculture and Livestock development are poor. There is no Medical Service. There are no facilities for Research. Housing is poor. Water supply is lacking. Wealth is privately owned. Means of Wealth Production and wealth are privately owned. There no public ownership. There is no Government Regulatory Control. Affluent States provide support infrastructures that help private investments, capital and wealth. Capital and wealth ownership protected by law. Adam Smith was Glasgow and Oxford trained political Economist and a strong supporter of Market Economy.

African Economy despite its Corrupt Nature seems to embrace Market Economy of Adam Smith, David Ricardo, Jean Baptise and John Stuart. Adam Smith wrote the Theory of Moral Sentiments, Enquiry into Natural and Causes of Wealth of the Nations. Adam Smith strongly disapproves of Market Mercantilism, "System of Natural Wealth Liberation in the wealth of the nation/1776. Adam Smith was born about June, 1723. He died around 17 July, 1790. He was a Scottish Moral Philosopher and Economist. John Maynard observed that Capitalist Economy could survive crises, unemployment, deep recession and Regulation could control rapid expansion. Shrinking or contraction of Economy is the fall in Gross Domestic Products (GDP). African Economy continuously shrinks as nobody cares to work hard to improve upon it. The Great Depression was caused by contraction of Money Supply by the Federal Reserve.

INVESTMENTS, COMMERCE, BANKING AND INSURANCE:

Investors are reluctant to invest in Africa. Africans are reluctant to invest in their continent. There is capital flight and money laundering. A survey by IMF and the World Bank showed that 40% of money the Africans take out of their continent is laundered in the Swiss Bank and at that time more money was laundered than the whole of African debts. Money laundering in safe Banking havens such as Cayman Islands, by African corrupt leaders is rampant and commonplace. Hence most of sub Saharan African money is invested in Markets outside Africa. Investors have no Business investing in Africa if Africans fail to invest in their homeland. The IMF and the World Bank step in during Emergency Crisis for rescue.

They lend money at punitive rates under very stringent and controversial conditions, such as the Structural Adjustment Programmes, (SAPs). SAPs turned out to act like RPGs of the African Bush fighters that caused the Economy to implode on itself. It devalued the currency and caused inflation beyond what the people could tolerate. It destroyed whatever was left in the sub-Saharan African global Economy. Hence IMF and WB loans are toxic to African Economy. Corruption and Crimes increased and made sub-Saharan Africa totally unattractive for investments. International Criminal Fraternities stepped in like vultures to mop up whatever they could get. Sub-Saharan Africa became detached from global Economy. Its leaders became content and complacent in carrying foreign currencies in plastic bags abroad for shopping. The Francophone zone has two Regional Banks in West Africa. They use these to supply the currency regulated by Bank Central, CFA . They are not investment or lending Banks.

COMMUNICATION, IT:

Sub-Saharan has twice the number of Cellular phones in Asia. This is endemic waste. It has the largest hot Desert and second largest tropical Forest with the richest fauna. These are said to impair the building of road and rail transports. This is a challenge to modern high Technology. Good Education, skills training and satisfactory apprenticeship for African youths to challenge them with building and construction needed in Africa would define what local indigenous hard work can do for Sub-Saharan Africa. Transcontinental roads and rails are essentially vital to develop sub-Saharan African Economy. Investments in them are worth all efforts. Their absence hampers Economic activities and closes the continent to the world and its citizens.

RIVERS:

Nile, Niger and Zambezi have seasonal Navigation periods. Transportation is erratic and sporadic. Roads are pliable in dry seasons but washed off in wet rainy seasons and full of potholes. Geography: Eco-environment is damaged by bush gorilla war fighters who deforestate the rainforest by reckless logging and poach the animals for bush meat and ivory and parts to sell to Asia for Oriental Medicine. Most areas in Africa are arid dry desert or Savannah but the volcanic range dust deposit of the Great Barrier Rift starting from Southern Africa and extending to the Cameroon is rich and fertile. The following authors, William, Masters, Jeffrey Sachs and Jared have all observed that sub-Saharan mineral resources, gold, diamond, copper and oil are mined by transnational corporations who control them for their shareholders. Poor and corrupt government cannot exercise good control and regulation and high tariffs on sub-Saharan African produce make them unattractive to traders.

Drug Manufactures:

HIV-AIDS and other tropical diseases, malaria and tuberculosis require large investments in Drug Manufacture but no funds are available. No indigenous local labour for support. Brain drain to industrialised Western countries renders manpower scarce. Very weak Economy makes Agricultural Development including livestock industry difficult. HIV-AIDS, TROPICAL DISEASES, Tuberculosis, malaria and Modern Diseases, Diabetes and Hypertension and cancer today affect Africa. There is no Drug Manufacture Basis. Africa is neither fit for Manufacture Basis nor for Market for Drug sales as there are no funds to pay for them.

COLONIAL COMPLEX:

Slave trade and slavery and brutal colonisation, racial segregation and suppression of substantial Economic Development, Education, Skills training and reliable apprenticeship all contribute to sap the confidence of sub-Saharan African Confidence in ability to do things for itself to improve its Economy. This has caused total loss of initiative. The leaders had been unable to re-integrate their continent to make it work them. They had been content in living in post colonial farmland plantation Bantustans with them as leaders. Linguistics, ethnic culture, religious cleavage frequently cause wars and violence and instability. The treatment of Robert Mugabe by the West is disgraceful. The British Press and Media deliberately subject him to raw intimidation and tyranny of greed. They deliberately bribed MDC leaders to de-stabilise Zimbabwe. No Western Nations would tolerate this state of Affairs. Yet Africa is spineless in the face of this type of provocation.

Africa accepts white farmers who do not want to take over our fertile farmlands. The world would expect the white farmers to sit down and sort out their problems with authorities instead of subverting the system and indulging in smear campaigns to damage individuals and the Economy. No sub-Saharan land is a colonial territory any more. Hence any form of harassment should stop. The people involved in it should be ashamed of their activities. This book of illustrative global History attempts to offer narration of events in the Western Atlantic and Mediterranean land for over five thousand years. It starts with African Egyptian Pharaoic civilisation that the Greeks admired and actually copied in intellectual development, Civil Engineering and Architecture. Later came the Romans that used its crack troops to crush everybody to have its way. The Romans engaged the African Carthaginians in war for several years. They signed several charters but none had any values to prevent war as long as the Roman power was on the ascent and increasing. Eventually Rome invaded Africa and with treachery, betrayal and bribery of corruption destroyed Carthage, a first class nation of the time in Africa.

Rome that initially was hesitant over Christ and his teachings, finally Emperor Constantine adopted Christianity. The Empire became the Holy Roman Empire. The Roman Empire prospered. Its nobles took pleasure in orgy and wild pursuits and failed in their duties to the Empire. The Empire finally collapsed under its weight of rapid and ambitious expansion and a changing world. The Greeks were by far more sophisticated and civilised people. The Romans were rustic farmers who found comfort and strength in their militaristic and aggressive character. Just as the Roman Empire was collapsing the Arabs fanned out on horse backs with swords in their right hands and the Quran in their left. They seized Israel Palestine from the Jews and the whole North Africa from native Africans.

Today, the Jews are fighting for their land. The world has the right to know this. The Arab occupiers of African land are embraced with equanimity but they must declare their loyalty to Africa. Then came the white people from Western Europe. They joined the Arabs and started aggressive and vicious slave trade and slavery. This can rightly be described as the Black Death and African holocaust. On the heels of this followed a vicious and brutal colonial rule. The colonial rule was mixed with racial discrimination and stigmatisation of black people. The frequency of destabilisation of Africa has contributed to its doom. Bantustanisation, very poor leadership and corruption had all led to failure of Africa. The current debate is judged from the Geography and Ecology of Africa de-Bantusnisation of Africa is the artery of its life line and survival. Two massive deserts and arid desert must be re-integrated into the fertile land of the continent to give them access to water and fertile land. Our relation with Europe is still a thorny issue. Should it be by subjugation or partnership? The answer lies on both Africa and Europe. The corrupt and ignorant African leaders are still very subservient without courage or any initiative. They call their timidity and cowardice silent diplomacy. The whole thing is stupidity. While you are not expected to howl like a mad dog you are expected to express your disapproval. Very few of the so-called African leaders have moral courage to speak and express what they stand for in the interest of Africa. This is demise of Africa.

The NGOs are the mouth-piece of Africa. Unless the spot the danger and announce it to the world no African leader has the ability to spot the danger, let alone bringing it to the world attention. The African leaders still have to tell us and the world what they are there for. The same applies to the whole mass of African people. We are very timid and cowardly. An African told me that his mortgage and slave labour were far more than his freedom, liberty and free speech. I have no reason to dispute his attitude in life. Unfortunately, my freedom, sound knowledge and sound skills are too invaluable to be enslaved by mortgage and salary. When I die the only truth that will survive will be my honest intellectual expression that is totally fearless and without restraints. Africa will have to remove post-colonial Bantustan borders and re-integrate in order to progress. It will have to accept that neither one man's progress, one ethnic group affluence is wealth of the community. Sectional prosperity does not make everybody rich nor make any impression on the wealth of the community. At the moment we have a lot of things but their developments are still at the Stone Age.

They have obstinately refused to join the Scientific, IT and high Technology age in development. Look at our animals their pasture is still subject to chance, Droughts are blights on them. They all die of drought hunger and thirst. The bulk of our population are dairy product dependent but our milking is primitive and unreliable. Trypanosomiasis from tsetse fly infestation is still scourge. This is why we have advocated for practical education and skills training. The people involved in animal husbandry should get to know their flocks and their flocks should know them. The African must have the moral courage to announce to the world and tell the world that he or she is not willing to compromise his basic principles of living. He does no longer accept the role of a slave that should be seen and heard.

We have a voice that has got to be respected. We will stand and fight till the last man is truly free. Apart from Hannibal there is no genuine record of African soldiers standing firm to confront and fight the enemies. Rather they had always been involved in fighting each other in fratricidal wars. They fight for foreigners and enemies to seize our land. They value life even under slavery and most dehumanising situations. We must learn to devalue our lives. We must pledge loyalty to our land and to defend it with our life and blood. Those who come to plunder us must be given a fight of their lives. We must know that after the fanfare of very noisy and intimidating war planes and bombs normal human being will become human again. They come down to earth to eat and wash. He becomes a man again for us to attack and fight. He is then prone to death in a fight. Therefore, we wait till our enemies come down to earth to be confronted with fight for their lives. We must endure hardship until we blow a fatal hole in the enemy war machine. If you do not want to be made a slave you maintain unity of your race and group. Make friends with dignity.

Our relationship with Europe and the West is still ambivalent and ambiguous. There is the group on the Straussite conservative right that still feel that the black man on earth should relate to the white man by slave and master bondage and strict racial stigmatisation and separation should be the norm. They may be in the minority but they are powerful and influential. They always deny and lie about their intention. There are equally those they describe as loony left that feel the black people should be free and be integrated into the community. This is not new. The Greeks from the onset stood for full integration and respect. The Marcus Cato faction of the Roman Senate and Octavia later known as Caesar Augustus stood firm for subjugation of the black people in Africa. Colonialism took the same factional argument and some colonisers were worse than beasts. The Belgians under the tyrant and butcher of Africans in the Belgian Congo, Leopold the second of Belgium were themselves bloody butchers. They continued to argue that every European coloniser abused and bullied Africans.

They were no exception. We therefore challenge Europe and the West to declare their policy and intention towards Africa and the black race. Even in Rome, we had Scipio Cornelius Publius, Julius and Marcus Antonio who argued against total subjugation of Africa and the black race. Their voices were always drowned by those of very powerful and influential minority in the Senate in Rome. The Africans unfortunately are timid cowards. They believe that escaping danger is by running away. That doctrine is now obsolete in the global IT high Technology village. We must stand our ground and fight until the powerful recognises our humanity and courage. We are the Carthaginians in the African Forest. We have been dehumanised several times over. We have no choice but to fight to be left alone to join modern world on our terms in liberty and our fundamental human rights in tact with freedom of speech in tact and respected. We reject sham and counterfeit democracy, starvation diet rationed democracy and selective freedom. True democracy is by free consultation of the citizens under the rule of law without buying support with money and respecting the voice of the citizenry. It is equality of opportunities, liberal and practical education and skills training. There is no such thing as exporting or importing democracy. Voting is not democracy. The type of Bush-Tony Blair Democracy in Iraq and Afghanistan are a sham. It is a scam.

Now that Europe under the British Prime Minister, Tony Blair and the West had brought this African debate from the back of the burner into the open hall for open and free debate, we just cannot fail to accuse African leadership of total failure. Timidity, cowardice, corruption and absolute ignorance are misleading Africa and the African people. To our white neighbours we ask them to grow up and acknowledge and recognise changes in the world. Give a little room to trial of sharing. Stop being greedy and selfish. Handouts of food and drug parcels in emergency are not genuine gestures of generosity. Stabilisation of the African situation requires correcting several millenniums of wrong doing and misconceptions both in the Africans themselves and among the white people in Europe and the West at large. The Africans must stop crossing their legs to ask for handouts.

They must genuine embrace practical Education and skills training and copy and compete with others on earth. We Africans must recognise that life itself is competition. We cannot win except we compete. History for five millenniums has shown that our repeated reluctance to compete and permanent and reliable friends and stand by them in emergencies had been detrimental to us. The Etruscans welcomed and embraced us into Europe. The Greeks appreciated our ways and were tolerant of us. The Spartan warriors trained our soldiers ready for war. Yet we were still facing the African rain forest as the ultimate hiding place. Now after two millenniums of enslavement in our forest retreat we have no choice but to correct the gross deficiency in the machinery of our very ignorant and corrupt leadership that has always misled us to tragic disasters. We must settle down to acquire very sound practical education and skills training. Religion is not bad. The human beings practising religion betray religion. It is the human adherents of religions that are bad. Excessive indulgence in anything including religion is bad. It is worst when religion is betrayed to achieve the evil desires of human beings.

This is a text of comparative History. It matches Africa and Africans against various lands, peoples, times and events. It also tries very hard to jog African memory to remind them that time changes but several generations of them had been here facing challenges but still behaving evasively. Now we have no choice but all of us have to link up with the times past and present and look up to the future. We must not pretend to have blank memory of the times particularly of events in our History. We are daft by pretending that we are the only Africans here in our life time and generations. There were several generations of us here long before our time. Their mistakes were our mistakes. We should vow not to commit the same mistakes again. We must resolve to sink our differences in times of danger, emergency, crisis, violence and danger and unite and fight any alien enemies at our doorstep. Collective freedom is better than individual selective democracy and rationed freedom. Any collaborator with alien invaders of our land is a traitor. Traitors must be shot at dawn. No honest, respectable and patriotic citizens should join alien invaders to subjugate the land of his or her birth. If the gene cannot join together to compete and defend the land that gene deserves elimination.

It is unsuitable for the land. A new concept of life in the Africans is. "Death will surely come whether from conflict illness or natural. Act of gallantry in war must not fear death we will all die. Death in defeat is a disgraceful death. We must defend our home land until we are no more here to defend it" A black man killing another black man for an alien invader of our land does not deserve to live and tread the soil of our birth. It has become a suicidal gene.

We do not advocate for war for aggression but attack on our land is attack on us. It requires a very harsh response. We must not be stupid or play the fool any longer. If we are rejected we have no reason to pretend that we have not received the message. Racial discrimination and stigmatisation had been here longer enough for us to know where we are not wanted. Those who hate us have no business to be in Africa our home. Racial acceptance should be reciprocal. Any black life wasted by racist must have replacement. In racial hatred life must be equal to life. We have to appreciate that life is life regardless of the colour of your skin. If anybody uses death to intimidate us let us use death to intimidate and bully him in return. We should respect peace among those who respect peace. The advocates of war and violence must not find peace by day or night. The world has enough for all but not enough for tyrants of greed. They it is that advocate for war and violence. They it is that we should stand our ground and fight in life and death until we have freedom from bullying and molestation. Bullying and molestation are a culture of colonisation. Africans should never again allow anybody to colonise our land. We are always ready to live in peace with all and we are always ready to share the world with all. We have no room for those who have no genuine respect for sharing.

IT and high Technological skills are not trademarks of civilisation. Civilisation is the degree of respect you have for the life of your fellow human beings. It is not the level of protection that you have for your land and fellow citizens rather it is the level of security and respect you have for the world, its environment and the earth. It is the level of self-respect and self-restraint. Obtrusive thinking and actions are acting by impulse. This is not a sign of mature civilisation. Any group that violates normal human behaviours and proceeds to defend its queer and strange behaviour with pseudo voo doo science is primitive and uncivilised. One man's civilisation and sophistication may be worse than rag to another. The Kukuli in Kenya, the Tuaregs in the Sahara Desert in Africa and the Bush men and Hottentots in the Kalahari Desert each has values for their civilisation. It is that intrinsic value of civilisation that matters to them. It is ignorance that makes people talk of our way of life and civilisation. Each one of us has a way of life. The world has enough for everybody but not enough for the greedy, jealous and envious.

Let us in religion be content that we are serving God by serving and saving our fellow human beings. In defending our ways of life let us be sure that we do not grab the poor man's goat to make sacrifice to God. Let the defence of our civilisation not find a home in the scarce resources of your weak neighbours. Democracy and other ideologies have very different meanings to different people. To some voting alone is democracy. To others it is a free speech that can be gagged when it is uncomfortable for the authorities. What you hear may be incisive and nasty but the danger comes from what you do not hear. Gagging free speech is dangerous. Any leaders that send troops to invade a place to slaughter civilians is a bloody dictator and murderer. The victims of one slaughter lose life as the victims of another slaughter. Let us not mock about and play with words. One trip of Hiroshima and Nagasaki damaged much more than five years. The monster might have taken twenty years to accomplish his purpose. In modern warfare you may take a few days to murder more people than in twenty years of dictatorial rule. God alone decides on life lost.

Since each of us passes through this world and will die and leave it alone, I will admonish each person to strive to do good and until his evil or good day of departure comes when he or she will be face to with his God. Peace and friendship are better than hostilities, violence and war. Re-integration of Africa would reduce the numbers of disasters in the continent. It will also avoid unnecessary wastage. It will also make it less cumbersome to manage the whole of Africa. It will facilitate doing business in Africa. Africa is not immune to poor leadership. Africa needs good leadership. Africa is worthy of all that is noble and good. Education and skills training are what Africa needs. Africa must not be encouraged to shy away from its responsibilities. It has to care of itself and its citizens and provide jobs for them. They must start with food production to prevent frequent starvation.

It has to plan for drought and malnutrition and diseases. It must be weaned off international community. Let us hear of the African community before the end of this century. No African Bantustans lose anything by coming together to re-integrate the continent. Once you are here you are African. The bond that binds us together is equality, liberty and pride in serving Africa and defending its honour. Neither colour of skin, language, religion, riches, race or ethnicity nor nobility of birth takes precedence over liberty and equality. The democratic world is the free world. Let no self-appointed regulator or policemen stifle the freedom of this democratic and free world. The creator made the world beautiful with diversity because uniformity is boring and monotonous. No culture, however, civilised and advanced should stifle other cultures and civilisations. Natural and creative uniformity rebuffs the artificial attempts at uniformity. No civilisation should ever attempt to stifle other cultures and civilisations on the grounds of superiority.

Human evaluation of cultures and civilisations is very faulty. It is fraught with mistakes. It is ignorantly destructive. It is furtive to allow ignorance to judge and decide on what it does understand. The preachers of "our way of life" do not understand the message they carry for their people or know how many ways of life they had destroyed in the world. They have no licence to go about the world destroying other peoples' ways of life. Nobody has a licence to discharge this duty in the world. The rule of law is universal for law and order. Criminal, damaging and destructive practices cannot be accepted as way of life. It should attract universal condemnation and penalty. The powerful and strong has no licence to launch rogue invasion of alien lands it deems it can subdue. This is unacceptable today. Since each of us is sure that once you are in this world you will die and leave this world alone, why do we not use our time to do good instead of going about killing innocent people and ending their times in the world prematurely for them before we take our turn to kiss death. Nothing is sure as death as each of us will take our turn to kiss its cold hands. It certainly does not want us to go about promoting it even though it is always ready to oblige our cruelties and atrocities. You fool and senseless killer do you know that you will finally also kiss the cold hands of death? Think my dear dispenser of death we all are passengers in the truck of recycle in the world riding slowly to our day to kiss death. It is sad we fail to acknowledge this fact but keep on deriding each other over what we do not own. We do not own the earth but the earth is in our custody for safe keeping and protecting of lives and properties and the environment.

Unfortunately the Western leaders from the Romans down to the current ones believe in prosecuting foreign wars to stabilise their regimes at home. The preach the message of hate of strangers in their midst to divert attention from their luxury wars to the hated aliens under suspicion Every intelligent person knows that in times of danger and war the citizens' nerves are on the edge. Unfounded suspicion can lead to lynching of innocent people, aliens and natives. Unfortunately the Western leaders that accredit themselves with civilisation and sophisticated deliberately preach the message of alien violation of generosity and repatriation. They dishonestly suppress the cause of friction and conflict in the population. Rather they accuse the hated soft target for the cause of chaos.

I love my adopted country Britain and will speak out against those who betray her because there are very many genuine people here despite some leaders who are ambitious, ambivalent and ambiguous leaders and devious. Gagging free speech is the demise of the dictators. They deny themselves the opportunity of hearing what other people think about them. Rather they rely on intelligence to gather adverse comments on their actions. I once said that the most unintelligent group in the community are the people in the intelligence. The whole array of events in the current US and UK Iraq has shown how faulty and unreliable the so called intelligence can be. It is fraught with fatal mistakes and flaws. The leaders who had blundered into a series of mistakes and avoiding killings and slaughters have no new allies. They have to make do with the ones they have including the so-called intelligence.

It is worth emphasizing that from the days of African Carthaginians in Spain Catalonia immigrants who voluntarily enter a foreign country do not go to change the way of lives of the natives. It is a hostile act to attempt to do this and is deliberate invitation to resistance friction and conflict. What I notice in ancient practices is that the immigrants had their low profile religious ceremonies and invited the native leaders to participate. The natives also invited the new comers to their religious festivities. Boasting that the immigrants want to replace the local deities with their own is an act of aggression and declaration of war. Paul was told in no uncertain terms the Diana of Ephesus was not his business. She was the guardian deity of the city of Ephesus. I would advise the would be immigrants to take note that they do not immigrate to create ghettos in their new adopted home. It is bad manners. They must accept to be converted into the new faith of the place of their adoption. It is wrong to place a taboo against your children and members of your group adopting the faith of your new home. The practice of honour killing stands to be condemned. Any group practising religious intolerance stands to be repatriated and sent back to their native homeland.

It is unfortunate that it has taken totally avoidable war and violence to make people conscious of this state of affairs.

The adoption and practice of faith should be absolutely free and beyond any religious edict. Any group that uses religious edict open or secret had overstayed its welcome and should be sent packing home to its native homelands. Religious freedom should be enshrined in the statutory books. This means that irrespective of what your parents and guardian worship you can join any religious faith of your choice. Religion should not constitute a platform to oppose the legitimate authority. Religious activities should be confined to the worshippers and their places of worship. These places must not be the rallying point for subversion and sabotage of your adopted new home. Gagging free speech is primitive. I would suggest that that the authorities should adopt a listening mood and explanation of its actions. The infallibility of the leaders should yield to acceptance of mistakes and promise to correct any obvious mistakes. The innocent should not be made victims of the mistakes of the leaders. Unfortunately the Reich and Nazi blaming of aliens in your midst for the mistakes of the leaders is dangerous. There is one thing unique about the UK as the conscience of the world, the good British population and people always finally stand up for the truth and justice. The leaders of this Island must always note this. You cannot manipulate our Island to Nazi hysteria and mania. We all came here to escape from poverty and hardship from our various homelands and to benefit from the education and skills training but not as missionaries to convert the natives.

Hence our religious activities should be compatible with our main objective in immigrating here. If we ignore our main purpose and take to religious mischief we have made null and void the objective of our being here. It is equally true that some die-hard local people would try to dehumanise us as easy soft target for bullying and abuse. With my finest skills and knowledge I will not sell my services to people under humiliation. This is slavery and the world derides slavery in all its forms. Human dignity stands to be respected in rendering services. We must hold each other in respect for the human person.

The Arab Israeli Palestinian conflict is playing to the gallery in the evacuation of Gaza. Are we human beings with human sympathy in our hearts? It is common sense that if these people love this land and want to live in it they must learn to forget the past and adopt a policy of sharing this land under the rule of law. They must not be emotional about their religious utopia. They must respect each others' faith. They must share the leadership and must adopt the motto of liberty and equality for all their citizens. The destruction of properties in scarce and limited resources world is madness and practical demonstration of hate. The Arabs must know that that the whole land of Palestine is not theirs. Alexander saw them in Gaza alone. Hence Gaza is their homeland. They chased out the Jews by force of arms to seize their land when the Jews were not strong enough. Now the Jews are strong enough to recover their land, the Arabs must be reasonable and rational. They must accept to share the land or be evicted and thrown. Right now they are slaughtering and seizing African land in Darfur. In two thousand years the descendants of victims of the current Arab ethnic cleansing and genocide may arrive back in for to recover their land. They who live in glass house should not throw stones.

The Arabs had been land grabbers in History riding on the back of their religion Muslim Islam, the Koran and Allah. In the name of Allah let the fanatical young Arabs recognise the injustice, suffering and humiliation the Jews went through. The Jews by their estimate had been cruel to them but the Arabs had been very cruel to the Jews by stealing their homeland and exposing them to all forms of suffering including holocaust. The Arab leaders must put on their thinking hat and tell us why the Jewish Temple is under their golden dome

Mosque in Jerusalem? The owner of this old Temple is the owner of this land. He owned the land and built that Temple before the Arab came with their religious myth. The Arabs also stole the whole of North Africa by aggressive land grabbing. The world is not saying that the Arabs should be evicted but they must abandon violence and provocative incitement and false religious myth and face the truth of the world in our time for peace to return to Palestine. Share the land and be governed and protected by the rule of law and be law-abiding. Adopt the policy of religious tolerance.

This land is too small for two states. Rather let Israel and the Arabs be autonomous entities under a common governance offering protection to both the Israelis and the Arabs and be in charge of foreign affairs and security. Short of this the two state theories are cells of violence and war. Continuous destabilisation and investment of the little money they have on explosives would continue to make the Arabs poor and offer room for incitement and propaganda. This will turn out to be no settlement of the conflict at all but creation of new cells of violence and war. Let the world not shrug off common sense because of timidity and total lack of courage. If we want to render a settlement of any conflict we must get the right History and have the wisdom and courage to tell the truth and ignore emotion and partisanship. We must equally examine the present condition realistically and look into the future for possibilities. In this case of Palestine Alexander found them in Gaza and there is a whole Jewish Temple under the golden dome Mosque and very many older Jewish settlements. Hence the Arab claim of the whole land cannot stand the test of time. They cannot superimpose Gaza as a carbuncle to swallow the whole land as theirs. They must recognise the right of Israel as the original owners of the land and share it.

One group observing forceful evacuation of the other to create room for the other may feel excited and happy but the distressed group creates enmity. This is not the right way of conflict resolution for peace or enduring harmony. The right way to resolve long lasting conflict is persuade the feuding parties to change their attitudes and learn to tolerate each other. Long lasting peace and resolution of conflict of this type must not distress or punish one group at the expense of the other. Good neighbourliness, trust and sharing in faith are what conflict resolution of the Arab-Israeli conflict resolution requires.

Making it blow like the wind destroying properties in one section while carrying freshness to the other is not very helpful. Religious fanaticism only fuels the conflict. It denies peace on earth to man and dishonours God or Allah. If we respect God we must respect His creation on earth. It is time the leaders of the Arabs and Israel stopped loathing at each other and seriously started to trust each other and tell their people that enmity must give place to friendship to help them all to live in peace and prosperity. Chaotic victory has no place for real peace. Genuine peace is by friendship and trust and the will to share and sacrifice. Conflict resolution distressing one group at time may be pleasing to the leaders but it will always fail to resolve the major conflict. The best way of resolving conflict is to obtain compromise from the warring groups that the leaders can sell to majority of their people.

The objective is to ensure that one group is not distressed at the expense of the other. In confined environment and land acceptance of sharing by the conflicting parties is important. They it is that will live together and cause conflicts. It is not only the leaders that will have to police the peace. Using the Armies and security forces indefinitely to keep the peace is policed peace. Policed peace is temporary and not permanent peace. Get the Arabs and the Israelis to accept to share this land and vital economic outlet services. As long as some people vow to fight on in the hope of driving some people out it is mere charade and not genuine peace. Sharing vital outlet economic services is sensible and economical. It avoids wasteful duplications and unnecessary wastes.

We African had always been a Matriarchal Society where the mother had very strong and powerful influence over the children and the father of her children, the husband. The female in the Pharaoh's family had strong influence on the family and in the state. Hence our women had franchise long before the other parts of the world allowed their women out. Hence the Queen of Sheba is a real story and not myths as our women were equal to men. Nigista Saba, Hebrew Melkart Shva in Arabic was a woman who ruled ancient kingdom of Sheba referred to in Habesham History of Hebrew Bible, the Torah. She was Queen of Sheba and Royalty and Biblical figure. She was born about 10th century BC just the time Rome and Greece were founded. The birthplace is speculated to be modern

Yemen. The Queen of Sheba had a son after her return to Sheba. Islam brought religious poisoned chalice and sadly separated women from the real society.

Cleopatra story was not a myth but real for our women had respectable place in the society including authority to lead. Cleopatra V11 was the last Hellenic ruler of Egypt. She was born 69-30 BC in Egypt. Originally she shared the throne with her father, Ptolemy X11, brothers and husband. She practised Egyptian Religion. She travelled with Julius Caesar to Rome. She had a son for Julius Caesar that was introduced to the Senate as his future heir. Julius Caesar was assassinated in 44 BC. Cleopatra returned to Egypt in the same year. She was to be protected by Marc Antonio but Octavius, Caesar Augustus defeated Marc Antonio. Cleopatra committed suicide. This is a demonstration of how advanced the degenerate Africa of today was. Religion should take the back seat in a secular society. It should feed the souls of the believers and the faithful. It should be free and must not be imposed on the society at large. It is this that will give religion respect. The behaviours of the believers in the society would do more to religion than human made religious laws.

We are appalled and very apprehensive of what is going on in assisted pregnancy in infertility treatment for women. Students were encouraged to donate sperms in lieu of payment in a consumer materialistic capitalist society. Some students donated sperms over fourteen times to earn extra cash at College. Anonymity was promised but now it has dawned on the authorities that Science may be successful but other human factors also affect human existence. It is not only Science and money but sociopsychogical factors of genetic bonding of Biological parents and children are also involved. It is now clear that the gene seems to retain the memory of its Biological parents. The offspring seems to be confused when the physical bonding fails to conform to psychobiological bonding. The offspring seems to feel something missing in life in a very uncanny way. This so far had forced the authorities to wave the anonymity law and blow the promised concealed identity made previously to sperm donors. Offspring is now free to know the Biological parents where it is possible. There is real danger of genetic in-breeding where brother may ignorantly fall in love and marry his sister. This will result in genetic in-breeding and risk of defective gene transfers from one generation to another. The risk of genetic in-breeding is a serious Medical and Scientific matter of grave concern in sperm and ovum donation in assisted pregnancies. Perhaps to prevent such overt mistakes this process may require better record keeping and full disclosures of the information to all the parties involved including the offspring. This will prevent a brother marrying a sister.

This exposition deals with world History starting from the times of the Pharaohs in Africa to the present time. I have deliberately omitted the Sumatrans, Babylonians, and Assyrians. Rather I have glossed over the reigns of individual Pharaohs. I have, however, not spared the time to emphasize what type of person was the Pharaoh. His role and status in the community were specific but never like those of the European or Arab feudal Kings. It also gave comparative accounts of the Greek influence in the world and the role of the Romans in the world. The arrival of the Western Europeans at the scene in the past five hundred years changed things completely. Africa and black people in the world had had very rough deal in the five thousand years because of their gross negligence and failure to pay attention to global changes and have vision of the future. We Africans have the weakness of cowardice, selfishness, divisiveness and failure to recognise the power of the community. This has led to complete failure of leadership. The leadership is degenerate and corrupt. We failed to observe the changes in times and persons. The times and changes left us behind. We are victims of our negligence in monitoring life and changes in the life styles of people on earth. We concentrated on our individual needs at the expense of the needs of the community and our land. Today, we have lost the community sense and soul. Now we are hopelessly dependent and parasitic in our lifestyle. We have to start life at the beginning. This is at the level of good practical education and effective skills training.

It is important to study world History in blocks of five thousand years or more. This reminds students that we are part of the various generations of human beings that had trodden the earth. Ours may be technologically more advanced but still we are part of the whole. We keep on repeating the mistakes the other made. Above all there are certain ingrained patterns of behaviours in certain groups in some regions of the world. Some people seem to think that they can ignore the signs of the times, change and get along with their former behaviours. Unfortunately past mistakes cannot be tolerated now. For the purpose of distinguishing times and people of the different ages we have decided to call ancient Egypt as distinguished from modern Arab Egypt, African Egypt. The same applies to ancient Libya, African Libya and Carthage, African Carthage. They were purely African and better integrated. The ancient Greece had always been eager to learn and they were good mariners and traders. They were averagely friendlier and better disposed to the Africans. They were law-abiding. The Romans were rustic farmers beyond the rule of law. They were aggressively military believed in conquest. Alexander, son and heir of Philip of Macedonia, Alexander the Great, a great General still carried Greek civilised methods with him.

In contrast with the Romans, Alexander respected the culture of the people he conquered but he still maintained discipline in his Army. The colonising militaristic culture of the West and Europe is from the Romans. The docile and cowardly behaviours of the black Africans had always been the rule. The Africans seem to lack the power of organisation to let things happen. They also seem to lack the potential to produce good leaders and their leadership potential had always been lacking. Hence they had been handicapped by poor leadership. In addition to this corruption and crimes had hindered the observance of rule of law. Fragmentation of the continent like salami to constitute current Bantustan rogue states which in majority are failed states or banana republics beyond the seam of law and order and viable economy make it a failed continent. The world conscience pleads that Africa should be opened up for stability of Globalisation. Clean up post-colonial dirt from Africa and open up the continent to the world. The UN should be given charge to re-unite Africa and open it up. Africans are Bantunistic, Atomistic, divisive and disunited. The world has no duty throwing money at Africa but let it rather tell Africans to get their acts together and co-operate with the world to rescue the continent.

Ignorance and poverty generate frequent conflicts, violence, civil strife and wars. Muslim Islam religion and Christianity now fast developing into native traditional religion both make things more complicated. At the moment the world seems genuinely concerned with the plight of Africa. Some of the Bantustans are in the middle of arid desert plagued by droughts and famines. This goes to emphasize re-integration of Africa and placing it under the rule of secular law and make the reign of law and order supreme. This will relieve the people of the burden of poverty and the world of the anxiety to rescue Africa from its dilemma. Perhaps it is fair to end this book by saying that wealth and prosperity are acquiring those good virtues lacking in your life and correcting past mistakes by learning them and preventing them taking place in future. If we view life as a continuity of successes and failures ever challenging us to learn from our past mistakes we may succeed to avoid past catastrophes. We would also know that we are not here to last for ever. We are perishable commodity and as such we would gain by doing good.

It is worth reminding the West and the world of the land mass the West alone had seized from others on earth: North and South America, Australasia and several Ocean islands on earth. All had been seized at the expense of lives and cultures of the native dwellers of those lands on earth. In Asia and Africa both nature and humans fought them back. In Africa slave trade and slavery and brutal colonisation damaged both the people and the land. In Asia the people fought back gallantly and bravely in Vietnam, Korea and several jungles. The West dropped nuclear weapons on Japan. Again the purpose of this book is not to put the West in the dock for trial. This is just to remind the global citizens that time is overdue for the Western leaders and governments to grow above brigandry. Lying over their real intentions for wars and violence is undignifying. The West is more respectable than lying over their activities. They are in the Middle East for oil. They now talk of democracy as an afterthought. Why did they not sell democracy to the world when they were ruling over them? Their past records of atrocities were atrocious and barbaric. Even in the process of tongue in cheek muttering democracy we still have Guantanamo Bay, Abu Graib Prison and Fallujah. It is total nonsense to talk of democracy in the face of these inhuman atrocities. It is equally difficult to differentiate between terrorists killing with missiles and bombs from the planes and terrorists killing us with exploding walking suicide bombs. I have always stated that death is death regardless of the means by which it touches its victims with its cold hands.

We cannot fail to remind the good Western citizens and the global audience that the West created Osama bin Laden from Soviet invasion of Afghanistan when the very West told the global Muslims to assemble in Kabul to defend their religion. The glorified Muslim Islam then and the words "radical and fanatics" were not in the Dictionary. The tyrant Saddam Hussein was bloomed and raised by the West to have bloated ego in the Iraq-Iran war. His violence was acceptable then. I am not professing dislike for the West or inciting people to hurt the West. I am eager to remind the West and its leaders that they should not keep on repeating the same mistakes to threaten their interest. I am just too ill and do not expect much of life left in me. The activities of the West in Iraq and Afghanistan are recruiting centres for the people who will constitute future threat to the West. The very friends of today will become the enemies of tomorrow. The West and its leaders are not too ignorant to tell me that they are not clever enough to know this.

Equally the West knows simple ways of working for world peace and security. It will be too dull and the West would not be able to sell arms to make huge fortunes from arms sales. Chaos promotes arms sales. Can the West with all its wealth and riches be honest to the world and share just peace with us the tormented global poor and the deprived? For those who count life in numbers and compare the life of one person with those of fifty seven, may I remind them all that life is not counted in numbers? One life is as precious as fifty seven lives. It is equally important to remind the commanders in Chief that it is wrong to wait for daily casualties to increase before taking action to save lives. It is arrogance of ignorance and tyranny of greed not to recognise these things to prevent them. Those who expect emerald from war in time would be shocked that History would not give the honour they expect.

Time has changed. IT Information Technology writes History as we go along and attempts at spin to falsify History to favour miscalculations will always fail. Time now recognises blunders and records them instantly. It is doing so now.

The Nigerian example is a clear case in question the way crises affect the social classes. There are two main social classes in Africa, the office workers all categories of workers: they form the middle class and the peasant farmers. The illiterate and ignorant leaders are drawn from this class. The wild and primitive soldiers were recruited from here as they constitute the majority. There is a flux between the minority and very weak middle class that draws its young members from this majority peasant group too. The peasant group feeds the middle class with newly educated people and workers. Most African peasant parents take to Chinua Achebe. They go full swing to ensure that their offspring do not join them in peasant farming as their holdings are small and scattered. They see the middle class workers as people with reliable and steady incomes. They want their offspring to join this group so that they can make steady income to support them and their families in their different villages. In any crises the weakly supported middle classes that rely on the peasant farmers suffer the most.

The Schools and Educational Institutions that form the outlet for the offspring of peasant farmers to join the middle class are disrupted. The stable Government and Administration that form the source of income for sustaining the working middle class is disrupted. The source of income is disrupted and there is no longer financial support for the Administration. The working middle class collapses first. Therefore any crises affect the working middle class most. They are the taxpayers in the place. Their taxes are deducted straight from their salaries. The collapse of this source of income ruins the Administration and the funds it can muster to run the services. It also destroys method of fund collection and even Banking. The middle class is the only group that reliably uses most of the facilities and pays for them. It also supervises their maintenance. Hence destroying them as it was in Nigerian situation destroys the country. It equally delays recovery for a very long time. The middle class depends on the modern facilities for survival. They die out faster when deprived of them. The post Nigerian crises have demonstrated that the middle class returning from top Western Universities to work in the country became rapidly wiped out. The peasants without its middle class drifts back to poverty and ignorance. The supporting facilities and services offered and supervised by the decaying middle class that supports developments die out with the middle class. I challenge the US and their satellites now in Iraq that this is what is going to happen after. I can equally say that this has affected development in Iran after the Muslim Islamic revolution. It is equally true of many places where there had been civil wars, crises and violence. The middle class dies out with developments. Those who deliberately target the middle class to eliminate them to start from the beginning as it was the case in Cambodia are destroying the bases of what they want, progress and development and prosperity.

I may go further to advise the people now interested in recovery of African to target genuine middle class to use as instruments of development. We must select our leaders from them. Enlightened leadership is better and essential for development and progress than the bogus alien counterfeit democracy and majority. It is fraud and deception. People who understand the principles of government and administration should run the administration and illiterate peasants drawn from peasants in the name of majority and false democracy should have their free votes but they just have no understanding of the complexity of modern administration. The people just do not understand. The meddlesome behaviour riding on the back of false democracy, free enterprise and bogus ideology must now give way to the truth about real life.

The truth is that the West has been dribbling us with all these false doctrines before. They used religion, law and order they fail to keep in going into sovereign states to kill their leaders to cause crises, ideology: free world which has now become a nightmare and a world in chains; capitalism versus socialism which is now the root of all evils particularly corruption and crimes. They are fast running out of the lists of false doctrines to use to deceive and fool the world. Fundamental human rights had become torture and killing chamber in Quantamo Bay in Cuba and ABU Graib Prison. Genocide trails the path of the West in the world like a bad smell of rotten eggs starting from the Romans in Carthage in Africa, in the Americas and Australia. The West has to be mindful of these its famous records and sympathize with the world. We are not anti-West. We want the West to behave like fellow human beings. We also find the West as perfect liars spinning perfect lies and deceiving its citizens and the world. They are insulting our reasoning by forcing lies down our throats and threatening us with punishment for complaining. It is nobody's business to hate the West or to go out to kill the Westerners. This would definitely be a gross violation of the rule of law. Equally the West has the greatest numbers of nuclear weapons. It will not be right to drop them on us as right of first strike in self defence. It will cause breakdown of law and order. It will replace daylight with the darkest night. Let us now use the power of reasoning to resolve all conflicts. Let us do away with emotions and incitements. We just cannot escape sharing this world. The West talks about competition but refuses to compete fairly or openly. Is it not time the West accepts free and open competition sincerely?

Most of the crises, conflicts and wars had taken place because the West does not accept free competition. It would fight rather than settle arguments over competition by discussion if it cannot cheat or has undue advantage. This is what it describes as Western interests. The West must recognise that others in the world also have interest.

This section deals mainly with the African middle class a minority section within it frequently joins the wild peasants in arms to destroy itself and their country. The real victims of such an uprising are people in the middle class. They destroy their jobs and means of living and facilities they use to support themselves as the middle class. The hardest hit section of the community in the long drawn Nigerian crises had been the middle class. Their life expectation has been shortened and drastically cut. The middle class should review its stand on national crises and ensure that that it takes the path of peaceful conflict resolution. It draws its young members from the peasant community. Naturally the loyalty of these young members lies with the peasants that find the middle class responsible for all its woes. But experience should offer all members of the middle class communities in Africa that national crises affects them most and destroys them.

The world seems to be flirting with Africa. Those who may be genuine in revived interest in the African continent should concentrate on the middle class to develop leadership subject to the rule of law. Such leadership must be taught the responsibilities of leadership to cater for the interest of all communities in the country regardless of their ethnic origin or religion. They must quickly recognise "impera et divide". They must avoid falling into this trap in the name of majority. The plates full on the table are better than starving majority dependent on the NGO's. It took much of my time to persuade my young friends and people to persuade them that the Igbos were not their major hindrance. Rather their major hindrance was their indolence and lack of entrepreneurial co-operative community spirit. Equally I warned them that it was necessary to start from the known to the unknown. We knew the Igbos. This is why we detested them for just and unjust reasons. Today, if our people are honest we would confess that we made mistakes. Our working middle class has been the price we had paid for our folly. I am strongly convinced that Africa should develop the African Union for home and protection for all the re-integrated parts of this vast continent. The multi-ethnic and multi-national groups can then constitute themselves into homogeneous groups for peace and stability under the AU and sharing common services under the AU that will be in charge of the rule of law, the CONSTITUTION. AU will maintain Law and Order. The Africans must stop being timid. They must stop feuding and think of positive actions to save their land and people. The primitive peasant farmers who are now leaders are gullible and believe in miracle from outside. They have the tendency to believe the hot air of foreign leaders promising non-existent aids to Africa still wriggling in pain of genocide in Rwanda and Darfur. We are still left to suffer the consequences of the international mafia of fund holders working for their share holders as multinational investors. They have no conscience.

If they do not care we have to tell them that we care. We have to make laws that protect our law and order and the rule of law. It is now obvious that the young Ibibio working middle class is more vulnerable to dislodgement crises violence and war. We have lost more in peace with deprivation, poverty and joblessness under false redundancy in the name of retirement. We do not need retirement age. It is forced redundancy. I propose that initially people should work in their home states to make room for the native indigenes who have no other places to work. The state employment law should be made by the state regardless of who is the employer. The state was created to cater for these people and their interest. Any employer must first obtain written permission from the state employment ministry before bringing in outsider to work in the state to state that it failed to find equivalent qualified personnel in the state. We cannot afford to be unemployed at the expense of outsiders. The so-called public servants and middle class have a duty to avoid provocation and incitement to crises. They fared very poorly in crises. Re-integrate Africa. Dismantle colonial Bantustans. Create Africa that is your home and fortress. Do not be timid. Make your home beautiful with great gardens. Give Africa hope. Give the world faith in Africa. Give the black race faith in themselves. The black Africans seem to be castrated in the senses, vision, hearing, smelling, feeling and tasting; in the brain and reasoning and in the genitals.

They are terrible cowards. They are too timid to defend their common interests. The hurricane, Katrina and flooding of Southern States of the US may have exposed not only the hypocrisy of the US authorities but also the stupidity and the timidity of the black people and their leaders. After the brutal murder of Martin Luther King, the black people seem to have gathered like vultures to gather the crumbs of the benefits of his self-sacrifice but all their leaders had failed to lead. They had taken to status symbols and cheap publicity stunts, and had fallen prey to the white trap of sham feeding the black with cosmetic roles that fool them to believe that they count.

Those people left behind to drown for five days before world opinion forced the Bush administration to intervene might have come from any part of Africa in crises of that dimension. How come that these people live in the midst of wealth and prosperity but yet are so poor? It means that there is an active and effective programme to keep down the black people in poverty and economic exclusion and deprivation. The black people were in the main stranded. Black people do not need anything from the white people but rewards for their labour from their ancestors as slaves but also till now all over the world. Pay us in kind with free good Education and productive skills training. The black people all over the world have no Economy to match the whites and other people. We have to pull ourselves together to develop one. The rule of law must prevail. We must have self-discipline.

They have to develop one based on the vastness of their re-integrated homeland Africa and all their squatting quarters scattered all over the world. The white slave masters had their compensation for losing this illegal slave labour. What is wrong in compensating the victims of free slave labour? You all Americans are living witnesses that slavery had damaged the black people economically, politically, socially and psychologically. The whole world bears witness to this. Those and their offspring responsible for the destruction of the black race in this way have all owed the whole world the responsibility to rehabilitate the black race on earth. Justice demands that you white ex-slave masters compensate your suffering post slavery victims. Do not evade justice by pleading that it has nothing to do with me and our generations. You all are reaping and enjoying the rewards of these ex-slaves' labour.

This labour had damaged them but it had improved your Economy and created wealth and made you prosperous. Bigotry Racial discrimination carries gun to protect itself. Justice carries sympathy. Sympathy alone can mend the sour relationship and suffering of the ex-black slaves. You do not know that slavery and Economic exclusion and deprivation had destroyed and damaged the basis of family as we all Africans know it. Economic power and family structure go hand and in hand. This is the basis of heritage. The black people must stage all their activities as a bundle. The loosened thread scatters the bundle and exposes individual black person to psychological and social trauma and madness that we saw on television screens on the way Hurricane Katrina affected the poor and deprived Southern black population.

You do not lose anything by uniting to form that critical mass essential for soliciting and working for your welfare. Welfare is not the weekly government payments of social security. It is your good education and good skills to work for your independent living. You must work as a bundle and the leaders must be part of the whole bundle and not timid traitors. Poor leadership is the scourge of the black race and Africa. Those who want to torture us must not find black people to hire to do so. Any black person hired to terrorise other black people to intimidate the group from building up and developing their destiny for their social security deserves to die. Black people in jobs to maintain law and order in the Society in general have no reason to fear and all black people should respect them. Recent hurricane and flood experience in Southern States of the US have shown the world the black person is vulnerable regardless of the location on earth. Black people fared worse in that natural tragic catastrophe. The people we saw on the telescreen could have been black people from any location on earth. Why do we continue to delude ourselves with the slogan while we are not participants in the feast? We are excluded from the feast. Can we team up in unity to create a feast for our children? There is no real genuine barrier except an imaginary demarcation between the Diaspora black African and African black. We have to overcome that false barrier. We must join hands to rebuild from the ruins we had been abandoned in. We need courage to overcome our inhibition. We need courage to cluster together and ignore the discouraging and disparaging comments from the very people who had tormented and abandoned us. The AU pretends to be seeking room in the UN but it has got a great problem in its hands to rehumanise dehumanised and abandoned black African. It has to rehabilitate Africans from the four corners of the world. Black Africans must remove artificial barriers deliberately used to divide them to weaken them to make them prone to abuses and bullying. We will overcome. We can overcome. We can work to set ourselves free. Today we are slaves by choice.

Tomorrow we may be free by choice. Nobody can make us free. It is we alone that can free ourselves from poverty and misery. We can be free from humiliation and mockery if we work hard by good and genuine education and practical skills training. We have no place in our hearts to hate anybody on earth. Hatred holds us back from progress and prosperity. We have to have the power of concentration ignoring the distractions of hate to concentrate and do what we feel is right for us to do. This is the incentive to success. Take the thought of self-doubt out of your system. Replace it with the strength and ability to organise and lead the bad and the good, the strong and the weak. Champion the cause of production and productivity and wealth generation and saving to proper. Africans in the Diaspora and Africans in Africa must join hands together to form that long chain that will attract global sympathy to them for the charitable and kind people to help them to overcome their impediments. The black Africans have a duty to overcome their inertia to change in their global status. They must convince the world that they are ready to overcome the status of working as the beasts of burden. They must show us that they are ready to bundle themselves together and unite to work for themselves for a common purpose. We have to turn 180 degrees to look in the opposite direction to see the gains we have been missing by disunity. We are ignoring the fact that those Southern black are not only American underclass but world universal underclass are global black people. We global black people deliberately bury ourselves in past History and make ourselves the world underclass regardless of the fact that we have the richest continent on earth. We continue to bury our heads in the sand and continue to tear away the barriers preventing us from coming together to rescue ourselves from permanent poverty trap.

Dr Rev Martin Luther is no more here to lead Southern black to expose US hypocrisy and hidden and subtle institutional racism responsible for destroying us black people. God sent Hurricane Katrina to expose this evil. The closed doors of white racial discrimination against black people were all flung open for the black Africans in the world and world to see. We cannot play politics with God. God or Allah is the truth and does not spin lies. All the specially stage-managed cosmesis of top isolated black people dressed in white gowns to do top jobs melted away. The black officials stood on a corroded base of very poor and desperate people to perform their state duties. They are two answers to solve this problem. They are two people to resolve this conflict and solve the anomalies.

The white people whose ancestors brought in these black people to work for them in slave labour must pay them at least in token good education and genuine skills training. They must accept the change of times and pay their descendants for the free labour of their ancestors. They must stop dehumanising them and abolish genuinely racial discrimination. The black people themselves must stop acting as slaves and thinking as slaves. They must use the IT high Technology to reach out to all global black people to plan their strategy together. They must unite to live or remain divisive and die out. The white people must help in this and stop to think of such efforts at unity subversive. They must see it as black survival strategy. Right now the black people in Africa do not have their blood chilled by the desperation of the abandoned Southern black. The events are not happening in their Bantustans. The Niger drought and famine earlier took no place in the US where hungry blacks are satisfied feeding on fat drippings from MacDonald and Burger King.

The reality of these two situations is that we are not in charge or in control of our lives. There is no such thing as complete independence. We still have mutual dependence on each other for mutual exchange of goods and services. But total parasitic dependence on others to rescue us from situations of life and death is suicidal. This is what changes us and the world to review critically re-integration of African Bantustans and closer interaction between black Africans in Africa and the Diaspora. They must develop a third Economy to have economic power. Again this requires white and black to co-operate. Massive construction begging to be tackle can generate work and create that third Economy. Road and rail network building in Africa has enormous potential for all black people. Water supply, provision of good shelters, organising wild life, forestry and Agriculture are very significant. Fund collection and storing must be attended to. These things are not too costly for the Africans and the world. We have to get rid of servant sit-tight despotic leaders who do not want to leave office even in extreme old age relying on powerful alien supporters. We must teach African youths self-less leadership.

One Radio commentator remarked: "The Katrina Hurricane had broken the under belly of American equal opportunity and racial separation of two separate groups: the privileged white and underprivileged and underclass black in two countries falsely operating as one. The hypocrisy of American white racial discrimination had been exposed." It is an issue of great sadness that this issue initiated by the Romans over two thousand years ago is still menacing mankind. This unfortunately is true of all European white people and Societies. Black immigrants in Paris and their children are being roasted and incinerated in nocturnal staircase arson-inspired initiated fires. A court Judge described as institutional racism the practice of discrimination in the London Metropolitan Police Force and several government Institutions. The world is yet to see any white society that does not practise subtle racial discrimination. There is equally a strong and valid argument in favour of the white people and detrimental to the black. The Asians and Hispanics came to the US just recently but they are making strong efforts to acquire economic power while the Africans do not. Unfortunately I can use myself to show the enormous hurdles and obstacles the black have to go through to escape.

I am a fine Consultant Specialist surgeon excluded and blocked by the hidden institution for criticising a system that exploits the talents of the skilful to augment the mediocrity of the non-talented by placing them under the mediocre. One can keep quiet at his or her peril on racial discrimination at work that would swarm the talents and skills of the highly talented and work for money. This suppresses one's conscience. Talk about it and be damned, isolated and excluded from a vicious system. The white people regard the black people as the lowest of the low. Even white women married to black regard their husbands as people hired to work for them. Hence the black people have mountain to climb in this system. Yet the black people have to unite and tackle disunity and its hindering of their efforts to achieve economic power. Corporate unity is Economic Power. The black people lack corporate power. The Banks respect corporate power.

The West should jointly pay the debts they owe to the black for several years of free slave labour and compensation for abuses of slavery and pay the money as collateral to the Banks for initiating construction projects in Africa for the black people. This will give the black people construction skills and earning and economic power. It is worth adding that Hurricane Katrina had called off the bluff of the US black people that they were better off than their African brothers and sisters. They are not. Katrina has punctured the under belly of African continuous pretence of economic power they essentially lack. It has exposed them as a failure in the system that had favoured all others. This is a challenge to two racial groups, white and black to co-operate for prosperity. I am not a religious fanatic but God the creator had visited us twice this year alone with tsunami and now with Katrina to emphasize interdependence of the creation. His strong emphasis is on the fact that we all have our feet firmly planted on earth. Danger to one is danger to all.

We all share death in common. We have to share wealth in common. We must share means of wealth creation in common education and skills and excellent Apprenticeship. The intriguing thing is that majority of black people give the impression that they are content with the situation but continue to grumble in silence. Globalisation compels us to speak out and reject the role of a second fiddle. Events have shown that Africa will continue to be part of the Western Atlantic that we belong by right. We will always share this with Europe and the West as slave dealings had planted the core of the black Africans among the white people in the US. Equally generations of both white and black leaders from Alexander of Macedonia to Julius Caesar and black leaders like Cleopatra had advocated for this. Equally we had been doing great things together in History but for the fact that colonial superiority needed to suppress our role to justify its action that it was out to tame savages. In the early Church you cannot ignore St Augustine of Hippo. The skin colour is beautiful but is just skin deep. What makes the man is his character. Character is the gene and environmental feedback. This constitutes education for maturity. This does not mean that one is born to be mediocre or bad but all must learn to adapt to the culture and norms of the community. Anyone ignores this at his peril. We all must learn to be part of the decent community. We must not opt out to be bad and a nuisance to the community.

The challenge to all true believers in God regardless of your faith and religious adherence is absolute belief in Him and patience to wait upon Him to execute His will for us. The Afghanistan–Iraq war is a disaster of human impatience and failure of human beings to wait upon God to execute His will. The Prophet Isaiah in the Holy Bible Chapter 40 states clearly in verses 30-31: "Even the youths shall faint and be weary, and the young men shall utterly fall: But they that wait upon the Lord shall renew their strength; they shall mount up with wings like eagles; they shall run and not be weary; and they shall walk and faint." Listen to the wise counsel regardless of its source. It is God only that gives wisdom and wise counsel. I told the US that going into Iraq was going to transform them into terrorists and erode their democratic and human rights potentials. Today these have become true. In addition an eye for eye was the law but Christians had been taught not to execute it to the full. September 11 was provocative and murderous. But how many people would die because it happened because September 11?

Two wrongs do not make one right. Now God to whom several years are just but a minute had decided to show His power and destructive forces to George W. Bush the suicide bombers, the Asian tsunami and the all destructive hurricane, Katrina to demonstrate how helpless we are on earth. We have to tolerate each other and wait upon the Lord. There is no such thing as water proof security. Our security comes from God the creator Himself. I am totally convinced that we are sophisticated walking chemical industries designed by nature Himself. Yet Science has no chance to replace the Creator, God. Neither George Walker Bush nor the suicide bombers have power to damage us. They can scare us but not damage us. In the twinkle of an eye God the creator by small measure can discipline us and can show us His Power and remind us that the power is in His hand. These two natural events have persuaded me that whatever we do God is in charge. Shall we be patient to wait upon him and let his will be done? The argument is raging over who is right, either Intelligent Designer or Darwinian Theory of Natural Selection. Charles Darwin is designated a Scientist. His theory is scientific observation but Intelligent Designer can equally use the two in the design and formulation of the creation. The creator, nature is not discriminatory. He has no go area. He extends beyond Science and Art of creation and its beauty. Who made the Genes to retain the patency in creatures? Who made matter? Who made the elements and selected the sequence they join to form the various creations in nature? We have to understand the nature of God the Supreme creator to be able to understand the creation. We must understand where our understanding and knowledge are incomplete.

We must equally appreciate what we know and look for more to expand our understanding. There may not be any conflict in our concept of the creation but we must recognise that religion at the beginning was intolerant of probing ideas except theories and concepts approved by the elders. Those who attempted to observe things to render some explanation were punished by excommunication or physical punishment. The Church was totally intolerant of Science. Astronomy suffered in the hands of the Church Authority. The Church bullied Galileo to denounce and withdraw his writings on Astronomy. Hence we will be making serious error of judgment by attempting to replace observations with decrees by the totalitarian Church Authorities who were by all intent desperate to hold unto members of their faith offered them perfunctory explanation of poorly conceived ideas deemed to come from God. Hence the Biblical story on the creation.

Despite this the Church Authorities had the message of resting on the day of Sabbath to worship God to give to their members. If God rested after the creation, they had no reason to reject resting on the Sabbath. They had to stop all work on the Sabbath to concentrate on worship. They were to keep the Sabbath holy. The Intelligent Designer Theory brings Arts to the creation in the same way the Darwinian Evolution and the Theory of Natural Selection. The Gene is Nature's Live Painting fitting both the Science and Arts. We must accept in this age of freedom, High Technology, Science, near perfect Democracy and mature reasoning and thought that Religious Books were written by wise followers of faiths to advise and teach their adherents the rights of God on earth. They were written to teach believers good conduct in the complex relationship between God, the community and fellow human beings. They are full of myths. They were to guide and direct believers. They were not meant to tell you how to live your life in a vast changing and expanding global world, business and Economy. On the other hand the faith books, Torah, the Bible, the Koran, that of the Confucius and Hindus all are perfect guide books on Righteousness. They never existed before the establishment of each of their faiths. We must not take them literally. We must accept them as good books to refer to for answer and advice on matters regarding our faiths and what God expects from us in faiths.

The Creator is not shy to use both Science and Arts to acquire the Genes for the Creation. The creator is not shy or restricted from using either the Intelligent Designer or Darwinian evolution of Natural Selection. None of the Contestants in methods of Creation has monopoly over the truth. None of them has full understanding of the materials and the way the world was created and they did not know the existence of the Universe and the Galaxy. Without comprehensive knowledge and understanding of these principles none of the contestants has the right to claim monopoly of having right theory of creation. The religious faiths are autocratic and intolerant and bullying their followers with punishments and ex-communications. They cannot sell their concept to us. The conclusion is that the creation is a dynamic Scientific Process involving the Environments and adaptability of Genes and Natural Selection to survive in different changing environments. Migrations from Africa show that those who remained behind showed minimum changes. The migrants on the other hand kept on changing until we had the whites and the Asians. Even animals and plants adapted too. Despite this heated argument the story of creation is a four-dimensional object. We have to see all the sides to comprehend its full size. We have guessed when it happened by carbon dating. The matter constituting the earth is not well known. We are unsure if the earth developed gradually or by spontaneity. The theories propounded for the origin of earth such as the big bang open new door for argument. Hence knowledge of the creation is still not comprehensive. The current big bang research may reveal more matter than we know at the moment. Trying to present a strong argument will demote the discussion from Science to politics.

Darwinian Theory of evolution of Natural Section is not the complete picture but it makes room to embrace new ideas while the religious faiths are too rigid to accommodate changing Scientific and Technological modern times. It would be risky and dangerous for the Darwinists to be paranoid and intolerant of other ideas. They must be open minded but critical of other ideas within Scientific analysis of concepts. Darwin never knew as much as we now know. His theory, however, is flexible to accommodate other ideas.

The job of the US President can be performed without war. The President can do a lot of good. The strange thing is that if the two combatants in this deliberate blood letting were together in the same places of these great natural events they would all be victims regardless of how they might hate each other. Humility is not beyond good leadership. Arrogance and flamboyance constitute the razzmatazz of high office but let them not corrupt the system or damage the innocent. We now need the resources we had wasted on avoidable war and violence to use in repair the Katrina damage. We equally have to pay a lot more fore gasoline and energy. It is a catastrophic disaster we should learn from to exercise patience in the face of extreme provocation. We must recall that this is not the only time nature had intervened with destruction of war and violence. Earthquake occurred in the battlefield while the Romans were fighting with the Africans led by RT noble Gen Hannibal Hamilcar Barca. God rejects our mutually assured self-destruction. Earthquake in superstitious way is just like nature is asking why are you slaughtering each other?

This is history with moral lessons on our world and duties to each other. Law and order can still regulate the chaotic world if we sincerely believe in them. The rule of law is still the perfect way to peaceful co-existence. We patiently believe in it and insist that the society respects and executes them. DIY security means war. IT high Technology unfortunately has created the global village. We cannot police it with violence. We must insist that everybody behaves responsibly with the rule of law. Let us not flirt with religion or bogus ideology to gain some advantage. Without religion or the type of democracy we now use as an afterthought to fool the world we still would exist.

If we want to package these things to sell to the world, let us do our serious home work before we do so. There are people who discard morality and conscience in politics and business deals. To them money has no conscience. They kill for money paper and metal and do not care. It is sad the ultra-conservative Straussite loony right have no value for life below the poverty. George Walker Bush's mother is quoted as saying that the poor black abandoned and left behind in Hurricane Katrina flooded New Orleans were actually done a favour to escape from their miserable lives. In the UK some politicians had suggested that the poor should have no children. Equally the British Immigrant Progress has been a good statistically but it failed to state that highly qualified black people are socially excluded and denied work opportunities. It failed to state that the white people eat rice and chicken curry and other Indian spices. They prefer to work with Indians because they sheepishly blunder in the name of doing their dirty jobs while Africans are meticulous.

They ask questions and refuse to be morons. We are not good cronies. Indians are very hard working intelligent people. But their culture seems to worship rulers and leaders. They advised Alexander to institute obeisance. This caused crisis in Alexander's camp. Alexander sentenced his loyal confidant to death for disloyalty but Greek sense and culture of freedom soon prevailed. Alexander abandoned Obeisance. Peace and Tranquillity returned to the camp. Docile adherence to rulers hinders progress and dwarfs initiatives. Progress in India would be faster than at present if it had not carried the weight of bulky Democracy to please the British that never practised it in the Raj. Any borrowed culture must be modified to suit the people and the environment. Corruption and crimes are embedded in Democracy to protect criminals. It leaves a loophole for the former colonial master to continue to exploit its former colonies. Such caps have to be blocked by local laws to allow Democracy function properly. Those who perform poorly are discriminated against at all levels in institutional racism. We black people can thrive if we create opportunities for ourselves in Africa in good education and practical skills training and create jobs. We need independent Economic development line to be free to compete at our own pace culturally. Africa can no longer afford to remain indifferent to the enormous development and changes taking place around the world.

The truth is that the white people do not trust us and we have no reason to trust them. The truth is that there had always been double image in our human relationship. George Walker Bush as Texan Governor signed and hanged more deprived poor black people permanently condemned to dehumanising life below the poverty line than any other Governor in the US. This could not be explained by duty to maintain law and order or protecting the rule of law. Negrophobic xenophobia and bloody taste for lynching the Negro as in the past seemed to have sharpened his zeal to know History and may explain his action. He seems to have a double image towards his relationship with the black people. His left hand accepts black people but his right hand pushes them away.

I am an optimist but doubt and pessimism had forced me to see a silver lining in the sky. We had co-existed long enough in this part of the Atlantic. We had interbred. Time had changed. We all must also change in order to co-exist in trust in modern times. Hate is not love or acceptance. We are yet to define the nature of good and evil of human beings. Why do we share together all natural processes of life while refusing to accept the truth that we are fallible and mortal human beings flowering in the morning and wilting away in evening? The arrogance of ignorance is gross in racial xenophobia but let it not deny us the truth. The truth is that we have no cause to hate each other but should accept and tolerate each other without any reticence. We are human beings in fortune or misfortune. In the morning we sprout and bloom but in the evening we droop and wilt and die. We must reject living in the past with all its emotions.

Children still cling to their parents' old jokes and resentment towards black people.

Recently a person commented that tourism is not trade or reliable business. I totally agree with him. In well developed countries, hospitality has very genuine place as business as locals, natives and foreigners use it. The European white male has every reason to fear of outsiders especially black people because of what their ancestors did to black people.

But those we find in the developing countries are investments relying on the unknown to exist and succeed. It is gambling of some sort. It is worth stating that good education means literate and able to read and understand and use the knowledge to communicate ideas. The Africans must know that the Continent was fragmented to salami by colonial masters to weaken it so that they could control it. It was possible to isolate Bantustan mini-state and control it. It caused disunity that is still haunting us till today and division. We are divisive and disunited. We must do everything to re-unite, integrate to regain our strength, control of our land, our strength, influence and leadership of our people in the world. This is a time the world is talking about the Eco-Environment. Nobody represents the wild fauna in these talks. Africans must discuss the management of their wildlife. The multinational corporations must know that any investments must include funds to rehabilitate wildlife.

Palmol in Borneo is logging wood and planting palm trees in pristine forests, home of the ape, Orangutan now facing extinction. African wildlife now needs people to speak for it. The Congo tropical rainforest is depleted by logging and mineral exploration and our precious forest gorillas are threatened. We must develop our wildlife tourist industry. We must make room for the wildlife as we live together with them on this continent.

Skills training mean that a child leaving Primary Elementary Education has mastered some trade, Carpentry or other Technical Trade. The child leaving High School has acquired substantial skills in building Technology and fixtures in the home. The students studying professional subjects study enough of practice in their profession that once completed their studies they can join the job market and excel. Practical skills should form fifty percent of studies at all levels. The practical skills guarantee security and employments. It is the bastion of development, the Economy and Prosperity. Overcoming the inertia of unemployment and poverty must always have alternative. The black people mischievously blackmail genuine white people who had opened their community to them. It is wrong to abuse privilege they have to live here among the natives. Criminality and corruption are not new ways to start new enterprise. Black youths are sabotaging the opportunities the white community offer them. The black youths have a duty to emancipate themselves. We must have a mind that rejects aggressive radicalism and massaging the system to get the best out of it. It is a shame that a section of Nigerians specialists in massaging the system had abused their system until it could not support them. They have now voted with their feet to the UK to continue the Arts. The mother of pregnant Nigerian girl drug trafficker in Laotian Gaol is typical of today's Nigerian criminal families. She denies that her daughter was guilty but failed to tell us why the daughter selectively went to Laos. It has been known for a long time now that Nigerian girls are drug couriers. The region of the country where this girl comes from is notoriously known to be involved in this.

Credit Crunch, Economic Crunch or Economic Collapse, Economic meltdown, deep recession, Banking crisis, Globalisation, global financial managers and fund administrators.

How could we get it so wrong? I spent my life exaggerating the fact that plastics, paper money and precious and base metal coins may fill the banks but they are not wealth. They are tokens of exchange of services and goods. Tokens are not money. We must define what Economy is and what money is before we can define what to keep and rely upon for savings and security. We have to broaden the definition of wealth. Mortgage Property must include the land the property stands on. Free lease or annual leases are elements of uncertainty and guarantee for confusion. The Mortgage lenders must have access to the lands as part of the security for the investment. There must also be community Property available for a fall back to for community rescue.

The total community wealth must be available to protect citizens and their Economic security. Absolute reliance on the tokens shatters people's confidence when the business collapses and the tokens scattered all over the tables. It is at this stage that we rise up to evaluate wealth and business. Economy is avoidance of wastage. Wastage has no concept of Economy. The lenders have enormous duty to perform their duties meticulously that no wastage is involved. We must not have realised that the integrated global wealth is involved in what the financial houses are doing. Agriculture, Education, Science, Technology, High Technology, Information Technology, (IT) Communications, by land, seas, and air, our core knowledge, our shelters, our groceries, our environments all depend on our financial houses. After Industrial Revolution little did it occur to us that we still had fellow human beings to look after. The relief we had from doing things with machines was electrifying. Yet Human beings and the environment were degraded. It took us time to realise the damage to make amend.

Globalisation, dictatorship of the free market had made us neglect the duty of care to our fellow human beings. We have withdrawn to hide behind HT abandoning the Financial Houses to do our jobs and duties to our citizens and the lands we love and have tools to look after. We have to do something to look after the dwellers of global village. We have seen that even the air requires to be regulated for good quality. Similarly the global village and the free market must be reined in. Globalisation is the Result of new Technology that must be regulated to absorb Human Beings to protect His means of Living and jobs. Economy inflicts heavy penalty on corruption, crime, wastage and fiddling. The Economy wants everybody to labour for his or her existence. Confucius says, "He who fails to labour will come to agony".

We must not abandon them. We must devise means to regulate them. While the collapse of the Financial Houses is a reminder to the employers in these Institutions and their important role they play in the global village. These people are key workers of the new IT and new HT global information Technology village. They need our support and regulation. The risk of allowing a few to use the power of Capitalism to control the free market is immense. It is not wealth that we should emphasise at the moment. Resources are limited. We should not boast about wealth. We should promise that we will engage global youth to work and sacrifice to replace what we have lost. The Bank Managers and Fund administrators overpaid huge bonuses to themselves even in poorly performing businesses. We must modify the Market and Capitalism to embrace all Participants.

Employers and employees and lay people in the community should be Board members and jointly manage enterprises. This is a new concept as the collapse of the business affects all of them. The sole business of the Board is to ensure that the Business is not abused to grind down due to malpractices or incompetence of the Managers. The Board should be the ear and the eye of the Community on the Business. Democracy is synonymous with corruption and crime. Demo dictatorship is constitutional rule. The well-written and easily understood and interpreted secular constitution approved in a referendum takes charge of law and order. Free and independent Judiciary uses the constitution to maintain law and order. The politicians and business leaders are watchdogs over the Judiciary to ensure that they are clean. A committee of equal numbers of politicians and business leaders and members of the Judiciary supervise both the Judiciary and Parliament. Everybody must be equal before the law and sustain the same penalty points.

The World of Finance:

The World of Finance is a jungle to most of us. We are facing global collapse. We are facing unsolicited global Economic collapse. We seem to have been fumbling into it. Global Economic recession seems to be laughing at us. What is money? These are guaranteed tokens selected and defined with certainty for use in trade and exchange of services and goods. The Jews pioneered the loan and lending business despite the fact that their religion rejects lending with usury. The Jews went through all manners of castigations. It soon became necessary that modern communities, city states, cosmopolitans needed modern Banking Facilities to make cash easily available for business.

Over the years Banking has become sophisticated and tends to follow the traditions of the holy knights. It is fast becoming a secret occult practice of mysticism. Yet Banking should be as transparent as possible. There is melt-down of our stock exchange and savings. The crises here are difficult to tract down. Very little human error may be highlighted. Very little group involvement can be fingered upon. It is implosion of the system. It is spontaneous. Free Market Capitalism requires regulation. It requires mixed Economy. It requires regulating body of honest people. The annual jamboree of shareholders meetings have got to change. Small investors must have their voice heard in these meetings. Big financial transactions must be approved by Board.

The CEO and his top officials must check and be sure that the borrowers are genuine. The collaterals must be verified, right and adequate. Each Bank must handle volume of business it can deal with. No Bank should exert itself beyond what it can afford to wreck in the margin. Orderly and sustainable method of doing business is essential. No panic is involved. Funds invested on Projects must be just adequate and each Project must be completed and used before making further investments.

The depositors pay their deposits to the Banks for safety to avoid malpractices and obtain good borrowing conditions to avoid loan sharks. Wholesale Banking had evolved from this. In addition to these sophisticated insurance methods had equally developed to provide additional security. Still people go further to establish off shore banking to hide their money from the tax men. The word security stands above all others. The age of plc and public shares liability had come to have share owners who rely on profits from their investments. Banking had never really been free from occasional frauds and misfortunes due to human errors. Do we have human beings with total commitment to security to run our Banks? Can we evolve a system that will give us authority to regulate these Banks? Modern businesses require speed but speed must not compromise security. How do we evolve regulatory security as blanket seal for our Banking business? How can we justify linking global money to the US dollar? Is it not time the world re-defines money and give us abstract value for money. It will mean that each person will know when he or she has money or not have money.

Subjecting ownership of money to deals must be resisted. Linking global money to the dollar is deal that reaps the belly of security in Banking. We have talked extensively about Banking reward. Bonuses should not fling the Bank door open to the top officials. The Authorities who design salaries Banking and Fund Managers have a duty to define their real remunerations. The Bonus Culture ill understood by Bank Employers and Government Officials and allowing Bank and Fund Managers free access to Depositors' Deposits. Definite salaries should be given to Managers in Banking and Fund holding without ambiguity and temptation to manipulate the market to generate private funds for their benefits. Lack of clarity had led to high handed practices in Banking and Financial Stock Exchange Market Fraudulent Practices. Significant losses had been treated with secrecy and profits declared in their places to report success to pay bonuses while piling up losses undeclared.

The culture of secrecy in Banking and Fund Management allows our Financial Institutions to be run as cults and old Knight Order. Regulation must tackle the Culture of Secrecy and Speculation. The bosses of the Financial Institutions, Bank Executives, Insurance Brokers and Fund Managers seem to be addicted to huge bonuses. Bonuses are open keys to the safes in the Banks. They allow financial Managers access to funds to take for personal use. People who work in Financial Sector must have standard fixed salaries for remuneration compatible with their work and experience. The spin and propaganda of head hunting are a ruse. These people are not egg-heads. They are workers in Finances. The Political and top Administrative officials seem to be short of ideas on how to regulate the Financial Institutions because they benefit from the lack or laxity of regulations. They are non-executive directors of these Institutions. They get their shares of the bonuses. They do not want to lose these.

Financial Institutions must be transparent and open in their conduct. Wealth must now be defined as the land and its resources, the education and skills of the people and crime free community. Crime ridden community is poor and not rich. Human beings have a duty to watch over their behaviours. Your freedom is as important as the freedom of others around you. Your business conduct must be transparent. Worldwide programmes must be embarked upon. Soft touch and dapping the soiling are not what we want. This is not time for asset mopping and stripping. We need integrated development. We may seize this opportunity to embark on radical development. Human character is important for law and order in the human community. There is no such thing as free. There is no free market. Creation is under natural laws.

Nature likes diversity. Even Charles Darwin's evolution of Natural Selection had not excluded Diversity. The genes predetermine the maintenance of balance and diversity. The intelligent designer concept equally respects diversity. Whatever is our concept of the creation is synonymous with maintenance of the Balance and Diversity. The market must be mixed and regulated. The dictatorship of the market is a recipe for chaos. The market traders must be under the rule of law. He has to justify his conduct of business in accordance to law. Where do we keep the Politicians who know little bits but claim tremendous experience and knowledge? Yes the Economic crises are serious. Yes the threat to Economy is serious. Obviously they are serious. They need urgent action. We cannot afford to sit over them any longer. We need immediate action to put out this fire burning and destroying our Economy and business. We have no time to wait. It is emergency. It requires immediate emergency response. The presence of predetermined genes makes free choice not free. Human regulation is by choice. Most cancers are familial. We cannot just opt out. This is good because we can cope with regulation. I appeal sincerely to all that nobody should take this as a tirade on them. Rather we should be magnanimous to accept our failures as fallible human beings. We all should unite and join hands together to rescue Africa. We must provide genuine education and adequate skills training to all Africans.

The Africans must work for the development of their continent and their plight. They must avoid duplications and wastage of their scarce funds and resources. They must devise practical means to tackle crimes and corruption. Nothing replaces orderly and sustainable development. Rash costly and wasteful projects are filthy drains consuming your resources. Avoid them even though they can be attractive and ensnaring. Good education, knowledge and productive skills and hard work shall certainly ferry us across this desolate sea and desert of want to the fertile land. Africa is rich and fertile but we just have to find the key to the barn and treasure house. We Africans are lazy and do not work. We run around the world looking for cheap money and wealth. A working nation has good maintenance service and well maintained farms and healthy livestock.

ANCIENT AFRICA:

The first origin of man took its root from Africa. History of Africa dates back further than all others on earth. Anthropology Palaeontology, andArchaeology had shown that the original human beings of the type we find on earth came fro Africa. They were initially not many. They lived in gatherings. They scavenged life out of what they gathered from the environment from kills by carnivorous animals. Gradually they used stone tools and fire in hunting and gathering food for themselves. They are located mainly to south-east Africa. Genetic evidence claims their existence to 60,000 years ago. Africa was the only place on earth modern humans inhabited about 60,000 years ago. They grew in numbers and spread around Arabian Peninsula and India and all the way to Australasia, several Ocean islands except Antarctica. Still a number of people remained in Africa. The advanced migrant populations took up habitations in several places and grew up and adapted to their new environments perhaps in response to Darwinian Theory of evolution of Natural Selection. Meanwhile the population staying back in Africa frequently migrated in waves to places where the initial migrants went to find settled and adapted populations. These may be friendly or receptive or frankly hostile. People still drifted across West Asia following animal herds and fertile lands.

The Ice Age came with climate change in Africa and other places became hot. The Sahara Desert started to develop. Food became scarce. Up to 6,000 BC people were herding animals and farming. As farming expanded the population grew. Clusters of people opted for groups with leaders and formed kingdoms to differentiate them from other groups. The first African kingdom was Egypt. The King was the Pharaoh. The Pharaoh built temples and Pyramids. They made decrees and controlled the people. They started trading with their neighbours, made friendship and treaties. They expanded by mutual travels and visits by war and annexation. They opened roads for trade. The kingdom of Kush (modern Sudan) developed along the Upper Nile.

They traded with Egypt, Babylon, Harapans and the Aryans in India. About 1550 BC Egyptians defeated Kush and formed a new Kingdom. They ruled for for 450 years before its collapse in 1100 BC. Kush again became free 715 BC under King Piankhy, an able leader conquered Egypt. African migrants returned from West Asia with skills in iron monger and were able to make new tools to conquer people without such tools. This is not accurate as the Egyptian civilisation seems to have predated most others. The Egyptians had crafts to explore the Mediterranean Sea. They had a lot of tools for farming and constructions. Hence Africans must have had skills in metallurgy and tools trade. It is hence very likely that they invented a number of common metals and very significant is the fact that the bellows for extracting metals seems to have been invented in Africa.

THE ANCIENT WORLDS GREAT CIVILISATIONS:

They all took this pattern in all global continents, Africa, Asia, Europe, Eurasia, Australasia, Several Ocean Islands and even at the fringes of frozen Arctic and Antarctica regions. We must observe that human population on earth has always been dynamic. People fan out and spread and they fan out and return to those they left behind in their first sojourn. Those who think of global population as static are mistaken. There is always forward and backward movement and population mixing. The habit gene seems to common origin of man on earth.

The Phoenicians returned to North Africa about 700 BC. During the age of expansion the Phoenicians had spread around the Mediterranean and had settlements in Sicily and other parts of Italy and North Africa that evolved into the city state of Carthage. There also some Greek settlers in North Africa, along the Balkan Sea coast and Sicily and Italy. These were people at the trading posts, disconnected youths looking for new and better life and people that left overcrowded cities in search of new settlements. They founded the City State of Carthage and dominated the Mediterranean Trade. The Assyrians from West Asia defeated Egypt about 664 BC. The Kushites learnt how to make iron tools from the Assyrians and became more powerful. The Persians, non-Maritime power conquered the Phoenicians a Maritime trading nation, Tyre, Siddon, Akka and Byblos (Lebanon) 539 BC. Carthage became an independent Kingdom ruling most of Western Mediterranean, Sicily, much of Spain and Catalonia. The population in Africa grew. By 300 BC Bantus population emerged along the River Niger in West Africa now Nigeria and Cameroons with small area of fertile land between the rain forest and the Sahara Desert. The Bantus spread out to other parts of Africa South and East through rain forest to grassland.

Europe too became overcrowded. The Romans invaded North Africa about 200s BC (146 BC). The Patriotic African Carthaginian General Hannibal Hamilcar Barca accepted call to duty and fought and tormented the Roman War Mongers. The Romans through corruption and bribery and traditional African failure to unite to fight invaders seriously the Romans defeated Carthage by brutal genocide and seized North Africa including Egypt. This single event changed the destiny of the world. It started the current global strife, violence and wars.

At the same time political changes took place in Africa south of the Sahara. A new kingdom called Aksum (modern Ethiopia) seized Kush. They traded with Parthians, India and the Romans. Recall Ethiopia had been part of the Judaic Religion long before the Romans accepted the Christian faith. Equally they were Christians before the Romans. Hence the Romans were trading with Christian Aksum. The Bantus took East Coast of Africa and some grassland in southern Africa in 400 AD. In West Africa there were relatively seasonal navigable rivers, the Niger, Senegal and the Volta. They made boats for fishing and transport. Malaria and Yellow fever became endemic and the people developed partial immunity to them. Most people in Nigeria had the skills of working with iron. They were iron smiths long before 400-200 BC. Bantus mean people in their languages. Bantus occupied South Africa-Khoikhot and San people farm their livestock, sheep and cattle. The hunters and gatherers were driven further into the desert. The farmers and livestock settled farmers built various types of sheds for their families and community started to grow. Leadership, politics, trade and commerce all started.

Some Bantus stayed back in West Africa. They developed Djenne, Djeno Mali and Niger in West Africa 250 AD. Djenne and Djeno Mali buried their dead in tall pots that they traded along the Niger. By 500 BC 20,000 people in Djenne Djeno Mali lived in small villages in clusters of ironsmiths coppersmiths and metal workers. They travelled between 1000 kilometres (600 miles) and 750 kilometres (450 miles). East Africa, Tanzania, Kenya traded with North Africa, India, West Asia, China and the Roman Guide Book Periplus Erythraen Sea written in Greek 50 AD showed Ports in Kenya. Shanga in 700 AD brought Muslim Islam and a Mosque existed in 800-900 AD with Swahili as the language of communication. By 1005 AD East Africa Coastal Ports traded with Fatimids in Egypt, Abbasids in West Asia and Muslim India. They minted gold, silver and copper coins. Some Fatimids Dinars (1066 AD) were found in Ntambe, Mkuu in Tanzania. They traded on produce of gold, furs from cattle, rock metals and ivory in exchange for cheap Asian jewellery, glass beads, Chinese porcelain and cotton goods. In 1320 AD African ruler, in Kilwa Tanzania, al-Hasan.ibn Suleiman built himself stone palace of coral. North African traveller and writer, ibn.Battula visited al-Hassan 1500 AD. The Portuguese had gradually invaded and taken over East African Coastal trade diminishing Muslim and Indian influence.

BERBERS:

These were the first inhabitants of the North African Coast. They were Nomadic shepherds and cattle herders. They spoke Hermitic language related to ancient Egyptian language and is a genetic mix from West Asia and Southern Africa. They frequently invaded Egypt and Libya. About 800 BC Phoenicians returned Western Asia to North Africa to set up the City State of Carthage (modern Tunisia). Carthage had good port and excellent military location and facilities. It was located in the narrowest part of the Mediterranean opposite Sicily. Its Navy controlled Sicily and Carthage and shipping in the Mediterranean. Carthage became independent State when the Persians defeated Phoenicia in 500s BC. Carthage controlled Sicily and Spain and made a lot of profits from silver mining in Spain. By 300 BC Carthage was actively involved in policing whole Mediterranean. It made treaties with the Etruscans in Italy to protect them from Greek pirates from Southern Italy. There was continuous war with Greeks in Sicily for control of the island. About 200s BC Carthage had to contain the expanding power and militarism of the Roman Empire. This led to the Punic Wars which should be described as European African Wars: 1st, 2nd, and 3rd Wars. These finally led to expulsion of African Carthaginians from Europe, Sicily and Spain and destruction of Carthage by genocide. The Romans seized North Africa. Julius Caesar by 50 BC a strong advocate of African-European integration and not conquest and subjugation restored Carthage to status of Roman City under all Emperors.

North Africa became important part of Roman Empire. Unfortunately this took place at the height of rivalry among the Roman leaders and Senators. Julius Caesar was eventually assassinated. North Africa supplied wheat, olive and pottery to Rome and all over the Western half of Roman Empire. This trade continued until 400s AD when the vandals defeated North Africa and set up their Kingdoms. Eastern Roman Empire reconquered North Africa in 500s AD but trade remained weak until the Muslim Islamic invasion and defeat of North Africa in 600s AD and the establishment of the Umayyad and then Fatimid dynasty. Under the Islamic Muslims, North Africa again became important trade centre again. Carthage was abandoned in favour of new Muslim cities like Tunis. Camel caravan trade developed across the Sahara and sub-Saharan Africa Ghana and Mali trading in gold, salt and slaves.

By 1100s AD North Africa became free under Almohad dynasty and about 1200s AD it broke up into smaller Kingdoms corresponding modern countries in North Africa under the Hafsids: in the East Libya, Tunisia, Abd-al- Wadids in the Middle (Algeria and Marinids), in the West (Morocco). All traded with Italy: Genoa, Piza, Venice. The Ottoman Empire annexed North Africa 1500s AD.

ANCIENT AFRICA BLACK KINGS:

As previously stated the world did not start in the West Europe, Rome, Asia, India as we may be tempted to assume. Rather Genetic Research, Anthropology and Archaeology Studies had revealed that first modern human beings appeared and lived in East-South Africa. From here they (Homosapiens) spread to cover the whole world except the Antarctica. The population of about 200,000 or 100,000 people, animal and plant food gatherers started to spread all over the global continents.

THE AFRICAN BLACK KINGS:

They featured mainly in the 25th dynasty of Egyptian Pharaoic reign. King Taharqa, one of the Nubians, ruled 690-664 BC. Timelines of Nubian Royalty Rulers of Egypt's 25th dynasty and ancient Nubian relates to Anu the first inhabitants of Egypt as stated by Swiss Archaeologists, Prof Bonnet and Dr Mathieu Honegger. They discovered palaces, temples and extraordinary tombs and massive ancient cities on the bank of the Nile in Northern Sudan (Kerma). Civilisation arose out of ancient pastoral culture that flourished in that part of Sudan since 7500 BC when the first settlements were established as confirmed by cemetery 3800-3100 BC. King Awawa one of the earliest Nubian rulers known by name 2000-1850 BC was a powerful Nubian ruler in Kerma. Under Nedjeh in the 13th dynasty of Egypt the kingdom underwent political upheaval and withdrew from Nubian. In the North the Hyksos took control of the lower Nile in the South. Some Egyptian soldiers stayed and served the Kushites. One inscription recovered an Egyptian soldier stated that he served as a gallant soldier washing his feet in company of Nedjeh.

Massive assault by the King of Kush and his allies from the land of Punt subdued Egypt and al Kab in the 17th dynasty 1575-1525 BC. Alara and Queen Kasaga (785-760 BC) united Upper Nubia and became founder of Nubian Power in Napalatan dynasty. In the beginning 25th dynasty King Kasta and Queen Pebatsma 760-747 BC brother of King Alara, Ruler of Napatan Kush and Egypt started to seize bit by bit Egypt from Libyan Pharaohs. Then there came an able leader el-Kurutsab 8, King Piankhy and his wife Queen Aqaluga and Tubing son of Kasta (747-706 BC) conquered all Egypt and retained it until his death. He preferred alliances and treaties. Piankhy ruled for about thirty years. He was buried in Egyptian styled pyramid with horses the Napatan Nubians prized highly. W M Flinders states in his History of Egypt part 31896p. 308 states that Daughter Chepmupe 11 and Qushata, Taharqa Napatan Nubian rulers represented the old civilisation of Upper Egypt. They were clear descendants of Amon Ore Osiris and rightful successors to the throne XV11 and X1Xth dynasties true Kings of Egypt rather than Libya (usurpers) from Nile Delta attempting to dominate Nile Valley from no man's land. Taharqa son and 3rd successor of King Pye was greatest Nubian Pharaoh. He smashed his way and seized Palestine to the confluence of the blue and white Nile about 684 BC. Nile floods and their fertile lands made Egypt very prosperous. The Christian Bible mentions Taharq (Tirhaka) in Isaiah 37 vv 8 and 9; 2nd King 9 vv 8 and 9). He was a great warrior. He fought battles for 20 years against the Assyrians from West Asia. Assyrians eventually conquered Egypt and Kush 667 BC and Nubia lost control of Egypt. Taharqa died 664 BCE. He was buried in Nuri Pyramid 150 ft high, the largest in Sudan. Egypt was very fertile area of Africa about 40, 000 years ago and was overcrowded around the Mediterranean. It needed Government to unite the whole land. Around 3000 BC (5000 years ago) Egypt united under a ruler called the Pharaoh. It remained united until it was defeated by Persia in 525 BC. Egyptian History is divided into 6 periods.

PERIODS IN EGYPTIAN HISTORY:

Old Kingdom
First Intermediate Period
Middle Kingdom
The Second Intermediate Period
Intermediate Kingdom Period
Third Intermediate Period.

Old Kingdom (2686-2160 BC) united Egypt about 3000 BC and created Pharaoic Rule in Egypt. The Pharaoh ruled over Upper Egypt in the south. He quickly took control over his subjects and the land. He ruled from the capital Memphis. He constructed irrigation

Projects, built palaces, temples and Pyramids. This is speculated to be associated with Sumer civilisation.

First Intermediate Period (2160-2040 BC) ended the Old Kingdom. The lower level of rich people revolted against the excessive power of the Pharaohs. The Pharaohs ruled through Government Officials who grabbed power and were autocratic at times and corrupt. Some Government Construction Projects collapsed. Institutional Anarchy prevailed. There was scarcity and the nobles were forced to go out and worked in the fields. Murders and crimes prevailed. It is speculated that drought and famine might have occurred.

Middle Kingdom Egypt (2040-1633 BC). After several years of wars between Upper Egypt (South) and Lower Egypt (North) Upper Egypt won and united Egypt again in 2000 BC with the capital sited at Thebes in the South a new capital south of Memphis. The Pharaohs ignored behaving as god-king but rather were shepherds of the people. The Nomarchs were powerful local officials and Jerusalem, Jericho and Syria first came under Egyptian jurisdiction. They traded with Byblos near Beirut in Phoenicia.

Second Intermediate Period (1786-1558):

Around 1786 BC the Hyksos from Western Asia invaded Egypt and set up the 2nd Intermediate Period. They took over control of Eastern Part of the Nile Delta (North Eastern Egypt) closest to Asia. They took the capital back to Memphis. The Hyksos spoke Semitic language which was related to the Hebrew language. It is speculated that they were Amorites from the region of Israel and Syria. The Hyksos ruled well for a hundred years but the rulers in Thebes reconquered North Egypt. The brothers Kamose and Ahmose fought both the Hyksos and the Nubian Africans who succeeded in re-uniting Egypt.

N Kingdom (1558-1085 BC)

Ahmose (Kamose) died before the re-unification but a new period took place in the 18th dynasty. There was trade with Western Asia. The Egyptian Army seized much of Israel and Syria fighting the

Hittites (Turks), from Anatolia, Assyrians, and built great Temples. There arose powerful Queens one of whom was Queen Hatshepsut actually became a Pharaoh 1490 BC. In 1363 BC the Pharaoh Akhenaton built himself a new capital at Amarna and introduced a new sun god. He declared the concept of one God and introduced new Arts. Akhenaton married Nefertiti but they had no children. Therefore at their demise the son in law Tutankhamen took over as the Pharaoh. In 1333 BC Tutankhamen returned the capital to Memphis and re-introduced the worship of Amon Ore Osiris. In 1303 BC a new Northern dynasty family of Pharaohs took over the 19th Egyptian dynasty and their first King was Ramses. He returned to Memphis in the North. Under Ramses the Priest became very powerful. They traded with Hittites in Western Asia. The 20th dynasty Pharaohs adopted the same policy were all called Ramses. They fought off assaults from Libya and West Asia the sea people and Hittites about 1100 BC. There was Economic collapse (Boom and Burst) Eastern Mediterranean and West Asia. The New kingdom collapsed.

Third Intermediate Period (1085-525 BC:

Hittites- Mycenaean cultures collapsed. The last Ramses died in 1085 BC and Egypt fell apart again. The sea peoples, Philistines, Lycians, Achaeans and (possibly Trojans) again assaulted Egypt. The sea peoples driven out but Egypt still collapsed. Egypt lost control over Israel and Lebanon. (Moses and uprising of the Jews took place during the rule of the Ramses). Different Kings ruled in the North and South. Nubia became independent and had its own king. Egyptian territories, Israel had its own King David and Solomon and Syria had its own king too. The Northern Kingdom grew richer and prosperous than the South. Egypt still remained militarily weak and Libya kept own harassing it. The Chief Priest of Amun Ore had his headquarters in Thebes. About 715 BC black Sudanese Kushite King from South of Egypt, Piankhy invaded and captured much of Egypt. He started the 25th Dynasty of Egyptian Pharaohs. The Kushite Rule lasted not long as the Assyrians from West Asia invaded and drove out the Kushites in 664 BC. The Assyrians could not control Egypt effectively as their capital NENIVEH was too far from Egypt. Soon another group of Libyan Kings with Greek allies Lydian soldiers succeeded in forming 26th dynasty at Saites in North

Egypt. In 609 BC the Assyrian Epire was collapsing and the Saites Kings managed to recaptured Israel and Syria. In 605 BC the Babylonian king Nebuchadnezzar defeated Egypt and Israel and Syria. In 525 BC Persia from West Asia defeated Egypt and took over its control.

GREEK RULE (332-30 BC):

In 332 BC Alexander, son of Philip of Macedonia marched against Persia. He drove them out of Greek Territories and seized all Territories of the Persian Empire including Egypt. Alexander made Egypt part of his new Empire. He, however, died of Malaria or typhoid feverish illness in Afghanistan, Pakistan or India 323 BC at about the age of 43 years. Alexander had no children. His Empire was divided among his Generals at his death. Ptolemy took Egypt. Ptolemy dynasty continued until Octavius, Caesar Augustus autocratic Roman Emperor nominated "god" by his sycophant Senators and cronies took over Egypt from the last Ptolemaic ruler, Cleopatra. The Ptolemy recaptured Israel and Syria and introduced Hellenistic culture into Egypt while the Egyptians were allowed to speak their language and worship their God.

Persian Rule in Egypt lasted 525-332 BC. They defeated the Libyans in 525 BC. Egypt revolted with the help of Athens in 484 and again in 460 BC but without success. Persia became weak and in 404 BC Egypt became free from Persia. Yet Egyptian Dynasties 28, 29, and 30 were weak. The 29th Dynasty made alliance with Sparta and Sparta was to be rewarded with wheat but Persia seized the wheat. Egypt and Sparta, however, defeated Persia. Athens weakened by Peloponnesian war. 30th Dynasty attempted to re-unite Egypt but Persia resubjugated it in 341 BC and retained it 63 years. In 332 BC Alexander sacked Persian Empire.

THE GREEKS AND THEIR CITY-STATES:

The Greeks had free citizens and slaves among their populations but they paid no attention to slave status. The slaves were frequently free while free people frequently lost their freedom and became slaves. The Greeks had always had

an Assembly in their city States and power rested only with free Greek adult male. The Greeks had overseas contact in the 6th and 7th century BC. They had several settlements in North Africa and in the East along the Black Sea. Oligarchs had power. One of them frequently became the tyrant and made laws for people to obey. External contacts developed trade. This brought wealth and prosperity. Great constructions took place. They built huge temples. They were polytheistic and had many deities and their temples such as the ones in Hera on Samos Artemis in Ephesus and Olympian Zeus in Athens. The discovery of new letters was a great incentive for both the city state assemblies and aspiring scholars and writers. The city states published laws on large stone tablets. Poetry flourished immensely. Iliad and Odyssey of Homer, the poems of Hesiod started to appear at the scene in the 7th century BC. The great lyric poets followed the trail. Among these were Archilochus, Ancreon and Sappho. Certain religious sanctuaries such as Olympia and Delphi sprang up and became places of pilgrimage for leaders of pan-Hellenic communities. In the last three decades of the 5th century BC saw the surge in Greek literary achievements in the works of Aeschylus, Sophocles and Euripides in the tragedy of Aristophanes and comedies for performance at festivals, such as City Dionysia and Lnaea. Herodotus, the famous Historian lived in Athens. Athens was the Greek maritime power in the Mediterranean and provided jobs and employments for the youths. It became the focal point for the sophists (teachers with fee-paying students), the philosophers, and rhetoricians. Thucydides was the Athenian city state historian. Herodotus reported with Greek flare, on most of the events in the Mediterranean areas. Ancient Greek culture reached its peak at about the 5th century BC. This period produced most fascinating relics of Western civilisation from the Bronze Age through the Hellenistic Period from the evidence the Palaeontologists and Archaeologists had found. Greek Myths are introduced by statutes, carvings and illustrations. Most Ancient Greek Books are rich in vivid colourful photographs for kids and adults. We can learn about politics, power and government in the City-State of Athens- the legendary Heracles, temples and home life. This Ancient culture has grown into modern life in Science, Medicine and the Olympic Games. The City-States had different types of

Governments. Greek people had different ideas about what made good Governments. Aristotle undertook the study of Governments various people used in the Mediterranean Region. He preferred the African Carthaginian system which had voting for the Committee of Hundred. He proceeded to divide the Ancient Greek Governments into Monarchy, Oligarchy, Tyranny and Democracy. All Greek City-States had Monarchies in late Bronze Age 2000-1200 BC. Homer's Iliad and Greek Mythology mention a series of Greek Kings such as Agamemnon and Theseus and some of their palaces had survived for Archaeologists to dig up for us to see. After the Dark Ages some of the Greek City-States and their Monarchies did not survived. Sparta, which, apparently, had two kings, one for war and the other for home administration, survived. In the Archaic Period Oligarchies ruled most City-States. The Oligarchies were rich aristocrats and traders. They gave orders to other citizens to do what the Oligarchy wanted. Tyrants ruled over most City-States in 600s-500s BC. Tyrants usually seized power from the Oligarchy by one of them bribing the commoners for support to rule alone. The ruled like Kings without authority. In 510 BC the State of Athens adopted Democracy and soon other Greek City-States also adopted it. It is clear that beyond Greece some outside City-States such as Carthage and some Regions in Africa practised Democracy before the Greek City-States. Even Rome experimented in Democracy by giving the poor more power.

Xerxes, King of Persia invaded Greece. This opened Greek eyes and brought the Greek city states together led by Athens that had the fleet. They stood together and fought Xerxes. After the war, Athens city state Empire developed and grew. The Peloponnese that included Sparta grew uneasy. Led by Sparta they started the Peloponnesian war. Each side enlisted Persian assistance in turn; the war lasted 27 years. In 387 BC the Persian king attempted to impose peace settlement on Greece. The subsequent thirty years witnessed a triumvirate of Athens, Sparta and Thebes each vying for power and dominance. The Peloponnesian war weakened both sides. In 359 BC Philip the 2nd became the king of Macedon. King Philip 2nd of Macedon seized the opportunity to unite both sides of

the city states into Greece. He gained control of Thrace in the east and Thessaly in the south. This enabled him to unite and control Greece. The Sacred War raged from 356-46 BC. Macedon became the focus of power in Greece. He defeated the Athenians and the Thebans at Chaeronea in 338 BC and imposed peace settlement on the whole of Greece. He died 2 years later and Alexander, his heir took over loosely united Greece.

ATHENIAN DEMOCRACY:

Athenian Democracy embraced free Athenian adult men but excluded women, children, slaves and foreigners and people from Athenian fringe empire. Most Greek City-States kept Monarchies, Oligarchies and Tyrannies.

ATHENS AND ITS PROGRESS IN GREEK CIVILISATION:

Athens was a town in Central Greece chosen because of its location with good seaport (at Piraeus) and a steep Hill that made it easy to defend. Athens was already important Greek City by Late Bronze Age. It appears in Homer's Iliad as a Kingdom of Theseus. Mycenaean Palace and pottery had been found in Athens. Athens like other Greek cities declined. The old palace was abandoned but the Athenians were happy as unlike others they were not sacked like Sparta and Corinth by alien forces. In the Archaic Period, about 900 BC Athens recovered again and emerged as Oligarchy after the Dark Ages. A group of rich men, aristocrats got together to form a government and make laws and decide everything in the community. The system of Government weighed down everybody but favoured the rich. In 631 BC DRACO was serving in the Athenian Government then called ARCHON. DRACO was a rich aristocrat. He ordered the poor to write down the laws for everybody. He wanted everybody to understand the laws and the rich people in the Oligarchy wouldn't just make laws that would favour them. The laws allowed killing the poor even for petty crimes like stealing cabbage. The poor had different penalties for the crimes from the rich. The rich had lighter punishment than the poor. A poor woman owing money to a rich man was to be sold into slavery to recover the debt. A rich man owing money to a woman was let go lightly. Most Athenians were deluded with the laws. They were angry and disapprove of the laws as unfair. They complained against the debt bondage- being sold into slavery to recoup debt.

In 594 BC Athenians chose another rich aristocrat, Solon to head the ARCHON. The Oligarchy warned him to do everything to prevent citizens becoming mad with them but to retain power for them. Herodotus, the Greek Historian wrote about DRACO and SOLON. Solon changed the law and abolished the debt bondage, nobody was to be sold to pay debt. He cancelled debts and re-distributed the land. The citizens were able to farm on their land and prosper. Solon abolished death penalty except for murder but the Oligarchy kept all their power and land. Solon started an Assembly where adult free Greek male could go and vote on any issue of concern to him. Solon elected to choose the judges by lottery. Women were excluded from the Assembly members and judges. Solon made it illegal for parents to abuse their children. People settled down and the aristocrats retained power. Solon laws gave the people lands and made them not owe. Then people started to subvert the laws. People started to lose their lands and debts returned and started to mount again. Citizens became enraged especially in defeat in wars.

In 560 BC another aristocrat, Pisistratus canvassed for support from other people for him to take over the Oligarchy to rule as a tyrant. He promised them that he would solve their problems. Pisistratus seized power and made good his promise to some extent even though the Oligarchy was struggling to get rid of him. Pisistratus levied equal taxes on all. He made Government lend money at fair rates of interest to farmers. He used tax money to build roads and new public water fountains and new temples. Pisistratus died in 528 BC. He was succeeded by his son Hippias (and possibly his brother, Hipparchus) as new tyrants. The name means Horse guys meaning they were rich people as only the rich had horses. Two people, Harmodius and Aristogliton attempted to get rid of the tyranny and seize power back to the Oligarchy. They requested for help from the Priest at the Festival of Athena's Birthday. They succeeded in murdering Hipparchus in 514 BC but Hippias became suspicious.

Eventually the Athenians got rid of the Tyranny in 508 BC. HIPPIAS escaped to Persia. They asked Aiconaeonids, the Priestess of Delphi to tell Sparta to help them get rid of Hippias. The Greeks got rid of Hippias and tyranny.

THE ALCONAEONIDS FAMILY:

CLEISTHENES started to institute his political system and Programme. Cleisthenes wanted power for himself but he just did not want another tyranny. He sold the new Government to free adult Greek male as their own. They could change things they did not like. Cleisthenes introduced DEMOCRACY to Athens. He did this after seeing Governments in other places including Carthage in Africa do it. Cleisthenes was very enthusiastic for Democracy. It is a bit of bias to give the credit for Democracy to the Greeks alone. Definitely the Greeks did a lot of Research by Aristotle before choosing DEMOCRACY as Government. It is speculated that Cleisthenes even gave the name Democracy to this new form of Government.

ATHENIAN DEMOCRACY:

It included free Greek adult male but excluded women, children, slaves, aliens and people in Greek Fringe Empire. Ordinary free Greek male adults voted in all important decisions including going to war. They attended the Greek Assembly (Greek Ekklesia) on a Hill Pnyx to take part in deciding all issues. Ekklesia had 6000 free adult men as members. The Ekklesia met monthly except in Emergency. The Athenians also chose 500 people by lottery to the Boule. The Boule met more frequently and drew bills that Ekklesia would deal with. The Boule enforced the laws, repaired the laws, public stoas, temples and build ships for the Navy at war. They also examined the quality of laws in the Statute Books and deleted them. The Greeks also appointed members of Special Committees who took care of Specific Matters. One of these was the Archon selected by lottery. They were nine in number and took care of Religious matters and Public Sacrifices. The Assembly elected ten Strategols (Generals) every year. The Strategols commanded the Athenian Navy and Army. The Strategols ruled over Athens during the Peloponnesian War just as the USA President. Pericles was the most famous Strategol known. Others include Themistocles and Alcibiades.

JUDICIARY:

Free Greek men volunteered to sit on the Jury. 6000 free Greek male sat in the Assembly every year. 500 free Greeks sat on the Jury daily to hear cases. The Jury deliberated on criminal and landed Property cases. They settled cases by simple majority. Socrates was tried in this manner. Plato had 30 silver to pay his fine but Socrates refused.

SPARTA was a town in Southern Greece. It was already there in late Bronze Age mentioned in Homer's Odyssey- kingdom of Menelaus. Sparta declined in the Dark Ages as other cities but recovered about 900 BC in the Archaic Period. Sparta had 2 kings. Sparta subjugated Messenia and brutally enslaved the. They called the "Helots". They forced them to farm for the so that male Spartans concentrated on practising Militarism. At 7 male children moved into Hostels. Their commanders exposed them to hardships underfeeding and scanty covering with blankets. They taught them the use of swords and spears. The females remained with their parents and were tough and practised house craft.

CORINTH was a Mycenaean town at the junction between Northern and Southern Greece. Mycenaean Pottery was found in excavations. Jason and Medea lived in Corinth in Greek Mythology. Corinth declined in the Dark Ages but recovered in the Archaic Period. Corinth had Oligarchy as its Government. Corinth traded in glass jars, perfumes, wines, pottery and furs with West Asia, other Greek cities and Italy. They hired Phoenician boats to convey some of their goods. Ships were towed across the road to cover 2 ports.

CENTRAL ASIANS IN ANCIENT INDIAN LITERATURE:

Ancient India and Central Asia have long tradition of social-cultural, religious, political and economic contact since recent antiquity. The two regions have common and contiguous border, climatic continuity, similar geographical features and geo-cultural affinity.

There have always been uninterrupted flows of people, material and ideas and ideas between the two. The relationship had been so close that ancient literary sources trace common lineage for Indians, Pakistan, Afghanistan, Iran and other nationalities of Central Asia.

The areas of information to look for are in:

Archaeological excavations, migrations from Central Asia into India, Central Asian people in Indian Classical Literature such as 3.1 Atharvaveda, 3.2 Sama Veda, 3.3 Aitereya Bramana, 3.4 Indian Epics (3.4.1Valmiki Ramayana & 3.4.2Mhabharata 3.5 Manusmriti, 3.6 Puranas 3.7 Madras Rakasdrahasa drama, 3.8 Raghuvamsha, 3.9 Rajtrangini, 3.10 Brahata Khataof Kshmendra, 3.11 Khata-Saritsagara of Somadeva, 3.12 Kavyamimamsa of Rajashekhara

4 References, 5. Books and Periodicals.

ARCHAEOLOGICAL EXCAVATIONS:

Archaeological excavations in the Amu valley of Uzbekistan, in Afrasiab on north-eastern edge of Samarkand some other places in Uzbekistan, Turkmenistan, Kazakhstan and Tak-mak in Kirghizstan all yield evidence between Ancient India and Central Asia within remote antiquity. Further extensive excavations had revealed remarkable results at Kara Tepa, Dalverzin Tepa Yer Kurgan, Ak-Beshin, Kranayerez and Isyk-Ata. Manuscripts discovered at Xinjiang (China) and several documents had revealed that India and Eastern Central Asia of Xinjiang were politically, culturally, and religiously linked together. Indian Dynasties came from Central Asia. Indian Dynasty ruled in Khortan and other Central Asian Cities. It is difficult to ascertain why Indian people like to be ruled over and controlled by authorities. Is it part of their socio-political culture of class, castes, Philosophy or Religion? Regardless of their background all rulers are acceptable and tolerated even with affection in India. The original rulers of India were universal monarchs and ruled over India from Khortan and other Central Asian cities. It seems India has a tradition of maintaining law and order. They see their rulers and leaders as instrument of authority to maintain law and order. It is this socio-political culture that has supported the Indian Democracy today.

The Emperors of the Sangoku, the "Three Kingdoms," of India, China and Japan are sources of Great Civilisations in Southern and Eastern Asia. They hence matched the pretence of the Roman Emperors in the West. Indian civilisation, however, suffered a setback from the collapse of the Indus Valley Civilisation. Chinese civilisation started later than the Middle Eastern Civilisations. The recovery of Indian civilisation took place at the same time as the onset of Greek Civilisation instead of that of other civilisations such as the Sumerian. Surprisingly China reached the same level of civilisation at the same time, "the axial era" (800-400 BC). At the time the West, India and China had contact, it was India through the influence of Buddhism that had great influence on China. Japan adopted the Buddhist Philosophy and made it its own while India had the ill fortune of Muslim Islamic invasion and conquest. This introduced cultural and political divisions into India. India was polytheist (Hindusm, Buddhism and Jain etc). It was tolerant of religions and obedient and tolerant of its leaders while Islam was Monotheist Religion and intolerant of other faiths. The Sultans and Mullahs ruled from the Caliphates and executed the Shariah Laws. The only disruptive influence in China was the advent of Communism in 1949. India adopted post colonial Democracy synonymous with corruption and graft of capitalism and prone to foreign interference. China has retained Communism but adopted very liberal attitude towards business. Japan has traditionally been an insular territory of very progressive ingenious people. It defeated Russian in 1905. Japan then fought wars of subjugation with China and Korea and took on the US in the 1941-45 War. US dropped the nuclear bombs in Japan. Japan surrendered and suffered post war trauma until its industry recovered in the 80s when its GNP grew to be the highest in the world and made Japan an Economic Power. The Indian Rule seemed to have started from about 322-184 BC when Mauryas ruled over India while Kings of Lanka and Kandy reigned over Ceylon. Despite the brief period Alexander of Macedonia had in Asia he was able to plant Macedonian Kings to rule over India from Batria 256-55 BC. The rule of Sakas/Parthians 97 BC-125 AD took India across the rule of the Kushans 20 BC-260 AD, the Guptas 320-550 AD, Vardhanas of Thanesar 500-647 AD;

The Deccan, Carnatic and Maharashtra, 543-1317 AD, Karkot as of Kashmir 725-810 AD; Gurjara-Pratiharas of Ujjain and Dantidurga 725-1017 AD, the Chola Kingdom 846-1279; the age of the rules of the Sultans of Delhi 1206-1555 AD; Then followed the era of the Rajas and Sultans of Mysore 1100-1949. Vijayanagar 1336-1660 and the Sikh Gurus and Khalsa 1469-1849 who attempted to evolve a new religion from both Hindusm and Islam to replace both but failed. Then came the Moghuls of Central Asia, Persia 1526-1540, 1555-1858 AD; Maratha (Mahratta) Confederacy/Empire 1674-1848, Mawwabs of Carnatic at Arcot, Mawwabs of Bengal 1704-1765 AD; Titular Mawwabs of Bengal till 1969. Then came British Governors General 1765-1858 AD, Mawwabs of Oudh 1722-1856, Nizams of Hyrabad 1720-1948, British coin of India 1835-1947 AD. Then the British Emperors and Viceroys 1876-1947 or (1858-1950) The British also ruled with Governors-Ceylon, Burma, Culmen Mundi, Himalayan Realms of Nepal, Bhutan & Sikkim. This was replaced with Prime Ministers in India, Pakistan and Ceylon. There is one thing obvious; the Indians seem to have the capacity to accommodate rulers irrespective of their origin. Is this culture, religion, philosophy or society that the caste system still exists? The Moghuls continued to pretend to have power as rulers even though they were virtually under British Protection but nobody raised an eyebrow.

The Second Century Kushian Empire:

Immigration from Central Asia into India and expansion of Central Asia Empire took place during this time. From Bronze Age Indo-Aryan migration to the Iron Age Kushan Empire dominated. Indo-Scythians, Indo-Greeks (Bactria) and the Mediaval Muslim Islamic Conquest of Indian subcontinent happened at this time. Intrusion usually took place across Hindukush. Population of intruders were in Punjab and Indus Valley expanding at times into Ganges Plain. The clans Shakas, Yavanas, Kambojas, Pahlavas, and Paradas also claim to have come as invaders from Central Asia in the Pre-Christian era. All of them were absorbed into Indian Society Community of Kshatriyas. The Shakas were formerly inhabitants of Hemodos---Shakadvipa of Puranas or Scythia. Lately evidence located them in Drangiana i.e. Shakasthana (modern Seistan) south of Herat. Periplus of the Erythraean Sea 1st and 2nd centuries

CE resided in Indo-Scythia as stated by Ptolemy attested to Indo-Scythia in lower Indus in western India. The Paradas previously inhabitants of Oxus and Sailoda (east Xinjiang) Ptolemy noted were Paradane in Sindhu or Gedrosia in western India. India and Central Asia were always at war. Hence most migrations to India came from Central Asia. There seems to be closer genetic mix in India than in Africa. The tragedy of India had been the Muslim Islamic Conquest. It planted seed of division and disunity. It dwarfed the desire for Progress. The Africans had double disaster. It was already in the business of disunity and divisiveness. Muslim conquest added its does of disunity and division. It also introduced indolent Psycho-social culture that relied on Allah that they were not sure of to do everything for them. The Africans spent all their time uniting and dividing their territories without making any Progress either in uniting and integration or permanent division to allow social Progress. They spent their energy and resources to chase and fulfil individual ambition; belief in either unity or disunity. They introduced permanent instability into their system of Progress. They moved in a circle and made no Progress. They lost out. This is the story of Africa even today. They must avoid individualism, corrupt and crime. They must forget the past not from their volition but because life is short and we have no time to wait to correct all the wrongs people had committed against them. They have to adopt culture of community development. They must integrate to create space for their development. They must adopt a Philosophy of community spirit and starting their development from where they find themselves. They must copy from others.

MIGRATION FROM CENTRAL ASIA INTO INDIA:

Immigration by peoples and tribes from Central Asia into India as well as expansion of Central Asian Empires into India is a recurring theme in the history of the region, from early Bronze Age from the sketchy but disputed Indo-Aryan to Iron Age Kushan Empire, Indo Scythians, Indo-Greeks (Batria), the medieval Islamic conquest of the Indian subcontinent. James Tod and other Western Scholars feel that all horse culture people of Central Asia are of Scythic or Saca races. The Kushanas, Hunas, Turks, Mongols and Pashtunss from Hindukush, Central Asia invaded and occupied mainland India in pre- Christian era. They were eventually absorbed Kshatriyas community of the Indian Society.

HISTORY OF CHINA:

The Silk Road of China was the legendary trade route from China through Central Asia.

Central Asian People in Indian Classical Literature are several such as Altharvaveda, Vamas Brahmana of Samveda. Central Asia is the Region of Asia from the Caspian Sea in the West to Central China in the East and from southern Russia in the north and from northern India in the south. Its people are nomads that spread along the Silk Road and were the early contacts between Europe, Western Asia, South Asia and East Asia. In recent times Central Asia consists of five former Soviet Republics of Kazakhstan, Kyrgyzstan, Tajikistan, and Turkmenistan. Other areas occasionally included in Central Asia are Afghanistan, north-eastern Iran, and parts of current China, Xinjiang, Mongolia, Kashmir, and northern Pakistan. Tibet, Qinghai, Gansu, Inner Mongolia and Siberia at times are included in Central Asia. Chinese Historical era extends from 2637 BC 1523-1028 BC Shang Dynasty; 1027-256 BC Chou Dynasty. Then there came Ch'n Dynasty 255-207 BC; early Han Dynasty 206 BC-25 AD & late Han Dynasty 25-220 AD. China adopted Monarchical System and a chain of Monarchs and diverse Dynasties rules various regions of the country until Manchu Ch'ing Dynasty took over and foreign intrusion into China took place 1644-1911 AD. Aliens intruded into Macao, Hong Kong, Kwanchouwan and Tibet. China then adopted Republican system; initially 1912-1928 AD as First Republic and from 1928 to the present day as Second Republic until it adopted Communism in the third Republic in 1949. The Chinese characters are based on the Mandarin Language.

JAPAN has shorter period of contact with the outside world perhaps due to its insularity. Legendary period of Japanese History; 660 BC-539 AD covers Hx Period, 539-645, Yamato Period, 645-711 AD, the Nara Period, 711-793, the Heian Period 793-1186 that ranged to the Fujiwara Chancellors and Imperial Regents 858-1868. The Genealogy of the Fujiwara started from Kamakura Period 1186-

1336 and continued until Edo Period 1603-1868. The Castle, Tokyo Imperial Palace is a Testimony to this Period. This led to Modern Period 1868 and the era of Prime Minister.

THE MONARCHS AND EMPERORS OF THE PERIPHERY OF CHINA AND THEIR VARIOUS SUCCESSORS ruled in;
Korea
Vietnam
Thailand
Laos
Cambodia
Burma
Tibet
Nepal, Bhutan and Sikkim.

The Mongol Khans Conquest was another influential intrusion that must not be ignored in the Hx of this Region of Asia. There is one thing unique about the people and their cultures in this global region. Despite all their travails, tragedies and catastrophes of Western particularly the US intrusion in their land and affairs, they had woken up to their role and responsibilities in the world. South America is soon adopting this attitude and the West has the responsibility of the duty of global leadership to encourage them and not to disrupt their Progress out of vanity, empty power and arrogance. Africa has duty to accept its global responsibilities. There are too many pleasure loving don't care Bantu Africans particularly in Nigeria. They have group culture and Philosophy that feel that they have to cheat to succeed. They fake everything and cheat in all their dealings. They do not believe in good conduct. They have a duty to care. We do not have others to blame for our plight. We must stand up and join others to create a comfortable room in the world for our people and children.

Migrations from Central Asia into India:

This section deals with origins of Ancient Peoples in each continent. It is obvious that Africans came from various parts of their continent and Western Asia and Palestine. Some of them had not lived long with each other. Hostility and hatred had heralded their interaction.

Diverse religion and cultures had made the community divisive. Trade had been based on hostility: slave trade and slavery. There was better trade with sound Economic basis with Europe before European slave trade and slavery and brutal colonisation. Boom and burst perhaps emanating from natural disasters that occasionally occurred.

In 700 AD the Arab Muslim Islamic Conquest of Palestine and North Africa took place and things had remained the same till today. The Arabs established a new Empire based in Syria. They replaced Christianity with Islam and language with Arabic, the language for teaching of Islam. Egyptian Christians are called Coptic. Egypt became free from Western Asia Muslim invaders 1000-1300 AD under Sheik Fatimid Dynasty, Sunni Ayyubids then Mama Luks 1500 AD as part of Ottoman Empire. It has remained so till today. Africans and Arabs must recognise that populations had been dynamic. Paranoid and emotional claim and attachment to Territories are delusion and not true. Compromise and genuine treaties and alliance to share lands and territories are what we need now. Avoidable and stupid wars are wasteful. They cause suffering among innocent people while fanatical ignorant religious extremists seize power and continue to rule by intrigues and terror. Time never started with their arrival in these lands. People were living here before they arrived. The Arabs must look for a compromise and accept to be good neighbours to other people. Let them keep their Religion and religious laws to themselves and accept to live under secular laws with their neighbours. They must come out of the past and its emotional attachment as past records would show that they were brutally cruel to their neighbours during the Arab Muslim Conquest of that lands. The world needs rational and reconciling and compromising decision from the Arabs mainly and Israel too. The Arabs and Israeli are all Semitic people divided by religion. Islam is a very young faith aggressive and pugnacious. Recently Pope Benedict was asked to apologise to the Muslims for quoting one Emperor who remarked that Islam was an aggressive religion. Everybody knows that the Prophet Mohammed was driven away from the temple in Mecca AD 200. He re-appeared with swordsmen on horses' backs. He used armed believers to spread his message. His became a religion with message by the sword. Some of the believers were forced to accept the faith by the sword. The Muslim cannot re-write their History to contain what is acceptable to them. They have to accept their History and modify their conduct to civilised standard compatible with religion and faith. Islam has done very well judging the fact that it is a very young religion established AD 200 after the message of Jesus of Nazareth.

Our fanatical adherence to the "TWO STATE SOLUTION" is attractive and persuasive it may not form safe permanent solution. Safe permanent solution lies on mutual trust between the Arabs and the Jews. They must abandon the emotions and the past and the urge to retaliate for their past sufferings. They must look to the future to replace hatred with love and friendship, violence and hostility with peace. How would they do this? Human anger and emotions make this difficult to conceive but human power to overcome human bitterness can overcome all. A strong secular Constitution drafted by these two hurt and brutalised relatives, the Semitic brothers and sisters, separated by religious fanatical extremism and wounds of past painful conflicts to ensure that there would be no hostility in future and to guarantee their future security acceptable to both of them the combatant groups should be written to generate mutual trust, guarantee the right of every citizen to be used in a "SINGLE STATE." The objective of one state is to prevent one group using autonomy to prepare for war to liquidate the other. If this happened the "TWO STATE SOLUTION" would not bring Peace. What would bring Peace is for the two groups to believe in the end of the war and have belief in mutual trust in one destiny for the land and peaceful co-existence. These are two resourceful people. They can be constructive and not destructive. Hence it is not completely safe to ignore Benjamin Netanyahu, the Israel. Simple thing like water would not cause hostility one state solution.

It is worth sounding Arab opinion on the "ONE STATE SOLUTION" for them to voice their objections. The place is too small for freedom of movements and goods. One state would allow free movement. Equally the cost of running either system needs to be considered. Israel and Arabs would destroy their opportunity for peace by hanging unto a programme of victory behind the "TWO STATE SOLUTION." Each State would be free to prepare for means of eliminating the other. We must recall that these are members of the Semitic Race who spoke Aramaic Language in the past. They had been split by fanatical religious extremism and subculture of ambivalence and deceit. They see the origins of events as when they started to occupy the lands either by brutal conquest war or religious faith implantation. Mohammed seemed to have done everything Jesus of Nazareth did in Jerusalem even though; records are vague if he ever lived there or set foot in Jerusalem. Yet the Palestinian Arab Muslims give us the impression that the land started with their conquest and Jerusalem had always been the home of Islam. Judaism dominated the land before the Muslim Arab conquest. Christianity made its roots by itinerant preacher and his disciples. All these happened long before Mohammed became Prophet in Arabian Peninsula to preach to the world. The world accepts and tolerates religious myths: the god-like natures of faith founders. Attachment to them and emotions to the past must not be allowed to overcome human common sense as to erupt into hostility, violence and war. The Arabs must know that even though they drove the Jews away by brutal conquest, the Jews were living on that land long before their conquest. The Semitic race was there before the origin of Judaism. Hence the Jews have full right to that land. It is a small territory but they can co-exist by good arrangement without violence and war. They are Semitic brothers and sisters. Religious intolerance and attachment to emotions of the past or present suffering must not be allowed to destroy the opportunity to end hostility, violence and war. They must replace hatred with friendship. They owe a duty to the land both Israel and they love; they should develop it and make it their peaceful and secure homeland. They will be wealthy and prosperous. The world can help them to achieve this goal if they listen to all who want to help them. End the Arab-Israeli conflict. The world is dynamic and time changes. We have to change. We and our religious faith have no reason to be inflexible in a fast changing globalised world.

SUMMARY:

The world has always been in a dynamic state. All living things including human beings had always had uncanny way of moving to and fro around the world. Even rocks have ways of moving with water from one place to the other. The Mycenaeans lived in Greece and said to have invaded Egypt. People invaded other territories for special reasons including capturing souvenir. Mycenaeans might have taken some artefacts of Ancient Egyptian civilisation back to Greece. Greek stood genuine advantage to exposure to Egyptian civilisation and borrowing heavily from it. Hence the concept of looking at the world as a static organ is wrong. Equally the attitude of feeling that this is exclusively mine is faulty. Equally the concept of pure race of human beings or any living thing is unsafe. Several living things had cross-bred. It is genetic natural selection that limits and restricts wild spread of species. The eco-ecology is part of the restrictive natural selection. Adaptation to new environments is equally an act of natural selection. In absolute ignorance and lack of information writers and scholars had frequently been mixed up and claim that African civilisation came from Asia. This is totally wrong. African civilisation stands out on its own. It had one significant culture and character. There were frequent struggle for power among ethnic groups. Egypt frequently integrated north and south and Kush but equally broke up again. This repeated itself and they wasted time on this nasty habit without consolidating on their gains. Human population is perpetually dynamic. People travel round with their cultures and mix with others and exchange cultures and civilisations.

HAITI AND WHAT RETARDS PROGRESS AMONG GLOBAL BLACK PEOPLE.

Haiti is one of the islands ninety miles from the USA just as Cuba and Cayman Islands. It was the first to be free both from slavery and to be independent from France. From the onset this was a country whose population still had memory of African culture. The Haitians still worship the Voo Doo god. Compared to Cuba and Cayman islands why is Haiti a total failure like Africa South of the Sahara? A couple of criminal mulatoes, the Papa Doc and Doc seized the leadership. They were corrupt and converted Haiti to criminal haven. They made Haiti remain a violent country with frequent murders and violent crimes.

Catalogue of what made Haiti a total failure: Total failure of law and order; the ruling cartel and their cronies were above the law; they could do what they wanted including killing their opponents. They used black Economy, smuggling drugs etc to USA.

The people seem to adopt hunter and gatherer's temporary culture ready to move away at any time. They feud with each other and indulge in violence and murders waiting for opportunities to move to the US. The population remains restless.

Crime and violence pervert the heart of darkness. The population seems divided into supporters of the rulers ready to kill for them and dispossessed poor who also fight their corners.

Lack of Unity and total loss of self-esteem seems to prevail.

Failure to love the land and develop a zeal for the land makes people ignore the land and working on it; failure to develop patriotism as compared to the US makes people feel as though they are squatters waiting for permanent settlement.

Failure to develop mature work habits and culture makes efforts people make to work on the land unsustainable and non-continuous.

Lack of leadership and total failure of leadership deprives the people of guidance and support.

Lack of motivation of the people and the will to solve their problems makes the people indifferent and not think of solution to them.

Failure to befriend the land and make it their own and plan to cultivate it and tackle problems such as hurricanes and floods that make people endure them when they occur and think of the menace and forget about them once they are gone without planning how to combat them.

Failure to develop genuine trade with the US and develop good policy towards the US that has no reason to trust its corrupt leaders has further made Haiti a failed state that knows no purpose for its existence. Failure to plan its Economy and cultivate the land to feed its people but relying on NGOs to feed them tantamount to self-neglect.

Regular feuding over the leadership; social and political violence;

Failure to accept their plight and settle down and makes it their home where they find themselves on earth like the US and Cuba seem to determine their unsettled behaviour.

The same behaviour can be seen in black people in sub-Saharan Africa. Their youths cannot cope with any honest genuine jobs. They are rather preparing to migrate to the West under any conditions. They pay human traffickers huge sums to put them in leaking sea unworthy crafts to cross over to Europe. Several perish enroute. Survivors quickly apply for refuge even though everybody knows they are Economic migrants. It is sad that Africa has lost its soul. Haiti failure is a copycat of African failure. Any people or nations without high sense of civic duties, self-respect and acceptance of responsibilities are dead. The Romans developed very high sense of duties and built an empire never known in world history before but when decadence set in and citizens neglected their civic duties nobody took responsibilities for the state seriously. The Empire collapsed in AD 476 and Rome threw the world into chaos. The direct consequence is the crises in the Middle East today. The world today has a duty to stand by the West and the rest to regulate the Globalisation and global institutions to build a world under the rule of law. The sub-Saharan Africans must be taught modern Agriculture and Livestock Farming to be able to feed their citizens. They must be weaned off depending on NGOs to feed them. They must be taught to care for their land. Care of the eco-environment equilibrium by not deforesting the tropical rain forest for timber and firewood. They must appreciate the concept of work and labour. They must be taught to develop the zeal to compete to catch up with the rest.

We need no magic wand for recovery. We must rid ourselves of ignorant corrupt Geriatric leaders and appeal to the world to help us to dislodge these criminal that we had found impossible to remove from office as they used all methods to keep themselves in Government. We must choose young ambitious and patriotic people to lead us in a free and fair election. We must work hard and be ready to make the sacrifices Economic development requires.

THE DEBATE ON PIONEERING OF CIVILISATION IS A WASTE OF TIME AND SPACE. IT DOES NOT EXIST BECAUSE HUMAN POPULATION IS DYNAMIC AND NOT STATIC.

People move to and fro different places for trade and curiosity of visiting places. There is always tremendous sharing of human assets. Natural selection of habits modified by eco-environment forms the diverse cultures of people. People in different parts of the world have different cultures. People travel from one place to another. While people also return from those places to the place the others travelled from. It is hence; wrong to ascertain Pioneering Civilisation to any Region or group. Africa seems to have pioneered early civilisation in Egypt but the Greeks were doing lots of Business with Egypt in trade, tourism and Educational Exchange. The Greeks loved Africa, Egypt. They even proclaimed that "the Africans were nearer to the gods". The Greeks loved knowledge and their scholars travelled frequently to learn and question old Masters in Egypt. Greek culture loved knowledge and open discussion on knowledge and philosophy. Alexander, the Great, son of Philip of Macedonia travelled extensively in his conquest of the world up to India where his brief period there made indelible mark till today but his great Greek love of Africa Egypt, enthralled him. He elected to make Alexandria in Egypt his capital and Headquarters of the world after the war but unfortunately Alexander died at 43 of febrile illness (malaria or typhoid) around Afghanistan before the war ended. He could not live to fulfil his ambition. Ptolemy took Egypt but he was not as visionary of Alexander.

Therefore, I discourage claiming monopoly of pioneering early civilisation. It seems Early Pioneering Civilisation moved from Africa from place to place and kept on improving from place to place. The Egyptians built their temples with stones cut and brought in badges on the Nile and supported their structures with several pillars to stand. The Greeks had limestone marble and needed not many pillars for support while volcanic eruption gave the Romans Cement who used Cement in their constructions. Hence environment improved the quality of early pioneering civilisation.

Wherever, we go on earth we see remnants of early pioneering civilisation. Archaeological excavations pottery is evidence with the type of clay found in the locality. Hence early pioneering civilisation travevelled with man round the globe and improved or lost some of it momentums. Africa has unique problems. Its central position has involved it in ancient and recent global crises from the Greeks, Romans, Arab Conquest of Palestine and North Africa, Islamic Conquest, even the Vandal sacking of the Roman Empire, Napoleonic march, the European brutal and looting colonisation of Africa and their two global wars. Muslims destroyed very many of our artefacts as idols. Today they claim that they are Arabs'. The Ancient Egypt was African through and through. It was frequently shared with Kush, Sudan and Pharaohs came from the two. They united and divided and re-united several times. The colonisers called us savages out of ignorance and to justify their actions for abuse of us. Most of the early colonisers were illiterate pack baggers in search of fortune. They were not scholars but rugged travellers. They saw their skin colour as mark of civilisation. Of course, to them that was the only difference they could see. They had to make capital of it. There is a place in the Old Testament of the Christian Bible that tells us that Moses was married to a Kushite (Sudanese) that is a Sudanese woman. Some people against grumbled against this but the religious myth says God smote one of them with leprosy. The victim was excluded from the camp for seven days and people of Israel had to wait for seven days before they resumed their journey. The significance of this story is that Moses was married to an African. Orthodox Jews should please refute this story from the Torah and justify their reason for Practise of exclusive and intolerant religion. Apparently the Sudanese are black people, the Nubians and Bashir is Arab by speaking Arabic language of the Koran and Muslim faith. The most significant other point is that Africans and the Jews are very close but a dynamic changing world had changed everything. The Jews went to Egypt to escape drought and famine. Jesus and his parent took refuge in Egypt. To the Jews Egypt was a second home. In our culture people shelter with relatives in disasters and in danger. Jews had Egypt as home of their distant relatives.

Following the train of arguments I find that even sophisticated Scholars fall into the temptation of waste of time in debating stories already present in Ancient Literature that do not deserve any debate and argument. We have nothing to claim. Our culture of internal strife restricted the consolidation of our gains and expansion of our influence. We kept on striving for power and position. The Kingdom united and divided several times, a sign of internal weakness. Bantu means several languages and this means divisiveness. It has made us unable to produce universal leaders. We seem to have produced some of the finest leaders in Europe. Perhaps Obama may be one of them and we always have much to share with the West either as leaders or vassals or even slaves. Hence the current generation may be amazed and excited but Obama is History repeating itself.

In some Literature we find that while old civilisations were declining, the new and recent ones were just rising up. Each ancient early civilisation had its dark ages and recovered. This is always period of decline in Progress. There had been no uniformity in Periods when Renaissance took place in the world. We cannot read about past global events in a four-walled room and feel that they happened there. Rather they happened in a rapidly changing dynamic world totally different from the current Globalisation. Events took place in different Regions among different peoples at different times because of continuous Human movements and interaction around the world.

African Studies is another Branch of Politics involving Researchers under maximum forty years. They are budding nationalists enthusiastic in the past of their Regions in the world. Pan-Africanism was a sustaining hope in our utter frustration in the past. Today while African Unity is important for Ecological and Environmental and Economic and Trade Purposes we are in a global village. We live in Western Atlantic where we have been doing business with Europe for a long time. We also live by the Indian Ocean and had long commercial dealings with Asia. Peoples from Western Asia, Assyrians, Hittites (Turks), Persia invaded Egypt frequently. We also share the Mediterranean Sea with Palestine and Europe. We have to abandon the past emotions and our current failures and frustrations. We must summons courage and rise up and join the race. Our efforts to nurture a viable Economy had remained disappointing due to our weakness in unity, leadership and fragmenting religious influence and ethnic loyalty and intruding foreign influence by our past colonial masters had not helped either. We must teach our children and youths Civic loyalty to Africa as our homeland. We must join the global Economic Race to make Africa self-sufficient on its land. India and China can feed itself. Africa can do the same if Africans pay attention to details and hard work. Today Economy is based on production from your land, manufacture and trade, Property on your land, Banking and Commerce. Education, Skills and excellent Apprenticeship Training support all these Economic Factors. Regulation and monitoring of these activities are the duties of patriotic and non-corrupt leaders. Corruptless and enthusiastic young and brilliant leaders take charge of things. The elders are rehabilitated in the House of Elders.

We are yet to know where the Arab invaders in Africa stand. Do they accept Africa as their home and be loyal to it? Do they feel that they are there as caliphate Sultans, Imams; Mullahs and followers of the Prophet. Some of them even muted the absurd idea of joining the European Union. The Europeans had made it in USA. The Arabs in co-operation with Africans can make it here. They must evolve a new culture with us and avoid advocating for Sharia laws. It is incompatible with the enormous changes that had taken place among human beings since the Prophet preached in the world AD 200 till it ended. It has taken away franchise from African women that they enjoyed over the ages and supplanted it with Arab Macho culture of disrespect to women. Islam should not be imposed on the community either directly by burning down their places of worship and property and murders spreading religion by terror or indirectly by imposing Sharia law on the Community and slamming unfair judgment on non-believers and deprivation of non-believers of their basic social privileges such denying their children entry and admission to elite Institutions. Non-believers accuse Islam of these practices but Muslim Islamic leaders have so far not come out to tell the world that they have dismounted the swordsmen on horse backs the world saw coming out of Medina, the home of Mohammed's mother to Mecca, his father's birthplace and spreading the Prophet's message by the sword and jihad all over the world. Rather they had resorted to bullying and shouting down anybody who mentions this Islamic History and demand an apology. Islam has a duty to announce a cease fire and promise the world that it would be tolerant of other religions and will spread the Prophet's Message peacefully and recruit new believers from volunteers to the faith. The world now knows that Islam is a great and fastest growing global religion. They must join hands with the Africans to develop secular laws that are compatible with modern times. They must tolerate other religions and accept their neighbours. They must abandon hidden territorial expansion to control mineral resources in Africa. Madrasah School type of indoctrination of children is bad for community and good neighbourliness. Religion is love, inclusive and not exclusive. Intermarriage should be allowed. Protracted and indefinite war of conquest idea is obsolete. It should be abandoned for live in peace with all thy neighbours. We need innovative new ideas, new philosophy and new concept of community life. It is dangerous to attempt to impose life in the times of HT. The Prophet lived several centuries ago but his message still has deep impression on the people. His firry religious message still has value for the human soul. Yes Islam just as other religions is a way of life a guide from Allah yet because time does not stand still; it changes, it has to adjust itself to accommodate the changing times. It is a fast expanding faith and must be modernised to attract more devotees.

I hope nobody would throw stones at me a dying man from terminal cancer of the Prostate or burn my book on a pile of bonfire. It is the voice of a departing man going to the place where all of us born into this world would finally go either violently or peacefully. In my youth I used to attend Muslim Festival to observe what the believers do. I do not understand Arabic but I knew what the Prayer caller was asking people to do as all the worshippers prostrated in great ovation to Allah and I did the same as we do on Christmas Day happy that God or Allah had sustained us to see another Christmas and another year. Nigeria then was a happy country full of hope until armed men arrived to slaughter men, women, pregnant women, children, and the invalid and confidants betrayed their friends to death that I began to fear. Nigeria collapsed and could not recover. The looters like the looting division of the Roman Army moved in to conduct thorough asset stripping of its resources. Its beautiful infrastructures and the country collapsed. It is we mortal human beings that will have to rebuild it. I sincerely advise the Geriatric leaders of Nigeria that now had forgotten the way back to their villages due Alzheimer or are addicted to power and wealth to have mercy on Africa and advocate for re-integration of colonial dismembered Africa (on the blackest day in the life of African Bantu Negro, 15th, Sept, 1884 in Berlin). Berlin and Germany had re-integrated what has Africa done to be abandoned by his own children? Why do your children love your resources and wealth but abandon you in wretchedness?

The real Asian civilisation is later than African civilisation. Indian culture is docile and they adore their leaders and authorities. Chinese culture is regimented institution and so is the Japanese culture. Hence it is erroneous to look at Africa as at present and think that they might have copied from others. I have repeatedly emphasised the importance that there had always been contact among all human beings and no group had lived in complete isolation. In some cases the contact had not been continuous but sporadic. The European civilisation took roots from African. The Greeks used to say that "the Africans nearer to the Gods". The Greeks love learning and freedom. They loved what they saw in Egypt. Greek love of freedom is exemplified by Socrates embracing death to be free to practise philosophy. The Romans learnt a lot from Carthage but they liked expansion supported by aggressive militarism. They had very high sense of civic duties. They also had a culture of cronyism and strife for power and leadership. They rewarded citizens for loyalty and civic responsibility. They were respected even by law. They could not be flogged. The Mediterranean became their lake and Europe and North Africa their domain. The Roman nobles became complacent and laxed in their duties. Their Empire collapsed. What of the advances in Science and Technology in Europe that led the tail end of European civilisation? The social and culture of Europe of Monarchy and Oligarchy (rich land owners and merchants) abandoned the poor who frequently used their ingenuity to probe the unknown and invented things that the community liked. Escape from poverty provided drive and incentive for European development. Equally the culture of sharing education and knowledge helped Science and Technology. Observations show that in every generation what was happening in one place was equally happening in other places in most European countries. The people in the World, USA formed the melting pot carved out life for themselves in their new home. They had the freedom to do things. They equally did things. Persistence and continuous practice improved skills and quality of products. The Christianity and its probing mind allowed mental development but the Christian dogma was hostile to most scientific observations in Astronomy. Galileo was threatened with excommunication and forced to recount his scientific observations and writings. Humans evolved as hunters and gatherers. They slowly adopted farming and livestock keeping. This seems to have split human beings into settlers and nomads. The settlers made up their communities. They appointed their leaders. They surveyed their environments. They made friends with their neighbours or fought and subjugated them. They established trade with their neighbours and built routes or roads for trade with their neighbours. The population of the communities increased breeding. Expansion into new territories and return of previous emigrants to their original communities equally increases the population. The concept of survival bonded people into communities. The safety and security of the community frequently forced people into violence and wars. Today the achievements of Science and Technology and Information Technology had brought people together including else while enemies in globalised village. We are challenged again to elect leaders that will devise regulations to maintain law and order in the new community. We Africans no longer have forests to hide away from the world. We cannot pretend any longer that we can enjoy the products of good Education, Science and Technology, good Skills Training and excellent apprenticeship and fail to contribute to sacrifice that others make to make the community function. At the moment the nations are scrambling for production of alternative fuel and energy sources. The Africans are busy selling oil and fossil fuels but when other parts of the world achieve success Africans would be left behind due to their indifference and indolence.

The Africans are not inferior to others but they lack leadership with foresight and the will to compete in good commerce and Economic Development. They have no skills in trading with money, Banking, Insurance and Commerce. They abandon these areas to the West to do it for them by Money laundering in alien Banks and Banking havens. The leaders slowly abandon their communities to rely on facilities and infrastructures of the developed world because they can access them. They neglect their communities and leave them without basic infrastructures. It sounds cruel but leaders of communities that are rich enough to have good Health Services similar to what Cuba has should not be entertained in foreign Hospitals abroad when they are sick as theirs are self-inflicted injury. They should not be allowed to block up these facilities built for the local people. They should use their resources to build and develop their own services. We know that trade would not allow this to happen but the world must harass Africans to wake up from somnolence and join others to do things for themselves without depending on others to do things for them. If Cuba under US sanctions can maintain such high standards, African Bantustans can if they care. The corruption in Nigeria today is pandemic. All youths and people under forty want well paid job, good house and car but none wants to work. They never worked at School and have questionable certificates. They are not qualified for any job but want good life.

THE PRESIDENCY IN NIGERIA.

This post has until recently been the monopoly of a mafia cartel of illiterate ex-Army officers. Most of them were hardened criminals and corrupt men. They had no idea about how to run a government. They controlled enormous government funds from oil royalties. They had no ideas on how government funds work. Through approaches from Asian Business men who persuaded them that they were fellow Muslims and could invest abroad for them, they opened the Nigerian treasuries to them. They gave them money to invest overseas for them. Equally the Swiss nose around the world for where they can smell money. Hence many of them became introduced to the Swiss Bank.

HOUSE OF OGRE:

Most Presidential Entourage were criminals and lawless men from the Nigerian civil war. They were drug abusers, barons, rapists, and female harassers, Paedophiles, sexual perverts, (homosexuals), sexual maniacs and people guilty of incest. A number of them were drunks despite their Islamic faith. Most of them spent twenty four hours in bed having various forms of sex in relay. They just had no time for things of governing. They were foul-mouth, swore and bullied. How can a country progress, if it is ruled by this mob? But this is what happened to Nigeria in recent past. Heads of State told young girls of the age band of their grand daughters, who approached them for help that they would help only when they accepted to have sex with them. Many of these Heads of State bred so many children that they just did not know how many children they had and who they were. A notorious former Criminal President was famous for in-house murders of his Court members and friends for plotting fictitious coups. He graduated in all manners of crimes, drugs, corruption, intrigues and murders. He plundered more than any other from the Treasury. He is said to be one of the richest Nigerians. He is one of the untouchables. Is there any doubt why Nigeria has remained the way it is?

These people rigged elections and openly boasted that it was better to die in office than to miss the post of President. Hence intra-court killings were rampant. What do say to a Military President who invited all his top Army Officers to meet him and gave them a Hercules plane to take home and the plane exploded in midair and fell into Delta slumps and he failed to send rescue team in until it was three or more days when all victims trapped in muddy slumps had died of hunger, exhaustion and respiratory failure from asphyxia from chests trapped in mud and could not breathe, who remarked that soldiers signed up to die? How can a commander in chief (CIC) make this remark without mourning for his men? It is rumoured that he was behind the crash to remove perceived threat to his rule. The Nigerian ex-colonial military officers are typically Idi Amin like, morally decadent and totally ignorant. They are mischievously cruel. They are very corrupt criminals.

Akpaneyen Akpan-Essien.

OBJECT OF WRITING THIS BOOK:

This is to remind all human beings that the world did not start with their religion or Scientific Achievements. The world had always been here before we came to achieve these great things. We are born into the world and will die and leave the world. We are wrong to claim monopoly of the world. Even the territories we fight to acquire at great costs in lives and resources had changed the boundaries and borders so frequently with generations that we are constrained to accept our efforts as wastage and investments in rapidly changing names of places that the lands remain unchanged are a waste. We fight to correct things according to what we see in our time but they may reverse to their former positions or other things when we die and leave the world. Our aggressive attitude and culture may suit our animal instinct but even animals have restrain and tolerance for each other. Standing in a static position to fight in a world that is dynamic and fluid is a display of ignorance. Inflexible attitude in conflicts and crises is a display of ignorance of the world. We are related to each other. The Jews and the Arabs are all Semitic race. The land we claim for our own might have changed hands several times. The Arab Muslim Conquest of Palestine and Northern Africa changed the face of the landmass. Nobody goes to take what belongs to them by force and conquest. The Arabs took the land by conquest. The Israeli owned this land.

They are not occupiers. Let Arabs not fool themselves and deceive their children and the world. They must accept that their ancestors did not do a nice job. They did not exterminate the Jews completely. The Jews are back and the Arabs must accept to share the land with them. This is the minimum Israel and the world can accept. Israel has to be magnanimous. The Arabs must know that Allah did not create Palestine on the date of Arab Muslim Islamic Conquest. Palestine existed before that day. Israel lived in Palestine before that day. The world is dynamic and rapidly changing. It is not static. The myth of God or Allah giving the land to Israel or Palestinian Arabs is nonsense. Zionism may be a propaganda stump but it is not worth going round the world to lecture on to upset people. No God takes part in conflicts between followers of different faiths. God takes no part in religious wars. All faiths belong to Him and they worship Him.

THE WRITER AGAIN:

Specialist Surgeon salvaged from Peasant Farming of his Parents by Education advises young people to have the strength of character to be obedient to your parents. Modernism sound attractive but the world changes not a lot. Drugs damage you because your body has been made by nature to reject and not to tolerate certain things. Certain lifestyles equally damage you. My parents were poor to support me financially at School but their moral support was magic. Scholarship and people's sympathy saw me through School. It was a miracle that I had a full Education judging from resources available to accomplish the feat. I owe tremendous gratitude to my loving parents. They brought me up to be a human being capable of acknowledging hardship in the world and enduring changing positions in life. I thank Prof Sam Agogbua, and the late Oguikes their sacrifice and physical support, and my teachers and mentors in the University of Nigeria who endured hardships to teach us at the end of the Nigerian Civil. I thank Professor Gilbert Onuaguluchi, The Foundation Dean of University of Nigeria. He used his family savings to feed over fifty of us the pioneer Medical students. He had no salaries at the onset but taught us free and ingeniously designed and built the equipment for our Practical work in Physiology and Pharmacology. I cannot complete the list without mentioning Prof Ruth Bowden who risked regular journeys to travel from her base in Royal Free Medical School to examine our students at Enugu, Nigeria. She took us as her children. She gave us references as her students here in London. I thank Helen Herbison that stood by me in the difficult days of studying and sitting examinations for the final FRCS. Finally I thank the Staff and teachers and officials in the Royal College of Surgeons particularly Dr Livingstone, the Dean of Nuffield College of Surgical Sciences. He gave us extra Anatomy Tuition free. He had a dry sense of humour to ease our frustrations in those days.

We were lucky the generation we met here were benign human beings ready to help without asking for any reward. That Civil war handed that rich country, Nigeria to corrupt and criminal rats. I thank all white and black who helped and stood by me in my difficult days. I use the privilege of my good education to advise the world it needs the restraining influence of a good and caring family. Both my parents were brutal to my tantrums and what they objected in me but this did not mean that they were bad parents. They were exceptionally good parents and all their actions were corrective in the circumstances of their social circumstances.

People would be surprised to learn that my mother came from the Royal Family of our clan and her forebears were rich and rulers of the place. The largest Market in our place is named after her great ancestor Ndueso Edem Ekong Udo Anwan. My mother's grandfather, Isong Ndueso was a Chief and respectable leader of our Clan. Her half brother was one of the first Doctors the British colonial Authorities trained at Yaba Medical School in Lagos. Unfortunately, he had CVA with severe hemiplegia at very tender age. My great grandfather was a warrior and local native Doctor. All of them were well to do but the changing times saw my parents exposed to poverty. Surprisingly, our own time saw us again in affluence with the clan educated and graduated. The active gene of hard work and leadership again adjusted to natural selection of the changing times.

Now advanced terminal hormonal refractory cancer of the Prostate Gland, scourge of males in our family is grasping my hand, I thank all Medical workers who had helped me in my ordeal. The world is exciting but it did not start with us and it will not end with us. We may witness the decline of our fortunes and the changes of our circumstances but this does not mean the world would collapse in our time. It will always recover and revitalise itself. Human beings will come and go but our duty to make our imprint on earth for promoting progress and peace and advancement of human beings on earth will always continue. Our life time cannot accomplish all. To my children and grandchildren I leave the message; "Whatever thy hand findest to do it with all thy strength." Avoid silly competitions. Do not lie about your status on earth. It is an expression of what you would like to be and may never be in life. It is an expression of Anxiety State. A successful worker plans his strategy silently until he reaches his objective. Empty boasting or bragging is fruitless lying. Humility is self-containment and restraint. The truth is the way the world sees you and not the way you see yourself. Bragging is confession that you will not be able to achieve what you long for. Silent contemplation and planning of strategy would help you to achieve your objectives provided you are ready to pay the price and sacrifice for your desire and objectives.

THRASHING RECALCITRANT NON-CONFORMING CHILDREN:

The breakdown of the family had been the price the developed countries had to pay for their travels in search of wealth in the world. The age of industrialisation and work came and separated families further apart. This eliminated parental influence in the upbringing of their children. Equally frequent chronic unemployment and redundancies in a capitalist bubble Economy affect family life and make parents lose control of their families. In addition to these the Child Welfare Department staffed in most cases with people without children of their own make family life redundant. Today the problem of child upbringing and family control is worldwide. We seem to have lost the skills of family control and upbringing and educating children to fit into the Community. Would it not be a better idea for part of training of all personnel involved in child care have part of their practical training by staying with families with children for a week or two to learn the practical responsibilities and problems of child care. They must learn the roles of mother and father and problems single parents have to deal with in bringing up children. It may even be wiser that senior personnel have staying with selected families with children abroad to learn the way children are brought up in other countries as their post graduate refresher course. It is vital people that people that deal with and take decisions on these matters know what they are doing in practical and not theoretical way only.

I strongly support corporal punishment at home, at School and Children's homes for child offenders. The fear of abuse of the cane is obvious. But what we fear is fear itself. Most of us in our sixties have experience of thrashing. I feel it made us appreciate what our mentors objected in us. Physical punishment will impress on the child the pain they inflict on their victims. The argument of Psychological intimidation and bullying by flogging will rage here. The criminal child does not feel the pain his victims feel when he stabs him to death or pulls the trigger of his modified gun to shoot down an innocent victim. Thrashing does not damage a child. What damages a child is abandoning the child to his or her wareward ways without cautioning the child against misbehaviour and antisocial conduct. Equally rehabilitating recalcitrant families in their homes is better than children's home. Reforming children's homes to act as families is important. The children in these homes must be treated the way good parents would bring up their children. They should not be there for three square meals and watching television. This makes the children feel isolated, abandoned and unloved. The young ones at School should have supplementary classes and encouraged to do their home work from School. The older ones must help out in the kitchen. They must learn how to tidy up and cook. They must take part in caring for the home. They must take part in games and athletics and drama. They must be taught to be responsible, imaginative and resourceful. Active participation in this way makes the children feel that they are part of the community. It stimulates positive competitive community spirit in the children. It gives them a sense of being valued as important members of the community (the family) and courage to grow in improving the community. They feel proud in making positive contribution to the community and living in peace with one another.

As a matter of fact many children of my generation are grateful to their mentors who even used corporal punishment to correct them as children. The adverse effects of corporal punishment are less than a child that grows up to be a criminal in the community. Caning a child in the Public in front of School Assembly is better than suspension and exclusion. Parental objection is a factor. Just as we do not allow traders to sell rotten fruits and food to the Public we object to Parents protecting criminal children to hurt us. Therefore bring back the cane and use it heavily on criminal children on drugs. There will be casualties. The community must either accept casualties or tolerate child crimes. I would rather eliminate child crimes than tolerate criminal children. Corporal punishment must be a major component of penalty for juvenile or child crimes even in combination with other forms of punishment. The criminal child must feel the physical pain before any other form of punishment. Regimental work houses including education suits these children. Failure to complete task must equally carry corporal punishment. The regime is corrective and to make confinement unattractive. Yes the child lives in fear but respects authority of the community. This is the objective of the regime.

To leaders of the world and all human races social exclusion dwarfs human progress and deny the society of individual talents. Allow talents to grow and shine. The Germans made this mistake with Jews. The whites made this mistake with the black. Let every qualified persons handle responsibilities he is capable to handle under good supervision and regulations. All will have opportunity of positive contribution to the community. Why should one human race endure the toxicity of inventions and industrial production while the rest enjoy the fruits of their labour? We should share these things equally. Also we have seen that intelligence does not depend on the race. It depends on concentration, education and persistent skills training and excellent apprenticeship and sociocultural discipline. In same spirit I sincerely appeal to all white racists who today feel uncomfortable having Barack Obama as the United States of America President, to be patient. In 146 BC, the fate of the World was seized by the Romans after defeating Carthage in Africa in a brutal blood-splitting genocidal war. In 476 AD the Vandals and Saxones sacked the Roman Empire. It fell and threw the World into crises and conflicts we are struggling to resolve in Religions and in the Middle East and in Racial Divide. Africans had always been loyal brothers and sisters to Europeans. European literatures and folktales speak of Melanesia marrying Europa; this alludes to friendship and not racial hostility or hatred. We have lived in this Western Atlantic Shore together and did business together. Events in a dynamic and convulsive world had changed the positions in our relationship. We had never been bitter as to wish to betray each other to extinction but had always remained loyal friends. When Rome defeated Carthage in 146 BC and initiated building its Empire Europe took up the mantle and baton of leading the world. The Europeans became masters of the world. They developed Education, Science and Technology. They later colonised the world and built further empires. Carthage and Africa had missed the opportunity of leading the world. Now USA a cosmopolitan country and with age-long pioneering contact and sharing of life with Africans had without knowledge of the age-long group of Europeans and Africans who had advocated for integration of Africa into the West as equals in Business and world affairs, had used Democratic Practice to achieve this, we Africans must prove to the world by supporting the US and its leaders and President. We must lead the USA in the path of friendship to the world. It is already playing the role but a lot of people do not know this. Its farmers feed most hungry people in the world through WFP. It can do more in world peace. As a friend and member of the world community the US can use a friendly world community to curb fanatical extremism and violence.

Despite the postcolonial chaos in Africa, a true African leader is a man of great dignity and virtue. His word is his bond. He respects treaties and keeps them. He believes strongly in peace as a safe platform for global development in trade, commerce and Economy. Wealth creation depends on peace. War and violence cut off people from changes and progress in civilisation. They block access to civilisation to some people and fragmenting civilisation into clusters excluding a large part of the world. It is good to be master but how many mouths would you work to feed? Let people be their own masters and look after themselves and families. Sub-Saharan Africans must know this; the NGOs must know this. The world should give us the chance and co-operate with us and let us see what we can do for ourselves and the world. Africa has to change its leadership and vision of the world.

Africans had played major roles in European crises, starting with the great Barcines, St Augustine in the early Catholic Church in the feuds and intrigues among the Emperors and Papal leaders, Generals leading Armies to wars and Abram Petrovich Gannibal, the Moor of Petersburg, the great ancestor of Pushskin, the great Russian Poet who is said to remotely related to most European Royalties including the Lord Mobatten, was an intellectual and a loyal servant to Peter the Great. He helped to build modern Russia. The collapse of the capitalist bubble Economy of boom and burst is a sad global event. Africans are exceptionally excellent leaders beyond their borders. There is no record of them being poor leaders in foreign lands. We have always regarded Europe as our home. This may be the time to achieve the desires of Alexander, the Great, son of Philip of Macedonia (taught by Aristotle, not fond of Africans but very fond of African enlightened culture), Julius Caesar and Cleopatra to integrate Africa with Europe to run as equals. Scipio Cornelius Publius insisted that Africa should not be destroyed and humiliated. He rejected Roman Noble burial funeral rights for heroes because of this. People like Marcus Cato and Octavius overambitious who accepted being made "god" by his cronies in the Senate and who later took the title, Caesar Augustus, insisted on subjugation and looting the riches in Africa. They had their way. They threw the world into near permanent crises and conflicts we are unlucky to deal with even when their dreamed Empire collapsed in 476 AD. A number of Western Media had started to be intrusive and plotting to show Barack Obama, as risk. They want him to panick and make mistakes to prove their case.

The Romanian now occupying the French Throne had to go through Democratic free election to be chosen by French people to rule over them as President. He did not have to be evaluated by George Walker Bush whose father was a President and he was a Governor before winning the Post of a President. The arrogant Romanian is not a very popular leader among the French people. Barack Obama does not need a lesson from him on how to be lowly rated as President among your citizens. He needs experience on how to meet the expectations of the American people and to make the US friendly to the world and not bullying its people with threats and wars, rendition and tortures. There is no dossier of experience; not even from this Romanian President of France for Obama to read for the type of experience he needs for his job. The type of Presidency he will offer to the world will be his experience and an example to the world. President Obama should never have deep conversation with the type of person who under wine would make the sort of gaffe or jibe President made on Presidents of other countries. Equally leaders are not to show their intelligence by answering questions from foreign leaders on domestic topics in their countries or foreign policy on certain issues. It is better to be seen as a fool and inexperienced than to impress others by overtly disclosing your country's secrets to nosy aliens in conversations. Is it not a great risk to open up to a foul-mouthed alien President like this one? It is avoidable risk.

The President orders in US Forces into areas of conflicts. The President's Orders are enough. He is not a fighting soldier. His able commanders are able to deploy troops and take action according to field situation. The President is not to stay on the phone to order for field action that he has no physical ideas about. Hence the Media people asking if the President authorised action are telling the pirates whom to go for and this is sad. The President of United States of America is not next to God. He alone cannot term the world or regulate it. He has a duty to make the US safe and protected and sell it to the world as a friend not a policeman. He has to use the Resources the US provides for its defence and security according to convention and the Presidential Role in this area in the Constitution. Perhaps God is handing the Baton to Obama to show the world what it had missed in what had happened in 146 BC.

Europe had taken the world to enormous development and progress never known in history of human beings before. The wealth has been outstandingly phenomenal and impressive. This has lost human relationship in its tract. We have to repair the damage and bring the human factor into all our development and progress. Obama must never attempt to be a macho man. He must be rational and level-headed. He must deal with Somali pirates crushingly as their activities do not affect the US alone but the whole world. The pirates say that people had violated their territory with illegal and dumping toxic wastes. They do deserve our hearing but we should not ignore their concern with environmental damage. Any group involved in this allegation must desist from their activities. It is criminal.

The world has to tell religious fanatics and extremists that they must choose us in the secular world or be excluded to isolation. They have to accept religious tolerance and reject religious intolerance. The world needs this to avoid conflicts. The manufacture, keeping and owning nuclear weapons should be made very costly. The members of these world potential destroyers must take enough high insurance capable of covering the damage by accidents. They must know that its use in war may mean extermination of the region involved in this use. The President has a duty to join other global leaders make laws to regulate the world in Globalisation. He must be ruthless with African war lords. He must persuade world leaders to bring out resources and skills to open up by rails and roads Africa to deny criminals the use of Africa as their haven. The world has the skills, Technology and Resources to do this. Organising African Resources can provide funds for this. The Africans must be ready to eliminate corruption and make sacrifices to achieve this. The world needs determination not to leave Africa as a dark continent any longer. Democracy and sovereignty of some Bantustans and fiefdoms have to be modified to accommodate this sort of construction. It is not for exclusive benefits to Africa but for benefits to the whole world. Obama is a hybrid of the whole world. He is a very Patriotic and loyal American Citizen. We must respect his sentiments. The doubters in Western Media should stop to portray him as an empty superman and toothless bulldog to panick him to make mistakes. We want a determined confident President ready to deal with reckless trouble-shooters with the understanding and sympathy of the world.

Akpaneyen Akpan-Essien.

The Africans should see how all their ancestors wasted time fighting to re-unite and divide again. Feuding over leadership and territorial control took much of their times and resources. We stagnated at where we reached; made no efforts to progress. We are even worst today. We must weed out those things that impair our Progress. We must compromise, make alliances and treaties. In the global village we must ignore our villages, ethnic groups and religious affiliations. We should settle down to expand our Education, skills training, good apprenticeship and genuine improvement in farming. We must be able to feed our people from our farms. We must invest to combat natural disasters affecting our farming. We must be constructive and not destructive, inclusive and not exclusive.

We must choose between living in a prosperous community in relative comfort for everybody and corrupt leaders holding us in fiefdoms to enjoy comfortable living for their families and friends. We must re-emerge and integrate Africa into a viable country. We must be prepared to accept the initial difficulties and problems of RE-UNIFICATION of Africa. Our ancestors endured the hardships of colonial division of this continent in Scramble for Africa that had no benefits for us. Re-unification will give us benefits. We must be ready to sacrifice for it. We must be ready to endure the initial hardship of Re-unification of Africa. We have four types of Governments, Monarchy, Oligarchy, Tyranny and Democracy. We can choose any system that will allow us to govern our people justly and weed out corrupt and criminal leaders. These leaders show signs of immaturity all over their lives. They are corrupt, paedophiles, rapists and worst sexual harassers of women, hard drug-abusers and drug barons and still want to rule even when they are Geriatric and need Old People's Residential Home instead of the State House. We must smash religious and ethnic influence and replace it with Secular African Constitution that will control the Judiciary, Political Conduct, Banking and Commerce, Contracts and Public Constructions, Freedom of Associations, the Right of Citizens, Ethnic and Religious Freedom not interfering in Politics and infringe on the Right of Government to govern, the Security (Army and the Police), Public Institutions and Administrations, Lands and Farming. The Constitution must be reviewed every ten years.

THE GLOBAL WESTERN ECONOMIC COLLAPSE AND DEEP RECESSION:

It is very disturbing to note that a broke West living on dud, fake, counterfeit notes printed by their Central Banks had given their quangos, the IMF and the World Bank (WB) would like to lend some of these worthless notes as loans to Africa to create phantom loans that would be refunded with gold, platinum, diamond, uranium and other valuable metals and energy. This is fraud and the quango, WTO has no credit in promoting this kind of fraud in trade. The West should trade by barter until it has genuine currencies to use for trade. African leaders must avoid being fooled to borrow valueless and worthless Western money from the IMF or WB. The West should endure its boom and burst without using intrigues and con to exploit poverty and ignorance to weave in Africa to share the burden of the CREDIT CRUNCH. Capturing and selling African Bantus for slave labour created Western capital. If the West is in trouble it should not return to Africa to look for capital. If it is to involve Africa it should be by significant construction work to open up Africa to the world for trade. The West must genuinely abolish money laundering and Off-shore Banking and dubious Hedge Funds. The West must eliminate dodgy money from their financial system. They must abolish unjustified rewards as bonuses above normal salaries paid to fund and Bank Managers. The West must not dupe Africa by selling Toxic Debts to its ignorant and corrupt leaders to weave Africa into current global Western deep recession. The President of Brazil, Lulu has spoken for the poor. The rich European white male inflicted this scam on their community in the middle of enormous wealth and prosperity. They should not play smart game by duping the poor they deem are not intelligent enough to pick up the bill for the repairing the damage in offering cheap IMF & WB loans of totally fake money. The West must seize this opportunity to help the poor resettle their community. There are no further free surplus resources among the poor that can be tapped into to resettle the rich West. We now know that the resources on earth are limited. It is our duty, rich and poor to manage them. We must give everybody, education, skills training, and apprenticeship training and working responsibility to support the community and the Economy. The community must supervise the Economy, legislate and regulate the Economy. Economic crimes must now be in the statute books. Stiff penalties must be administered to the culprits. We must examine the quality of wealth an individual has and ensure that the rich is not defrauding the poor. Life on earth is dynamically changing and never static.

Human being should be able to adapt to this changing dynamism. We should be content with what we have. One person should not aspire to own the whole world. The wealthy must not aim at making the world static so that his fortune cannot change. He should be able to bear changes in life. Conditions may change in evolutionary natural selection and the rich may become poor. The rich in a changed condition must learn to endure poverty. He should not lose his head, kill and commit suicide. He may become rich again if he learns to endure poverty. The poverty confronting him may be a learning curve and a short spell in life to mature his learning. Wealth is not the only source of happiness. The hermits, monks and religious people in the Abbeys and Monasteries are happy and contented. There should be a limit to wealth a person gets. Beyond this limit the wealthy should have share holders and run plc and pay taxes.

The West and the whole world have a duty to restore the family back to its previous status in the human community. Parents like every living thing including the wild animals look after their young and teach them how to live in this world. The community must support parents, father and mother, stop practising undeclared social exclusion for certain groups, and give them opportunity to work to support their families. The global people must work to provide for the world population and its various communities. Darwinian evolution states that natural selection allows the rich to exploit the poor but the poor must have what the rich wants. We are at that level where the rich and poor have got to help each other. We have brought our globe to a very precarious state threatening its very existence. It is our duty to join hands and rescue our world together. We must avoid phantom families of Modernism of homosexual lifestyle which is a vogue. It may allow consumer-materialistic capitalism to commercialise and monetarise reproduction method but this is fraud as we still need ova and sperms from Nature and female womb to achieve our purpose. Yet we claim patency for our doubtful discovery. We are attempting to integrate human reproduction into the Market and Capitalism. Capitalism is mean by attempting to commercialise means of human reproduction perhaps to make it available to the rich only and stop the poor from having children. IVF is a great Science that helps the infertile but it is not for the homosexual pervert lifestyle infertile or rich people selecting the sex of their children and choosing fashion babies infertile? No they can pay for their services. Sadly the traders here are Doctors. They are said to be regulated by politicians but the politicians are not Doctors. Doctors have ethics not to dupe nature or act against their conscience. Commercialising human reproduction is unethical and against good conscience. Anything we do here should be free.

There should be no patency in this line of research. It should be funded by Public. The individuals involved in the research should be rewarded by the Public fund and given commendation as a mark of appreciation. We have not gained full control of means of human reproduction. We should not abuse it to make money and encourage the devious lifestyle of weird perverts. Capitalism would like to commercialise and monetarise all means of Production for the Market to gain control. Nature and the instrument of natural selection are opposed to this plot. The Human Community may be fooled to accept it as the wonders of advances in Science and Technology. GM Foods are said to have yielded increased production and better quality foods in spin and will feed the poor third world but yet the poor is still starving. Further any new inventions and discoveries must be monitored for acute and chronic long term toxicity. GM foods have yet to go through this. Its effects on the environment are yet to be known. We do not object to Research in this field but it should be spared from spin and strong lobby and sale. The knowledge should be free and available to all consumers in the globe. It should not constitute the means to dispossess the poor of the means of production. There is enormous fear that capitalism and the Market want to use Science and Technology to commercialise natural methods of breeding and producing things by claiming better quality produce. Why do we write Patency for these Produce while we use Nature to complete stages we least understand?

Finally I wish the world would listen to me, a dying man who at above sixty years following global events and listening to various messiahs with magic solutions to global problems I have come to the conclusion that solution to global problems neither lies in ideology, communism, capitalism, socialism, free market, regulated or unregulated market, private ownership or public ownership, nor in the type of government that is present in the community or a country, Tyranny, Oligarchy, Monarchy or Democracy or in multiple suggestions I have included in this book and even religion has no solution to global problems the solution to global problems lies in the people who operate the systems; if they are honest and completely abandon, ignore and exclude individual interest in the performance of their daily public duties, the method they use will work. If individual interest sneaks in, here and there, any system fails to work. It is individualism that makes any method not work. It is the individual integrity, virtue and honesty, commitment and very high sense of duty that make the system work.

The recent economic collapse of Western Economy in the hands of corrupt, criminal and greedy Financial and Fund Managers and Administrators has exposed capitalism at its worst practice. The fiddle in claiming allowances by the British Parliamentarians in the Heart of mother of Parliament and Democracy, exposed by the Daily Telegraph has shown human greed and selfishness and malpractices in capitalism. No system is exempt from human greed and malpractices. It is the fault and fallibility of human beings that make any system fail. There is the story of Pottery and China Store. The Manager had promised the Assistant that he will take over when he goes. The Assistant became restless and wanted the Manager to go so that he could tidy up and rearrange things. The Manager already tired and exhausted left and handed over to the Assistant. The job became enormous for Assistant. When people told him to get on with it he told them the pottery and china would break. He was frightened out of breath. He was afraid of breaking things. He left everything untouched. This is the sad story of capitalism, free market and Democracy. The job looked damn easy to the ambitious assistant from a distance. He has been given the mantle to carry on with it. Fear took over; he failed to move any of the items for fear of breaking them. He lacked courage in doing things. His leadership went into crisis and chaos. Leadership requires courage to do things and effect changes. Leadership requires transparent honesty, integrity, Patience, personal initiative, consistency, persistence, reliability and ability to carry the people along in his honest decisions. Selfless leadership is visionary. It is void of selfishness and individualism and its actions are purely in public interest. A good leader is humble but conscientiously active in performing his duties and carrying out his responsibilities.

Despite strong lobby and defence of capitalism with plenty of funds and force at times, it is fraught with corruption and crimes. Those attracted to Democracy and capitalism give us the impression that they like them because they give them free access to public assets and ways for them to take home the assets they strip from the public coffer. Communism is bad because it is committed to provide jobs and comforts of infrastructures to citizens who take permanent holidays and refuse to work normally to support the system. Rather they take to mischief of drug and alcohol abuse. The leaders make themselves tyrants neglecting their duties. They take to the bottle and are chronic alcoholics and hunt down their opponents to protect their individual position and interest. The other two systems, Oligarchy and Democracy suffer from the same plight from human beings. Any system will work if human beings are sufficiently honest to work hard and operate it to work. No farm produces good yield if the farmers abandon it, and fail to care for it. Similarly if the people involved in operating a system return home and fail to do their duties and expect the system to work automatically and provide for them the system will fail to work. Hence those who have preference for any system must know that any system has the stench of human beings. It is not the system that fails but it human beings that fail. Therefore my proposal the community must trump both the private business and corporations through community appointed civil servants that play the roles of housekeepers in businesses and in governments. The proposal is not suggesting revolution but modifications to guarantee the security of funds for the Public to prevent frequent sudden changes destabilising jobs and employments. This causes redundancies and unemployment. Housekeepers take the burden of financial management off the shoulders of the politicians to allow them to concentrate on the duty of governance. In the business sector the housekeepers serve as Public guardians and regulators in attendance to prevent the business leaders under stress of business management making mistakes that can damage the businesses. This can cause redundancies and unemployment. The whole duty of this concept of housekeepers is to prevent overspending and careless mistakes causing sudden collapse of businesses to throw the community into economic crisis and confusion as the current financial meltdown and deep recession have done.

As for you African Bantus it is simple to keep, maintain, improve, and value the good thing you have. Do not neglect the good things you have and run away with funds for their maintenance and improvement. Turn your good infrastructures into valuable treasures and national assets. It is on record that illiterate Northern coup-sponsored heads of state like Ibrahim Babangida and Mohammed Abacha out sheer envy, jealousy and complete ignorance destroyed the sound foundation of Education Nigeria had. They did this with active collaboration of southern decadent illiterate Geriatric military leaders who spend twenty fours in bed with girls of their grand daughters' age. They are jealous and envious of the educated Nigerians. They never bothered to have good education even though our past colonial masters and the missionaries offered all of us opportunities to do so. Late Fela Ransom Kuti, the famous and ingenious Nigerian musician and Moshed Abiola who were School mates of Odusekun Obasanjo used to make fun of him as military Head of State of Nigeria for his poor performance at School. Yet this class of people had been ruling Nigeria for the last near fifty years. Is it any wonder that Nigeria had degenerated into a failed criminal rogue state despite its rich energy resources and the good efforts by past colonisers to make a showpiece of colonial rule. These mediocre illiterate leaders messed up and ran down every good thing the British colonisers left behind in Nigeria. They destroyed all the jobs they created. They have evolved a homogeneously poor and deprived semiliterate people without means to challenge them. The deprived youths had turned to depend on their patronage. They use them for their criminal purposes to secure them in power. Nigeria is in Anarchy and a den of international and local criminals.

They used to boast that they were to make southerners especially Easterners eat their certificates and truly they had done it but what they had done damaged Nigeria. The Education your children have abroad is not first class. It cannot be classified in planning Economic

Development of Nigeria. It is cowardice, corruption, crimes and intrigues embedded in religion and ethnicity and active intimidation and atrocities that force the military on Nigeria. Re-integration of colonial dismembered Africa is the main solution to African Bantu Economic problems but Nigeria must get rid of its rotten illiterate wild military. There are a lot of fine educated Nigerians in the military but it is led and dominated by illiterate wild Geriatric old colonial soldiers ignorant of the law and order; they are above the law. They call themselves the untouchable. They teach the young ones bad manners. They have no clue about what makes a modern Community beyond what Idi Amin knew as an old colonial soldier.

Finally all global people have seen a lot of things to take in at the same time but it appears God, Allah, the creator has at last descended to teach us earthly people that we are all people of his creation and family. He had taught us that we do not have to waste the scarce resources on earth to destroy ourselves in wars as He can do it by natural disasters, volcanic eruptions, earthquakes, tsunamis, floods (Katrina), destructive wild bush fires, land slides etc. Then our pride in wealth had been dealt a fatal blow even with the computers and our sophisticated IT and high Technology gadgets keeping records and maintaining high level of security for the rich in the West the great Western global Economy collapsed in very competent hands. African Bantus with poor education and skills had been notoriously corrupt and selfish. Now the world knows that regardless of our colour, the level of wealth and affluence, we are all, to some degree, greedy human beings; why do we in the Western Atlantic region not rise up and rescue Africa and open it up for the world? It is worth doing in our interest. We should not leave Africa behind for others to go and filter whatever is left of its wealth. If the world continues to exclude and ignore Africa in its scheme of things, Africa may finally become acute global problem. Everybody knows that the longer we allow the problem to last and be longstanding and protracted the more it would cost to fix it. In a situation the current global warming has extended the Sahara Desert, it would affect the world climate. This would need a lot of money to fix. Equally African may become a crime haven. The whole world would be affected. For eight years the West has been battling the Al-Qaida and Taliban. Could you imagine how long it would take and the amount it would need to confront such a situation in Africa in the hands of criminals as their safe haven?

Even Mrs Clinton, American Secretary of State for Foreign Affairs has complained about the new Asian Tiger Economies rushing round Africa and South America to buy anything on the cheap in sight from the illiterate corrupt and criminal leaders. It would be a great shame and a disaster for anybody to think that Asian wealth would be created from African resources by unfair deals. Secondly it would be very sad indeed when African Intellectuals are advocating for integrating Africa into Western Atlantic Economy and Industrial Base and not to subjugate and humiliate and abandon Africa again. It would be a real tragedy if the West abandon us to the mercy of Asia with their population. We are not afraid of the new Asian Tiger Economy coming to do business with us in Africa provided they come to do equal business to help us to develop. But the policy of "quick bug and take it home while it exists" is damaging to Africa. Yes the mere mention of Africa makes it revolting because of its illiterate corrupt leaders' criminal tendency. Despite its enormous resources investments are not safe. Determined and honest Africans can clean the Aegean Stable and make African work. Africa is central in the world and in the Southeast of Western Atlantic. There has been religious brainwashing by some Asians using Muslim brotherhood to lure and attract Africa through influence of the leaders who are in the main Muslims from Sultan of Sokoto Stock some of whom trace their Genealogy to the Prophet Mohammed. Re-integration of colonial dismembered Africa would allow viable new countries to be formed along the lines they were before the European colonisers salamised it on 15th September, 1884 in Berlin, Germany. This will also bring religious and ethnic groups together. It would allow better control of lawless and criminal groups on the continent than at present. The world would know the ethnic groups prone to commit crimes and flouting the law. They run about in the world and ruin the reputation of Africa and black people and teaching our youths all manners of crimes. Such ethnic groups should b known by the world by their ethnic identity not by country's name as it is now. This may curb corruption and crimes to some extent.

The problem of Africa is Economic and neither religious nor political. We have seen recently that after burning just one consignment of cocaine in the Sierra Leone the price of the drug jumped in Europe and the dealers had to adulterate it to sell to the abusers and addicts. This is the fear that Africa abandoned with its corrupt leaders would fall into the hands of criminals who would convert it into their haven. We sincerely feel that the whole world, everybody of good will, compassion and sympathy for Africa, all genuine global Africans of concern for the African continent including Africans on the continent and the Diaspora, members of the African Union ashamed of the deplorable state of Africa would treat it as a matter of urgency to come to the rescue of Africa from selfish, corrupt and irresponsible individual leaders whose patriotism and public service are buried in their irrepressible greed and insatiable desire to plunder the continent. The UN, EU, the West as whole and the United States of America with serious stake in Africa currently destroyed by its corrupt and criminal leaders should please realise that this is the time for everybody to join forces to rescue Africa from its corrupt leaders and their alien collaborators. The world cannot abandon Africa at the mercy of these people who ruin the continent and harvest its rich resources to store in their barns. Every minute, Africans and African children are dying of all manners of infections, malaria and AIDS, tuberculosis and Typhoid, starvation and malnutrition and drinking infected and contaminated water while their corrupt leaders continue to build up their stolen assets in various Banking havens abroad. Is the world doing the right thing by abandoning Africa in the hands of these corrupt and criminal leaders while it picks up the bills for the disasters, tragedies and catastrophes the criminal actions of these leaders had caused? All global people of good conscience and good will should join genuine patriotic Africans and Africans in the Diaspora to salvage and rescue Africa from these shameless and unrestrainedly corrupt and criminal people who hold the continent to ransom. The world in global recession is seriously considering review of world Financial Management, Banking and Economy. Africa has a pool of rich natural and mineral resources that its leaders take as their private property while relying on the NGOs to take care of its people. The world must take courage and challenge the illiterate, corrupt and criminal African leaders to allow re-integration of colonial dismembered Africa to allow African resources to be pooled together to invest in the development of the continent. We cannot continue to allow African wealth to remain in private pockets of its illiterate and corrupt criminal leaders to distort its Economy while abandoning Africa to remain as the "heart of darkness" and a dark continent. (Joseph Conrad) Africans and the world must determine to open up Africa. A BBC interviewer interviewing Zimbabwean Prime Minister, Morgan Tsvangirai was very rude. He was bent on weeping up emotions to incite the poor man against his President Robert Mugabe. It was consoling that the Prime Minister told him that resolution of land conflict was a consensus of the three Parties. I can say, "It is a consensus of all Africans on earth. Do these white males know that what they would not accept in their land is what others reject and object to in their land now free from colonialism and racial xenophobic segregation? Britain has been fighting several wars for over one millennium to secure its land and secure its freedom. What would it do with these greedy and selfish white male farmers if it were in Zimbabwean position? Would it offer over ninety per cent of fertile land to alien white male farmers with flag of convenience as Zimbabwean citizens to use proud British people at peanut salaries to crop the land with maize tobacco, vegetables and other reach food crops for human consumption and supermarket sales and animal food export to other countries to make fortunes while its people are condemned to settle and crop infertile land?

Let them look for farmland in other places in the world. The interviewer and his employer, the BBC know that they should not weep up emotions to fan up conflict and crises among leaders in a country. Can Britain entertain aliens coming to incite its people against its leaders and Parliamentarians now sorting out misappropriation of funds in their claims of allowances? There is one thing the Anglo-American alliance should do. Take your long nose out of other people's affairs. You have a lot of problems at home. Solve your problems first. You go about testing your arms on innocent people and slaughtering them in large numbers. You violate basic human rights in Iraq, Afghanistan and Guantanamo Bay. You conducted rendition and kidnapped innocent people to be tortured and locked up in alien false Prisons you bribe the unscrupulous tyrannical leaders to do the nasty jobs for you. You fix, manage and rig elections at gun point to intimidate the people for your hand-picked so-called moderates and supporters you acquire by bribery. Are these the actions of civilised people and believers in world order and the rule of law in the world? "Don't do as I do but do what I order you to do" is not a good way to sell Democracy to people. Do the Western leaders and their citizens know that theirs is not the only interest in the world? They can reduce tension and conflicts in the world if they recognise other people's interests. Weeping up emotions and stirring up crisis, violence and wars are just obnoxious and inacceptable.

BBC taking up announcing demonstrations in Iran under the pretext of reporting international affairs is deplorable. It betrays the neutrality of the BBC and exposes its journalists to risk and danger. The UN can expand its Human rights charter to include the imposition of religious laws, like the Sharia that it is violation of human rights. The UN should make binding secular constitution and laws embracing human rights as a condition for acceptance for membership. Subversion is not the way to spread Democracy in the world. The Anglo-American alliance should tell the world how many Anglo-American inspired crises in Iran would lead to freedom and stability in that country. Are they going to make it in cycles of temporary peace and crises eliminating its leaders all the time?

They should recall that they fought against each other in American war of Independence because of "right of man and taxation without consent without consent". Anglo-American alliance should abandon the ambition of ruling Iran by proxy by lobbying for votes in the UN Security Council and UN Atomic Agency. Are their nuclear warheads for fighting alien invaders? If this is so why should North Korea and Iran not get it to use in the defence of the earth against alien invaders? If they are for deterrent, bullying and intimidation of other nations then other nations deserve to get them. When USA dropped these nasty WMDs on Japan it was neither a rogue nor mad unstable State but very stable USA. It was all powerful rich USA. Hence all the world should regulate the use of the nuclear weapons in conflicts and avoidance of accidents. The Insurance for cleaning up and compensating victims in accidents should be above the roof top. The nuclear nations should deposit the Insurance Certificates with the UNAA. There must be evidence that such nations are paying their premiums by confirmation by UNAA direct communication with the Insurance Company owned by the honestly neutral UN. No Insurance no nuclear weapons as the UNAA is authorised to seize such weapons and its factory for destruction as serious risk to people. People who want to bomb can go in bomb such manufacturing facilities and go in and seize the weapons if the owners refuse to surrender them peacefully. The Security Council and UN should establish this by international binding statute.

For the new rich nations who want to join the club they should apply to the UNAA for permission and inspection of their sites and facilities. If it is a small overcrowded country approval is denied permanently. If the site would blow nuclear wind across neighbouring countries it is permanent disapproval. Any secret installations are located and destroyed. A continent like Africa without one can get one if the location is suitable in seismic and geological structure without threat of contaminating surface drinking water. Every old bomb keeper must equally comply with the regulations and stringent conditions. Anybody that cannot comply with the regulations is free to surrender the facilities and the weapons to UNAA. Anybody new or old nation possessing the weapons and storing them in unsuitable locations like the French still sprawling around the Sahara Desert with the overt and covert consent of corrupt African leaders should open their door to the UNAA.

Finally when everybody agrees to truly verifiable total disarmament and denuclearisation the Security Council and the UN should by international statute signed by all nuclear nations should authorise the UNAA to collect the weapons and destroy and the bomb making facilities. The Insurances should then mature to afford the funds to pay for the job of getting rid of these deadly weapons and their manufacturing facilities.

This book is written not to criticise any people, nations and certain global alliances but to extol the dignity and freedom of various people to live without molestation by people who do not understand the problems various people have in their homelands in the world. Sponsoring crises everywhere in the world does not give the West any credit as Democratic and law-abiding people.

FINAL SUMMARY:

“The war against Terrorists” is a rubbish, vague and ambiguous spin to confuse the unwary and innocent people. Normal wars have fronts and rears. Where are these vital landmarks in the war against Terrorists? The West hired the Mujahidin alias Taliban Al-Qaida as Mercenaries to fight and defeat the now defunct Soviet Union. Ancient History reveals that Carthage frequently fought wars against disaffected mercenaries. Are we sure that the West alias NATO is not fighting against disaffected mercenaries in the war against Terrorists? The war is now complicated. It now involves socio-political, cultural and religious differences. The world has got to know that despite Banki Moon photo appearance with Ahmed Kazai and President Obama and Prime Minister Gordon Brown's approval of this trusted friend of Anglo-American Alliance, NATO should admit their failure in Afghanistan if this is the only friend they could find in Afghanistan in eight years. Using this man to endorse their stay and illegal actions in Afghanistan is fraud and forgery. Is this licence to shed part of the population in war? The security of the West is not on the mountains, in the valleys and caves of Afghanistan. It is in the streets of the cities in the West and Europe. The safety of the European citizens in the world is in the neutrality of the UN and its Secretary in engaging in genuine conflict resolution and warning all the combatants that security and safety in the world is mutual. They have to protect Europeans and Europeans would protect them in return.

The West said the Iraqi Arabs were content with receiving money they offered them as bribe to constitute them into opposing factions. They accepted that the Western formed puppet government and the partisan Army of semi-mercenaries from the local people to take over the fighting to allow the West to consolidate their grip on their land while pretending that they had withdrawn. Those who know the Arabs would not be surprised; they are fun-loving very mercenary opportunistic people. Their behaviour in Africa was a revelation of this habit. They sold all our vital artefacts and precious treasures as idols unwanted and disapproved by Islam and Allah. They went on the rampage for tomb robbery and stole all burial treasures from the tombs. The European colonisers expressed interest in mummies. The Arabs exhumed and sold all the mummies. They proceeded to make fake mummies to sell to Europeans to make money when they exhausted the original stock. They, finally, settled down to slave gathering and land grabbing religious (jihad) wars. The Arabs sell their war plans and wars. They rely on the West to interfere with their internal politics and fight their civil wars. The world hopes the West would realise this and free itself from Arab feuds.

The black Africans do not recognise their enormous potentials. They are leaderless and disunited. If they had a uniting leader with genuine leadership skills and they sincerely agree and accept to unite under a uniting leader and abandon individual vested interest and selfishness, they would realise their potential and global influence. Are they not pathetic in allowing the Arabs to share their land and tell them where to live? The hope of Africa lies on re-integration of Africa, having a credible selfless uniting leader and all citizens uniting and working in communities as united and peaceful people. They must start on a clean slate. They must develop a Secular powerful uniting Constitution religiously, ethnically, racially and socially neutral. Equality of opportunities and acknowledgement of talents must be the hallmark of social elites and celebrities. Recognition of individual achievement should not be taken for granted. Religion should be free as long as it is confined to the worshippers and believers in the faith. It should not go beyond its place of worship. Internal Feuding over the doctrine within the faith spilling into Public disorder is strictly prohibited. It is invitation to government to step in and band the sect and groups so involved. A re-integrated united Africa must have a crack Army training under the harshest conditions to fight as a crushing fighting machine. Its motto should be that of the Spartan Army. "We African children would hold this ground until the enemy is routed". The Army should never interfere with politics and stage coups. Anybody or military unit breaking this law is inviting the severest of penalty including death by firing squad.

The Army should have access to the leader and his cabinet to discuss problems in secret. They may resist military action in cases the politicians should handle in conflict resolution. They can refuse orders in secret discussion with the leaders if they are not combat ready due to shortage of equipment. The Army should never be used to quell civilian riots. No security force should be developed to rival the Army. Civilian Police should deal with the Public. The Army top brass must discuss any issues at stake in secret and decide on the direction to take. If fighting and war are to be involved they must plan their strategy and obey the order. The order would come from the national military council of non-partisan wise men and women. Everybody in the Army is personnel of the national crack forces of fighting machine well trained in land, water and air combat. They must train in fighting in the roughest terrains, on mountains, in valleys and caves. They must learn how to live with hardships. "The world is a dangerous place", they say. Who makes it dangerous? Africa cannot standby any longer; they must fight back if they are provoked. Africa is in the South of Western Atlantic. Western Atlantic defence is non-existent and defenceless with Africa without effective fighting force. This is why all wars in the world always affected Africa. The Africans do not know this; all the wars in the world had always involved fighting on African soil. The reason is that Africa has no credible Army. Africa should not allow this to continue any longer. Africa re-assures everybody in it that it is the original home of all human beings on earth and cannot discriminate against all its children scattered all over the earth. Everybody is equally safe in Africa. Its security is for protection of all in Africa regardless of colour, language or race. Africa is a rainbow nation and colour blind. It is determined to enforce its laws. Everybody must live within the rule of law.

Law and order must be strictly maintained and observed. Nobody should be above the law. Corruption and crimes ruin and sell Africa on the cheap to total strangers. It is important to stress that many people had written on the information in this book with different objectives. This one is to emphasize the continuity of life on earth. It is to trace the relationship that existed among different peoples. It also shows the role of religion, race, and colour of skin, ethnicity, Social class, human greed and selfishness had played in human relationship. It appeals to human conscience if nature sent us here to do these things; can human beings change with the dynamically changing times to accept that each person on earth has a right to be here? Therefore, nobody has the right to fight and kill off the other; human beings should respect nature's decision to decorate the earth with diversity. All people should appreciate nature's artistic skills to make the world so beautiful. Inclusion of human beings in natural diversity is to make people conscious of nature's choice of diversity to make the world less boring. This book is written not to provide a platform for people to foment trouble and attempt vengeance against those they feel had ill-treated them. It is recalling these incidents for everybody to swear that never again would they allow their relationship to degenerate as low as to make them do these things to fellow human beings and each other. People must control their acquisitive instinct. Human beings need tolerance and patience. They must treat fellow human beings decently. They must acknowledge that they and their offspring are not to stay here permanently. They would die and leave the world in their own times. They must stop hoarding global wealth and must share wealth.

The Computer Model Research Conclusion is giving Scientific, Biological and Medical Research a bad name. The current row on cannabis between the Home Minister and the Scientific Drug Advisory Group is a feud that should not arise. The T expert Advisory group misled the politicians to declassify cannabis. The Computer Model experts are totally ignorant of the effects of cannabis in man. They fail to acknowledge that any drugs cannabis, alcohol and tobacco affect human beings differently. Some people are affected and seriously damaged by some drugs; others, may be a tiny minority, abuse the same substances and drugs but they are not damaged. Selected small population or Laboratory rats and animal experiments and Statistical computer Model may give a false result and interpretation. The Media publications of Scientific Research results, common in these days, completely complicate matters. The journalists go for sensation and not for scientific reasoning in publishing the results to sell their Media.

The truth is that if the expert scientific advisers bothered to go around the world they would learn more about the damage cannabis (ibbo) does to several teenagers in Africa. It is the fuel drug in several youth violence, armed robbery, all African bush wars, coups and violent overthrow of governments. Go to Africa and mix with these groups of people you will return with better results of acute toxicity of cannabis. It may be cannabis has different effects on black African youths and child soldiers from those in white youths. Chronic toxicity of cannabis causes imbecility. A descent young chronic abuser becomes scruffy, unkempt and living rough. They develop mental disease. The effect of this drug on these mental patients is brain damage. Do you know those who would tell you the cause of their mental disease? Their young colleagues who had known their lifestyle will confess to you. These Computer

Models statistically imposed on the wider population without active human population studies are very misleading. Have the British Drug experts investigated some black scruffy and unkempt mental patients in Brixton and other black areas of London?

REFERENCES:

AFRICA IN THE 21st CENTURY: Towards a New Future.

Mazama, Alma (Ed)

Brings together leading Pan African and Afrocentric intellectuals to discuss the possibilities of a new future where the continent claims its own agency in response to the economic, social, political and cultural problems present in every nation. In areas of 1. African Unity and Consciousness, Assets and Challenges, 2. Language, Information and Education and Education 3. African Women, Children and Families 4.Political and Economic Future of the African World UK ROUTLEDGE, 2007 9780415957731

AFROCENTRISM: Mythical Pasts and Imagined Homes

Howe, Steven

Argues that the necessary redress to racist, colonial and Eurocentric attitudes has created a misleading counter mythology that proclaims the innate superiority of African descended peoples. The Author challenges the Afrocentric movement……Index, bib, notes, x, 337pp, UK VERSO, 1859842283

THE AFROCENTRIC PARADIGM

Mazama, Ama (Ed)

A collection of essays focusing on the intellectual dimensions of afrocentricity index refs, v 293pp, USA AFRICA WORLD PRESS

AFROCENTRIC THOUGHT AND PRAXIS: An Intellectual History

Gray, Cecil Conteen

A history of African-centred thought looking at its external and internal anatomy and development across the Diaspora index bib, notes, xv, 204pp USA AFRICA WORLD PRESS, 0865438269

AFRICAN DIASPORA: African Origins and New World Identities

Okpewho, Isidore, Mazrui, Ali & Davies, Carol B. (Eds)

New World Black Cultures. The first is that Africa is the homeland of all blacks and defines their identity, the second that black culture in the Diaspora owes more to the hybrid climate that has become home than to ancestral origin. B/w ill, notes, refs, index, xxvii, 566pp, USA, INDIANA UNIVERSITY PRESS. 0253213947

BLACK ATHENA WRITES BACK:

Martin Bernal Responds to his Critics

Bernal, Martin

The author tackles his critics by providing additional information to back up his thesis that Greek culture was influenced by Afro-Asiatic civilisations, Maps, notes bib inde xvi 550pp USA DUKE UNIVERSITY PRESS 2001 822327171

BLACK, CULTURE, IDEOLOGY AND DISCOURSE: A Comparative Study

Abodunrin, Femi

New revised edition. Explores theca of Blackness and its manifestations in creative writing Index bib notes 476pp NIGERIA DOKUN PUBLISHING HOUSE, 2008, 1996, 9789783796263

BLACK IDENTITY IN THE TWENTIETH CENTURY: Expressions of the US and UK African Diaspora

Christian, Mark (Ed)

A collection of essays which examine the forces which shape black identity in the UK and in the US in the twentieth century. Index, notes refs xx 267pp UK HANSIB PUBLISHING. 2002 187051887x

BLACK ROUTES: Legacy of African Diaspora

Belton, Brian A Collection of commetaries and biographies featuring a distinguished group of black theorists, writers and influential revolutionaries viz Berni Grant and Kwame Toure, Stuart Hall, Gwendolyn Brooks, Ericka Huggins, Assata Shakur, Michael Akintaro, Nawal El Saadawi, Eldridge Cleaver, Henan Ashrawi. Peter Mokoba and Clive Charles. Index bib b/w photos 212pp UK HANSIB PUBLISHING 2007 9781870518925

CONTMPORARY AFRICANA THEORY; THOUGHT AND ACTION:

A to African Studies.

Hudson-weems, Clenora (Ed)

A collection of essays covering myriads of Panafricanist fields of theory...

Index, 476pp, USA, AFRICA WORLD PRESS. 2007 9781592213108

THE CONTINENT OF BLACK CONSCIOUSNESS: On the History of the African Diaspora from Slavery to the Present Day.

Brodber, Ema

A collection of seven lectures by the author addressing the issues of slavery, of Marcus Harvey, Claude McKay, George Padmore and

C.L.R. James. The author discusses two novels by Merle Hodge and Paule Marshall. Index, notes, xiv 194pp, UK NEW BEACON BOOKS LTD, 1873201176

DIASPORIC AFRICA: A Reader presents most recent research on history of African descent outside of African continent....352pp, USA NEW YORK UNIVERSITY PRESS 2005 081473166X

EGYPT vs. GREECE AND THE AMERICAN ACADEMY: The Debate Over the Birth of Civilisation

Asante, Molefi Kete and Mazama, Ama

Contributors respond to many of key arguments formulated in Gorge James "Stolen Legacy" (No 21842) Refs, v, 186pp USA AFRICAN AMERICAN IMAGES 0913543772

FREEDOM DREAMS:

Imagination

Kelly Robin D. G.

A Hx of renegade intellectuals and artists of the African Diaspora in the twentieth century focusing on the visions of activists from C.L.R. James Aime Cesaire and Malcolm X... Communism and surrealism, radical feminism in terms of black culture Index xii, 248pp, USA BEACON PRESS, 0807009776

GROUNDING WITH MY BROTHERS

Rodney, Walter & Small, Richard (Ed)

Political Tract by the activist murdered by the Burnham government in Guyana in 1980 68pp UK BOGLE L'OUVERTURE

1990 1969 0904521567

THE HISTORY OF AFRICA: The Quest for Eternal Harmony

Asante, Molefi Kete

A wide-ranging history of Africa from early Pre-history to the present day…

Index, bib, apps, 397pp, UK, ROUTLEDGE

2007 9780415771399

AN INTRODUCTION TO AFRICANA PHILOSOPHY

Gordon, Lewis

Offers the first comprehensive treatment of Africana philosophy… .288pp, UK. CAMBRIDGE UNIVERSITY PRESS 2008 9780521675468

MARVELS OF AFRICAN THE AFRICAN WORLD:

African Cultural Patrimony, New World Connections and Identities

Afolabi Niyi (Ed) An Examination of cultural and spiritual connections between Africa and the New World….Afro-Brazilian Identity. Index, xiii, 644pp USA. USA AFRICA WORLD PRESS, 159221021X

NEGRO WITH A HAT

Grant, Colin

Marcus Garvey contemporary and rival of WEB Dubois placed under close observations by Intelligence of the USA under J. Edgar Hoover, Director of Bureau of Investigation (FBI) index, notes, b/w photos, 530pp, UK JONATHAN CAPE 2008 9780224078689

PANAFRICANISME: Les Nouvelles

Perspectives

Sim Remy

New Perspectives on Pan-African ideologies......Text in French, bib notes b/w illus map, 369pp, UK NEKHEN

PAN AFRICANISM:

The idea and movement, 1776-1991

Esedebe P Olisanwuche

Looks at the development of Pan-Africanism. USA. HOWARD UNIV PRESS 0882581864

PAN AFRICANISM AND INTEGRATION IN AFRICA

Mandaza Ibbo (Ed)

A collection of papers presented to the Southern African Political Economy Series Trust in 2000 which are aimed at finding solution to the problems of regional integration and in Africa generally. Index, notes, refs, 352pp, ZIMBABWE SAPES, 1779051492

PAN-AFRICAN HISTORY:

Adi, Hakim & Sherwood Marika (Ed)

A guide to figures of Pan-Africanism from 1797-present day. Index xi, 203pp UK ROUTLEDGE 0415173531

ROOTS OF BLACK HISTORY: A Comprehensive Guide to the Ancient and Medieval History of Africa

Walker, Robin

Discusses the civilisations of the Nile Valley North Africa, West Africa, the western, the Central Sahara, East Africa, and Southern Africa, as well as civilisations of early Asia and African influences in Ancient America and Medieval Spain Illus; maps, notes, bib, index 167pp UK L'OUVERTURE

2000 0904521338

THE SPIRIT AND THE WORD: A Theory of Spirituality in Africana Literary Criticism

Montgomery, Georgenes Bess

Utilising a method informed by ideas world view of Ifa

Index bib 243pp USA. AFRICA WORLD PRESS

2008 9781592215676

STOLEN LEGACY: Greek Philosophy is Stolen Egyptian Philosophy

James, George G.M.

A New edition of the controversial text originally appeared 1954 Index 191pp

USA AFRICAN AMERICAN IMAGES, 0913543780

TRUTH CRUSHED TO THE EARTH WILL RISE AGAIN: The East Organisation and the Principles and Practice of Black Nationalist Development

Konadu, Kwasi

Examines the historical, socio-political and cultural significance of the East..

Black Nationalist thought. Index bib, 183pp USA. AFRICA WORLD PRESS 1592212808

WHAT'S MY NAME?

Black Vernacular Intellectuals

Farred, Grant

Four Diaspora African citizens, Muhammad Ali, C.L.R. James, Stuart Hall and Bob Marley...challenge external and internal injustices Index notes, x, 316pp

USA, UNIVERSITY OF MINNESOTA PRESS,

08166333177

WHEN WE RULED: The Ancient and Medieval History of Black Civilisations

Walker, Robin Pan-Africanist Hx......Egypt. Index bib timeline 713pp UK EVERY GENERATION MEDIA 2006 095510680X

Burghardt Du Bois, W.E. The World and Africa; An inquiry into the part which Africa has played in world history.

Barnes, H. Gannibal, The Moor of Petersburg; Abram Petrovich Gannibal; First published in Great Britain in 2005, Profile Books Ltd, 3A Exmouth House, Pine Street, London EC1R 0JH.

Bull, G. Niccolo Machiavelli, THE PRINCE. Published by arrangement with Penguin Books, Ltd. 1961, 1975, 1981, 1995, 1999.

Paine, T Rights of Man. December, 1792. Reproduced by Permission of Penguins Books Ltd. Introduction M.R.D. Foot. 2007.

Russell, B. History of Western Philosophy and its connection with political and social Circumstances from the earliest times to the present day. 1996. The Bertrand Russell Peace Foundation. Introduction A. C. Grayling.

Quigley, M Ancient West African Kingdom: Ghana, Mali and Songhai, 2002.

Patricia and Frederick McKissach, The Royal Kingdom of Ghana, Mali and Songhai, 1995.

Man, K. Life in Medieval Africa; 1996.

Cynthia, L, Jenson-Elliott, East Africa; 2002.

Thomas, H. W. City States of Swahili Coast; 1998.

Diouf, S. A. Kings and Queens of East Africa; 2000.

Ayoub, A, Binous, J. Gragaleb, A. Umm El Madayan. Islamic City through the ages; 1994.

Green, R. Hannibal (First Book).

Henty, G. A. The Young Carthaginian 1860s (reprinted 2001).

Frank, M.C. The Late Roman West and Vandals; 1993.

Bessire, M. Great Zimbabwe (First Book).

Carpenter, A. Hughes, J. W. Uganda (Enchantment of Africa); 1973.

Turnbull, C. M. Uganda, the Enchantment of Africa, 1960s republished, 1987.

Hart, G. Ancient Egypt.

Shaw, I. The Oxford History of Ancient Egypt; 2002.

Hornung, E. History of Ancient Egypt: An Introduction; 1999.

Stiebing, W. H. Ancient Near Eastern History and Culture; later History of Aksum & Meroe; 2002.

Service, P. F. Ancient African Kingdom of Kush (Sudan); Past Cultures; 1998.

Caba, J. R. A Place in the Sun; 1998.

Bianchi, B. Daily Life of the Nubians; 2004.

Steyn, H. P. The Bushmen of Kalahari; 1989.

Hart, G. Ancient Egypt (for kids).

Kaplan, L. Politics and Government in Ancient Egypt (for kids); 2004.

Casson, L. Everyday Life in Ancient Egypt; (revised edition, 2001).

Southern, P. The Fall of Rome (476 AD).

Heathe, P. The Fall of Roman Empire – the Decline of the Roman Empire (Moral Decline of the Romans).

Pearsons, A. Ancient Greece (for kids).

Taones, R. Ancient Greek Children (People in the past series-Greece); 2002.

Rees, R. The Ancient Greeks (understanding people in the past); 2001.

Flaceliere, R. Daily Life in Greece the time Pericles; 2002.

Burrell, R. and Connolly, P. Oxford First Ancient History; 1997.

Parton, S. Cleisthenes, Founder of Athenian Democracy; 2002.

Jones, A. H. M. Athenian Democracy; (reprinted 1986).

Brock, R. Hodkinson, H. Alternatives to Athens: Political Organisations, Community in Ancient Greece; types of Governments-Monarchy, Oligarchy, Tyranny and Democracy; 2003.

Millar, F. Cotton, H. M. Rogers, R. Rome, the Greek World and the East, Government Society and Culture; 2004.

Lord Kinross A Short introduction to Ottoman Government for non-specialist; 1979.

Legge, J. Philosophy of Confucianism, Mandate of Heaven, selections from Shu Jing (classical history; 6th century BCE).

Mueller, F. M. (editor) The Sacred Books of the East, 50 vols (Oxford Clarendon, 1879-1910), vol 3; pp 92-95, reprinted in

Andrea, A. J. Overfield, J. H. The Human Record: Sources of global History vol 1, vol 2 ed in

Mafflin, B. H. Selection from the writings of Han Feitzu c 230 BCE (London: Arthur Probathain 1939 from W. L. Liaotrans).

Gardew, Sir Alan, Egypt of the Pharaohs pp131, 199, 285 (Clarendon Press, Oxford); 1964.

Redmount, C. A. Bitter Lives, Israel in Egypt in Oxford History of the Biblical Word (ed Michael Coogan; Oxford University Press).

Baines, J and Malek, J Atlas of Ancient Egypt, Oxford; 1984.

James, T. G. H. An Introduction to Ancient Egypt, London; 1979.

James, T. G. H. Pharaohs' People, scenes from life in Imperial Egypt; Oxford University Press; 1985.

Kemp, B. H. Ancient Egypt, Anatomy of civilisation, Routledge, London; 1989.

Pierre, M. Lives of the Pharaohs, Spring Books; London, 1974.

Romer, J. Ancient Lives, the story of the Pharaoh's Tombmakers, London; O'Mara; 1984.

Stead, M. Egyptian Life, British Museum Publications, 1986.

Stroul, E. Life in Ancient Egypt, Cambridge University Press; 1992.

Prof Bradley, K. Resistance to Slavery.

Dr Berry D. Ancient Roman Time, 753-509 BC, Rome gained control of over the whole Italy, 264-241.

Alerunni,sIndia, 2001, p19-21, Edward C. Sachau – History, Dates of the Buddha, 1987, p126, Shriram Sathe; foundations of Indian Culture, 1984, p20 sqq, Dr Govind Chandra Pande- History, India and Russia, Linguistics and Cultural Affinity,1982, Weer Rajendra Rishi; Geographical and Economic Studies in Mahabharata: Upayana Parva, 1945, Dr Moti Chandra – India; Linguistics and Cultural Affinity, 1982, Weer Rajendra Rishi; Racial Affinity of Early North Indian Tribes, 1973, Myths of Dog-Man, 1991, David Gordon White- Social Science; Sudhar Chattopadyaya – Ethnic Groups. History and Culture of Indian People, The Vedic Age, pp286-87, 313-14.

Mahabharata II.27.25

Rawlinson, H. G. Cf. Interaction between India and Western World, pp75-93

Journal of Royal Asoiatic Society, 1906, p215

History & Culture of Indian People, The Age of Imperial Unity, p121

Annals and Antiquities of Rajashthan, pp 53-54, 64.

Dr Witzel, M. AV-Par, 57. 2. 5; cf Persica-9, 1980, p 106.

Dr Law, B. C. Vedic Index, 138; Some Kshatriya Tribes of Ancient India, 1924 pp 230-231.

Kenoyer, J. M. Heuston, K. Ancient South Asian world; Oxford University Press, May 2005. ISBN 195174224. OCLC 56413341

Rendell, H. R. Dennell, R. W. and Halim, M. Pleistocene and Palaeolithic Investigations in the Soan Valley, Nortern Pakistan, British Archaeological Reports, International Series.

Jarrige, C. Jarrige, J. F. Meadow, R. H. and Quivron G. Mehrgarth Field Reports from the Neolithic to Indus Civilisation; Dept of Culture and Tourism. Govt of Sindh and Ministry of Foreign Affairs, France. 1975-85.

Feuerstein, G. Subhash, K. Frawley, D. In search of the cradle of civlisation: new light on Ancient India. Wheaton, Illinois: Quest Books, pp147 ISBN 0835607208.

Lawrence, S. The Harappan "Port" at Lothal; (Another View); American Anthropologist new series 70 (5) 911-922. Retrieved 2007-05-06.

Kenoyer, J. Ancient cities of Indus Valley Civisation, USA; Oxford University Press p96. 15 Sept 1998. ISBN 0195779401.

Goldman, R. P. (ed) The Ramayana of Valmiki: An Epic of Ancient India, ol. 1 Balakanda Ramayana of Vamilki. Princeton New Jersey; Princeton University Press, pp 23. March, 1990. ISBN069101485X.

WItzel, M. Early Sanskritization. Origins and development of the Kuru State (B. Kolver ed) The State, Law and Administration in classical India. Munchen. Dec 1995.

Fisher, M. P. In Living Religions: An Encyclopaedia of the World's faiths (I. B. Tauris) London. ISBN 1860641482.

Fuller, J. F. C. "Alexander's Great Battles"; Generalship of Alexander the Great; New York, Da Capo Press pp188-199; 3 Feb. 2004; ISBN 0306813300.

Innes, M. J. The Spice Trade of Roman Empire: 29 BC – 641 AD; Oxford University Press, 1969; special edition for Sandpiper Books, 1998 ISBN)0-19-814264-1.

STRABO, 11.5.12 At any rate, when Gallus was prefect of Egypt, I accompanied and ascended the Nile, as far as Syene and the frontiers of Ethiopia, and I learnt that as many as one hundred and twenty vessels were sailing from Myos Hormos to India whereas formerly, under Ptolemies only a very few ventured to undertake the voyage and to carry on in Indian merchandise. Pliny, Historia Naturae; 12. 41. 84.

"Vasco da Gama: Round Africa to India, 1497-1498 CE" Internet Modern History Sourcebook. Paul Halall. June 1998. Retrieved on 2007-05-07.

The Great Moghul Jahangir: Letter to James 1 King 1617 AD, Indian History Sourcebook: England, India and East India, 1617 CE Internet Indian History Sourcebook, Paul Halsall. June 1998.

Pryor, F. Overview: From Neolithic to Bronze Age, 8000-800 BC.

Richards, J. Overview: Iron Age, 800- AD 43.

Keys, D. Mummification in Bronze Age Britain

Moorhead, T. S. N. and Hill, J. D. Iron Age Sites in Britain.

Jundi, S. Life in Iron Age Village.

Bennett, P. Reconstructing Iron Age Buildings.

Hill, J. D. Surving Iron Age Britain.

Fitzpatrick, P. Amesbury Archer. The King of Stonehenge?

Dr James, S. Peoples of Britain. (Over 10,000years ago. Post-Roman Anglo-Saxon and the Vikings. Julius Caesar invaded Britannia 55-54 BC; inhabitants, Silures, Comovii, Selgovae). Britons, AD 1000.

Kreis, S. (ed) The History: Lectures on Ancient and Medieval European History. 1996.

David, L Five Great Battles of Antiquity (GNU Free Documentation Licence) Ancient History online from Wikipia.

Race and History: Ancient Greek and Roman Civilisations.

Gill, N. S. Ancient History Blog online

Hal, P. Internet Ancient History Sourcebook; April 1998-October, 2000.

Prof Wallace-Hadrill, A. Roman Empire: Ancient/Classical History, Romans.

Achebe, A.C. Things Fall Apart, 1958.

Montaigne, M. Essays; Moral, Politics and Military, March, 1580. (Vols 1-3).

Akpaneyen Akpan-Essien 21st April, 2009. BK ID 63229, Au ID 871158.

Lightning Source UK Ltd.
Milton Keynes UK
06 February 2010

149675UK00001B/17/P